Java™ 1.2 and JavaScript™ for C and C++ Programmers

Michael C. Daconta

Al Saganich

Eric Monk

Martin Snyder

WILEY COMPUTER PUBLISHING

John Wiley & Sons, Inc.

New York • Chichester • Weinheim • Brisbane • Singapore • Toronto

Publisher: Robert Ipsen
Editor: Robert M. Elliott
Managing Editor: Brian Snapp
Electronic Products, Associate Editor: Mike Sosa
Text Design & Composition: Publishers' Design and Production Services, Inc.

This book is printed on acid-free paper. ♾

Published by John Wiley & Sons, Inc.

Published simultaneously in Canada.

Library of Congress Cataloging-in-Publication Data:

ISBN: 0-471-18359-8

Printed in the United States of America.

10 9 8 7 6 5 4 3 2 1

Contents

Acknowledgments

Behind every project and product there are stories to tell. This one is no exception. There are so many "behind the scenes" events and people that come together over a span of months and give of themselves in ways great and small. That is what this book really is: a mosaic of faces seen and unseen, of thoughts light and deep, and of actions direct and indirect. Here I'd like to take a brief moment to thank and acknowledge those faces seen and unseen.

First is family. To my wife Lynne who supports me in everything. To my children, Samantha, Gregory, and CJ. To my parents, Joseph Daconta and Josephine Worner. To my inlaws, Buddy and Shirley Belden. To my brothers and sisters, Frank, Kristine, Joe, Lori, John and Christian. To my grandparents who call me and encourage me, Frank and Vera Daconta. Thank you all for your support and guidance.

Second is the people who worked to produce this book. First to my great collaborators and co-authors, Al Saganich, Martin Snyder, and Eric Monk. To my editors at John Wiley & Sons, Bob Elliott and Brian Calandra. To the production editor, Brian Snapp. And to the publisher, Robert Ipsen, who takes care of his technical writers. Thank you all for your hard work and trust in my abilities.

Third is friends and co-workers. To my long-standing friends, John Sweeney, Colm Magner, and Robert McDonnell. To my co-workers at Mystech Associates, Dave Young, Bob Cotter, and Maria Shugars. Special thanks to Jodi Johnson and her fabulous HR department for helping me produce wonderful Java training based on the book. To my co-workers at TMAC, Liz Dugger, Meredith Sivick, Vishal Kakkad, Everett Nelson, Mark Chapman, and Karen Sears. Thanks to Ken Cohen for making TMAC a reality. Special thanks to Rich O'Hanley and the folks at Newbridge Communications who produce my monthly Java column in *Tech Talk*. And very special thanks to my Java training partners at /training/etc. who provide Internet and Java training based on the book, Mike and Susan Saltzman. Thank you for your patience, advice, encouragement, and the many good times.

Finally, I'd like to thank the many readers of my books who have e-mailed me or send me letters. Your enthusiastic e-mails give me the courage and desire to keep doing what I'm doing. Thank you for your support.

To those not mentioned here, but who have also helped me in my pursuits—thank you.

—Michael C. Daconta

First I'd like to thank my wife Becky and my children. AJ and Jackie, for their support during the long hours of writing, rewriting, and development. I'd also like to thank all my friends who helped me (wittingly or otherwise) retain my focus when necessary and distracted me when *that* was necessary!

I'd also like to thank Mike Daconta for allowing me to be involved with this book in the first place. His reviews of my work and his attention to detail have caused this book to be more than a good book but perhaps a great book. I'd also like to thank Eric Monk and Martin Snyder whose contributions filled all the right areas and whose work contributed greatly to both the quality and the depth of the book. And of course, Bob Elliot, Brian Calandra, and the rest of the John Wiley staff who helped pull the project together.

Lastly, I'd like to thank Jay Cross who introduced me to Java in the first place.

—Al Saganich

I would like to thank my wife Audra, and my children Madeline and Cameron for Supporting me during the writing of this book. I would also like to thank my parents Edison and Helen Monk, my brother Mark, my sister Julie, and my in-laws, Jim and Serena Powell.

I would also like to thank Mike Daconta for getting me started in Java and giving me and opportunity to coauthor this book. Thanks to our other co-authors, Al Saganich and Martin Snyder. Thanks also to my friends and co-workers at TMAC, Mystech, PEC, and to my friends from UMBC.

—Eric Monk

I would like to take this opportunity to thank my family which, through no fault of my own, has grown to the extent that I cannot mention them all. However, I will mention the most direct members of my family. I'd like to thank my grandfather, also Martin Snyder, and my grandmother Jeanne Church, my father and stepmother Marty (yes, another one) and Ann Snyder, my mother and stepfather Susan and Tom Moore, and my brothers and sisters Becky, Pearson, Nicholas, and Sarina.

I'd also like to thank Al Saganich and Michael Daconta for their generous offer to work on this book with them. I'd also like to thank Eric Monk for his contributions as well as everyone at Wiley. Obviously, I could have done any of this without them.

To everyone I've worked with at OneWave, especially Geoff Charron, Paul Curtin, Andrew Goodale, and Mary Harvey, thank you for everything you've taught me along the way, and for your patience while I've been completing this book. There have been so many others over the past two years that I couldn't possibly mention you all.

Finally, I'd like to thank everyone who read this far, but weren't mentioned above. Thank you for purchasing this book, thank you for your interest, and thank you for your support.

—Martin Snyder

Welcome to *Java™ 1.2 and JavaScript™ for C and C++ Programmers*

Every technology goes through three stages: first, a crudely simple and quite unsatisfactory gadget; second, an enormously complicated group of gadgets designed to overcome the shortcomings of the original and achieving somewhat satisfactory performance through extremely complex compromise; third, a final proper design therefrom.

—Robert A. Heinlein

In a move that's seen as a capitulation to emerging Internet software standards, Microsoft Corporation announced plans to license a new, universal programming language called Java.

—CNN correspondent Brian Nelson

OBJECTIVE

My objective is to show you how this book is your *fastest ticket to the future of programming*. We will cover the techniques I have refined over the years in my previous books to deliver the best learning environment to you. For instance: the book's extensive use of nontrivial and complete programs, the conversational (easy-reading) style, the complete coverage of all major topics, and the side-by-side comparisons of C and C++ to Java. I will also discuss the impact of Java 1.2 and JavaScript on the software industry and why you should not hesitate to get involved in this software revolution!

Welcome to *Java™ 1.2 and JavaScript™ for C and C++ Programmers!* We will begin this section by covering the characteristics of the Java programming language and platform. Java has galvanized the entire software industry to produce a distributed computing environment for the next century. Then we will briefly examine the role of the JavaScript scripting language as the glue for the current generation of Web-top applications. Lastly, we will close with a description of the organization of the book and highlight its key features. I hope this section motivates you to see that this is the right time for you to learn these new skills. The discipline of learning new languages requires an underlying motivation to do so. Of course, this is true of all discipline. It is this motivation, this understanding of the real progress of these new inventions, and the excitement of discovery that I wish to impart here.

WHAT IS JAVA?

The first fundamental point to understand about Java is that it was born out of necessity. In 1991, a small team of Sun Microsystems engineers set out to develop a distributed system for the consumer electronics market. They started by using the most popular language of the day, a language that was both familiar and object oriented: the C++ programming language. After trial and error they realized that the inherent historical flaws and complexity in the evolution of C and C++ were holding them back. Their solution was to design a simple, more refined language, and an easily portable virtual machine that could interpret this new language on many consumer devices. That solution became Java the language and the beginnings of Java the platform. The fact that Java is both a language and a platform has caused some confusion for those who try to pigeonhole it into one or the other. We will separate our discussion of Java between the language and the platform.

The Java language has the following characteristics:

- **Familiar**. This is the most important characteristic for C and C++ programmers. Change is always difficult; however, small changes are much more readily accepted than large leaps. Java is derived from C and C++ and many of the keywords are identical to those in C and C++. In fact, all of Java's language features have been implemented in some other language. There are features borrowed from Smalltalk, Eiffel, Objective-C, Ada, Lisp, Cedar, and Mesa. Many programmers see this as Java's greatest strength: It is an intelligent integration of the best features of many existing languages. This means that at the concept level, Java is not only familiar to C and C++ programmers but to almost all programmers. Of course, C and C++ programmers will feel most comfortable with this language. Java code "Looks like" C++ code. You will immediately recognize it and feel comfortable around it.
- **Simple**. This was one of Java's overriding design goals. Java is based on the so-called KISS principle—Keep It Small and Simple (or "Keep It Simple, Stupid!"). The Java development team removed many C and C++ features that were redundant, sources of numerous confusion, or sources of unreliable code. Examples of such reduction are: no pointers, no multiple inheritance, no operator overloading, and no need to explicitly free memory. This paring down to the essentials reduces the complexity of the language while increasing the reliability.

- **Object oriented**. Unlike C++, Java is a pure object-oriented language. This is one of the areas where Java needed to be free from the shackles of compatibility. Everything in Java is an object and a descendant from a root object. Everything in a Java program except the primitive types is an object. C programmers should not be overly concerned about this. Object-oriented concepts are discussed in detail in Chapter 3. You will find that Java makes the transition from procedural to object-oriented programming easy.
- **Threaded**. Modern, networked applications are often required to perform multiple tasks simultaneously, like scrolling a window while downloading a file and playing background music. Java has built-in support for threads via a Thread class that makes it simple to construct programs using these powerful techniques.
- **Robust and secure**. Java is a robust language in its many safeguards to ensure reliable code. First, there is no Java preprocessor or operator overloading, which often lend themselves to programmer error on large projects. In Java, the program will execute just as it is written without worry that a variable is defined to mean something else. Second, Java has strict compile time and runtime checking for the proper use of the type system. Third, Java programmers are free from the numerous memory bugs that haunt C and C++ programmers because Java is a garbage-collected language. Java garbage collection frees the programmer from worrying about explicitly de-allocating memory. Also, since there are no pointers in Java, array overruns and memory overwrites are impossible. The portable nature of Java programs has opened an entire new area of development: applets in Web pages. Up until now, the World Wide Web was composed of client browsers automatically downloading static text and images from Web servers around the globe. The portable and secure nature of the Java bytecodes, combined with Java-powered browsers, enable a new level of interactivity on the World Wide Web by allowing Java programs to be transported over the Internet and executed on the client browser. The "automatic downloading" of programs across the unsecure Internet made security a very high priority for the Java development team. That is why the Java interpreter and environment were designed with numerous security features built in. The key security features are: First, computer memory is not directly accessible by any Java program. Memory layout decisions for the program are postponed until run time. Second, all bytecodes are verified for accuracy and tested for security violations. Third, the class loader always checks for local classes first and thereby protects against "class spoofing." Lastly Java's Security Manager class allows users to set the level of access (and therefore protection) for their systems.

Java the platform has the following key characteristics:

- **Architecture neutral, portable, and interpreted**. Java was designed to thrive in a heterogeneous, networked environment. Java applications will run on multiple hardware systems and operating systems. JavaSoft produces runtime environments for Solaris, Windows NT, Windows 95, and the Mac OS. Ports also exist for AIX, HP-UX, IRIX, and LINUX (and every other major operating system not mentioned here). How does Java accomplish this? The answer is architecture-neutral bytecodes and the Java interpreter. The Java compiler translates Java code into an intermediate format called bytecodes. This format is very compact and can easily be transported efficiently to multiple hardware and software platforms. These bytecodes are then verified and executed by the Java interpreter. The best way to think about the Java interpreter is as a virtual machine that represents a "generic computer." The portability of Java is one of its most exciting features. The ability to take a Java program written on a Solaris workstation and run it unmodified on a Macintosh or a Windows PC has enormous potential. This portability even extends to the Graphical User Interface which has long been the bane of crossplatform development. As you'll discover, throughout this book, the wealth of the Java environment (i.e., file I/O, system functionality. Abstract Window Toolkit, networking classes . . .), you will be excited at the potential of all that power being portable. With the release of the Java Foundation Classes, JavaSoft has achieved its goal of making a state-of-the-art interface full cross platform. Java programmers do not have to sacrifice a sophisticated interface to achieve "write once, run anywhere."

- **Extensible to incorporate legacy code**. The Java Virtual Machine can be extended to load native shared libraries and call native methods (methods written in non-Java languages). This allows you to preserve your investment in existing source code bases while making the transition to cross-platform, dynamic and distributed object-oriented programming via Java. We demonstrate linking to C and C++ using the Java Native Interface (JNI) mechanism.
- **High performance**. Although most interpreted languages are much slower than compiled languages, Java maintains a high level of performance using many techniques. First, the Java language supports multithreading at the language level that improves the interactivity and response of applications performing multiple, simultaneous tasks. Second, much effort and a special patented algorithm (performed instruction replacement to "quick" instructions after an initial pass) made the original Java interpreter run faster than most previous interpreters. Third, applications requiring even more speed have the option of rewriting computer-intensive portions of the code in a native language like C. Fourth, there currently exists "just-in-time" compilers (JITs) for all major platforms that translate the architecture-neutral bytecodes into machine code at run time. Lastly, the "hotspot" virtual machine will use runtime optimization techniques that will eliminate the need for JITs and native code. JavaSoft's goal is to make the interpreter as fast, or faster, than statically compiled executables.

One key characteristic of both the language and platform that must be stressed:

- **Strategic**. It is my belief that Java represents a milestone in the evolution of programming languages. It is evolution without forced compatibility, which is true progress. It takes the best of what we know about object-oriented programming. It takes a bold step in putting reliability and robustness above "nifty features."

Because of these reasons and all the characteristics just listed, Java will achieve phenomenal acceptance and growth. Part of this fantastic growth will be fueled by Java's role as the first and premier application language of the World Wide Web. But this will not be the only use for Java. Java will also soon become the premiere language for standalone applications. In essence, Java is the successor to C and C++.

WHY IS JAVA 1.2 SIGNIFICANT?

The Java Development Kit 1.2 is the fastest, most stable and feature-complete Java platform ever released. This is the release that will move Java from pilot projects into mainstream corporate development. This is also the release where the tool vendors and browser vendors have caught up to JavaSoft so that all the major industry players support the same version of the platform. For JavaSoft, this release marks a point in the history of Java where they were able to move away from furious functionality development to concentrate on the quality of the product. JavaSoft plans to continue this trend by slowing down the release of new versions of the platform to one per year. This is good news for vendors and developers trying to adjust to this new technology.

Some of the key features of Java 1.2 are:

- **JavaBeans™ Components**. Robust software component model for Java. This model makes it simple to reuse Java objects in a graphical, drag-and-drop application builder. Chapter 11 covers this exciting new feature.
- **CORBA Integration**. The Common Object Request Broker architecture (CORBA) is a standard for interconnecting objects written in different languages across a heterogenous network. You can now integrate your Java objects with all other CORBA objects. Chapter 13 demonstrates this.
- **Enhanced Security**. Java has support for digital signatures, message digests, encryption, and access control lists. Chapter 17 demonstrates this.
- **Server-side Java**. An optional extension to the Java platform enables you to replace Common Gateway Interface (CGI) programs with server-side Java objects called servlets. Chapter 20 demonstrates this.
- **Java Media**. You can now integrate time-based media like audio and video into your Java applications! Chapter 21 shows you how.
- **Java Foundation Classes**. JavaSoft has created a new paradigm for cross-platform user interface development: pluggable look and feel. This robust set of user interface components will give your applications a sophisticated look and feel with support for tree controls, toolbars, sliders, tabbed panels, styled text editing, and much more! Chapter 23 covers this.

This Java platform is the one that you, and your company, can feel confident supporting. The platform is feature rich and stable. The development tools are plentiful and refined. Lastly, a software component industry focused around JavaBeans is available to speed your project development by integrating prebuilt components.

WHAT IS JAVASCRIPT?

JavaScript is a standard cross-browser scripting language. The basic idea is that all the functionality of a browser is scriptable, and all content within a browser is manipulable by scripts. JavaScript is a good glue language between applets, plugins, and HTML content.

The World Wide Web and the browsers that navigate it have been and continue to be the killer application of the 1990s. The newly released MacOS 8 was shipped with both major browsers bundled with the operating system. Since browsers have taken such a prominent place on the desktop, JavaScript has become increasingly important. For the near future, browsers and the World Wide Web will continue to dominate the desktop. JavaScript will continue to be a good vehicle to program new browser features like push content, cascading style sheets, new mime types and the resulting new plugins, and the eXtensible Markup Language (XML).

Once you learn Java, JavaScript will be familiar to you, which is the approach we take to teaching the new language. You learn Java first since JavaScript is derived from Java. Many of the keywords and most of the operators are identical. Then you learn how to integrate the two. How to call Java from JavaScript and JavaScript functions from Java applets.

ORGANIZATION OF THIS BOOK

This book is designed to teach the Java language and runtime environment to C and C++ programmers by revealing the language as an evolutionary step up from C and C++. This approach builds on your existing base of knowledge to rapidly have you coding nontrivial Java programs. The goal of this book is to be both a transition book and the premiere Java tutorial; the book you turn to first and then repeatedly until the pages are dog-eared and smudged from use.

This book is divided into four major parts:

- Part 1 focuses on explaining and demonstrating all of the language features; how those features compare to C and C++; and what other OOP languages influenced those features. We start with an introduction, compare Java to ANSI C, compare Java to C++, learn features not shared with C or C++, and learn how to interface Java to existing C and C++ code.
- Part 2 covers the Java equivalent of the C and C++ Standard Library, which is inseparable from any discussion of C and C++. this is the largest part of the book in that it covers every package in the Java Development Kit. This part includes Chapter 6 to Chapter 24.
- Part 3 compares JavaScript to Java. Here you learn the fundamentals of JavaScript. We then devote a chapter to how to interface Java and JavaScript using Netscape's LiveConnect.
- Part 4, the shortest part, is on style and reference. Here we present coding conventions and references of glossary terms, keywords, and resources on the Internet. This part resides only on the CD-ROM.

The style of text and code in this book has been refined over the last decade. It has received much praise from the programming community. The commitment to a conversational, non-stuffy tone, insightful diagrams and complete, working and nontrivial examples has been carried out throughout this book.

WHY A POINTER EXPERT CHOSE JAVA

At first glance it seems strange for someone who has published two books on pointers and dynamic memory management to be writing about a language that has not pointers and is garbage collected[1]; however, it is precisely because I understand pointers and dynamic memory that I deliberately chose to program and teach the Java language. Pointers can be wonderfully elegant and expressive tools; however, that elegance has a very high price. In fact, the countless number of buggy C and C++ applications stresses the fact that the price of those complex features is just too high.

The Java language sacrifices nothing. In these pages you will learn that the huge gains of this simple and robust object-oriented language and environment far outweigh the few features removed from C and C++. In fact, I will show you how to implement the same powerful techniques I highlighted in my first two books in the Java language.

As a practicing programmer, I have worked hard at providing code examples that are exciting, reusable, and nontrivial. I write a Java column for the Library of Computer and Information Science book clubs an the Small Computer Book clubs that focuses on real-world uses for Java. the column is called "Java from the trenches." This is not an academic exercise for me. I am building real-world systems using Java and JavaScript and therefore practice what I preach. It is in this spirit that I present every complete and nontrivial program in this book. A few examples are:

- An implementation of the dining philosopher's problem to demonstrate deadlock in threads.
- A drawing program that demonstrates selectable and resizable drawing objects (i.e., squares). This example uses double-buffered animation, popup menus, and printing.
- A Dvorak keyboard tutorial that demonstrates dirty rectangle animation.
- A greyscale image tester.
- A robot war simulation that dynamically loads any number of robot participants.
- A bank simulation where each simulation entity runs in its own thread.
- A JavaBean that displays both text and images from a Web address (Uniform Resource Locator).
- A custom layout manager.
- A search applet that communicates with search server on the host it is downloaded from.

---

[1]Garbage collection is a language technique that eliminates the need for memory management by periodically reclaiming unused memory.

- A Remote Method Invocation (RMI)-based Web page visit counter.
- An online book service servlet and Web site example that makes extensive use of Java Database Connectivity (JDBC).
- And lots more; the book and CD-ROM are jam-packed with over 200 source code files!

We believe you will find these examples exciting, challenging, and useful in your development projects!

INVITED COMMENTS

This book is written *by* a programmer *for* programmers. All comments, suggestions, and questions from the entire computing community are greatly appreciated. I can be reached electronically:

America Online: MikeDacon@aol.com
Internet: mdaconta@mystech.com

Or you can write to:

Michael Daconta
c/o Robert Elliott
John Wiley & Sons, Inc.
605 Third Avenue
New York, NY 10158

Best wishes,

Michael C. Daconta
Bealeton, VA

CHAPTER 1

Introduction to Java

Reality isn't static anymore. It's not a set of ideas you have to either fight or resign yourself to. It's made up, in part, of ideas that are expected to grow as you grow, and as we all grow, century after century.

—Robert M. Pirsig, *Zen and the Art of Motorcycle Maintenance*

OBJECTIVE

This chapter will give you a tutorial introduction to the Java language. This chapter is not meant to explain all of the concepts presented—that will be done in following chapters. Instead, this chapter gives you a "feel" for the language and its potential. We will close the chapter with an examination of Sun Microsystems' Java Development Kit (JDK) 1.2.

We will begin in the same manner as Brian Kernighan and Dennis Ritchie in their landmark book, *The C Programming Language*. "The only way to learn a new programming language is by writing programs in it. The first program to write is the same for all languages: Print the words "Hello, World."[1] Source 1.1 lists the program.

[1]Brian W. Kernighan and Dennis Ritchie, *The C Programming Language*, (Englewood Cliffs, N.J.: Prentice Hall, 1988), p. 5.

SOURCE 1.1 HelloWorld.java

```
class HelloWorld
{
     public static void main(String args[])
     {
       System.out.println("Hello, World.");
     }
}
```

Let's dissect the program line by line and thereby slowly begin wading into this new language.

Line 1: `class HelloWorld`

This is a class declaration, which is an object-oriented construct. A class declaration defines a template for an object. By this, I mean that an object is an instantiated class or, in more C terms, a variable definition for a class. Java is a pure object-oriented language so everything must be inside an object. In this simple program, we are just wrapping an object around the main function. C programmers should not be overly concerned about objects. In general they are just more powerful structures. Figure 1.1 shows the key characteristic of a class: the combining together (also called encapsulation) of data and the functions that act on that data. We will go into classes in great detail in Chapter 3.

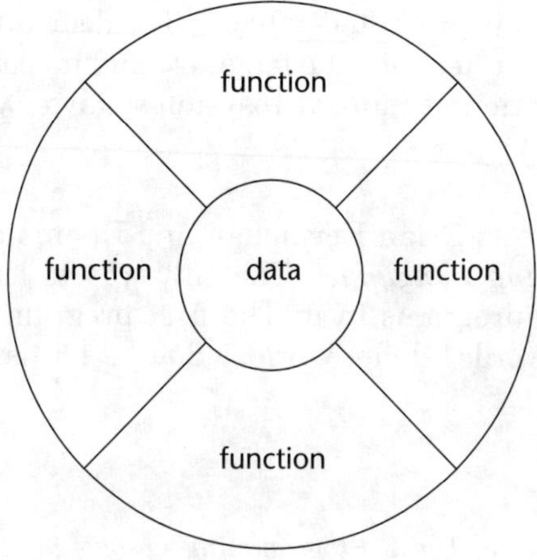

FIGURE 1.1 An object.

Line 2: `{`

Line 2 is identical to the C/C++ braces to begin a block of code. This, of course, is familiar to both C and C++ programmers.

Line 3: `public static void main(String args[])`

Line 3 is conceptually identical to the C/C++ main() function. The differences are the modifiers (public, static) and the String class array for the command line arguments. The public modifier is an access modifier that declares this function as unprotected and open to all other classes. The public modifier behaves the same as the C++ public modifier. The static modifier declares this function as being part of the entire class and not part of objects of the class. This is also a feature of C++. As you can see, the arguments to main are slightly different than in ANSI C; however, they are functionally equivalent. String is a class in Java that implements immutable (non-changing) strings. C programmers can think of a class as wrapping a whole slew of utility functions around a common data structure. This is the case with the String class. So, in Java the command line arguments come to us in an array of strings. We will discuss arrays in Java in the next chapter.

Line 5: `System.out.println("Hello World.");`

Line 5 is the Java equivalent of a printf(). Remember, since Java is object oriented, every function must be part of an object (called an object's method). The function println() is a function (also called a method) of the out object, which is similar to stdout. The out object is a data member of the System object. Thus the concatenation of System.out.println(). The dot operator (.) separating elements in the class is familiar to C/C++ programmers because it is identical to how structure or class elements are accessed.

Now that we have typed the "Hello, World" program into a text file, let's review the process of compiling and running the program. You compile the program into architecture-neutral bytecodes by using the Java compiler (named javac):

```
javac <filename>
```

which for the "Hello, World" program is:

```
javac HelloWorld.java
```

The Java compiler produces one file for every class. The compiler names the file <classname>.class. The file contains the bytecodes for that class. A detailed specification of the Java class file format can be found in *The Java Virtual Machine Specification*, published by Addison Wesley. The Java interpreter (named java) executes the bytecodes. You run the interpreter on the class you just compiled like this:

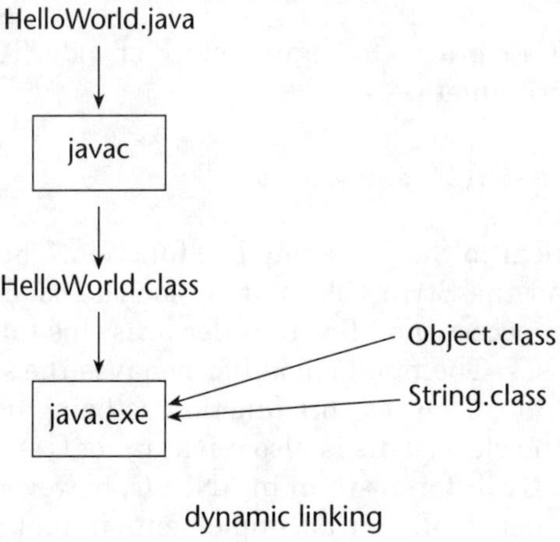

FIGURE 1.2 Compiling HelloWorld.

```
java <classname>
```

which for the HelloWorld class is:

```
java HelloWorld
```

When this is typed the console displays:

```
Hello, World.
```

Figure 1.2 visually depicts the process just described. How the virtual machine performs dynamic linking will be described later in Section 1.4. Detailed information on installing and setting up the Java Development Kit (JDK) 1.2 is found in Section 1.5. Before you compile and run HelloWorld yourself, you will need to read that section and install the JDK. Now let's move on to how familiar Java is to C/C++ programmers.

1.1 INSTANT RECOGNITION

One of the recurring themes you will see pop up in this book is that Java is "familiar" to C and C++ programmers. This will be even more apparent as we compare Java to ANSI C in the next chapter. For now, let's look at a simple program coded in both C and Java. Source 1.2 is a C implementation of that old high-school bus song, "99 Bottles of Beer on the Wall."

SOURCE 1.2 bottles.c

```
/* 99 bottles of beer */
#include <stdio.h>
#include <stdlib.h>

void main(int argc, char *argv[])
{
     int i=0;

     for (i=99; i > 0; i–)
     {
          printf("%d bottles of beer on the wall,\n",i);
          printf("%d bottles of beer.\n",i);
          printf("If one of those bottles should happen to fall,\n");
          printf("%d bottles of beer on the wall.\n", i-1);
     }
}
```

The output of this program is:

```
99 bottles of beer on the wall,
99 bottles of beer.
If one of those bottles should happen to fall,
98 bottles of beer on the wall.
98 bottles of beer on the wall,
98 bottles of beer.
If one of those bottles should happen to fall,
97 bottles of beer on the wall.
...
If one of those bottles should happen to fall,
1 bottles of beer on the wall.
1 bottles of beer on the wall,
1 bottles of beer.
If one of those bottles should happen to fall,
0 bottles of beer on the wall.
```

Source 1.3 is the Java version of the same program. Although the program only has a few constructs like the main function, variable declaration, for loop and output, each one of those constructs is nearly identical in C and Java.

The only significant difference between the C and Java versions is the Java method used to output strings to the console. The Java function System.out.println() outputs a Java string to the console. Java strings are different from C strings, as discussed in detail in Chapter 2. Let's briefly dissect one of the output statements:

```
System.out.println(i + " bottles of beer on the wall,");
```

SOURCE 1.3 bottles.java

```
/* 99 bottles of beer */

class bottles
{
    public static void main(String args[])
    {
        int i=0;

        for (i=99; i > 0; i–)
        {
            System.out.println(i + " bottles of beer on the wall,");
            System.out.println(i + " bottles of beer.");
            System.out.println(
                "If one of the bottles should happen to fall,");
            System.out.println(i-1 + " bottles of beer on the wall.");
        }
    }
}
```

There are two important points to note about the preceding statement:

1. The integer i is automatically converted to a string.
2. The Java compiler overloads the + operator to allow concatenation of Java strings. This is the only operator overloaded in Java, and it is not overloaded by the programmer but as part of the language specification. So the result of the two actions shown is the creation of two strings, and the concatenation of those two strings into a single Java string that is then output to the console.

C programmers will find it very straightforward to port their favorite utilities and programs to Java. Secondly, C and C++ programmers will find that their learning curve in this language is very short, on the order of a few days to begin programming nontrivial applications.

1.2 OBJECT ORIENTED

Java is a pure object-oriented language. This means that everything in a Java program is encapsulated in objects, and all objects are descended from a single Object class. Let's now look at a program that implements and uses objects. As with my previous two books, the source code may be a little long, but I feel it is better to have meaningful examples that you can reuse in your code. Also, I always include a full running program and never just a "snippet of code." Our example program will be the start of a personal book inventory program. Like all object-oriented programs, the program is focused around a number of objects that communicate and perform actions. In our book inventory program we will have three objects: a book, a bookshelf, and a wrapper object for the main() function called bookMain. It is pretty clear that we are trying to model our program after real-world objects that you find in the home. This is the key power of object-oriented programs. Of course, you need to complete the analogy by making your object behave as closely as possible to the real-world object. Source 1.4 demonstrates my implementation of a book object. C++ programmers will be very

SOURCE 1.4 book.java

```
// book.java
import java.io.InputStreamReader;
import java.io.BufferedReader;
import java.io.IOException;

/**
 *  A class that represents a single book.
 *  @version 1.1
 *  @author Michael C. Daconta
 */
public class book
{
    /** Title of the book. */
    protected String title;

    /** Author of the book. */
    protected String author;

    /** Publisher of the book. */
    protected String publisher;

    /** A reference to the next book object in the list. */
    book next;

    /**
     * Constructor to create an "empty" book.
     * Class data members initialized by JVM.
     */
    public book() { }

    /**
     * A constructor to create a new book given title, author, and
     * publisher.
     */
    public book(String aTitle, String anAuthor, String aPublisher)
    {
        title = aTitle;
        author = anAuthor;
        publisher = aPublisher;
    }

    /**
     * This method prompts the user for the information necessary
     * for a valid book object.
     */
```

```
    public void getBook()
    {
        try
        {
            InputStreamReader isr = new InputStreamReader(System.in);
            BufferedReader br = new BufferedReader(isr);
            System.out.print("Enter title    : ");
            System.out.flush();
            title = br.readLine();
            if (title.equals("done"))
                return;
            System.out.print("Enter author   : ");
            System.out.flush();
            author = br.readLine();
            System.out.print("Enter publisher: ");
            System.out.flush();
            publisher = br.readLine();
        } catch (IOException ioe)
          {
            System.out.println(ioe.toString());
            System.out.println("Unable to get the book data.");
            return;
          }
    }

    /**
     * A method to display the contents of a book object.
     */
    void showBook()
    {
        System.out.println("Title    : " + title);
        System.out.println("Author   : " + author);
        System.out.println("Publisher: " + publisher);
    }

    /** Accessor method to get the title. */
    String getTitle() { return title; }

    /** Accessor method to get the author. */
    String getAuthor() { return author; }

    /** Accessor method to get the publisher. */
    String getPublisher() { return publisher; }

    /** Mutator method to set the title. */
    void setTitle(String aTitle) { title = aTitle; }

    /** Mutator method to set the author. */
    void setAuthor(String anAuthor) { author = anAuthor; }

    /** Mutator method to set the publisher. */
    void setPublisher(String aPublisher) { publisher = aPublisher; }
}
```

familiar with the class construct, constructors, and methods. C++ programmers will also note the lack of a destructor. This is a side effect of garbage collection, which we will discuss more in Chapter 2.

The only readily noticeable difference is the new comment form that begins with a slash and two asterisks:

```
/** This is a javadoc comment. */
```

This new comment form is used to automatically generate Hyper-text markup language (HTML) documents on the source by running a program called javadoc.exe. We will discuss javadoc in detail in Section 1.5.

The bookshelf class is an example of a container class. Source 1.5 contains the implementation of the bookshelf. This is actually a very important example in that it highlights a key difference between Java and C++. It demonstrates how Java can create self-referential data structures (linked lists, trees, etc.) with references instead of pointers. This will be explained in detail in the section on data types in the next chapter; however, for now suffice it to say that Java uses object references, which are essentially pointers without pointer arithmetic. C++ programmers should see the detailed discussion in Chapter 3 comparing Java object references to C++ references.

The main() function is again wrapped in its own class. Source 1.6 is the implementation. The main function processes the input from the user and creates our linked list of books on our bookshelf. We then print the list and exit.

Here is a run of the bookMain program:

```
Enter your books.
Type 'done' when finished.
Enter title    : Jonathan Livingston Seagull
Enter author   : Richard Bach
Enter publisher: Avon
Enter title    : The Grapes of Wrath
Enter author   : John Steinbeck
Enter publisher: Bantam
Enter title    : done
Number of books in bookshelf: 2
Book: 1
Title    : Jonathan Livingston Seagull
Author   : Richard Bach
Publisher: Avon
Book: 2
Title    : The Grapes of Wrath
Author   : John Steinbeck
Publisher: Bantam
```

We have already seen some of the built-in classes like System.out.println() in the preceding programs; however, there are hundreds of classes in the Java Class Libraries. The next program demonstrates some of them.

SOURCE 1.5 bookShelf.java

```
// bookShelf.java
import book;

/**
 * Class which represents a bookshelf and stores books in a singly
 * linked list.
 * @version 1.1
 * @author Michael C. Daconta
 */
public class bookShelf
{
    /** Reference to first and last book objects. */
    protected book first,last;

    /** Count of books in bookShelf. */
    protected long count;

    /** Method to add a book object to the list. */
    public void add(book aBook)
    {
        if (first != null)
        {
            last.next = aBook;
            last = last.next;
        }
        else
        {
            first = aBook;
            last = first;
        }
        count++;
    }

    /** Method to get the size of the linked list. */
    public long size() { return count; }

    /** Method to print all books in the bookShelf. */
    public void print()
    {
        book curBook = first;
        int cnt=1;

        while (curBook != null)
        {
            System.out.println("Book: " + cnt++);
            curBook.showBook();
            curBook = curBook.next;
        }
    }
}
```

SOURCE 1.6 bookMain.java

```
// bookMain.java
import book;
import bookShelf;

/**
 * Wrapper class for main() method.
 * @version 1.1
 * @author Michael C. Daconta
 */
public class bookMain
{
    /**
     * main method to create a bookShelf object and fill it
     * with book objects.
     */
    public static void main(String args[])
    {
        bookShelf mybooks = new bookShelf();
        boolean done = false;

        System.out.println("Enter your books.");
        System.out.println("Type 'done' when finished.");
        while (!done)
        {
            book curBook = new book();
            curBook.getBook();
            if (!(curBook.getTitle()).equals("done"))
                mybooks.add(curBook);
            else
                done = true;
        }

        System.out.println("Number of books in bookshelf: " +
                           mybooks.size());
        mybooks.print();
    }
}
```

1.3 THE JAVA CLASS LIBRARIES

The current version of the Java Class Libraries (functionally equivalent to the C and C++ Standard Libraries) includes hundreds of classes and methods in twelve major functional areas. All of these are covered in great detail in Part 2, "The Java Packages."

- **Language Support.** A collection of classes and methods that support the robust language features in Java like strings, arrays, system-dependent functionality, threads, and exceptions. Chapter 6 covers this package (called lang).

- **Utilities.** A collection of classes to provide utility functions like random number generation, date and time functions, and storage classes like a Vector and Hashtable class. Source 1.7 demonstrates the use of the Vector class. Chapter 7 covers this package (called util).
- **Input/output.** A collection of classes to get input from multiple sources and manipulate that input in numerous ways as well as output to multiple sources and in varying ways. The classes include filter classes, sequential and random access to files, and dozens of methods to read and write data of all types. Chapter 8 covers this package (called io).
- **Networking.** A collection of classes to connect to other computers over either a local network or the Internet. Classes include Socket, InternetAddress, and URL (Uniform Resource Locator) processing. Chapter 9 covers this package (called net).
- **Abstract Window Toolkit (AWT).** A collection of classes that implements a platform-independent graphical user interface. Source 1.7 demonstrates the use of some of the AWT classes. Chapter 10 is dedicated entirely to the abstract window toolkit. Chapter 10 covers this package (called awt).
- **Java Beans.** A collection of classes to create reusable components suitable for a drag-and-drop application builder. Chapter 11 covers this package (called beans).
- **Applet.** A class that allows you to create a Java program that can be downloaded from a Web page and run on a client browser like HotJava, Netscape, and Internet Explorer. Chapter 12 covers this package (called applet).
- **Math.** Two classes that support numbers of any size. Chapter 15 covers this package (called math).
- **Remote Method Invocation (RMI).** A collection of classes that provide a remote procedure call mechanism in Java. This is a form of distributed computing. Chapter 16 covers this package (called rmi).
- **Security.** A collection of classes that provide security features for applets and applications. Allows digital signing of applets, creation of digital signatures, encryption of content, and access control lists. Chapter 17 covers this package (called security).
- **Structured Query Language (SQL).** A set of classes that support database access from Java. Chapter 18 covers this package (called sql).
- **Text.** A set of classes that perform formatting of text and storage of program resources. Chapter 19 covers this package (called text).

Source 1.7 is based on the same principles as the bookShelf class shown earlier with two important differences: First, we present a graphical user interface to input, display, and browse the books; second, instead of storing the books in a linked list, we store the books in a Vector. A Vector is a dynamic, growable array.

A run of Source 1.7 produces the output shown in Figure 1.3.

The key points to note about Source 1.7 involve understanding the basics of the AWT classes and the Vector class. The purpose of the program is to display a window that lets you both enter and display records that are stored in the Vector class. Instead of giving a detailed explanation of the classes and all their methods (which is done in great detail later), let's walk through the required functionality and point out how it is implemented.

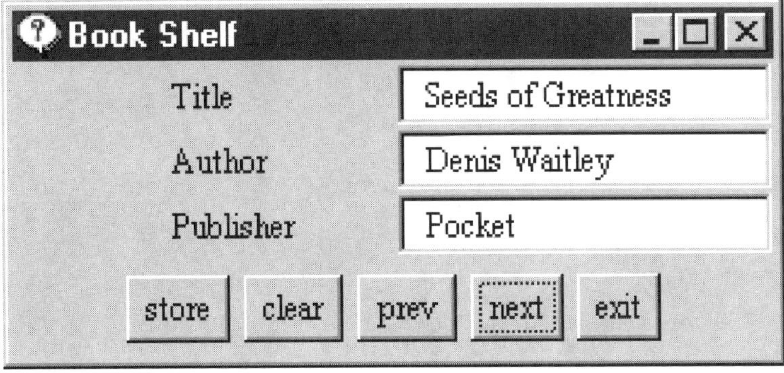

FIGURE 1.3 A graphical bookshelf.

SOURCE 1.7 bookWindow.java

```
// bookWindow.java

// import the Graphical User Interface (GUI) classes
import java.awt.*;
import java.awt.event.*;

// our book class
import book;

// a utility class
import java.util.Vector;

/**
 * Class to implement a graphical window into a
 * bookshelf.
 * @version 1.2
 * @author Michael C. Daconta
 */
public class bookWindow extends Frame implements ActionListener
{
    /** book title. */
    TextField title;
    /** author of the book. */
    TextField author;
    /** publisher of the book. */
    TextField publisher;
    /** book store. */
    Vector theBooks;
    /** current index. */
    int iCurrentIdx;
```

```
/** bookWindow constructor. */
public bookWindow()
{
    super("Book Shelf");
    setLayout(new BorderLayout());

    // initialize the growable array
    theBooks = new Vector(3);
    iCurrentIdx = 0;

    Panel centerPanel = new Panel();
    centerPanel.setLayout(new GridLayout(0, 2));

    centerPanel.add(new Label("Title"));
    centerPanel.add(title = new TextField(20));

    centerPanel.add(new Label("Author"));
    centerPanel.add(author = new TextField(20));

    centerPanel.add(new Label("Publisher"));
    centerPanel.add(publisher = new TextField(20));

    add("Center", centerPanel);

    Panel bottomPanel = new Panel();
    bottomPanel.setLayout(new FlowLayout());
    // create buttons
    Button b1 = new Button("store");
    b1.addActionListener(this);
    Button b2 = new Button("clear");
    b2.addActionListener(this);
    Button b3 = new Button("prev");
    b3.addActionListener(this);
    Button b4 = new Button("next");
    b4.addActionListener(this);
    Button b5 = new Button("exit");
    b5.addActionListener(this);
    bottomPanel.add(b1);
    bottomPanel.add(b2);
    bottomPanel.add(b3);
    bottomPanel.add(b4);
    bottomPanel.add(b5);
    add("South", bottomPanel);

    setLocation(200, 100);
    pack();
    setVisible(true);
} // end of constructor

/** necessary to implement ActionListener. */
public void actionPerformed(ActionEvent evt)
```

```
    {
        String command = evt.getActionCommand();
        if ("store".equals(command))
        {
            book aBook = new book(title.getText(),
                                  author.getText(),
                                  publisher.getText());

            theBooks.addElement(aBook);
            iCurrentIdx = theBooks.size();
            title.setText("");
            author.setText("");
            publisher.setText("");
        }
        else if ("clear".equals(command))
        {
            title.setText("");
            author.setText("");
            publisher.setText("");
        }
        else if ("prev".equals(command))
        {
            if (iCurrentIdx > 0)
            {
                    book aBook = (book) theBooks.elementAt(–iCurrentIdx);
                    title.setText(aBook.getTitle());
                    author.setText(aBook.getAuthor());
                    publisher.setText(aBook.getPublisher());
            }
        }
        else if ("next".equals(command))
        {
            if (iCurrentIdx < (theBooks.size()-1))
            {
                    book aBook = (book) theBooks.elementAt(++iCurrentIdx);
                    title.setText(aBook.getTitle());
                    author.setText(aBook.getAuthor());
                    publisher.setText(aBook.getPublisher());
            }
        }
        else if ("exit".equals(command))
        {
            System.exit(0);
        }
    } // end of actionPerformed

    /** main method to invoke from JVM. */
    public static void main(String args[])
    {
        new bookWindow();
    }
}
```

All functionality is from the graphical user interface, which is why the main function of Source 1.7 only contains the constructor for the bookWindow(). The bookWindow class extends the Frame class (extends is the keyword for inheritance, which is discussed in detail in Chapter 3). The Frame class is a GUI component that implements a Window with a border. A Window is not only four corner points with a border. It is also a container that can hold other graphical user interface components (widgets to X programmers). We therefore need to create the rest of our graphical components and add them to the Frame with the add() method. You will notice that we also add something called a panel. Panels are used to group graphical components together. You use panels to break up your window into functional parts. Source 1.7 uses two panels, one to hold the record information and one to hold and lay out the buttons. The "center" panel uses a special layout called a grid layout. A grid layout allows you to create a matrix of rows and columns that form equal size cells in which to place a graphical component. We place the field label in one component (i.e., Title, Author, etc.) and a text field in the adjacent cell of our grid. A text field is a graphical component that implements an editable text string. Once we have added all the components, we can move the window to where we want and size the window using either width and height or the pack() method, which sizes the window the minimum size to display all the components. Last, we call the setVisible() method to display the window and all its components.

All graphical user interfaces are programmed using the event-driven programming model. This model structures a program as a series of event handlers that respond to events triggered by the user (i.e., mouse moves, button push, menu choice, etc.).

Java uses a Delegation Event Model to handle event processing. The Delegation Event Model consists of a "source" object and a "listener" object. Events are generated by source objects and received by listener objects. Source objects are AWT components that are capable of generating AWT events. Here is a list of all AWT events: ActionEvent, AdjustmentEvent, ComponentEvent, ContainerEvent, FocusEvent, InputEvent, ItemEvent, KeyEvent, MouseEvent, PaintEvent, TextEvent, and Window Event. Our GUI is mostly concerned with button pushes, which generate ActionEvents. In order to capture and process these events, we need to send the generated events to a listener object. Using the addActionListener() method we can add listeners to a component. The frame itself is an action listener since it implements the ActionListener interface (we will discuss interfaces in detail in Chapter 4). Therefore, we can write code to handle the button clicks in the actionPerformed() method. This is the method that will be called each time a button is pushed in our GUI. All the main functionality of the program is driven by responding to the button pushes. The Store button stores the current text in the textfields as a book record in the Vector. We use the Vector addElement() method to store a book class. That same record can be retrieved with the elementAt() method by providng the array index of the record. The Clear button clears the text fields. The Next and Prev buttons display the next and previous book object stored in the vector respectively. The Exit button exits the application (which also destroys the window).

As I demonstrated earlier, the Java class libraries provide a rich and robust programming environment that makes it a joy to program in! I think Arthur Van Hoff, one of the key members of the Java development team (and now Chief Technical Officer of Marimba, Inc.), describes this sentiment best in the way he signs off in his e-mail. He always finishes with "Have Fun." We will!

1.4 DEVELOPMENT CYCLES

The development cycle in Java is slightly different than the one in C or C++. In this section we will discuss some of the differences between developing and running programs in C/C++ versus Java. There are three primary areas of divergence:

- Simpler source code management
- Faster development via dynamic linking (versus static)
- No "fragile" superclass problem

Source Code Management

In C and C++ the declaration of a class or function is separated from the actual implementation of the class or function. The declaration portion is put into a header file, and the implementation is placed in a source file. The #include keyword is used to include the header file in the source code. Using the declarations in the header file, the compiler can determine if function calls used in the source code are using the correct parameters. There is not a one-to-one correspondence between header files and source files; in fact, header files can contain multiple class or function declarations (which can be in one or more source files), and source files can include more than one header file.

There are no header files in Java. When you code a Java class, you code only the implementation of the class; there is no separate declaration information. You might be wondering "If there are no header files, how I do reuse existing classes? And if there is no separate declaration information, how will the compiler know if I am using the classes and methods correctly?" The answer to the first question is the import keyword. Using the import keyword you can declare another Java class for use in your own class. Here is an example:

```
import jwiley.chp10.Grid;
```

This particular statement will declare the Grid class contained in the jwiley.chp10 package. Refer to Chapter 4 for more information on packages. Now the Grid class can be used in my class. When I use constructors and methods in the Grid class the compiler will check the Grid.class file to see if I am using the calls properly. Pretty convenient, eh? So the answer to the second question is that the class files themselves contain the necessary information to check constructor and method calls versus the actual implementation. If the Grid.class file does not exist or is older than the Grid.java file, the Java compiler will automatically compile it.

In order to find the Grid class, the CLASSPATH environment variable must be set. This is similar to the INCLUDE and LIB environment variables in C and C++. The CLASSPATH variable contains a list of paths that are checked for class files. Here is an example classpath for Windows 95:

```
CLASSPATH=.;c:\java\classes\classes.zip;c:\myprog\classes
```

The compiler would first check the current directory, then the classes.zip file (contains an archive of class files), and finally the directory c:\myprog\classes looking for the Grid class. Note that since the Grid class is in the jwiley.chp10 package, the Grid class must be located in the jwiley\chp10 subdirectory under one of the specified classpath directories. The compiler will find the Grid class if it is located here:

```
c:\myprog\classes\jwiley\chp10\Grid.class
```

Static versus Dynamic Linking

One thing you will notice right away is that compiling is less complicated in Java. Let's examine Figure 1.4.

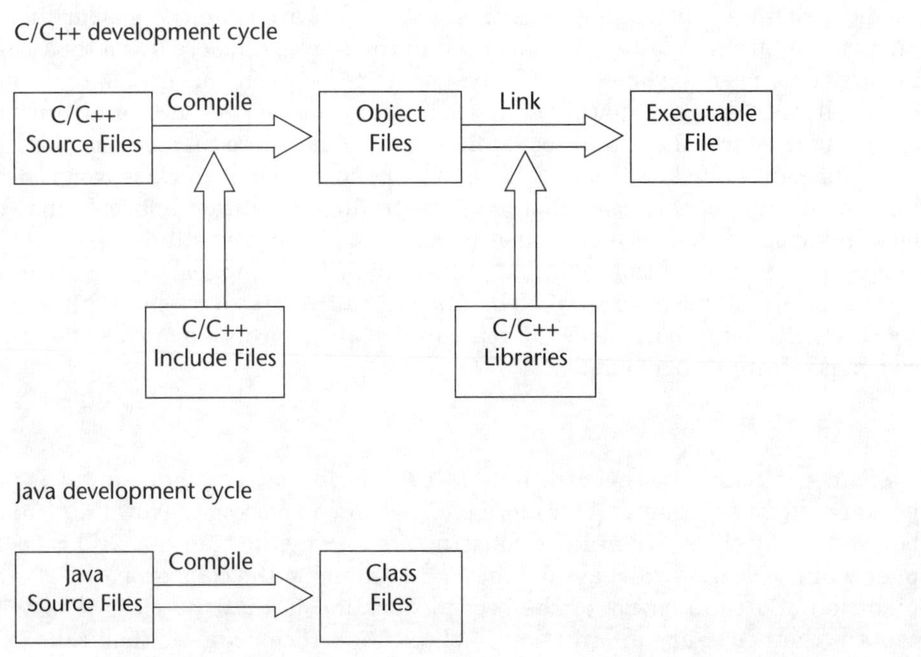

FIGURE 1.4 Compiling source code in Java and C/C++.

As you see in Figure 1.4, both Java and C/C++ have a compilation phase, but Java eliminates static linking. Java eliminates this static linking in favor of dynamic linking by the virtual machine.

In the C/C++ development cycle the source code module is first compiled to an intermediate object file, and then all object files are linked to form an executable file. The executable file itself is a binary file that contains microprocessor-specific instructions. This executable file will only run on the microprocessor it was compiled for, or a compatible one.

In Java, source code modules are compiled to a class file. A class file consists of bytecodes that represent Java Virtual Machine instructions. To run your class file, you must invoke the Java interpreter with your class file as an argument. The Java interpreter, or Java Virtual Machine (JVM), will load the class file and translate the Java bytecodes into operating system calls. Since the JVM acts as an intermediate between the class files and the operating system, your compiled class files will run on any platform that has a JVM.

The link phase in the C/C++ environment takes code from static libraries and includes it in the executable file. In Java there is no link phase to link class files to an executable. Every Java class has a corresponding .class file and is loaded during runtime when it is needed.

TIP In C and C++ all source files are compiled and linked during a build. This ensures that the executable program is concurrent with the source code. In Java it is easy to run into problems caused by outdated class files because the source was not recompiled. Since each source file is compiled independently, there are times when class files do not get updated. An example of this is changing the public methods (known as the "contract") of a super (parent) class that has been subclassed. The class will compile fine, but the subclass will not be recompiled because the superclass does not know it exists. Adding things to a superclass is fine, but if you change or delete things you should make sure you go back and recompile all subclasses.

C and C++ programs are launched in the same manner as other programs for your operating system. In order to run a Java program, the Java Virtual Machine must be invoked. The JVM will look for the following method in your class:

```
public static void main (String args[])
```

If this method is not found, the JVM will print out an error message and exit. This is similar to the main function in C and C++. Command line arguments are passed in using the args[] string array. The argument count can be obtained by checking the args.length variable.

When the Java interpreter encounters a class that has not been loaded into memory, it uses the class loader to load the new class into memory. The class is verified before it is put into use by the JVM. The class loading process is very similar to loading a dynamic link library (Windows) or a shared library (Unix). The difference is that in a C or C++ program the programmer must explicitly load and free the library, but in Java the process of loading classes is automatically handled by the JVM.

The Java interpreter translates the bytecodes contained in the class files into operating-system-specific calls. In a C or C++ program, the executable file already contains the operating system calls and can therefore perform at a much higher speed. But this is a key trade-off—do you need a high-performance program or a program that can be executed on a machine that has a JVM? The speed of executing Java programs is increasing as the technology evolves. Just-in-time (JIT) compilers already exist that perform much faster than just a straight interpretive JVM, and soon compilers that do on-the-fly optimization will be available. Figure 1.5 graphically depicts the Java Virtual Machine and just-in-time compilers.

JIT compilers are available in some JVMs. The way classes are handled is different on a JVM with a JIT as opposed to handling classes on a plain interpretive JVM. When handling classes with a JIT compiler present, the JVM will pass the class files it loads to the JIT. When a method is called in the class the JIT will compile the method into native code. If the same method is called again, the method will run much faster since it can be executed as native code. Even the process of compiling and running the method can be faster than interpreting the method. The JIT compiler gets its "just-in-time" name from doing this compilation in response to a method call during runtime. The speed improvements vary depending on your program and the

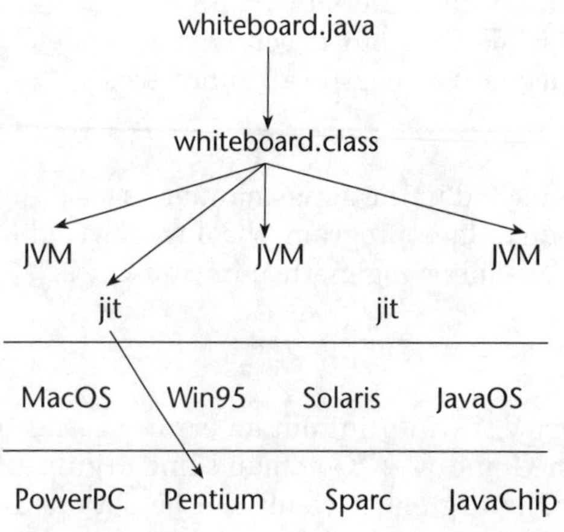

FIGURE 1.5 Running Java programs.

JIT you are using, but some JITs claim performance improvements of up to 50 times faster.

No "Fragile" Superclass Problem

In most implementations of C++, any time you change a class you need to recompile all classes that depend on or use that class. That is especially true for superclasses. One reason for this is that the object file produced for the C++ class creates a static table of pointers to methods called a vtable. Since each subclass has its own static table of method pointers, if both the superclass and subclasses are not recompiled, the subclasses could point to incorrect methods in the superclass. Java resolves methods dynamically at runtime instead of statically. This allows greater flexibility to programmers to freely change superclasses as long as you do not break the "contract" that other classes depend upon. By "contract," I am referring to the public data members and methods of a class. We will discuss these object-oriented concepts in detail in Chapter 3.

1.5 THE JAVA DEVELOPMENT KIT (JDK)

The JDK can be freely downloaded from Sun Microsystems' Web site at: http://java.sun.com/products/jdk/.

Installation instructions are also available on the Web site for your particular platform. Please note that the JDK documentation must be downloaded separately from the JDK.

The JDK comes with everything you need to get started as a Java programmer. Before we start looking at the tools, let's go over the environment variables that need to be set:

- **CLASSPATH.** This variable specifies where to look for Java classes during compilation and run time. At a minimum this variable needs to include the path of the Java standard libraries and the path where you will store your classes. The Java libraries will be located in %javaroot%\lib\classes.zip where %javaroot% is the base path of your Java installation.
- **PATH.** In order to run the compiler, the interpreter, and all of the other tools, you must include the %javaroot%\bin path in this variable.

The JDK comes with a rich set of tools that include the compiler, interpreter, debugger, and others. Following is a listing of the tools with a brief description of what they do, and what the key parameters are for the tool. A complete description of the tools can be found in the JDK documentation.

javac

```
javac [options] filename.java ...
```

This is the Java compiler. Javac will compile a .java file (Java source) into a .class file (Java class). Multiple source files can be specified on the command line. You can also use wildcards with the javac command. To compile all the Java files in a directory you could use this statement:

```
javac *.java
```

Some of the most useful parameters are:

- **classpath <path>.** This parameter allows you to specify the classpath on the command line. The specified classpath will override the classpath specified by the system variable CLASSPATH.
- **verbose.** Causes the compiler to print out which class files are being compiled and which ones are being loaded.
- **deprecation.** Causes the compiler to print out deprecation warnings for methods that have been deprecated. Deprecated methods are methods that are still available, but their use is frowned upon.

java

```
java [ options ] classname <args>
```

This is the Java interpreter. Class files that you have compiled that contain a static main method may be run using the Java interpreter. Any command line arguments to your program should be passed after the specified class. Here is an example of running the fictitious PrintArg class.

```
java PrintArg ThisIsTheOnlyArgument
```

In this example one argument is passed in on the command line. Here are some of the key parameters that can be used with Java.

- **classpath <path>.** This parameter allows you to specify the classpath on the command line. The specified classpath will override the classpath specified by the system variable CLASSPATH.
- **prof.** Starts profiling on the Java run time. Results are stored in the java.prof file in the current directory.
- **mx <x>.** Maximum size of the memory allocation pool. This is the amount of memory that can be allocated by this instance of Java. You should increase this if you start running out of memory.
- **verbosegc.** Prints messages to the console whenever the garbage collector runs. It also tells how many objects and bytes were freed.

On Windows platforms, you may find the javaw tool useful. It allows you to run the Java interpreter without creating a console window.

appletviewer

```
appletviewer [ options ] urls ...
```

The appletviewer is used to run Java applets. The url parameter can be a file located in the current directory or it can be a standard URL used to access an HTML page. Here are some examples of using the appletviewer command:

```
appletviewer SearchForm.html
appletviewer
```

The HTML file specified on the command line must contain an APPLET tag.

jdb

```
jdb [ options ]
```

This is the Java debugger. The Java debugger is used to analyze Java source files during run time for errors. The Java debugger is a terminal-based debugger. A list of commands can be listed by typing the help command at the java debugger prompt. You can start the Java debugger by using it to launch a class file, or you can use the debugger to connect to a Java interpreter that is already running. Here is an example of launching the debugger with a class:

```
jdb ClassToDebug
```

javadoc

```
javadoc [ options ] [ package | source.java ]
```

Javadoc is used to document Java source files. A package or a source file must be specified on the command line. Javadoc will generate an HTML file for each Java file, as well as an HTML file for the package; one that includes all documented classes, methods, and variables, and one that generates an object hierarchy.

By default, all public classes, interfaces, methods, and variables are documented by Javadoc. You can also specify your own comments to appear in Javadoc documentation by using the following comment syntax:

```
/**
 *  This is a Javadoc test
 *
 *  @version 1.0
 */
```

The comment is just like a C comment except that it has a double asterisk at the beginning. Having the double asterisk will flag this comment to be included in the Javadoc documentation. Special tags are also available such as the version tag just shown. All of these special tags begin with the @ symbol. In a Javadoc comment you may also include HTML tags. Since the end result will be an HTML file, any HTML tags you specify will be used to format the documentation.

javah

```
javah [ options ] classname. . .
```

This tool is used to create C header files and source files needed to implement native methods. You can use javah on Java source files that contain method declarations with the Java keyword, native. The C header files contain the function declaration for the functions you have to write in C. Here are some of the key parameters:

- **jni.** This will cause javah to create a header file that contains JNI-style function prototypes. JNI stands for Java Native Interface and is the standard way for interfacing Java code to platform-specific code.
- **stubs.** For those of you who implemented native methods in Java 1.0, this parameter is provided for backward compatibility. Stub files are no longer needed if you use JNI, so this parameter should be avoided.

javap

```
javap [ options ] class. . .
```

This tool is used to disassemble Java class files. The output produced depends on which parameters are used. Here are a few of the key parameters:

- **public.** Outputs only public classes and members.
- **protected.** Outputs only protected and public classes and members.
- **package.** Outputs only package, protected, and public classes and members. This is the default.
- **private.** Outputs all classes and members.

jar

```
jar [ options ] [manifest] destination input-file [input-files]
```

This tool is used to combine multiple files into a JAR file, or Java Archive file. The jar tool is useful for combining all files necessary to run an applet or application in a single archive file. The files included in the archive file are compressed using the ZLIB compression library. The JAR file can also include a manifest file, which is used for signing applets. Here is an example of using the jar command:

```
jar cf myarchive.jar *.class
```

This example will create a new JAR file called myarchive.jar and include all class files in the current directory. Here are some of the key parameters:

- **c.** Creates a new or empty archive on standard output. Use this option with the f option to produce an archive file.
- **t.** Lists the table of contents from standard output. Use this option with the f option to list an archive file.
- **f.** Specifies that the second argument is the name of a JAR file to process. If this parameter is used with the c (create) parameter, the specified file will be created. If used with the t (table) or x (extract) parameters, the specified file will be processed.

javakey

```
javakey [ options ]
```

This tool is used to generate digital signatures for use with Java archive files. To use javakey you need to have an understanding of signers, identities, and certificates, as well as private and public key pairs. Refer to Chapter 17 for a discussion of javakey.

rmic

```
rmic [ options ] package-qualified-class-name(s)
```

This tool generates stub and skeleton files for remote objects. Java classes that implement the java.rmi.Remote interface are used to instantiate remote objects. The command shown here will generate the myRemoteClass_Skel.class and the myRemoteClass_Stub.class. Refer to Chapter 16 for more discussion on rmic.

```
rmic myPackage.myRemoteClass
```

rmiregistry

```
rmiregistry [port]
```

This tool creates and starts a remote object registry on the specified port. The registry will start on port 1099 if port is omitted. A remote object registry is a naming service used to bind remote objects to names. Clients can use the registry to lookup remote objects and make remote method invocations. Refer to Chapter 16 for more discussion on rmiregistry.

serialver

```
serialver [ options ]
```

This tool returns the serialVersionUID for one or more classes in a form suitable for copying into an evolving class. The serialVersionUID is used in object serialization to determine if an old class can be used to handle a class that has evolved (i.e., new methods or variables have been added).

native2ascii

```
native2ascii [options] [inputfile [outputfile]]
```

This tool converts native character encodings into Latin-1 or UNICODE characters. In order to use the Java compiler and other tools, files must be encoded using Latin-1 or UNICODE characters. Here are the parameters:

- **reverse.** Causes Latin-1 or UNICODE characters to be converted to a native character encoding.
- **encoding <encoding_name>.** Specifies the encoding to be used to convert the native characters into Latin-1 or UNICODE characters.

1.6 SUMMARY

In this chapter you have received a "taste" of the key aspects of Java: the familiarity of the language, its object-oriented nature, and its rich environment. We have also examined how the Java development cycle is faster and simpler than development in C/C++. And lastly, we examined the development tools found in the Java Development Kit. Now you are ready for a more structured examination of the language in comparison to C and C++.

CHAPTER 2

Comparing Java to ANSI C

When a feature that exists in both Java and ANSI C isn't fully explained in this specification, the feature should be assumed to work as it does in ANSI C.

—*The Draft Java Language Specification*

If you like C, we think you will like Java.

—*The Java Language Specification*

OBJECTIVE

This chapter will compare and contrast the Java language to ANSI C. All major elements of ANSI C will be examined and all differences highlighted.

Comparing Java to ANSI C is important because the constructs that these languages share will make up the lion's share of your code. You will learn that the keywords and operators that Java inherited from ANSI C—particularly the data types, control flow constructs, and all the operators—are the bulk of all your applications. The rest of a Java application is the object-oriented constructs that we will discuss in the next chapter; however, those familiar with object-oriented programming will agree that the OOP constructs are more about the framework and design of a program than the implementation. You can think of the OOP constructs as the skeleton and ANSI C as the organs, muscles, and tendons. So, let's examine those vital organs.

2.1 PROGRAM STRUCTURE

In its simplest form, a Java program contains classes with one or more of those classes implementing a main() method. Each Java source file (also called a compilation unit) may contain one or more Java classes. Java classes must be fully defined within a single source file; a single class cannot span multiple files. Each source file ends with a ".java" suffix. Classes contain data members (data type declarations) and methods (functions that operate on the data members of a class). Class methods contain data type declarations and statements. Source 2.1 is the skeleton of a Java standalone program (the format of an applet is different and will be discussed in Chapter 12).

At first glance, this program structure may not be familiar to a C programmer. This is because a Java program has an object-oriented structure that is more familiar to C++ programmers; however, I will explain these features from a C programmer's viewpoint (in the next chapter we will examine them again from a C++ viewpoint). Let's discuss all the components of the Java skeleton program just shown.

SOURCE 2.1 Skeleton.java

```
// Skeleton.java
package jwiley.chp2;      /* OPTIONAL: these classes may belong to a named
                             package */
import java.util.Vector; /* OPTIONAL: import a single class for use in this
                             class */
import java.net.*;        /* OPTIONAL: import all public classes in a
                             package. */

/* OPTIONAL: an interface is a group of methods */
interface InputOutput{
    void read();
    void write();
}

/* OPTIONAL: multiple classes per file. */
class aCLass
{
    /* data members and methods */
}

class mainClass
{
     public static void main(String args[])
     {
         /* code here executed first by interpreter */
     }
}
```

- **Package statement.** This declares the classes in this compilation unit to be part of a package called jwiley.chp2. A package is a collection of related classes. This means that all the classes in the file actually have the name: jwiley.chp2.<classname>.

  A package name is a hierarchical construct. To be explicit, all the classes in the file belong to the chp2 package that is a subpackage of the jwiley package. The package statement must be the first non-whitespace, non-comment statement in the compilation unit. The benefit of packages is that they allow the namespace of a program to be divided into functional components. This makes it easier to avoid name conflicts when importing third-party classes. As stated in the comment, the package statement is optional because your classes do not have to be part of an explicitly named package. By default, they are part of an unnamed package. Packages are discussed in detail in Chapter 4. The Java compiler implicitly imports all classes that belong to the package of the Java class being compiled.

  All public classes and interfaces in the java.lang package are implicitly and automatically imported. This makes sense because all the classes in the java.lang package are considered part of the Java "language." This is identical to the statement:

  ```
  import java.lang.*;
  ```

  Chapter 6 describes all the classes in the java.lang package.
- **Comments.** Java uses the same comment syntax as ANSI C (/* */); however, Java also uses two additional syntaxes for comments:

  // The C++ style comment for single-line comments.

  /** */ As demonstrated in Section 1.5, this is a special comment form that can precede class declarations, class member declarations, and class method declarations, and is used by javadoc to generate HTML documentation.

- **Import statement.** This is similar to the #include preprocessor statement in C. It is important to understand that the similarity is only in effect and not implementation. In effect, both techniques can bring new type declarations into the scope of your program; however, the implementation differs significantly.

  The #include statement in C instructs the preprocessor to include another file. That second file can contain other preprocessor directives, type declarations, and function prototypes. The import statement declares a public class, its public data members, and methods into the namespace of the compilation unit. The compiler verifies the existence of the class, and will perform syntax checking whenever the class is used, but no inclusion occurs. The class file simply includes these references to the other classes. All classes are dynamically linked at run time. As we will discuss later on, this is the only similarity to the C preprocessor because there is no preprocessor in Java. This sticks to the Java design goal for simplicity. One final point on import is to notice the two methods for importing other classes: an explicit import of a single class or an import of all classes in a package. The latter is called a "type-import-on-demand" declaration. This means that all public types declared in the package will be imported as needed. Import always works on a single class or package; when an entire package is specified, only classes in that package will be imported, not classes in any subpackages. For example, importing the Java package will not import classes in any of the subpackages such as java.net, java.io, java.util, and so forth.

The use of import is never required. As stated previously, a class in a package actually has the name <packages>.<name>. You can always specify a class using its complete name. In some cases, this is advisable because it can resolve ambiguity, such as when two packages both have a class with the same name.

- **Interface declaration.** This is an object-oriented construct that we will discuss in Chapter 4.
- **Class declarations.** You can declare multiple classes within a compilation unit. Classes are the primary and essential component of a Java program. Without at least one class you do not have a Java program. All the other constructs discussed so far are mere supporting characters to the class construct. Although I have shown how it is possible to model your Java programs after C programs, I would not advise this. I believe that object-oriented programming is better than procedural programming and therefore it would behoove you to learn it. We will cover the primary OOP constructs in Java and how they compare to C++ in the next chapter.
- **Main method.** Every Java standalone program requires a main function as its starting point. Although I say "main function," it is actually more technically correct to say "main method." Java does not support separate functions, only class methods. The difference is that a method is a function bound to a class. This is yet another distinction where Java has taken the object-oriented path; however, in this chapter I will still often use the term function because it is more familiar to C programmers. The requirement for a main function is identical to C and C++ programs; however, the precise syntax of a Java main function is slightly different. The Java main function must have this format:

```
public static void main(String args[])
{
    ...
}
```

This is the format the Java compiler looks for to denote the function to execute first and the function that should receive any command-line arguments from the operating system. When main() completes, the program terminates and control passes back to the operating system.

If your program is a multithreaded program, it may not exit upon the completion of the main() method. It would only exit after all non-daemon threads have completed. This is discussed in detail in Chapter 4.

2.2 KEYWORDS AND OPERATORS

To me, the keywords and operators of a language give the computer language its "feel and expressiveness." In this, it is very obvious that Java has retained the "feel and expressiveness" of C. And this is a good thing. Programming in C, although procedural, has a very concise and quick feel to it. As a programmer's language, it has been honed to a fine edge. As we cover the keywords and operators of Java, you will appreciate the fact that Java retains the "feel" of a carefully crafted, concise, and quick programmer's language.

First let's examine the keywords common to both Java and C. Figure 2.1 graphically depicts this.

TIP The keywords const and goto are reserved but not used in Java. They are reserved to provide better error messages.

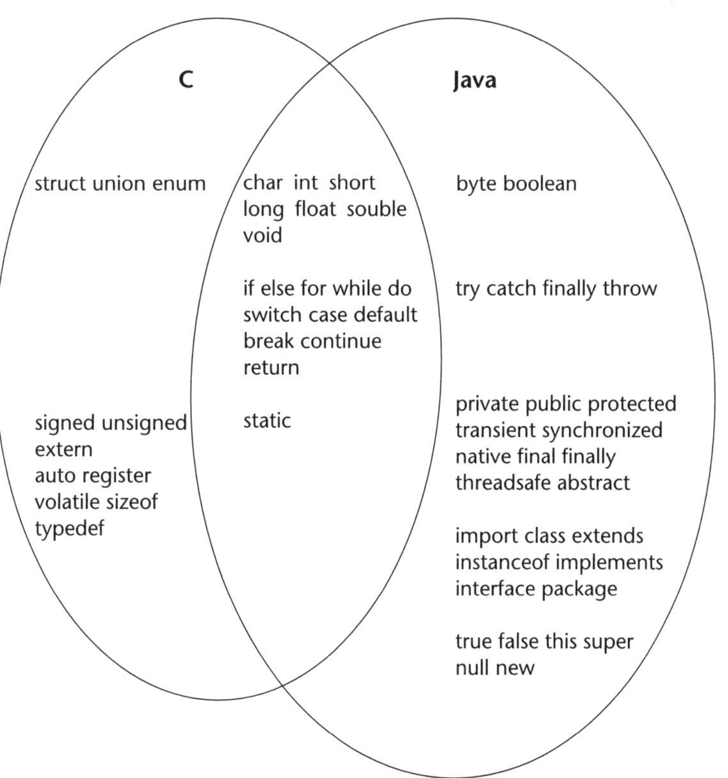

FIGURE 2.1 Common C and Java keywords.

The important item to note about the keywords common to both Java and C is that these are the keywords that make up the bulk of your programming. These keywords, combined with the operators (discussed next), make up the majority of statements that fill your functions. The framework may be object oriented but the implementation is very close to C. A detailed description of all the Java keywords can be found in the Appendix, "The Java Reference." Now let's examine the operators in Java.

Operators are divided into several types: mathematical, relational, logical, and bitwise. In each category, Java supports all of the C operators in those categories except the comma operator. The comma operator allows multiple expressions in a statement. You can achieve the same result with multiple statements. The comma does have uses in Java, for instance it is used to separate multiple interfaces in an "implements" declaration. See Chapter 4 for more details on interfaces. The comma can also be used in a for statement to separate declarations and statements, as we will see later in this chapter.

Here are the operators common to Java and C (with each line being a different precedence, with the first being the highest precedence). On the right side of each line I have listed the associativity of the operators. This tells you the order in which operators of equal precedence are processed.

```
( ) [ ] .                               Left to right
! ~ ++ — + - (cast)                     Right to left
* / %                                   Left to right
+ -                                     Left to right
<< >>                                   Left to right
< <= > >=                               Left to right
== !=                                   Left to right
&                                       Left to right
^                                       Left to right
|                                       Left to right
&&                                      Left to right
||                                      Left to right
?:                                      Left to right
= += -= *= /= %= &= |= ^= <<= >>=       Right to left
```

C programmers should be familiar with all of the operators just shown. We will not demonstrate each operator, but will instead use them in examples throughout the book.

Java has added six new operators:

```
new, instanceof , >>>, >>>=, + (String)
```

Let's discuss each operator in turn:

- **new.** We have already seen the new operator that is used to allocate a new object. The new operator is very familiar to C++ programmers and is loosely similar to the function of malloc(). Unlike malloc(), new returns allocated memory that has been initialized and is ready to use. In Java, new can only be used to create objects.
- **instanceof.** This operator is used for runtime-type identification (RTTI), and we will discuss it when we compare Java to C++.

- **>>>.** The >>> operator is a right shift with zero fill. It is necessary because all types are signed in Java; therefore, the >> operator does a right shift with a sign extension. This means that if the number is negative, it will shift in 1s. No matter what the sign of the number, >>> will shift and fill in 0s on the left-hand side.
- **>>>=.** The zero-fill, right-shift assignment operator that is analogous to all the other assignment operators (like +=, -=, etc.).
- **+.** Used with strings, this operator concatenates String objects together and produces a single String object. We will see this demonstrated later in this chapter.

Source 2.2 is a simple program that demonstrates the use of some Java operators.

SOURCE 2.2

```
// LeapYear.java
package jwiley.chp2;

import java.io.BufferedReader;
import java.io.InputStreamReader;
import java.io.IOException;

/**
 * Class to accept a year and state if it is a leapyear.
 * @author Michael C. Daconta
 */
class LeapYear
{
    /** The main method. */
    public static void main(String args[])
    {
        BufferedReader br = new BufferedReader(new
                                  InputStreamReader(System.in));
        String Syear=null;
        System.out.print("Enter a year: ");
        System .out.flush();
        try
        {
            Syear = br.readLine();
        } catch (IOException ioe)
          {
            System.out.println(ioe.toString());
            System.exit(1);
          }

        long year = Long.parseLong(Syear);
        System.out.println("year is " + year);
        if ( ((year % 4 == 0) && (year % 100 != 0)) || (year % 400 == 0) )
            System.out.println(year + " is a leap year!");
        else
            System.out.println(year + " is NOT a leap year.");
    }
}
```

A run of Source 2.2 produces the following:

```
Enter a year: 1992
year is 1992
1992 is a leap year!
```

Source 2.2 allows you to enter a year and then uses the Java mathematical and logical operators to determine if that year is a leap year. The key expression in the program is:

```
( ((year % 4 == 0) && (year % 100 != 0))  ||  (year % 400 == 0) )
```

which translates to: If the year is divisible by 4, AND if year is NOT divisible by 100, OR if year is divisible by 400, THEN it is a leap year. The modulus operator returns the remainder of an integer division operation and can be used to answer whether the number is evenly divisible by another number. The logical operators provide the boolean logic (AND, OR, etc.).

In Java, unlike C, all conditional expressions must evaluate to a boolean value (see Section 2.4, "Data Types" for a description of the boolean type). In particular, if you wanted to check a value for null, you must explicitly compare the value to null as follows:

```
if (val != null)
```

instead of

```
if (val)
```

This may seem restrictive at first, but you will find that this dramatically reduces errors in code. Among others, the common C error:

```
if (a = 5)
```

is no longer possible. If you need to convert a number to a boolean value, you must use the logical operators to compare the number to some other number.

2.3 IDENTIFIERS

Identifiers are the programmer-defined names used to label variables, classes, functions (methods), packages, and interfaces in a program. Java identifiers follow the same rules as C with a few beneficial additions that you will appreciate. Source 2.3 both lists and demonstrates the rules associated with identifiers.

By far the most valuable Java improvement with identifiers is the ability to make identifiers as long as you wish. It is common knowledge that long, descriptive identifiers improve both code readability and maintenance.

SOURCE 2.3

```
// IdentifierTest.java
package jwiley.chp2;

/**
 * Class to demonstrate the properties of Java identifiers.
 * @author Michael C. Daconta
 */
class IdentifierTest {
    /** Main method to invoke class from a JVM. */
    public static void main(String args[])
    {
        /* 1) C rule, names can be letters and digits, MUST
              start with a letter. */
        int legal_name1;
        /* int 1_illegal; ILLEGAL */

        /* 2) C rule, underscores count as a letter */
        int _123_name;

        /* 2a) Java addition to rule 2: dollar sign counts as a letter */
        int $123_name;

        /* 3) C rule, upper case and lower case are distinct */
        int Legal_name1;

        /* 4) Java allows identifiers greater than 32 characters */
        int The_number_of_dark_haired_children_in_family;
    }
}
```

2.4 DATA TYPES

A data type denotes both a storage area in memory for a class of data and the legal operations that can be performed on a variable of this type. An identifier names this storage area to produce a variable. Therefore, a variable is a named storage area that can store a precise set of values and have a precise set of operations performed on it. In other words, a variable is a named data type. C programmers are familiar with declaring variables a certain type, like this:

```
int myInteger;
```

This creates a storage area that can store a single integer. The program accesses and manipulates this integer by referring to its name "myInteger." The C programming language has five categories of data types: primitives, arrays, structures, unions, and pointers. Java is much simpler in that it has only two categories of data types:

primitives and references. The primitive data types are nearly identical to their C counterparts. Here is a description of each Java primitive type:

byte. A basic data type that represents a single byte as an 8-bit signed value. This is useful in moving C ASCII characters to Java UNICODE characters when implementing native methods or reading ASCII files. A native method is a C function linked to a Java program and called from a Java program.

boolean. A basic data type that represents only two values: true or false. Both true and false are also keywords. The boolean data type only uses 1 bit of storage. The boolean type in Java eliminates the need for the common C and C++ practice of using #define to allow true and false to stand for 1 and 0, respectively.

char. A basic data type used to declare character variables. A Java character is different than an ASCII character. Java uses the UNICODE character set that is a 16-bit unsigned value. UNICODE is an international character set that includes European and Asian characters. Figure 2.2 graphically portrays the UNICODE character set. Java is very explicit about the size of all types. The Java Virtual Machine guarantees that all data types have the same size on all platforms. Because the size of all data types is constant, the C sizeof() operator is obsolete.

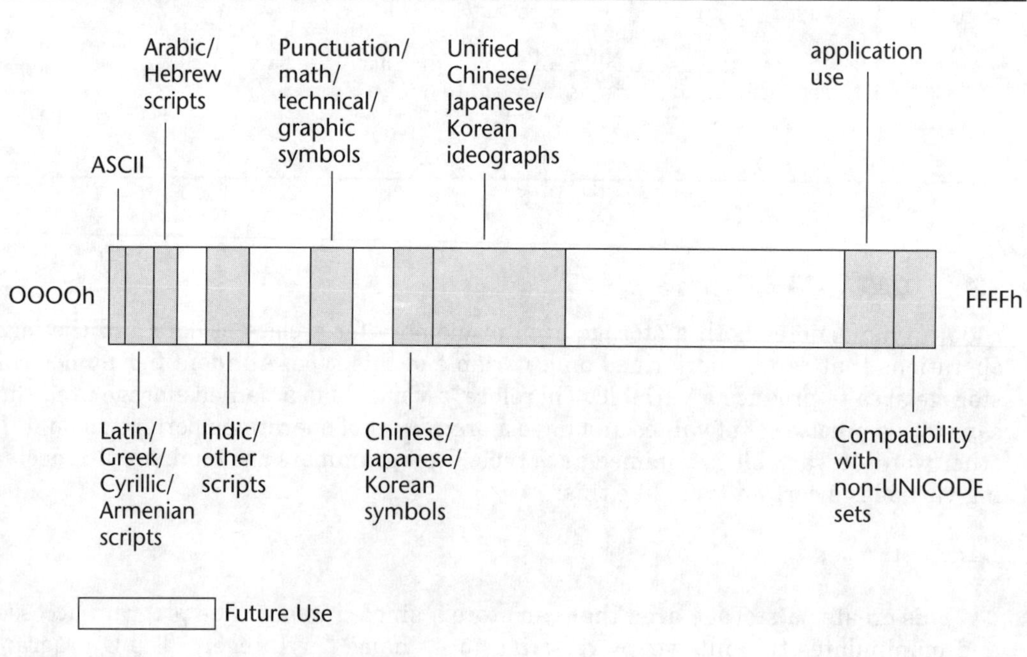

FIGURE 2.2 The UNICODE character set.

double. A basic data type used to declare double variables. A Java double is 64 bits and conforms to the Institute of Electronic and Electrical Engineers (IEEE) Standard 754 (IEEE 754).

float. A basic data type used to declare float variables. A Java float is 32 bits and conforms to IEEE 754.

int. A basic data type used to declare integer variables. A Java integer is a 32-bit signed value.

long. A basic data type used to declare long integer variables. A Java long is a 64-bit signed value.

short. A basic data type used to declare short integer variables. A Java short is a 16-bit signed value.

In addition to the new types, boolean and byte, you will notice that all Java types have fixed sizes. There is no ambiguity and all Java types are platform independent.

Java references are essentially "safe pointers" to Java objects. All Java objects are allocated from the heap and accessed via references. You cannot declare variables that are objects, you can only declare variables that are references to objects. This is analogous to only being allowed to declare pointers to structures and never being allowed to declare a structure.

Java references are dereferenced automatically so, for all intents and purposes, a reference can be treated as an object is in C. For example, to access a data member of an object, the familiar dot operator is used on the variable that refers to the object. This simplification in the number of data types makes the language easier to use for development. In addition, it is easier to create compilers for the language and virtual machines to execute the compiled code. Source 2.4 demonstrates the two categories of Java data types.

SOURCE 2.4

```
// TestDataTypes.java
package jwiley.chp2

/**
 * class to demonstrate Java data types.
 * @author Michael C. Daconta
 */
class TestDataTypes
{
    /** main method. */
    public static void main(String args[])
    {
        // primitives (space allocated)
        int localInt = 10;
        double localDoub = 20.459;
```

```
        System.out.println("Primitive types");
        System.out.println("localInt has the value: " + localInt);
        System.out.println("localDoub has the value: " + localDoub);

        // references types
        int [] intArrayReference = null;
        similar2Struct classReference = null;
        String stringReference = null;
        Double doubleObjectReference = null;

        System.out.println("Reference type");
        System.out.println("intArrayReference has the value: " +
                           intArrayReference);
        System.out.println("classReference has the value: " +
                           classReference);
        System.out.println("stringReference has the value: " +
                           stringReference);
        System.out.println("doubleObjectReference has the value: " +
                           doubleObjectReference);

        // only other valid value for a reference type
        intArrayReference = new int[5];
        classReference = new similar2Struct();
        stringReference = new String("mike");
        doubleObjectReference = new Double(20.459);

        System.out.println("Allocated references.");
        System.out.println("intArrayReference has the value: " +
                           intArrayReference);
        System.out.println("classReference has the value: " +
                           classReference);
        System.out.println("stringReference has the value: " +
                           stringReference);
        System.out.println("doubleObjectReference has the value: " +
                           doubleObjectReference);
    }
}

/**
 * A sample class.
 */
class similar2Struct
{
    int dmInt;
    Float dmFloat;
    Long dmLong;
}
```

A run of Source 2.4 produces:

```
C:\1-1update\newSrc>java jwiley.chp2.tstDataTypes
Symantec Java! ByteCode Compiler Version 1.02a
Copyright (C) 1996 Symantec Corporation
Primitive types
localInt has the value: 10
localDoub has the value: 20.459
Reference type
intArrayReference has the value: null
classReference has the value: null
stringReference has the value: null
doubleObjectReference has the value: null
Allocated references.
intArrayReference has the value: [I@1393a70
classReference has the value: similar2Struct@1393a78
stringReference has the value: mike
doubleObjectReference has the value: 20.459
```

There are three key points to note about Source 2.4:

1. The declaration and definition of primitive types is identical to C.

```
int localInt = 10;
```

2. It is important to understand that the declarations of all Java objects and arrays do not declare an object, but a reference to an object. This is analogous to declaring a pointer to the object in C.
3. We are able to print out the objects because every Java object has a default toString() method that is executed when the object is in a concatenation expression. We will discuss how all Java objects share these common characteristics when we cover Inheritance in Chapter 3.

Figure 2.3 graphically portrays the two Java data types.

2.5 LITERALS

Literals are a sequence of characters, digits, or both that represent an exact or "literal" value. Java literals are identical to C literals with a few exceptions and a few additions. Source 2.5 demonstrates the Java literals as compared to C literals.

Literals are most often used for setting final variables (similar to constants) in Java. You should note the new Java literals (null, true, and false). The literal null denotes a reference that points to "nothing" or "no object." The literals true and false are the values for the boolean type. Now let's talk about another Java language feature that is nearly identical to C: Expressions.

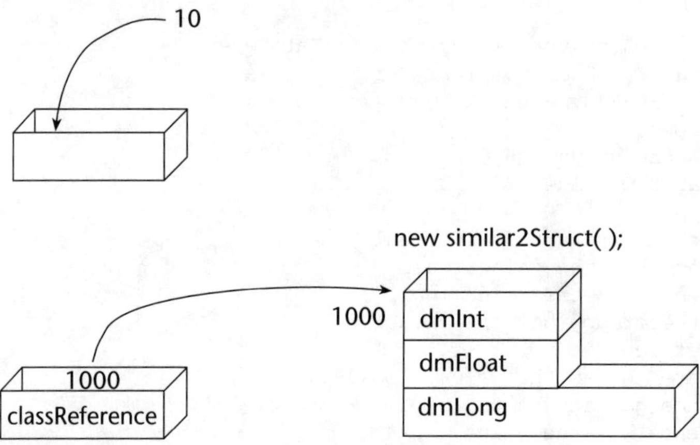

FIGURE 2.3 Primitive type versus a reference.

SOURCE 2.5

```
// LiteralTest.java
package jwiley.chp2;

/**
 * Class to demonstrate Java literals.
 * @author Michael C. Daconta
 */
class LiteralTest
{
    /** Main method to invoke from JVM. */
    public static void main(String args[])
    {
        int myint = 123;         /* C-style int literal         */
        long mylong = 123L;      /* C-style Long literal        */
        int hexnum = 0x1ac;      /* C-style Hexadecimal literal */
        int octnum = 037;        /* C-style Octal literal       */
        double mydouble = 3.12;  /* C-style double literal      */

        char mychar = 'c';       /* C-style character literal   */
        char newline   = '\n';   /* C-style escape sequence     */
        char backspace = '\b';
        char formfeed  = '\f';
        char cr        = '\r';
        char tab       = '\t';
        char backslash = '\\';
        char snglequote= '\'';
        char doubquote = '\"';
```

```
        char Octal      = '\032';
        char Unicodeltr= '\u0391'; /* Greek capital A         */
        String myname  = "Mike";   /* C-style string literal  */
        float javaFloat = 2e3f;
        float javaFloat2 = 2E3f;
        double javaDouble = 1e1;

        boolean done = false; /* Java-specific. */
        String nullRef = null;

        /* Illegal in Java - compile time error.
        char bell       = '\a';
        char vertTab    = '\v';
        char question   = '\?';
        */
    }
}
```

2.6 EXPRESSIONS

An expression is any combination of operators, literals, and variables that can be evaluated to produce a value. An expression may consist of subexpressions that may themselves have subexpressions, ad infinitum. Each expression and subexpression has a type as its result. The resulting type is based upon the types of its subcomponents and the rules of its operators. Programming gains its power from the use of mathematics and logic, and it cannot be emphasized enough that expressions are the primary tools to "express" them.

To its credit, Java has adopted C's powerful expression facilities in whole with only a few exceptions. Java expressions combine the Java types with the Java operators in different ways as demonstrated in Source 2.6.

SOURCE 2.6

```
// ExpressionTest.java
package jwiley.chp2;

/**
 * Class to test Java expressions.
 * @author Michael C. Daconta
 */
class ExpressionTest
{
    /** Main method to invoke from a JVM. */
    public static void main(String args[])
    {
```

```
        System.out.println("Arithmetic expressions");
        float fahr=60.0f, celsius =0;
        celsius = (5.0f/9.0f) * (fahr-32.0f);
        System.out.println("fahrenheit: " + fahr + " celsius: " +
                           celsius);
        System.out.println("");
        System.out.println("Relational and logical expressions");
        System.out.println(fahr > 20.0);
        /* System.out.println((fahr < 20.0) && (1));
           Legal in C but ILLEGAL in Java. */
        System.out.println(((fahr < 20.0) && (true)));
        System.out.println("");

        System.out.println("Casts and conversions in expressions");
        int age=10;
        float gpa = age;
        double salary=30000.3;
        System.out.println(gpa + salary);
        System.out.println((int)(gpa + salary));
        System.out.println("");

        System.out.println("Bitwise expressions");
        System.out.println(100 >> 1); // division by 2
        System.out.println(age << 1); // multiplication by 2
        int memoryBlock = (12 + 7) & ~7;
        System.out.println("12 rounded to a power of 8 is " +
                           memoryBlock);
        System.out.println("");

        System.out.println("Order of Evaluation in Expressions");
        int a = 5 & 1 + 2;
        System.out.println(a);
        a = (5 & 1) + 2;
        System.out.println(a);
    }
}
```

A run of Source 2.6 produces:

```
Arithmetic expressions
fahrenheit: 60 celsius: 15.5556

Relational and logical expressions
true
false

Casts and conversions in expressions
30010.3
30010
```

```
Bitwise expressions
50
20
12 rounded to a power of 8 is 16

Order of Evaluation in Expressions
1
3
```

TIP All Java logical expressions must evaluate to one of the literals true or false. This is different from C where the integer 0 denotes false and any non-zero integer denotes true.

One final point about expressions is automatic type conversions in Java expressions. These conversions are also called "numeric promotions" because the "lower" type is promoted to the "higher" type before the operation proceeds. For example, if one type is an int and one a long, the int will be converted to a long before the operation is executed. For the analogous Java data types, these conversion rules are identical in C and Java.

You will happily discover that C expressions port very easily to Java. The next language element we will discuss is another cornerstone of programming: Control Flow.

2.7 CONTROL FLOW

Control flow constructs provide a language with the ability to perform branch selection via decision points and repetition also known as loops. The control flow constructs are the first items mastered in C and the most often used. Java adopted C's control flow constructs with only a few minor modifications. Source 2.7 demonstrates the Java control flow constructs.

SOURCE 2.7

```
// ControlFlowTest.java
package jwiley.chp2;

/**
 * A class to demonstrate Java control flow constructs.
 * @version 1.1
 * @author Michael C. Daconta
 */
class ControlFlowTest
{
    /** main() method to invoke from JVM. */
    public static void main(String args[])
    {
```

```
    int a = 1, b = 2, c = 3;

    System.out.print("The ");

    /* if statement. */
    if (a > 1)
      System.out.print("old ");
    else
      System.out.print("young ");

    System.out.print("man ");

    /* switch construct. */
    switch (b)
    {
      case 1:
        System.out.print("is ");
      break;
      case 2:
        System.out.print("was ");
      break;
      case 3:
        System.out.print("can ");
      break;
      default:
        System.out.print("will ");
    }

    System.out.print("singing ");

    /* for loop. */
    for (int i=0,j=0; i < c; i++, j++)
      System.out.print("FaLaLa, ");

    System.out.println("and ");

    /* while loop. */
    while (c– > 0)
      System.out.print("TaDeDa, ");

    /* do-while loop. */
    do
    {
      System.out.print("all ");
    } while (c == 3);

    System.out.println("the way home.");
  }
}
```

A run of Source 2.7 produces:

```
\The young man was singing FaLaLa, FaLaLa, FaLaLa, and
TaDeDa, TaDeDa, TaDeDa, all the way home.
```

All of the control flow constructs just shown should be familiar to C programmers. The for construct is identical to C except for its restrictions on the comma operator. Java only supports a comma operator in the initialization and increment sections of the for loop. Now that we've seen how the majority of control flow constructs are identical to C, let's examine the differences.

Java did omit one control flow construct—the goto. The keyword is reserved but not used. It is reserved only for the possibility of providing richer error messages. I think Dennis Ritchie and Brian Kernighan said it best:

> "Formally, the goto is never necessary, and in practice it is almost always easy to write code without it. We have not used goto in this book."[1]

The Java development team, and James Gosling in particular, found that people predominantly used the goto construct to exit out of nested loops. To provide this one capability, Java allows a labeled break and labeled continue. Labeled break and continue transfer control to a strictly limited place, namely to an enclosing block. Source 2.8 demonstrates labeled continue and labeled break.

SOURCE 2.8

```
// ContinueAndBreak.java
package jwiley.chp2;

/**
 * Class to test labeled continue and break.
 * @version 1.2
 * @author Michael C. Daconta
 */
class ContinueAndBreak
{
    /** main method to invoke program from JVM. */
    public static void main(String args[])
    {
        int i=0, j=0;
```

[1]Brian W. Kernighan and Dennis M. Ritchie, *The C Programming Language*, p. 65.

```
        System.out.println("*** Continue test ***");
        outaHere:
        while (i++ < 3)
        {
            while (j < 50)
            {
                System.out.println("i: " + i + " j: " + j);

                if (j++ < 2)
                {
                    System.out.println("Continuing on.");
                    continue;
                }
                else
                {
                    System.out.println("Continuing outaHere.");
                    continue outaHere;
                }
            }

            i++;
        }

        i=0; j=0;

        System.out.println("*** Break test ***");
        outerLoop:
        for (i = 0; i < 4; i++)
        {
            for (j=0; j < 4; j++)
            {
                if (i != 0 && i % 2 == 0)
                {
                    System.out.println("Breaking from outerLoop.");
                    break outerLoop;
                }
                if (j != 0 && j % 2 == 0)
                {
                    System.out.println("Breaking from inner loop.");
                    break;
                }
                System.out.println("i: " + i + " j: " + j);
            }
        }
    }
}
```

A run of Source 2.8 produces:

```
C:\1-1update\newSrc>java jwiley.chp2.continueAndBreak
Symantec Java! ByteCode Compiler Version 1.02a
Copyright (C) 1996 Symantec Corporation
*** Continue test ***
i: 1 j: 0
Continuing on.
i: 1 j: 1
Continuing on.
i: 1 j: 2
Continuing outaHere.
i: 2 j: 3
Continuing outaHere.
i: 3 j: 4
Continuing outaHere.
*** Break test ***
i: 0 j: 0
i: 0 j: 1
Breaking from inner loop.
i: 1 j: 0
i: 1 j: 1
Breaking from inner loop.
Breaking from outerLoop.
```

Source 2.8 demonstrates how to write a labeled break and what happens when execution jumps to that label; however, it is a very boring example. The next section will diverge into a more interesting example. Those who wish to get right to the next language feature should skip the next section.

A More Interesting Example of Labeled Break

This next example is inspired by a problem I had to solve in the Telemedicine system I am developing. The problem is a fairly easy one to solve once you understand the RGB color model. I needed to distinguish between greyscale and color images. Source 2.9 uses a labeled break in determining whether an image is color or greyscale. Before examining the source code, let me ask you to concentrate on the part with the labeled break and not worry about classes that you don't understand. We will cover all of these classes later in the book. For now, all I want you to understand is the RGB color model and the labeled break. Figure 2.4 graphically depicts the RGB color model. You should notice that all the greyscale values in the RGB color model are on a diagonal line between (0,0,0) and (255,255,255). This means we can easily test for greyscale if every pixel in the image has red, green, and blue values that are equal. The value can fall anywhere between 0 and 255 as long as the red, green, and blue component of the pixel have the same value.

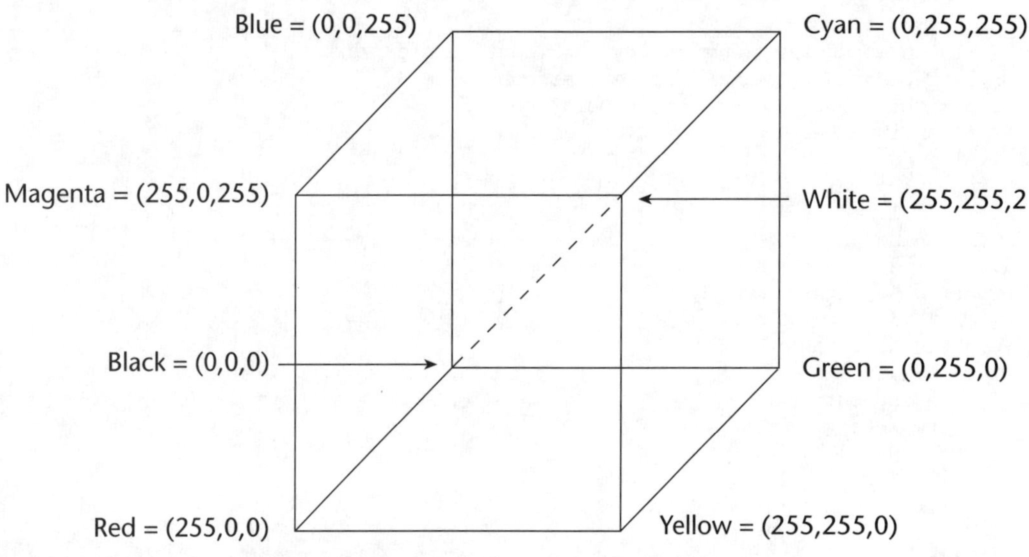

FIGURE 2.4 The RGB color model.

SOURCE 2.9

```
// GreyScaleTest.java
package jwiley.chp2;
import java.awt.image.*;
import java.awt.Image;
import java.awt.MediaTracker;
import java.awt.Toolkit;
import java.awt.Frame;

/**
 * Class to demonstrate break to a label by way of
 * testing whether an image is greyscale or color.
 * @author Michael C. Daconta
 */
class GreyScaleTest
{
    /** Main method to invoke from JVM. */
    public static void main(String args[])
    {
        if (args.length < 1)
        {
            System.out.println("USAGE: java GreyScaleTest <imgFileName>");
            System.exit(1);
        }
```

```
String imgTitle = args[0];
boolean isGreyScale = true; // optimist
Image img1=null, img2=null;

/* load gifs into program. */
img1 = (Toolkit.getDefaultToolkit()).getImage(imgTitle);
System.out.println("Loading " + imgTitle + "...");

/* wait until image is fully loaded. */
Frame dummyFrame = new Frame();
MediaTracker imgTracker = new MediaTracker(dummyFrame);
imgTracker.addImage(img1,0);
try
{
    imgTracker.waitForAll();
} catch (InterruptedException ie)
  {
    System.out.println(ie.getMessage());
    System.exit(1);
  }
if (imgTracker.isErrorAny())
{
    System.out.println("Error loading image.");
    System.exit(1);
}

/* get height and width of image. */
int imgWidth = img1.getWidth(dummyFrame);
int imgHeight = img1.getHeight(dummyFrame);
System.out.println("imgWidth : " + imgWidth);
System.out.println("imgHeight: " + imgHeight);

/* create an array of integers to hold the pixels */
int [] pixels = new int[imgWidth * imgHeight];

/* now image is loaded, extract pixels. */
PixelGrabber pg = new PixelGrabber(img1,0,0,imgWidth,imgHeight,
                                   pixels, 0, imgWidth);

try
{
    pg.grabPixels();
} catch (InterruptedException ie)
  {
    System.out.println(ie.getMessage());
    System.exit(1);
  }

outerLoopLabel:
for (int i=0; i < imgHeight; i++)
{
```

```
            for (int j=0; j < imgWidth; j++)
            {
                int pixel = pixels[(i * imgHeight) + j];
                int red   = (pixel >> 16) & 0xff;
                int green = (pixel >>  8) & 0xff;
                int blue  = (pixel      ) & 0xff;

                if (red != green || red != blue || blue != green)
                {
                    isGreyScale = false;
                    break outerLoopLabel;
                }
            } // end of for(int j=...
        } // end of for (int i= ...

        if (isGreyScale)
            System.out.println("Image is a greyScale image.");
        else
            System.out.println("Image is a color image.");

        System.exit(0);
    }
}
```

Two separate runs of Source 2.9 produce:

```
C:\1-1update\newSrc>java jwiley.chp2.GreyScaleTest javabk.gif
Symantec Java! ByteCode Compiler Version 1.02a
Copyright (C) 1996 Symantec Corporation
Loading javabk.gif...
imgWidth : 365
imgHeight: 465
Image is a color image.
C:\1-1update\newSrc>java jwiley.chp2.GreyScaleTest greybk.gif
Symantec Java! ByteCode Compiler Version 1.02a
Copyright (C) 1996 Symantec Corporation
Loading greybk.gif...
imgWidth : 1500
imgHeight: 600
Image is a greyScale image.
```

2.8 ARRAYS AND STRINGS

In the Java language, arrays and strings are objects and are no longer prone to the errors or confusion common to arrays and strings in C. Let's first examine arrays and then cover strings.

In C, an array is a group of contiguous, homogeneous data types that are accessed as offsets from a single name (which corresponds to an address). In C, there is no array bounds checking. In C, a pointer may be substituted for the array name to access array elements. The preceding attributes of an array have caused much confusion among programmers as well as being a source of numerous bugs. Java arrays are simpler than C arrays and protected from misuse. Java arrays are different from C arrays in three ways:

1. Like all objects in Java, arrays are created by using the new operator. As a result, you do not enter a size of the array in the declaration. You enter the size in the new expression:

   ```
   int intArray[] = new int[5];
   ```

2. All arrays store the allocated size in a variable named length. You can access this at any time using:

   ```
   int intArraySize = intArray.length;
   ```

3. Java arrays are protected from array overruns and underruns. An exception (the Java error-handling facility uses exceptions) is thrown if you attempt to index an element beyond the end of an array or try to use a negative index.

Source 2.10 demonstrates the basics of declaring and allocating single and multi-dimensional arrays.

SOURCE 2.10

```
// ArrayBasics.java
package jwiley.chp2;

/**
 * Class to demonstrate the basics of array creation and access.
 * @version 1.1
 * @author Michael C. Daconta
 */
class ArrayBasics
{
    /** Main method to invoke from the JVM. */
    public static void main(String args[])
    {
        /* 1) cannot put dimension in declaration.
              This declares a reference to an array. */
        int myArray[];

        /* 2) must allocate an array object using new. */
        myArray = new int[3];
```

```
        /* 3) You can get the size of the array */
        System.out.println("myArray size is : " + myArray.length);

        /* 4) for multi-dimensional arrays you allocate
              an array of array references. */
        int multiArray[][];
        multiArray = new int[3][4];

        /* 5) with multi-dimensional arrays you do can
              allocate the size of each "row" later. */
        int dynamicMulti[][];
        dynamicMulti = new int[3][];

        dynamicMulti[0] = new int[5];
        dynamicMulti[1] = new int[10];
        dynamicMulti[2] = new int[20];

        /* 6) array overruns and underruns are impossible. */
    }
}
```

The dynamic allocation of Java arrays gives you the same flexibility that pointers do without the risk. Accessing an element of an array is identical to how it is done in C by indexing into the array. Also identical to C, the first element of a Java array is stored at index 0. Source 2.11 demonstrates array indexing and the Java runtime protection against array overruns.

SOURCE 2.11

```
// ArrayOverrun.java
package jwiley.chp2;

/**
 * Class to demonstrate runtime array bounds checking.
 * @version 1.1
 * @author Michael C. Daconta
 */
class ArrayOverrun
{
    /** Main method to invoke from JVM. */
    public static void main(String args[])
    {
        int myArray[];

        myArray = new int[3];
        myArray[0] = 10;
        myArray[1] = 20;
        myArray[2] = 30;
        myArray[3] = 40; /* Oops! */
        myArray[-1] = 50; /* double Oops! */
    }
}
```

A run of Source 2.11 produces:

```
Exception in thread "main" java.lang.ArrayIndexOutOfBoundsException
        at ArrayOverrun.main(C:\hotjava\bin\ArrayOverrun.java:9)
```

Source 2.11 exits after the ArrayIndexOutOfBoundsException is thrown. Exceptions are a mechanism for error handling, and when used properly can significantly increase an application's robustness. When the Java Virtual Machine or any Java code encounters an error, it signals this by throwing an exception. The exception can be caught and handled in a single location. Exceptions make the process of signaling, identifying, and handling errors much simpler, mainly because they allow programmers to isolate their error-handling core from the rest of the program. In the next chapter we will discuss the exception model and exceptions in detail. The Java exception model is very similar to the C++ exception model.

Java single and multidimensional arrays can be initialized just as C arrays. Java arrays of objects (similar to arrays of structures) require an extra allocation step similar to the method used to allocate dynamic two-dimensional arrays (my two previous books cover allocation of dynamic two-dimensional arrays in detail). When allocating an array of objects, it is important to remember that you are actually creating an array of object references. The objects themselves must be created separately. Source 2.12 demonstrates array initialization and arrays of objects.

SOURCE 2.12

```
// ArrayTest.java
package jwiley.chp2;

/**
 * Simple class (similar to structure) to use in
 * arrayTest example.
 * @version 1.1
 * @author Michael C. Daconta
 */
class testObject
{
    /** integer data member. */
    int anInt=0;
    /** string data member. */
    String aString="";

    /** constructor to create and initialize an object. */
    testObject(int theInt, String theString)
    {
        anInt = theInt;
        aString = new String(theString);
    }
```

```
    /** method to print a testObject. */
    void printObject()
    {
        System.out.println("anInt   : " + anInt);
        System.out.println("aString : " + aString);
    }
}

/**
 * Simple class to demonstrate array operations.
 * @version 1.1
 * @author Michael C. Daconta
 */
class ArrayTest
{
    /** Main method to invoke from JVM. */
    public static void main(String args[])
    {
        int a[] = { 1, 2, 3 };
        int b[];
        int c[];

        b = a;
        c = new int[3];
        c = a;

        for (int i=0; i < b.length; i++)
        {
            System.out.println("a[" + i +"] is " + a[i]);
            System.out.println("b[" + i +"] is " + b[i]);
            System.out.println("c[" + i +"] is " + c[i]);
        }

        testObject objArray[];
        testObject anObject;
        testObject realObject = new testObject(1,"Mike");

        objArray = new testObject[3];
        for (int i=0; i < objArray.length; i++)
            objArray[i] = new testObject(i,"person"+i);

        anObject = realObject;

        for (int i=0; i < objArray.length; i++)
            objArray[i].printObject();

        realObject.printObject();
        anObject.printObject();
    }
}
```

A run of Source 2.12 produces:

```
a[0] is 1
b[0] is 1
c[0] is 1
a[1] is 2
b[1] is 2
c[1] is 2
a[2] is 3
b[2] is 3
c[2] is 3
anInt   : 0
aString : person0
anInt   : 1
aString : person1
anInt   : 2
aString : person2
anInt   : 1
aString : Mike
anInt   : 1
aString : Mike
```

Notice the assignments of one array object to another as in:

```
b = a;
```

This highlights the fact that Java arrays are implemented with pointers like this:

```
int a[];
```

is equivalent to

```
int *a;
```

This continues with two-dimensional arrays where

```
int a[][];
```

is equivalent to:

```
int **a;
```

You will notice that all Java objects are accessed through references. A reference is a restricted pointer in that a programmer cannot directly manipulate a reference. In C, programmers can perform arithmetic on pointers and use pointers to access random blocks of memory. In Java, a reference can only be used to access members (data and methods) of the object it points to. You were introduced to this with the linked list example in Chapter 1. We will cover this in greater detail later in this chapter.

Multidimensional arrays in Java are identical to C's multidimensional arrays. Java also uses "array of arrays" to implement multidimensional arrays. Source 2.13 is an example of using multidimensional arrays in Java.

SOURCE 2.13

```
// Rotate.java
package jwiley.chp2;

import java.io.BufferedReader;
import java.io.InputStreamReader;
import java.io.IOException;

/**
 * Class to demonstrate multi-dimensional arrays via
 * matrix rotation.
 */
class Rotate
{
    /** Main method to invoke from the JVM. */
    public static void main(String args[])
    {
        /* enter number of coordinates to rotate. */
        BufferedReader br =
                new BufferedReader(new InputStreamReader(System.in));
        System.out.print("Enter number of Coordinates: ");
        System.out.flush();
        String numStr = null;
        try
        {
            numStr = br.readLine();
        } catch (IOException ioe)
          {
            System.out.println(ioe.toString());
            System.exit(1);
          }
        int numCoords = Integer.parseInt(numStr);

        /* create a matrix of 2-d coordinates. */
        int coords[][] = new int[numCoords][2];

        /* Fill the matrix */
        for (int i=0; i < numCoords; i++)
        {
            boolean badInput=false;
            do
            {
                try
                {
                    System.out.println("Coordinate #" + i);
                    System.out.print("Enter x: ");
```

```
                System.out.flush();
                String xStr = br.readLine();
                coords[i][0] = Integer.parseInt(xStr);

                System.out.print("Enter y: ");
                System.out.flush();
                String yStr = br.readLine();
                coords[i][1] = Integer.parseInt(yStr);
                badInput=false;
            } catch (IOException ioe)
              {
                System.out.println(ioe.toString());
                System.exit(1);
              }
              catch (NumberFormatException nfe)
              {
                System.out.println("Must enter a number.");
                badInput=true;
              }
        } while (badInput);
    }

    /* get the degree of Rotation */
    boolean badDegree=false;
    int degrees = 0;
    do
    {
        System.out.print("Enter degree of rotation (1-360): ");
        System.out.flush();
        String degStr = null;
        try
        {
            degStr = br.readLine();
            degrees = Integer.parseInt(degStr);
            badDegree=false;
        } catch (IOException ioe)
          {
            System.out.println(ioe.toString());
            System.exit(1);
          }
          catch (NumberFormatException nfe)
          {
            System.out.println("Enter number between 1 and 360.");
            badDegree=true;
          }
    } while (badDegree);

    /* translate degrees to radians */
    double radians = ((double)degrees/180.0) * Math.PI;
    System.out.println(degrees + " degrees is " + radians +
                       " radians.");
```

```
        /* create rotation Matrix */
        double rotMatrix[][] = new double[numCoords][2];

        /* perform the rotation */
        for (int i=0; i < numCoords; i++)
        {
            /* new X */
            rotMatrix[i][0] = Math.cos(radians) -
                              coords[i][1] * Math.sin(radians);

            /* new Y */
            rotMatrix[i][1] = Math.cos(radians) +
                              coords[i][0] * Math.sin(radians);
        }

        /* print the Rotation matrix */
        for (int i=0; i < numCoords; i++)
        {
            System.out.println("Rotated Coordinate #" + i);
            System.out.println("x :" + rotMatrix[i][0]);
            System.out.println("y :" + rotMatrix[i][1]);
        }
    }
}
```

A run of Source 2.13 produces:

```
C:\hotjava\bin>java jwiley.chp2.Rotate
Enter number of Coordinates: 7
Coordinate #0
Enter x: 2
Enter y: 5
Coordinate #1
Enter x: 4
Enter y: 7
Coordinate #2
Enter x: 2
Enter y: 9
Coordinate #3
Enter x: 7
Enter y: 9
Coordinate #4
Enter x: 7
Enter y: 4
Coordinate #5
Enter x: 5
```

```
Enter y: 6
Coordinate #6
Enter x: 3
Enter y: 4
Enter degree of rotation (1-360): 90
90 degrees is 1.5708 radians.
Rotated Coordinate #0
x :-5
y :2
Rotated Coordinate #1
x :-7
y :4
Rotated Coordinate #2
x :-9
y :2
Rotated Coordinate #3
x :-9
y :7
Rotated Coordinate #4
x :-4
y :7
Rotated Coordinate #5
x :-6
y :5
Rotated Coordinate #6
x :-4
y :3
```

A graphical representation of the rotation is depicted in Figure 2.5.

Just as arrays and strings are similar in C, Java arrays and strings are similar in how they differ from their C counterpart. In Java, strings are implemented using two classes: String and StringBuffer. The String class is used for immutable (nonchangeable) strings and the StringBuffer class is used for mutable (changeable) strings. We will first discuss Strings and then String Buffers.

In C, strings are simple NUL-terminated character arrays. There is a critical reliance on the ASCII NUL character being there to terminate the string. In fact, in the standard header <string.h>, the majority of string manipulation functions depend on the NUL-terminator to complete processing. Due to C's lack of bounds checking, the ability to overwrite the NUL terminator is a cause of numerous program bugs. This potential hazard is also magnified by the fact that string manipulation is the most common and pervasive part of most programs. Java strings fix the deficiencies of C strings to deliver safe, predictable, and reliable string manipulation. A Java string is an instantiated object of the String class. The String class provides numerous constructor and manipulator functions. Source 2.14 demonstrates both construction and manipulation of Java strings.

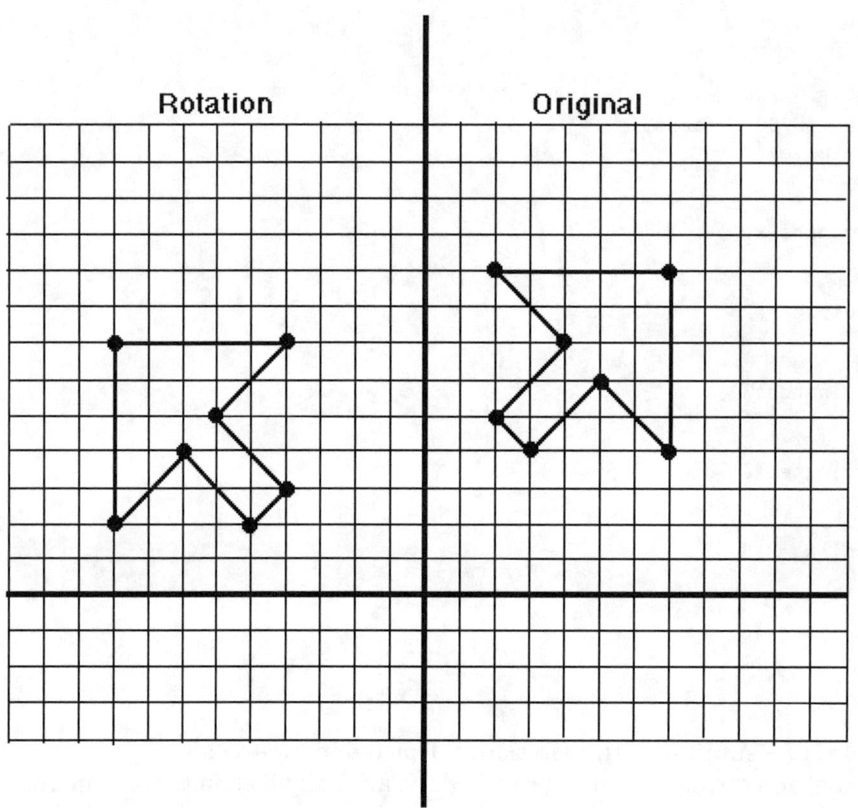

FIGURE 2.5 Matrix rotation.

SOURCE 2.14

```
// StringBasics.java
package jwiley.chp2;

/**
 * Class to demonstrate the basics of Java Strings.
 * @author Michael C. Daconta
 * @version 1.1
 */
class StringBasics
{
    /** Main() method to invoke from JVM. */
    public static void main(String args[])
    {
```

```
        /* 1) a String is NOT a character array. */
        // char charArray[] = "mike"; ILLEGAL
        char charArray[] = new char[4];
        charArray[0] = 'm';
        charArray[1] = 'i';
        charArray[2] = 'k';
        charArray[3] = 'e';
        // a Java character array is NOT NUL terminated. */
        System.out.println("charArray is " + charArray);
        System.out.println("length of charArray is " +
                           charArray.length);

        /* 2) creating a String object. */
        String myName = "Michael";
        String sentence = new String("I live in a small town.");

        /* 3) get the string length. */
        System.out.println("Length of " + myName +
                           " is " + myName.length());

        /* 4) character access, char is UNICODE NOT ASCII! */
        for (int i=0; i < myName.length(); i++)
                System.out.println("char #" + i +
                                   " is " + (int) myName.charAt(i) +
                                   " which is " +
                (new Character(myName.charAt(i))).toString());

        /* 5) String concatentation. */
        String fullName = myName + " Corey " + "Daconta";
        System.out.println("my fullName is " + fullName);

        /* 6) String comparison */
        if (myName.equals("Michael"))
                System.out.println("My name is Michael.");

        if ("Michael".equals(myName))
                System.out.println("... and Michael is my name.");

        /* 7) String manipulation */
        int idx = sentence.indexOf("small");

        if (idx > 0)
        {
            System.out.println("sentence is : <" + sentence + ">");
            System.out.println("small starts at index: " + idx);
            String smallStr = sentence.substring(idx, idx +
                                                 "small".length());
            System.out.println("smallStr is " + smallStr);
        }
    }
}
```

A run of Source 2.14 produces:

```
C:\hotjava\bin>java jwiley.chp2.StringBasics
charArray is mike
length of charArray is 4
Length of Michael is 7
char #0 is 77 which is M
char #1 is 105 which is i
char #2 is 99 which is c
char #3 is 104 which is h
char #4 is 97 which is a
char #5 is 101 which is e
char #6 is 108 which is l
my fullName is Michael Corey Daconta
My name is Michael.
... and Michael is my name.
small starts at index: 12
smallStr is e in a
```

It is important to understand that the Java character set is UNICODE and not ASCII. UNICODE is an international character set that encompasses all the characters in the majority of languages in the world. A UNICODE character is a 16-bit unsigned value. To bridge the gap between 1-byte ASCII strings and the UNICODE characters used in Java strings, the String class has the ability to convert between byte arrays and Java strings. Source 2.15 shows how to read an ASCII text file and store it in a Java string.

SOURCE 2.15

```
// ASCIIFileReader.java
package jwiley.chp2;

import java.io.FileInputStream;

/**
 * Class to load an ASCII file using Java.
 * @version 1.1
 * @author Martin C. Snyder
 */
class ASCIIFileReader
{
    public static String readFile(String strFilename)
    {
        try
        {
            StringBuffer sb = new StringBuffer();
            FileInputStream fs = new FileInputStream(strFilename);
            int len = fs.available();
```

```
            for (int i = 0; i < len; i++)
            {
                byte ASCIIChar = (byte)fs.read();
                char JavaChar = (char)ASCIIChar;
                sb.append(JavaChar);
            }

            return sb.toString();
        }
        catch (Exception x)
          {
            System.out.println(x);
            return "";
          }
    }

    /** Main method to invoke from JVM. */
    public static void main(String args[])
    {
        System.out.println(readFile(args[0]));
    }
}
```

A run of Source 2.15 produces:

```
C:\hotjava\bin>java jwiley.chp2.ASCIIFileReader message.txt
There is no message of the day today.
```

Another Java string feature unfamiliar to C programmers is overloading the functionality of the + operator for the purpose of concatenating strings. You have already seen numerous examples of this in conjunction with the System.out.println() method. The last part of Source 2.14 demonstrates some of the string manipulation features. A more thorough introduction into the String class will be covered in Chapter 6.

A Java StringBuffer is similar to a Java string in its bounds checking; however, you have the ability to modify and extend a StringBuffer. You can also construct a StringBuffer from a Java string. Lastly, you can convert a StringBuffer back to a Java String by using the toString() method. Source 2.16 demonstrates the most common functions of a StringBuffer.

SOURCE 2.16

```
// StringBufferBasics.java
package jwiley.chp2;

/**
 * Class to demonstrate the basics of Java's mutable
 * Strings.
```

```
 * @author Michael C. Daconta
 * @version 1.1
 */
class StringBufferBasics
{
    /** Main() method to invoke from JVM. */
    public static void main(String args[])
    {

        /* 1) initialize */
        StringBuffer aSentence = new StringBuffer("Mary had a ");
        System.out.println("The sentence is " + aSentence);

        /* 2) modify chars */
        aSentence.setCharAt(5,'w');
        aSentence.setCharAt(7,'s');
        System.out.println("Modified sentence is " + aSentence);

        /* 3) append to end */
        aSentence.append("little girl.");
        System.out.println("Appended sentence is " + aSentence);

        /* 4) insert in middle */
        String aWord = new String(aSentence.toString());
        int idx = aWord.indexOf("little");

        if (idx > 0)
                aSentence.insert(idx,"very ");
        System.out.println("Inserted sentence is " + aSentence);
    }
}
```

A run of Source 2.16 produces:

```
C:\hotjava\bin>java jwiley.chp2.StringBufferBasics
The sentence is Mary had a
Modified sentence is Mary was a
Appended sentence is Mary was a little girl.
Inserted sentence is Mary was a very little girl.
```

Since arrays and strings are so common to programming, I provide one more example that combines the two concepts. Source 2.17 implements a simple CheckBook register. Remember that a class is similar to a structure. In fact, in Source 2.17 I make a class even more similar to a C structure by making the class data members have public access. This allows you to access the data members directly just as you would access structure data members (using the dot operator).

SOURCE 2.17

```
// CheckBook.java
package jwiley.chp2;

/* this program will demonstrate both Strings and Arrays */
import java.io.InputStreamReader;
import java.io.BufferedReader;
import java.lang.Integer;
import java.io.IOException;

/**
 * Class to represent a single check.
 * @author Michael C. Daconta
 * @version 1.1
 */
class Check
{
    /** check number. */
    public int number;
    /** payable to. */
    public String to;
    /** amount of check. */
    public Float amount;
    /** memo field of check. */
    public String memo;

    /** Method to get check data. */
    void enterCheck()
    {
        try
        {
            System.out.print("Check number: ");
            System.out.flush();
            String numStr = CheckBook.br.readLine();
            number = Integer.parseInt(numStr);
            System.out.print("Check to: ");
            System.out.flush();
            to = CheckBook.br.readLine();
            System.out.print("Check amount: ");
            System.out.flush();
            String amtStr = CheckBook.br.readLine();
            amount = Float.valueOf(amtStr);
            System.out.print("Check memo: ");
            System.out.flush();
            memo = CheckBook.br.readLine();
        } catch (IOException ioe)
          {
            System.out.println(ioe.toString());
            System.out.println("Unable to get Check data.");
            return;
          }
    }
}
```

```
/**
 * Class to represent a check book.
 * @author Michael C. Daconta
 * @version 1.1
 */
class CheckBook
{
    /** buffered reader of standard input stream. */
    static BufferedReader br =
            new BufferedReader(new InputStreamReader(System.in));

    /** Main() method to invoke from JVM. */
    public static void main(String args[])
    {
        Check theCheckBook[];

        /* enter the checks */
        System.out.print("Enter number of checks used this month: ");
        System.out.flush();
        String numStr = null;
        try {
                numStr = br.readLine();
        } catch (IOException ioe)
          {
                System.out.println(ioe.toString());
                System.exit(1);
          }
        int numChecks = Integer.parseInt(numStr);

        theCheckBook = new Check[numChecks];

        for (int i=0; i < numChecks; i++)
        {
            theCheckBook[i] = new Check();
            theCheckBook[i].enterCheck();
        }

        /* print out check register.
           First print the header. */
        System.out.println("Check #\t       Payee        \t Amount" +
                           " \tMemo");
        System.out.println("———————————————————" +
                           "—————————");
        for (int i=0; i < numChecks; i++)
            System.out.println(theCheckBook[i].number + "\t" +
              pad(theCheckBook[i].to,20,' ') + "\t" +
              theCheckBook[i].amount + "\t" +
              theCheckBook[i].memo);

        /* calculate total expenses */
        double total=0.0;
```

```
        for (int i=0; i < numChecks; i++)
        {
            total += theCheckBook[i].amount.doubleValue();
        }
        System.out.println("Total expenses for month: $" + total);
    }

    /** method to pad strings. */
    static String pad(String inString, int desiredLength, char padChar)
    {
        if (inString.length() >= desiredLength)
            return new String(inString);

        StringBuffer newStr = new StringBuffer(inString);
        for (int i=inString.length(); i < desiredLength; i++)
            newStr.append(padChar);

        return newStr.toString();
    }
}
```

A run of Source 2.17 produces:

```
C:\hotjava\bin>java jwiley.chp2.CheckBook
Enter number of checks used this month: 5
Check number: 101
Check to: Quality TV & Appliance
Check amount: 65.40
Check memo: TV Repair
Check number: 102
Check to: Smiths
Check amount: 99.45
Check memo: groceries
Check number: 103
Check to: Dr. Schaus
Check amount: 45.20
Check memo: office visit
Check number: 104
Check to: Livingstons Books
Check amount: 15.10
Check memo: Entertainment
Check number: 105
Check to: Southwest Gas
Check amount: 20.20
Check memo: gas bill
```

```
Check #      Payee                     Amount     Memo
___________________________________________________________
101          Quality TV & Appliance    65.4       TV Repair
102          Smiths                    99.45      groceries
103          Dr. Schaus                45.2       office visit
104          Livingstons Books         15.1       Entertainment
105          Southwest Gas             20.2       gas bill
Total expenses for month: $245.35
```

Another important point to note is the creation of the static utility function to pad the Java string to the proper length. You should notice that the function is not attached to any particular object through the use of the static keyword. We will cover this in more detail in the next section.

2.9 FUNCTIONS

Functions are the cornerstone of modular code and procedural programming and should not be underestimated in the age of object orientation. Functions are more than just a language feature, they are the implementation of a common-sense, problem-solving methodology. The idea is that you functionally decompose a large system into smaller subcomponents, and further divide those subcomponents into smaller components until no further decomposition is possible. The end result is a hierarchical organization that describes the functioning of a system in a sufficient amount of detail to implement it. It also makes it easy to divide the implementation work by parceling out branches of the hierarchy.

Java follows the object-oriented programming methodology whereby functions only exist as a part of an object. In this role, the term function has been replaced by the term method. The key difference between object-oriented programming and procedural programming—and thus the difference between methods and functions—is the focus on data. In procedural programming, data is something you act on and functions are the tools you use to act on that data. In that arrangement, however, data is taking a back seat to the functions. Over the years, the programming community has realized that the data is the most important part of the program. The data should be protected. The primary method to protect data has been to restrict access to it and to surround it with methods (functions) that are the outside world's only access to the precious data inside. This "wrapping" of functions around data in a tight little ball is where the idea "encapsulation" comes from. An instantiation of this encapsulated data and functions in memory is then called an object.

In general, I support the object-oriented approach to program design. I do believe that the "data is king"; however, there are times when separate, standalone utility functions come in handy. C++ allowed both methods and standalone functions. Java has simplified things by only allowing methods; however, utility functions are possible by making a method static. A static method can be called from anywhere in a Java program, without requiring an object. You can call a static method by using the dot operator with the class name to specify the method. Source 2.18 demonstrates both class methods and static class methods.

SOURCE 2.18

```
// Coord.java
package jwiley.chp2;

/**
 * A simple, 3 dimensional coordinate class.
 */
class Coord
{
    /** components. */
    int x,y,z;

    /** constructor. */
    Coord(int inX, int inY, int inZ)
    {
        x = inX; y = inY; z = inZ;
    }

    /** accessor. */
    int getX()
    { return x; }

    /** accessor. */
    int getY()
    { return y; }

    /** accessor. */
    int getZ()
    { return z; }

    /** mutator. */
    void setX(int inX)
    { x = inX; }

    /** mutator. */
    void setY(int inY)
    { y = inY; }

    /** mutator. */
    void setZ(int inZ)
    { z = inZ; }

    /** print out a String representation. */
    public String toString()
    {
        return "x: " + x + " y: " + y +
               " z: " + z;
    }

    /** method to scale this point. */
    void scalePt(int Scale)
```

```
    {
        x *= Scale;
        y *= Scale;
        z *= Scale;
    }

    /** static utility function */
    static Coord scalePt(Coord inCoord, int Scale)
    {
        int aX, aY, aZ;
        /* use methods */
        aX = inCoord.getX();
        aY = inCoord.getY();
        aZ = inCoord.getZ();
        aX *= Scale;
        aY *= Scale;
        aZ *= Scale;
        Coord outCoord = new Coord(aX, aY, aZ);
        return outCoord;
    }

    /** main method to invoke from JVM. */
    public static void main(String args[])
    {
        Coord aCoord = new Coord(4,5,2);

        /* use method */
        String coordStr = aCoord.toString();
        System.out.println("aCoord holds " + coordStr);

        /* use utility function */
        Coord scaleCoord = Coord.scalePt(aCoord,10);
        coordStr = scaleCoord.toString();
        System.out.println("scaleCoord holds " + coordStr);
    }
}
```

A run of Source 2.18 produces:

```
C:\hotjava\bin>java jwiley.chp2.functionTst
aCoord holds x: 4 y: 5 z: 2
scaleCoord holds x: 40 y: 50 z: 20
```

The key difference between methods and static methods is how you are able to invoke the method (function). With methods you can only invoke the method via an instantiated object. In this sense, the object "owns" the method. It is inextricably part of the object's repertoire of actions. When you declare a method static, it is not instantiated with each object but is part of the entire class. Therefore, you invoke the method by preceding it with the class name. In essence, this allows you to make utility functions that belong to a class. If the class is public, then you have in essence created standalone functions.

An Interesting Example of Static Methods

If you are anxious to learn the other Java features, feel free to skip this section. Here I will diverge slightly to show you an interesting example of static methods. We will examine how you can encode a binary file (image file, application, data, or executable) into a text format suitable for sending via e-mail. In this example we will create a base 16 (hexadecimal) encoder and decoder. A base 16 encoder is not as efficient as a base 64 encoder; however, it is simpler and demonstrates the same concepts.

SOURCE 2.19

```
// Base16.java
package jwiley.chp2;

import java.io.*;
import java.net.Socket;
import java.net.*;

/**
 * Class to convert from binary to text format.
 * @version 1.1
 * @author Michael C. Daconta
 */
class base16Encoder
{
    /** global constant indicating whether
        or not we are in debug mode */
    public static final boolean debug = false;

    /** global encoding between binary
        and text characters */
    static final char encoding[] = { '0', '1', '2', '3', '4',
                                     '5', '6', '7', '8', '9',
                                     'A', 'B', 'C', 'D', 'E',
                                     'F' };

    /**
     * Converts from binary to text
     */
    public static void encodeStream(InputStream is, OutputStream os)
                       throws IOException
    {
        DataInputStream dis = new DataInputStream(is);
        PrintStream ps = new PrintStream(os);
        int lineLength=0;
        long byteCount=0;
        long charCount=0;
```

```
        try
        {
            while (true)
            {
                byte b = dis.readByte();
                byteCount++;
                int upper = (b >> 4) & 0xf;
                int lower = (b & 0xf);

                ps.write(encoding[upper]); // writes a byte (not char)
                ps.write(encoding[lower]);
                charCount += 2;
                lineLength += 2;
                if (lineLength >= 76)
                {
                    ps.write('\n');
                    lineLength = 0;
                }
            }
        } catch (EOFException eof)
          {
            // OK, do nothing
            if (debug)
            {
                System.out.println("base16Encoder, byteCount: " +
                                    byteCount);
                System.out.println("base16Encoder, charCount: " +
                                    charCount);
            }
          }
          catch (IOException ioe)
          {
            throw new IOException(ioe.getMessage());
          }
    }
}

/**
 * Class to convert from text to binary format.
 * @version 1.1
 * @author Michael C. Daconta
 */
class base16Decoder
{
    /** global constant indicating whether
        or not we are in debug mode */
    public static final boolean debug = false;

    /**
     * Method that converts a character to binary
     */
```

```
private static int decodeChar(int ch)
{
    if ( (ch >= '0') && (ch <= '9') )
        return ch - '0';
    else
        return ch - 'A' + 10;
}

/**
 * Method that converts from text to binary
 */
public static void decodeStream(InputStream is, OutputStream os)
                     throws IOException
{
    DataInputStream dis = new DataInputStream(is);
    DataOutputStream dos = new DataOutputStream(os);
    int lineLength=0;
    long charCount = 0;
    long byteCount = 0;
    try
    {
        while (true)
        {
            char upperC = (char) dis.readByte();
            if (upperC == '\n')
                continue;
            char lowerC = (char) dis.readByte();
            charCount+=2;
            int upperB = decodeChar(upperC);
            int lowerB = decodeChar(lowerC);
            byte b = (byte) (upperB << 4);
            b |= lowerB;
            dos.writeByte(b);
            byteCount++;
        }
     } catch (EOFException eof)
       {
         // OK, do nothing
         if (debug)
         {
             System.out.println("base16Decoder, charCount: " +
                                 charCount);
             System.out.println("base16Decoder, byteCount: " +
                                 byteCount);
         }
       }
       catch (IOException ioe)
       {
         throw new IOException(ioe.getMessage());
       }
 }
```

```
}

/**
 * Class to convert between text and binary formats.
 * @version 1.1
 * @author Michael C. Daconta
 */
class Base16
{
    /**
     * Main method to be called by JVM
     */
    public static void main(String args[])
    {
        if (args.length < 2)
        {
            System.out.println("USAGE: java base16 inputFile outputFile");
            System.exit(1);
        }

        String inputFileName = args[0];
        String outputFileName = args[1];

        try
        {
            // encode
            FileInputStream fis = new FileInputStream(inputFileName);
            int dotIdx = inputFileName.indexOf('.');
            String tmpFileName = inputFileName.substring(0,dotIdx)
                                 + ".enc16";
            System.out.println("Writing: " + tmpFileName);
            FileOutputStream tmpFos = new FileOutputStream(tmpFileName);
            base16Encoder.encodeStream(fis,tmpFos);
            fis.close();
            tmpFos.close();

            // decode
            fis = new FileInputStream(tmpFileName);
            FileOutputStream fos = new FileOutputStream(outputFileName);
            base16Decoder.decodeStream(fis,fos);
            fis.close();
            fos.close();
        } catch (Exception e)
          {
            e.printStackTrace();
            System.exit(1);
          }
    }
}
```

A run of the preceding program will take any file, like a binary executable file or a graphics file, and create a file of printable ASCII text that is suitable for e-mail. The idea behind the program is simple: take a byte and split it into two hexadecimal digits. Then map each hexidecimal digit to its character equivalent and write that character to the output file. The only drawback in the program just shown is that the size of the output file it creates is exactly double the size of the input file. It does this by mapping every byte into two characters. A base 64 encoder is more efficient in that it maps every three bytes in a file into four characters.

Just as functions have been slightly modified due to Java's object-oriented focus, so have command line arguments. Let's see how.

TIP You can define variables that are similar to global variables using the static keyword. Static has the same effect on data and methods in Java.

2.10 COMMAND LINE ARGUMENTS

Command line arguments allow you to pass parameters to a program when it is run from the operating system. In C, this is implemented by the main() function being passed two arguments: argc and argv. In C, main() looks like this

```
int main(int argc, char *argv[]);
```

The integer variable argc represents the number of arguments passed into the program. The variable argv is a pointer to an array of character strings that contain the arguments. In C, there is always at least one argument (argv[0]), which is the name of the program being executed.

Java also allows command line arguments from the operating system; however, the interface is simpler and makes use of the String class discussed earlier. In Java, the command line arguments are passed to the main function as an array of Java strings. The argc variable is unnecessary since all Java arrays have a length data member. Source 2.20 demonstrates a program processing the three most common types of command line arguments.

SOURCE 2.20

```
// CmdLineTest.java
package jwiley.chp2;

/**
 * Class to demonstrate the basics of Java command line
 * arguments.
 * @author Michael C. Daconta
 * @version 1.2
```

```
 */
class CmdLineTest
{

    /** Main() method to invoke from JVM. */
    public static void main(String args[])
    {

        /* 1) no need for argc because arrays have the
           length data member. */
        System.out.println("Number of command line args is " + args.length);

        /* 2) command line args in Java are just
           an array of Strings. */
        for (int i=0; i < args.length; i++)
                System.out.println("arg #" + i + " is " +
                                          args[i]);

        /* 3) IMPORTANT: java arguments do NOT include
           the program name as in C and C++. */

        /* 4) flag arguments. */
        for (int i=0; i < args.length; i++)
        {
            if (args[i].startsWith("-"))
            {
                switch (args[i].charAt(1))
                {
                    case 'a':
                            System.out.println("a flag."); break;
                    case 'b':
                            System.out.println("b flag."); break;
                    case 'c':
                            System.out.println("c flag."); break;
                    default:
                            /* normally error,
                            here do nothing to allow other
                            tests */ ;
                }
            }
        }

        /* 5) word arguments. */
        for (int i=0; i < args.length; i++)
        {
            if (args[i].equals("-verbose"))
                    System.out.println("Set the verbose flag.");
        }
```

```
        /* 6) arguments that require arguments. */
        for (int i=0; i < args.length; i++)
        {
            if (args[i].equals("-getNext"))
            {
                String nextArg = new String(args[++i]);
                System.out.println("next Arg is " + nextArg);
            }
        }
    }
}
```

A run of Source 2.20 produces:

```
C:\hotjava\bin>java jwiley.chp2.CmdLineTst -a -b -verbose -getNext hello -c
Number of command line args is 6
arg #0 is -a
arg #1 is -b
arg #2 is -verbose
arg #3 is -getNext
arg #4 is hello
arg #5 is -c
a flag.
b flag.
c flag.
Set the verbose flag.
next Arg is hello
```

The first point to stress about Source 2.20 is the fact that Java differs from C and C++ by not including the program name in the command line arguments. This is very important for people porting C and C++ applications to Java as it will require a modification to the command line processing code. This also means that if there are no command line arguments the length of the args array will be 0.

Processing Java command line arguments is very simple due to the rich array of class methods in the String class. In Source 2.20 I demonstrate processing of one-letter flags, command words, and arguments that require further arguments.

We have now covered the majority of identical and similar features between the C language and Java. Now we will turn to features in C but purposefully left out of Java.

2.11 ENVIRONMENT VARIABLES

In C, environment variables are passed to the main function in much the same way that command line arguments are. In Java, the mechanism for accessing environment variables is very different. Java provides a class named System that allows programmers to access one or more of the system environment variables. In addition to allowing access to the platform's environment, Java provides two additional mechanisms for specifying environment variables. Environment settings can be specified on the command line when the Java Virtual Machine is started as follows:

```
Java -D<propname>=<value> <classname>
```

Environment settings can also be specified in the properties file. The properties file is a file named properties found in the .hotjava directory. The format of the properties file is very simple. It consists of a series of lines of the format <propname>=<value>. Any line beginning with a # is treated as a comment and ignored. Source 2.21 shows an example properties file. Source 2.22 gives an example of using the System class to access environment variables.

A run of Source 2.22 produces:

```
C:\java\bin>java jwiley.chp2.SystemProperties
— listing properties —
user.language=en
java.home=C:\JDK1.1.1\BIN\..
awt.toolkit=sun.awt.windows.WToolkit
file.encoding.pkg=sun.io
java.version=1.1.1
file.separator=\
line.separator=

user.region=US
file.encoding=8859_1
java.vendor=Sun Microsystems Inc.
user.timezone=EST
user.name=unknown
os.arch=x86
os.name=Windows 95
```

SOURCE 2.21

```
# Default properties used by the appletviewer
appletloader.disposed=Applet disposed.
appletloader.exception2=exception: %0: %1.
appletloader.started=Applet started.
# Our own custom properties
favoritecolor=blue
jarfiles=c:\jars
```

SOURCE 2.22

```
// SystemProperties.java
package jwiley.chp2;

import java.util.Properties;

/** Class to demonstrate the System class. */
public class SystemProperties
{
    /** main() method to invoke from JVM. */
    public static void main(String args[])
    {
        Properties props = System.getProperties();

        // list the properties
        props.list(System.out);

        // access an individual property
        System.out.println("\n Accessing individual properties.");
        String fileSeparator = System.getProperty("file.separator");
        System.out.println("File Separator is <" + fileSeparator +
                                    ">");
    }
}
```

```
java.vendor.url=http://www.sun.com/
user.dir=c:\src\jwiley\chp6
java.class.path=c:\jdk1.1.1\lib\classes.zip;c:\src;c:...
java.class.version=45.3
os.version=4.0
path.separator=;
user.home=C:\JDK1.1.1\BIN\..

Accessing individual properties.File Separator is <\>
```

2.12 FEATURES REMOVED FROM C

We will focus on four key areas where functionality was removed from Java. Those areas are: keywords, global variables, pointers, the preprocessor and variable arguments. We will also discuss why these items were removed and how the same or similar functionality exists in Java.

Keywords

C unique statement keywords removed from Java:

goto. In C, a control flow keyword that allows unconditional branching to a label farther down in the current function. There have been many studies on the harmful effects of using gotos in code. The most obvious is the hard-to-follow "spaghetti code" produced by overusing gotos. The elimination of goto simplified the Java language. The fact that the Java language takes a firm stance on many programming issues is very refreshing. The Java language was designed to be clear, straightforward, and without ambiguity.

sizeof. In C, a compile-time operator that returned the size, in bytes, of its argument (a data type or variable). Since the Java language precisely specifies the size of all the basic types, there is no need for the sizeof operator. Again, Java has set its stake in the ground and is sticking to it. Why is this so important? Because it is an area where the language designers have taken on the responsibility of an imperfect decision (all decisions are inherently imperfect), so that the language users (programmers) do not have to worry about it. This allows programmers to concentrate on creating useful programs and less on how to work the tools of their trade.

typedef. In C, a declaration keyword that allows a type to be given an alias. This directly violates the Java design principle of simplicity. The problem with typedefs, header files, and #defines is that they cause a program to be uninterpretable without having examined the entire "hidden context" behind the program. A Java program is a Java program and all types and operators mean exactly what they should.

C-unique data types removed from Java:

struct, union, enum. In C, these keywords are used to create user-defined data types. The Java class gives you the same facilities as structs so they are redundant. Unions allow the same memory area to be accessed in multiple ways. Such behavior is inherently unsafe and is therefore not supported. Structs and unions could have been removed from C++; however, the desire for strict backward compatibility to C forced these redundancies on C++. You can obtain the same effect as enums by using constants. These are good examples of how Java stuck to its design philosophy of being a simple language by removing redundancies in C++.

C unique modifier keywords removed from Java:

auto. A data type modifier that gives a variable only scope and lifetime within a block. In Java, just like C++, you can declare data types anywhere in the program (not just at the start of new blocks).

extern. A data type modifier that tells the compiler that the definition of the global variable or function is found in another compilation unit. In Java, there are no global variables and all external classes are loaded dynamically by the runtime interpreter.

register. A data type modifier that requests the compiler store a local variable in a register of the CPU rather than in main memory. Since Java is portable across different platforms, the number of available registers is not known and therefore this type of optimization is up to each platform-dependent implementation of the interpreter.

signed, unsigned. These data type modifiers specify whether an int or char is signed or unsigned. In Java all integer types are always signed.

volatile. A type modifier that tells the compiler a variable may be externally modified unpredictably. This will prevent the compiler from performing certain optimizations. Being portable across platforms, there is no equivalent of this in Java.

Global variables were removed from Java because they violate object-oriented design concepts and cause naming conflicts. Since all Java code is part of a class, and the Virtual Machine only loads and executes classes, global variables would introduce unnecessary complexity to the system. For instance, how would a global variable be loaded into the namespace? Where would the memory for the global variable be allocated? Instead, Java requires that all variables be associated with classes. By declaring a class variable to be static, you can achieve the same benefits of a global variable without the hazards.

Pointers

Having written two books on pointers, I obviously feel they are a very important part of C and C++. However, as I stated in the Introduction, we are at a point in the software industry where reliability and portability far outweigh any gains in speed or flexibility through the use of pointers. The risks of pointers are well documented. In my first book, *C Pointers and Dynamic Memory Management*, I documented many pitfalls of pointer programming, like dangling pointers, memory leaks, forgetting the NUL terminator in a string, requesting the wrong number of bytes from malloc(), array overruns, incorrect operator precedence in malloc() calls, and dereferencing a NULL pointer.

Java does not support a pointer variable type, but it does support object references that are very similar. Much of the requirements of a pointer can be satisfied with a reference. Source 2.23 demonstrates how Java's object references can be used to perform some of the same functions performed by C pointers.

SOURCE 2.23

```
// PointerEquiv.java
package jwiley.chp2;

class simpleObject {
    int a;
    public simpleObject left, right;

    simpleObject(int inA)
    {
        a=inA;
        left = right = null;
    }

    int getA()
    {
        return a;
    }

    void setA(int inA)
    {
        a = inA;
    }

    public String toString()
    {
        return new String("a: " + a);
    }
}

class PointerEquiv {
    static void swap(Object a, Object b)
    {
            Object tmp = a;
            a = b;
            b = tmp;
    }

    public static void main(String args[])
    {
        /* 1) Like pointers, all objects and arrays
              are dynamically allocated. (Arrays are a special type
              of object) */
        int arr[] = new int[10];
        simpleObject myObj = new simpleObject(5);

        /* 2) An object reference can point to an object
              of the specified class, or to nothing */
        int arr2[] = arr;
        simpleObject yourObj = myObj;
        System.out.println("yourObj is " + yourObj.toString());
```

```
        /* 3) null is a reserved keyword identical to
              NULL in usage. */
        int arr3[] = null;
        arr = null; /* causes arr to point to null */

        /* 4) Object references are passed to Java methods by value
              The original object can be modified, but a method cannot
              Change what the original reference points to. */
        simpleObject otherObject = new simpleObject(20);
        System.out.println("Before swap, myObj is " + myObj.toString() +
                           " otherObject is " + otherObject.toString());
        swap(myObj, otherObject);
        System.out.println("After swap, myObj is " + myObj.toString() +
                           " otherObject is " + otherObject.toString());

        /* 5) There is no explicit free or delete. Java
              memory is garbage collected. */
        System.gc(); /* force garbage collection to occur NOW. */

        /* 6) Since all Java objects are descendants of a
              single Object class. An unitialized Object
              can act like a void pointer. */
        Object voidp = otherObject;
        ((simpleObject) voidp).setA(100);
        System.out.println("voidp points to " +
                           ((simpleObject) voidp).toString());
        System.out.println("Just as otherObject now is " +
                           otherObject.toString());

        /* 7) Self-referential structures are possible by
              using object references. An object can even point
              to itself */
        simpleObject root = new simpleObject(1000);
        root.left = new simpleObject(500);
        root.right = root;

        /* 8) There is NO equivalent to function pointers
              in Java. Safety prevailed as a design goal. */
    }
}
```

A run of Source 2.23 produces:

```
C:\hotjava\bin>java jwiley.chp2.PointerEquiv
yourObj is a: 5
Before swap, myObj is a: 5 otherObject is a: 20
After swap, myObj is a: 5 otherObject is a: 20
voidp points to a: 100
Just as otherObject now is a: 100
```

So, as you see demonstrated in Source 2.23, Java's heap-based arrays and objects give you the following pointer functionality:

1. Dynamic initialization.
2. The ability for multiple references to refer to the same object.
3. The ability to represent no object using the null keyword.
4. Freedom from worrying about explicitly freeing memory by using garbage collection. This allows rapid, yet safe, prototyping.
5. Since all objects are inherited from a single root Object (we will discuss inheritance in more detail in the next chapter), a reference to a java.lang.Object can in fact point to any Java object.
6. Self-referential abstract types like linked lists, trees, and graphs can be implemented.

Java has no way of implementing two current pointer functions:

1. **Pass by reference.** Although all arrays and objects are accessed via references, Java only supports pass by value. The need for pass by reference is minimized through the use of objects and object-oriented design whereby most methods act on the object's data members and do not need to modify variables in the caller. If it is necessary to modify a caller's variable, the method's return value can be used.
2. **Function pointers.** Although very useful as callbacks in GUI functions, and in parser dispatch tables, some of the benefit of function pointers can be gained through using virtual functions and inheritance (discussed more in the next chapter). In general, however, Java interfaces can be used to solve all problems solved by function pointers. Java interfaces will be explained in more detail in Chapters 3 and 4.

Preprocessor

The C preprocessor manipulates a C source file before it is passed to the compiler. It generally provides two capabilities: text replacement and conditional compilation. It is important to understand that both of these capabilities have been criticized as not truly being benefits at all, especially since the majority of a code's lifetime is spent in the maintenance phase.

Bjarne Stroustrup, creator of C++, gives the following warning about preprocessor macros:

> "Don't use them if you don't have to. It has been observed that almost every macro demonstrates a flaw in the programming language, in the program, or in the programmer. Because they rearrange the program text before the compiler proper sees it, macros are also a major problem for many programming tools, so when you use macros you should expect inferior service from tools such as debuggers, cross reference tools, and profilers."[2]

[2]Bjarne Stroustrup, *The C++ Programming Language*, *Second Edition*, (Reading, MA: Addison-Wesley, 1991), p. 138.

The primary problem with a preprocessor can be summed up with the expression, "seeing is not believing." That means that C source code cannot be trusted until all header files have been read (including the headers that the headers include) and all macros expanded. This chore becomes impractical in very large programming projects. Source 2.24 is an example of source code that is not what it appears to be through the misuse of macros.

A run of Source 2.24 produces:

```
b is less than a.
a is less than b.
```

SOURCE 2.24

```
/* obfuscate.c */
#include <stdio.h>
#include "obfuscate.h"

void _funcB(void)
{
    println("What function am I?");
}
void main()
{
    int a=10, b=5;

    if (b < a)
    {
        printf("b is less than a.\n");
    }
    else
    {
        printf("a is less than b.\n");
    }
}

/* obfuscate.h */
#define a b
#define b a
#define else ;
#define PI 6.28

#ifdef configureB
#define _funcA _funcB
#else
#define _funcB _funcA
#endif
```

As is evident, Source 2.24 is not only ridiculous but produces ridiculous output that doesn't make sense. This is an exaggeration, however, I have seen real code that comes close to being that bad. Many modern compilers allow you to preprocess your source code and examine the product. Source 2.25 is the tail end (without all the preprocessed macros for the header files) of the preprocessed version of Source 2.24.

SOURCE 2.25

```
void _funcA(void)
{
println("What function am I?");
}
void main()
{
int a=10, b=5;
if (b < a)
{
printf("b is less than a.\n");
}
;
{
printf("a is less than b.\n");
}
}
```

C macros are often used to implement program constants. In Java, constants are specified with the final keyword, and variables that can be accessed globally are specified with the static keyword. Not only do these two keywords combine to provide the exact same functionality that C macros do, but Java constants defined this way also benefit from type checking. A C macro is merely text; it doesn't have an associated data type. A class that contains global constants will look like this:

```
Class A
{
    public static final int constantInt = 5;
    public static final String constantString = "I am constant."
    // Other constants here
}
```

The other capability that the preprocessor gave C programmers was conditional compilation. This is performed using #ifdefs and was useful in debugging. This same functionality can be performed in Java by using a boolean variable as a debug flag. Not having to worry about what the preprocessor will do to your code speeds up the programming process and will increase productivity. When the Java compiler encounters a code fragment that can never be reached, such as:

```
if (false)
{
    ...
}
```

the compiler will ignore the code entirely. By using a constant debug variable you can easily conditionally compile sections of code by merely modifying the value of the constant. The C preprocessor allows programmers to conditionally compile not just code fragments, but entire functions. Java provides no parallel mechanism to achieve this. This is actually a benefit because there is never any confusion about whether or not a method is actually available on a class. All methods are always available whatever the build parameters were.

Variable Arguments

Variable arguments give C and C++ programs the ability to pass an unspecified number of arguments to a function. The C standard library routines printf, sprintf, and fprintf all use variable arguments. Source 2.26 is a C program that demonstrates the use of variable arguments.

SOURCE 2.26

```
#include <stdio.h>
#include <stdarg.h>

long sum(int numInts, ...)
{
     long total = 0;
     int i=0;
     va_list args;
     va_start(args, numInts);

     for (i = 0; i < numInts; i++)
          total += va_arg(args, int);

     va_end(args);
     return total;
}

int main(int argc, char *argv[])
{
     long theTot = sum(4, 5, 10, 20, 30);
     printf("The total is %d.\n", theTot);
}
```

A run of the C Source 2.26 produces:

```
The total is 65.
```

Variable arguments are especially useful in creating generic utility functions in C. The flexibility that variable arguments provide in C can be achieved in Java through the use of the Vector class. The Vector class is a Java implementation of a generic, dynamic array. A Vector can hold objects of any type and does not have to be homogenous. A Vector turns out to be perfect to achieve all the benefits of variable arguments. Source 2.27 demonstrates the use of the Java Vector class for passing a variable number of arguments to a method.

TIP If you need to store a primitive such as a short or long in a Vector, you should use the reference data types in java.lang (java.lang.Short, java.lang.Long, etc.). Every Java primitive has a corresponding class in the java.lang package.

SOURCE 2.27

```
import java.util.Vector;
class VarArgs {
        static long sum(Vector ints)
        {
                long total = 0;
                for (int i=0; i < ints.size(); i++)
                        total += ((Integer)ints.elementAt(i)).intValue();
                return total;
        }
        public static void main(String args[])
        {
                Vector intVec = new Vector(3);
                intVec.addElement(new Integer(5));
                intVec.addElement(new Integer(10));
                intVec.addElement(new Integer(20));
                intVec.addElement(new Integer(30));
                long theTot = sum(intVec);
                System.out.println("The total is " + theTot);
        }
}
```

A run of Source 2.27 produces:

```
C:\hotjava\bin>java jwiley.chp2.VarArgs
The total is 65
```

Although it takes a few extra lines of code to set up the Vector, the use of the Vector class proves simpler than the variable argument macros. As for length, there are 18 lines of code in the C program and 20 lines of code in the Java program. Again Java maintains its simplicity yet does not sacrifice any functionality.

Forward References

The final aspect of C that has been removed is the use of header files and function prototypes. In C, headers and prototypes were used to specify the interfaces of a series of functions that were either located in a separate compilation unit (source file), or located in a source file somewhere after they are used. Java removes the need for function prototypes because the compiler parses the source file multiple times. On one of the first passes, the compiler determines what methods are available. Because of Java's object-oriented design, all functionality is clearly broken down into separate classes. Rather than require the programmer to build a header file to specify the contents of a class, the Java compiler looks at the class itself to determine the interface. These two features of Java greatly reduce code maintenance time, and make it much easier to move blocks of code within a file or between files.

Although this chapter covered C language features removed from Java, I believe we have shown how these features were redundant or how similar functionality is provided via another Java language feature. Now that we have finished covering the similarities and differences between the languages, we need to see how the Java class hierarchy gives you identical or similar functionality as the C Standard Library.

2.14 THE C STANDARD LIBRARY

"The Standard C Library is fairly ambitious."[3]

Although C is not an object-oriented language, the C Standard Library is probably the greatest reuse success story to date. The C Standard Library has provided a wealth of useful functions used in every C program for nearly 20 years. The library consists of 15 header files that roughly divide the library into functional parts as well as declare all the functions accessible to the C programmer. We will discuss each header file, some of the more commonly used functions, and follow up with how that functionality is achieved in the Java Standard Library. The Java Standard Library (also known as the Java Environment or Java Core API) is demonstrated in great

[3]P.J. Plauger, *The Standard C Library*, (Englewood Cliffs, N.J.: Prentice Hall, 1980), p. 5.

detail in Chapter 3. References to Chapter 3 for specific code examples will be made instead of duplicating the code here.

<assert.h>

The purpose of this header is solely to implement the assert macro. The assert macro allows a diagnostic predicate (an expression that evaluates to true or false) to be put in your code. The assert macro is used like this:

```
assert( i < 10);
```

If the assert expression evaluates to false, a text line is printed ("Assertion failed: expression, file xyz, line nnn") and the program terminates abnormally. The utility of assert expressions is for testing and debugging of source code. You can turn off assertions by defining the macro NDEBUG.

Since Java is not preprocessed there is no direct correlation for the assert macro. It is also debatable whether it is needed at all in an object-oriented language that supports encapsulation and exception handling. There is no reason to sprinkle your code with assertions about the values of variables because data members of properly implemented objects are always in a stable state.

<ctype.h>

The purpose of this header is to define a set of macros that perform tests on a character and translation of a character (i.e., toupper(c)). This header is very common in any program that parses or manipulates text. The three most common macros in the set are: isalpha(c), isdigit(c), and isspace(c). It is important to remember that this header only works on the ASCII character set, which is normally an 8-bit representation of a character. The impact of this is that these macros cannot be used for international characters that are part of the UNICODE standard.

The Java Character class (see section 3.2) provides some of the same functionality as the macros in ctype.h for the UNICODE character set. The Character class has methods for isDigit(c), isSpace(c), toLowerCase(c), and others.

<errno.h>

The purpose of this header is to provide macros for the reporting of errors. Unfortunately, the only reliable use of the errno macro is a test where equality to zero means no error and equality to any non-zero value means error. Beyond that, the actual error codes for different functions vary widely by implementation. The Java exception model (see section 3.5) is far superior for both the reporting and handling of errors. In fact, the Java language has taken a bold step forward in error handling by forcing a function that throws an exception to add a throws clause to the function declaration like this:

```
public int read() throws IOException
{
     ...
}
```

<float.h>

The purpose of this header is to define properties of floats, doubles, and long so that your programs can avoid overflow, underflow, and significance loss during floating-point arithmetic. Java's implementation of float and double is fixed and in conformance with IEEE 754 Standard for floating-point arithmetic.

<limits.h>

This header is used to define macros for the ranges of numeric types in C. This is unnecessary in Java since all types are of fixed, platform-independent sizes.

<locale.h>

This header declares two functions and one type, and defines several macros that store information on properties related to a local culture (i.e., monetary formatting, time, and numeric formatting). The contents of the type lconv will also affect other library functions with respect to scanning input and formatting output. Java 1.1 automatically supports many of the internationalization services provided by locale.h.

<math.h>

This header serves the purpose of providing common mathematical functions to C programmers like sin(), exp(), and sqrt(). The Java Math class (see section 3.2) serves the same purpose and almost all of the functions are identical.

<setjmp.h>

> "Exceptions are an evolution of the setjmp/longjmp function pair of Standard C, which has been on the scene for much longer."[4]

The purpose of this header is to define a macro setjmp, a type jmp_buf, and a function longjmp() that implement a nonlocal goto (a goto outside of the current function). In practice, the two main uses of setjmp and longjmp were the implementation of

---

[4]Alessandro Vesely, "Debugging with Exceptions," C/C++ User's Journal, October 1995, p. 22.

exceptions and the implementation of threads. Since Java provides both exceptions and threads, there is need for setjmp and longjmp in Java.

<signal.h>

The purpose of this header is to define a function, type, and macros for the handling and raising of signals. A signal is an extraordinary event (also known as an exception) that can occur because of erroneous actions in your program (i.e., divide by zero) or from the operating system (a termination signal from a control-c typed at the console). The signals common to all implementations are:

SIGABRT. (signal ABORT) abnormal termination

SIGFPE. (signal Floating-Point Exception) an erroneous arithmetic operation

SIGILL. (signal Illegal) an illegal instruction

SIGINT. (signal Interrupt) receipt of an interactive attention signal

SIGSEGV. (signal Segmentation Violation) an invalid access to memory

SIGTERM. (signal Terminate) a termination request sent to the program

The functionality of signal.h is covered by the Java Exception classes. Java exceptions can be thrown by both your Java code and the Java run time.

<stdarg.h>

The purpose of this header is to declare a type and define three macros that process a variable number of arguments passed into a function. The three macros defined are va_start(), va_arg(), and va_end(). As discussed in section 2.12, although Java does not currently support variable arguments, it is easy to replicate this functionality by using the Vector class (see section 3.2).

<stddef.h>

The purpose of this header is to define macro definitions that do not fit into the specific areas covered by floats.h, limits.h, and stdarg.h. Synonyms for the primitive types are defined like ptrdiff_t, size_t, and wchar_t. Since all Java types are platform-independent fixed sizes, this header is unnecessary in Java.

<stdio.h>

The purpose of this header is to define a large assortment of functions that perform input and output. This is a large and very well-known (and very popular) portion of the standard library. C programmers will be happy to know that Java supports the full range of I/O provided in the stdio.h. The Java io package (see section 3.2) has a wealth of classes that implement reading and writing to streams and files. Java also has System.in and System.out that are identical to stdin and stdout.

<stdlib.h>

This header serves a variety of purposes for functions and macros that did not fit into other headers in the standard library. Dr. Plauger, in his classic book, *The Standard C Library* organizes the functions of this header into six groups:

- **Integer math (abs, div, labs, and ldiv).** Some of these functions (the abs() functions) are implemented in the Java Math class (see section 3.2).
- **Algorithms (bsearch, qsort, rand, and srand).** The rand functions are implemented in the Java's Random class (see section 3.2). The search and sort algorithms are not currently part of the Java class hierarchy.
- **Text conversions (atof, atoi, atol, strtod, strtol, and strtoul).** These conversions from strings to primitive types are implemented in the Java type wrappers (i.e., Integer, Float, ... see section 3.2) and java.lang.String.
- **Multibyte conversions (mblen, mbstowcs, mbtowc, wcstombs, and wctomb).** These type of conversions are not necessary in Java due to its support of the UNICODE character set.
- **Storage allocation (calloc, free, malloc, and realloc).** Dynamic allocation is performed in Java with the new operator. Explicit deallocation (like free()) is not necessary due to Java's runtime automatically reclaiming unused allocated memory via garbage collection.
- **Environmental interactions (abort, atexit, exit, getenv, and system).** This functionality is provided by the Java System class (see section 3.2).

<string.h>

The purpose of this header is to provide a set of functions to manipulate text as arrays of characters. Commonly used functions in this header are: strcpy(), strcmp(), strstr(), and strtok(). The weakness of all these functions is their use of pointers (which also makes them efficient) and their reliance on the NUL-terminator. If an array overrun has stomped on memory and removed the NUL-terminator, these routines' behavior is undefined. Java supports all the functionality supported by this header with the String and StringBuffer classes (see section 3.2).

<time.h>

The purpose of this header is to define structures, macros, and functions for representation and manipulation of times and dates. C programmers will be very satisfied with the Java Date class (see section 3.2), which provides all the functionality of this header and is structured almost identically like the tm_struct.

C Header	Java Package or Class
assert.h	Not Applicable
ctype.h	Character class
errno.h	Exception class
float.h	inherent in language definition
locale.h	System Properties
math.h	Math class
setjmp.h	Exception class
signal.h	Exception class
stdarg.h	Vector class
stddef.h	inherent in language definition
stdio.h	io Package
stdlib.h	Math class
	Random class
	type wrapper classes
	System class
string.h	String class
	StringBuffer class
time.h	Date Class

FIGURE 2.6 Correlation of the C Standard Library to the Java Core API.

Figure 2.6 summarizes the previous discussion and compares the C Standard Library to the Java Standard Library.

2.14 SUMMARY

Java has very much in common with C. Many of the operators, expressions, and syntax remain the same. Java has added some object-oriented, thread-specific, and error-handling constructs that will be explained in later chapters. At the same time Java has removed some of the more error-prone and misused aspects of C, including pointers and the goto expression.

Java is an object-oriented programming language. The ramifications of this are discussed in much greater detail in Chapters 3 and 4. However, all data and functionality must belong to a class or object. A class is a definition of an object that implements global methods and data using the static keyword. An object is a combination of data and functions to manipulate that data.

Java features two types of data types: primitives and references. Primitives include the standard numeric and character data types. References provide many of the same features that pointers do in C, without the associated danger. All references point to either a valid object or a special value called null. All objects in Java are created with the new operator, which is similar to malloc. Java has no operator similar to free, however. Java implements a mechanism called garbage collection that automatically frees unreferenced objects.

Arrays in Java are a special type of object. They are created using the new operator, and the size is specified upon creation. Arrays can hold either primitives or objects. Multidimensional arrays are easily implemented as arrays of arrays.

Strings and characters in Java are very different than in C. First, Java uses UNICODE, which is a wide character encoding encompassing characters from most languages throughout the world. Second, Java implements strings as objects rather than as nul-terminated arrays.

The Java Core API provides many of the capabilities of the C Standard Library as well as many other features of C, including: command line arguments, access to the underlying file system, access to the standard input and output streams, and access to the local machine's environment.

CHAPTER 3

Comparing Java to C++

Design. As I write a program, I should use a language that minimizes the distance between the problem-solving strategies that I have in my head and the program text I eventually write on paper.

—Jon Bentley, *Programming Pearls*

OBJECTIVE

This chapter will compare and contrast the Java language to C++. All major elements of C++ will be examined and all differences will be highlighted. This chapter will also serve as a good foundation on object-oriented programming for C programmers.

The C++ programming language was designed and developed by Bjarne Stroustrup in the Computer Science Research Center at AT&T Bell Labs in Murray Hill, New Jersey. Originally called C with Classes, C++ is a superset of the C language that adds object-oriented facilities. C++ has maintained backward compatibility with C. In general, by introducing object-oriented programming constructs to the large audience of C programmers, C++ performed a valuable service and thereby achieved broad success among developers. On the downside, C++ has inherited all the difficulties of programming in C and added some new complexities with features like operator overloading, multiple inheritance, and templates. This chapter will introduce C programmers to object-oriented programming as well as compare and contrast all of the major features of C++ to Java.

3.1 OBJECT-ORIENTED PROGRAMMING

There is a very basic idea behind object-oriented programming: Make the computer language resemble the way things work in the real world. Real-world objects like people, places, and things are what our programs are about. If your program tracks office supplies, then your computer language should talk about office supplies. Most real-world objects are defined in terms of characteristics (or attributes) that describe the object and behaviors (or actions) the object can perform. The object-oriented technique that allows us to model real-world objects in our programs is called *encapsulation*.

The real-world objects like people, animals, and motorcycles are often understood by grouping them in a set of objects that all share common characteristics and behaviors. Humans are part of the group called mammals because we share characteristics and behaviors with other mammals. Expressed another way, a human *is* a mammal. The object-oriented technique that allows us to organize objects hierarchically is called *inheritance* and is modeled after biological inheritance.

The last major contribution of object-oriented programming is its mimicking of how real-world objects describe the actions they perform. Real-world objects often perform the same type of action yet perform it in their own slightly different way. A boy runs, a dog runs, a stream runs, and a car runs. All those real-world objects use the verb "run" to describe one of their actions. The object-oriented technique that allows us to use one name for many different implementations of an action is called *polymorphism*. Now that we have an intuitive understanding of the three characteristic traits of all object-oriented languages (encapsulation, inheritance, and polymorphism), we will examine each in more technical detail.

Encapsulation

Encapsulation is a technique that extends the concept of abstraction from a strictly data phenomena to both data and functions. If you think of the data abstraction used in C, the structure, then it is easy to grasp the idea that a class encompasses what a structure did and then extends the concept to include the binding of functions into the single entity. See Source 3.1 for a comparison of a C structure to a C++ class. A class binds both data and functions into a single entity, creating a brand new abstraction called an object.

There is a very definite relationship between a C structure and a C++ class. In fact, in C++ the structure concept has been expanded to include member functions. This was elegantly stated in the *Annotated C++ Reference Manual*:

> Thus the C++ class concept can be seen as a generalization of the C notion of a structure or—looking at it the other way—the C concept of a structure is a simple variant of the C++ class concept. In particular, C structures do not support member functions of any kind. Having a C struct be a simple variant of a C++ class has important implications for cooperation between C and C++ programs.[1]

[1]Margaret A. Ellis and Bjarne Stroustrop, *The Annotated C++ Reference Manual* (Reading, M.A.: Addison-Wesley Publishing Company, 1990), p. 165.

SOURCE 3.1 encapsulate.cpp

```
// encapsulate.cpp

// a C structure is only an abstraction of attributes
struct car {
     char make[60];
     char model[60];
     int top_speed;
     float price;
};

// a C++ class is an abstraction of both attributes and actions
class automobile {
     private:
          // some attributes
          char make[60];
          char model[60];
          int top_speed;
          float price;

     public:
          // some actions
          int run()
          {
               int travelling_speed=0;

               // do something

               return travelling_speed;
          }

          void breakDown()
          {
               // fix it
          }
};

int main(int argc, char **argv)
{
     struct car data_abstraction;
     automobile a_real_world_object;
     return 0;
}
```

After examining Source 3.1 you may have noticed that a Java class is slightly different from a C++ class. Source 3.2 is an example of a Java class.

A run of Source 3.2 produces:

```
C:\java\bin>java jwiley.chp3.Loan
Enter Principal of Loan: 150000
Enter annual Interest rate percentage (i.e., 9.5): 7
Enter number of years of Loan: 30
Your monthly payment is : 997.9537457710456
```

SOURCE 3.2 Loan.java

```
// Loan.java
package jwiley.chp3;

import java.io.BufferedReader;
import java.io.InputStreamReader;

/**
 * Class to represent a commercial loan.
 * @author Michael C. Daconta
 * @version 1.2
 */
class Loan
{
    /** principal of loan. */
    private float principal;
    /** interest rate of loan. */
    private float interestRate;
    /** term of loan. */
    private int numYears;

    /** constructor. */
    Loan(float thePrincipal, float theInterest,
            int theYearsToRepay)
    {
        principal = thePrincipal;
        interestRate = theInterest;
        numYears = theYearsToRepay;
    }

    /** accessor. */
    float getPrincipal()
    { return principal; }

    /** accessor. */
    float getInterestRate()
    { return interestRate; }

    /** accessor. */
    int getYears()
    { return numYears; }
```

```
    /** method to calculate the payment
        of this loan. */
    double calculatePayment()
    {
        // assuming monthly payments
        double interest = interestRate/100;
        double payment = (interest * principal/12) /
                         (1 - Math.pow(interest/12 + 1,
                                       -12*numYears));
        return payment;
    }

    /** main() method to invoke from JVM. */
    public static void main(String args[])
    {
        Float principal = new Float(0);
        Float interest = new Float(0);
        int theYears = 0;
        try
        {
            BufferedReader br = new BufferedReader(new
                                InputStreamReader(System.in));
            System.out.print("Enter Principal of Loan: ");
            System.out.flush();
            String principalStr = br.readLine();
            principal = Float.valueOf(principalStr);
            System.out.print("Enter annual Interest rate percentage" +
                             " (i.e. 9.5): ");
            System.out.flush();
            String interestStr = br.readLine();
            interest = Float.valueOf(interestStr);
            System.out.print("Enter number of years of Loan: ");
            System.out.flush();
            String yearsStr = br.readLine();
            theYears = Integer.parseInt(yearsStr);
        } catch (java.io.IOException e)
          {
            System.out.println("IO error. Rerun program.");
            System.exit(1);
          }

        Loan theLoan = new Loan(principal.floatValue(),
                                interest.floatValue(),
                                theYears);

        double monthlyPayment = theLoan.calculatePayment();
        System.out.println("Your monthly payment is : " +
                                monthlyPayment);
    } // end of main()
} // end of class Loan {}
```

You will notice in Source 3.2 that Java variables and methods can be separately type-modified with the public, private, or protected keywords. We will go into more detail on access modifiers in the next section.

The last general concept to understand about an object is that a class definition is not an object. A class is the definition (or description) of what makes up an object. A class describes the encapsulation. It is often helpful to think of the class definition as a template or blueprint for an object. The actual object comes into existence when the class is instantiated into an actual implementation of the class in memory. Many objects can be instantiated from a single class description. So, it is easy to see how encapsulation of data and functions together gives us the ability to create new data types that very closely resemble the characteristics and behaviors of real-world objects. An object's characteristics and behaviors may be very similar to other objects that are related closely to it. An example of this is how your characteristics (hair color, eye color, body type, and facial features) may be very similar to those of your father or mother. In the real world, we would say that you inherited some of your characteristics and behaviors from your parents. The real-world concept of inheritance has been included in object-oriented programming.

Inheritance

Inheritance is the ability for a class, called a derived class or subclass, to acquire the characteristics and behaviors of another class, called a base class or superclass. The most common method of using inheritance is to create class hierarchies that move from the most general concept at the root of the tree to the most specific representation of that generic concept at the leaves of the tree. Figure 3.1 is an example of a class hierarchy.

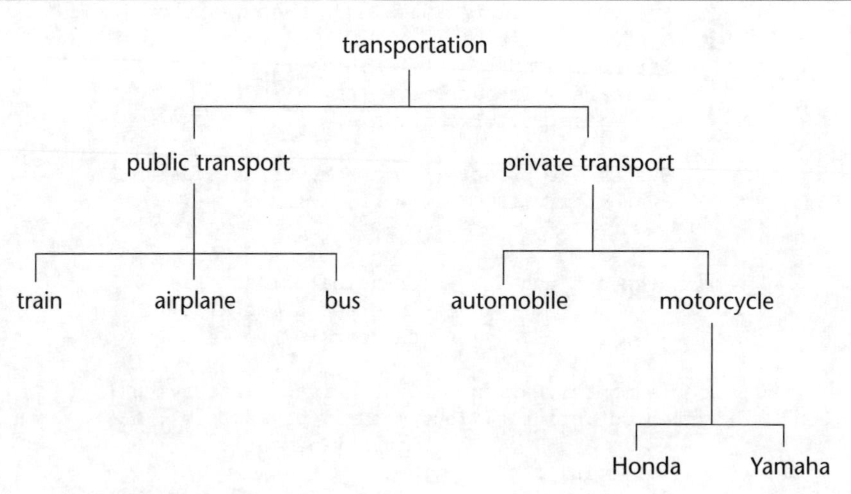

FIGURE 3.1 A class hierarchy.

Figure 3.1 demonstrates a class hierarchy that describes different modes of transportation. It is very important to understand the relationship between classes in the class hierarchy. Starting from the "leaves" of the tree, each subclass has an "is a" relationship to its parent or superclass. A Yamaha is a motorcycle. A motorcycle is a private transport. A private transport is a form of transportation. We will examine the "is a" relationship again in section 3.3. Source 3.3 demonstrates inheritance using Cartesian coordinates.

A run of Source 3.3 produces:

```
C:\java\bin>java jwiley.chp3.Coordinate3d
x: 10
y: 20
z: 30
```

There are three key points to understand about Source 3.3:

1. Coordinate is the superclass and Coordinate3d is the subclass. The keyword super is a special reference to the superclass methods and data members; however, a subclass is not a "two-part" object. It is a single new object that consists of the superclass and any extensions made by the subclass.
2. Java uses the keyword extends to signify that the subclass is inheriting the capabilities and characteristics of the superclass. The keyword extends is significant in that it clearly denotes the purpose of inheritance: code reuse. In a well-designed class hierarchy, subclasses reuse all characteristics of their superclasses while extending those characteristics to fit a specific situation. Building a class hierarchy that is designed with reuse in mind is no trivial task; however, once accomplished it will pay for itself many times over.
3. The Coordinate3d class has access to the Coordinate methods just as if they were part of Coordinate3d. This is demonstrated by the call to getX() and getY() from the variable myCoord.

Polymorphism

Polymorphism, the last major tenet of object-oriented programming, is a fancy word that stands for "many forms." In C++ and Java it is a technique that implements a "single interface" for "many implementations." Just as with the other object-oriented concepts, the whole idea of polymorphism is based on very common real-world phenomena. In real-world languages, it is very common to use a single action verb with many different nouns. For example,

The Army sergeant barked the orders.

The dog barked at the passing cars.

In both of the preceding sentences, the verb is barked. Of course, how that action would be carried out is unique to each subject of the sentence. Source 3.4 implements

SOURCE 3.3 Coordinate3d.java

```
// Coordinate3d.java
package jwiley.chp3;

/**
 * Class to represent a 2d coordinate.
 */
class Coordinate
{
    /** components. */
    protected int x,y;

    /** constructor. */
    Coordinate(int inX, int inY)
    {
        x = inX; y = inY;
    }

    /** accessor. */
    int getX()
    { return x; }

    /** accessor. */
    int getY()
    { return y; }
}

/**
 * Class to represent a 3d coordinate.
 */
class Coordinate3d extends Coordinate
{
    /** 3rd dimension. */
    protected int z;

    /** constructor. */
    Coordinate3d(int inX, int inY, int inZ)
    {
        super(inX, inY);
        z = inZ;
    }

    /** accessor. */
    int getZ()
    { return z; }

    /** main() method to invoke from JVM. */
    public static void main(String args[])
    {
        Coordinate3d myCoord = new Coordinate3d(10,20,30);
        System.out.println("x: " + myCoord.getX());
        System.out.println("y: " + myCoord.getY());
        System.out.println("z: " + myCoord.getZ());
    }
}
```

polymorphism in Java by creating an array of Animal references and then passing a message to each Animal reference that asks it to speak (actually invoke its speak() method). The object-oriented behavior lies in the fact that the program has no idea at compile time which actual speak() method will be called. The speak method that is called is determined at run time and is based on whatever subclass of Animal was actually assigned to the Animal reference. This is uniquely object-oriented behavior and directly supports the metaphor that we are passing a message to an object. The polymorphic behavior of this message passing is that we leave it up to the object to determine how to implement that message.

SOURCE 3.4 Polymorphism.java

```
/** Polymorphism.java */
package jwiley.chp3;

import java.util.Random;

/** abstract class that represents a "generic" animal. */
abstract class Animal
{
    public abstract void iAmA();

    public void speak()
    { System.out.println("Burp!"); }
}

/** specific type of animal. */
class Bird extends Animal
{
    public void iAmA()
    { System.out.println("I am a Bird."); }

    public void speak()
    { System.out.println("Cheep!"); }
}

/** specific type of animal. */
class Dog extends Animal
{
    public void iAmA()
    { System.out.println("I am a Dog."); }

    public void speak()
    { System.out.println("Bark!"); }
}

/** specific type of animal. */
class Snake extends Animal
{
    public void iAmA()
    { System.out.println("I am a Snake."); }
```

```
    public void speak()
    { System.out.println("Ssssss!"); }
}

/** specific type of animal. */
class human extends Animal
{
    public void iAmA()
    { System.out.println("I am a human."); }
}

/** Class to demonstrate polymorphism. */
public class Polymorphism
{
    static Random dice = new Random();

    /** method to randomly catch an animal for our "zoo". */
    static Animal catchAnimal()
    {
        int iRoll = Math.abs(dice.nextInt() % 3);
        switch (iRoll)
        {
            case 0:
                return new Bird();
            case 1:
                return new Dog();
            case 2:
                return new Snake();
        }
        return null;
    }

    /** main method to invoke from JVM.
        We catch a bunch of animals, put them in
        the zoo (an array) and let them speak! */
    public static void main(String args[])
    {
        Animal zoo[] = new Animal[6];
        for (int i=0; i < 6; i++)
            zoo[i] = catchAnimal();

        for (int i=0; i < 6; i++)
        {
            zoo[i].iAmA();
            zoo[i].speak();
        }

        human aHuman = new human();
        aHuman.iAmA();
        aHuman.speak();
    }
}
```

A run of Source 3.4 produces:

```
C:\1-1update\src11\jwiley\chp3>java Polymorphism
I am a Snake.
Ssssss!
I am a Dog.
Bark!
I am a Bird.
Cheep!
I am a Bird.
Cheep!
I am a Bird.
Cheep!
I am a Snake.
Ssssss!
I am a human.
Burp!
```

There are four key points to note about Source 3.4:

1. All of the subclasses must implement the iAmA() method of the Animal class as it is declared abstract. We will go into more detail about the abstract keyword later in the chapter. Secondly, all except the human class have their own speak() method. This is called "overriding" the superclass method.
2. The catchAnimal() method of the Polymorphism class creates the specific instances of the subclasses (i.e., new bird()) yet returns a reference to the Animal class. This works because bird is a subclass of Animal.
3. The zoo array is an array of Animal references. We then iterate through this array and pass the speak() message to each object. The object implements the speak() method if it knows how (which it translates to if it has overriden the superclass method).
4. Since the human class did not override the speak() method, when we pass it the speak() message it invokes its superclasses speak method.

This completes your introduction to the key principles of object-oriented programming. We will now move on to a detailed comparison of the major elements of C++ with Java.

3.2 CLASSES

The Java class is identical to the C++ class in general form. Both Java and C++ classes have data members, methods, and access specifiers. We will examine each of these "class basics" in the following paragraphs. The most visible syntactical differences between Java classes and C++ classes are the omission of the scope resolution operator from Java and the C++ ability to list multiple variables under a single C++ access specifier. Figure 3.2 shows a C++ class and Java class side by side.

As is very clear from Figure 3.2, C++ programmers will feel very comfortable with

C++ Class	*Java Class*

C++ Class

```
class Entity
{
protected:
     char*name;
     int x,y;
public:
     Entity();
     ~Entity();
     void setName(char *inName);
     void setXY(int inX, int inY);
};

Entity::Entity()
{
     x=y =0;
     name = NULL;
}

Entity::~Entity()
{
     // Code here
}

Entity::setName(char *iName)
{
     // Code here
}

Entity::setXY(int inX, int inY)
{
     // Code here
}
```

Java Class

```
class Entity
{
     protected String name;
     protected int x;
     protected int y;
     public Entity()
     {
        x=y =0;
        name=null;
     }

     public void finalize()
     {
        // Code here
     }
     public void setName(String iName)
     {
        // code here
     }
     public void setXY(int inX, int inY)
     {
        // code here
     }
}
```

FIGURE 3.2 Comparing a C++ class to a Java class.

the fact that Java classes are nearly identical to C++ classes. The object-oriented community is in agreement that the concept of a class is the central tenet of object-oriented programming. As *The C++ Annotated Reference Manual* states, "'Class' is the key concept of C++."[2] The class will be central to every Java program you create. For C++ programmers this is the central reason why Java code is immediately recognizable and "looks like C++." Let's now compare the basic constructs of a Java and C++ class as displayed in Figure 3.2. The basic constructs are the class declaration, class data members, access specifiers, and class methods.

[2]Margaret A. Ellis and Bjarne Stroustrop, *The Annotated C++ Reference Manual*, p. 165.

Class Declaration

Both the C++ and Java versions in Source 3.2 declare the Entity class. A class declaration is the template that describes all of the data members or instance variables and methods of an object. You can instantiate many objects from one class declaration.

Now we are ready to discuss the individual components of a class: data members, access specifiers, and methods.

Data Members

Just as in C++, a Java class can have both primitive data types and other classes as data members. The data members of a class are identical to the data members of a C structure except in how class data members can be hidden and protected. Data hiding is a very important principle of object-oriented programming. The best way to think of this is that an object is composed of a private internal state (composed of its private data members) and a public set of operations it can perform.

An important difference between Java and C++ is the way that class data members are initialized. First, all data members in Java are automatically initialized to default values. Numeric data types are initialized to zero and reference data types are initialized to null. Programmers can override this behavior in two ways. They can provide new initial values in a constructor, as in C++, or they can specify an initial value when the member variable is declared as follows:

```
public class MyClass
{
    int myInt = 18;
    int myString = new String("");
}
```

Now let's examine how we hide and protect the data members using the access specifier keywords.

Access Specifiers

Access specifiers are similar in meaning for both C++ and Java. The *private* specifier denotes a variable or method as being private to the class and may not be accessed outside the class. The only way to gain access to the variable or method is by calling one of the public class methods. The *protected* specifier denotes a variable or method as being public to subclasses of this class but private to all other classes outside the current package. This allows derived classes the ability to directly access protected variables of its parent. This is a good idea as it makes extending classes easier. The concept of a Java package has changed the meaning of the protected access specifier. All classes within the same package have access to protected variables regardless of whether they are subclasses. Packages are discussed in detail in section 4.1. The *public* specifier denotes a variable or method as being directly accessible from all other

Access Specifier	*Accessible by classes in the same package*	*Accessible by classes in other packages*	*Accessible by subclasses in the same package*	*Accessible by subclasses in other packages*
Public	Yes	Yes	Yes	Yes
Protected	Yes	No	Yes	Yes
Default	Yes	No	Yes	No
Private	No	No	No	No

FIGURE 3.3 Properties of the Java access specifiers.

classes. Public data members of a class are accessed just like structure variables; however, public data members violate the principle of data hiding and are not recommended for object-oriented programming. Remember that the "data is king" and we must protect it. If no access specifier is used, then the class member has default access, otherwise known as package access. Members with package access are available to all classes in the same package, but are not available to any classes in other packages, even subclasses. In C++ terms, it is useful to consider all classes in the same package as friends. Figure 3.3 details the properties of the Java access specifiers.

Methods

The methods (or member functions) are the actions that a class can perform. There are some special class methods called constructors and destructors that we will discuss later. The regular class methods (the methods setName() and setXY() in Figure 3.2) are identical in Java and C++, except for the omission of the scope resolution operator (::) in Java. In C++ the scope resolution operator is most often used to separate the function definitions from the function declarations. In C++ it is common to put the class declarations in the header file and the function definitions in the source file. In Java, all methods in a Java class must be declared within the class; therefore, the scope resolution operator is unnecessary. In Java, namespacing issues are handled through the use of packages and classes. Every data element or method is a member of a class. Because there are never global variables or methods, Java does not require anything similar to the C++ scope resolution operator.

In C++, programmers can tell the compiler to embed the body of a function in place of every call to that function. This process is called *inlining* and speeds execution. C++ programmers can use the inline keyword to specify that which functions the compiler should perform this optimization on. In addition, by specifying the body of a class method in a class definition, C++ programmers implicitly specify that the method be inlined. Java does not support the inline keyword, nor does it allow the programmer to implicitly specify an inline method. The Java compiler has the option of automatically inlining any methods declared with the final keyword. The final keyword will be discussed in detail in Chapter 4. The rules for whether or not this optimization takes place varies from compiler to compiler. In general, inline functions make your program run faster, but the class files for the program will be a little larger.

Let's examine a complete example of a Java class. Source 3.5 demonstrates a line segment class.

SOURCE 3.5 LineSegment.java

```
// LineSegment.java
package jwiley.chp3;
import java.awt.Point;

/**
 * Class to represent a line segment.
 */
class LineSegment
{
    /** points in line segment. */
    protected Point pts[];

    /** constructor */
    LineSegment(int x1, int y1, int x2, int y2)
    {
        pts = new Point[2];
        pts[0] = new Point(x1,y1);
        pts[1] = new Point(x2,y2);
    }

    /** accessor method. */
    Point getPoint(boolean first)
    {
        return (first ? pts[0] : pts[1]);
    }

    /** mutator method. */
    void setPoint(boolean first, int inX, int inY)
    {
        if (first)
        {
                pts[0].x = inX;
                pts[0].y = inY;
        }
        else
        {
                pts[1].x = inX;
                pts[1].y = inY;
        }
    }
```

```
    /** calculate slope. */
    double calculateSlope()
    {
        return ( (pts[0].y - pts[1].y) /
                 (pts[0].x - pts[1].x) );
    }

    /** calculate the length of the line segment. */
    double length()
    {
        int a = Math.abs(pts[0].x - pts[1].x);
        int b = Math.abs(pts[0].y - pts[1].y);
        double c = Math.sqrt( (a*a) + (b*b) );
        return c;
    }

    /** main method to invoke from JVM. */
    public static void main(String args[])
    {
        LineSegment aSegment = new LineSegment(0,0,4,4);
        Point one = aSegment.getPoint(true);
        Point two = aSegment.getPoint(false);
        double segSlope = aSegment.calculateSlope();
        double segLength = aSegment.length();
        System.out.println("Slope of segment is  :" + segSlope);
        System.out.println("Length of segment is :" + segLength);
    }
}
```

A run of Source 3.5 produces:

```
C:\java\bin>java jwiley.chp3.LineSegment
Slope of segment is  :1
Length of segment is :5.656854249492381
```

Source 3.5 demonstrates four basic topics about Java classes: overloading constructors, accessor and mutator methods, the new operator and object creation, and how to call class methods. Let's discuss each topic in detail.

Overloading Class Constructors

A constructor is a special class method that is run automatically when an object is instantiated. In C++, the purpose of a constructor is to insure that an object is always properly initialized before the object is used in any way. A very common error in C and C++ is to use a pointer variable before it is properly initialized, causing either an immediate or delayed program crash. The constructor is to be used to insure that an object is ready for use once it is instantiated. The format of a constructor (as demonstrated by the lineSegment() methods in Source 3.5) is the class name and optional function arguments. There is no return type from a constructor. Java constructors are identical to C++ constructors except are not used for initialization. Java class data members have default initial values and can also be explicitly initialized upon creation. Therefore, the Java constructor is primarily used for other initialization tasks.

Before performing any specific initialization, all Java constructors must do one of two things; they must call a specific constructor on their superclass or they must call some other constructor in the current class. In order to call a constructor on the superclass, use the super variable with the following syntax:

```
class MyClass extends MySuperClass
{
    public MyClass()
    {
        super(args…);
        … other initialization
    }
    …
}
```

To call another constructor in the same class, use the *this* variable with the following syntax:

```
class MyClass extends MySuperClass
{
    public MyClass()
    {
        this(args…);
        … other initialization
    }
    …
}
```

If the programmer does not explicitly specify a constructor (either on the current class or on the superclass), the Java compiler will insert a call to the default constructor of the superclass. A default constructor is any constructor for a class that takes no arguments. In both C++ and Java, the compiler will insert a default constructor into any class that has no constructors defined. Once a constructor is defined for a class, however, Java will no longer automatically insert a default constructor. As a result of this, when extending a class that has no default constructor, you are required to implement a constructor which, at a minimum, calls one of the constructors on the superclass.

We already discussed how function overloading is a form of polymorphism. In the same manner a constructor can be overloaded to provide different ways to construct an object. Source 3.6 demonstrates the overloading of constructors with two ways to create a lineSegment object.

SOURCE 3.6 SillyMath.java

```
// SillyMath.java
package jwiley.chp3;

/**
 * Class to demonstrate one form of
 * polymorphism.
 */
class SillyMath
{
    /** an integer. */
    int a;

    /** constructor. */
    SillyMath(int inA)
    {
        a = inA;
    }

    /** method to add. */
    int add(int b)
    {
        return a + b;
    }

    /** overloaded add. */
    float add(float b)
    {
        return ((float)a + b);
    }

    /** overloaded add. */
    double add(double b)
    {
        return ((double)a + b);
    }

    /** main() method to invoke from JVM. */
    public static void main(String args[])
    {
        SillyMath num = new SillyMath(10);
        int c=10;
        float d = 30.2f;
        double e = 459998.8;

        System.out.println("adding an int  : " + num.add(c));
        System.out.println("adding a float : " + num.add(d));
        System.out.println("adding a double: " + num.add(e));
    }
}
```

Overloading Class Methods

In Java, as in C++, you can overload methods to provide different implementations for different arguments to the method. Source 3.6 implements function overloading.

A run of Source 3.6 produces:

```
C:\java\bin>java jwiley.chp3.SillyMath
adding an int  : 20
adding a float : 40.2
adding a double: 460008.8
```

Source 3.6 implements function overloading in a single class by allowing one method name, add(), to be used for multiple implementations of the add operation. The way the compiler distinguishes between add functions is based on the type of the arguments. The return type is not considered and cannot be used to differentiate between two methods with the same name. Additionally, two methods with the same name must have arguments that vary in either type or number.

Accessors and Mutators

Although not required, there are two categories of class methods that aid data hiding and protection in object-oriented programming. These categories are accessor methods and mutator methods. Accessor methods are methods that retrieve the current value of class data members. Mutator methods are methods that allow internal state variables to be modified. You should be cautious when providing mutator methods and only provide them if there is a valid requirement for an external class to know about and be able to influence the internal state of the object. Most objects should not need mutator functions.

The New Operator and Object Creation

In C++ there are generally three different ways to create an object: define a global object that is created at the program startup, define an object at the beginning of a function that is created on the application stack, and define a pointer to the object and allocate the object in the free store (known as the heap in C). Java simplifies object creation by providing only one method to create all objects: on the heap via the new operator. The syntax of the new operator is very similar but not identical to the C++ new operator. The Java new operator must specify an object's constructor, whereas a C++ new can just have the class name (which defaults to calling the no argument constructor). Source 3.5 demonstrates the creation of a lineSegment object using the new operator.

Calling Class Methods

Calling a class method in Java is identical to the way C++ methods are accessed from an instantiated object. Java uses the "dot operator" (.) in conjunction with the object name to specify which class method is to be called. In Source 3.5 the class method getPoint() is invoked in this fashion:

```
Point one = aSegment.getPoint(true);
```

In C++ there is a different way to access class methods from a class pointer which uses the "arrow operator" (->). This method does not exist in Java since Java consciously did not include pointers in the language.

Now we will discuss several other characteristics of classes to include: class assignment, the this variable, static members and methods, and runtime type information.

Class Assignment

In C++ and Java, the definition of a class is the defining of a new data type that has many of the same properties as the primitive data types. We will learn that Java differs from C++ in not adding features to the language that make classes have the ability to exactly mimic the primitive data types. We will explain this later, when we talk about how Java consciously left out operator overloading. For now, let's examine one commonality between user-defined types and primitive types: class assignment.

In C++ and Java you may assign classes of the same type to one another. Source 3.7 demonstrates class assignment in Java.

A run of Source 3.7 produces:

```
C:\java\bin>java jwiley.chp3.ClassAssign
myObject a: 10
yourObject a: 20
yourObject a: 10
myObject a: 10
trueCopy a: 30
```

SOURCE 3.7 ClassAssign.java

```
// ClassAssign.java
package jwiley.chp3;

/**
 * Simple demonstration object.
 */
class simpleObject implements Cloneable
{
    /** integer. */
    private int a;
```

```
    /** constructor. */
    simpleObject(int inA)
    { a = inA; }

    /** accessor. */
    int getA()
    { return a; }

    /** mutator. */
    void setA(int inA)
    { a = inA; }

    /** clone method. */
    public Object clone()
    {
        Object copy = null;
        try
        {
            copy = super.clone();
        } catch(CloneNotSupportedException cne)
          {
            cne.printStackTrace();
            System.exit(1);
          }
        return copy;
    }
}

/**
 * Class demonstrating both shallow and deep copies.
 */
class classAssign
{
        public static void main(String args[])
        {
            simpleObject myObject = new simpleObject(10);
            System.out.println("myObject a: " + myObject.getA());
            simpleObject yourObject = new simpleObject(20);
            System.out.println("yourObject a: " + yourObject.getA());

            // reference assignment
            yourObject = myObject; // assignment
            System.out.println("yourObject a: " + yourObject.getA());

            // true copy
            simpleObject trueCopy = null;
            trueCopy = (simpleObject) myObject.clone();
            trueCopy.setA(30);
            System.out.println("myObject a: " + myObject.getA());
            System.out.println("trueCopy a: " + trueCopy.getA());
        }
}
```

Although Source 3.7 would be nearly identical in C++ and Java, the languages arrive at the same solution via different paths. In C++, a default assignment operator would be called to copy the values of myObject into yourObject. In Java, there are no default assignment operators or copy constructors because all objects are accessed via references. This means that the previous assignment of one object to another is actually a copying of the reference to myObject into the reference to yourObject. The effect of this references copying is that you have two references to Objects pointing at the same instantiation of an object. In Java, there is a tremendous difference between copying a reference and copying an object. This is parallel to the difference between copying a pointer and copying the contents of that pointer in C and C++. In Java, a reference can be copied using the assignment operator (=). In order to copy the object itself, programmers should call the clone method that is available on all objects. Clone returns a deep copy of the object it is called on. This means that not only is the object itself copied, but any objects that it has references to are copied as well. Not all objects support the clone operation. Those that do not will throw a CloneNotSupportedException whenever clone is called.

Implementing a clone method is a two-step process. The object must implement the java.lang.Cloneable interface and the object must provide an implementation of the clone method itself. Objects that do not implement this interface cannot be cloned, even if they have a clone method. The first step in every clone method is to create a new object of the same type as the object being cloned. It is the responsibility of the clone method to create this destination object for the information being copied. Next, all primitive values should be copied from the object being cloned to the destination object. This is a simple process, because the assignment operator automatically copies primitives. Finally, the object references contained in the object being cloned must be copied. It is here that most of the confusion occurs. For each reference, there are three ways to handle the clone operation. The reference can simply be copied, the object the reference points to can be cloned, or the destination reference can be set to null.

There are three common reasons to copy a reference without cloning the object it refers to. When the reference is to an immutable object, like a string, it makes no sense to clone the object. In fact, cloning the referenced object in this case is wasteful. Another time the reference should simply be copied is when the referenced object does not support the cloning operation. Finally, when the object being cloned has a reference to a system object, or an object such as an Applet, it makes more sense to just copy the reference. The destination reference should only be set to null if the reference represents temporary information, such as a working space, or data cache. In those situations, the data can be cloned at the discretion of the programmer. Everything else falls into the most common category where the object referred to is simply cloned.

Typically, programmers don't need to explicitly throw a CloneNotSupportedException, as it is thrown automatically when such a situation is detected. There are still some circumstances where it may be appropriate to explicitly throw the exception. For instance, if the object is only cloneable when it is in certain states, then it would make sense to throw the exception when it occupies a non-cloneable state. For example, an object that performs some distributed functionality may not be cloneable while it is communicating with a remote server. Also, a reference to a base class or abstract class may point to an object that doesn't actually support the cloneable operation, even though the base class does. In these situations, the derived class should simply throw a CloneNotSupportedException in the body of the clone method.

Now let's move on to another Java class feature that is similar in both Java and C++: the this variable.

The This Variable

In Java and C++, the this variable is used in exactly the same manner. The this variable represents the currently executing object. In C++, the this variable is a pointer to the current object. In Java it is a reference to the current object. The this variable is very useful in allowing you to pass the current object to another object's constructor or method. Source 3.8 demonstrates multiple uses of the this variable. Although Source 3.8 is longer than normal examples, it is a much more useful example that you can reuse in your own coding efforts.

SOURCE 3.8 ThisDemo.java

```
// ThisDemo.java
package jwiley.chp3;

/**
 * Class to represent an automobile. Demonstrates
 * the use of the this reference.
 */
class Automobile
{
    /** model of car. */
    String sModel;
    /** Capacity of fuel tank in gallons. */
    int iTankCapacity;
    /** miles car has travelled. */
    int iOdometer;
    /** fuel efficiency of car. */
    int iMilesPerGallon;
    /** gas tank. */
    FuelTank gasStorage;

    /** no-arg constructor. NOTICE use of this. */
    Automobile()
    {
        this("Unknown",10, 20);
    }

    /** overloaded constructor. */
    Automobile(String sModelName)
    {
        this(sModelName,10, 20);
    }
```

```
    /** overloaded constructor. */
    Automobile(String sModelName, int iNumGallons)
    {
        this(sModelName,iNumGallons, 20);
    }

    /** overloaded constructor. */
    Automobile(String sModelName, int iNumGallons, int MPG)
    {
        sModel = sModelName;
        iTankCapacity = iNumGallons;
        iMilesPerGallon = MPG;
        gasStorage = new FuelTank(this, iTankCapacity);
        System.out.println("Auto, model: " + sModel + ", capacity: " +
                           iTankCapacity + ", MPG: " + iMilesPerGallon);
    }

    /** method to move (drive) the auto. */
    void move(int iMiles)
    {
        for (int i=0; i < iMiles; i++)
        {
            if (gasStorage.gasLeft())
                iOdometer++;
            else
            {
                System.out.println("Ran out of gas.");
                System.out.println("Odometer: " + iOdometer);
                break;
            }

            if (iOdometer % 50 == 0)
            {
                System.out.println("Odometer: " + iOdometer);
                System.out.println("Gallons : " +
                                   gasStorage.getCurrentGallons());
            }
        }
    }
}

/**
 * Class to represent a fuel tank.
 */
class FuelTank
{
    /** capacity of fuel tank in gallons. */
    int iCapacity;
    /** current # of gallons in the tank. */
    float fCurrentGallons;
    /** Last odometer reading of "parent" automobile. */
    int iLastOdometerReading;
    /** The reference to the parent automobile. */
```

```
    Automobile parent;

    /** constructor. */
    FuelTank(Automobile theParent, int iInitialCapacity)
    {
        parent = theParent;
        iCapacity = iInitialCapacity;
        fCurrentGallons = iInitialCapacity;
        iLastOdometerReading = parent.iOdometer;
    }

    /** accessor. */
    float getCurrentGallons()
    { return fCurrentGallons; }

    /** calculates the current fuel in the tank. */
    float currentCapacity()
    {
        int iDistance = parent.iOdometer - iLastOdometerReading;

        if (iDistance > 0)
        {
            float fGallonsWasted = (float)iDistance /
                                   parent.iMilesPerGallon;
            if (fGallonsWasted > 0 && fCurrentGallons > 0)
            {
                fCurrentGallons -= fGallonsWasted;
            }
        }

        iLastOdometerReading = parent.iOdometer;
        return fCurrentGallons;
    }

    /** method to determine if there is any gas left? */
    boolean gasLeft()
    {
        return (currentCapacity() > 0) ? true : false;
    }
}

/**
 * Wrapper class to drive the demo.
 */
class ThisDemo
{
    /** main() method to invoke from a JVM. */
    public static void main(String args[])
    {
        Automobile newCar = new Automobile("Chevy");
        newCar.move(300);
    }
}
```

A run of Source 3.8 produces:

```
C:\java\bin>java jwiley.chp3.ThisDemo
Auto, model: Chevy, capacity: 10, MPG: 20
Odometer: 50
Gallons : 7.5499907
Odometer: 100
Gallons : 5.049981
Odometer: 150
Gallons : 2.5499787
Odometer: 200
Gallons : 0.049979996
Ran out of gas.
Odometer: 200
```

Source 3.8 illustrates the two main uses of the this variable. In the beginning of the source file, you can see how this is used to call from one constructor to another. The this reference can be used to pass a reference to the current object to another object. We see an example of this when the FuelTank object is created. ThisDemo is also a good example of data encapsulation. The Automobile object hides all the data that defines a car and only exposes one method, move. By calling move, programmers can interact with the object without having to worry about modifying all the internal variables themselves. The Automobile object is able to protect its data so that its member variables never reach an inconsistent state.

Now let's move on to static members and methods of a class.

Static Members and Methods

Static methods were discussed in Chapter 2 as a way to implement utility functions within Java's object-oriented framework. In this section, we will examine how static variables and methods work in C++ and in object-oriented programming in general. Last, we will examine a program that demonstrates both static class data members and methods.

If a member of a class is defined as static, it means that that data member or method belongs to the entire class. The storage space for the static data member is reserved in the static or global space and not reserved with each instantiation of the object, as is the case with nonstatic data members. There is a slight difference between static data members in C++ versus Java. In C++, you may only declare static data members and then define them outside of the class. In Java, since there are no declarations, you define the static data member right in the class definition. Source 3.9 demonstrates the use of static variables and methods.

A run of Source 3.9 produces:

```
C:\java\bin>java jwiley.chp3.TstStatic
Case 1: use of static variables.
Total # of entities: 1
Total # of entities: 2
Total # of entities: 3
Total # of entities: 4
Total # of entities: 5
```

SOURCE 3.9 TstStatic.java

```
// TstStatic.java
package jwiley.chp3;

/**
 * Simple class to demonstrate a static variable.
 */
class Entity
{
    /** Total number of Entity instantiated. */
    static long totalEntities = 0;
    /** Unique entity Id. */
    private long eId;

    /** constructor. */
    public Entity()
    {
        eId = totalEntities++;
        System.out.println("Total # of entities: " +
                           totalEntities);
    }
}

/**
 * Class to demonstrate a static method.
 */
class myMath
{
    /** method to calculate the fibonacci sum. */
    static int fibonacci(int n)
    {
        if (n == 0 || n == 1) return n;
        return (fibonacci(n - 1) + fibonacci(n - 2));
    }
}

/**
 * Wrapper class to test both uses of static.
 */
class TstStatic
{
    /** main() method to invoke from JVM. */
    public static void main(String args[])
    {
        System.out.println("Case 1: use of static variables.");
        Entity eArray[] = new Entity[5];
        for (int i=0; i < eArray.length; i++)
                eArray[i] = new Entity();

        System.out.println("Case 2: use of static methods.");
        System.out.println("fibonacci(14) is : "
                          + myMath.fibonacci(14));
    }
}
```

```
Case 2: use of static methods.
fibonacci(14) is : 377
```

Source 3.9 uses both a static data member and a static method. Static data members are used to store information about a class that is not specific to a single instance of that class. In the Entity class we use a static data member to count the total number of entities that have been instantiated. With this same logic, we could have written a static method called getTotalEntities() that returned the number of entities. Because static methods do not have an associated object instance, they cannot access the this variable, and therefore cannot access instance data or methods of the class. Instance methods, however, can access static data and methods.

Source 3.9 also demonstrates a static "utility" function in the myMath class. A static method is needed when a method has no relation to a specific object. In our example, our utility function works on the primitive types and therefore has no relationship to any user-defined object. Given a desired number, the utility function returns the value of that position in the fibonacci sequence. The fibonacci sequence is a sequence of numbers defined by Leonardo of Pisa where each successive number is formed by the addition of the two previous numbers. The fibonacci sequence holds a mystique in the mathematical community, as is clear from the book *The Joy of Mathematics*, where Theoni Pappas states that the fibonacci sequence appears in:

I. The Pascal triangle, the binomial formula & probability
II. The golden ratio and the golden rectangle
III. Nature and plants
IV. Intriguing mathematical tricks
V. Mathematical identities[3]

Run Time Type Information (RTTI)

Run time type information is the ability to determine the type of an object at run time. In the forthcoming C++ standard, Run Time Type Information is supported using the typeid operator. Source 3.10 demonstrates the use of RTTI in C++. Pay particular attention to the use of the typeid operator.

A run of Source 3.10 produces:

```
Display a GIF file.
Display a PICT file.
```

As you can see from Source 3.10, the program has the ability to tell what type of object you passed the function using RTTI. Java also implements RTTI using the instance of operator. In Source 3.11 we implement the exact same program as in Source 3.10 in Java.

---

[3]Theoni Pappas, *The Joy of Mathematics* (San Carlos, CA: Wide World Publishing, 1986), p. 29.

SOURCE 3.10 RTTI.cpp

```
// RTTI.cpp - a demonstration of RTTI in C++
#include <typeinfo.h>
#include <iostream.h>
#include <stdlib.h>
#include <stdio.h>
#include <string.h>

class graphicImage {
        protected:
          char name[80];
          int pixelsHigh, pixelsWide;
          unsigned char **bitmap;

          public:
        graphicImage()
        {
                pixelsHigh = pixelsWide = 0;
                strcpy(name,"graphicImage");
        }

        graphicImage(char * filename)
        {
                // process file, store bitmap
                cout << "Process " << filename << endl;
        }

        virtual void display()
        {
                    cout << "Display a generic image." << endl;
                for (int i=0; i < pixelsHigh; i++)
                        for (int j=0; j < pixelsWide; j++)
                                ; // draw each pixel
        }

        char* getName()
        {
                return name;
        }
};

class GIFimage : public graphicImage {
        // GIF data members

         public:
        GIFimage()
        {

                // GIF constructor
                strcpy(name,"GIFimage");
        }
```

```
        void display()
        {
                // display the GIF file in a GIF-specific way
                cout << "Display a GIF file." << endl;
        }
};

class PICTimage : public graphicImage {
        // PICT data members

         public:
        PICTimage()
        {
                // PICT constructor
                strcpy(name,"PICTimage");
        }

        void display()
        {
                // display the PICT in a PICT-specific way
                cout << "Display a PICT file." << endl;
        }
};

void processFile(graphicImage *type)
{
     if (typeid(GIFimage) == typeid(*type))
     {
           ((GIFimage *)type)->display();
     }
     else if (typeid(PICTimage) == typeid(*type))
     {
          ((PICTimage *)type)->display();
     }
     else
         cout << "Unknown type! <" << (typeid(*type)).name()
              << ">" << endl;
}

void main(int argc, char **argv)
{
     graphicImage *gImage = new GIFimage();
     graphicImage *pImage = new PICTimage();

     processFile(gImage);
     processFile(pImage);
}
```

SOURCE 3.11 TstRtti.java

```
// TstRtti.java
package jwiley.chp3;

import java.awt.Color;

/**
 * Class to demonstrate a parent class.
 * Not a complete implementation.
 */
class graphicImage
{
    /** name of image. */
    protected String name;
    /** width and height of image. */
    protected int pixelsHigh, pixelsWide;
    /** 2d array of colors. */
    protected Color bitmap[][];

    /** method to decode an image. */
    void decode()
    {
        System.out.println("Decode a generic image.");
        for (int i=0; i < pixelsHigh; i++)
                for (int j=0; j < pixelsWide; j++)
                        ; // get each pixel
    }

    /** accessor. */
    String getName()
    { return name; }
}

/**
 * Specific subclass of graphic image.
 */
class GIFimage extends graphicImage
{
    // GIF data members

    /** constructor. */
    GIFimage()
    {
        // GIF constructor
        name = "GIFimage";
    }

    /** method to decode  a .GIF file. */
    void decode()
    {

        // decode the file in a GIF-specific way
        System.out.println("Decode a GIF file.");
    }
}
```

```
/**
 * Specific subclass of graphic image.
 */
class PICTimage extends graphicImage
{
    // PICT data members
    /** constructor. */
    PICTimage()
    {
        // PICT constructor
        name = "PICTimage";
    }

    /** method to decode a PICT image. */
    void decode()
    {
        // decode the file in a PICT-specific way
        System.out.println("Decode a PICT file.");
    }
}

/**
 * Wrapper class to demonstrate Java Run Time Type
 * Identification (RTTI).
 */
class tstRtti
{
    /** method to process some graphic file. */
    static void processFile(graphicImage type)
    {
        type.decode();
    }

    /** main() method to invoke from the JVM. */
    public static void main(String args[])
    {
        GIFimage gImage = new GIFimage();
        PICTimage pImage = new PICTimage();

        processFile(gImage);
        processFile(pImage);
    }
}
```

A run of Source 3.11 produces:

```
C:\java\bin>java jwiley.chp3.TstRtti
Decode a GIF file.
Decode a PICT file.
```

As you can see, the functionality of the two programs is identical. In fact, except for the liberal use of pointers in the C++ program, the code looks very similar.

3.3 INHERITANCE

In object-oriented programming, inheritance is the ability for a derived class to acquire the non-private data members and methods of a base class. Although the implementation works the same way in C++ and Java, the syntax used is different. Figure 3.4 is an example of C++ inheritance and Java inheritance side by side.

C++ inheritance

```
//inherit.cpp
#include <iostream.h>
class Coordinate {
  protected:
    int x,y;
  public:
    Coordinate(int inX, int inY)
    { x = inX; y = inY; }
    int getX() { return x; }
    int getY() { return y; }
};

class Coordinate3d: public Coordinate {
  protected:
    int z;
  public:
    Coordinate3d
     (int inX,int inY,int in Z):
        Coordinate(inX,inY)
     { z = inZ; }

    int getZ() { return z; };
};


void main (int argc, char **argv)
{
    Coordinate3d myCoord(10,20,30);
cout << "x: " << myCoord.getX() << endl;
cout << "y: " << myCoord.getY() << endl;
cout << "z: " << myCoord.getZ() << endl;
}
```

Java inheritance

```
//inherit.java
class Coordinate {
  protected int x,y;
  Coordinate (int inX, int inY)
  {x = inX; y + inY;}
  int getX()
  { return x; }
  int getY()
  { return y; }

}

class Coordinate3d: extends Coordinate {
  protected int z;


  Coordinate3d(int inX,int inY,int in Z)
  {
      super(inx, inY);
      z = inZ;
  }
  int getZ() { return z; };
}

class coordTst {
  public static void main(String args[])
  {
    Coordinate3d myCoord =
        new Coordinate3d(10,20,30,);
    System.out.println("x: " +
      myCoord.getX());
    System.out.println("y: " +
      myCoord.getY());
    System.out.println("z: " +
      myCoord.getZ());
  }
}
```

FIGURE 3.4 Comparing C++ inheritance to Java inheritance.

As stated earlier, the only glaring differences are the syntax used to implement inheritance and the syntax used to call the base classes constructor. Java has the more intuitive of the approaches: Java uses the keyword extends to denote that the derived class is "extending" the base class (also referred to as a superclass in other object-oriented languages). Second, Java uses the keyword super as a variable that points to the parent (or superclass) in order to call the parent's constructor. C++ overloads the colon operator for both of these purposes; however, in defense of C++, this was primarily sticking with the C language's terse tradition.

Single Inheritance

We will examine a good example of single inheritance: how a warning dialog is created via inheritance of a class hierarchy of graphical user interface elements in Java's abstract window toolkit (AWT). Figure 3.5 is a graphical representation of the inheritance hierarchy for the creation of a warning dialog. Notice that each class only has one "parent." This is called single inheritance.

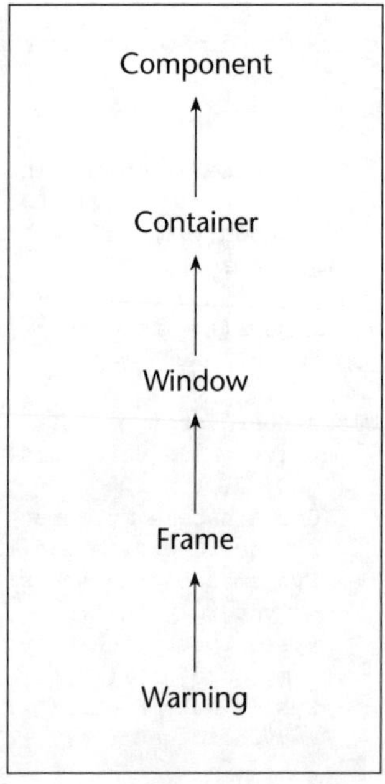

FIGURE 3.5 Single inheritance in AWT.

Let's start at the top and work our way down to the Warning class:

- **Component.** A component is an abstract class that represents a generic graphical user interface (GUI) object. Everything displayed in an abstract window toolkit GUI is a graphical component. The component class has data members and methods common to all graphical components, such as a screen coordinate, size, or color.
- **Container.** A component that can contain or hold other components, responsible for storing all the components in the display and laying them out on the screen in accordance with a chosen layout manager. The different layout managers will be discussed in detail in Chapter 10.
- **Window.** A top-level window that has no title, no border, and no menubar.
- **Frame.** A window that has a title and also has the ability to contain a menubar.
- **Warning.** A frame that displays a Warning message.

Thus, the reason inheritance is so useful is because a Warning IS A frame, which IS A window, which IS A container, which IS A component. And, of course, our simple Warning class benefits by inheriting all of the characteristics and methods of every class above it. That's like adding the hubcaps to a Ferrari and saying, "Look what I built!"

Source 3.12 implements the Warning class using inheritance.

SOURCE 3.12 Warning.java

```
// Warning.java
package jwiley.chp3;

import java.awt.Frame;
import java.awt.event.ActionEvent;
import java.awt.event.ActionListener;
import java.awt.Button;
import java.awt.Graphics;
import java.awt.Color;
import java.awt.Panel;
import java.awt.Point;

/**
 * Simple class to demonstrate inheritance.
 */
class Warning extends Frame implements ActionListener
{
    /** Warning message. */
    private String message;

    /** constructor. */
    Warning(String title, String WarningMessage)
    {
```

```
        super(title);
        message = new String(WarningMessage);
        Panel p = new Panel();
        Button okButton = new Button("OK");
        okButton.addActionListener(this);
        p.add("Center", okButton);
        add("South",p);
        setSize(200,100);
        setLocation(new Point(50,50));
        setForeground(Color.black);
        setBackground(Color.white);
        setVisible(true);
    }

    /** event handler. */
    public void actionPerformed(ActionEvent evt)
    {
        if ("OK".equals(evt.getActionCommand()))
        {
            System.exit(1);
        }
    }

    /** paint() method. */
    public void paint(Graphics g)
    {
        g.drawString(message,10,40);
    }

    /** main() method to invoke from JVM. */
    public static void main(String args[])
    {
        Warning anError = new Warning("Error", "A serious Error");
    }
}
```

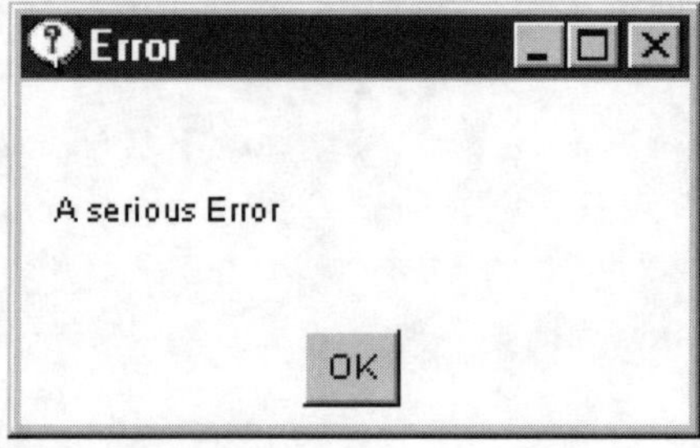

FIGURE 3.6 A warning alert box.

A run of Source 3.12 produces the output shown in Figure 3.6.

Source 3.12 demonstrates single inheritance in Java. For now do not concern yourself with the specific implementation of the windows and event handling. That is covered in great detail in Chapter 10, "Abstract Window Toolkit." So, by now you should know the two key Java constructs to implementing single inheritance: the extends keyword and the super variable. The super variable contains a reference to the superclass of the current object. It is conceptually identical to the this variable.

One last point to understand about inheritance is how it differs from containment. As I have said earlier, inheritance establishes an "IS A" relationship between a parent and child object. An "IS A" relationship is a relationship characterized by belonging to the same group and therefore sharing the same characteristics and behaviors. Inheritance forms a relationship of membership; however, there are other relationships between objects. If you are designing a program with a car object, a steering wheel object, a Honda Civic object, and a wheel object, what relationships do these objects have to each other? Should the steering wheel object extend the car object? I hope you said no. The relationship between a car and a steering wheel is a "HAS A" relationship. A car HAS A steering wheel. Putting the objects in English sentences with "has a" or "is a" will quickly tell you whether you should use inheritance or not. Figure 3.7 depicts both the IS A and HAS A relationships between objects.

The diagram shows that a Honda Civic is a car but contains (or has) a steering wheel. The other interesting thing to note about the "car" in Figure 3.7 is that it is

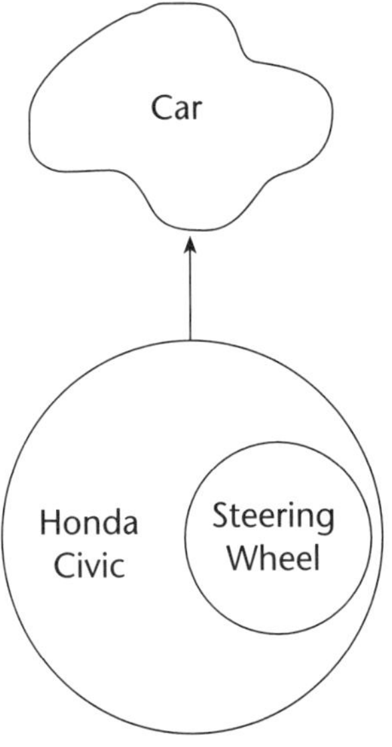

FIGURE 3.7 IS A versus HAS A relationships.

depicted with an amorphous shape. This graphically represents that car is an abstract idea that would do well to be implemented as an abstract class. This brings us to our next section.

Abstract Classes and Virtual Functions

An abstract class is a class created solely for the purpose of being extended. It is akin to an abstract idea that a physical implementation is derived from. You cannot instantiate an object from an abstract class. If you attempt to, a compiler error will result. Java has both abstract classes and abstract methods. A Java abstract method is a method that has no body and MUST be overriden in all subclasses derived from the class with the abstract method. A Java abstract class is any class that has at least one abstract method. In C++, abstract methods are called pure virtual functions and are declared like this:

```
class B {
     public:
          B();
          virtual int getNum() = 0;    // a pure virtual function
};
```

In C++, like in Java, a class that has one or more virtual functions in it is considered abstract, although there is no abstract keyword in C++. As you can see, Java is simpler in that an abstract class and method both use the abstract keyword as they are similar concepts.

Source 3.13 demonstrates both an abstract Shape class and an abstract method. The program then extends the shape class with three specific shape classes: a square, a triangle, and a hexagon. To make this program more interesting, I made it graphical. Again, do not worry about not understanding all the aspects of the graphical user interface. It is explained in detail in Chapter 10 (If you can't wait, go ahead and jump ahead to that chapter).

A run of Source 3.13 produces the output shown in Figure 3.8.

The square shape is not shown, as its implementation is trivial. All the shapes shown are subclasses of the abstract Shape class. Our abstract definition of a shape is nothing more than an array of points. It is up to the specific shape to determine how many points (using the Point class) and where those points are located. That is why we made the calculatePoints() method abstract so that it must be overridden. The calculatePoints() function for the triangle and hexagon involves some trigonometry.

SOURCE 3.13 DrawShapes.java

```
// DrawShapes.java
package jwiley.chp3;

import java.awt.*;
import java.awt.event.ActionListener;
import java.awt.event.ActionEvent;
import java.lang.Math;
import java.util.Random;

/**
 * Abstract class representing a generic shape.
 */
abstract class Shape
{
    /** Number of points in shape. */
    protected Point pts[];
    /** Center of shape. */
    protected Point Center;

    /** abstract method, MUST be implemented in subclasses. */
    abstract void calculatePoints();
}

/**
 * Subclass of shape. Represents a square.
 */
class Square extends Shape
{
    /** the drawing window. */
    drawWindow dw;
    /** The width of the square. */
    int theWidth;

    /** constructor. */
    Square(drawWindow win, Point center, int width)
    {
        dw = win;
        pts = new Point[4];
        Center = center;
        theWidth = width;

        for (int i=0; i < pts.length; i++)
                pts[i] = new Point(0,0);
    }

    /** Method to calculate the points of the square. */
    void calculatePoints()
    {
        int radius = theWidth/2;
        pts[0].x = Center.x - radius;
```

```
        pts[0].y = Center.y - radius;
        pts[1].x = Center.x - radius;
        pts[1].y = Center.y + radius;
        pts[2].x = Center.x + radius;
        pts[2].y = Center.y + radius;
        pts[3].x = Center.x + radius;
        pts[3].y = Center.y - radius;
        dw.setPoints(pts);
    }
}

/**
 *  Subclass of Shape. Represents a Triangle.
 */
class Triangle extends Shape
{
    /** Drawing window. */
    drawWindow dw;
    /** Base and Height of triangle. */
    int Base, Height;
    /** angle of lower left corner. */
    int Angle;

    /** Constructor. */
    Triangle(drawWindow win, Point center, int base, int height,
                              int baseAngle)
    {
        dw = win;
        Center = center;
        Base = base;
        Height = height;
        Angle = baseAngle;
        pts = new Point[3];
        for (int i=0; i < 3; i++)
            pts[i] = new Point(0,0);
    }

    /** Method to calculate the points of the triangle. */
    void calculatePoints()
    {
        int halfBase = Base/2;
        int halfHeight = Height/2;

        // create base
        pts[0].x = Center.x - halfBase;
        pts[0].y = Center.y + halfHeight;
        pts[2].x = Center.x + halfBase;
        pts[2].y = Center.y + halfHeight;

        // now the apex
        if (Angle == 90)
        {
```

```
            pts[1].x = Center.x - halfBase;
            pts[1].y = Center.y - halfHeight;
        }
        else if (Angle < 90)
        {
            int adjacent_angle = 90 - Angle;
            int opposite_angle = 180 - (adjacent_angle + 90);
            double radians = ((double)opposite_angle/180.0 * Math.PI);
            double theTan = Math.tan(radians);
            pts[1].x = (int) (pts[0].x +
                        ((double)(Height)/theTan));
            pts[1].y = Center.y - halfHeight;
        }
        else if (Angle > 90)
        {
            int adjacent_angle = 180 - Angle;
            double radians = (double)adjacent_angle/180.0 * Math.PI;
            double theTan = Math.tan(radians);
            pts[1].x = (int) (pts[0].x -
                        ((double)(Height)/theTan));
            pts[1].y = Center.y - halfHeight;
        }
        dw.setPoints(pts);
    }
}

/**
 * Subclass of Shape.  Represents a Hexagon.
 */
class Hexagon extends Shape
{
    /** The drawing window. */
    drawWindow dw;
    /** Base and Height of triangle. */
    int triangleBase, triangleHeight;

    /** constructor. */
    Hexagon (drawWindow win, Point center, int base, int height)
    {
        dw = win;
        Center = center;
        triangleBase = base;

        // *** triangle height is half the height of the Hex
        triangleHeight = height;

        pts = new Point[6];
        for (int i=0; i < pts.length; i++)
            pts[i] = new Point(0,0);
    }
```

```
    /** Method to calculate the points of the hexagon. */
    void calculatePoints()
    {
        int halfBase = triangleBase/2;

        // upper and lower side are trivial
        pts[0].x = Center.x - halfBase;
        pts[0].y = Center.y - triangleHeight;
        pts[5].x = Center.x + halfBase;
        pts[5].y = Center.y - triangleHeight;

        pts[2].x = Center.x - halfBase;
        pts[2].y = Center.y + triangleHeight;
        pts[3].x = Center.x + halfBase;
        pts[3].y = Center.x + triangleHeight;

        // get points to connect sides
        double radians = 60.0/180.0 * Math.PI;
        double theTan = Math.tan(radians);
        int right_triangle_adjacent = (int)
                    ((double)triangleHeight/theTan);
        pts[1].x = pts[0].x - right_triangle_adjacent;
        pts[1].y = Center.y;
        pts[4].x = pts[5].x + right_triangle_adjacent;
        pts[4].y = Center.y;
        dw.setPoints(pts);
    }
}

/**
 * Class to draw the shapes in a window frame.
 */
class drawWindow extends Frame implements ActionListener
{
    /** Points of the shape to draw. */
    private Point dPts[];
    /** Random number. */
    Random dice;

    /** Constructor. */
    drawWindow()
    {
        super("draw Shapes");
        setBackground(Color.white);
        setForeground(Color.red);

        // initialize the random number seed
        dice = new Random();

        // add a menuBar
        MenuBar mBar = new MenuBar();
        setMenuBar(mBar);
```

```
    Menu FileMenu = new Menu("File");
    MenuItem itemRef = new MenuItem("Quit");
    itemRef.addActionListener(this);
    FileMenu.add(itemRef);
    mBar.add(FileMenu);
    Menu ShapeMenu = new Menu("Shapes");
    itemRef = new MenuItem("Square");
    itemRef.addActionListener(this);
    ShapeMenu.add(itemRef);
    itemRef = new MenuItem("Triangle");
    itemRef.addActionListener(this);
    ShapeMenu.add(itemRef);
    itemRef = new MenuItem("Hexagon");
    itemRef.addActionListener(this);
    ShapeMenu.add(itemRef);
    mBar.add(ShapeMenu);

    // size and show
    setSize(200,200);
    setLocation(new Point(50,50));
    setVisible(true);
}

/** Method to implement ActionListener. */
public void actionPerformed(ActionEvent evt)
{
    String command = evt.getActionCommand();
    if ("Quit".equals(command))
    {
        dispose();
        System.exit(0);
    }
    else if ("Square".equals(command))
    {
        setPoints(null);
        repaint(); // clear window

        // roll a random # between 10 and 100
        int roll = dice.nextInt() % 100;
        if (roll < 0) roll = -roll;
        if (roll < 10) roll = 10;

        Square aSquare = new Square(this,new Point(100,100),roll);
        aSquare.calculatePoints();
        paint(getGraphics());
    }
    else if ("Triangle".equals(command))
    {
        setPoints(null);
        repaint(); // clear window
```

```
            // roll 2 random #'s between 10 and 100
            int base = dice.nextInt() % 100;
            if (base < 0) base = -base;
            if (base < 10) base = 10;

            int height = dice.nextInt() % 100;
            if (height < 0) height = -height;
            if (height < 10) height = 10;

            // roll a random angle between 1 and 179
            int angle = dice.nextInt() % 179;
            if (angle < 0) angle = -angle;
            if (angle < 1) angle = 1;

            Triangle aTriangle =
                    new Triangle(this, new Point(100,100),
                                    base, height, angle);
            aTriangle.calculatePoints();
            paint(getGraphics());
        }
        else if ("Hexagon".equals(command))
        {
            setPoints(null);
            repaint(); // clear window

            // roll a random #'s between 10 and 100
            int base = dice.nextInt() % 100;
            if (base < 0) base = -base;
            if (base < 10) base = 10;

            /* calculate the height of the
                    equilateral triangle  */
            int right_triangle_adjacent = base/2;
            double radians = 60.0/180.0 * Math.PI;
            double theTan = Math.tan(radians);

            int equilateral_height = (int)
                            (theTan * right_triangle_adjacent);

            Hexagon aHexagon =
                    new Hexagon(this, new Point(100,100),
                                    base, equilateral_height);
            aHexagon.calculatePoints();
            paint(getGraphics());
        }
    }

    /** Method to set the points in the drawing window. */
    void setPoints(Point inPoints[])
    {
        dPts = inPoints;
    }
```

```
    /** Method to paint the window. */
    public void paint(Graphics g)
    {
        if (dPts != null)
        {
            for (int i=0; i < dPts.length - 1; i++)
                    g.drawLine(dPts[i].x, dPts[i].y,
                               dPts[i+1].x, dPts[i+1].y);

            g.drawLine(dPts[dPts.length-1].x,
                       dPts[dPts.length-1].y,
                       dPts[0].x,dPts[0].y);
        }
    }
}

/**
 * Wrapper class to demonstrate abstract classes.
 */
class DrawShapes
{
    /** main() method to invoke from JVM. */
    public static void main(String args[])
    {
        new drawWindow();
    }
}
```

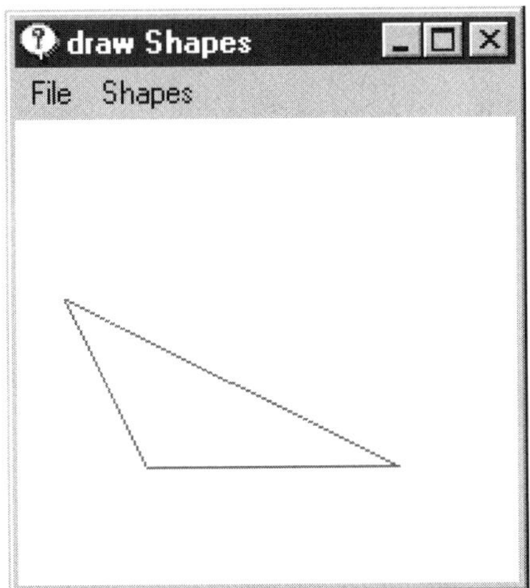

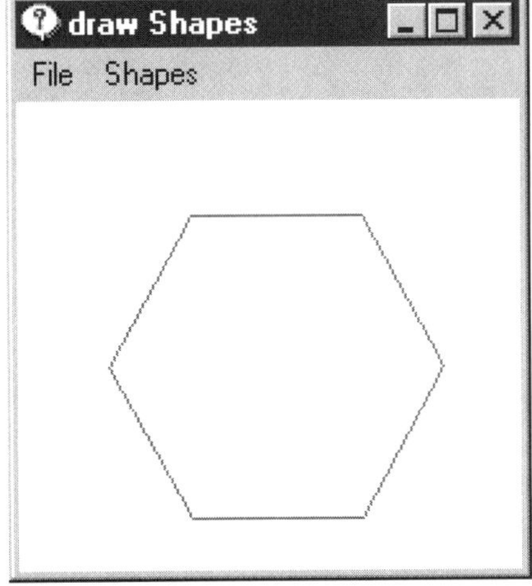

FIGURE 3.8 The drawShapes GUI.

Figure 3.9 depicts the trigonometric functions necessary to calculate the location of the apex point of the triangle given the base, height, and an angle greater than 90 degrees. Since we have the height of the triangle, we already have the Y coordinate of the apex point. We need to determine the length of the adjacent side of the right triangle that is adjacent to the triangle we wish to draw. Remembering the simple phrase my high school math teacher taught me for defining the trigonometry functions, SOH CAH TOA (say it out loud), this tells us that the sine of the angle equals the opposite over the hypotenuse, the cosine equals the adjacent over the hypotenuse, and the tangent equals the opposite over the adjacent. Knowing that we have the length of the opposite side, it is apparent that we can use the tangent of the adjacent angle to determine the length of the adjacent side. The length of the adjacent side will give us the X coordinate of the apex point of our triangle.

We perform very similar trigonometry to calculate the apex of triangles with a base angle of less than 90 degrees and also to calculate the center left and right points of the hexagon. I hope you enjoy experimenting with this program—it was certainly fun writing it to demonstrate abstract classes and methods!

Although we have discussed abstract classes and abstract methods, we have not demonstrated how Java supports virtual functions in the way that C++ does. In C++, every object has a table of function pointers called a vtable. The vtable stores the addresses of all the virtual methods supported by the class that object is an instance of. When a virtual method is called, the address of the function is looked up in the vtable at run time. Through this mechanism, calling a method on two objects does not necessarily execute the same function. The call may be different for each object, depending on their vtables. For nonvirtual methods, the address of the method is bound at compile time, so the same function will be executed regardless of the type of object the method is called on.

In Java, all methods are virtual and are therefore bound at run time. Source 3.14 demonstrates this virtual method behavior in Java.

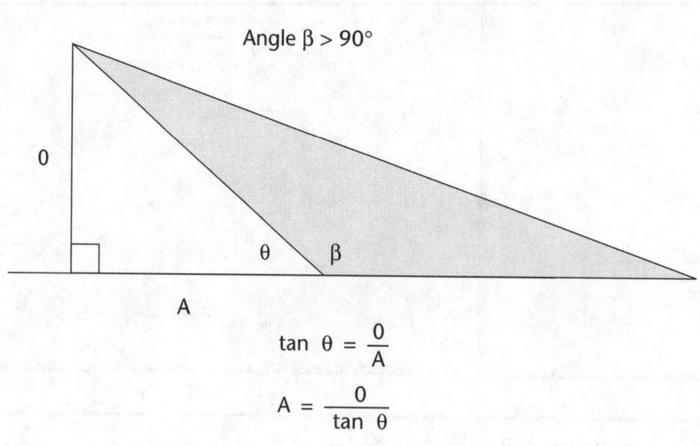

FIGURE 3.9 Calculating the apex of a triangle.

SOURCE 3.14 TstVirtual.java

```
// TstVirtual.java
package jwiley.chp3;

import java.util.Random;

/**
 * Class to represent a generic car.
 */
class car
{
    /** top speed of car. */
    int top_speed;
    /** number of gallons of gas. */
    int fuel_in_gallons;

    /** constructor. */
    car(int inSpeed, int inGallons)
    {
        top_speed = inSpeed;
        fuel_in_gallons = inGallons;
    }

    /** method to print how much fuel left in tank. */
    void howMuchFuel()
    {
        System.out.println("There is " + fuel_in_gallons +
                           " left.");
    }
}

/**
 * Specific type of car.
 */
class Honda extends car
{
    /** Model of car. */
    String model;
    /** constructor. */
    Honda(String theModel, int inSpeed, int inFuel)
    {
        super(inSpeed, inFuel);
        model = new String(theModel);
    }

    /** method to print out how much fuel left in tank. */
    void howMuchFuel()
    {
        System.out.println("My Honda " + model +
                           " has " + fuel_in_gallons +
                           " left.");
    }
}
```

```
/**
 * Specific type of car.
 */
class Dodge extends car
{
    /** Model of car. */
    String model;
    /** constructor. */
    Dodge(String theModel, int inSpeed, int inFuel)
    {
        super(inSpeed, inFuel);
        model = new String(theModel);
    }

    /** method to print out how much fuel left in tank. */
    void howMuchFuel()
    {
        System.out.println("My Dodge " + model +
                           " has " + fuel_in_gallons +
                           " left.");
    }
}

/**
 * Wrapper class to demonstrate virtual methods.
 */
class TstVirtual
{
    /** Random number class. */
    static Random dice = new Random();

    /** method to get a random type of car. */
    static car get_a_car()
    {
        if (dice.nextInt() % 2 == 0)
                return new Dodge("Caravan",90,20);
        else
                return new Honda("Civic",70,10);
    }

    /** main() method to invoke from JVM. */
    public static void main(String args[])
    {
        car theCar;
        for (int i=0; i < 5; i++)
        {
            theCar = get_a_car();
            theCar.howMuchFuel();
        }
    }
}
```

A run of Source 3.14 produces:

```
C:\java\bin>java jwiley.chp3.TstVirtual
My Dodge Caravan has 20 left.
My Dodge Caravan has 20 left.
My Honda Civic has 10 left.
My Dodge Caravan has 20 left.
My Honda Civic has 10 left.
```

The key point to understand in Source 3.14 is that the type declaration of the variable theCar is as a type of base class car; however, the object instantiated is one of the subclasses (Honda or Dodge). Since the instantiated object is one of the subclasses, the subclass howMuchFuel() method is called. This is identical to the behavior of virtual functions in C++. Now we can move on to another area in which C++ and Java are similar: exceptions.

3.4 EXCEPTIONS

Exceptions are a robust error-handling mechanism that functions equally well in C++ and Java. In the latest draft language specification from the standards committee, C++ exception handling has been expanded and improved, resulting in a system nearly identical to Java's. You will notice that C++ and Java each have unique features in their exception handling mechanisms. In general, the exception handling facilities of both languages are good. Let's now examine the main elements of exception handling in both languages and demonstrate them in code.

Try Blocks and Handling Exceptions

The cornerstone of exception handling in both C++ and Java involves a try block and catch expression. The keyword try precedes a block of code that may throw an exception. In Java, any method that throws an exception must explicitly state so in its function declaration using the throws keyword. C++ also allows exception specifications in its function declaration, but the absence of an exception specification can mean that the function can throw all exceptions. The closing brace of a try block must be followed by a catch expression. This catch expression is the type of the exception that the following block of code can handle. Both C++ and Java allow a catchall feature by using the following code:

```
in C++:     } catch (...)

in Java:    } catch (Exception e)
```

The catch expressions are followed by an exception handler block of code for that exception. Source 3.15 demonstrates throwing and catching exceptions as well as some C++ unique facilities for exception handling (i.e., set_unexpected()).

SOURCE 3.15 exceptions.cpp

```
#include <iostream.h>
#include <stdlib.h>
#include <stdio.h>
#include <string.h>
#include <stdexcept.h>

class ResultTooLarge : public exception{
    char message[80];

    public:
    ResultTooLarge(char * msg)
    {
        strcpy(message,msg);
    }

    const char *what()
    {
        cout << "Exception: " << message << endl;
        return message;
    }
};

void my_unexpected()
{
    cout << "Catching unexpected exceptions." << endl;
}

void my_terminate()
{
    cout << "If unexpected not handled, call me." << endl;
    exit(1);
}

void badboy()  // can throw all exceptions
{
    throw ResultTooLarge("I'll throw any exception I like.");
}

void goodboy() throw (ResultTooLarge)
{
    throw ResultTooLarge("You can expect me only to throw ResultTooLarge");
}

void greatboy() throw()
{
    cout << "I don't throw ANY exceptions." << endl;
}

void main()
{
```

```
    set_unexpected(my_unexpected);
    set_terminate(my_terminate);

    int a=100, b=2;
    try {
         int result = a/b;
         if (result > 5)
         {
                char msg[80];
                sprintf(msg,"%d is too Large.", result);
                throw ResultTooLarge(msg);
         }
    } catch (ResultTooLarge e)
         {
                cout << "Caught the result too large." << endl;
                e.what();
         }
      catch (...)
         {
               cout << "Caught any exception." << endl;
         }
}
```

A run of Source 3.15 produces:

```
Caught the result too large.
Exception: 50 is too Large.
```

There are three key points to note about Source 3.15:

- *The class ResultTooLarge is a subclass of the standard exception class.* There are several types of standard exceptions defined in the proposed C++ standard and they are broken down into two types: logic exceptions and runtime exceptions. These two types are identical to the function of the Exception and RuntimeException classes in Java. Those Java classes are discussed in detail in the later section, The Java Standard Library.
- *The functions badboy(), goodboy(), and greatboy() demonstrate exception specifications.* In my opinion, the fact that lack of a specification denotes that the function may throw any exceptions weakens the utility of the C++ exceptions specification facility as well as opening it up to abuse. This, of course, is the most severe drawback of C++: The majority of safety features and object-oriented protections can be circumvented via either casting or pointers.
- *The function set_unexpected() and set_terminate() allow you to provide last-ditch event handlers to cover two specific conditions.* The unexpected() function will be

called if an exception is thrown in a function that has an exception specification where the exception being thrown is not part of the specification. The terminate() function is called if no handler is found for an exception.

Now let's examine the Java exception handling facility and compare it to the code in Source 3.15. Source 3.16 demonstrates exception handling and throwing in Java.

SOURCE 3.16 TestExceptions.java

```
// TestExceptions.java
package jwiley.chp3;

/**
 * Class to represent an erroneous result exception.
 */
class ResultTooLarge extends Exception
{
    /** constructor. */
    ResultTooLarge(String msg)
    {
        super(msg);
    }
}

/**
 * Class to demonstrate throwing and catching exceptions.
 */
class TestExceptions
{
    /** main() method to invoke from JVM. */
    public static void main(String args[])
    {
        int a=100, b=2;
        try
        {
            int result = a/b;
            if (result > 5)
            {
                throw new ResultTooLarge(result + " is too Large.");
            }
        } catch (ResultTooLarge e)
          {
            System.out.println("Caught the result too large.");
            System.out.println(e.getMessage());
          }
          finally
          {
            System.out.println("Finally will always be run.");
            System.out.println("Even if exceptions are caught.");
          }
    }
}
```

A run of Source 3.16 produces:

```
C:\java\bin>java jwiley.chp3.TestExceptions
Caught the result too large.
50 is too Large.
Finally will always be run.
Even if exceptions are caught.
```

Finally will always be run. Even if exceptions are caught!

Before we get into the specific variations of Java exception handling, it should be evident that the facilities are very similar. I feel that is a good thing. Both seem to be well thought out and should be taken very seriously by every programmer.

There are three key points to understand about Source 3.16:

- The exception ResultTooLarge is a subclass of the Exception class. The Exception class extends the Throwable class. Any class that extends throwable can be thrown and caught. Classes derived from the Exception class fall into the category of errors that can be recovered from, whereas classes derived from the Runtime-Exception class generally cannot be recovered from.
- The Java try, throw, and catch constructs are nearly identical to their C++ counterparts.
- The Java finally keyword allows a block of code to be executed, even if any exceptions are thrown within the try block and catch blocks.

Although we have shown that Java has adopted many parts of C++, there are also many parts of the language intentionally left out. We discuss these in section 3.6. But first let's look at C++'s nested and Java's inner classes.

3.5 INNER AND NESTED CLASSES

Both Java 1.1 and C++ share the concept that classes can be contained within other classes. Java calls these *inner* classes while C++ terms them *nested* classes. Figure 3.10 shows a C++ and Java nested class side by side. The most notable differences are those differences that we have already seen between Java and C++, again the absence of the scope resolution operator and C++'s allowing of multiple variables under a single access specifier. Basically all the same rules apply to inner classes as normal or *enclosing* classes. However, some differences do exist, both within C++ and Java, the most important of which is that classes defined within the scope of another are invisible outside the enclosing class. This new feature of Java allows classes to be defined in any scope, within an enclosing class anonymously within an expression or within a block of code. The following sections show exactly what inner classes are, how they can be used, and where they differ from C++.

Both inner and nested classes share other common traits. Classes defined within another class may access the variables and methods of the enclosing class without qualification. However, Java inner classes can extend or implement another class.

C++ Nested Class	***Java Inner Class***

C++ Nested Class

```
Class BufferedIO
{
protected:
    int iRead;
    int iWrite;
public:

    BufferedIO() { };
    class BufferedInput
    {
    public:
        BufferedInput() { };
        int read();
        // Other methods
    ...
    };

    class BufferedOutput
    {
    public:
        BufferedOutput() { };
        int write();
        // Other methods
    ...
    };
};
BufferedIO::BufferedInput::read()
{
    // Implementation of read
}
```

Java Inner Class

```
Class BufferedIO
{
    protected int iRead;
    protected int iWrite;

    public BufferedIO() { };
    class BufferedInput
    {
        public BufferedInput()
        {
        }
        public int read()
        {
        // Implementation
        }
        // Other methods
    ...
    };

    class BufferedOutput
    {
        public BufferedOutput()
        {
        }
        int write()
        {
        // Implementation
        }
        // Other methods
    ...
} // End of class Buffered IO
```

FIGURE 3.10 Inner classes.

Such a class is called an *adapter* class. Adapter classes are so called because they adapt or translate one class method to another. As we shall see in Chapter 10, Java 1.1 introduces a new event model that is based on adapting an action performed on an object (graphic or otherwise) to a method in another class. Those of you familiar with the earlier Java event model saw how you needed to define large switch statements to capture events and process them. With adapter classes and the new event model programmers can define event behavior much closer to where it makes sense and in a much more elegant fashion! Source 3.17 shows an example of a simple adapter class.

As you can see there were only minor additions to the bookshelf class to accommodate the inner class. But why the inner classes at all? One behavior of the bookshelf class was supporting listing the books and a *java.util.Enumeration* does this nicely.

SOURCE 3.17 bookShelf2.java

```
//
// bookshelf2.java
//
package jwiley.chp3;

/**
 * Class to implement a real-world bookshelf
 */
public class Bookshelf {
.
. // Entire bookshelf class here with the addition of the enumerator class
.
        class Enumerator implements java.util.Enumeration
        {
            book current = first;
            book toBeReturned;
            public boolean hasMoreElements()
            {
                return current != null;
            }
            public Object nextElement()
            {
                if ( current == null)
                    return null;
                toBeReturned = current;
                current = current.next;
                return toBeReturned;
            }
        }

        public java.util.Enumeration elements()
        {
            return new Enumerator();
        }
}

/**
 * Class to provide a main routine for the bookshelf application
 */
class bookMain2 {
        public static void main(String args[])
        {
                Bookshelf mybooks = new Bookshelf();
                java.util.Enumeration myEnumeration;
                boolean done = false;
                System.out.println("Enter your books.");
                System.out.println("Type 'done' when finished.");
                while (!done)
                {
```

```
                    book curBook = new book();
                    curBook.getBook();
                    if (!(curBook.getTitle()).equals("done"))
                    {
                            mybooks.add(curBook);
                    }
                    else
                            done = true;
            }
            // print the books in the shelf using the enumeration
            System.out.println(
                    "Number of books in bookshelf(by enumeration): " +
                     mybooks.size());

            int cnt = 0;
            myEnumeration = mybooks.elements();
            while (myEnumeration.hasMoreElements())
            {
                book aBook = (book) myEnumeration.nextElement();
                System.out.println("Book: " + cnt++);
                aBook.showBook();
            }
        }
} // End class bookMain2
```

However, the bookshelf should not implement this enumeration directly; after all it's a bookshelf. So the implementation of an enumeration allows for listing the books as required, but does not compromise the design of the bookshelf class. In C++ we might have done the same thing with a friend class, but the inner class is much simpler and more elegant. There is still a somewhat sizeable problem with our enumeration related to the fact that our enumeration of the bookshelf and the bookshelf itself can both be accessed at the same moment. We shall address this problem shortly.

Classes need not be quite so complex; Source 3.18 shows a useful but very simple inner class.

This particular example illustrates how an inner class simplifies normal code. By placing the runnable object within the main method we eliminate the need for another class and simplify parameter passing, if required, between the two.

Local and Inline Classes

Java allows for classes defined within the scope of a block of code. Such a class is called a *local* or *inline* class. Java also allows for classes defined within an expression. Such a class is called an *inline* class. Source 3.18 shows an example of a local class, whereas Source 3.19 shows an inline class. Both local and inline classes allow a class to be

SOURCE 3.18 ASimpleClass.java

```
// ASimpleClass.java
package jwiley.chp3;

/**
 * A class to demonstrate inner classes
 */
public class ASimpleClass
{
    public static void main( String args[])
    {
        for (int i = 0; i < args.length; i++)
        {
            final String anArg = args[i];
            class printArg implements Runnable
            {
                public void run()
                { System.out.println(anArg); }
            }
            new Thread (new printArg()).start();
        }
    } // end main
} // end ASimpleClass
```

SOURCE 3.19 LocalClass.java

```
// LocalClass.java
package jwiley.chp3;

/**
 * A class to demonstrate local classes
 */
public class LocalClass
{
    public static void main( String args[])
    {
        // Note the use of final below!
        final int someVar = 1;
        final int anotherVar = 3;
        class foobar
        {
            int ctFoobars = someVar + anotherVar;
            public void printStuff()
            {
                System.out.println("Value is " +ctFoobars);
            }
        }
        foobar foo = new foobar();
        foo.printStuff();
    }
}
```

defined exactly where it is needed and are used extensively in adapters. A local class might be defined as shown here.

The primary difference between local/inline classes and nested classes is their location within the code and their scope. A local class, as just shown, is contained within an existing block of code, but not necessarily within another class, whereas inner classes are defined within the scope of another class. You can think of local classes just like you do local variables. They exist only within the scope of the block of code in which they are defined. Nested classes, on the other hand, exist for the lifetime of instances of the class they are defined within. Source 3.20 shows another example of an inline class and how they are used in adapters. Source 3.20 specifically shows how classes can be defined within an expression.

SOURCE 3.20 AdptrTst.java

```
// AdptrTst.java
package jwiley.chp3;

import java.awt.Button;
import java.awt.Frame;
import java.awt.FlowLayout;
import java.awt.event.ActionEvent;
import java.awt.event.ActionListener;

/**
 * A class to demonstrate adapters
 */
public class AdptrTst
{
     public AdptrTst(String args[]) { }
     void ButtonAPushed()
     {
          System.out.println("Button A pushed");
          System.out.flush();
     }

     void ButtonQuitPushed()
     {
          System.out.println("quitting!");
          System.out.flush();
          System.exit(1);
     }
     static public void main (String args[])
     {
          AdptrTst app = new AdptrTst(args);
          GUI gui = app.new GUI();
     } // End main
```

```
    // Now define the inner class which represents the gui
    // and is defined within the application.
    class GUI extends Frame
    {
        public GUI()
        {
            setLayout(new FlowLayout());
            Button a = new Button("Button A");
            Button quit = new Button("Quit");
            add(a); // Insert into frame
            add(quit);

            // Now use a local adapter class to hook the button press
            a.addActionListener
                (
                    new ActionListener()
                    {
                        public void actionPerformed(ActionEvent e)
                        {
                            ButtonAPushed();
                        }
                    }
                );
            // Likewise the other button
            quit.addActionListener
                (
                    new ActionListener()
                    {
                        public void actionPerformed(ActionEvent e)
                        {
                            ButtonQuitPushed();
                        }
                    }
                );
        pack();
        show();
        }
    } // Close the frame class extention
} // close the app itself.
```

Anonymous Classes

In addition to inner classes, both Java and C++ support the concept of anonymous classes. Anonymous classes are those which define a class that has no explicit name. In the previous example, the class name lent little to the understanding of what the class is and how it is used. With an anonymous class you need not give a name. Anonymous classes are really just a short-hand way of creating a simple local instance of an object, by wrapping it in a new expression. Most often, anonymous classes are used to

C++ Anonymous class	*Java Anonymous class*

```
// A C++ anonymous class
class SomeClass
{
     class {
     public: int a,b,c;
     } IntegerData;
     class{
     public: float d,e,f;
     } FloatData;
};
```

```
// A Java anonymous class
class canEnumerate
{
    // Other methods

  Enumeration anEnumeration()
  {
    // Internal data if required
    return new Enumeration()
    {
    public boolean hasMoreElements()
    {
       // Code based on class
    }
    public Object nextElement()
    {
       // Code based on class
    }
   }
  }
}
```

FIGURE 3.11 Comparison of anonymous classes.

create simple callback methods or adapters. Significant differences exist between C++ anonymous classes and those in Java. Quite simply, C++ classes are more akin to structures and cannot contain static data or member functions.

As we can see from Figure 3.11, the C++ anonymous class is really just an embedded structure with no methods associated with it. The Java class, on the other hand, is actually a complete class with data and methods just like any other class.

An anonymous class may have initializers but cannot have a constructor. Basically, the argument list of the associated new expression is implicitly passed to the constructor of the superclass. This stems from the fact that explicit *implements* are illegal in anonymous classes. When a class is defined from some interface, the actual superclass is *Object* and the class does not extend the interface but only implements it. Since the argument list of *Object* is null, the constructor is not required.

If we revisit our bookself example and assume that books can be linked backward and forward, we could define an anonymous enumeration for walking from the last book to the first as shown in Source 3.21.

Scoping. Both C++ and Java support resolving class names using scoping operators. C++ uses the :: (double colon) as in BufferedIO::BufferedInput::read(), whereas Java uses dot notation. For example, BufferedIO.BufferedInput.read().

SOURCE 3.21 bookBack.java

```
// bookback.java
Enumeration Backwards()
{
     return new Enumeration()
     {
          book current = last;
               book toBeReturned;
          public boolean hasMoreElements()
          {
               return current != null;
          }
          public Object nextElement()
          {
               if ( current == null)
                    return null;
               toBeReturned = current;
               current = current.previous;
               return toBeReturned;
          }
     }
}
```

Access Specifiers. All the normal access protections and modifications apply to inner classes. Classes, interfaces, and data members within an inner class can have any mix of specifiers. However, the same is not quite true of classes defined within a block of code, which are by definition local to the code they are contained within.

Any named class can be defined as final or abstract. Likewise, accessible nonfinal classes and interfaces can serve as superclasses.

Static. The static keyword takes on special meaning when used with an inner class. As the reader will remember, the static keyword was designed to allow a method to apply to a class as a whole and not to a specific instance of a class. A restriction on inner classes is that they may not define any static members at all (think about it for a moment, does a static member of an inner class make sense, given how inner classes are scoped?). Inner classes, on the other hand, may be defined as static. This has the effect of causing the class to be a *top-level* class.

Local* final *Variables. Version 1.1 of Java introduced a new feature to Java: local *final* variables. Local variables used by inner classes must be declared final. Because of inherent synchronization issues there is no way for two objects to share access to a changeable local variable.

Synchronization. In the Bookshelf2.java example we saw a simple enumeration that listed the elements (books) in our bookshelf. However, one problem was overlooked, that of synchronization. Because of the thread-based nature of Java there is nothing to prevent one thread from creating the bookshelf and another thread from processing it. Because the first thread may be adding entries while another thread enumerates these entries, there is nothing to stop one of the processes from accessing the bookshelf while an add or delete operation is in progress; potentially undermining the bookshelf, the enumeration, or both. Enter synchronization. We can solve this problem by using the *synchronized* keyword as follows:

```
//
// Update the enumerator to support synchronization!
//
class Enumerator implements java.util.Enumeration
    {
    book current = first;
    book toBeReturned;
    public boolean hasMoreElements()
    {
         synchronized(bookshelf.this)
         {
             return current != null;
         }
    }
    public Object nextElement()
    {
         synchronized(bookshelf.this)
         {
             if ( current == null)
                 return null;
             toBeReturned = current;
             current = current.next;
             return toBeReturned;
         } // end synchronized block.
    }
}
```

Of course, any other methods which add or remove entries from our bookshelf object would need to be synchronized as well! The synchronized block specifier easily makes our code thread-safe!

Parameter Masking

It is possible for a newly defined class to define variables that mask those in the parent or enclosing class. Java allows inherited names to mask those defined in an enclosing block or inner class, but requires they be qualified before they can be used.

Static Classes and "Packages"

Through the use of the static keyword, a developer can give a package-like orientation to his or her classes, allowing a set of inner classes access to all the private variables of the enclosing class. Don't forget that inner classes can make use of their own instance variables (the this variable), whereas static classes have no instance information and apply to ALL instances of the class.

3.6 FEATURES OMITTED FROM C++

C++ is a large language that is growing larger with its standardization. Part of this is due to the fact that C++ has grown from being extensions to C into being a whole separate language on top of C (sort of how Windows was implemented on top of DOS). The draft standard just released by the C++ standards committee has seen the Standard Library leap from just iostreams and the C Standard Library into 10 separate libraries. In a word, the C++ Standard Library is now huge (we will discuss this more in section 3.7).

Being large is not necessarily a problem, especially in relation to library routines. However, the C++ language has also grown increasingly complex. Features like operator overloading, multiple inheritance, and templates can generate very complex code that can only be enhanced or maintained by the person who created it. If that person leaves the company, the code becomes practically useless.

Lastly, not only did C++ inherit certain flaws and dangers from C—like the preprocessor and pointers—but added its own dangers and redundancies such as multiple inheritance and references. All the features to be discussed here do not include all the new features and ambiguities in the new draft C++ standard.

The following C++ features were intentionally omitted from Java or significantly modified.

- **Destructors**. The Java language has changed the concept of an object's destruction to its finalization. The reason for this is that object destruction is most often associated with the explicit freeing of dynamic memory allocated for the object. Since Java performs garbage collection, the programmer does not explicitly deallocate memory. However, there may be some resources (ports, files, devices) that need to be released, closed, or cleaned up before they are garbage collected by the system. Therefore, Java has replaced the object's destructor with a finalize() function. Source 3.22 demonstrates finalization in Java.

  A run of Source 3.22 produces:

```
C:\java\bin>java jwiley.chp3.TstFinalize
Setting data member.
Finalizing simpleObject.
```

In Source 3.22 the object had to be forced to be finalized. Normally, objects would not be garbage collected until either the program was idle (the Java garbage collector is a low-priority thread), or a memory request could not be satisfied. Since neither situation applied in our simple program, I forced the system to garbage collect via a call to System.gc(). However, just because the garbage collector ran, there was still no need for the program to immediately finalize the object. Instead, it sat on the finalization queue awaiting finalization if the resource was needed (which it wasn't). Therefore, to force finalization I called System.runfinalization().

SOURCE 3.22 TstFinalize.java

```
// TstFinalize.java
package jwiley.chp3;

/**
 * Simple object for demo purposes only.
 */
class simpleObject2
{
    /** an integer data member. */
    int a = 5;

    /** mutator. */
    void setA(int inA)
    {
        System.out.println("Setting data member.");
        a = inA;
    }

    /** finalize method. */
    protected void finalize()
    {
        System.out.println("Finalizing simpleObject.");
        a = 0;
    }
}

/**
 * Wrapper class to demonstrate use of finalize().
 */
class TstFinalize
{
    /** main() method to invoke from JVM. */
    public static void main(String args[])
    {
        simpleObject2 myObject = new simpleObject2();

        myObject.setA(100);
        myObject = null;
        System.gc();
        System.runFinalization();
    }
}
```

- **Operator Overloading.** This is a C++ construct that allows the primitive operators to be overloaded to work with classes. This can lead to elegant code that lets you use the + operator to add matrix classes, coordinates, and other objects where addition makes sense. However, all of a sudden you have programmers getting carried away with the feature and overloading the minus operator to remove components from a GUI. Or you have an overloaded right-shift operator (>>) used to mean fast-forward through a linked list because "it sort of resembled the fast-forward button on my VCR." The bottom line is that it is actually more intuitive and not open to interpretation to use descriptive method names for operations involving objects. And with Java allowing method and variable names of any length, there is no excuse not to be descriptive.

- **Templates.** The idea behind templates is an excellent one, allowing classes and methods to be type independent or generic. Unfortunately, many of the other C++ features like multiple inheritance, references, and operator overloading can make a template overly complicated and difficult to understand. It is as if the language polluted a fine idea that was implemented in Ada long before being implemented in C++. You may have noticed that the keyword generic is reserved for future use in Java. It is highly probable that you will see generic become either a method modifier or a new type. Since every Java object is inherited from the root Object class, it is not necessary to have a class be generic. The Container classes can already store a generic object by storing a uninstantiated Object. This is exactly the methodology of the Vector and other container classes.
- **Multiple Inheritance.** A C++ feature that allows inheritance from more than one parent or base class. This is another feature where the concept is sound but the implementation proves difficult and adds complexity to the language. In the end, a simpler solution like Java interfaces (explained in section 5.2) provides most of the same benefits.
- **References.** The C++ concept of references is different than it is in Java. In Java, all variables that point to objects are actually references. In C++, references are actually a layer on top of the standard data type system, including pointers. In C++, a variable can be a reference to a primitive, an object, or a pointer. C++ references are more powerful than Java references for two reasons. First, they allow primitives to be passed by reference. In Java, primitives must be wrapped in objects. Also, in C++, by passing a pointer to an object by reference, a function can change which object that pointer points to. In Java, a method can alter the contents of an object but it cannot replace the object completely. To accomplish either of these C++ capabilities in Java you must either pass the argument as an element of an array, or pass the argument as a content of a special container class.
- **Friend Classes.** A feature that allows one class to have access to protected and private data members and methods of another class. This feature is implemented through packages (see section 6.1). In a Java package, when you do not explicitly put in an access specifier, the default access specifier is "friendly," which means that all classes and methods within the package have access to friendly methods and data.

3.7 THE C++ STANDARD LIBRARY

I mentioned in the previous section that the new C++ Standard Library was getting huge. Let me give you a little detail on exactly what the new library contains (from the draft standard specification):

54 standard macros from the C library

45 standard values from the C library

19 standard types from the C library

2 standard structures from the C library
208 standard functions from the C library
66 standard template classes
86 standard template operator functions
24 standard template structures
28 standard classes
144 standard template functions
12 standard operator functions
78 standard functions in the C++ library
16 additional structures in the C++ library
28 additional types in the C++ library
8 standard objects

This gives a grand total of 818 items in the C++ Standard Library, all accessed via 18 C library headers and 32 C++ headers.

Naturally, no compiler vendor has yet implemented the entire C++ Standard Library as specified in the latest draft standard. Some have only a very small portion implemented. Regardless, it is not the primary domain of this book and is far too large to discuss. The draft specification divided the library into 10 categories. We will describe each category in general terms and then refer the reader to a similar capability or package in the Java standard library if one exists.

Language Support Library

This library implements macros, objects, and functions used in other parts of the library and in the C++ language. The majority of this library is composed of C Standard Library headers already discussed in section 2.11. The C Standard Library headers are:

```
<cstddef> <climits> <cfloat> <cstdlib>

<cstdarg> <csetjmp> <ctime> <csignal> <cstdlib>
```

There are four C++ headers:

- **<limits>.** This header provides detailed information on the implementation of the primitive types. This type of information is platform independent in Java and fixed.
- **<new>.** This header implements the C++ dynamic allocation functions new, delete, and the array forms of the operators. The Java new operator and built-in garbage collection provide the same functionality.
- **<typeinfo>.** This header provides the C++ Run Time Type Information as demonstrated for C++ and Java previously in this chapter.

- **<exception>.** This header defines the bad_exception class, the unexpected(), terminate(), set_unexpected(), and set_terminate() functions. Due to Java's stricter implementation of exceptions, these functions are not necessary in Java.

Diagnostics Library

The diagnostics library offers basically the standard exception classes added to the existing C library headers for reporting errors. The C headers are:

```
<cassert> <cerrno>
```

The C++ header that declares the standard exceptions is <stdexcept>. The standard exceptions are the following classes: exception, logic_error, domain_error, invalid_argument, length_error, out_of_range, runtime_error, range_error, and overflow_error. While this is a good start, the Java Standard Library has many more standard exceptions in each package of the library. We will discuss every Java exception in the next chapter.

General Utilities Library

This library has utility classes and functions that can be used both by the C++ library and user programs. There is one C header in this category, the <ctime> header, which provides date and time function. In general, this category has some similarities to the Java util package (see Chapter 7).

There are three C++ specific headers in this category:

- **<utility>.** This header defines numerous template operators. There are no templates in Java.
- **<functional>.** This header also defines numerous templates for basic operations (minus, plus, logical operations, etc.); no correlation to Java.
- **<memory>.** This header provides templates for allocators and allocator support functions. There is no correlation to Java, which is garbage collected.

Strings Library

In addition to the C string and character headers shown here

```
<cctype> <cwctype> <cstring> <cwchar>
```

This category also includes template classes for a basic_string class in the C++ <string> header. The functionality is very similar to the Java String and StringBuffer classes discussed in Chapter 2.

Localization Library

In addition to the C header <clocale> previously discussed, this category adds a C++ header <locale>. These headers provide internationalization support for character classification and string collation, numeric, monetary, and date/time formatting and parsing. Java's new internationalization support is built into the Core API. All operations that vary from locale to locale allow programmers to either rely on default behavior or specify a precise locale to operate in. This is most important when handling multibyte strings. Because Java uses UNICODE characters, all multibyte strings must be converted before they can be used. When converting between UNICODE and multibyte strings, the language being converted must be specified or the conversion can produce incorrect results.

Containers Library

It is important to give credit where credit is due, and the next three sections (mostly derived from the Standard Template Library (STL) developed by Alex Stepanov, Meng Lee, and David R. Musser) are incredible achievements. It would not surprise me if Sun did not add generics just to have the STL. Hewlett-Packard has released its implementation into the public domain; you can obtain the source code via anonymous ftp from butler.hp1.hp.com.

The containers library is the part of the STL that is completely implemented already in Java. In fact, an even greater number of containers can be found at www.gamelan.com. The containers category has eight headers:

- **<vector> <deque> <list> <queue> <stack>.** These containers are all sequences. A sequence is a finite set of elements arranged in a linear fashion. Java currently implements a Vector class and Stack class. (See Chapter 4.)
- **<map> <set>.** These implement an associative container that maps keys to values. Java provides a Dictionary and HashTable class described in Chapter 7.
- **<bitset>.** A sequence of individual bits. Java has a BitSet class as described in section 4.2.

Iterators Library

In one sense, iterators are another bandaid to avoid the dangers of pointers. I admit pointers can be dangerous in the wrong hands (just like power tools), but they are worth the effort to learn. After you learn them, you will see why it is better to not program with them explicitly. This is what both Java and iterators do for you. They allow you to implicitly program with pointers instead of explicitly. And that is fine because safety and reliability should outweigh control and efficiency for most (not all) programming situations.

There is only one <iterator> header. An iterator is described in the standard as a generalization of pointers that allow data structures to be sequenced through in a uniform manner. This same definition could be used to describe the Enumeration interface in section 4.2. I also demonstrate in Chapter 5 how to implement the Enumeration interface for a list package.

Algorithms Library

This is probably the only area where the C++ library outshines the Java standard library (again, thanks to the STL). This category has four types of generic algorithms: nonmutating sequence operations, mutating sequence operations, sorting operations, and the C standard library algorithms (binsearch, quicksort, etc.). I expect all of these to be implemented and incorporated into the Java standard library as new interfaces (along with some new containers).

This category consists of the <cstdlib> header and one C++ header called <algorithm>. The <algorithm> header is fairly large and packed with over a hundred useful algorithms. The header contains generic algorithms to search, sort, compare, transform, merge, unique, fill, count, copy, swap, randomly access, partition, and many other operations on container elements.

Numerics Library

The numerics library performs many functions for the manipulation of numbers. Some of this capability is also in Java but not all. In addition to the <cmath> header and <cstdlib> header, this category has three C++ headers:

- **<complex>.** A comprehensive header that provides templates and functions to manipulate complex numbers. Complex numbers are numbers that can be written in the form a + bi, where a and b are real numbers and i is the imaginary unit (defined by i2 = –1). There is no corresponding class or function currently in Java.
- **<valarray>.** This header defines five different types of arrays (valarray, slice_array, gslice_array, mask_array, and indirect_array). Some of these capabilities are in Java's array, being a first-call object, but not close to all of them. A Java array is very similar to the val_array template class. There are no corresponding classes in Java for the slice and gslice class in this header.
- **<numeric>.** This header provides generic mathematical algorithms for operations such as accumulate, calculating the inner product, partial sum, and adjacent difference. There is no corresponding interface currently in Java.

Input/Output Library

Besides the C headers <cstdlib>, <cstdio>, and <cwchar>, this category has nine C++ headers:

```
<iosfwd> <iostream> <ios> <streambuf> <istream>

<ostream> <iomanip> <sstream> <fstream>
```

We do not need to discuss the C++ io classes in detail. Suffice it to say that both C++ and Java have robust Input/Output facilities. The Java io package is described in detail in Chapter 8.

3.8 SUMMARY

In this chapter, we learned about Object-Oriented Programming and its implementation in both C++ and Java. The three main elements of object-oriented programming are encapsulation, inheritance, and polymorphism. Encapsulation is the technique of protecting data within an object. Each object represents a real-world object and presents an interface that represents how one would interact with that object in real life without exposing the data directly. Inheritance is the ability for one class to start with the capabilities of another class and extend those capabilities. Polymorphism is when a base class provides one method, and multiple subclasses provide their own implementations of that method. Programmers can invoke the same method with different results without having to worry about the exact type of the object they are referencing.

Classes are the enabling programming structure for object-oriented programming. The main elements of a class are: data members, constructors, and methods. All elements of a class have an associated access specifier. The access specifier determines whether or not a specific element is accessible outside of the class and the Java package. Java supports two special variables for writing class methods. This always refers to the current object, and super always refers to the parent class of the current object. Static data and methods are not associated with particular object instances, but rather are associated with the class itself. This and super are not available to static methods.

In Java, all methods are virtual, meaning that they are bound at run time to the referenced object. A method is termed abstract when its implementation is not provided. Typically, abstract methods are implemented by one or more child classes. If a class has at least one abstract method, then the class is called an abstract class.

Objects are always created by using the Java new operator to call a specific class's constructor. New cannot be used to create objects for abstract classes.

Java uses exceptions to implement error handling. Exceptions are characterized by the try/catch statement. Try is used to designate a block of code that can generate an exception, and catch is used to define an error handling for that block. A finally clause can designate a block of code that always executes whether or not an exception was actually thrown.

While many of the constructs from C++ have parallels in Java, there are some features that are not implemented in Java. Destructors in C++ have been replaced with Java finalizers. This was done because destructors imply an explicit freeing of memory, but Java uses a garbage collection system where no such explicit freeing occurs. The Java designers also chose not to implement operator overloading, mainly because it is often misused and can lead to confusing, unmaintainable code. Finally, Java doesn't support anything like C++ templates.

CHAPTER 4

Language Features Not in C or C++

If I have seen further than other men, it is because I have stood on the shoulders of giants.

—Sir Isaac Newton

OBJECTIVE

This chapter describes characteristics of Java that are not part of the C or C++ programming languages. It also explores the influence of other object-oriented languages on Java.

The evolution of a programming language follows the same process of natural selection as does biological evolution. In his magnificent science fiction series, *Dune*, Frank Herbert explored the potentiality of humanity through an order of women, called the Bene Gesserit, who attempted to create a perfect human through the careful control of breeding in order to magnify certain traits and suppress others. This analytical selection (called the analytical knife by Robert Persig) of beneficial characteristics that should survive and flourish over other characteristics is analogous to the language designer playing Bene Gesserit. The developers of Java began with a pared down C/C++ base stock and then grafted characteristics from other object-oriented languages into their creation. This is genetic engineering of the second degree. In Java, you will find influences of Ada, Objective-C, Smalltalk, and Eiffel. We will examine these new Java features in light of their presence in other languages.

4.1 PACKAGES

The Ada language was developed for the Department of Defense (DoD) in the late 1970s with the ANSI standard published in January 1983. Also, a new object-oriented version called Ada 95 was released in 1995. The Ada language was named in honor of Augusta Ada Byron, the Countess of Lovelace (1815–1852). Ada was the assistant and patron of Charles Babbage and worked on his mechanical analytical engine, which is generally thought of as the first mechanical computer. Because of her work with Charles Babbage, Ada is considered the world's first programmer.

Although Ada has not been widely adopted outside of DoD circles, it has proven itself to be a robust and reliable procedural language with many language features that object-oriented languages have just begun to exploit. Some of those features are private types (similar to the private access specifier), exceptions, generics (similar to C++ templates), and tasks (similar to threads). The Ada 95 standard has added such facilities as single inheritance, constructors, destructors, and improved generics and tasking. Unfortunately, since Ada was derived from Pascal, C and C++ programmers often feel the syntax is wordy and clunky. Also, like C++, it is a procedural language with object-oriented additions and not a pure object-oriented language like Java.

Compared to Java, Ada packages have more similarity to a class than to a Java package. Ada packages are primarily used for data hiding by placing a wall around a group of declarations and only permitting access to those that you intend to be visible. The Ada package comes in two parts: the specification, which describes the interface to the package user, and the body, which gives the hidden implementation. Another example of Ada packages being analogous to modern classes is that Ada private types are private to the whole package and not to any type.

In Java, a package is primarily used for managing namespaces; however, Java does allow default "friendliness" among all classes inside a package. So the Java package is actually a blend of C++ namespace declaration and an Ada package. A Java package can be thought of as a container for related classes and interfaces. As will be shown in later chapters, the Java standard library was divided into packages.

Sources 4.1 through 4.6 demonstrate both aspects of a Java package. Implementing a new package called List does this. The List package also implements two interfaces (discussed in the next section): the Enumeration interface and a new interface called the Traverse interface. We will examine each source of the List package to understand its purpose and functionality.

Source 4.1 is a simple program to demonstrate how to use the list package. Notice how the import statements are of the form <package>.<class>. That form of the import statement imports the specific class. In order to import ALL the classes in a package you use the following import statement:

```
import List.*;
```

The program also demonstrates how class data members by default are friendly within a package but not accessible (unless declared public) to any class outside the package.

SOURCE 4.1 TestList.java

```
/** TestList.java. */
import List.ListHead;

/** class to test our generic linked list. */
class TestList
{
    /** main method to invoke from JVM. */
     public static void main(String args[])
     {
          ListHead myList = new ListHead(false);

          myList.addElement(new Integer(10));
          myList.addElement(new Integer(20));
          myList.addElement(new Integer(30));

          myList.printAll();

          myList.showFriendly();
     }
}
```

A run of Source 4.1 produces:

```
C:\java\bin>java tstList
Calling singleLink Link
Calling singleLink Link
Node #0 : 10
Node #1 : 20
Node #2 : 30
Inside the package,
 a class can access another class's
 variables, unless they are private.
 node1.next.data is : 200
```

Source 4.2 is the ListHead class in the List package. This is the "list manager" class and the only class a program needs to import to get the functionality of a list.

- **Classes:**

  1. ListHead. This class manages a list of ListNodes (see ListNode class in Source 4.3). Data members of the class are a pointer to the head and tail of the list, a node count, and a few variables used to keep track of the current position and direction of the Enumeration (see Chapter 4) and Traverse (see Source 4.8) interface.

- **Key methods:**

  2. public ListHead (boolean isDoubly). A class constructor that allows you to construct either a doubly linked or singly linked list. The benefit of a doubly linked

list is that it allows list traversal in both directions (forward and backward). The way this list class can manage either type of node is that both the singleLink class and the doubleLink class are derived from an abstract parent class called ListNode.

3. public addElement(Object data). This method allows you to store ANY Java object in the linked list. It is similar to the addElement method in the Vector container (see Source 1.7). This method creates a new ListNode and attaches it to the list. The "attaching" processing is considerably easier and faster by maintaining a tail pointer (remember by pointer we mean an uninstantiated ListNode object) to the end of the list. The tail pointer makes it unnecessary to traverse the list.
4. public int size(). This method returns the number of elements in the list; also identical to the Vector class.

The rest of the methods in the class implement the Enumeration and Traverse interfaces. The code is self-explanatory.

SOURCE 4.2 listHead.java

```
/** ListHead.java. */
package List;
import java.util.Enumeration;
import java.util.NoSuchElementException;

/** Class to implement a linked list manager. */
public class ListHead implements Enumeration, Traverse
{
    /** flag to denote type of nodes this list contains. */
     boolean doubly;
     /** reference to head of linked list. */
     ListNode head;
     /** reference to last node in linked list. */
     ListNode tail;
     /** number of nodes in list. */
     int count;

     /** Used to implement Enumeration. */
     int current;
     /** reference to current node. */
     ListNode curNode;

     /** Used to implement Traverse. */
     boolean forward;

    /** constructor. */
     public ListHead(boolean isDoubly)
     {
```

```
        /* "typing" the list in this fashion will
           insure a homogenous list. */
        doubly = isDoubly;
    }

  /** Add a data element to this linked list. */
    public synchronized void addElement(Object data)
    {
        ListNode inNode;

        if (doubly)
            inNode = new DoubleLink(data);
        else
            inNode = new SingleLink(data);

        if (head == null)
        {
            head = tail = inNode;
        }
        else
        {
            ListNode tmp = tail;
            tail = inNode;
            inNode.Link(tmp);
        }
        count++;
    }

  /** remove first element of the list. */
    public synchronized Object removeFirst()
    {
        if (head != null)
        {
            ListNode tmp = head;
            if (tail == head)
                tail = head.next();
            head = head.next();
            count-;
            return tmp.data;
        }
        return null;
    }

    /** get size of list. */
    public int size() { return count; }
    /** The Enumeration Interface */
    public boolean hasMoreElements()
    {
        if (count > 0 && current < count)
            return true;
```

```
        else
            return false;
    }

    /** implements the enumeration interface. */
    public Object nextElement()
    {
        forward = true;
        if (count > 0 && current == 0)
        {
            curNode = head;
        }
        else if (current > 0 && current < count)
        {
            if (forward)
                curNode = curNode.next();
        }
        else
            throw new NoSuchElementException();

        if (forward)
            current++;
        return curNode.data;
    }

    /** print all nodes in the list. */
    public void printAll()
    {
        ListNode traverse = head;

        for (int i=0; i < count; i++)
        {
            System.out.println("Node #" + i + " : "
                               + traverse.data);
            traverse = traverse.next();
        }
    }

    /** demonstration of package friendliness. */
    public void showFriendly()
    {
        SingleLink node1 = new SingleLink(new Integer(100));
        SingleLink node2 = new SingleLink(new Integer(200));

        node1.next = node2;
        System.out.println("Inside the package, ");
        System.out.println("  a class can access another classes ");
        System.out.println("  variables, unless they are private.");
        System.out.println("  node1.next.data is : " + node1.next.data);
    }
```

```
// the Traverse interface...
/** am I at the beginning? returns false for an empty list.*/
public boolean atStart()
{
     if (count > 0 && current <= 0)
     {
          forward = true; // only possible direction
          return true;
     }
     else
          return false;
}

/** am I at the end?. */
public boolean atEnd()
{
     if (count > 0 && current == count)
     {
          forward = false; // only possible direction
          return true;
     }
     else
          return false;
}

/** access the next list element. */
public Object next()
{
     forward = true;
     if (count > 0 && current == 0)
     {
          curNode = head;
     }
     else if (current > 0 && current < count)
     {
          if (forward)
               curNode = curNode.next();
     }
     else
          throw new NoSuchElementException();

     if (forward)  // handle direction change
          current++;
     return curNode.data;
}

/** access the previous list element. */
public Object prev() throws IllegalListOpException
{
     if (doubly)
     {
```

```
                if (count > 0 && current == count)
                {
                     curNode = tail;
                }
                else if (count > 0 && current > 0)
                {
                     if (forward == false)  // moving backward
                     {
                          try {
                          curNode = curNode.prev();
                          } catch (Exception e) { }
                     }
                }
                else if (count == 0 || current == 0)
                {
                     throw new IllegalListOpException(
"Prev() invalid for empty list.");
                }
                else
                     throw new IllegalListOpException("Prev() invalid.");
          }
          else
          {
                // undefined for singly linked lists
                throw new IllegalListOpException(
"Prev() invalid for singly linked list.");
          }

          if (!forward)  // handle direction change
                current-;
          forward = false;
          return curNode.data;
     }

     /** jump to the head of the list. */
     public Object start()
     {
          if (count > 0)
          {
               current = 0;
               curNode = head;
               forward = true;
          }
          else
               throw new NoSuchElementException();
          return curNode.data;
     }

     /** jump to the last element of the list. */
     public Object end()
     {
```

```
        if (count > 0)
        {
            current = count - 1;
            curNode = tail;
            forward = false;
        }
        else
            throw new NoSuchElementException();
            return curNode.data;
    }
}
```

Source 4.3 is the abstract ListNode class in the List package. This is the abstract parent of the singleLink and doubleLink classes. Notice the abstract classes that BOTH children must implement. The Link() class is the key class that actually "links" or "connects" this node to the list. For a complete list implementation, this class needs two other abstract methods: a delete() method and an insert() method. These are left for you as an exercise.

SOURCE 4.3 ListNode.java

```
/** ListNode.java */
package List;

/** Generic linked list node. */
public abstract class ListNode
{
    /** data in node. */
    Object data;

    /** constructor. */
    public ListNode(Object inData)
    {
        data = inData;
    }

    /** method to link a node to the list. */
    abstract void Link(ListNode prev);
    /** access next node in list. */
    abstract ListNode next();
    /** access previous node in list. */
    abstract ListNode prev() throws IllegalListOpException;
}
```

SOURCE 4.4 SingleLink.java

```
/** SingleLink.java. */
package List;

/** Class to represent a node in a singly linked list. */
public class SingleLink extends ListNode
{
    /** reference to NEXT node in list. */
     SingleLink next;

    /** constructor. */
     public SingleLink(Object theData)
     {
          super(theData);
     }

    /** Method to connect this node to previous node. */
     public void Link(ListNode prev)
     {
          ((SingleLink)prev).next = this;
     }

    /** Method to access the next node in the list. */
     public ListNode next()
     {
          return this.next;
     }

    /** Method to access the previous node in the list. */
     public ListNode prev() throws IllegalListOpException
     {
          throw new IllegalListOpException("No prev() in singly" +
                                                    " linked lists.");
     }
}
```

Source 4.4 is the singleLink class in the List package. This class extends ListNode. This class is a representation of a node in a singly linked list. The key feature of a singly linked list is a single connection to the list in the form of a next pointer. Notice the use of the this pointer in the Link() method. The Link method is passed in a "pointer" to the previous node in the list. It then makes the previous node's next pointer point to "this" node. This package also defines a generic List exception called an illegalListOpException. This exception is thrown if an attempt is made to call the prev() method for a singly linked list.

Source 4.5 is the illegalListOpException in the List package. This class extends Exception. The exception represents an illegal list operation—for example, an attempt

SOURCE 4.5 illegalListOpException.java

```
/** IllegalListOpException.java. */
package List;

/** Class to represent a list-specific exception .*/
public class IllegalListOpException extends Exception
{
    /** constructor. */
     public IllegalListOpException(String msg)
     {
          super(msg);
     }
}
```

to get a previous node in a singly linked list. This exception could also be thrown for an attempt to delete a node from an empty list or delete a node when the current node points to the end of the list.

Packages and CLASSPATH

Now that we have seen a simple package let's understand a little bit more about packages in general and how they impact CLASSPATH.

In a manner of speaking, packages are collections of classes within a directory structure. Packages normally contain groups of related classes, although it's not a requirement, but why group together classes that have nothing in common? As you've no doubt noticed, a Java class must be in a file that matches the name of the class and has a .java extention. Packages take this one step further. For example, consider a class a defined in a directory b within a directory c within a directory d. The structure of the directory would look something like:

```
D
|-->C
     |—>B
           |--> a.class
```

Within class a we could structure the package as

```
package b;
package c.b;
package d.c.b;
```

Notice that the directory structure separator ("\" under Windows and "/" under Unix) is replaced with a dot; otherwise, the structures are identical.

For most of the source code within this book you will see packages defined as package jwiley.chpx, where x is the chapter number of the source. You will also notice that the source is layered to match this directory structure exactly. Chapter 4 is the only exception to this rule and is placed in a directory called list so that the examples make more sense.

TIP While it's not a requirement, packages are often structured to match the reverse Internet domain of the provider. If you look at the Sun classes packaged with the JDK you will see that they all start with "Sun." As an example, if you worked for a department called Sorting within a company BitsRUS whose Internet domain was Sorting.BitsRUS.Com you would create packages as COM.BitsRUS.Sorting. If you follow this rule you are likely to avoid any naming conflicts with other packages.

Classpath. There are three elements that work together when a class is being loaded. The first two we have already encountered-Classes and Packages. The final player is the CLASSPATH environment variable. The CLASSPATH variable is an environment variable normally set in either some shell initialization file like .csh (under Unix) or within autoexec.bat (under Windows 95). Windows NT will normally have a system-wide version of CLASSPATH which is "inherited" by all users.

When locating a class the JVM employs the following algorithm,

1. Starting with the entire class name, including package, replace the dots with the appropriate slash. d.c.b.a would become d\c\b\a under Windows.
2. Take the result of the prior step and append it to each of the directories defined in the CLASSPATH and attempt to load the class. If our classpath was c:\jdk\lib;c:\myclasses, and we were searching for aClass.class in package somedir.apackage, the search would be for c:\jdk\lib\somedir\apackage\aClass.class, and c:\myclasses\somedir\apackage\aClass.class, and .\somedir\apackage\aClass.class.

If the class was not found in any of the directories then an error would occur and the application would either stop running or never start up in the first place.

Although we have used interfaces in our List package, they have not yet been formally introduced; however, you should have a feeling that they are an obviously useful feature since we have already discussed them several times to include the Persistent interface, the Enumeration interface, and the Traverse interface. The next section explains them in detail. A final note before we move on to interfaces: You never "need" to use an import specification, you can always completely qualify your classes and variables explicitly. For example, if you wished to use a class java.lang. Someclass you could simply qualify the class variable as java.lang.Someclass instanceofSomeclass rather than import java.lang.Someclass; and then Someclass instanceofSomeclass. The import statement can be considered a shortcut to the class.

4.2 INTERFACES

Objective-C is a superset of the C programming language developed by Brad Cox, formerly of the Stepstone Corporation. Objective-C has received a considerable amount of success due to its adoption by Steve Jobs, the founder of NeXT Computer, Inc., for the development of the object-oriented NeXTStep operating system. On April 4, 1995, NeXT Computer acquired all the rights and trademark for the Objective-C language. It is important to note that many of the goals of Objective-C are identical to the goals of Java. In fact, Brad Cox produced a white paper and software (called TaskMaster) to extend Objective-C to include exception handling and lightweight multitasking (threads). There is currently not a standard implementation of Objective-C; however, NeXT now plans to lead the standardization effort.

One of NeXT's extensions to Objective-C is protocols. Protocols were added to specifically address some of the benefits of multiple inheritance without the complexity or implementation problems of multiple inheritance. Protocols allow you to group related methods into a high-level behavior that numerous classes can implement. Here is a simple protocol definition for archiving objects:

```
@protocol Archiving
- (int) readInt: (Stream *) stream;
- (void) writeInt: (Stream *) stream;
@end
```

In Java the archiving interface would look like this:

```
public interface Archiving
{
     int readInt(InputStream stream);
     int writeInt(OutputStream stream);
}
```

Now we can discuss Java interfaces in detail. There are two ways to view interfaces. The first is as a set of methods that describe a high-level behavior. As an example, DataInput describes methods that perform data input in a machine-independent manner. Second, an interface is an abstract class that can point to any class that implements the interface. This means that an interface provides the same benefits with multiple classes that virtual functions provide to a singly inherited class hierarchy. The more you work with interfaces, the more you will understand their power and elegance.

Source 4.7 demonstrates the List package using the Enumeration interface. Remember, the two methods of the Enumeration interface are hasMoreElements() and nextElement().

SOURCE 4.7 TestEnumeration.java

```
/** TestEnumeration.java */
import List.ListHead;

/** Class to demonstrate the linked list implementation of
    the Enumeration interface. */
public class TestEnumeration
{
    /** main() method to invoke from JVM. */
     public static void main(String args[])
     {
          ListHead myList = new ListHead(true);

          myList.addElement(new Integer(10));
          myList.addElement(new Integer(20));
          myList.addElement(new Integer(30));

          while (myList.hasMoreElements())
               System.out.println(((Integer)myList.nextElement()));

     }
}
```

A run of Source 4.7 produces:

```
C:\java\bin>java TestEnumeration
10
20
30
```

Source 4.8 is the definition of the Traverse interface. Let's for a moment think about the benefits for creating this interface. The action we are describing is sequencing through a set of elements. However, if that were all, our requirement would be satisfied by the Enumeration interface. Our List container is different in that it allows both forward and backward list traversals. Secondly, with the head and tail pointer we can rapidly jump to the start or end of the list. Therefore, we can see how the Enumeration interface is not complete enough for what we want to accomplish; therefore, we needed a new interface. In fact, it would be wise to modify the Vector class to also implement the Traverse interface. The Traverse interface consists of six functions: two testing functions (atStart and atEnd) and four traversal functions: (next, prev, start, and end).

SOURCE 4.8 Traverse.java

```
package List;

/**
 * Traverse is an interface that is an abstraction for
 *    free-flow viewing of a connected list of objects.
 *    By free-flow viewing, I mean six operations:
 *    atStart(), atEnd(), next(), prev(), start() , end()
 */

public interface Traverse
{

     // check if at the start of list
     public boolean atStart();

     // check if at the end of list
     public boolean atEnd();

     // access the next list element
     public Object next();

     // access the previous list element
     public Object prev() throws illegalListOpException;

     // jump to the head of the list and return it
     public Object start();

     // jump to the end of the list and return it
     public Object end();
}
```

Source 4.9 demonstrates the use of the Traverse class with our List package. It clearly demonstrates some of the unique capabilities of the interface.

SOURCE 4.9 TestTraversal.java

```
/** TestTraverse.java -  tests the Traverse interface. */
import List.ListHead;
import List.IllegalListOpException;

/** Class to demonstrate the linked list implementation of
    the Traverse interface. */
public class TestTraverse
{
```

```
/** main() method to invoke from JVM. */
 public static void main(String args[])
 {
      ListHead myList = new ListHead(true);

      myList.addElement(new Integer(100));
      myList.addElement(new Integer(200));
      myList.addElement(new Integer(300));
      myList.addElement(new Integer(400));
      myList.addElement(new Integer(500));
      myList.addElement(new Integer(600));

      System.out.println("List size: " + myList.size());

      System.out.println("Forward...");
      while (!myList.atEnd())
            System.out.println(((Integer)myList.next()));

      System.out.println("Backward...");
      while (!myList.atStart())
      {
           try
           {
                System.out.println(((Integer)myList.prev()));
           }
           catch (IllegalListOpException iloe)
           {
                System.out.println(iloe.toString());
                System.exit(1);
           }
      }

      System.out.println("Go forward three nodes.");
      for (int i=0; i < 3; i++)
      {
           if (!myList.atEnd())
                System.out.println((Integer)myList.next());
      }

      System.out.println("Go Back three nodes.");
      for (int i=0; i < 3; i++)
      {
           if (!myList.atStart())
           {
                try
                {
                     System.out.println(((Integer)myList.prev()));
```

```
                    }
                    catch (IllegalListOpException iloe)
                    {
                         System.out.println(iloe.toString());
                         System.exit(1);
                    }
               }
          }

          System.out.println("Jump to Start...");
          System.out.println((Integer)myList.start());

          System.out.println("Jump to End...");
          System.out.println((Integer)myList.end());
     }
}
```

A run of Source 4.9 produces:

```
C:\java\bin>java TestTraverse
List size: 6
Forward...
100
200
300
400
500
600
Backward...
600
500
400
300
200
100
Go forward three nodes.
100
200
300
Go Back three nodes.
300
200
100
Jump to Start...
100
Jump to End...
600
```

SOURCE 4.10 TestTraverse2.java

```
/** TestTraverse2.java. */
import List.ListHead;
import List.Traverse;

/** Class to demonstrate a reference to an interface. */
public class TestTraverse2
{
    /** main() method to invoke from JVM. */
     public static void main(String args[])
     {
          ListHead myList = new ListHead(true);

          for (int i=100; i <= 600; i+= 100)
               myList.addElement(new Integer(i));

          Traverse t = myList;
          while (!t.atEnd())
               System.out.println((Integer)t.next());
     }
}
```

Source 4.10 demonstrates using an interface as a type similar to an abstract class. As an abstract class, you cannot instantiate it directly. Instead, assign it or instantiate a class that implements the interface. In the next example we declare a variable t of type Traverse that we assign myList to. This is legal since the ListHead class implements the Traverse interface.

A run of Source 4.10 produces:

```
C:\java\bin>java TestTraverse2
100
200
300
400
500
600
```

Although not demonstrated in the preceding code, interfaces can even have variables. This should reaffirm your understanding of an interface as an abstract class. When an interface has a variable, that variable is final, public, and static by default. Methods in an interface are public and abstract by default.

4.3 USING OBJECTS AND INTERFACES DYNAMICALLY

There are two remaining areas that we haven't covered in any detail yet: using interfaces dynamically and creating objects dynamically. So far we have used interfaces to solve compile time issues resolving class behavior. An additional use of an interface is as a parameter to a function. What we are doing here is dynamically providing an instance of a class that implements our interface and then using that instance to do something.

Using Interfaces Dynamically

As we shall see in the next section there exists a class, Thread, which takes as a parameter to one of its constructors an object that implements the Runnable interface. The internals of the object then start this object when the start method is called on the object. Source 4.11 shows an example of using an interface dynamically. It also has another interesting feature that we will examine in a moment: using objects dynamically.

The whatis method of the tstanInterface class expects an instance of an object that implements the AnInterface interface. Notice that we have not defined any objects that implement this interface. What we have done is defined a method which expects an instance of an object that implements the interface. Within that method we can use the methods that the interface defines.

This happens in the following steps:

1. An interface is defined that defines a set of methods that an object must implement. In our case,

   ```
   public interface anInterface { String ImA(); }
   ```

2. Then we define a method that expects objects that have implemented this interface.

   ```
   somemethod(anInterface a);
   ```

We then build our classes normally, perhaps storing them in a package.

1. At some point we define one or more classes that implement the interface. ImAClassA.java shows a simple class that implements the anInterface interface.

   ```
   Class SomeClass implements anInterface …
   ```

2. Finally we create objects of the required type, either dynamically, or normally and pass them to the method.

   ```
   SomeClass instanceofSC;
   . . .
   somemethod(instanceofSC);
   ```

The interesting part of this example is that the object that implements the interface may have existed when the class that uses it was developed! It's not unusual in software development to partition projects into components that are developed by different groups. Using interfaces in this fashion, two groups could agree on the interface and then one could go off to use it while the other went off to develop the implementation.

SOURCE 4.11 tstanInterface.java

```
package List;
import java.lang.Class;

class tstanInterface
{
    public void whatis(int which,
                        anInterface anInstanceofanInterface)
    {
        System.out.println("Instance " + which + " is a " +
                             anInstanceofanInterface.ImA());
    }
    public static void main (String args[])
    {
        anInterface a;
        tstanInterface me = new tstanInterface();
        for ( int i = 0; i < args.length; i++)
        {
            try
            {
                Class instanceOf = Class.forName(args[i]);
                a = (anInterface) instanceOf.newInstance();
                me.whatis(i,a);
            }
            catch (Exception e)
            {
                e.printStackTrace();
            }
        }

    }
}
```

A run of Source 4.11 produces:

```
C:\java\bin>java tstanInterface ImAClassA ImAClassB Foobar
Instance 0 is a ClassA Object
Instance 1 is a ClassB Object
java.lang.ClassNotFoundException: Foobar
      at List.tstanInterface.main(tstanInterface.java:19)
```

You'll notice that nowhere did we expressly define or import any object that implemented our interface.

Using Objects Dynamically

The java.lang package contains a class known as "Class" which supports a method forName which causes the class loader to load a named class. In Source 4.11 we forced the class loader to load an instance of a class by name using:

```
Class instanceOf = Class.forName(args[i]);
```

In addition we created an instance of the object using the newInstance method, which works exactly like we called new on the object with no arguments.

```
a = (anInterface) instanceOf.newInstance();
```

If the class cannot be found, the forName method throws a ClassNotFoundException.

The java.lang.Class class contains other interesting methods, some of which are:

- **IsInstance(Object).** Equivalent to the instanceof operator.
- **GetSuperClass.** Returns the superclass of the object.
- **GetInterfaces.** Determines the interfaces implemented by the class or object.
- **GetSigners.** Returns the signers of the class. See Chapter17, "Java and Security", for more information about signers.

There are other methods for getting information on the interfaces, types, methods, fields, and modifiers of a given class. We will cover the Class class in more detail in Chapter 6 under the reflection package. For now, let's look at a useful example of dynamically loading classes. The idea is that we can define an interface to a class that tells us all we need to know to use the class effectively. In Source 4.12 we define a Robot interface that defines an interface that would allow us to create and manipulate a robot.

SOURCE 4.12 Robot.java

```
/** Robot.java. */
package jwiley.chp4;

public interface Robot
{
    public final int ACTION_OFFENSIVE_ATTACK = 0;
    public final int ACTION_DEFENSIVE_BLOCK = 1;
    public final int ACTION_FLEE = 2;

    public final int TOTAL_ACTIONS = 3;

    public void setInitialCapital(int units);
    public int getArmor();
    public int getFirePower();
    public int getSpeed();
    public void setArmor(int curArmor);
    public void setFirePower(int curFirePower);
    public void setSpeed(int curSpeed);
    public int getNextAction();
    public void assessOpponent(int currentUnits);
    public String toString();
    public String getName();
}
```

Now we can create a simulation that dynamically loads classes that implement the Robot interface and makes them fight. Source 4.13 is such a simulation.

SOURCE 4.13 RobotBattle.java

```
/** RobotBattle.java */
package jwiley.chp4;

import java.io.File;
import java.util.Random;

public class RobotBattle
{
    Robot [] robots;
    String sPackageName = "jwiley.chp4.Robots";
    Random dice = new Random();

    Robot [] getRobots()
    { return robots; }

    public void loadRobots()
    {
        String sCurrentDir = System.getProperty("user.dir");
        File fDir = new File(sCurrentDir + File.separator + "Robots");
        String [] sFileList = fDir.list();

        int iRobotCount=0;
        for (int i=0; i < sFileList.length; i++)
        {
            if (sFileList[i].endsWith(".class"))
                iRobotCount++;
        }

        robots = new Robot[iRobotCount];
        int iCnt=0;
        for (int i=0; i < sFileList.length; i++)
        {
            if (sFileList[i].endsWith(".class"))
            {
                try
                {
                    String sClassName = sPackageName + "." +
                                        sFileList[i].substring(0,
                                        sFileList[i].length() - 6);
                    System.out.println("Loading " + sClassName + "...");
                    Class robotClass = Class.forName(sClassName);
                    robots[iCnt++] = (Robot) robotClass.newInstance();
                } catch (Exception e)
                  {
                    System.out.println("Failed to instantiate class from "
                                      + sFileList[i]);
                    continue;
                  }
            }
```

```
    }
}

int getRobotsAssessment(Robot r)
{
    return r.getFirePower() + r.getSpeed() + r.getArmor();
}

boolean coinToss()
{
    int iNum = Math.abs(dice.nextInt() % 100);
    return (iNum > 50);
}

public static void main(String args[])
{
    // get initial Robot building funds from command line
    if (args.length < 1)
    {
        System.out.println(
            "USAGE: java RobotBattle #\n The # represents" +
                           " initial robot building funds.");
        System.exit(1);
    }

    int iFunds = Integer.parseInt(args[0]);

    RobotBattle ww3 = new RobotBattle();
    ww3.loadRobots();

    // get the robots
    Robot [] contestants = ww3.getRobots();

    // initialize the robots
    for (int i=0; i < contestants.length; i++)
        contestants[i].setInitialCapital(iFunds);

    // introduce the contestants
    System.out.println("Introducing the contestants...");
    for (int i=0; i < contestants.length; i++)
        System.out.println(contestants[i].toString());

    // make the first two fight
    if (contestants.length < 2)
    {
        System.out.println("Need two robots to fight!");
        System.exit(1);
    }

    Robot robot1 = contestants[0];
    Robot robot2 = contestants[1];

    while (robot1.getArmor() > 0 && robot2.getArmor() > 0)
    {
        robot1.assessOpponent(ww3.getRobotsAssessment(robot2));
```

```
robot2.assessOpponent(ww3.getRobotsAssessment(robot1));

int iAction1 = robot1.getNextAction();
int iAction2 = robot2.getNextAction();
switch (iAction1)
{
    case Robot.ACTION_OFFENSIVE_ATTACK:
        boolean handToHand = false;
        System.out.println(robot1.getName() + " Attacks!");
        if (robot1.getFirePower() > 0)
        {
            System.out.println(robot1.getName() +
                                            "'s weapons blaze!");
            robot1.setFirePower(robot1.getFirePower() - 20);
        }
        else
        {
            System.out.println(robot1.getName() +
                                 " uses hand " +
                                "to hand combat!");
            handToHand = true;
        }

        if (iAction2 == Robot.ACTION_DEFENSIVE_BLOCK)
        {
            System.out.println(robot2.getName() +
                                " BLOCKED IT!");
        }
        else if (iAction2 == Robot.ACTION_FLEE)
        {
            // check if successful
            if (ww3.coinToss())
                System.out.println(robot2.getName() +
                                        " Dodged it!");
            else
            {
                System.out.println(robot2.getName() +
                                        " got grazed!");
                robot2.setArmor(robot2.getArmor() - 10);
            }
        }
        else // BOTH ATTACK
        {
            // gets hit?
            if (ww3.coinToss())
            {
                System.out.println(robot1.getName() +
                                        " SCORED a DIRECT HIT!");
                if (handToHand)
                    robot2.setArmor(robot2.getArmor() - 2);
                else
                    robot2.setArmor(robot2.getArmor() - 50);
            }
            else
            {
```

```
                        // missed - return FIRE!
                        System.out.println(robot1.getName() +
                                           " MISSED!");
                        int iReturnFire = 0;
                        if (robot2.getFirePower() > 0)
                        {
                            System.out.println(robot2.getName() +
                                               " RETURNS FIRE!");
                            iReturnFire = 50;
                            robot2.setFirePower(robot2.getFirePower()
                                                - 20);
                        }
                        else
                        {
                            System.out.println(robot2.getName() +
                                           " Fights hand to hand!");
                            iReturnFire = 2;
                        }

                        // check for return fire hit
                        if (ww3.coinToss())
                        {
                            System.out.println(robot2.getName() +
                                               " LANDED a blow!");
                            robot1.setArmor(robot1.getArmor()
                                            - iReturnFire);
                        }
                    }
                }
            break;
            case Robot.ACTION_DEFENSIVE_BLOCK:
                System.out.println(robot1.getName() +
                                   " Defensive block.");
                // logic left as exercise
            break;
            case Robot.ACTION_FLEE:
                System.out.println(robot1.getName() +
                                   " Fleeing...");
                // logic left as exercise
            break;
            default:
                System.out.println("Unknown action: " + iAction1);
        }

        // stats
        System.out.println("STATE: " + robot1.toString());
        System.out.println("STATE: " + robot2.toString());
    }

    if (robot1.getArmor() <= 0)
        System.out.println(robot2.getName() + " has WON!");
    else
        System.out.println(robot1.getName() + " has WON!");
  }
}
```

A run of Source 4.13 produces:

```
C:\1-1update\src11\jwiley\chp4>java RobotBattle 100
Loading jwiley.chp4.Robots.RandomRobot...
Loading jwiley.chp4.Robots.ToughRobot...
Introducing the contestants...
RandomRobot: Armor(41) Speed(34) FirePower(25)
ToughRobot: Armor(50) Speed(0) FirePower(50)
RandomRobot Fleeing...
STATE: RandomRobot: Armor(41) Speed(34) FirePower(25)
STATE: ToughRobot: Armor(50) Speed(0) FirePower(50)
RandomRobot Attacks!
RandomRobot's weapons blaze!
RandomRobot MISSED!
ToughRobot RETURNS FIRE!
STATE: RandomRobot: Armor(41) Speed(34) FirePower(5)
STATE: ToughRobot: Armor(50) Speed(0) FirePower(30)
RandomRobot Defensive block.
STATE: RandomRobot: Armor(41) Speed(34) FirePower(5)
STATE: ToughRobot: Armor(50) Speed(0) FirePower(30)
RandomRobot Attacks!
RandomRobot's weapons blaze!
RandomRobot MISSED!
ToughRobot RETURNS FIRE!
ToughRobot LANDED a blow!
STATE: RandomRobot: Armor(-9) Speed(34) FirePower(-15)
STATE: ToughRobot: Armor(50) Speed(0) FirePower(10)
ToughRobot has WON!
```

There are two key points to note about Source 4.13:

- Classes are loaded from a Robots directory. The program has absolutely no idea how many classes are in this directory. It simply loads all the .class files in that directory. This is similar to the way a browser loads plugins. In this same fashion you could create a drawing program that dynamically loads its drawing tools. The key benefit to this technique is that it lets you add robots, plugins, or drawing tools at any time. The addition of an added capability required no new coding. It should be obvious how a program could take advantage of this. You could have a word processor that connected to a Web site for the user to buy additional functionality. The class would be downloaded and dynamically loaded into the running application after the user had paid.
- The remainder of the main() method in the RobotBattle class revolves around invoking the methods of the Robot interface to have the robots fight. You should notice how we declare a reference to the Robot interface and not to any specific class. This makes sense in that all we know about is the methods in the Robot interface, and therefore that is all we will invoke. In Chapter 6 we will discuss Reflection, which allows you to query an unknown class to determine its attributes and methods.

As you can see from the run of Source 4.13, we have two simple classes that implement the Robot interface. They are RandomRobot.java and ToughRobot.java. We will only display one of them here. The other (ToughRobot.java) can be found on the CD-ROM. Source 4.14 is our RandomRobot class that implements the Robot interface.

Dynamic object loading is a powerful mechanism that neither C nor C++ support. Let's now take a look at another feature in that category: multithreading.

SOURCE 4.14 RandomRobot.java

```
/** RandomRobot.java */
package jwiley.chp4.Robots;

import jwiley.chp4.Robot;

import java.util.Random;

public class RandomRobot implements Robot
{
    Random dice = new Random();
    int iValue;
    int iArmor;
    int iSpeed;
    int iFirePower;

    public void setInitialCapital(int units)
    {
        iValue = units;

        // randomly distribute expenditures
        int iRoll = Math.abs(dice.nextInt() % units);
        iArmor = iRoll;
        int iLeft = units - iArmor;
        if (iLeft > 0)
        {
            iRoll = Math.abs(dice.nextInt() % iLeft);
            iSpeed = iRoll;
            iLeft -= iSpeed;
            iFirePower = iLeft;
        }
        else
        {
            iSpeed = iFirePower = 0;
        }
    }

    public int getArmor()
    { return iArmor; }
    public int getFirePower()
    { return iFirePower; }
```

```
    public int getSpeed()
    { return iSpeed; }
    public void setArmor(int curArmor)
    { iArmor = curArmor; }
    public void setFirePower(int curFirePower)
    { iFirePower = curFirePower; }
    public void setSpeed(int curSpeed)
    { iSpeed = curSpeed; }
    public int getNextAction()
    {
        return Math.abs(dice.nextInt() % (Robot.TOTAL_ACTIONS + 1));
    }

    public void assessOpponent(int currentUnits) { }

    public String toString()
    {
        return "RandomRobot: Armor(" + iArmor + ") " +
               "Speed(" + iSpeed + ") " +
               "FirePower(" + iFirePower + ")";
    }

    public String getName()
    { return "RandomRobot"; }
}
```

4.4 MULTITHREADING

Multithreading is the ability of a single process to spawn multiple, simultaneous execution paths. As discussed previously, multithreading is similar to multiprocessing; however, with multithreading all execution contexts share the same memory. This makes sharing data between threads simpler than sharing data between processes. See Sources 4.12 and 4.13 for a demonstration of threads sharing classes.

The benefits of multithreading are most apparent in graphical user interfaces and in applets. You do not want the user to be forced to wait on an applet (when running a browser) or a GUI function when he or she has decided to quit the application. Threads provide this asynchronous execution. Two other areas that benefit greatly from multithreading are servers and simulations. A multithreaded server can spawn a new thread for each incoming client request and is therefore always ready for a new connection. Also, a multithreaded server will never make a high-priority client service wait for a low-priority one as a nonthreaded server would do. Simulations benefit by threading because they often model autonomous, interacting entities. A threaded simulation is demonstrated later in this chapter.

As stated earlier, multithreading has been part of the Ada language, via the task construct, since its inception. In fact, in Ada 95 a form of synchronization has been added called a "protected type." Of course, in Ada a task is merely a procedure as a lightweight process, whereas in Java a thread is a class that implements the Runnable interface. Being a class, a Java thread can have an unlimited number of methods. In the next section we will examine the Java implementation of threads in detail.

Thread Characteristics

Threads in Java have five characteristics that define their behavior. We will discuss each characteristic individually.

- **Thread Body.** This is the sequence of instructions for the thread to perform. This is defined by a run() method. There are two ways for you to supply a run() method to a thread.

  1. Extending the Thread class and overriding the run() method in Thread.
  2. Creating a thread with a Runnable class as its target. A class can implement the Runnable interface and then be passed to a thread constructor. The Runnable interface is simply implementing the run() method.

- **Thread State.** A thread can be in one of four states: new, runnable, nonrunnable, or dead. The thread's methods and the Java run time control what state a thread is in. A thread's state also determines what methods are legal to run. For example, you cannot stop() a thread that is not running. If you attempt to run a method incompatible with the thread's state, an IllegalThreadStateException will be thrown.

  1. new Thread(). When a constructor is called, the thread is created but is not yet run(). Therefore, the thread is in the new state. In the new state the only legal methods are start() and stop().
  2. start(). This method switches the thread into the runnable state and the Java run time will schedule the thread to run by invoking its run() method.
  3. stop(). This method switches a thread's state to the dead state. A thread will also move to the dead state naturally when it reaches the end of its run() method.
  4. destroy(). Stops a thread without any cleanup; ignores the thread state.
  5. suspend(). Causes a thread to move to the nonrunnable state. The target thread will stay in the nonrunnable state until resume() is called.
  6. resume(). Causes a thread to return to being runnable. See suspend().
  7. sleep(long millis). Causes a thread to be nonrunnable for a specific number of milliseconds.
  8. wait(). This is a method of Object. A thread can call the wait() method of an object that it is waiting on to change state. If it calls wait, it moves itself into a nonrunnable status. The only way the thread can then become runnable is when a synchronized method in the object has changed state and calls notify().
  9. yield(). Only called when a thread is runnable and executing. Does not change the thread's state but instead allows other threads of the same priority to be executed.

- **Thread Priority.** Every thread has a priority. When threads are created, they are given the priority of their parent (if one exists, else a normal priority of 5). A thread's priority can be between 1 and 10, and determines how it will be scheduled. The scheduler follows a simple rule: At any given time the thread with the highest priority will be running. When a thread is running, it will not be preempted by a thread with the same priority. The Java run time does not time slice between threads of the same priority; instead, a thread may yield its execution to another thread of the same priority. A low-priority thread will be interrupted when a higher-priority thread becomes runnable.

  1. setPriority(int newPriority). Sets the priority of this thread.
  2. int getPriority(). Gets the priority of this thread.

- **Daemon Threads.** This denotes that a thread is a "server" thread. A server thread is a thread that services client requests (by invoking one of the servers methods). Calling a server a "daemon" is based on Unix tradition where these background server processes were considered mysterious and hidden things that could often cause you trouble (just like a "demon"). The Java run time treats daemon threads differently than normal threads. The run time will not exit until all normal threads have terminated. Not so with daemon threads. Since daemons are service providers (servers), if there are only daemon threads running, then the run time can exit. This makes sense because there are no more clients running for the daemon to provide a service to.

  1. setDaemon(). Sets a flag that denotes this thread as a daemon thread.
  2. isDaemon(). Returns true if this thread is a daemon, else returns false.

- **Thread Groups.** For large programs that spawn many threads, Java allows you to group similar threads and manage them as a group. A ThreadGroup is a class distinct from the Thread class. A ThreadGroup is a group of threads or other thread groups. A thread does have the ability to access information about its ThreadGroup and the other threads in its group. The ThreadGroup has methods to manipulate the group as a whole like setDaemon(), setMaxPriority(), stop(), suspend(), remove(), and others.

Now that you understand the major characteristics of threads, let's examine a nontrivial program that uses threads.

A Multithreaded Bank Simulation

Source 4.15 is a time-stepped simulation of the queueing problems that a bank faces in handling customers. The purpose of the simulation is simply to determine how many tellers would be necessary to adequately handle a typical busy day at the bank. The program uses threads to represent the autonomous actions of all the major simulation entities: the customers and tellers. Let's now discuss the major classes and methods in the simulation while highlighting the use of threads.

The class simData is a simple class to get the number of seconds to run the simulation and the number of tellers to put on duty.

SOURCE 4.15 BankSim.java

```
import java.lang.Thread;
import java.io.BufferedReader;
import java.io.InputStreamReader;
import java.io.IOException;
import java.lang.Runnable;
import java.util.Random;

import List.ListHead;

/** Class to get and store key simulation data. */
class SimData
{
    /** number of tellers on duty at the bank. */
    int numTellers;
    /** number of seconds to run the simulation. */
    int secondsToRun;

    /** constructor. */
    SimData() throws Exception
    {
        String secStr=null;
        String numStr=null;

        System.out.println(" ");
        System.out.print("Enter number of tellers on duty: ");
        System.out.flush();
        try
        {
            numStr = BankSim.dis.readLine();
        }
        catch (IOException ioe)
        {
            System.out.println(ioe.toString());
            System.exit(1);
        }

        if (numStr != null && numStr.length() > 0)
            numTellers = Integer.parseInt(numStr);
```

```
          else
               throw new Exception("Invalid number of tellers.");

          System.out.println("Time is compressed for this Sim.");
          System.out.println("One second equals one minute.");
          System.out.print("Enter number of seconds to run Sim: ");
          System.out.flush();
          try
          {
               secStr = BankSim.dis.readLine();
          }
          catch (IOException ioe)
          {
               System.out.println(ioe.toString());
               System.exit(1);
          }

          if (secStr != null && secStr.length() > 0)
               secondsToRun = Integer.parseInt(secStr);
          else
               throw new Exception("Invalid number of Seconds.");

     }

     /** accessor. */
     int getnumTellers() { return numTellers; }

     /** accessor. */
     int getsecondsToRun() { return secondsToRun; }
}

/** Thread for running the sim. */
class SimRun extends Thread
{
    /** current sim time. */
     public long simTime;
     /** flag. */
     public boolean quitting_time;
     /** timer thread. */
     Thread clockThread;
     /** random number generator. */
     public Random dice;
     /** data for sim. */
     SimData sData;
     /** simulation statistics. */
     SimStats sStats;
     /** bank queue. */
     ListHead bankLine;

     /** calculate probably that a customer will walk in
       the door. */
```

```
static int customerProbability(long minute_in_day)
{
    /* uses a Parabola mapped to an 8-hour day.
       x-axis is minutes.
       y-axis is probability. */

    return (int) - ( ( (minute_in_day - 240) *
                        (minute_in_day - 240) ) -
                        (3 * 240 * 98) ) /
                        (3 * 240);
}

/** constructor. */
SimRun(SimData theData, SimStats theStats)
{
    simTime = 0;
    quitting_time = false;
    dice = new Random();
    sData = theData;
    sStats = theStats;
    bankLine = new ListHead(false);
}

/** implements runnable. */
public void run()
{
    int duration = sData.getsecondsToRun();

    // generate tellers
    int numTellers = sData.getnumTellers();

    // update stats
    sStats.numTellers = numTellers;
    sStats.simDuration = duration;

    for (int i=0; i < numTellers; i++)
    {
            Teller aTeller = new Teller(bankLine, this, sStats);
            aTeller.start();
    }

    // kick off clock thread
    Clock aClock = new Clock(this);
    clockThread = new Thread(aClock);

    // set clock priority as the highest in group
    clockThread.setPriority(6);
    clockThread.start();

    // sleep a sec
    try { sleep(1000); } catch (Exception e) { }
```

```
          while (!quitting_time)
          {
               // generate customers based on function
               int probability = customerProbability(simTime);

               //System.out.println("Probability: " + probability);

               // roll dice
               int roll = Math.abs(dice.nextInt() % 100);

               if (roll <= probability)
               {
                    System.out.println("A customer just walked in...");

                    // update stats
                    sStats.totalNumCustomers += 1;

                    // generate customer thread
                    Customer aCustomer = new Customer(bankLine);
                    aCustomer.start();
               }

               // update line size stats
               if (bankLine.size() > sStats.maxLineSize)
                         sStats.maxLineSize = bankLine.size();

               try
               {
                    sleep(1000);
               }
               catch (Exception e) { }


               if (simTime >= duration)
                         quitting_time = true;
          }
          System.out.println("Simulation complete.");
     }
}

/** clock thread. */
class Clock implements Runnable
{
     SimRun theRun;

     Clock(SimRun aRun) { theRun = aRun; }

     public void run()
     {
          while (!theRun.quitting_time)
          {
```

```
                try
                {
                    Thread.sleep(1000);
                    theRun.simTime++;
                    if (theRun.simTime % 10 == 0)
                        System.out.println("CLOCK: " +theRun.simTime);

                }
                catch (Exception e) { }
            }
        }
}

/** abstract action class. */
abstract class Action
{
    abstract int execute();
}

/** specific action. */
class OpenAccount extends Action
{
    int execute()
    {
        System.out.println("open an account...");
        return 5;
    }
}

/** specific action. */
class CloseAccount extends Action
{
    int execute()
    {
        System.out.println("close an account...");
        return 3;
    }
}

/** specific action. */
class RobBank extends Action
{
    int execute()
    {
        System.out.println("rob the bank...");
        return 20;
    }
}

/** specific action. */
class DepositCheck extends Action
```

```
{
     int execute()
     {
          System.out.println("deposit a check...");
          return 4;
     }
}

/** specific action. */
class CashCheck extends Action
{
     int execute()
     {
          System.out.println("cash a check...");
          return 7;
     }
}

/**
 * Thread per customer.
 *  The concept of each entity in a Simulation being a
 *  separate thread has great potential for creating
 *  Autonomous, Polymorphous Entities (APE).  This would be a
 *  large breakthrough for the modeling of computer
 *  generated forces (cgf) and human intelligence collection.
 */
class Customer extends Thread
{
    /** count of all customers generated. */
     public static int customerCount = 0;
     /** unique id of this customer. */
     private int Id;
     /** bank line to join. */
     ListHead bankLine;
     /** action to perform. */
     Action myAction=null;

     /** constructor. */
     Customer()
     {
          customerCount++;
          Id = customerCount;
     }

     /** constructor. */
     Customer(ListHead theLine)
     {
          customerCount++;
          Id = customerCount;
          bankLine = theLine;
     }
```

```
/** accessor. */
Action getmyAction() { return myAction; }

/** accessor. */
int getId() { return Id; }

/** implements runnable. */
public void run()
{
    /* be busy a random number of sim minutes before
     * entering the bank line.
     */
    Random dice = new Random();
    int busy = Math.abs(dice.nextInt() % 10);

    try { sleep(busy * 1000); } catch (Exception e) { }

    /* after this "thinking" the customer knows
     * what they came to do.
     */
    int decide = Math.abs(dice.nextInt() % 5);

    switch (decide)
    {
            case 0:
                    myAction = new OpenAccount();
                    break;
            case 1:
                    myAction = new CloseAccount();
                    break;
            case 2:
                    myAction = new RobBank();
                    break;
            case 3:
                    myAction = new DepositCheck();
                    break;
            case 4:
                    myAction = new CashCheck();
                    break;
            default:
                    myAction = new OpenAccount();
                    System.out.println("Unknown action.");
    }

    // now wait on line
    bankLine.addElement(this);
    System.out.println("Customer #" + Id +
                        " is now waiting on line.");

    // sleep a little to allow println
    try { sleep(2000); } catch (Exception e) { }
```

```
    }
}

/** Thread for teller. */
class Teller extends Thread
{
    /** count of all tellers. */
    public static int tellerCount = 0;
    /** unique id of this teller. */
    private int Id;
    /** bank line. */
    ListHead theLine;
    /** simulation environment. */
    SimRun sRun;
    /** sim statistics. */
    SimStats sStats;

    /** constructor. */
    Teller(ListHead aLine, SimRun aRun, SimStats inStats)
    {
        tellerCount++;
        Id = tellerCount;
        theLine = aLine;
        sRun = aRun;
        sStats = inStats;
    }

    /** implements runnable. */
    public void run()
    {
        // pause a second to allow menu println to finish
        try { sleep(1000); } catch (Exception e) { }

        // if free, pops a customer and serves the customer
        boolean stillWaiting = false;
        while (!sRun.quitting_time)
        {
            if (theLine.size() > 0)
            {
                stillWaiting = false;
                Customer currentCustomer =
                    (Customer) theLine.removeFirst();
                System.out.print("Teller #" +
                                  Id + " is helping " +
                                  "Customer #" +
                                  currentCustomer.getId() +
                                  " to ");
```

```
                System.out.flush();
                int helping =
                        (currentCustomer.getmyAction()).execute();

                // update the stats
                sStats.totalCustomersServed += 1;

                try
                {
                    sleep(helping * 1000);
                }
                catch (Exception e) { }
            }
            else
            {
              if (!stillWaiting)
                System.out.println("Teller #" + id +
                               " is waiting to help someone.");
              stillWaiting = true;
            }

            try { sleep(2000); } catch (Exception e) { }
        }
    }
}

/** simulation statistics. */
class SimStats
{
    public int numTellers;
    public int simDuration;
    public int totalNumCustomers;
    public int totalCustomersServed;
    public int maxLineSize;
    // exercise: maxCustomerWait, maxTellerWait

    /** method to print the statistics. */
    void printStats()
    {
        System.out.println(" ");
        System.out.println("<<<<< SIM STATISTICS >>>>>");
        System.out.println("# Tellers             : " + numTellers);
        System.out.println("# minutes simulated   : " + simDuration);
        System.out.println("Tot customers entered: " +
                        totalNumCustomers);
        System.out.println("Tot customers served : " +
                        totalCustomersServed);
        System.out.println("Maximum line size     : " + maxLineSize);
    }
}
```

```
/** Class to present a simple menu-driven interface to control
    the bank simulation. */
public class BankSim
{
static BufferedReader dis = new BufferedReader(
new InputStreamReader(System.in));

     /** main method to invoke from JVM. */
     public static void main(String args[])
     {
          boolean done = false;
          SimData sData = null;
          SimRun sRun = null;
          SimStats sStats = new SimStats();
          while (!done)
          {
               System.out.println(" ");
               System.out.println("<<<<<< Bank Sim >>>>>>");
               System.out.println("   1) Enter Simulation Data.");
               System.out.println("   2) Run Simulation.");
               System.out.println("   3) Stop Simulation.");
               System.out.println("   4) Print Simulation Stats.");
               System.out.println("   5) Exit.");
               System.out.println(" ");
               System.out.print("Enter choice: ");
               System.out.flush();
               String choiceStr=null;
               try
               {
                    choiceStr = dis.readLine();
               }
               catch (IOException ioe)
               {
                    System.out.println(ioe.toString());
                    System.exit(1);
               }

               if (choiceStr != null && choiceStr.length() > 0)
               {
                    int choice = Integer.parseInt(choiceStr);
                    switch (choice)
                    {
                         case 1:
                              try
                              {
                                   sData = new SimData();
                              }
                              catch (Exception e)
                              {
```

```
                        System.out.println(e.toString());
                        sData = null;
                    }
                    break;
                case 2:
                    if (sData != null)
                    {
                        sRun = new SimRun(sData,sStats);
                        sRun.start();
                        System.out.println("Sim started.");
                    }
                    else
                        System.out.println(
                            "Must enter sim data first.");
                        break;
                case 3:
                    if (sRun != null)
                    {
                        System.out.print("Stopping...");

                        sRun.quitting_time = true;
                        try
                        {
                            Thread.sleep(1000);
                        }
                        catch (Exception e) { }
                        System.out.println("Done.");
                        sRun.stop();
                        System.out.println("Sim stopped.");
                    }
                    else
                        System.out.println(
                            "Sim must be running to stop.");
                        break;
                case 4:
                    sStats.printStats();
                    break;
                case 5:
                    done = true;
                    break;
                default:
                    System.out.println("Invalid choice");
            }
        }
        else
            System.out.println("Invalid choice.");
    }
    System.exit(1);
  }
}
```

The class simRun extends Thread. The run() method of the thread executes the simulation. The simulation first kicks off the teller threads, then the clock thread. The clock thread is an endless loop that updates simulation time every second. This simulates time compression where one second simulates one minute of the day. You should notice that the clock class does not extend Thread. Instead it implements the Runnable interface. Examine how the simRun class creates the Thread for this "runnable" target. The rest of the simulation revolves around time-stepping through the day and generating customers based on a customer-probability function. The important thing to understand is that the customer and teller threads are executing the major parts of the simulation asynchronously and autonomously. In a nonthreaded synchronous program the simRun loop would control everything. The occurrence of many simultaneous autonomous activities is much closer to real life.

The class customer extends thread. The customer thread simulates a customer entering the bank, spending a few minutes filling out forms or thinking about what he or she needs to do, and then waiting in line to perform a specific activity. The activity to perform is a subclass of an abstract action class. Executing the activity takes a certain number of minutes for the teller.

The teller class extends Thread. The teller thread checks if there are any customers waiting. If so, the teller calls a customer over (retrieves from the list) and assists the customer with his or her banking activity. The teller is busy for however many minutes the customer's action takes. The teller thread simulates being busy by sleeping the appropriate number of simulated minutes.

A run of Source 4.15 produces:

```
C:\java\bin>java BankSim

<<<<<< Bank Sim >>>>>>
   1) Enter Simulation Data.
   2) Run Simulation.
   3) Stop Simulation.
   4) Print Simulation Stats.
   5) Exit.

Enter choice: 1

Enter number of tellers on duty: 3
Time is compressed for this Sim.
One second equals one minute.
Enter number of seconds to run Sim: 120

<<<<<< Bank Sim >>>>>>
   1) Enter Simulation Data.
   2) Run Simulation.
   3) Stop Simulation.
   4) Print Simulation Stats.
   5) Exit.

Enter choice: 2
```

```
Sim started.

<<<<<< Bank Sim >>>>>>
   1) Enter Simulation Data.
   2) Run Simulation.
   3) Stop Simulation.
   4) Print Simulation Stats.
   5) Exit.
Enter choice: Teller #2 is waiting to help someone.
Teller #3 is waiting to help someone.
Teller #1 is waiting to help someone.
A customer just walked in...
A customer just walked in...
Customer #1 is now waiting on line.
Teller #3 is helping Customer #1 to
CLOCK: 10
Customer #2 is now waiting on line.
Teller #1 is helping Customer #2 to cash a check...
close an account...
Teller #1 is waiting to help someone.
A customer just walked in...
Teller #3 is waiting to help someone.
CLOCK: 20
A customer just walked in...
A customer just walked in...
A customer just walked in...
Customer #4 is now waiting on line.
Teller #3 is helping Customer #4 to deposit a check...
Customer #3 is now waiting on line.
A customer just walked in...
Customer #6 is now waiting on line.
Teller #2 is helping Customer #3 to rob the bank...
Teller #1 is helping Customer #6 to rob the bank...
A customer just walked in...
...
Teller #3 is helping Customer #28 to cash a check...
A customer just walked in...
Customer #54 is now waiting on line.
Customer #58 is now waiting on line.
CLOCK: 120
Simulation complete.
Customer #57 is now waiting on line.
Customer #59 is now waiting on line.
4

<<<<< SIM STATISTICS >>>>>
# Tellers            : 3
# minutes simulated  : 120
Tot customers entered: 59
Tot customers served : 27
Maximum line size    : 29
```

$$y = -\frac{\left((x - 240^2) - (3 \cdot 240 \cdot 98)\right)}{3 \cdot 240}$$

FIGURE 4.1 Parabola formula.

```
<<<<<< Bank Sim >>>>>>
   1) Enter Simulation Data.
   2) Run Simulation.
   3) Stop Simulation.
   4) Print Simulation Stats.
   5) Exit.

Enter choice: 5
```

Examining the statistics of the simulation run, you can tell that our three tellers were extremely overworked that day. This is a very busy bank in a big city. Obviously, an important criterion for the accuracy of this simulation is how you determine when a customer enters the bank. I chose to map a simple curve to our 8-hour day and then determine the probability of a customer entering the bank to our position on the curve. The formula for the parabola mapped to our 8-hour day is shown in Figure 4.1.

Figure 4.2 is a graph of the same curve.

I recommend experimenting with this simulation by modifying the customer probability (I recommend lowering it), adding new actions for the customer to perform, and allowing the bank manager to increase staff at peak bank periods. Also, it is important to determine the maximum number of minutes a customer had to wait on line. Another possible enhancement would be to determine the number of minutes a teller sat idle. These are left to you as an exercise.

Now we need to discuss how threads can share data in a controlled fashion.

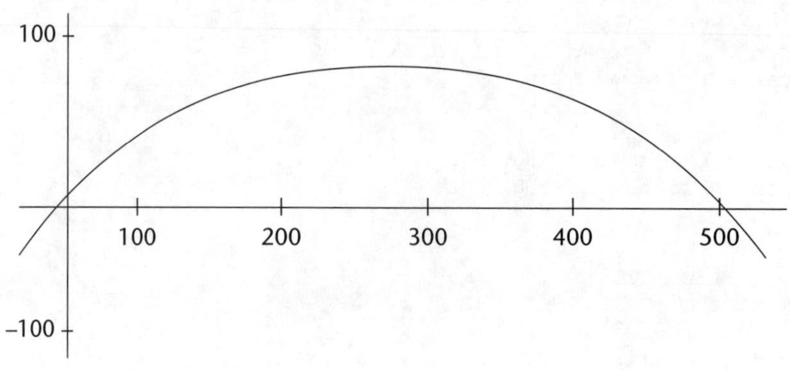

FIGURE 4.2 Parabola graph.

Sharing Data between Threads

As stated earlier, all threads share the same memory space and therefore have access to objects created in other threads and the main process. When you share data among threads it is necessary to insure that two threads do not update the shared variables simultaneously. Historically this was done using semaphores or mutexes or similar software. The obvious drawback to managing synchronization yourself was that if you made a coding error you were in trouble. Java's built-in thread support provides the synchronized keyword that insures that multiple threads will NOT run ANY synchronized method in a class concurrently. This is accomplished by the Java run time placing a software "lock" on the object that only allows one thread access at a time. Source 4.16 demonstrates threads sharing an object that uses synchronized methods. The object that uses synchronized methods is the Stack class.

SOURCE 4.16 TestSync.java

```
// TestSynch.java
import java.lang.Thread;
import java.lang.Exception;
import java.lang.Integer;
import java.util.Stack;
import java.util.Random;

/** Class Producer puts items in shared data store. */
class Producer extends Thread
{
     int Rest, qty, myNumber;
     Stack theStorage;
     static int ProducerCount = 0;

     /** constructor. */
     Producer(int millisRest, int numberToProduce, Stack aStack)
     {
          Rest = millisRest;
          qty = numberToProduce;
          ProducerCount++;
          myNumber = ProducerCount;
          theStorage = aStack;
     }

     /** implements runnable. */
     public void run()
     {
          int i=qty;

          while (i > 0)
          {
```

```
                System.out.println("Producer: " + myNumber +
                                        " created and stored a product.");
                Integer anInt = new Integer(myNumber);
                theStorage.push(anInt);
                try { sleep(Rest); } catch (Exception e) { }
                i–;
            }
        }
}

/** a Consumer class pulls from shared data store. */
class Consumer extends Thread
{
        static int ConsumerCount = 0;
        int myNumber, delay, count;
        Stack theStorage;

        /** constructor. */
        Consumer(int millisToConsume, int numberToConsume, Stack aStack)
        {
            delay = millisToConsume;
            count = numberToConsume;
            theStorage = aStack;
            ConsumerCount++;
            myNumber = ConsumerCount;
        }

        /** implements runnable. */
        public void run()
        {
            int i=count;
            while (i > 0)
            {
                System.out.println("Store holds " + theStorage.size() +
                                                    " products.");
                if (theStorage.size() > 0)
                {
                    Object o = theStorage.pop();
                    System.out.println("Consumer: " + myNumber +
                                            " consumed a product.");
                    try { sleep(delay); } catch (Exception e) { }
                }
                else
                {
                    System.out.println("Consumer: " + myNumber +
                                        " could NOT get any product!");
                    break;
                }
                i–;
            }
```

```
    }
}

/** Class to test synchronization.  The Stack data object uses
    synchronized push() and pop() methods. */
public class TestSynch
{
    /** main() method to invoke from JVM. */
    public static void main(String args[])
    {
        if (args.length < 2)
        {
            System.out.println(
                "Usage: java tstSynch #producers #consumers");
            System.exit(1);
        }

        int producers = Integer.parseInt(args[0]);
        int consumers = Integer.parseInt(args[1]);

        // create the stack
        Stack theStore = new Stack();

        Random dice = new Random();

        for (int i=0; i < producers; i++)
        {
            int produceCount = Math.abs(dice.nextInt() % 5);
            int millis = Math.abs(dice.nextInt() % 500);
            System.out.println("ProduceCount " + produceCount);
            Producer p = new Producer(millis, produceCount, theStore);
            p.start();
        }

        try { Thread.sleep(200); } catch (Exception e) { }

        for (int i=0; i < consumers; i++)
        {
            int hunger = Math.abs(dice.nextInt() % 5);
            int timeToEat = Math.abs(dice.nextInt() % 500);
            System.out.println("hunger: " + hunger);
            Consumer c = new Consumer(timeToEat, hunger, theStore);
            c.start();
        }

        try { Thread.sleep(2000); } catch (Exception e) { }

        System.out.println("Active threads: " + Thread.activeCount());
    }
}
```

Here is a run of Source 4.16.

```
C:\java\bin>java TestSynch 2 2
ProduceCount 4
ProduceCount 2
Producer: 2 created and stored a product.
Producer: 1 created and stored a product.
Producer: 2 created and stored a product.
Producer: 1 created and stored a product.
hunger: 0
hunger: 2
Store holds 4 products.
Consumer: 2 consumed a product.
Producer: 1 created and stored a product.
Store holds 4 products.
Consumer: 2 consumed a product.
Producer: 1 created and stored a product.
Active threads: 1
```

The Producer and Consumer threads share the same Stack object. The synchronized methods in the Stack object insure that only one thread accesses the Stack object at a time. It also allows threads to wait for a certain condition in the object (like the Consumer waiting for the Producer to put a product on the shelf). As an experiment, you should modify the preceding program to make a Consumer wait for a product if the Stack is empty. This is left for you as an exercise.

Deadlock and Starvation

One of the problems that can potentially occur when two or more processes interact to perform a task is *Deadlock*. Deadlock is a situation that occurs when a thread or process is prevented from executing because it requires a resource that will never become available. *Starvation* is a similar process to deadlock. Starvation occurs when a process if prevented from accessing a resource due to scheduling.

The Dining Philosophers. We can illustrate the concept of deadlock by examining a well-known computer science problem known as *The Dining Philosophers* problem.

It's a well-known fact that all modern day philosophers do is philosophize, think, and eat. However, what most people don't realize is that in order for a philosopher to eat, he or she must have two forks. Hence the problem.

Five philosophers (the actual number is unimportant) sit around a table. In the middle of the table is a large bowl of spaghetti. Between each set of philosophers is a fork. That is, for five philosophers there are five forks. Each philosopher sits around and thinks for a while and then talks for a while and then eats for a while. Since there are only five forks, each philosopher must reach for first one fork and then the other. In addition, once a philosopher has a fork he or she holds onto it (after all, he or she's hungry) until he or she can get the other fork. The problem occurs when all the philosophers grab a right or a left fork at once. Each then has one fork and waits forever to obtain the other. The requirements for deadlock can be summed up by the following four requirements.

- **Mutual exclusion.** Only a single process can hold a resource or modify shared information at one time. In our example, a fork can only be held by a single philosopher at a time.
- **Circular waiting.** A thread *A* can wait for a process *B*, which in turn waits on *C*, which in turn waits on *A*. So the chain from *A* to *C* back to *A* forms a loop.
- **Piecemeal allocation.** Resources can be allocated piecemeal or one at a time. For example, each philosopher can grab a fork one at a time.
- **Lack of preemption.** Once a resource has been granted to a thread it cannot be taken away. In *The Dining Philosophers* problem, once a fork is obtained it cannot be taken away.

Source 4.17 implements a version of *The Dining Philosophers* problem. Since the example contains all of the four requirements for deadlock, it hangs almost immediately.

SOURCE 4.17 Philosopher.java

```
package jwiley.chp4;

import java.lang.*;
import java.lang.Math;
import java.util.Random;
import java.util.Date;

/**
 * A simple implementation of the dining philosophers problem which
 * results in deadlock.
 *
 * The table class represents the table that the philosophers will sit at.
 *
 * @author  A. Saganick
 * @version 1.0
 *
 */
class Table
{
     final int FREE = -1;
     int philosopherCount = 0;
     int forks [];
     Philosopher phils[];
     /** The names of a few of my favorite philosophers */
     String names[] = {"Plato",
                       "Aristotle",
                       "Socrates",
```

```
                                    "Alan Turing",
                                    "Mr Bill",
                                    "Sluggo",
                                    "Mr Ed",
                                    "Decartes",
                                    "St. Augustine",
                                    "Occam",
                                    "Nietzsche"};

    /* Create a table and seat philosphers at it */
    Table (int howMany)
    {
         philosopherCount = howMany;
         forks = new int[howMany];
         phils = new Philosopher[howMany];
         for ( int i = 0; i < howMany; I++)
         {
              forks[i] = FREE;
              phils[i] = new Philosopher();
              phils[i].init(this,names[i],i);
              phils[i].start();
         }
    }

    /* Put down the allocated forks */
    synchronized public void  putDownForks(int which)
    {
         int left = which;
         int right = (which + 1) % philosopherCount;
         forks[left] = FREE;
         forks[right] = FREE;
    }
    /* Pick up the right fork */
    synchronized public boolean  pickUpRightFork(int which)
    {
         int right = (which + 1) % philosopherCount;
         if (forks[right] != FREE)
              return false;

         forks[right] = which;
         return true;
    }
    /* Pick up the right left */
    synchronized public boolean  pickUpLeftFork(int which)
    {
         int left = which;
         if (forks[left] != FREE)
              return false;

         forks[left] = which;
         return true;
    }
```

```
    /** Start the simulation and then let it run for a while */
    public static void main (String[] args)
    {
        Table table = new Table(5); // Five philosophers

        try { Thread.sleep(10000*5); }
        catch (Exception e) { System.exit(1); };

        for ( int I = 0; I < 5; I++)
        {
            table.phils[i].stop();
        }
    }

} // end class Table

/**
 * Each philosopher is a thread.
 *
 * @author  A. Saganich
 * @version 1.0
 *
 */
class Philosopher extends Thread
{
    final int timeSlice = 10000;  // Max time anything can happen for.
    int         thinkTime;
    int   eatTime;
    int   talkTime;
    String      name;
    int   which;
    Random      dice;

    Table table = null;

    public Philosopher()
    {
        init(null,"Unknown",-1);
    }
    public Philosopher(Table table, String name, int which)
    {
        init(table,name,which);
    }

    int getRand()
    {
        return Math.abs(dice.nextInt()) %timeSlice;
    }
    int getRand(int modifier)
    {
        return Math.abs(dice.nextInt()) %modifier;
```

```
}
public void init(Table table, String name, int which)
{
     dice = new Random();
     this.name = name;
     this.which = which;
     this.table = table;
     thinkTime = getRand();
     eatTime   = getRand();
     talkTime  = getRand();
}

void thinking()
{
     Date currentTime = new Date(System.currentTimeMillis());
     int howLong = getRand(thinkTime);
     System.out.println(name + " is thinking for " + howLong +
          "ms at " + currentTime);
     try { sleep(howLong); } catch (Exception e) {} ;
}

void eating()
{
     Date currentTime = new Date(System.currentTimeMillis());
     int howLong = getRand(eatTime);
     System.out.println(name + " is eating for " + howLong + "ms at "
                    + currentTime);
     try { sleep(howLong); } catch (Exception e) {} ;
}

void talking()
{
     Date currentTime = new Date(System.currentTimeMillis());
     int howLong = getRand(talkTime);
     System.out.println(name + " is talking for " + howLong + "ms at "
                    + currentTime);
     try { sleep(howLong); } catch (Exception e) {} ;
}

/**
 * The run method does all the work by thinking for a while
 * and then talking for a while to build up an appetite and
 * then obtaining forks and finally eating.
 * The process then repeats itself.
 */

public void run()
{
     Date currentTime = new Date(System.currentTimeMillis());
     System.out.println(name +" sat in seat " + which + " at " +
                    currentTime);
```

```
        do
        {

            System.out.println(name +
                " attempting to pick up left fork");
            while (table.pickUpLeftFork(which) == false)
            {
                try { sleep(100); } catch (Exception e) {} ;
            }
            System.out.println(name + " obtained left fork");
            System.out.println(name +
                " attempting to pick up right fork");
            while ( table.pickUpRightFork(which) == false)
            {
                try { sleep(100); } catch (Exception e) {} ;
            }
            System.out.println(name + " obtained right fork");
            eating();
            table.putdownForks(which);
            thinking();
            talking();
        }while (true);
    }
} // End class Philosopher
```

A run of Source 4.17 produces.

```
C:\java\bin>java Table
Alan Turing sat in seat 3 at Thu Jul 24 22:46:09 EDT 1997
Socrates sat in seat 2 at Thu Jul 24 22:46:09 EDT 1997
Alan Turing attempting to pick up left fork
Plato sat in seat 0 at Thu Jul 24 22:46:09 EDT 1997
Alan Turing obtained left fork
Aristotle sat in seat 1 at Thu Jul 24 22:46:09 EDT 1997
Plato attempting to pick up left fork
Plato obtained left fork
Plato attempting to pick up right fork
Alan Turing attempting to pick up right fork
Mr Bill sat in seat 4 at Thu Jul 24 22:46:09 EDT 1997
Socrates attempting to pick up left fork
Socrates obtained left fork
Socrates attempting to pick up right fork
Aristotle attempting to pick up left fork
Aristotle obtained left fork
Aristotle attempting to pick up right fork
Mr Bill attempting to pick up left fork
Mr Bill obtained left fork
Mr Bill attempting to pick up right fork
```

As you can see from the result, the example deadlocks almost immediately because the philosophers all come to the table and grab their left fork. Since each grabs his or her left fork, no philosopher can obtain two forks and then eat, and the example deadlocks. Listed here are the three methods commonly used to avoid deadlock.

The three methods used to prevent deadlock are:

- **Avoidance.** Do not enter a state where deadlock can occur. In our example, don't pick up a fork unless you can pick up two. Or alternately, if you cannot pick up a second fork, put down the first.
- **Detection and recovery.** If the current state is a deadlock state, then back up.
- **Prevention.** Prevent deadlock by removing one of the previously mentioned conditions.

Java is, by its very nature multithreaded, and as such deadlock will always be possible. Of the three-deadlock prevention methods, prevention is often the best method for avoiding deadlock. Often it's obvious that two threads are attempting to use the same resources and deadlock can be overcome by simply allowing one to preempt the other. Avoidance is a close second, and detection and recovery last. Avoidance and prevention are certainly the simplest methods to implement, especially if the developer keeps the requirements for deadlock firmly in mind. Detecting and preventing deadlock is a large and complex topic, weighing heavily in graph theory and considerably beyond the scope of this chapter.

4.5 SUMMARY

In this chapter we have covered several features of Java that do not exist in C or C++. We examined packages, interfaces, dynamic object loading, and multithreading. As we examined these features we first explored how other languages implemented the same feature. This is one of Java's strongest claims: most or all of its features are borrowed from other languages. There is nothing necessarily new in Java, it just borrowed the best features available from other languages while retaining a simple and pure object-oriented foundation.

CHAPTER 5

Connecting to Legacy Code

OBJECTIVE

This chapter will give you an introduction to the Java Native Interface (previously known as Native Methods) and explain how and why you might want to use them. The JNI is, in its simplest form, an API for allowing the Java Virtual Machine to call applications and libraries written in other languages. As C and C++ native methods are the most common, they are the ones we will demonstrate.

5.1 OVERVIEW

The Java Native Interface, or JNI as it is more commonly called, is a description and an API on how Java applications can call external functions or *Native Methods*. Simply stated a Native Method is one that is not written in Java but rather in the native language of the platform. While it's entirely possible to write your application completely in Java, there may be reasons not to do so; the most compelling of which may be that you have some sort of library or set of functions that you simply cannot do without, or execution speed simply cannot be compromised, or some critical application feature simply does not exist in the standard libraries. While you should go to great lengths to avoid native code there may be times when native methods are simply unavoidable.

With the JNI you can:

- Write methods in C/C++ or other languages
- Create and manipulate Java Objects
- Call Java methods from other languages
- Process and throw exceptions
- Load and examine classes

TIP—Native Methods Should Be Avoided! While the JNI makes calling native methods more manageable it's still a method of last resort. In most cases you can find an alternate way to access your native code. The JNI circumvents most of Java's most important features, weakening security, confusing memory management, and worst of all, losing the portable nature of Java. The JNI is really to be avoided unless you simply have no choice!

Other Alternatives to Native Methods

There is almost always a way to do without native methods. Here are just a few suggested alternatives.

- Create two separate executables: one in Java and one in C and communicate using sockets.
- Create two separate executables: one in Java and one in C and communicate using disk files.
- Use ActiveX components in your Java Applications.
- Get Sun's package for connecting to CORBA (See Chapter 13, "Programming with CORBA and Java").

These are just some of the ways to avoid native methods. There are most certainly others and possibly third-party tools which may make this type of development easier or not required. In any case, before you commit to native methods consider your options and then choose wisely.

5.2 PROGRAMMING TO THE JNI

If you were previously programming using the JDK 1.02 native methods, then you should immediately transition your code to instead use the JNI. If you were using some other form of native method interface, such as Microsoft Windows COM, Raw Native Interface, or Netscape's JRI, then it is in your best interest to learn and understand the new JNI.

How the JNI Works

Native method calls work simply by loading a shared library (.so under Sun's Solaris) or a Dynamic Link Library (.DLL under Windows 95 or Windows NT) using the System.loadLibrary call. Users of the JDK1.0 native method interface will find no differences here. Native methods are "stored" within the dynamic library and referenced within Java via the native keyword. Source 5.1 shows a simple example of a native method.

SOURCE 5.1 myNativeMethods.java

```
package chp5;
class myNativeMethods
{
     native long aMethod(long aLong);
     native void aNotherMethod(long aLong);
     native void aNotherMethod(short aShort);
     public void aNotherMethod()
     {
          System.out.println("Standard Java aNotherMethod called!");
     }
     static { System.loadLibrary("chp5_myNativeMethods"); }
}
```

Let's examine what Source 5.1 demonstrates:

- **native.** The native keyword flags the method as being external and from a dynamically loadable library.
- **System.loadLibrary.** The loadLibrary method causes the dynamically loadable library chp5_myNativeMethods to be actually loaded. This is done under Win32 using the Win32 calls and under Sun Solaris using load paths. Other operating systems most certainly will use other methods.

Underlying Implementations. The underlying type of the dynamically loadable library is determined by the operating system in use. Windows 95 and Windows NT loadLibrary calls will be loaded based on DLLs, whereas under Sun Solaris the library will be assumed to be a shared object. Other operating systems that do not support dynamic object loading may require that the actual external classes be linked with the Java Virtual Machine. And don't forget that the operating system must be able to find the loadable library.

Writing Native Method Code

We've seen how a simple Java class that uses native method is defined. But how do we actually structure the to-be-called code. And how does the Java class name and the c/c++ function names get linked together? Let's look at each of the steps required to write a Java/native method application.

1. Write your Java application code noting, with the keyword native, those methods not implemented in Java.
2. Compile the code normally.
3. Run Javah on the resulting class file with the –jni switch to produce a .h file. Unlike the 1.0 native methods, you don't generate stub code.

4. Write the appropriate C or C++ code for your methods and compile/link into a DLL or shared object.
5. Run your application!

Write the Java Application. This is the simplest part of all the steps. Let's write a simple Java class that has a set of methods that display one type of Java argument per call to System.out.

As you can see, very little differs from a standard Java class. With the exception of the native keyword on the methods and the System.loadLibrary call, our class looks almost identical to any other Java application. Once you've developed your class, compile it with javac normally.

Once you've written your class you need to develop the underlying native methods. To do this you need to understand how Java expects the underlying calls to look. Anyone who has seen the result of generating a C++ mangled method name knows this is no trivial feat. Yet we must know exactly how the method calls will look on the C–C++ side. Javah to the rescue!

Run Javah on the Resulting Class File. Javah is a utility that ships with the JDK and creates a header file from your class file. As we saw in Source 5.2 this is no trivial feat! In Source 5.3 we will see a sample of the header file output from javah. Here is the command line used to generate it.

```
javah -jni tstNative
```

SOURCE 5.2 tstNative.java

```
// tstNative.java
package chp5;
class tstNative
{
     native public void dump(long aLong);
     native public void dump(float aFloat);
     public void dump(String aString)
     {
          System.out.println("String:"+aString);
     }
     static { system.loadLibrary("chp5_tstNative"); }

     public void main( String args[])
     {
          tstNative tst = new tstNative();
          tst.dump(1);
          tst.dump(3.0);
          tst.dump("A string!");
     }
}
```

The javah utility will examine a class file and extract from it the native methods and then build appropriate header files entries for you. Remember that this is a generated file and you should never edit it!

Javah has a number of command line arguments. Figure 5.1 is a listing of the arguments.

The only switch of interest is the –jni switch that instructs javah to generate a JNI-specific header file. Other switches, such as –o, -d, –v, or –classpath, may occasionally be of interest for changing the name of the result file, output directory, or the class path search order. For more information see the JDK1.1 or newer documentation.

TIP—Older Switches and Backward Compatibility Javah, when run without switches, with the –stubs or the –trace switch, supports Version 1.0 native methods. This was done to support backward compatibility. You should not be using these and can ignore their existence!

How Javah generates function names. Determining the correct signature for a method is an error-prone and tedious job. Javah takes the pain out of determining native method call names. While it's tedious it's still instructional to understand how javah actually generates the names and header file entries for native methods.

Javah generates function names as follows:

1. Prefix the native method name with Java_.
2. Append the fully qualified mangled class name plus an underscore separator.
3. Append the mangled method name.

One additional step exists for overloaded method:

4. Append two underscores and then the mangled argument signature.

```
Usage: javah.exe [-v] [-options] classes...
where options include:
    -help       print out this message
    -o          specify the output file name
    -d          specify the output directory
    -jni        create a JNI-style header file
    -td         specify the temporary directory
    -stubs      create a stubs file
    -trace      adding tracing information to stubs file
    -v          verbose operation
    -classpath  <directories separated by colons>
    -version    print out the build version
```

FIGURE 5.1 Javah's command line arguments.

One of our prior examples call

```
native long aMethod(long aLong);
```

would result in

```
Java_chp5_myNativeMethods_aMethod
```

The overloaded methods are significantly more messy and would result in

```
Java_chp5_myNativeMethods_aNotherMethod__J
```

and

```
Java_chp5_myNativeMethods_aNotherMethod__S
```

Source 5.3 shows a complete listing of the header file covering our sample class when run on a Win32 platform.

SOURCE 5.3 chp5_myNativeMethods.h

```
/* DO NOT EDIT THIS FILE - it is machine generated */
#include <jni.h>
/* Header for class chp5_myNativeMethods */

#ifndef _Included_chp5_myNativeMethods
#define _Included_chp5_myNativeMethods
#ifdef __cplusplus
extern "C" {
#endif
/*
 * Class:     chp5_myNativeMethods
 * Method:    aMethod
 * Signature: (J)J
 */
JNIEXPORT jlong JNICALL Java_chp5_myNativeMethods_aMethod
  (JNIEnv *, jobject, jlong);

/*
 * Class:     chp5_myNativeMethods
 * Method:    aNotherMethod
 * Signature: (J)V
 */
JNIEXPORT void JNICALL Java_chp5_myNativeMethods_aNotherMethod__J
  (JNIEnv *, jobject, jlong);


#ifdef __cplusplus
}
#endif
#endif
```

TABLE 5.1 Java VM Type Signatures

Signature	*Java Type*
Z	boolean
B	byte
C	char
S	short
I	int
J	long
F	float
D	double
L fully qualified class	Fully qualified class (i.e., java.lang.String)
[type	type[]
(arg-types) return type	method return type

If you look closely at the overloaded methods you will see that the generated signatures differ based on the trailing characters. Table 5.1 shows the list of signatures used by the Java VM to differentiate overloaded methods.

Native and Normal Methods. The sharp-eyed reader will have noticed that we mixed normal Java methods with native methods. There is no reason that you cannot mix and match regular Java methods and native methods in the same class. Other classes will not, and should not, know that they are any different!

Develop the C/C++ Code

Now the hard part. You've developed your class and created a header for it. It's time to fill in the actual functionality. With version 1.0 native methods you could use the –stubs switch to generate a set of stub source code, which you could then modify to suit your needs. Under version 1.1 and later you need to actually write this code yourself. Source 5.4 shows a simple example of this.

Compile and Link the Code to Create a DLL

The next step is to create the loadable library. How you actually create the callable DLL or shared object is dependent on the operating system you are using. In the case of Windows 95/Windows NT using Visual C++ 5.0 or better at the DOS prompt, type:

```
cl /I c:\jdk1.1\include /I c:\jdk1.1\include\win32 chp5_tstNative.c -MD -LD
javai.lib
```

SOURCE 5.4 chp5_tstNative.c

```
/* chp5_myNativeMethods.c
 * Simple C implementation of two overloaded functions to dump a long
 * and a double.
 * Al Saganich, Java for C/C++ programmers.
 */
#include "chp5_tstNative.h"
#include <stdio.h>
JNIEXPORT void JNICALL Java_chp5_tstNative_dump__J
  (JNIEnv *pEnv, jobject jObject, jlong inLong)
 {
     printf("long: %ld\n",inLong);
 }
JNIEXPORT void JNICALL Java_chp5_tstNative_dump__D
  (JNIEnv *pEnv, jobject jObject, jdouble inDouble)
 {
     printf("double: %e\n",inDouble);
 }
```

On Sun/Solaris using the standard C compiler type:

```
cc -G -I/usr/local/java/include -I/usr/local/java/include/solaris
chp5_tstNative.c -o chp5_tstNative.so
```

The Windows case will produce a file named chp5_tstNative.dll. The Sun/Solaris case will produce a file called chp5_tstNative.so. In either case, the Java interpreter will dynamically load the library when called for via the System.loadLibrary method.

Run Your Application

You can now run your Java application normally. If all went well it should produce the output shown here.

```
C:\jdk1.1\bin\java tstNative
string:A string!
long: 1
double: 3.000000e+000
```

Common Mistakes. There are two common exceptions that you may need to debug. The first is a **NullPointerException** with an **UnsatisfiedLinkError**. Most often this error is a result of not having correctly established a library path. The second is just an **UnsatisfiedLinkError**. This error is normally a result of misnaming the dynamic load library in the System.loadLibrary statement. Having misnamed the dynamic load library itself or not having the dynamic load library in one of the directories described by the PATH statement under Windows 95/NT are both common mistakes.

A Simple Development Technique. So you've decided that you have to use the JNI, written your Java class(es) and have started to debug. You will find it hard, or impossible, to step into your native code to determine what is wrong when something fails. A simple technique to ease this pain is as follows. Develop each of your native methods as a function that can be called by a normal C or C++ test application, that is completely separate from Java. Develop, test, and debug these functions and methods outside of the Java environment using Visual C++ or the Solaris equivalent, and then when they are complete, integrate them with your Java class. While this will not solve all your debugging problems it will certainly reduce them down to a manageable set!

Now that we are JNI experts, let's take a few moments and look closer at our native methods and argument passing.

Method Arguments

All JNI native methods have two or more arguments. The first two arguments are really support and state information that your method can draw on. While there are always at least two arguments, they are not necessarily the same two.

Looking back we see that the first argument to all JNI methods is a pointer to a JNI environment structure. This structure contains a set of functions that provide some basic levels of support for manipulating Java objects and the Java environment. The functions fall into the following categories.

- **Version information.** Return version information about the JNI Interface.
- **Class operations.** Define a class, get class(es) super, etc.
- **Exceptions.** Throw an exception, test if an exception has been thrown, etc.
- **Global and local references.** Create local and global references to objects, etc.
- **Object operations.** Allocate objects, create new objects, get object class information, access object data and fields, etc.
- **Calling instance methods.** Return method information, call object methods, etc.
- **Accessing static fields.** Access static object fields and data and methods, etc.
- **String operations.** Manipulate strings.
- **Array operations.** Manipulate arrays.
- **Registering native methods.** Register native methods with a class.
- **Monitor operations.** Provides synchronization support.
- **Java VM interface methods.** Allows access to the calling Java Virtual Machine.

TIP—For More Information on JNI Environment Methods. An exact description of each of the JNI environment functions is beyond the scope of this chapter. If you would like more information on JNI environment functions, including detailed descriptions, arguments, and general info, see the JNI spec available at www.javasoft.com/products/JDK/.

TABLE 5.2 Type Mappings from Native Types to Java Types

Native Type	*Java Type*	*Description*
Jboolean	boolean	unsigned 8 bits
jbyte	byte	signed 8 bits
jchar	char	unsigned 16 bits
jshort	short	signed 16 bits
jint	int	signed 32 bits
jlong	long	signed 64 bits
jfloat	float	32-bit floating point
jdouble	double	64-bit floating point
void	void	not applicable

The second argument can be one of two things and is dependent on whether the method is static or nonstatic. For static methods the second argument is a reference to the Java class the method is defined within. For nonstatic methods the second argument is a reference to the instance of the Java object the method is defined within.

The third and subsequent arguments are simply the method arguments described in the class. Table 5.2 lists all the primitive types and their mappings between native and Java types.

Referencing Java Objects

Often times you will not be passing a Java primitive object to your underlying native method but rather an object derived from one of the known types. The JNI provides for many types of objects. All references to Java objects have type jobject. For convenience and to reduce programming errors a set of java "objects" is provided for within the JNI interface, all of which can be thought of as derived from jobject. The object hierarchy supported by the JNI is:

- -jobject supports all Java objects
  - -jthrowable supports Java exceptions (java.lang.Throwable)
  - -jclass supports Java class objects (java.lang.Class)
  - -jstring supports Java strings (java.lang.String)
  - -jarray supports Java arrays
    - -jbooleanArray supports boolean arrays
    - -jbyteArray supports byte arrays
    - -jcharArray supports char arrays

-jshortArray supports short arrays
-jintArray supports int arrays
-jlongArray supports long arrays
-jfloatArray supports float arrays
-jdoubleArray represents double arrays
-jobjectArray supports arrays of objects

Without getting in too deep, let's look at a simple example of how to access an object of type java.lang.String from within a native method.

If we define a method as follows:

```
native void someMethod(java.lang.String inString);
```

then within the native method we access the string by using one of the environment methods:

```
const char *pString=(*pJNIEnv)->GetStringUTFChars(pJNIenv,inString,0);
printf("String:%s", pString);  // Manipulate the string
(*pJNIEnv)->ReleaseStringUTFChars(pJNIenv, inString, pString);
```

Java Objects Are Passed by Reference. Primitive types passed to native methods are copied between the Java VM and the underlying native method. Java objects, on the other hand, are passed by reference. So, when your native method receives an object and changes it, that change will be seen by the caller. This is not a side effect, nor a bug, nor a mistake, but by design! It takes a long time to copy a large object or structure. It takes little or no time to create a reference to an object!

Parameters and the JNI Environment Pointer. One important point to understand with respect to the JNI Environment functions is that they perform little or no error checking on their parameters. This was a compromise to keep the overhead of accessing class methods and data to a minimum. When calling a JNI Environment function be absolutely sure you passed valid arguments!

Calling Methods and Accessing Data

The JNI API would be incomplete without a way to access the data and methods of the calling class. Two steps are required to call a class method or access a class variable. First you must obtain an id to the method or field, after which you can then call the method using the CallxyzMethod set of calls. Similar calls exist for accessing the data members of the calling class.

Source 5.5 shows a Java class, dateTime.java, which both calls a native method and is called by a native method.

SOURCE 5.5 dateTime.java

```
/**
 * dateTime.java
 * This class calls a c function which determines the current
 * data and time and formats it as a string.
 * The c function then accesses the dataTime variable and fills it.
 * Next it calls the method javaPrintDateTime which prints the contents.
 *
 */
package jwiley.chp5;

class dateTime
{
     native void nmFillDateTime();
     String dateTime;
     void javaPrintDateTime(String aDateTime)
     {
          System.out.println("Java:Current data and time is " + aDateTime);
     }
     static  { System.loadLibrary("dateTime"); }
     public static void main(String args[])
     {
          dateTime dtObject = new dateTime();
          dtObject.dateTime = "Original value";
          System.out.println("Java:Calling java method");
          dtObject.javaPrintDateTime(dtObject.dateTime);
          System.out.println("Java:Calling native method");
          dtObject.nmFillDateTime();
          System.out.println("Java:returned from native method");
          System.out.println("Java:Current dataTime from java is "
                                   + dtObject.dateTime);
     }
}
```

This class is almost identical to the previous example; however, the C code is quite different. Source 5.6 shows the associated C code.

Let's examine how our C method is structured to support accessing a local reference and calling a Java method.

Global and Local References. The JNI support two types of references, Local and Global. As you might imagine, local references are created when the native method is called and freed when the method returns. Global references, however, must be explicitly allocated and freed.

In Source 5.6 we wish to access one of the local variables within the dateTime class. The way this is done is shown in the numbered steps following Source 5.6.

SOURCE 5.6 dateTime.c

```
/**
 * dateTime.c
 * C function which is called by java, updates a java variable and
 * then calls a java method.
 *
 * Al Saganich, Java for C/C++ programmers.
 */

#include <stdio.h>
#include <jni.h>
#include <time.h>
#include "dateTime.h"  // Header file produced by javap -s -p someclass
JNIEXPORT void JNICALL Java_dateTime_nmFillDateTime (JNIEnv *pJNIEnv ,
                                                    jobject jObj)
{
    jclass jclsContainingClass;
    jmethodID methodID;
    jfieldID fieldID;
    jstring jString;
    const char *pCStr;
    time_t ltime;

    /*
    * Get a handle to the containing class.
    */
    jclsContainingClass = (*pJNIEnv)->GetObjectClass(pJNIEnv, jObj);

    /* java.lang.String dateTime;
    * Ljava/lang/String;
    */
    printf("C:Getting handle to data member dateTime\n");
    fieldID = (*pJNIEnv)->GetFieldID(pJNIEnv, jclsContainingClass,
                                "dateTime", "Ljava/lang/String;");
    if (fieldID == 0)
    {
        printf("C:Error field  dateTime not found!\n");
        return;
    }
    // Access the java string
    jString = (*pJNIEnv)->GetObjectField(pJNIEnv, jObj, fieldID);
    // get a c-string pointer
    pCStr = (*pJNIEnv)->GetStringUTFChars(pJNIEnv, jString, 0);

    printf("C:Original value of dateTime = %s\n",pCStr);

    // Done with it
    (*pJNIEnv)->ReleaseStringUTFChars(pJNIEnv, jString, pCStr);
```

```
    // Now update the java field with the current time.
    time( &ltime );
    printf("C:setting dateTime = %s\n",ctime( &ltime ));
    // Allocate a java string to contain the new value
    jString= (*pJNIEnv)->NewStringUTF(pJNIEnv, ctime( &ltime ));
    // set the value into our string
    (*pJNIEnv)->SetObjectField(pJNIEnv, jObj, fieldID, jString);
    /*
    *      Get a handle to the method to call
    *      void javaPrintDateTime(java.lang.String);
    *         (Ljava/lang/String;)V
    */
    methodID = (*pJNIEnv)->GetMethodID(pJNIEnv, jclsContainingClass,
                                       "javaPrintDateTime",
                                       "(Ljava/lang/String;)V");
    if (methodID == 0)
    {
        printf("C:Error method javaPrintDateTime not found!\n");
        return;
    }

    (*pJNIEnv)->CallVoidMethod(pJNIEnv, jObj, methodID, jString);
    printf("C:Called Java method returning to Java.\n");
}
```

1. Variables are accessed via field ids. This is done for two reasons. First, a variable accessed through classes is expensive; second, it's tedious to code. The JNI Environment pointer provides a function for determining the field ID of a field. Once we have obtained a field id it is valid until the method returns.

   Before we can get a field id we need a reference to the class that the field is contained within. The JNI provides a method, GetObjectClass, which returns a reference to the Java class containing the variable we wish to access.

   ```
   jclsContainingClass = (*pJNIEnv)->GetObjectClass(pJNIEnv, jObj);
   ```

2. Next we obtain a field id using the JNI method GetField ID.

   ```
   fieldID = (*pJNIEnv)->GetFieldID(pJNIEnv, jclsContainingClass,
                                    "dateTime", "Ljava/lang/String;");
   ```

   GetFieldID takes four arguments. First is a pointer to the JNI Environment variable. All JNI functions use this variable for context. Second is the class containing the variable. The third argument is a string containing the name of the class, and the last is a string that differentiates our dateTime function from other functions by signature. More on this in a moment.

3. Once we have a field id we can obtain a reference to the actual field using GetObjectField.

```
jString = (*pJNIEnv)->GetObjectField(pJNIEnv, jObj, fieldID);
```

4. Finally, we get a C-style pointer to the string using the GetStringUTFChars function.

```
pCStr = (*pJNIEnv)->GetStringUTFChars(pJNIEnv, jString, 0);
```

We can do as we wish with the C pointer. In our case, simply print its contents to standard out.

```
(*pJNIEnv)->ReleaseStringUTFChars(pJNIEnv, jString, pCStr);
```

One additional step that we need to examine is how we set a value back into our string. This is accomplished by populating a new Java string and using it to set our original string.

```
jString= (*pJNIEnv)->NewStringUTF(pJNIEnv, ctime( &ltime ));
(*pJNIEnv)->SetObjectField(pJNIEnv, jObj, fieldID, jString);
```

Certainly not straightforward, but then again not difficult either.

We would also like to call back into our Java class. To call back into our class we use a method similar to the one we used to access our field using GetMethodID.

```
methodID = (*pJNIEnv)->GetMethodID(pJNIEnv, jclsContainingClass,
                                   "javaPrintDateTime",
                                   "(Ljava/lang/String;)V");
```

The arguments to GetMethodID are identical to those of GetFieldID except that GetMethodID returns a method id that can be used to refer to our method. Next we use one of the JNI support functions to indirectly call the java method.

TIP Be careful when caching field IDs or method IDs. If you store a field ID, for example in a static variable external to any function, and the underlying object is destroyed, your field ID will be invalid and its use could (and most likely will) crash your application. If you do cache IDs make sure the objects that are referenced remain available for the life of the library they are used in!

Java methods can return any of a number of data types. A set of JNI methods exists that support basic Java types as return codes. Since our class returned void we will use CallVoidMethod. However, we could have just as easily used CallFloatMethod or CallDoubleMethod or one of the other similar methods and caught the return code into an appropriate variable.

```
(*pJNIEnv)->CallVoidMethod(pJNIEnv, jObj, methodID, jString);
```

The Java method we are testing with is not quite as trivial as it looks. It intentionally contained a stack variable. We need to pass a Java version of the variable to the CallXYZMethod so that the Java method gets a local reference to the variable on its stack. The normal method of calling a Java method is to just push the Java variable types onto the stack by listing them in the CallXYZ method. The call signature, which we will discuss momentarily, tells the underlying call what arguments to expect. Other methods exist based on var_args processing and using Java unions. See the JNI section of the JDK Documentation set for more information on alternate parameter-passing methods.

TIP While we have concentrated on nonstatic methods we could have just as easily called a static method by replacing the GetMethodCall with GetStaticMethodID; Likewise, the GetFieldID with GetStaticFieldID. An additional example is packaged with the Chapter 5 code, AccessData.c and AccessData.java. This example exercises the access methods for both static and nonstatic fields.

The Javap Tool. The last argument to both GetMethodID and GetField ID was a method or variable signature. The JDK provides a tool, javap, that can be used to generate the signatures we need to pass to GetMethodID and friends. Source 5.7 shows the result of running javap on our dateTime.class.

The important portions of this file are the ones referring to our dateTime variable and the javaPrintDateTime method. In each case, we can see the signature we needed for our method and field calls following the variable and method descriptions themselves.

Two important arguments to javap are:

- **-s.** Print internal signatures
- **-p.** Print private methods as well as public

Exceptions within Native Methods

The last section of the JNI API worth noting supports exceptions. Everyone makes mistakes and coding errors. When I stop making mistakes it will be time to retire. Native methods and JNI Environment functions may raise and process exceptions just like normal Java classes. An important point to note is that JNI functions will often return an error as well as raise an exception! You should always check the result of JNI functions for success. When a function does fail you can get more data via the ExceptionOccurred function.

SOURCE 5.7 dateTime.signature

```
c:\jdk\bin\javap -s -p dateTime > dateTime.signature
Compiled from dateTime.java
synchronized class dateTime extends java.lang.Object
    /* ACC_SUPER bit set */
{
    java.lang.String dateTime;
     /*   Ljava/lang/String;   */
    native void nmFillDateTime();
     /*   ()V   */
    void javaPrintDateTime(java.lang.String);
     /*   (Ljava/lang/String;)V   */
    public static void main(java.lang.String[]);
     /*   ([Ljava/lang/String;)V   */
    dateTime();
     /*   ()V   */
    static static {};
     /*   ()V   */
}
```

There are two ways exceptions can be raised without an error code being returned. They are:

- Calls to Java methods, which throw exceptions and return the result of a method call.
- Array accessor functions, which may throw ArrayIndexOutOfBounds or Array-Store exceptions.

Don't think that just because you didn't get an error result back you didn't have an error!

Exception Handling. Once it has been determined that an exception has occurred the Native method may do one of two things: return immediately, normally with an error code; or clear the exceptions and run its own exception code, perhaps even raising a difference exception. The JNI functions exist for handling exceptions once they have occurred. They are:

- **ExceptionOccured.** Determines if an exception has occurred.
- **ExceptionDescribe.** Prints an exception report and a stack to some system output (normally stderr).
- **ExceptionClear.** Clears an currently thrown exception.

In addition, the native method may generate and throw its own exceptions using the following JNI functions:

- **Throw.** Throw a java.lang.Throwable object to be thrown.
- **ThrowNew.** Creates a new exception object from its arguments and then throws the exception.

5.3 SUMMARY

That concludes our whirlwind tour of the JNI API. As we have seen, the JNI infrastructure is both large and powerful. But native methods are still fraught with peril. Tread lightly in this area as there be dragons here!—the dragons of C, C++, and playing outside the Java Sandbox! All of which we originally strove to avoid by choosing Java in the first place!

For further information you should download the JNI API PDF file from www.javasoft.com or look at the JNI tutorial www.javasoft.com/products/jdk/1.1/docs/guide/jni.html. Both are excellent sources of additional information about the JNI functions and provide further examples.

CHAPTER 6

The Java Language Classes and Reflection

OBJECTIVE

This chapter details the contents of the java.lang and java.lang.reflect packages, explaining the concept of reflection in the process. The purpose and usage of many of the classes are explained and demonstrated through a set of examples. Finally, the hazards of reflection are explained to help Java programmers from misusing it and adding unnecessary complexity to their programs.

6.1 INTRODUCTION

There are many packages in the Java 1.2 Core API. The language package is the only one that contains fundamental language elements, and is thus required for any and all Java programs. Because of their nature, all classes in the java.lang package are implicitly imported into every Java source file.

Reflection is a concept that was added to Java 1.1. Reflection allows Java programs to examine and interact with classes that were not available when the program was compiled. In Java 1.02, programs could load new classes dynamically, but in order to interact with the object it had to be typecast to an object or interface that was known when the program was compiled. This requirement was too restrictive for the proper development of *Java Beans*, the Java component model. For a more detailed explanation of Beans, please refer to Chapter 11. In order for applications to arbitrarily access Beans, a mechanism must be provided to interact with unknown classes without compiling.

The purpose of reflection is to allow the examination of class structures and the invocation of methods by running Java objects. Reflection enables a Java programmer to enumerate the three types of contents of a class: Fields, Constructors, and Methods. In addition, reflection can be used to identify which members of a class are defined on the class itself, and which are inherited from superclasses.

6.2 THE JAVA.LANG PACKAGE

This package supports the Java language and provides access to various Virtual Machine and System operations. It is not required to import these classes since they are part of the language.

Primitive types as classes. The classes listed here are more than just wrapper classes, as can be seen in the code that demonstrates them. In addition to providing objects for all the primitive types, these wrapper classes provide numerous utility methods.

- **Character.** A wrapper class for a character. Remember that Java characters are in the 16-bit UNICODE format. This class provides some of the useful methods in the C <ctype> header like isDigit() and isSpace(). For a demonstration of the Character class see Source 6.4.
- **Byte.** A wrapper class for a byte.
- **Boolean.** A wrapper class for a boolean.
- **Number.** An abstract superclass for the Double, Long, Float, and Integer classes. A very common use of all the wrapper classes is to convert a string input into a number.
- **Double.** A wrapper class for a double precision floating-point number. Source 6.1 is an example of using the number wrapper classes.
- **Long.** A wrapper class for a long integer. See Source 6.1.
- **Float.** A wrapper class for a floating point number. See Source 6.1.
- **Integer.** A wrapper class for an integer. See Source 6.1.
- **Short.** A wrapper class for a short.
- **Void.** An unistantiable class that represents the Java primitive void.

Source 6.1 demonstrates use of the wrapper functions for types.

SOURCE 6.1 TestNumTypes.java

```
// TestNumTypes.java
package jwiley.chp6;

import java.io.BufferedReader;
import java.io.InputStreamReader;
import java.util.Vector;
import java.io.IOException;

/** Class to demonstrate type wrapper classes. */
public class TestNumTypes
```

```
{
    /** main() method to invoke from JVM. */
    public static void main(String args[])
    {
        BufferedReader br = new BufferedReader(
                                new InputStreamReader(System.in));
        int myInt;
        String IntString = null;
        String FloatString = null;

        System.out.print("Enter an Integer: ");
        System.out.flush();
        try
        {
          IntString = br.readLine();
        } catch (IOException ioe)
          {
                System.out.println("IO Exception");
                System.exit(1);
          }
        myInt = Integer.parseInt(IntString);
        System.out.println("myInt : " + myInt);

        System.out.print("Enter a Float: ");
        System.out.flush();
        try
        {
          FloatString = br.readLine();
        } catch (IOException ioe)
          {
                System.out.println("IO Exception.");
                System.exit(1);
          }
        Float myFloat = Float.valueOf(FloatString);
        System.out.println("myFloat : " + myFloat);

        Integer intObject = new Integer(myInt);

        // stuff num objects into a Vector
        Vector numbers = new Vector(2);
        numbers.addElement(intObject);
        numbers.addElement(myFloat);

        Integer anInt = (Integer) numbers.elementAt(0);
        Float aFloat = (Float) numbers.elementAt(1);

        System.out.println("At Vec element 0 : " + anInt);
        System.out.println("At Vec element 1 : " + aFloat);
    }
}
```

A run of Source 6.1 produces:

```
C:\java\bin>java jwiley.chp6.TestNumTypes
Enter an Integer: 10
myInt : 10
Enter a Float: 230.333
myFloat : 230.333
At Vec element 0 : 10
At Vec element 1 : 230.333
```

There are two key points that Source 6.1 demonstrates:

1. How to convert a string to a number using the valueOf() method or parseInt() method. There is also a parseLong() in the Long class.
2. How to convert the primitive types to objects for use in other Java classes (i.e., the Vector class). You will find this absolutely essential when using the container classes in the util package.

Abstract classes and interfaces. These classes represent the root of the class hierarchy, as well as a commonality between all Java objects.

- **Class.** This class is a runtime description of a class. This is the key class for providing reflection. Each object in the Java runtime is an instance of some class. Each class has a corresponding instantiation of the Class class that acts as a class descriptor. Source 6.2 demonstrates the use of a class descriptor to find out the names of all the superclasses for the input class. You will examine the use of this class in detail in section 6.3, "Reflection."

SOURCE 6.2 ClassHierarchy.java

```
// ClassHierarchy.java

import java.io.BufferedReader;
import java.io.InputStreamReader;
import java.io.IOException;

/** Class to demonstrate the Class class. */
public class ClassHierarchy
{
    /** main() method to invoke from JVM. */
    public static void main(String args[])
    {
        try
        {
            BufferedReader br = new BufferedReader(
                                    new InputStreamReader(System.in));
            System.out.print("Enter class to print hierarchy: ");
            System.out.flush();
            String ClassName = br.readLine();
            Class aClass = Class.forName(ClassName);
            System.out.println("Class name: " + aClass.getName());
            Class superClass;
```

```
            do
            {
                    superClass = aClass.getSuperclass();
                    if (superClass != null)
                    {
                            aClass = Class.forName(superClass.getName());
                            System.out.println("Class name: " +
                                                superClass.getName());
                    }
                    else
                    {
                            System.out.println("No superclass.");
                            break;
                    }
            } while (!superClass.getName().equals("java.lang.Object"));
        } catch (ClassNotFoundException cfe)
          {
            System.out.println("Class Not Found: " + cfe.getMessage());
          }
          catch (IOException ioe)
          {
            System.out.println("IO Exception.");
            System.out.println(ioe.getMessage());
          }
    }
}
```

A run of Source 6.2 produces:

```
C:\java\bin>java jwiley.chp6.ClassHierarchy
Enter class to print hierarchy: java.awt.Frame
Class name: java.awt.Frame
Class name: java.awt.Window
Class name: java.awt.Container
Class name: java.awt.Component
Class name: java.lang.Object
```

- **Object.** All objects in the Java runtime are descendants (subclasses) of the Object class. It is important to understand that every class you create extends Object by default. You don't even have to specify it. Aobj is defined in Source 6.3:

```
class Aobj
{
     ...
}

Which is translated to:
class Aobj extends Object
{
     ...
}
```

This gives you many advantages in manipulating objects at run time. One of the most obvious is the ability to supply any object for a method that requires an object of type Object. This makes creating generic container classes simple. The Object class also has a getClass() function that will return the Class descriptor for the current object.

Source 6.3 demonstrates some of the methods provided by the Object class.

SOURCE 6.3 TestObject.java

```
// TestObject.java
package jwiley.chp6;

/** simple test object. */
class Aobj implements Cloneable
{
    /** int data member. */
    int inum;
    /** one arg constructor. */
    Aobj(int inNum) { inum = inNum; }

    /** accessor. */
    int getNum() { return inum; }

    /** clone method. */
    public Object clone()
    {
        try
        {
            Object result = super.clone();
            return result;
        } catch (Exception e) { return null; }
    }
}

/** simple test object. */
class Bobj
{
    /** float data member. */
    float fnum;
    /** constructor. */
    Bobj(float inNum) { fnum = inNum; }
    /** accessor. */
    float getNum() { return fnum; }
}

/** Simple class to test the Object class. */
public class TestObject
{
```

```
    /** main() method to invoke from the JVM. */
    public static void main(String args[])
    {
        Aobj a1 = new Aobj(10);
        Aobj a2 = new Aobj(20);
        Bobj b1 = new Bobj((float)5.0);

        if (a1.equals(a2))
            System.out.println("a1 equals a2");

        if (a1.equals(b1))
            System.out.println("a1 equals b1");
        else
            System.out.println("a1 does NOT equal b1");

        Aobj a3 = (Aobj) a1.clone();
        System.out.println("a1 is              : " + a1.toString());
        System.out.println("a3 is an a1 clone: " + a3.toString());
    }
}
```

A run of Source 6.3 produces:

```
C:\java\bin>java jwiley.chp6.TestObject
a1 does NOT equal b1
a1 is            : jwiley.chp6.Aobj@1cc738
a3 is an a1 clone: jwiley.chp6.Aobj@1cc747
```

- **Throwable.** The base class for all errors and exceptions. Throwable objects are used to transfer execution from one place to another. All throwable objects store the stack frame when they are thrown.
- **Cloneable.** An interface implemented by all objects that support the clone operation. The clone operation copies an object and all of its fields into a new object.
- **Runnable.** An interface implemented by all objects that have the ability to execute code, such as Thread.

Strings. You will find Java's string classes extremely robust.

- **String.** The String class was discussed in Chapter 2. The primary purpose of the String class is to store and manipulate immutable (nonchangeable) strings. Source 6.4 demonstrates both Strings and StringBuffers.
- **StringBuffer.** A StringBuffer is used for mutable (changeable) strings. See Source 6.4.

SOURCE 6.4 TestStrings.java

```
// TestStrings.java
package jwiley.chp6;

import java.io.BufferedReader;
import java.io.InputStreamReader;
import java.io.IOException;

/** class to demonstrate String and StringBuffer class. */
public class TestStrings
{
    /** main() method to invoke from JVM. */
    public static void main(String args[])
    {
        if (args.length < 1)
        {
                System.out.println("USAGE: java tstStrings someString");
                System.exit(1);
        }

        String clString = new String(args[0]);
        System.out.println("Command line string is : " + clString);

        // count characters and digits
        int charCount = 0;
        int digitCount = 0;
        for (int i=0; i < clString.length(); i++)
            if (!Character.isDigit(clString.charAt(i)) &&
                !Character.isWhitespace(clString.charAt(i)))
                    charCount++;
            else if (Character.isDigit(clString.charAt(i)))
                    digitCount++;

        System.out.println("# of Chars : " + charCount +
                           " # of Digits: " + digitCount);

        // construct a sentence
        BufferedReader br = new BufferedReader(
                             new InputStreamReader(System.in));
        System.out.println("Hit <ret> after each word, to exit type" +
                           " a '.'");
        String word=null;
        StringBuffer sentence = new StringBuffer();
        do
        {
          try
          {
```

```
                word = br.readLine();
            } catch (IOException ioe)
              {
                  System.out.println("IOException.");
                  break;
              }
              if (!word.equals("."))
                sentence.append(word + " ");
              else
                sentence.setCharAt(sentence.length() - 1, '.');
          } while (!word.equals("."));

          System.out.println("Sentence : " + sentence);
      }
}
```

A run of Source 6.4 produces:

```
C:\java\bin>java jwiley.chp6.TestStrings
StringsAndStringsBuffers111222areFun333444
Command line string is : StringsAndStringsBuffers111222areFun333444
# of Chars : 30 # of Digits: 12
Hit <ret> after each word, to exit type a '.'
Every
Good
Boy
Does
Fine
.
Sentence : Every Good Boy Does Fine.
```

System info. This category of classes provides both information from the operating system as well as access to some operating system services.

- **System.** You have seen a demonstration of one aspect of the System class in almost every program in this book. You may have guessed that I was referring to the call to System.out.println(). The method println() actually belongs to the PrintStream class; however, the variable out is a public and static member of the System class. In addition to having the in, out, and error streams (known as stdin, stdout, and stderr in C or as cin, cout, and cerr in C++), the System class provides a system-independent method of accessing system functionality and information. Source 6.5 demonstrates accessing System information with the System class.

SOURCE 6.5 SystemProperties.java

```
// SystemProperties.java
package jwiley.chp6;

import java.util.Properties;

/** Class to demonstrate the System class. */
public class SystemProperties
{
    /** main() method to invoke from JVM. */
    public static void main(String args[])
    {
        Properties props = System.getProperties();

        // list the properties
        props.list(System.out);

        // access an individual property
        System.out.println("\n Accessing individual properties.");
        String fileSeparator = System.getProperty("file.separator");
        System.out.println("File Separator is <" + fileSeparator +
                           ">");
    }
}
```

A run of Source 6.5 produces:

```
C:\java\bin>java jwiley.chp6.SystemProperties
- listing properties -
user.language=en
java.home=C:\JDK1.1.1\BIN\..
awt.toolkit=sun.awt.windows.WToolkit
file.encoding.pkg=sun.io
java.version=1.1.1
file.separator=\
line.separator=

user.region=US
file.encoding=8859_1
java.vendor=Sun Microsystems Inc.
user.timezone=EST
user.name=unknown
os.arch=x86
os.name=Windows 95
java.vendor.url=http://www.sun.com/
user.dir=c:\src\jwiley\chp6
java.class.path=c:\jdk1.1.1\lib\classes.zip;c:\src;c:...
java.class.version=45.3
os.version=4.0
```

```
path.separator=;
user.home=C:\JDK1.1.1\BIN\..

Accessing individual properties.
File Separator is <\>
```

- **Process.** A class instantiated from a call to the exec() method in the runtime class. The exec() call is very common in Unix programming where it is used to spawn a new process. Remember that Unix is a multitasking and multiuser system so that the CPU is constantly running many background and interactive processes like servers, shells, and user-command programs. This will become more common in low-end systems with the preemptive multitasking capabilities now in Windows 95 and being added to the Mac OS. The process class provides methods that let you get the standard input and standard output of the process, kill the process, and get the exit value if the process has terminated.
- **Runtime.** This class is an adjunct class to the System class. In fact, the System class uses the Runtime class to perform some of its functions. Source 6.6 demonstrates some of the functions of the Runtime class.
- **Compiler.** A placeholder to enable support for Just In Time (JIT) compilers. JIT compilers dynamically translate class files to machine code to speed execution. If no JIT compiler can be found, then this class does nothing.

SOURCE 6.6 SystemRuntime.java

```
// SystemRuntime.java

/** Class to demonstrate the Runtime class. */
public class SystemRuntime
{
    /** main() method to invoke from JVM. */
    public static void main(String args[])
    {
        Runtime sysRun = Runtime.getRuntime();
        System.out.println("Free Memory (in bytes) : " +
                           sysRun.freeMemory());
        System.out.println("Total Memory (in bytes): " +
                           sysRun.totalMemory());
    }
}
```

A run of Source 6.6 produces:

```
C:\java\bin>java jwiley.chp6.SystemRuntime
Free Memory (in bytes) : 926512
Total Memory (in bytes): 1048568
```

- **SecurityManager.** This class is an abstract class that allows a security policy to be created and enforced in your Java code. This class has methods that allow checks to the ClassLoader, to file creation, to applet access of packages, and much more. With security being such a ripe area of concern, this topic alone requires several chapters if not an entire separate book. This class is discussed in detail in Chapter 17, "Java and Security."
- **ClassLoader.** This is an abstract class that can be extended to allow the loading of classes either from a file or over a network. This mechanism will allow true dynamic distribution of objects to any machine on the network that has a Java runtime (which is soon to be all or most computers out there).

Math functions. All of the math functionality resides in a single class called Math.

- **Math.** The Math class has already been used in many of the programs in this book. Source 6.7 demonstrates using the exp() static method in the Math class to calculate exponential growth.

SOURCE 6.7 Growth.java

```
// Growth.java
package jwiley.chp6;

import java.io.BufferedReader;
import java.io.InputStreamReader;
import java.io.IOException;

/** class to calculate exponential growth and demonstrate
    the Math class. */
public class Growth
{

    /** main() method to invoke from JVM. */
    public static void main(String args[])
    {
        try
        {
            BufferedReader br = new BufferedReader(
                                    new InputStreamReader(System.in));
            System.out.print("Enter initial Deficit: ");
            System.out.flush();
            String popStr = br.readLine();
            long initPopulation = Long.parseLong(popStr);

            System.out.print("Enter number of years elapsed: ");
            System.out.flush();
            String yearStr = br.readLine();
            int years = Integer.parseInt(yearStr);
```

```
            double growth = Math.exp((double)years);
            long newPopulation =
                    Math.round(( (double)initPopulation * growth));
            System.out.println("Exponential growth : " +
                               newPopulation);
        } catch (IOException ioe)
          {
            System.out.println("IO Error");
            System.exit(1);
          }
    }
}
```

A run of Source 6.7 produces:

```
C:\java\bin>java jwiley.chp6.Growth
Enter initial Deficit: 100000
Enter number of years elapsed: 7
Exponential growth : 109663316
```

Threads. The Thread classes implement priority-based multiple execution contexts in a single program. This facility is one of the strongest features of Java that simplifies many programming tasks and makes GUI programming simpler and more responsive.

- **Thread.** This class is subclassed to produce a Thread. You must override the run() function of the Thread class with the code you want your thread to run. Source 6.8 demonstrates how to create a Thread.
- **ThreadGroup.** Allows you to group threads and manipulate them as an entire group. For example, you could change the priority of the whole group and enumerate through all the threads in a group. As your experience grows with threads, you will begin using the ThreadGroup class in your "thread management" strategy. Source 6.8 demonstrates accessing information about a ThreadGroup.

SOURCE 6.8 TestThreads.java

```
// TestThreads.java
package jwiley.chp6;

import java.util.Random;

/** simple class to demonstrate a Thread. */
class DummyThread extends Thread
{
```

```
    /** Count of all threads created. */
    static int dummyThreadCount = 0;
    /** number of seconds thread should sleep. */
    int Seconds;
    /** unique id for this thread. */
    int id;

    /** constructor. */
    DummyThread()
    {
        id = ++dummyThreadCount;
        Random dice = new Random(System.currentTimeMillis() +
                                 dummyThreadCount);
        Seconds = Math.abs(dice.nextInt() % 100);
    }

    /** runnable method. */
    public void run()
    {
        System.out.println("Dummy Thread # " + id +
                           " is sleeping for " + Seconds +
                           " seconds.");
        try { sleep(Seconds * 1000); } catch (Exception e) { }
        System.out.println("Thread # " + id + " is awake.");
    }
}

/** Class to demonstrate the Thread class. */
public class TestThreads
{
    /** main() method to invoke from JVM. */
    public static void main(String args[])
    {
        Random generator = new Random();
        int numThreads = Math.abs(generator.nextInt() % 10);

        System.out.println("Number of Threads to start: " +
                           numThreads);
        for (int i=0; i < numThreads; i++)
        {
            DummyThread d = new DummyThread();
            d.start();
        }

        Thread currentThread = Thread.currentThread();
        ThreadGroup theGroup = currentThread.getThreadGroup();
        theGroup.list();  // list all threads in the group
    }
}
```

A run of Source 6.8 produces:

```
C:\java\bin>java jwiley.chp6.TestThreads
Number of Threads to start: 6
Dummy Thread # 1 is sleeping for 28 seconds.
Dummy Thread # 2 is sleeping for 94 seconds.
Dummy Thread # 3 is sleeping for 45 seconds.
Dummy Thread # 4 is sleeping for 16 seconds.
java.lang.ThreadGroup[name=main,maxpri=10]
Dummy Thread # 5 is sleeping for 37 seconds.
Dummy Thread # 6 is sleeping for 93 seconds.
    Thread[main,5,main]
    Thread[Thread-1,5,main]
    Thread[Thread-2,5,main]
    Thread[Thread-3,5,main]
    Thread[Thread-4,5,main]
    Thread[Thread-5,5,main]
    Thread[Thread-6,5,main]
Thread # 4 is awake.
Thread # 1 is awake.
Thread # 5 is awake.
Thread # 3 is awake.
Thread # 6 is awake.
Thread # 2 is awake.
```

Runtime errors. The following classes extend the Throwable class and are thrown by the Java runtime when an abnormal event occurs. In general, you should not bother catching these Errors unless you have an intimate knowledge of the Java runtime. Unless you are writing programs that stress the limits of your machine, you will probably never see any of these errors thrown. However, these errors could also be triggered from buggy applets or malicious applets. It is good to see the Java runtime have extensive error checking. This will allow browser vendors to better protect your machine from viruses disguised as applets. Some of these errors could be thrown from the Java bytecode verifier. You will notice that most of these errors fall into two major categories: a virtual machine error or some type of linkage error when trying to load a class.

- **Error.** A generic error class that other runtime errors extend. Allows the storing of a detailed error message.
- **ThreadDeath.** This class extends Error. It is thrown when thread.stop() is called. You should not catch this error since it should be thrown.
- **VirtualMachineError.** This class extends Error. It signals that either the Virtual Machine has run out of resources or it has an unrecoverable internal error.
- **StackOverflowError.** This class extends VirtualMachineError. It signals an error that indicates the Java virtual machine's runtime stack has overflowed. There are usually only two ways this can be caused: passing very large objects on the stack by value, which is currently impossible in Java; or runaway recursion. Source 6.9 demonstrates runaway recursion.

SOURCE 6.9 BadRecurse.java

```
// BadRecurse.java
package jwiley.chp6;

/** Class designed to exhaust the stack. */
class BadRecurse
{
    /** number of function calls. */
    static long numCalls=0;
    /** Method to invoke. */
    static void badFunc(long dummy)
    {
        numCalls++;
        if (numCalls % 1000 == 0)
                System.out.println("numCalls : " + numCalls);
        badFunc(numCalls);
    }

    /** main() method to invoke from JVM. */
    public static void main(String args[])
    {
        try
        {
            badFunc(0);
        } catch (Error e)
          {
            System.out.println(e.toString());
          }
    }
}
```

A run of Source 6.9 produces:

```
C:\java\bin>java jwiley.chp6.BadRecurse
numCalls : 1000
numCalls : 2000
numCalls : 3000
numCalls : 4000
numCalls : 5000
numCalls : 6000
numCalls : 7000
numCalls : 8000
java.lang.StackOverflowError
```

TIP You can modify the behavior of Source 6.9 by setting the –oss parameter when invoking the java virtual machine. The –oss parameter allows you to specify the size of each stack within a Thread.

- **OutOfMemoryError.** This class extends VirtualMachineError. It occurs when the Java runtime cannot satisfy a memory request. Source 6.10 demonstrates a program gobbling an extraordinary amount of memory and causing the VM to run out.

SOURCE 6.10 BadGobble.java

```
// BadGobble.java
package jwiley.chp6;

/** Class designed to exhaust the heap. */
class BadGobble
{
    /** total # of bytes gobbled. */
    static long totalMemRequested=0;
    /** # bytes gobble this time. */
    static int numBytes=0;
    /** array to gobble to. */
    static char cArray[];
    /** method to gobble memory.*/
    static void badGobble()
    {
        numBytes += 1000;
        totalMemRequested += numBytes;
        cArray = new char[numBytes];
        if (numBytes % 100000 == 0)
                System.out.println("numBytes : " + numBytes);
    }

    /** main() method to invoke from JVM. */
    public static void main(String args[])
    {
        try
        {
          while (true)
            badGobble();
        } catch (Error e)
          {
            System.out.println(e.toString());
            System.out.println("Total memory requested was: " +
                                    totalMemRequested);
          }
    }
}
```

A run of Source 6.10 produces:

```
C:\java\bin>java jwiley.chp6.BadGobble
numBytes : 100000
numBytes : 200000
numBytes : 300000
numBytes : 400000
numBytes : 500000
numBytes : 600000
numBytes : 700000
numBytes : 800000
numBytes : 900000
java.lang.OutOfMemoryError
Total memory requested was: 476776000
```

TIP You can also modify the behavior of Source 6.10 by setting the –mx parameter when running the java virtual machine. The –mx parameter allows you to set the maximum heap size for the java virtual machine.

- **UnknownError.** This class extends VirtualMachineError. An unknown error with the Virtual Machine. This error should never occur. If you get this error, file a bug report with JavaSoft at http://www.javasoft.com.
- **InternalError.** This class extends VirtualMachineError. An unexpected internal error within the Virtual Machine. This error should never occur. If you get this error, file a bug report with JavaSoft at http://www.javasoft.com.
- **LinkageError.** This class extends Error. Many subclasses extend this class. This class and all its subclasses indicate that a class has a dependency on another class; however, the latter class has incompatibly changed after the compilation of the first class. This only occurs if you change the class in some abnormal way. Normally a class is neatly defined into a private implementation and public interface. As long as the public interface does not change (often known as the "contract"), or classes outside the package do not access the private implementation, you should not have any problems. However, if you violate the rules just given you could see a subclass of Linkage error be thrown.
- **ExceptionInInitializerError.** This class extends LinkageError. An unexpected exception was thrown in a static initializer.
- **NoClassDefFoundError.** This class extends LinkageError. The Virtual Machine cannot find a class. This could occur if the <classname>.class file existed during compilation but was later accidentally deleted or moved (moved outside of the CLASSPATH environment variable). Source 6.11 demonstrates this situation.

SOURCE 6.11 NoClass.java

```
// NoClass.java
package jwiley.chp6;

import noExist;

/** Class designed to not find noExist class. */
public class NoClass
{
    /** main() method to invoke from JVM. */
    public static void main(String args[])
    {
        noExist aClass = new noExist();
        aClass.noMethod();
    }
}
```

A run of Source 6.11 produces:

```
C:\java\bin>java noClass
Exception in thread "main" java.lang.NoClassDefFoundError: noExist
        at
```

- **ClassCircularityError.** This class extends LinkageError. A circular reference has been detected while initializing a class. If the static initializer of class A uses a class B that has not been loaded, the run time then loads class B and tries to initialize it. If class B uses class A, an impossible to fulfill circular dependency has been created (a classic Catch 22).
- **ClassFormatError.** This class extends LinkageError. It indicates the detection of an invalid file format while attempting to load a class.
- **VerifyError.** This class extends LinkageError. A verification error has occurred when verifying the bytecodes of a class being loaded.
- **UnsatisfiedLinkError.** Extends LinkageError. This class is thrown if a native was declared native but the runtime cannot find the dynamic library to link to, or has linked to the specified library but the method is not part of that library.
- **IncompatibleClassChangeError.** This class extends LinkageError. Several classes extend this one. Again, the basic reason for this error is when a class with dependencies is changed in an incompatible way. Four specific changes will cause this exception:

  1. A variable is changed from static to non-static without recompiling other classes that still use the variable as static.
  2. A variable is changed from non-static to static without recompiling other classes that use the variable as a non-static.

3. A field is deleted but is still used in other classes that access the field.
4. A method is deleted but classes that use it are not recompiled.

- **NoSuchMethodError.** Extends IncompatibleClassChangeError. A method could not be found. See IncompatibleClassChangeError for the reason why.
- **NoSuchFieldError.** Extends IncompatibleClassChangeError. A field could not be found. See IncompatibleClassChangeError for the reason why.
- **AbstractMethodError.** This class extends IncompatibleClassChangeError. This is thrown if there was an attempt by the runtime to call an abstract method.
- **IllegalAccessError.** This class extends IncompatibleClassChangeError. An illegal access has occurred.
- **InstantiationError.** This class extends IncompatibleClassChangeError. This class is thrown if the interpreter attempts to instantiate an abstract class or interface.

Exceptions. The purpose and use of Exceptions have already been discussed in section 3.4. Here we will examine the Exception classes thrown by either the Java lang classes or the Java virtual machine.

- **Exception.** An exception is an abnormal condition that programs should attempt to catch and handle. All classes that extend this class are "checked exceptions." A checked exception must either be handled, or specified in the method prototype that this method throws such an exception.
- **InterruptedException.** This class extends Exception. It is thrown by a thread when a thread with a higher priority has interrupted it.
- **ClassNotFoundException.** This class extends Exception. It is thrown if a class cannot be found.
- **InstantiationException.** This class extends Exception. It is thrown when a method attempts to dynamically create an object using Class.newInstance() or some similar mechanism on an Abstract class.
- **IllegalAccessException.** This class extends Exception. It is thrown when a method attempts to dynamically create an object using Class.newInstance() or some similar mechanism but doesn't have the proper access privileges to create objects of that class.
- **NoSuchFieldException.** This class extends Exception. A field could not be found.
- **NoSuchMethodException.** This class extends Exception. A method could not be found.
- **RuntimeException.** An exception thrown by the Virtual Machine that can reasonably occur. You are not forced to catch these exceptions as you are with exceptions that extend the Exception class. Source 6.12 demonstrates the requirement for catching Exceptions but not RuntimeExceptions. Classes that extend this class are referred to as "unchecked exceptions." Since these exceptions can be common (like running out of memory), nearly every class would be forced to handle these types of exceptions. This would overly burden programmers. All exceptions that you create should subclass Exception and not RuntimeException.

SOURCE 6.12 ThrowException.java

```
// ThrowException.java
package jwiley.chp6;

/** Class to represent a RuntimeException. */
class SeriousException extends RuntimeException
{
    /** constructor. */
    SeriousException()
    { super("A really bad exception."); }
}

/** Class to represent an exception we can handle. */
class RecoverableException extends Exception
{
    /** constructor. */
    RecoverableException()
    { super("catch this"); }
}

/** Class to throw both types of exceptions. */
public class ThrowException
{
    /** main() method to invoke from JVM. */
    public static void main(String args[]) throws RecoverableException
    {
        try
        {
            throw new SeriousException();
        } catch(Exception e)
          {
            e.toString();
          }
          finally
          {
            throw new RecoverableException();
          }
    }
}
```

A run of Source 6.12 produces:

```
C:\1-1update\src11>java jwiley.chp6.ThrowException
jwiley.chp6.RecoverableException: catch this
        at jwiley.chp6.ThrowException.main(ThrowException.java:35)
```

It is very important to note that when creating exceptions you should extend the Exception class. The RuntimeException class is reserved for exceptions that the Virtual Machine can throw. The only difference a runtime exception makes is that you are not forced to "propagate" the exception if you do not catch it; however, to produce extremely reliable code you should catch and handle all exceptions to include the runtime exceptions.

- **ArithmeticException.** This class extends RuntimeException. It is thrown when an arithmetic exception like a divide by zero occurs.
- **ClassCastException.** This class extends RuntimeException. It is thrown when an attempt is made to cast an Object of type A into an Object of type C when A is not a C nor a subclass of C. Source 6.13 demonstrates legal and illegal casts.

SOURCE 6.13 TestCast.java

```
// TestCast.java
package jwiley.chp6;

/** Class to represent a super class. */
class A
{
    /** data member. */
    int a;
    /** constructor. */
    A()
    { System.out.println("I am A"); }
}

/** Class to represent subclass of A. */
class Ason extends A
{
    /** data member. */
    int b;
    /** constructor. */
    Ason()
    { System.out.println("I am son of A"); }
}

/** Class to represent another class. */
class C
{
    /** data member. */
    int c;
    /** constructor. */
    C()
    { System.out.println("I am C"); }
}

/** Class to demonstrate casting types. */
public class TestCast
{
```

```
    /** main() method to invoke from JVM. */
    public static void main(String args[])
    {
        A anA = new A();
        Ason B = new Ason();
        C aC = new C();

        A A2 = (A) B;                // legal
        // Ason B2 = (Ason) anA;     // invalid cannot downcast
        // Ason B3 = (Ason) aC;      - invalid cast
        // C C2 = (C) anA;           - invalid cast
    }
}
```

A run of Source 6.13 produces:

```
C:\1-1update\src11>java jwiley.chp6.testCast
I am A
I am A
I am son of A
I am C
```

- **ArrayStoreException.** This class extends RuntimeException. It is thrown when an attempt is made to store the wrong type in an array.
- **NullPointerException.** This class extends RuntimeException. This is one of the most common exceptions thrown. It is thrown any time a null object is used to access a method. Source 6.14 demonstrates this.

SOURCE 6.14 UseNull.java

```
// UseNull.java
package jwiley.chp6;

/** Class to demonstrate illegal reference use. */
public class UseNull
{
    /** main() method to invoke from JVM. */
    public static void main(String args[])
    {
        String myName = null;

        // oops forgot to assign it a valid String
        System.out.println("My name is " + myName);

        // cannot trim a null
        myName.trim();
    }
}
```

A run of Source 6.14 produces:

```
C:\java\bin>java jwiley.chp6.UseNull
My name is null
Exception in thread "main" java.lang.NullPointerException
        at useNull.main(useNull.java:10)
```

- **NegativeArraySizeException.** This class extends RuntimeException. It is thrown if an attempt is made to create an array with a negative size.
- **IllegalArgumentException.** This class extends RuntimeException. It is extended further by other, more specific exceptions. In general, it indicates an illegal argument has occurred. See NumberFormatException for a specific example.
- **IllegalMonitorStateException.** This class extends RuntimeException. It is thrown whenever a thread synchronization routine is called on an object by a thread that doesn't own the monitor of that object. As an example, it will be thrown if you call Object.wait() without explicitly synchronizing on that object.
- **IllegalStateException.** This class extends RuntimeException. It is thrown when a method is called at an inappropriate time.
- **IllegalThreadStateException.** This class extends the IllegalArgumentException class. It is thrown if a thread is not in the proper state for the requested operation. As an example, it will be thrown if you try call Thread.stop() before a call to Thread.run().
- **NumberFormatException.** This class extends IllegalArgumentException. It is thrown if an invalid number format occurs. This is a very common exception that is easily thrown. Source 6.15 demonstrates this exception being thrown. You should always catch and handle this exception.

SOURCE 6.15 BadFormat.java

```
// BadFormat.java
import java.io.BufferedReader;
import java.io.InputStreamReader;
import java.io.IOException;

/** Class designed to demonstrate incorrect formatting. */
public class BadFormat
{
    /** main() method to invoke from the JVM. */
    public static void main(String args[])
    {
        BufferedReader br = new BufferedReader(
                                 new InputStreamReader(System.in));
        System.out.print("Enter an Integer: ");
        System.out.flush();
        String numStr = null;
```

```
        try
        {
            numStr = br.readLine();
        } catch (IOException ioe)
          {
            ioe.printStackTrace();
            System.exit(1);
          }

        System.out.println("numStr is : " + numStr);
        int theNum = Integer.parseInt(numStr);
    }
}
```

A run of Source 6.15 produces:

```
C:\java\bin>java jwiley.chp6.BadFormat
Enter an Integer: abc
numStr is : abc
Exception in thread "main" java.lang.NumberFormatException: abc
        at java.lang.Integer.parseInt(Integer.java:139)
        at java.lang.Integer.parseInt(Integer.java:159)
        at badFormat.main(badFormat.java:21)
```

- **IndexOutOfBoundsException.** This class extends RuntimeException. It is thrown if an index is out of bounds. This class is extended by specific classes for strings and arrays.
- **ArrayIndexOutOfBoundsException.** This class extends IndexOutOfBoundsException. It is thrown if an array index is out of range.
- **StringIndexOutOfBoundsException.** This class extends IndexOutOfBoundsException. It is thrown if a string index is out of range.
- **SecurityException.** This class extends RuntimeException. It is thrown if there is a violation of the security policy set by the SecurityManager class (see Chapter 17).

6.3 THE JAVA.LANG.REFLECT PACKAGE

The classes in java.lang.reflect together implement Reflection. As mentioned previously, Reflection is the ability for a class to expose its interface at run time to other objects. Reflection can be used to write a Java program that can interact with classes that are not available when the program itself is written. Such mechanisms are inherently difficult to use because while it is possible to identify the interface of a class, it is impossible to determine its meaning. Programs that use reflection will typically need to accept some user input to help interpret the meaning of a class.

TIP: **Advanced Users Only** Reflection is an advanced Java concept, and difficult to use correctly. Most developers will never need to use these classes, unless they are implementing a JavaBean container application.

Interfaces. There is only one interface in the java.lang.reflect package.

- **Member.** An interface to be shared by all classes that represent members. This interface describes methods that can be used with any reflected member.

Member Classes. A member class is a reflection class that is used to represent a member (field, method, or constructor) of a Java class.

- **Constructor.** Represents a constructor of a Java class. Constructor objects can be used to create new instances of the class they belong to.
- **Field.** Represents a field of a Java class. Field objects can be used to access static fields of a class as well as instance fields of an object.
- **Method.** Represents a method of a Java class. Method objects can be used to invoke static methods of a class as well as instance methods of an object.

Utility classes. These classes provide additional reflection functionality that is not directly related to class structures.

- **Array.** A utility class for dealing with arrays. Array objects can be used to create new arrays as well as access the elements of an existing array.
- **Modifier.** A utility class for interpreting member and class modifier information. Reflection uses integers to indicate which modifiers apply to a given member. The modifier class implements methods that indicate whether specific modifiers are represented by such integers.

Exceptions. There is only one reflection exception. It is used to represent all possible conditions that can occur through reflection.

- **InvocationTargetException.** A generic exception that indicates some failure during a reflection operation. This exception usually contains another exception that caused the initial failure.

Using Reflection to Examine a Class

With the addition of reflection to the Java specification, Class representation becomes more important. As in Java 1.02, the core Java class java.lang.Class is used to represent classes; however, the use and functionality of this class has been greatly expanded. In Java 1.02, java.lang.Class objects represented only Java classes and interfaces. In Java 1.2, Class objects represent classes, interfaces, arrays, and primitives including the special type void. The methods isPrimitive, isArray, and isInterface can be used to distinguish between the different types of Class objects. All three methods return a boolean indicating whether or not the Class object satisfies the condition.

At most one of the three methods will return true for a particular Class object. If all three methods return false, then the Class object represents a regular Java class.

Reflection allows programmers to examine four types of members of class structures: fields, constructors, methods, and inner classes. The following table details which members exist for each of the four types of Class objects.

Class Type	*Fields*	*Constructors*	*Methods*	*Inner Classes*
Class	Yes	Yes	Yes	Yes
Interface	No	Yes	Yes	No
Array	Yes	No	Yes	No
Primitive	No	No	No	No

Members of a class fall into two categories: public and declared. Public members are all public members defined on a class or any superclass or inherited interface. Declared members are all public, protected, private, and package (default) members defined on a class, ignoring any inherited members.

The java.lang.Class methods getField, getMethod, and getConstructor search a class for a particular public member and return it if it is found. If the member is not found, then a NoSuchMethodException orNoSuchFieldException is thrown. GetFields, getMethods, and getConstructors return arrays of all public members of a class. A valid array is always returned; however, if no valid members exist, a zero length array is returned.

The java.lang.Class methods getDeclaredField, getDeclaredMethod, and getDeclaredConstructor search a class for a particular declared member and return it if it is found. If the member is not found, then a NoSuchMethodException or NoSuchFieldException is thrown. GetDeclaredFields, getDeclaredMethods, and getDeclaredConstructors return arrays of all public members of a class. A valid array is always returned; however, if no valid members exist, a zero length array is returned.

The use of the methods just discussed is subject to security restrictions imposed by the security manager. If the examination of a class structure is disallowed, then a SecurityException is thrown.

All classes and class members (fields, methods, and constructors) have a name and some modifiers. The name is simply the identifier of the field, constructor, or method. For constructors, the name is always the same as the name of the class.

Modifiers indicate which of the Java behavior modifying keywords were used in the definition of the class or member. Valid modifiers are abstract, final, interface, native, private, protected, public, static, synchronized, transient, and volatile. Modifiers are represented as integers; the class java.lang.reflect.Modifier can be used to interpret these integers. For each object type, only a subset of the modifiers can exist. For instance, fields can be final, private, protected, public, static, transient, or volatile, but not abstract, interface, native, or synchronized. For more information on the use and meaning of these modifiers, see Chapter 3.

There are four cases where data type information can be examined. All fields have a corresponding data type, all methods have a return value data type, and all constructors and methods have parameter data type lists and exception data type lists. Parameter and exception data type lists are represented as arrays of Class objects (which can be zero length), whereas field data types and method return data types are represented as singular Class objects.

Source 6.16 illustrates the use of the java.lang.Class class to iterate through the contents of a class. The class jwiley.chp6.ClassInspector displays to the console the public members of any Java class.

SOURCE 6.16 ClassInspector Implementation

```
// ClassInspector.java
package jwiley.chp6;

import java.lang.reflect.*;

/**
 * Class to enumerate all fields, methods and constructors of a Java class.
 * The output of this class is similar to the JDK utility javap
 */
public class ClassInspector
{
    /**
     * Translates an array of exceptions into a throws clause
     */
    public static void PrintExceptions(Class exceptions[])
    {
        if (exceptions.length != 0)
            System.out.print(" throws ");

        for (int i = 0; i < exceptions.length; i++)
        {
            if (i != 0)
            {
                System.out.print(", ");
            }
            System.out.print(exceptions[i].getName());
        }

        System.out.println();
    }

    /**
     * Converts an array of classes into a parameter list for a function
     */
    public static void PrintParameters(Class params[])
    {
        System.out.print("(");
        for (int i = 0; i < params.length; i++)
```

```
    {
        if (i != 0)
        {
            System.out.print(", ");
        }
        System.out.print(params[i].getName());
    }
    System.out.print(")");
}

/**
 * Prints all fields for a class as they would
 * appear in a java source file
 */
public static void PrintFields(Field fields[])
{
    System.out.println("Fields:");
    if (fields.length == 0)
    {
        System.out.println("\tNo public fields");
    } else {
        for (int i = 0; i < fields.length; i++)
        {
            System.out.println("\t" +
                Modifier.toString(fields[i].getModifiers()) + " " +
                fields[i].getType().getName() + " " +
                fields[i].getName());
        }
    }
}

/**
 * Prints the signatures of all methods in a class as they
 * would be displayed by javap
 */
public static void PrintMethods(Method methods[])
{
    System.out.println("Methods:");
    if (methods.length == 0)
    {
        System.out.println("\tNo public methods");
    } else {
        for (int i = 0; i < methods.length; i++)
        {
            System.out.print("\t" +
                Modifier.toString(methods[i].getModifiers()) +
                " " + methods[i].getReturnType().getName() + " " +
                methods[i].getName());
            PrintParameters(methods[i].getParameterTypes());
            PrintExceptions(methods[i].getExceptionTypes());
        }
    }
}
```

```
    /**
     * Prints the signatures of all constructors in a class as they
     * would be displayed by javap
     */
    public static void PrintConstructors(Constructor constructors[])
    {
        System.out.println("Constructors:");
        if (constructors.length == 0)
        {
            System.out.println("\tNo public constructors");
        } else {
            for (int i = 0; i < constructors.length; i++)
            {
                System.out.print("\t" +
                        Modifier.toString(constructors[i].getModifiers()) +
                        " " + constructors[i].getName());
                PrintParameters(constructors[i].getParameterTypes());
                PrintExceptions(constructors[i].getExceptionTypes());
            }
        }
    }

    /**
     * Examines the structure of a class and prints
     * the structure to the console
     */
    public static void Inspect(Class c)
    {
        System.out.println("Contents of class " + c.getName());
        PrintFields(c.getFields());
        PrintConstructors(c.getConstructors());
        PrintMethods(c.getMethods());
    }

    /**
     * Allows users to invoke the ClassInspector from the command
     * line.  This routine expects the name of the class to inspect
     * to be entered as a command line argument
     */
    public static void main(String[] argv) throws ClassNotFoundException
    {
        if (argv.length == 0)
        {
            System.out.println("USAGE: java ClassInspector <class name>");
            return;
        }

        Class c = Class.forName(argv[0]);
        Inspect(c);
    }
}
```

A run of Source 6.16 produces:

```
C:\java\bin>java jwiley.chp6.ClassInspector java.lang.Number
Contents of class java.lang.Number
Fields:
     No public fields
Constructors:
     public java.lang.Number()
Methods:
     public final native java.lang.Class getClass()
     public native int hashCode()
     public boolean equals(java.lang.Object)
     public java.lang.String toString()
     public final native void notify()
     public final native void notifyAll()
     public final native void wait(long) throws
java.lang.InterruptedException
     public final void wait(long, int) throws
java.lang.InterruptedException
     public final void wait() throws java.lang.InterruptedException
     public abstract int intValue()
     public abstract long longValue()
     public abstract float floatValue()
     public abstract double doubleValue()
     public byte byteValue()
     public short shortValue()
```

Using Reflection to Create an Object

Java 1.02 had the ability to create instances of any class types through the newInstance method on the java.lang.Class object. This ability, however, was limited because it could only be used on classes implementing a zero argument constructor.

Reflection provides an alternative mechanism to create object instances, but can work for all constructors, not just those that take no arguments. Calling constructors through reflection is subjected to the same privilege restrictions that are enforced in the language. For example, you cannot use reflection to create an object that only has private constructors.

The first step in creating an object using reflection is to acquire a reference to desired constructor object. The newInstance method is then called on that constructor object. Assuming an exception is not thrown, newInstance returns an object created by that constructor. NewInstance takes a single argument, an array of objects. This array should contain the parameters to be passed to the constructor. If the desired constructor takes no arguments, then the argument to newInstance is ignored, and can be null. The contents of the object array must match the signature of the constructor being called with a few exceptions. If a parameter has a primitive type (such as int, float, etc.) then the Class corresponding to the primitive should be used (i.e., java.lang.Integer, java.lang.Float, etc.). In addition, a less precise data type may be substituted for a more precise type. Specifically, a short may be substituted for an integer or long, an integer may be substituted for a long, a float may be substituted for a double, and so forth.

There are four different exceptions that can be thrown when invoking constructors through this mechanism: InstantiationException, IllegalAccessException, IllegalArgumentException, and InvocationTargetException. An InstantiationException occurs when the class being constructed is an abstract class. An IllegalAccessException occurs when the constructor is not available due to the Java language access control. An IllegalArgumentException occurs when the incorrect number of arguments is supplied, or when one or more arguments are of the incorrect data type and cannot be coerced to the required type. An InvocationTargetException indicates that the constructor being invoked threw an exception. Calling the method getTargetException on an InvocationTargetException will return the actual exception thrown by the constructor.

TIP: Proper Use of Reflection The problem with this mechanism is that it forces the programmer to make assumptions about the meanings of the arguments to a constructor. In an actual application, it is likely that some user intervention will be required in order to construct objects through this mechanism. As mentioned previously, reflection is an advanced topic and should not be used by most Java programmers.

Source 6.17 uses reflection to create objects of an arbitrary class specified on the command line. The program first attempts to use a default constructor (one which has no arguments). If no such constructor exists, then the program attempts to locate a constructor that takes one string argument. For these constructors, an empty string is supplied as the lone argument. If neither of these two constructor types can be located, or the constructors are not public, then the program throws an Exception indicating that the class cannot be instantiated.

SOURCE 6.17 ClassCreator Implementation

```
// ClassCreator.java
package jwiley.chp6;

import java.lang.reflect.*;

/**
 * Class which creates objects of arbitrary types as long
 * as either a default constructor or a constructor which
 * takes a single string argument is available
 */
public class ClassCreator
{
```

```
/** Private constructor for demonstration purposes
 */
private ClassCreator(String strArg) {}

/**
 * Creates and returns an object of an arbitrary type.
 * If the class doesn't have a default constructor or
 * a constructor which takes a single string argument
 * then an exception is thrown.
 */
public static Object CreateClass(String strClassName) throws
  IllegalAccessException,
  InvocationTargetException,
  InstantiationException,
  ClassNotFoundException
 {
    // First we need to load the class
    Class c = Class.forName(strClassName);

    // Now, enumerate the constructors
    Constructor constructors[] = c.getDeclaredConstructors();

    // first look for a constructor which takes zero args
    for (int i= 0; i < constructors.length; i++)
    {
        if (constructors[i].getParameterTypes().length == 0)
        {
            return constructors[i].newInstance(null);
        }
    }

    // Ok, that didn't work, now look for a constructor which
    // takes a single string.  We'll pass in an empty string ""
    for (int i= 0; i < constructors.length; i++)
    {
        Class classString = Class.forName("java.lang.String");
        Class paramTypes[] = constructors[i].getParameterTypes();

        if (paramTypes.length == 1 &&
            classString.equals(paramTypes[0]))
        {
            Object args[] = new Object[1];
            args[0] = new String("");
            return constructors[i].newInstance(args);
        }
    }

    throw new InstantiationException(
        "Couldn't find appropriate constructor");
 }
```

```
    /**
     * Main routine so the class can be tested from the command line.
     * A class name is expected to be passed in on the command line
     */
    public static void main(String argv[]) throws Exception
    {
        if (argv.length == 0)
        {
            System.out.println("USAGE: java ClassCreator <class name>");
            return;
        }

        try
        {
            Object obj = CreateClass(argv[0]);
            System.out.println("Class created successfully!");
        } catch (Exception ex)
          {
            ex.printStackTrace(System.out);
          }
    }
}
```

A run of Source 6.17 produces:

```
C:\java\bin>java jwiley.chp6.ClassCreator java.lang.ClassLoader
java.lang.InstantiationException: java/lang/ClassLoader
     at jwiley.chp6.ClassCreator.CreateClass(ClassCreator.java:36)
     at jwiley.chp6.ClassCreator.main(ClassCreator.java:72)
C:\java\bin>java jwiley.chp6.ClassCreator java.lang.String
Class created successfully!
```

Using Reflection to Invoke a Method or Access a Field

Invoking a method on an object is very similar to calling a constructor on a class. Again, one must start with a reference to the desired method object. The invoke method on a method object is similar to the newInstance method on a constructor object with two important differences. First, invoke returns an object that is the return value from the method being invoked instead of a reference to a new object. Second, invoke takes two arguments instead of one. The first argument is an object, the second is an array of objects. For static methods, the first argument is ignored, and can be null. For instance methods, the first argument must be a reference to an object that is either an instance of the class that implements the method or a reference to an object that inherits from the class or interface that implements the method.

Because instance method invocations are dynamically looked up based on the actual class of the object, invoking a method object may result in an overloaded version of that method being called.

The second argument is an array of objects. This array should contain the parameters to be passed to the method. If the desired method takes no arguments, then this argument is ignored, and can be null. The contents of the object array must match the signature of the method being called, with a few exceptions. If a parameter has a primitive type (int, float, etc.) then the Class corresponding to the primitive should be used (i.e., java.lang.Integer, java.lang.Float, etc.). In addition, a less precise data type may be substituted for a more precise type. Specifically, a short may be substituted for an integer or long, an integer may be substituted for a long, a float may be substituted for a double, and so forth.

There are three different exceptions that can be thrown when invoking constructors through this mechanism: IllegalAccessException, IllegalArgumentException, and InvocationTargetException. An IllegalAccessException occurs when the method is not available due to the Java language access control. An IllegalArgumentException occurs when the incorrect number of arguments is supplied, or when one or more arguments are of the incorrect data type and cannot be coerced to the required type. An InvocationTargetException indicates that the method being invoked threw an exception. Calling the method getTargetException on an InvocationTargetException will return the actual exception thrown by the constructor.

TIP: Proper Use of Reflection The problem with this mechanism is that it forces the programmer to make assumptions about the meanings of the arguments to a method. In an actual application, it is likely that some user intervention will be required in order to invoke methods through this mechanism. As mentioned previously, reflection is an advanced topic and should not be used by most Java programmers.

Source 6.18 uses reflection to invoke a method on an arbitrary class specified on the command line, using a field of that class as an argument to the method. The program only works for classes that have an instance method that takes a single string as an argument. The class must also have an instance variable that is a string. The example program creates an object of this class, looks up the value of the field, and supplies it as an argument to the method. If the class does not meet these precise conditions, then the program will throw an exception indicating why the class was not acceptable.

In general, it is much easier to use interfaces to access classes in a generic way. Reflection should only be used when there is absolutely no compile-time information available about a class.

SOURCE 6.18 ClassInvoker Implementation

```
// ClassInvoker.java
package jwiley.chp6;

import java.lang.reflect.*;

/**
 * Uses reflection to examine the structure of a class for specific features
 * if the class has all of the expected features, then an
 * object is created, a field is examined, and a method is
 * invoked.  For simpler testing, this class implements the
 * exact features it requires in order to invoke the method.
 */
public class ClassInvoker
{
    /**
     * String data member for ClassInvoker.  This member only
     * exists so that ClassInvoker will support the features required
     * of classes it will work with.
     */
    public String strMsg = "This is a very complex way to call a method!";

    /**
     * A method which takes a single string as an argument.  This
     * method only exists so that ClassInvoker will support the
     * features required of classes it will work with.
     */
    public void TestMethod(String strArg)
    {
        System.out.println(strArg);
    }

    /**
     * Uses reflection to examine a class for the following two properties:
     * 1) An instance variable which is a String reference
     * 2) A method which takes a single string as an argument
     * If the class meets those criteria, then an object is created,
     * and the method is called, using the string field as an argument
     * to the method.
     */
    public static void InvokeClass(String strClassName) throws Exception
    {
        Object obj = ClassCreator.CreateClass(strClassName);
        Class c = Class.forName(strClassName);
        Class classString = Class.forName("java.lang.String");

        Field theField = null;
        Method theMethod = null;
```

```
        // find the first instance variable on the class which is a string
        Field fields[] = c.getFields();
        for (int i = 0; i < fields.length; i++)
        {
            if (!Modifier.isStatic(fields[i].getModifiers()) &&
                classString.equals(fields[i].getType()))
            {
                theField = fields[i];
                break;
            }
        }

        if (theField == null)
        {
            throw new InstantiationException(
                        "Could not find a valid field");
        }

        // find the first method which takes a single string argument
        Method methods[] = c.getMethods();
        for (int i = 0; i < methods.length; i++)
        {
            if (!Modifier.isStatic(methods[i].getModifiers()))
            {
                Class params[] = methods[i].getParameterTypes();
                if (params.length == 1 && classString.equals(params[0]))
                {
                    theMethod = methods[i];
                    break;
                }
            }
        }

        if (theMethod == null)
        {
            throw new InstantiationException(
                        "Could not find a valid field");
        }

        Object args[] = new Object[1];
        args[0] = theField.get(obj);

        theMethod.invoke(obj, args);
    }

    /**
     * Allows users to invoke the ClassInspector from the command
     * line.  This routine expects the name of the class to inspect
     * to be entered as a command line argument
     */
```

```
    public static void main(String argv[]) throws Exception
    {
        if (argv.length == 0)
        {
            System.out.println("USAGE: java ClassInvoker <class name>");
            return;
        }

        InvokeClass(argv[0]);
    }
}
```

A run of Source 6.18 produces:

```
C:\java\bin>java jwiley.chp6.ClassInvoker jwiley.chp6.ClassInvoker
This is a very complex way to call a method!
```

6.4 SUMMARY

The java.lang package provides classes that are fundamental elements of the Java language. It is impossible to write a Java application or applet without using at least some of these classes. There are wrapper classes for all of the primitive data types as well as two classes used to implement strings. Java.lang packages implement key features of the Java language including threads and exceptions. Finally, classes in this package provide platform-independent access to the underlying operating system, allowing Java programmers to create and manage processes, access environment variables, and access low-level Java mechanisms such as the Java classloader.

The java.lang.reflect package provides classes that implement reflection, the ability of a class to expose its interface at run time, as opposed to compile time. Reflection can be used to access static fields and static methods. Reflection also enables Java programs to create objects of arbitrary classes, even if the class has no default constructor. Finally, reflection can be used to access instance fields, and invoke instance methods on those fields.

Reflection is a very advanced mechanism that most users should never use. Using reflection is difficult, cumbersome, and can lead to all sorts of unnecessary problems. Reflection was added to the Java language specification in order to support Java Beans, more specifically to support the creation of container applications for Java Beans. In most cases, using Java interfaces is a more suitable alternative to reflection.

CHAPTER 7

Package java.util

OBJECTIVE

This package is a utility package of classes that provides common storage classes, date and time classes, locale and resource classes, and a subpackage that contains compression classes. In this chapter you will learn how to use the classes in each of these categories, and why they are useful to a Java programmer.

The java.util package provides a wealth of classes that come in handy when developing applications. Classes for object storage and retrieval, resource management, date retrieval, and others, are all included in the java.util package. It makes life so much easier having a utility package instead of having to fish through obscure include files to find the functions you want. The java.util package can be divided up into the following major categories:

- **Containers.** This category of classes consists of classes that perform efficient storage and retrieval of other objects.
- **Date/Time.** This category provides date and time retrieval classes. The classes have been designed with internationalization in mind, so they are flexible enough to handle different calendar systems and different time zones.
- **Resource.** This category provides classes for managing resources. Resources can be as simple as text strings used in your program, or as complicated as user-defined objects used in your program. In conjunction with the Locale class, the Resource class can be used to manage different resources for different languages and countries.
- **Miscellaneous utilities.** The rest of the utilities in this package do not belong to a specific category.

A separate package, java.util.zip, provides compression utility functions. The functions in this package give the programmer the ability to compress and decompress information using the ZLIB compression library.

7.1 CONTAINERS

Containers are classes that store and retrieve objects. All of the containers except BitSet can operate on ANY Java object. There is no requirement for the containers to hold a homogeneous sequence of objects. When you need to recall an object from a container you can use Java safe-casting to cast to the type of object you want. Let's take a look at the containers provided in this package:

- **Dictionary.** An abstract class that describes an associative set. An associative set maps keys to values. This class is the abstract parent of HashTable.
- **HashTable.** This class extends Dictionary. A hash table is an efficient random access storage technique that uses a hash function (the method hashCode() in this class) to change the key into an array index. If two keys map to the same index a collision list is created.
- **Properties.** This class extends HashTable. A persistent hash table is created that can be saved to a stream and loaded from a stream. This class is often used to save or recall parameters for an application. Source 7.1 shows an example of recalling a parameter from a property file.

SOURCE 7.1 TestProperties.java

```
package jwiley.chp7;

import java.io.FileInputStream;
import java.io.IOException;
import java.util.Properties;

public class TestProperties
{
    public static void main (String args[])
    {
        if (args.length != 1)
        {
            System.out.println("Usage: java TestProperties <prop>");
            System.exit(0);
        }
```

```
        try {
            FileInputStream fis = new FileInputStream("family.txt");
            Properties props = new Properties();
            props.load(fis);

            String sValue = props.getProperty(args[0]);
            if (sValue == null)
                System.out.println("Property not found.");
            else
                System.out.println("Value: " + sValue);

            fis.close();
        } catch (IOException ioe)
          {
            System.out.println(ioe.toString());
          }
    }
```

A run of Source 7.1 will produce the following:

```
c:\jwiley\chp7>java jwiley.chp7.TestProperties Daughter

Value: Madeline
```

- **Vector.** A growable array class. This class is one of the most useful containers. It provides methods for adding, removing, and accessing elements. The remove methods are especially handy because you can remove objects by specifying the object to remove, or by specifying the index of the object. The Vector class is used in Source 1.7 and in code samples throughout the book.
- **Enumeration.** An interface (section 4.2 describes interfaces in detail; in general they are a set of methods that specify a protocol that one or more classes can implement) that describes the protocol for sequencing through a set of elements until there are no more. There are two methods declared in this interface: hasMoreElements() and nextElement(). Similar in concept to the C++ iterator described in Chapter 3.
- **Stack.** This class extends Vector. It implements a First-In-First-Out queue. A stack is a common data structure that lets you push() and pop() elements from a single side of queue. Source 7.2 demonstrates the use of a Stack in a simple postfix calculator.
- **EmptyStackException.** This class extends RuntimeException. It is thrown when you try to pop() an empty Stack. This can be avoided by testing the empty() method of the Stack as demonstrated in Source 7.2.

SOURCE 7.2 PostFix.java

```
// PostFix.java
package jwiley.chp7;

import java.util.Stack;
import java.io.BufferedReader;
import java.io.InputStreamReader;
import java.io.IOException;

/** Class that represents a PostFix calculator.
    Designed also to demonstrate the Java stack container class. */
class PostFix
{
    /** main() method to invoke from the JVM. */
    public static void main(String args[])
    {
        BufferedReader br =
           new BufferedReader(new InputStreamReader(System.in));
        System.out.println("Simple PostFix calculator.");
        String input=null;

        System.out.println("Valid operations are + - / *");
        System.out.println("Enter 'q' to quit.");

        Stack numberStack = new Stack();

        do
        {
            System.out.print(": ");
            System.out.flush();
            try
            {
                input = br.readLine();
            } catch (IOException ioe)
              {
                System.out.println("IO Error.");
                System.exit(1);
              }

            if (input.equals("+"))
            {
                if (numberStack.size() >= 2)
                {
                    Integer a = (Integer) numberStack.pop();
                    Integer b = (Integer) numberStack.pop();
                    int total = a.intValue() + b.intValue();
                    System.out.println(total);
                    numberStack.push(new Integer(total));
                }
                else
                {
```

```
            System.out.println("In Postfix notation " +
                               "there must be 2 numbers " +
                               "and then an operator.");
        }
    }
    else if (input.equals("-"))
    {
        if (numberStack.size() >= 2)
        {
            Integer a = (Integer) numberStack.pop();
            Integer b = (Integer) numberStack.pop();
            int total = b.intValue() - a.intValue();
            System.out.println(total);
            numberStack.push(new Integer(total));
        }
        else
        {
            System.out.println("In Postfix notation " +
                               "there must be 2 numbers " +
                               "and then an operator.");
        }
    }
    else if (input.equals("/"))
    {
        if (numberStack.size() >= 2)
        {
            Integer a = (Integer) numberStack.pop();
            Integer b = (Integer) numberStack.pop();
            if (a.intValue() != 0)
            {
                    int total = b.intValue() / a.intValue();
                    System.out.println(total);
                    numberStack.push(new Integer(total));
            }
            else
                    System.out.println("Divide by 0 is " +
                                       "illegal.");
        }
        else
        {
            System.out.println("In Postfix notation " +
                               "there must be 2 numbers " +
                               "and then an operator.");
        }
    }
    else if (input.equals("*"))
    {
        if (numberStack.size() >= 2)
        {
            Integer a = (Integer) numberStack.pop();
            Integer b = (Integer) numberStack.pop();
```

```
                    int total = a.intValue() * b.intValue();
                    System.out.println(total);
                    numberStack.push(new Integer(total));
                }
                else
                {
                    System.out.println("In Postfix notation " +
                                       "there must be 2 numbers " +
                                       "and then an operator.");
                }
            }
            else if (input.equals("="))
            {
                // show top of stack
                if (!numberStack.empty())
                {
                    Integer tot = (Integer) numberStack.pop();
                    System.out.println("Total : " + tot);
                }
                else
                {
                    System.out.println("Stack is empty!");
                }
            }
            else if (Character.isDigit(input.charAt(0)))
            {
                int num = Integer.parseInt(input);
                numberStack.push(new Integer(num));
            }
            else if (!input.equals("q")) // unknown input
            {
                System.out.println("Unknown input <" +
                                   input + ">");
            }
        } while (!input.equals("q"));
    }
}
```

A run of Source 7.2 produces:

```
C:\java\bin>java jwiley.chp7.postFix
Simple PostFix calculator.
Valid operations are + - / *
Enter 'q' to quit.
: 10
: 20
: +
30
: 10
: -
20
: 10
```

```
: *
200
: 2
: /
100
: =
Total : 100
: q
```

- **Observer.** An interface that allows the class to be observable by an instance of class Observer.
- **Observable.** A representation of an object or "data" that is being observed by a set of observers. If the object changes, all observers are notified by calling their update() routine (the update() is part of the Observer interface).
- **BitSet.** A growable set of bits. These bits can be set, cleared, read, ANDed, ORed, and XORed.

The Observer/Observable relationship lends itself well to the Model-View-Controller (MVC) paradigm introduced by SmallTalk. In the MVC paradigm the model, view, and controller portions are all separate objects. The model maintains and manages some set of data, the view is a graphical representation of the data, and the controller is used to accept input from the user to update the model. Using the Observer interface and the Observable class it is easy to implement the MVC paradigm in Java. The Observable class can be used to implement the Model, and the Observer interface can be used to implement the View. The Controller class will have to be written separately. Figure 7.1 depicts the Model-View-Controller paradigm with the Java equivalents.

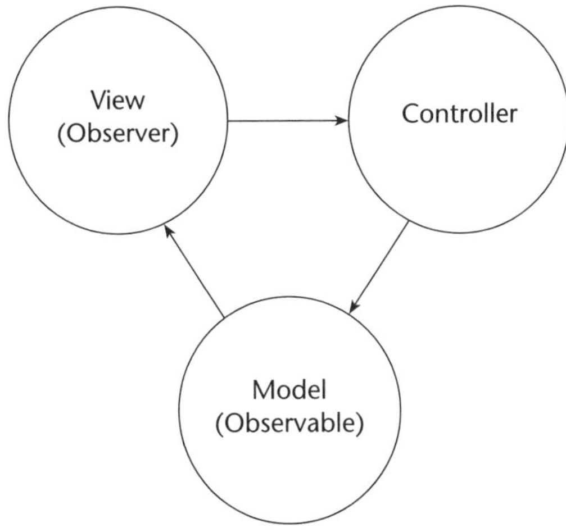

FIGURE 7.1 Model-View-Controller paradigm.

Using the MVC paradigm or the Observable/Observer relationship gives you the flexibility to change the view without affecting the model. The new Swing set of GUI components contained within the JFC allow the MVC architecture to implement a pluggable look and feel for the components. The components can have multiple views and multiple controllers associated with one model. In the following example, we will implement the MVC paradigm and use three different views to display our model. Before we list the code, let's take a look at each class and find out what its role will be. This example makes use of components provided in the AWT. You do not need to know the AWT classes to understand the use of Observer and Observable in this example. For a discussion of the AWT, see Chapter 10.

- **ControllerFrame.** This frame acts as a container for all of the other components. This class in conjunction with the ModelUpdater class serves as the controller.
- **ModelUpdater.** This class in conjunction with the ControllerFrame acts as the controller. When a button is pressed, this class updates the model continuously until the button is released.
- **PositionModel.** This class is the model for our MVC implementation. This class extends Observable and therefore can notify its Observers when a change occurs. This model represents a point being moved around inside of a rectangle. If you use your imagination, you can imagine that it is a person running around a large field.
- **AerialView.** This class is one of the views of our MVC implementation. It uses a GUI component, SimplePositioner, to display the model. This class implements the Observer interface and will receive updates when the model has changed.
- **SideView.** This class is another view of the MVC implementation. It uses a GUI component, SimpleSlider, to display the model. This class implements the Observer interface and will receive updates when the model has changed.

Source 7.3 lists the code for these five classes. The source for SimpleSlider and SimplePositioner are not listed here since they are AWT components, but are included on the CD for your reference.

SOURCE 7.3 ControllerFrame.java

```
// ControllerFrame.java
package jwiley.chp7;

import jwiley.chp10.Grid;
import java.awt.*;
import java.awt.event.*;

/**
 * This class is used as the container for all of the components
 * It relays button presses to ModelUpdater so the PositionModel
 * can be updated.
 *
 * @author Eric Monk
```

```
 * @version 1.0
 */

public class ControllerFrame extends Frame implements MouseListener
{
    Button cmdWest = new Button("W");
    Button cmdNW = new Button("NW");
    Button cmdNorth = new Button("N");
    Button cmdNE = new Button ("NE");
    Button cmdEast = new Button("E");
    Button cmdSE = new Button("SE");
    Button cmdSouth = new Button("S");
    Button cmdSW = new Button("SW");

    PositionModel  pm;
    Thread         t;
    ModelUpdater   modelUpdater;

    public ControllerFrame (String sTitle)
    {
        super(sTitle);

        modelUpdater = new ModelUpdater(this);
        t = new Thread(modelUpdater);
        t.start();

        setLayout(new Grid(3,1));
        setBackground(Color.lightGray);

        // Control Panel
        Panel pnlControl = new Panel();
        pnlControl.setLayout(new Grid(3,5,2,2));

        pnlControl.add("1,3", cmdWest);
        pnlControl.add("1,2", cmdNW);
        pnlControl.add("2,2", cmdNorth);
        pnlControl.add("3,2", cmdNE);
        pnlControl.add("3,3", cmdEast);
        pnlControl.add("3,4", cmdSE);
        pnlControl.add("2,4", cmdSouth);
        pnlControl.add("1,4", cmdSW);

        cmdWest.addMouseListener(this);
        cmdNW.addMouseListener(this);
        cmdNorth.addMouseListener(this);
        cmdNE.addMouseListener(this);
        cmdEast.addMouseListener(this);
        cmdSE.addMouseListener(this);
        cmdSouth.addMouseListener(this);
        cmdSW.addMouseListener(this);
```

```
        // View Panel
        Panel pnlView = new Panel();
        pnlView.setLayout(new Grid(3,5,2,2));

        pm = new PositionModel(new Rectangle(400,400), new Point(200,200));

        AerialView aerialView = new AerialView(pm);
        SideView topView = new SideView(SideView.TOP_BOTTOM_VIEW, pm);
        SideView leftView = new SideView(SideView.LEFT_RIGHT_VIEW, pm);

        pm.addObserver(aerialView);
        pm.addObserver(topView);
        pm.addObserver(leftView);

        pnlView.add("1,1", new Label("Aerial View"));
        pnlView.add("2,1,2,3", aerialView.getCanvas());

        pnlView.add("1,4", new Label("Top View"));
        pnlView.add("2,4,2,1", topView.getCanvas());

        pnlView.add("1,5", new Label("Left View"));
        pnlView.add("2,5,2,1", leftView.getCanvas());

        // Layout Panels
        add("1,1,2,1", pnlView);
        add("3,1", pnlControl);

        setSize(400,250);
        show();
    }

    public void mouseClicked(MouseEvent evt)    {  }
    public void mouseEntered(MouseEvent evt)    {  }
    public void mouseExited(MouseEvent evt)     {  }

    public void mousePressed(MouseEvent evt)
    {
        modelUpdater.setTarget(evt.getsource());
        modelUpdater.setRun(true);
    }

    public void mouseReleased(MouseEvent evt)
    {
        modelUpdater.setRun(false);
    }

    public static void main (String args[])
    {
        new ControllerFrame("Observable/Observer example");
    }
}

// ModelUpdater.java
package jwiley.chp7;
```

```
/**
 * This class is used to update the model based on user input
 *
 * @author Eric Monk
 * @version 1.0
 */

public class ModelUpdater implements Runnable
{
    ControllerFrame controllerFrame;
    Object          target;
    boolean         bRun = false;
    int             iIncrement = 4;

    public ModelUpdater (ControllerFrame controllerFrame)
    {
        this.controllerFrame = controllerFrame;
    }

    public void setTarget (Object target)
    {
        this.target = target;
    }

    public void setRun (boolean bRun)
    {
        this.bRun = bRun;
    }

    public void run ()
    {
        while (true)
        {
            if (bRun)
            {
                if (target == controllerFrame.cmdWest)
                {
                    controllerFrame.pm.moveLeft(iIncrement);
                }

                else if (target == controllerFrame.cmdNW)
                {
                    controllerFrame.pm.moveLeft(iIncrement);
                    controllerFrame.pm.moveUp(iIncrement);
                }

                else if (target == controllerFrame.cmdNorth)
                {
                    controllerFrame.pm.moveUp(iIncrement);
                }
```

```
                else if (target == controllerFrame.cmdNE)
                {
                    controllerFrame.pm.moveRight(iIncrement);
                    controllerFrame.pm.moveUp(iIncrement);
                }

                else if (target == controllerFrame.cmdEast)
                {
                    controllerFrame.pm.moveRight(iIncrement);
                }

                else if (target == controllerFrame.cmdSE)
                {
                    controllerFrame.pm.moveRight(iIncrement);
                    controllerFrame.pm.moveDown(iIncrement);
                }

                else if (target == controllerFrame.cmdSouth)
                {
                    controllerFrame.pm.moveDown(iIncrement);
                }

                else if (target == controllerFrame.cmdSW)
                {
                    controllerFrame.pm.moveLeft(iIncrement);
                    controllerFrame.pm.moveDown(iIncrement);
                }

                try {
                    Thread.sleep(50);
                } catch (InterruptedException ie)  {  }
            }
            else
                Thread.yield();
        }
    }
}

//PositionModel.java
import java.util.Observable;
import java.awt.Point;
import java.awt.Rectangle;

/**
 * This class is a simple model of a point inside a rectangle
 *
 * @author Eric Monk
 * @version 1.0
 */
```

```
public class PositionModel extends Observable
{
    Point       pPostion = new Point();
    Rectangle   rectFieldSize;

    public PostionModel (Rectangle rectFieldSize, Point pInitPosition)
    {
        // check bounds
        pPosition.x = pInitPostion.x
        pOostion.y = pInitPosition.y;
        this.rectFieldSize = rectFieldSize;
    }

    public Rectangle getFieldSize ()
    {
        return (rectFieldSize);
    }

    public Point getPosition ()
    {
        return (pPosition);
    }

    public void moveLeft (int iIncrement)
    {
        pPosition.x -= iIncrement;
        setChanged();
        notifyObservers(this);
    }

    public void moveRight (int iIncrement)
    {
        pPosition.x += iIncrement;
        setChanged();
        notifyObservers(this);
    }

    public void moveUp (int iIncrement)
    {
        pPosition.y -= iIncrement;
        setChanged();
        notifyObservers(this);
    }

    public void moveDown (int iIncrement)
    {
        pPosition.y += iIncrement;
        setChanged();
        notifyObservers(this);
    }
}
```

```
// AerialView.java
import java.awt.Canvas;
import java.util.Observable;
import java.util.Observer;

/**
 * This class displays an aerial view of the given model
 *
 * @author Eric Monk
 * @version 1.0
 */

public class AerialView implements Observer
{
    SimplePostitioner   sp;

    public AerialView (PositionModel pm)
    {
        sp = new SimplePositioner(calculatePercent(pm), new Rectangle(6,6));
    }

    public Canvas getCanvas()
    {
        return (sp);
    }

    public void update(Observable o, Object arg)
    {
        PositionModel pm = (PositionModel) arg;
        Point p = calculatePercent(pm);
        sp.setMarker(p.x, p.y);
    }

    Point calculatePercent(PositionModel pm)
    {
        Rectangle r = pm.getFieldSize();
        Point p = pm.getPosition();

        int iXPercent = (int) (((float)p.x / (float)r.width) * 100);
        int iYPercent = (int) (((float)p.y / (float)r.height) * 100);

        return (new Point(iXPercent, iYPercent));
    }

}

// SideView.java
package jwiley.chp7;

import java.awt.Point;
import java.awt.Rectangle;
import java.awt.Canvas;
```

```
import java.util.Observable;
import java.util.Observer;

/**
 * This class displays a side view of the given model
 *
 * @author Eric Monk
 * @version 1.0
 */

public class SideView implements Observer
{
    public static final int LEFT_RIGHT_VIEW = 1;
    public static final int TOP_BOTTOM_VIEW = 2;

    Simpleslider    ss;
    int             iView;

    public SideView (int iView, PositionModel pm)
    {
        this.iView = iView;
        if (iView != LEFT_RIGHT_VIEW)
            iView = TOP_BOTTOM_VIEW;

        ss = new SimpleSlider(calculatePercent(pm), 6);
    }

    public Canvas getCanvas()
    {
        return (ss);
    }

    public void update(Observable o, Object arg)
    {
        PositionModel pm + (PositionModel) arg;
        ss.setMarker(calculatePercent(pm));
    }

    int calculatePercent(PositionModel pm)
    {
        Rectangle r = pm.getFieldSize();
        Point p = pm.getPosition();

        int iPercent = 0;
        if (iView == LEFT_RIGHT_VIEW)
            iPercent = (int) (((float)p.y / (float)r.height) * 100);
        else
            iPercent = (int) (((float)p.x / (float)r.width) * 100);

        return (iPercent);

    }
}
```

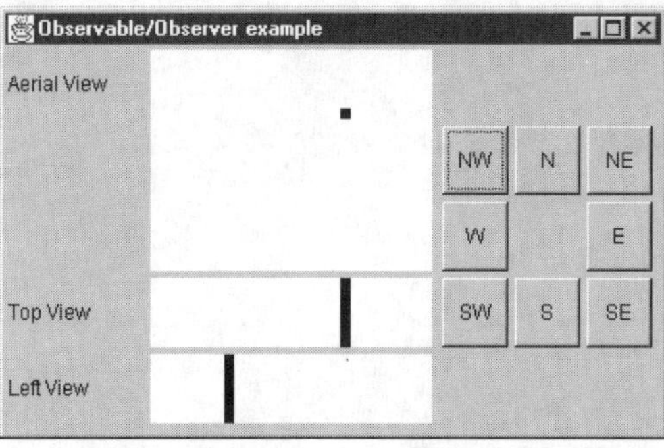

FIGURE 7.2 ControllerFrame Observable/Observer example.

A run of Source 7.3 produces Figure 7.2.

By pushing the directional buttons on the right of the frame, you change the underlying model, which causes the views to be updated. The Aerial View represents looking at the field from a bird's-eye view. The left and top views represent looking at the field from the left and top, respectively.

Let's examine the interaction between the model, view, and controller. Based on the input received from you by clicking buttons, the controller updates the position model. If you click the N button, the model gets updated by calling the moveUp() method. If you click the S button, the model gets updated by calling the moveDown() method. Each time one of the move methods is called in the position model, it calls the methods setChanged() and notifyObservers(). The setChanged() method indicates that an observable change has occurred in the model. Since an observable change has occurred, calling notifyObservers() will call the update() method for each observer. The three objects, aerialView, topView, and leftView, were added as observers to the position model by calling the addObserver() method. Now each time an observable change has occurred and the notifyObservers() method is called, the observers will have their update() methods called. In this example, each observer acts as a different view for the position model. New views can be created, or different controllers can be created to be used with the model.

Using the MVC paradigm is good practice if you have a generic or widely used model that might need different representations. To get a feel for the flexibility of the MVC architecture, I recommend that you create new views or a different controller for the example just given.

7.2 DATE/TIME

This category provides classes for working with dates and times. Java 1.1 introduced major changes in the way dates were handled. In Java 1.02, creating an instance of the Date class gave you all the methods necessary for computing and setting individual date fields. However, this locked us in to the Gregorian Calendar system because that is how the Date class calculated its date fields. This did not lend itself well to the internationalization of Java since there are other calendar systems in the world. To solve the problem of handling multiple calendar systems, an abstract Calendar class was created to handle the interpretation of dates. For a particular calendar system, a subclass of Calendar should be created to handle the rules for that calendar system. Java provides one implementation of the Calendar class, the GregorianCalendar.

In addition to the Calendar class, Java also comes with a TimeZone abstract class. The TimeZone class will enable the Calendar implementation to make the necessary adjustments for a particular time zone. Java provides one implementation of the TimeZone class, the SimpleTimeZone. Here is a description of the java.util classes that pertain to date and time.

- **Calendar.** An abstract base class that provides methods for getting standard date and time fields (such as hour, day, year), setting the current date in the calendar, and various other utility methods.
- **Date.** Used to get the system date and time. All methods that get or set a particular date field have been deprecated.
- **GregorianCalendar.** An implementation of Calendar for the Gregorian calendar system. This class should be used instead of Date to get particular date fields.
- **SimpleTimeZone.** An implementation of the TimeZone class. It includes methods for setting daylight savings time rules.
- **TimeZone.** An abstract base class that provides methods for computing time zone offsets.

Source 7.4 is an example of how to print out the current date.

SOURCE 7.4 PrintCurrentDate.java

```
package jwiley.chp7;

import java.util.GregorianCalendar;
import java.util.Calendar;

public class PrintCurrentDate
{
    public static void main (String args[])
    {
        Calendar cal = new GregorianCalendar();

        int iYear = cal.get(Calendar.YEAR);
        int iMonth = cal.get(Calendar.MONTH) + 1;
        int iDay = cal.get(Calendar.DAY_OF_MONTH);

        System.out.println("Today's Date is: " +
                iMonth + "/" + iDay + "/" + iYear);
    }
}
```

7.3 RESOURCES

Resources were introduced to isolate locale-specific information. Using resources allows the program to be translated into different languages more easily, because the translation is done only on the resource files themselves, not on the entire program. The Resource class is designed to handle multiple locales easily. Given a particular locale the Resource class will search for a ResourceBundle implementation for that locale and dynamically load the class if it exists.

The Locale class is used in conjunction with the ResourceBundle class to handle locale-specific resources. A new Locale can be created with the following constructors:

```
Locale(String language, String country)
Locale(String language, String country, String variant)
```

The first argument, language, is a valid ISO Language Code as defined in ISO-639. The second argument, country, is a valid ISO Country Code as defined in ISO-3166. In the second constructor the argument variant is used to specify more detailed information. Variant could relate to a particular region or dialect, or it could be used to specify operating system or vendor-specific information. None of the arguments are validated when constructing a new locale.

So how does ResourceBundle use Locale? Let's say you have a class called ComputerTerms that extends ResourceBundle. ComputerTerms will be used as the default resource. To specify a locale-specific instance of ComputerTerms you could create the class ComputerTerms_en_UK, which would specify the language as English and the Country as the United Kingdom. Now if you used a locale object with the same language and country codes to access this resource, an instance of ComputerTerms_en_UK is returned. Source 7.5 provides an example of using resources.

SOURCE 7.5 JavaStatements.java

```
// JavaStatements.java
package jwiley.chp7;

import java.util.ListResourceBundle;

public class JavaStatements extends ListResourceBundle
{
    public Object[][] getContents ()
    {
        return contents;
    }

    static final Object[][] contents = {
        {"JavaFun", "Java is fun."},
        {"JavaPower", "Java is powerful."},
        {"JavaFlex", "Java is flexible."}
    };
}
```

```
// JavaStatements_en_US_CubaGooding.java
package jwiley.chp7;

import java.util.ListResourceBundle;

public class JavaStatements_en_US_CubaGooding extends ListResourceBundle
{
    public Object[][] getContents ()
    {
        return contents;
    }

    static final Object[][] contents = {
        {"JavaFun", "Show me the Java."},
        {"JavaPower", "Java is the 'Quan'."},
        {"JavaFlex", "Java is as flexible as my agent."}
    };
}

// JavaStatements_en_US_ForrestGump.java
package jwiley.chp7;

import java.util.ListResourceBundle;

public class JavaStatements_en_US_ForrestGump extends ListResourceBundle
{
    public Object[][] getContents ()
    {
        return contents;
    }

    static final Object[][] contents = {
        {"JavaFun", "Java is a fun drink."},
        {"JavaPower", "Mama always said: don't drink too much Java."},
        {"JavaFlex", "Flexible is as flexible does."}
    };
}

// JavaStatements_en_US_HomerSimpson.java
package jwiley.chp7;

import java.util.ListResourceBundle;

public class JavaStatements_en_US_HomerSimpson extends ListResourceBundle
{
    public Object[][] getContents ()
    {
        return contents;
    }
```

```
    static final Object[][] contents = {
        {"JavaFun", "Java is like beer."},
        {"JavaPower", "Doh! Java is strong."},
        {"JavaFlex", "Java goes good with donuts and cake."}
    };
}

// ReasonsToCodeInJava.java
package jwiley.chp7;

import java.util.ResourceBundle;
import java.util.Locale;

public class ReasonsToCodeInJava
{
    public static void main (String args[])
    {
        ResourceBundle  bundle = null;
        Locale          locale = null;

        if (args.length == 1)
        {
            if (args[0].equals("-ForrestGump"))
            {
                locale = new Locale("en", "US", "ForrestGump");
            }
            else if (args[0].equals("-CubaGooding"))
            {
                locale = new Locale("en", "US", "CubaGooding");
            }
            else if (args[0].equals("-HomerSimpson"))
            {
                locale = new Locale("en", "US", "HomerSimpson");
            }
        }

        if (locale == null)
            bundle = ResourceBundle.getBundle("JavaStatements");
        else
            bundle = ResourceBundle.getBundle("JavaStatements", locale);

        System.out.println("Reasons to code in Java:");
        System.out.println(bundle.getString("JavaFun"));
        System.out.println(bundle.getString("JavaPower"));
        System.out.println(bundle.getString("JavaFlex"));
    }
}
```

A run of Source 7.5 will produce the following:

```
c:\jwiley\chp7>java ReasonsToCodeInJava -HomerSimpson

Reasons to code in Java:
Java is like beer.
Doh! Java is strong.
Java goes good with donuts and cake.
```

In the preceding example I created multiple classes that extended ListResourceBundle, which is an implementation of ResourceBundle. When running the program using the different arguments, the getBundle method will load and instantiate the locale-specific object that I requested. The getString method will return the string value based on the supplied key. Note that here I am using String resources, but the ResourceBundle class can handle objects as well. Let's take a look at the four classes pertaining to resources.

- **Locale.** This class is used to access specific resources focused on a specific geographical, political, or cultural region. The constructors for this class accept a language code, a country code, and optionally a variant code. When used in the ResourceBundle.getBundle() call it will cause a ResourceBundle specific to this locale to be loaded (if one exists).
- **ResourceBundle.** This is an abstract class used to store information focused on a specific geographical, political, or cultural region. The class name of an implementation of ResourceBundle should contain a language code, a country code, and optionally a variant code. These codes were described earlier. This class contains methods for loading resource bundles as well as accessing individual resources within a bundle.
- **ListResourceBundle.** This is an abstract class that extends ResourceBundle. Resources are stored in a list format. Subclasses must override the getContents() method to supply their own resource contents. Source 7.4 demonstrates subclassing ListResourceBundle.
- **PropertyResourceBundle.** This is an abstract class that extends ResourceBundle. Resources are stored as a set of strings in a property file. You do not need to subclass this like ListResourceBundle to create resources. Resources should be created as property files and should be named with the correct language, country, and variant codes. Property files need to end with '.properties' extension in order to be loaded properly. An example available on the attached CD called ReasonsToCodeInJava2 changes the getBundle(JavaStatements) call to getBundle(JavaProps). Here are the names of the property files for this example:

```
JavaProps.properties
JavaProps_en_US_CubaGooding.properties
JavaProps_en_US_ForrestGump.properties
JavaProps_en_US_HomerSimpson.properties
```

- **MissingResourceException.** This class extends java.lang.RuntimeException. This exception is thrown when the specified resource cannot be found. The getKey() and getClassName() methods can be called to obtain the key that caused the error or the class that caused the error.

7.4 MISCELLANEOUS

The classes contained in this category do not fit in any other category. Let's examine each class in this section.

- **EventObject.** This class is the root of all AWT Event classes. Its main purpose is to store a reference to the source object when generating an event.
- **TooManyListenersException.** This class is declared to indicate that a particular event handling interface can only have one listener.
- **Random.** A class that creates a psuedo-random number generator. You can either provide a seed or use the default, which is the System time in milliseconds. You can choose between a uniform distribution and a gaussian (bell curve) distribution.
- **StringTokenizer.** This class implements the Enumeration interface. This class will tokenize (separate into meaningful units, like words or keywords) a String. This is a more robust version of the Standard C Library function strtok(). This class is demonstrated in Source 7.5.
- **NoSuchElementException.** This class extends RuntimeException. It is thrown when an attempt is made to get another element in an enumeration that is empty. This can be avoided by testing the hasMoreElements() method as demonstrated in Source 7.6.

SOURCE 7.6 SimpleTokenizer.java

```
package jwiley.chp7;

import java.util.StringTokenizer;

public class SimpleTokenizer
{
    public static void main (String args[])
    {
        if (args.length != 2)
        {
            System.out.println("java SimpleTokenizer " +
                               "<string> <separators>");
            System.exit(0);
        }

        int iTokenCount = 0;
        StringTokenizer st = new StringTokenizer(args[0], args[1]);
```

```
        while (st.hasMoreElements())
        {
            iTokenCount++;
            System.out.println("Token " + iTokenCount + ": " +
                                          st.nextToken());
        }
    }
}
```

A run of Source 7.6 will produce the following output:

```
c:\jwiley\chp7>java SimpleTokenizer "12/31/1999 11:59 PM Party Time!" "/: "
Token 1: 12
Token 2: 31
Token 3: 1999
Token 4: 11
Token 5: 59
Token 6: PM
Token 7: Party
Token 8: Time!
```

Note that the StringTokenizer can take multiple delimiters in its constructor. If you do not specify any delimiters the standard whitespace delimiters are used. The whitespace delimiters are space, tab, new line, and carriage return.

7.5 PACKAGE JAVA.UTIL.ZIP

The java.util.zip package contains classes for lossless compression and decompression. The compression and decompression routines are implemented using the ZLIB compression library. The ZLIB library was designed to be free to use and is not covered by any patents; therefore, Javasoft decided to incorporate it in its JDK 1.1 release. For more information on ZLIB see the ZLIB homepage at www.cdrom.com/pub/infozip/zlib/zlib.html.

Let's take a look at the classes contained in this package. First we will describe the classes used to create and extract your own Zip files.

- **InflaterInputStream.** This class extends FilterInputStream. This class is used to uncompress data that is stored in a compressed format. It is used as the basis for other decompression filters such as GZIPInputStream and ZipInputStream.
- **DeflaterOutputStream.** This class extends FilterOutputStream. This class is used to take uncompressed data and compress it. It is used as the basis for other compression filters such as GZIPOutputStream and ZipOutputStream.
- **ZipInputStream.** This class extends InflaterInputStream. This class is used to read files stored in the Zip format. Using the read() method will take the compressed data and uncompress it into the specified buffer. The getNextEntry() method will move the stream to the beginning of the next file contained in the Zip stream. Source 7.6 demonstrates the use of ZipInputStream.

- **ZipOutputStream.** This class extends DeflaterOutputStream. This class is used to store files in the Zip format. Using the write() method will take uncompressed data and write it out compressed. The putNextEntry() method will begin writing a new Zip file entry. Source 7.6 demonstrates the use of ZipOutputStream.
- **ZipEntry.** This class represents an entry in a Zip file. This class provides many methods for setting and getting information associated with the Zip file entry. The getCompressedSize() and getSize() methods will return the compressed and uncompressed sizes of the entry. The getMethod() method is used to return the compression type, either STORED or DEFLATED. The ZipInputStream and ZipOutputStream classes use ZipEntry to compress and decompress files. Source 7.6 demonstrates the use of ZipEntry.
- **ZipFile.** This class represents a Zip file. A Zip file can contain multiple Zip entries. The entries() method can be used to obtain an enumeration of all entries contained in the Zip file. Individual entries can be accessed using the getEntry() and getInputStream() methods. Source 7.6 demonstrates the use of ZipFile.
- **ZipException.** This class extends java.io.IOException. This exception is thrown in numerous methods in the ZipFile, ZipInputStream, and ZipOutputStream classes. The exception denotes that some Zip format or file error has occurred.

Source 7.7 demonstrates a simple Zip utility program. Three options are available in the program: deflate, inflate, and list. The deflate option creates a Zip file with the files specified on the command line. The inflate option will extract all files contained in the specified Zip file. The list option will list files contained in the Zip file.

SOURCE 7.7 ZipUtil.java

```
// ZipUtil.java
package jwiley.chp7;

import java.util.zip.ZipInputStream;
import java.util.zip.ZipOutputStream;
import java.util.zip.ZipEntry;
import java.util.zip.ZipFile;
import java.util.Enumeration;

import java.io.File;
import java.io.FileInputStream;
import java.io.FileOutputStream;
import java.io.IOException;

public class ZipUtil
{
    public static final int BUFFER_SIZE = 2048;

    public static void main (String args[])
    {
        if (args.length < 2 || args.length > 3)
```

```
    {
        System.out.println("Invalid number of arguments!");
        printUsage();
        System.exit(0);
    }

    String sFileList = null;
    String sZipFile = null;

    if (args[0].equals("-l"))
    {
        listZipFiles(args[1]);
    }

    else if (args[0].equals("-d"))
    {
        if (args.length == 3)
        {
            makeZipFile(args[1], args[2]);
        }
        else
        {
            System.out.println("Invalid use of -d parameter.");
            printUsage();
            System.exit(0);
        }

    }

    else if (args[0].equals("-i"))
    {
        unpackZipFile(args[1]);
    }

    else
    {
        System.out.println("Invalid argument: " + args[0]);
        printUsage();
        System.exit(0);
    }
}

static void listZipFiles(String sZipFile)
{
    try
    {
        ZipFile zipFile = new ZipFile(sZipFile);
        Enumeration enumZipFile = zipFile.entries();

        while(enumZipFile.hasMoreElements())
        {
```

```
            ZipEntry zipEntry = (ZipEntry) enumZipFile.nextElement();

            System.out.println(zipEntry.getName() + " is " +
                               zipEntry.getSize() + " bytes.");
        }

        zipFile.close();

    } catch (IOException ioe)
        {
        System.out.println("Error with zip file: " + sZipFile +
                           ".\nError: " + ioe.toString());
        }
}

static void makeZipFile(String sFileList, String sZipFile)
{
    try
    {
        File fCurrentDir = new File(".");
        String sFiles[] = fCurrentDir.list();

        FileOutputStream fosZipFile = new FileOutputStream(sZipFile);
        ZipOutputStream zosZipFile = new ZipOutputStream(fosZipFile);

        byte buffer[] = new byte[BUFFER_SIZE];

        for (int iCount = 0; iCount < sFiles.length; iCount++)
        {
            if (fileMatches(sFiles[iCount], sFileList))
            {
                try
                {
                    // add to zip file
                    System.out.println("Adding " +
                        sFiles[iCount] + " to " + sZipFile + "...");
                    FileInputStream fisFileToAdd =
                            new FileInputStream(sFiles[iCount]);

                    ZipEntry zipEntry = new ZipEntry(sFiles[iCount]);
                    zosZipFile.putNextEntry(zipEntry);

                    int iNumBytesRead = 0;
                    while (true)
                    {
                        iNumBytesRead = fisFileToAdd.read(buffer);
                        if (iNumBytesRead == -1)
                            break;

                        zosZipFile.write(buffer, 0, iNumBytesRead);
                    }
```

```
                    fisFileToAdd.close();
                    zosZipFile.closeEntry();

                } catch (IOException ioe1)
                  {
                    System.out.println("Error adding " +
                        sFiles[iCount] + " to zip file.\nError: " +
                        ioe1.toString());
                  }
            }
        }

        zosZipFile.close();

    } catch (IOException ioe2)
      {
        System.out.println("Error making zip file.\nError: " +
                                            ioe2.toString());
      }


}

static void unpackZipFile(String sZipFile)
{
    try
    {
        FileInputStream fisZipFile = new FileInputStream(sZipFile);
        ZipInputStream zisZipFile = new ZipInputStream(fisZipFile);

        byte buffer[] = new byte[BUFFER_SIZE];

        while (true)
        {
            ZipEntry zipEntry = zisZipFile.getNextEntry();
            if (zipEntry == null)
                break;

            try
            {
                // get from zip file
                System.out.println("Extracting " +
                                        zipEntry.getName() +
                                      " from " + sZipFile + "...");
                FileOutputStream fosFileToExtract =
                            new FileOutputStream(zipEntry.getName());

                int iNumBytesRead = 0;
                while (true)
                {
                    iNumBytesRead = zisZipFile.read(buffer,
                                                    0, buffer.length);
```

```
                    if (iNumBytesRead == -1)
                        break;

                    fosFileToExtract.write(buffer, 0, iNumBytesRead);
                }

                fosFileToExtract.close();
                zisZipFile.closeEntry();

            } catch (IOException ioe)
              {
                System.out.println("Error extracting " +
                        zipEntry.getName() + " from zip file." +
                        "\nError: " + ioe.toString());
              }
        }

        zisZipFile.close();

    } catch (IOException ioe2)
      {
        System.out.println("Error making zip file.\nError: " +
                                                ioe2.toString());
      }
  }

  static boolean fileMatches(String sFileName, String sWildcardPattern)
  {
      // currently only handle asterisks at beginning of string
      if (sWildcardPattern.equals("*"))
          return (true);
      else
      {
          // get last part of WildcardPattern
          String sExtension = sWildcardPattern.substring(1);
          if (sFileName.endsWith(sExtension))
              return (true);
      }

      return (false);
  }

  static void printUsage()
  {
      System.out.println();
      System.out.println("Usage: java ZipUtil [-i | -d | -l]");
      System.out.println("\tinflate\t-i <zip file>");
      System.out.println("\tdeflate\t-d <file(s)> <zip file>");
      System.out.println("\tlist\t-l <zip file>");
  }
}
```

A run of Source 7.7 with the deflate option produces:

```
C:\jwiley\chp7\images>java jwiley.chp7.ZipUtil -d *.tif images.zip
Adding fig3.tif to images.zip...
Adding grid.tif to images.zip...
Adding fig_scut.tif to images.zip...
Adding fig_pop.tif to images.zip...
Adding skull.tif to images.zip...
```

This compressed every .tif file in the current directory into the images.zip file. Running the source with the list option produces:

```
C:\jwiley\chp7\images>java jwiley.chp7.ZipUtil -l images.zip
skull.tif is 249226 bytes.
fig_pop.tif is 8568 bytes.
grid.tif is 230574 bytes.
fig3.tif is 260014 bytes.
fig_scut.tif is 7676 bytes.
```

This listed all the files in the images.zip file and printed their original size. You can run the program with the inflate option to extract the files out of the images.zip file. Let's discuss the three key methods in Source 7.6:

- **makeFZipFile.** This method will create a new Zip file given a list of files. Currently, only limited wildcard support is available in the file list specification. This method will create a new file and open a ZipOutputStream on top of it. A ZipEntry object is created and placed in the ZipOutputStream using the putNextEntry() method for each file specified in the file list. After a ZipEntry is added the data from the input file is read in and written to the ZipOutputStream with the write() method. The write() method does the actual compression on the input data. After writing all data the entry is closed, and the process is repeated for the next file. After all files have been processed the close() method is called to close the Zip file. The close() method will also close the underlying stream.
- **unpackZipFile.** This method will extract entries contained in a Zip file. This method will open the Zip file and open a ZipInputStream on top of it. The getNextEntry() method is called on the ZipInputStream to obtain the next entry in the Zip file. If no more entries exist, null is returned and we can stop processing the Zip file. For each entry the name of the file is retrieved and is used to create a file in the current directory. The read() method is used to extract the data from the current entry. The read() method handles the decompression of the data, so the data buffer read in can be written out to the file we just created. After all reading is done, we close the current entry and repeat the process for all entries in the Zip file. After all files have been processed the close() method is called to close the Zip file.
- **listZipFile.** This method will list the files stored in the Zip file. This method creates a ZipFile object with the specified Zip file name. An enumeration of Zip entries is returned by a call to the entries() method. Each element in the enumer-

ation is cast to a ZipEntry object and the appropriate information is printed out. After processing is complete, the Zip file is closed.

In the remainder of this section we will describe the rest of the classes contained in the java.util.zip package.

- **Checksum.** This is an interface that represents a data checksum. A checksum is used to verify the integrity of a set of data.
- **Adler32.** This class implements the Checksum interface. It will compute the Adler checksum for a given set of data.
- **CRC32.** This class implements the Checksum interface. It will compute the CRC checksum for a given set of data.
- **CheckedInputStream.** This class extends FilterInputStream. This is an input stream that maintains a checksum of all data being read.
- **CheckedOutputStream.** This class extends FilterOutputStream. This is an output stream that maintains a checksum of all data being written.
- **Deflater.** This class provides general-purpose compression using the ZLIB compression library. The deflate(), needsInput(), and setInput() methods work in conjunction to deflate data. The finish() method can be called to force compression to complete with the current contents of the input buffer.
- **Inflater.** This class provides general-purpose decompression using the ZLIB decompression library. The inflate(), needsInput(), and setInput() methods work in conjunction to inflate data. The finished() method can be called to see if the end of the compressed data stream has been reached.
- **GZIPInputStream.** This class extends InflaterInputStream. This class is used to read compressed data stored in the GZIP format.
- **GZIPOutputStream.** This class extends DeflaterOutputStream. This class is used to write compressed data in the GZIP format.
- **DataFormatException.** This class extends java.lang.Exception. This exception is thrown when a data formatting error has occurred.

7.6 SUMMARY

The util package contains utility classes that provide generic containers, date and time classes, storage of application resources, and miscellaneous helper classes (like a random number generator). It is important for you to learn all of the classes and how they save you time. Do not reinvent the wheel; instead, use these classes for the functionality they provide.

The util.zip subpackage provides lossless compression and decompression to your application. This is a very powerful package that will allow you to easily compact your program's data. Take your time and study the example provided.

CHAPTER 8

Package java.io

OBJECTIVE

This package contains classes that provide input/output functionality. In this chapter you will learn how to create and use streams to read and write Java primitive types and Java objects. You will also learn how to perform file input and output, and how to serialize Java objects.

8.1 OVERVIEW

The java.io package provides classes that perform input and output functionality. Using these classes you can read and write information to a file, to the console, or to some other object that supports streams (such as a socket). In the JDK 1.02 the classes in this package worked on byte streams, and using the DataInputStream and DataOutputStream classes you could read and write Java primitives and Strings. In the JDK 1.1 many new classes were added to support character streams, and to support the serialization of objects. Figure 8.1 shows the logical breakdown of the input/output classes.

At the lowest level of the figure are classes that access physical devices. These classes can create and manipulate files, or perform network I/O using sockets. This package contains the classes for file access. See Chapter 9 for a discussion of creating and using sockets.

On top of the base classes are logical input and output stream classes. These classes can be created on top of a class that accesses a physical device. The logical input and output classes are used to implement finer control over the raw data. The classes in each section are further divided up into byte streams, character streams, and object streams. Byte stream classes operate on bytes, character streams on char-

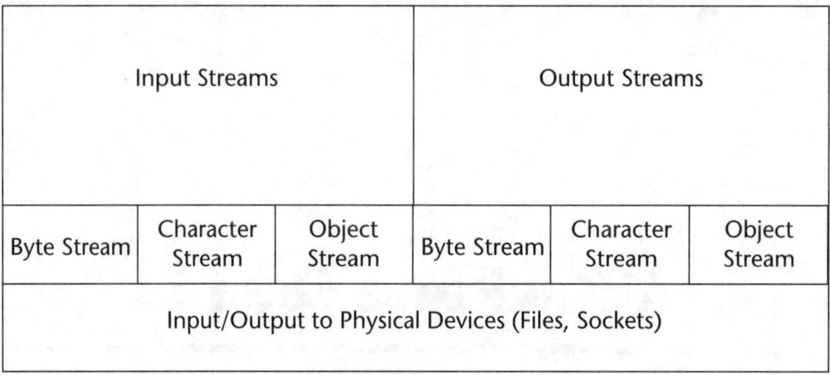

FIGURE 8.1 Input/Output package organization.

acters, and object streams on objects. At the lowest level of I/O everything must be converted into bytes, which makes the character and object stream classes especially useful. These classes will translate characters and objects into bytes automatically so you do not have to do the work yourself. Let's examine character streams and object streams more carefully before we move on.

Character Streams

In the JDK 1.1 classes to support character streams were added. Character streams are just like byte streams except character streams operate on 16-bit UNICODE characters and byte streams operate on 8-bit bytes. Allowing UNICODE I/O is very important for the internationalization of Java. UNICODE is a worldwide character encoding standard used to support languages used around the world. The text and script characters of different languages are stored as binary codes. Since UNICODE uses 16 bits for its base unit of storage, more than 65,000 characters can be encoded.

Those classes that operate on byte streams all end with either InputStream or OutputStream. Those classes that operate on character streams end with either Reader or Writer. Listed here is a comparison of the available byte streams and character streams:

- An equivalent Reader class exists for the InputStream classes and an equivalent Writer class exists for the OutputStream classes shown in Table 8.1:
- Two classes exist for converting a byte stream into a character stream: InputStreamReader and OutputStreamWriter.
- The implementation of PrintStream has changed to incorporate an OutputStreamWriter. This allows the System.out and System.err variables to use character streams without affecting existing code.

TABLE 8.1 **Character Stream Equivalents to Existing Byte Streams**

Byte Input	*Char Input*	*Byte Output*	*Char Output*
BufferedInputStream	BufferedReader	BufferedOutputStream	BufferedWriter
ByteArrayInputStream	CharArrayReader	ByteArrayOutputStream	CharArrayWriter
FileInputStream	FileReader	FileOutputStream	FileWriter
FilterInputStream	FilterReader	FilterOutputStream	FilterWriter
InputStream	Reader	OutputStream	Writer
LineNumberInputStream	LineNumberReader	(none)	(none)
PipedInputStream	PipedReader	PipedOutputStream	PipedWriter
(none)	(none)	PrintStream	PrintWriter
PushbackInputStream	PushbackReader	(none)	(none)
StringBufferInputStream	StringReader	(none)	(none)

The only three byte stream classes that do not have an equivalent character stream class are DataInputStream, DataOutputStream, and SequenceInputStream. DataInputStream and DataOutputStream use the byte stream to construct and deconstruct Java primitives; therefore, there is no corresponding character stream class. For those of you who need a character equivalent to SequenceInputStream, you should try constructing an InputStreamReader with the SequenceInputStream as the argument.

When you need to perform I/O in your programs you will have to decide which type of stream to use. If your I/O is strictly character based, then you should definitely use character streams. For all other type of I/O use byte streams.

Object Serialization

Object serialization allows an object to be written to or read from a stream. If you are using file streams your object can be stored and retrieved from a file. If you are using sockets you can send an object over a socket just as easily as you can send an integer. Using object serialization will free you from having to worry about breaking an object down into its primitive components, writing those to a stream, and then reconstructing the object once you have read in its primitive components from an input stream. Object serialization makes it possible to do Remote Method Invocation (RMI), object storage and retrieval, and distributed computing using objects. A source code demonstration of object serialization occurs later in this chapter.

You can allow your objects to be serialized by making them implement either the Serializable interface or the Externalizable interface. The easiest way to make your object serializable is to implement the Serializable interface. This interface does not define any methods but it is needed as a marker to mark the class as serializable. Note that all subclasses of a serializable class are themselves serializable.

How does your object become serialized? When you write your object to an ObjectOutputStream Java will write out all data fields declared in your object with two exceptions: fields marked as transient or static are not serialized or deserialized. All other fields will be written out to the stream using appropriate methods for the data type. Integers will be written out using writeInt(), floats will be written out using writeFloat(), and so forth. How does Java handle writing out data fields that are objects? It will write out objects by serializing them in the same manner it is handling your object. Java will traverse references to other objects in the object graph to create a serialized representation of the object. Note that if an object that is not serializable is contained in your object, a NotSerializable exception will be thrown if you try to serialize your object.

Besides implementing the Serializable interface, a class may also become serializable if it implements the Externalizable interface. The Externalizable interface defines two methods, readExternal and writeExternal, that can be used to provide your own serialization implementation. These methods will be called to serialize and deserialize your object instead of the default mechanism. This provides greater control over the external representation of your object. Using the Externalizable interface you could provide security enhancements for your object such as omitting sensitive data fields when writing your object, or encrypting the data before it gets written. Another benefit of using your own methods for serialization would be to provide compression and decompression for an image class, or a class that contains a large amount of data.

8.2 INPUT STREAMS

The purpose of the input stream classes is to read in data. The classes in this section support not only the reading of data but also the manipulation of data as it is read in. The read() methods available in these classes read from an underlying stream and perform custom processing before it is returned in a buffer.

- **InputStream.** An abstract class that represents an input stream of bytes. All input streams extend this class.
- **Reader.** An abstract class for reading character streams. All input readers extend the class.
- **InputStreamReader.** This class extends Reader. This class translates a byte stream into a character stream given a specified encoding.
- **ByteArrayInputStream.** This class extends InputStream. The class implements a byte buffer that can be used as an input stream. Very useful for reading persistent objects. See Source 8.4 in the database package for a demonstration of this class.
- **CharArrayReader.** This class extends Reader. This class is the character equivalent to ByteArrayInputStream.
- **FilterInputStream.** This class extends InputStream. This class allows multiple input streams to be chained together. This concept will be very familiar to Unix users who often insert filters between an input and output stream using pipes.

Source 8.1 demonstrates the use of a FilterInputStream to strip comments from a Java source file. The program optionally lets you save the comments to a separate file.

- **FilterReader.** This class extends Reader. This class is the character equivalent to FilterInputStream.

SOURCE 8.1 CommentFilter.java

```
// CommentFilter.java
package jwiley.chp8;

import java.io.FilterInputStream;
import java.io.FileInputStream;
import java.io.FileNotFoundException;
import java.io.FileOutputStream;
import java.io.PrintWriter;
import java.io.InputStream;
import java.io.PushbackInputStream;
import java.io.IOException;
import java.util.Stack;
import java.lang.Character;

/** Class to demonstrate FilterInputStream. */
public class CommentFilter extends FilterInputStream
{
    /** flag to determine whether to output comments to a file. */
    private boolean OutputComments=false;
    /** Stream to store comments. */
    private FileOutputStream fos;
    /** Stream to format outgoing text. */
    private PrintWriter pw;
    /** characters in the stream. */
    private static char currentChar=0, lastChar=0, nextChar=0;
    /** flag to determine if in a single line comment. */
    private static boolean inLineComment=false;
    /** flag to determine if in a multiLineComment. */
    private static boolean inMultiLineComment=false;

    /** one arg constructor. */
    CommentFilter(InputStream src)
    {
        super(src);
        PushbackInputStream pis = new PushbackInputStream(src);
        in = pis;
    }

    /** open a potential output stream for comments
       if output flag is set */
    CommentFilter(InputStream src, String outFileName)
```

```
{
    super(src);
    PushbackInputStream pis = new PushbackInputStream(src);
    in = pis;
    OutputComments = true;

    try {
        fos = new FileOutputStream(outFileName);
        pw = new PrintWriter(fos);
    } catch (IOException e)
      {
        System.out.println("IO Error on " + outFileName);
        System.exit(1);
      }
      catch (Exception e)
      {
        System.out.println("Unable to filter input");
        System.exit(1);
      }
}

/** override the read() method in FilterInputStream. */
public int read()
{
    int input=0;
    boolean peekAhead = false;

    try {
        input = super.read();
        if (input == -1)
            return -1;
        currentChar = (char) input;
    } catch (IOException ioe) { return -1; }

    if (currentChar == '/' && !inLineComment &&
        !inMultiLineComment)
    {
        // peek ahead
        try {
            input = super.read();
            if (input == -1)
                    return -1;
           nextChar = (char) input;
           peekAhead = true;
        } catch (IOException ioe) { return -1; }

        if (nextChar != '/' && nextChar != '*')
        {
            // push it back on the stream for next read
            try {
              ((PushbackInputStream)in).unread(nextChar);
```

```
            } catch (IOException ioe) { return -1; }
        }
    }

    if (currentChar == '/' && nextChar == '*')
    {
        if (!inLineComment)
            inMultiLineComment = true;
    }
    else if (currentChar == '/' && nextChar == '/')
    {
        if (!inMultiLineComment)
            inLineComment = true;
    }

    if (inLineComment || inMultiLineComment)
    {
       while (inLineComment || inMultiLineComment)
       {
          if (OutputComments)
          {
               pw.print(currentChar);
               if (peekAhead)
               {
                   pw.print(nextChar);
                   peekAhead = false;
               }
               pw.flush();
          }

          // check if comment is over
          if (inMultiLineComment && lastChar == '*' &&
               currentChar == '/')
          {
               inMultiLineComment = false;
               if (OutputComments)
               {
                   pw.print('\n');
                   pw.flush();
               }
          }

          if (inLineComment &&
               (currentChar == 10 || currentChar == 13))
          {
               if (OutputComments)
               {
                   pw.print('\n');
                   pw.flush();
               }
```

```
                inLineComment = false;
                lastChar = currentChar;
                return currentChar;
            }

            lastChar = currentChar;

            // get next character
            try {
                input = super.read();
                if (input == -1)
                    return -1;
              currentChar = (char) input;
            } catch (IOException ioe) { return -1; }
        }
    }
    else
        return currentChar;

    return currentChar;
}

/** close the file prior to object destruction. */
public void finalize()
{
    try
    {
        fos.close();
    } catch (Exception e) { }
}

/** main() method to invoke from JVM. */
public static void main(String args[])
{
    // Get command line argument
    if (args.length < 1)
    {
        System.out.println("USAGE: java CommentFilter " +
                           "fileToRead [-output commentFile]");
        System.out.println("  -output flag is optional.");
        System.exit(1);
    }

    String fileName = null;
    String commentFileName = null;
    boolean captureComments = false;
    for (int i=0; i < args.length; i++)
    {
        if (args[i].equals("-output"))
        {
            if (args.length > i + 1)
```

```
                {
                    commentFileName = new String(args[i+1]);
                    i++;
                    captureComments = true;
                }
                else
                {
                    System.out.println("No output file specified.");
                    System.exit(1);
                }
            }
            else
                fileName = new String(args[i]);
        }

        System.out.println("fileName is " + fileName);

        FileInputStream fis=null;
        // open the input file
        try
        {
            fis = new FileInputStream(fileName);
        } catch (FileNotFoundException fnf)
          {
            System.out.println("Unable to open " + fileName);
            System.exit(1);
          }

        if (captureComments)
            System.out.println("Comment File is " + commentFileName);

        CommentFilter cf=null;
        if (captureComments)
            cf = new CommentFilter(fis, commentFileName);
        else
            cf = new CommentFilter(fis);

        int in=0;
        while ( (in = cf.read()) != -1)
        {
            System.out.print((char)in);
            System.out.flush();
        }

        try
        {
          fis.close();
        } catch (Exception e) { }
    }
}
```

A run of Source 8.1 produces:

```
// Copyright (c) 1995 by Michael C. Daconta
// check if file exists
// philosophy & credits
// define DB
// select DB
// add record
// view records
// close DB
// exit
```

- **PushbackInputStream.** This class extends InputStream. This is an input stream with a 1-byte pushback buffer. Source 8.1 uses the PushbackInputStream to allow a one-character peek ahead in the input stream when checking for comments.
- **PushbackReader.** This class extends Reader. This class is the character equivalent to PushbackInputStream.
- **StringBufferInputStream.** This class extends InputStream. It allows a StringBuffer to be used as an input stream. Deprecated.
- **StringReader.** This class extends Reader. It allows a String to be used as input for a character stream.
- **DataInput.** An interface to read all Java primitive types in a machine-independent way.
- **DataInputStream.** This class extends FilterInputStream and implements DataInput. This is one of the most commonly used streams in Java programs. It allows the reading of Java primitive types (i.e., integer, floats, strings) in a machine-independent way. Almost every program in this book that accepts input uses DataInputStream.
- **BufferedInputStream.** This class extends FilterInputStream. It implements a byte buffer to improve the performance of reads. This is similar to the C Standard Library fread() versus the nonbuffered Unix read().
- **BufferedReader.** This class extends FilterReader. This class is the character equivalent to BufferedInputStream.
- **LineNumberInputStream.** This class extends FilterInputStream. Deprecated.
- **LineNumberReader.** This class extends FilterReader. This class is the character equivalent of LineNumberInputStream. This is an input stream that keeps track of the line number. This class is very useful for debugging source code. Source 8.2 demonstrates a source code listing utility that comes with many compilers. The LineNumFilter in Source 8.2 creates a source code listing that includes the line number. For the majority of debugging this utility is sufficient to isolate the error. In fact, this simple utility was used throughout this book instead of using the Java debugger (jdb).

SOURCE 8.2 LineNumFilter.java

```
// LineNumFilter.java
package jwiley.chp8;

import java.io.FileInputStream;
import java.io.FileOutputStream;
import java.io.InputStream;
import java.io.InputStreamReader;
import java.io.LineNumberReader;
import java.io.IOException;
import java.io.PrintWriter;
import java.io.FileNotFoundException;

/** Class to demonstrate the LineNumberReader class as a filter. */
public class LineNumFilter extends LineNumberReader
{
    /** text to add to stream. */
    private static String lineNumber=null;
    /** Current position within string version of line number. */
    private static int StrPos=0;
    /** Current character in stream. */
    private char currentChar;

    /** constructor. */
    LineNumFilter(InputStreamReader src)
    {
        super(src);
        lineNumber = new String((getLineNumber()+1) + " ");
    }

    /** override the read method of the stream to act as
        a filter. */
    public int read()
    {
        int input=0;

        if (lineNumber != null && lineNumber.length() > 0
            && StrPos < lineNumber.length())
        {
            currentChar = lineNumber.charAt(StrPos++);

            if (StrPos == lineNumber.length())
            {
                // dumped line number - reset
                StrPos = 0;
                lineNumber = null;
            }
        }
        else
        {
            try
            {
                input = super.read();
```

```
            } catch (IOException ioe) { return -1; }

            if (input == -1)
                    return input;
            currentChar = (char) input;
            if (currentChar == '\n')
            {
                // set up lineNumber
                lineNumber =
                    new String((getLineNumber()+1) + " ");
            }
        }

        return currentChar;
    }

    /** main() method to invoke from JVM. */
    public static void main(String args[])
    {
        if (args.length < 1)
        {
            System.out.println("USAGE: java runLineNumFilter " +
                                 "fileToRead [-output lineFile]");
            System.out.println("  -output flag is optional.");
            System.exit(1);
        }

        String fileName = null;
        String lineFileName = null;
        boolean captureLines = false;
        for (int i=0; i < args.length; i++)
        {
            if (args[i].equals("-output"))
            {
                if (args.length > i + 1)
                {
                    lineFileName = new String(args[i+1]);
                    i++;
                    captureLines = true;
                }
                else
                {
                    System.out.println("No output file specified.");
                    System.exit(1);
                }
            }
            else
                fileName = new String(args[i]);
        }

        System.out.println("fileName is " + fileName);

        FileInputStream fis=null;
        // open the input file
        try {
```

```
            fis = new FileInputStream(fileName);
        } catch (FileNotFoundException fnf)
          {
            System.out.println("Unable to open " + fileName);
            System.exit(1);
          }

        if (captureLines)
            System.out.println("Line File is " + lineFileName);

        LineNumFilter lf = new LineNumFilter(new InputStreamReader(fis));
        FileOutputStream fos = null;
        PrintWriter pw = null;

        if (captureLines)
        {
          try {
                fos = new FileOutputStream(lineFileName);
                pw = new PrintWriter(fos);
            } catch (IOException e)
            {
                System.out.println("IO Error on " + lineFileName);
                System.exit(1);
            }
            catch (Exception e)
            {
                System.out.println("Unable to filter input");
                System.exit(1);
            }

        }

        int in=0;
        while ( (in = lf.read()) != -1)
        {
            if (captureLines)
            {
                pw.print((char)in);
                pw.flush();
            }
            else
            {
                System.out.print((char)in);
                System.out.flush();
            }
        }

        try {
          fis.close();
          fos.close();
        } catch (Exception e) { }
    }
}
```

- **SequenceInputStream.** This class extends InputStream. It converts a sequence of input streams into a single input stream.
- **PipedInputStream.** This class extends InputStream. This is an input stream that must be connected to a pipedOutputStream before use. This is useful for communication between threads.
- **PipedReader.** This class extends Reader. This class is the character equivalent of PipedInputStream.
- **StreamTokenizer.** A class used to transform a stream of bytes into a stream of tokens. This class has numerous methods to define the lexical analysis of tokens. This class is extremely useful for creating parsers.

8.3 OUTPUT STREAMS

The purpose of the output stream classes is to write out data. Numerous streams are provided for outputting data in a variety of formats and to a variety of sinks. The write() methods available in these classes perform custom processing on input data before it is written to the underlying stream.

- **OutputStream.** An abstract class that represents an output stream of bytes. All output streams extend this class.
- **Writer.** An abstract class that represents an output stream of characters. All writers extend this class.
- **OutputStreamWriter.** This class extends Writer. This class translates a character stream into a byte stream given a specified encoding.
- **FilterOutputStream.** This class extends OutputStream. This is an abstract filter for an output stream. This allows you to chain together output streams with each filter, potentially modifying the stream.
- **FilterWriter.** This class extends Writer. This class is the character equivalent to FilterOutputStream.
- **DataOutput.** An interface for outputting all the Java primitive types in a machine-independent way.
- **DataOutputStream.** This class extends FilterOutputStream and implements the DataOutput interface. This stream allows you to output all the primitive types in a machine-independent way. This is useful especially when combined with DataInputStream. This will let you write data to a file, network, or any other sink in a machine-independent manner. Since every major software and hardware vendor has thrown their support behind Java, this will open up a new era in sharing data between software applications! Source 8.4 demonstrates the use of DataOutputStream.
- **BufferedOutputStream.** This class extends FilterOutputStream. This class implements a byte buffer to improve the performance of writes. This is similar to the fwrite() function in the C Standard Library as compared to the unbuffered write() function in Unix.
- **BufferedWriter.** This class extends FilterWriter. This class is the character equivalent to BufferedOutputStream.

- **PrintStream.** This class extends FilterOutputStream. The structure of this class has been changed to handle character streams instead of byte streams. PrintStream can still be used for debugging, like when you use the System.out and System.err variables. Both constructors for this class have been deprecated. You should try to use PrintWriter instead.
- **PrintWriter.** This class extends FilterWriter. This class should be used instead of PrintStream for all purposes other than debugging.
- **ByteArrayOutputStream.** This class extends OutputStream. This class allows the use of a byte buffer as an output stream. This is very useful for creating persistent objects that can be accessed using ByteArrayInputStream. In fact, I demonstrate a flexible database package that does just this! Specifically, Source 8.4 demonstrates the use of this class.
- **CharArrayWriter.** This class extends Writer. This class is the character equivalent to ByteArrayOutputStream.
- **PipedOutputStream.** This class extends OutputStream. It is an output stream that must be connected to a PipedInputStream. This is useful for interthread communication.
- **PipedWriter.** This class extends Writer. This class is the character equivalent to PipedOutputStream.
- **StringWriter.** This class extends Writer. This class will collect output in a string buffer, which can be used to construct a String.

8.4 FILES

This category of classes allows streams to be connected to file objects, to read from files, and to write to files.

- **File.** A class that represents a file on the host system. There are numerous methods to get the filepath, check if the file exists, check if it is a directory, list the files in the directory, and many more. It is a very useful class. Source 8.3 demonstrates the use of the File class. This class is even more exciting when you think of the cross-platform utilities you could create. I expect to see some very cool shells produced using the file and system utilities that will run on all major operating systems.
- **FileInputStream.** This class extends InputStream. It allows a file to be an input stream, and is very useful in conjunction with DataInputStream. Source 8.7 demonstrates the use of FileInputStream.
- **FileReader.** This class extends Reader. This class is the character equivalent to FileInputStream.
- **FileOutputStream.** This class extends OutputStream. This class allows a file to be an output stream. It is very useful, especially in conjunction with DataOutputStream and PrintStream. Source 8.5 demonstrates the use of FileOutputStream.
- **FileWriter.** This class extends Writer. This class is the character equivalent to FileOutputStream.

- **RandomAccessFile.** This class implements both the DataOutput and DataInput interfaces. It gives you the ability to create a random-access file equivalent to the C binary file type. It allows seeking to, reading, and writing to any position in the file. It is similar to the C Standard Library fseek(), fwrite(), and fread() functions; the only crucial difference being that the Java RandomAccessFile is in a machine-independent format. The database application below uses a RandomAccessFile as a platform-independent database to store variable-length, user-definable records. See Source 8.8 for a demonstration of using RandomAccessFile.
- **FilenameFilter.** An interface that provides a common method to filter filenames.

A Database Package, Application, and Persistent Objects

I have always disliked snippets of code in technical books. I would rather see a short working program than a snippet. I also would like to see nontrivial examples instead of trivial, throwaway ones. In order to really demonstrate the power of the Java io package, I ported a freeware program that I had coded in C to Java. Source 8.3 consists of a database application and a database package that the application uses. I will describe the design and functioning of each module of the package and application. While porting the code, I realized the need for Persistent objects and devised an interface to accomplish them. This example uses "lightweight" persistence, meaning that only the data is stored and not the whole object. Object serialization will be discussed in the next section. I hope you will find this code useful from the learning standpoint as well as to experiment with and add capabilities to. I hereby give you the right to use this code on a royalty-free basis as long as you clearly cite the source in your resulting program. Now let's examine the design and functionality of the application in detail.

Let's begin by examining all the files in the application and the database package. This will give us the "big picture." There is only one file for the application, called EZDB.java. EZDB stands for Easy Database. This program is a simple, command-line driven database program that lets you define databases with any number of fields (String, float or integer). Once a database is defined and the definition stored in a schema file, you are able to add records to the database and view records in the database. At the end of this section I will discuss how to extend the capabilities of this application.

Before we discuss the four Java files that make up the database package, you need to understand the general idea of what the package considers a database. A database consists of a schema file that describes all the fields in a database record, a data file that stores all the variable-length records, and one or more index files that store indexes into the data file. Therefore, our definition of a database consists of three or more files. Each file has a specific purpose and is necessary to implement a variable-length record, flexible database system that can create numerous different databases, each with a different record format. Of course, there is much room for improvement of this application in terms of user interface, capabilities (modify, delete, search), and performance, but Source 8.3 will give you a good starting point. The six files in the database package are:

- **Schema.java.** The code to define a database, generate and parse a schema file.
- **DB.java.** A class that represents a container for all the parts of a database (schema, data file, and index files). In the original C program, there was no "wrapper" structure, which limited the program to only opening a single database at a time. All the pieces were managed separately. The DB class is an improvement on this concept that will allow multiple databases to be opened simultaneously. I leave this modification to the EZDB program for you as an exercise.
- **DbHeader.java.** This is the class that represents all the relevant information in a database. This header information also keeps track of the current state of a database. The database header is also stored in the data file of the database. The header is always the first record in the index file.
- **IdxRecord.java.** This is the class that represents index information. It is used in conjunction with DbFiles to facilitate data recovery.
- **DbFiles.java.** This class performs all the actual writing and reading to and from the database. The current implementation only uses a single index file; however, for large databases, index files sorted on a particular field value are necessary.
- **LightPersistence.java.** This is an interface designed to implement light persistence. A byte array is written out to store the data for the object, and a constructor is used to reconstitute the object. The Externalizable interface could be used instead by implementing the writeExternal and readExternal methods.

We will describe the classes and key methods (excluding intuitive ones like constructors) of each Java file:

- Source 8.3 is the EZDB application.

  —**Classes.** None.

  —**Key methods.**

  1. public static void main(). This method presents a menu to the user and dispatches to the appropriate function based on the user's choice. The options are define a DB, select a DB, add a Record, view Records, and close a DB.
  2. DbHeader select_db(). This method prompts the user for a database name to select. It checks if a schema file exists for the database (created by choosing the define a DB option). If so, it creates a DbHeader object by calling the DbHeader constructor and returns the object.

SOURCE 8.3 EZDB.java

```
// Copyright (c) 1995 by Michael C. Daconta
package jwiley.chp8;

import java.io.RandomAccessFile;
import java.io.BufferedReader;
import java.io.InputStreamReader;
import java.io.DataInputStream;
import java.io.IOException;
import java.io.File;
import java.io.PrintStream;
import java.util.Vector;
import jwiley.chp8.database.*;

/** Main program that allows the creation of simple,
    single-table databases. */
class EZDB
{
    /** buffered reader to receive input. */
    static BufferedReader br = new BufferedReader(
                               new InputStreamReader(System.in));

    /** method to select which db to operate on. */
    static DbHeader select_db()
    {
        DbHeader outHeader=null;
        System.out.print("Enter the database name: ");
        System.out.flush();
        String buf=null;
        try {
                buf = br.readLine();
        } catch (Exception e) { return null; }

        if (buf.length() > 0)
        {
            buf.replace(' ', '_');

            // check if file exists
            File afile = new File(buf + ".schema");
            if (afile.exists())
                outHeader = new DbHeader(buf + ".schema");
            else
                return null;
        }
        else
            System.out.println("Invalid db name.");

        System.out.println(buf + " selected...OK");
        return outHeader;
    }
```

```
/** main() method to invoke from JVM. */
public static void main(String args[])
{
    boolean done = false;
    DB theDB = null;
    Schema DBschema = null;

    while (!done)
    {
        PrintStream out = System.out;   // save typing space
        out.println(" ");
        out.println("<<<<<<<<<<<<<<<<<<<<>>>>>>>>>>>>>>>>>>>>>>>");
        out.println("<<<<<<<<<<<< EZ DB 1.02J >>>>>>>>>>>>>>>");
        out.println("<<<<<<<<<<<<<<<<<<<<>>>>>>>>>>>>>>>>>>>>>>>");
        out.println(" ");
        out.println("          0) Philosophy & Credits");
        out.println("          1) Define DB");
        out.println("          2) Select DB");
        out.println("          3) Add Record");
        out.println("          4) View Records");
        out.println("          5) Close DB");
        out.println("          6) Exit");
        out.println(" ");
        out.print("Enter choice : ");
        out.flush();            String choiceStr=null;
        try {
          choiceStr = br.readLine();
        } catch (IOException ioe)
          {
            System.out.println("Error reading choice.");
            System.exit(1);
          }

        int choice = -1;
        if (choiceStr.length() > 0)
            choice = Integer.parseInt(choiceStr);

        switch (choice)
        {
          case 0:
            // philosophy & credits
            out.println(" ");
            out.println("<<<<<<<<<<< EZDB Philosophy >>>>>>>>>>");
            out.println("This program is based on the idea that");
            out.println("most people do not need an expensive, ");
            out.println("feature-packed database. What the common ");
            out.println("person needs is a simple, efficient ");
            out.println("database to help them keep track of the");
            out.println("people, places, and things in their");
            out.println("lives.  EZDB is a free solution. Enjoy!");
            out.println(" ");
```

```
          out.println("The Original EZDB was in C and had more");
          out.println("options (i.e. find, delete, modify...).");
          out.println("There was also a version with a GUI.");
          out.println("This is just a demonstration of the");
          out.println("concepts in Java.");
          out.println(" ");

          out.println("Press Enter to continue: ");
              try { br.readLine(); } catch (Exception e) { }
              break;
        case 1: // define DB
          DBschema = new Schema();
          if (DBschema.buildSchema())
          {
              DBschema.outputSchema();
              System.out.println("Schema stored as : " +
                                      DBschema.getFileName());
          }
          break;
        case 2: // select DB
          if (theDB == null)
          {
             DbHeader aHeader = select_db();
             if (aHeader != null)
             {
                  theDB = new DB();
                  theDB.setHeader(aHeader);
             }
             else
                  System.out.println("DB does not exist.");
          }
          else
             System.out.println("Close current DB first. " +
                                         "Choose Option 5.");
          break;
        case 3: // add record
          if (theDB != null)
          {
              System.out.println("Enter Record data...");
              Vector recVals = theDB.createRecord();

              if (!theDB.addRecord(recVals))
                 System.out.println("Unable to add Record to DB.");
              else
                 System.out.println("Successfully added " +
                                          "Record to DB.");
          }
          else
              System.out.println("MUST selecte a DB. " +
                                         "Choose option 2.");
          break;
```

```
            case 4: // view records
              if (theDB != null)
                  theDB.viewRecords();
              else
                  System.out.println("MUST selecte a DB. " +
                                                      "Choose option 2.");

              break;
            case 5: // close DB
              if (theDB != null)
              {
                  theDB.close();
                  theDB = null;
              }
              break;
            case 6: // exit
              done = true;
              if (theDB != null)
                  theDB.close();
              break;
            default:
              System.out.println("Choice must be between 0 and 10.");
          }
      }
   }
}
```

A run of Source 8.3 produces:

```
C:\jwiley\chp8>java jwiley.chp8.EZDB

<<<<<<<<<<<<<<<<<<<<<<>>>>>>>>>>>>>>>>>>>>
<<<<<<<<<<<< EZ DB 1.02J >>>>>>>>>>>>>>>
<<<<<<<<<<<<<<<<<<<<<<>>>>>>>>>>>>>>>>>>>>

          0) Philosophy & Credits
          1) Define DB
          2) Select DB
          3) Add Record
          4) View Records
          5) Close DB
          6) Exit

Enter choice : 1
Defining a database consists of two steps:
1) Name the database.
2) Describe the fields of the database.

Hit Return to continue, else type 99 to return to main menu.
Enter the database name: employee
```

```
To describe the fields in your database.
There are two pieces of information for each field.
1) The field name.  This is what you call the data,
   for example, an address database would have names
   like - name, street, city...
2) The data type.  This is what type of data the field
   holds.  There are currently only three (3) choices:
   string (text), number (whole numbers), decimal.

Enter the field name: name
Choose the field type:
1) String (text - alpha and numbers)
2) Long (whole numbers)
3) Double (decimals)
Enter choice:
...
<<<<<<<<<<<<<<<<<<<<>>>>>>>>>>>>>>>>>>>>
<<<<<<<<<<<< EZ DB 1.02J >>>>>>>>>>>>>>>
<<<<<<<<<<<<<<<<<<<<>>>>>>>>>>>>>>>>>>>>

          0) Philosophy & Credits
          1) Define DB
          2) Select DB
          3) Add Record
          4) View Records
          5) Close DB
          6) Exit

Enter choice : 3
Enter Record data...
name : Mike Daconta
department : Telemedicine
Salary : 100500.99
Database successfully initialized.
Successfully added Record to DB.

<<<<<<<<<<<<<<<<<<<<>>>>>>>>>>>>>>>>>>>>
<<<<<<<<<<<< EZ DB 1.02J >>>>>>>>>>>>>>>
<<<<<<<<<<<<<<<<<<<<>>>>>>>>>>>>>>>>>>>>

          0) Philosophy & Credits
          1) Define DB
          2) Select DB
          3) Add Record
          4) View Records
          5) Close DB
          6) Exit

Enter choice : 4
> 2 records in the DB.
name : Mike Daconta
department : Telemedicine
Salary : 100501
Hit Return to continue or 99 to return to main menu.
```

```
name : Samantha Daconta
department : training
Salary : 45000
Hit Return to continue or 99 to return to main menu.
```

- Source 8.4 is the DB class in the database package. Due to the length of the source code, this class resides on the CD-ROM. Access the CD-ROM to view the source listing.

  —Classes.

  1. DB. A representation of a database. Has data members for a Schema class, a DbHeader class, a DbFiles class, and a recordCount.

  —Key methods.

  1. public synchronized Vector createRecord(). This method displays each field-name in the database and prompts the user for the value. The string input by the user is converted to the proper field type as defined by the Schema and stored in the DbHeader class. The method returns the values in a Vector.
  2. public synchronized void displayRecord(Vector RecVals). Displays the field-names and field values of the Vector passed in.
  3. public synchronized byte[] RecValsToByteArray(Vector RecVals). Converts the record Vector into an array of bytes. Uses ByteArrayOutputStream and DataOutputStream to do this. This is a very important method as well as the methodology used to create a persistent object in Java. The DbHeader class and IdxRecord class implement the LightPersistence interface (Source 8.6). It would be smart to have every new class you create implement the LightPersistence interface (just as you should always implement the toString() method). The LightPersistence interface is described later in the chapter.
  4. public synchronized Vector ByteArrayToRecVals(byte bytes[]). This method uses ByteArrayInputStream and DataInputStream to translate a byte array into a database record. This method and its opposite are the key translation functions that go between a file representation of our record and its viewable (human-readable) representation.
  5. public void initDBfiles(). This method either creates a new database or opens an existing one. It either creates the header (for an initialization) and stores it in the database or retrieves it from the existing database.
  6. public void close(). Writes the current DbHeader to the data file and closes all open files.
  7. public boolean addRecord(Vector RecVals). This method adds the current Record to the database. To do this it converts the record to a byte array, calls initDBfiles() if this is the first write, then calls the DbFiles method writeBytes() to actually write the byte array to the appropriate files. It is important to understand how this routine will need to change when you implement record deletion. Since all record lengths and positions in the data file are stored in the master

index file (which is what allows us to store records of variable length), the easiest way to delete a record is to just set its index record to some special deletion marker (i.e., a -99 in the length and position field). This deletion marker would cause you to skip the record during viewing or searching through the database. Before you write the deletion marker to the index file, you first record the record position and length in a Free List of space available to be reused. Then before you add a record to the end of the database (also known as growing the database), you check the Free List to see if there are any available "holes." This implementation of record deletion is left for you as an exercise.

8. public void viewRecords(). This method sequences through all the records in the database. This is a good example of a class that should implement the Enumeration interface. See Source 4.2 for a demonstration of a List package implementing the Enumeration interface.

- Source 8.5 is the Schema class in the database package. Due to the length of the source code this "supporting" class resides on the CD-ROM. Access the CD-ROM to view the source listing.

  —Classes.

  1. Schema. A representation of a description of a database record.

  —Key methods.

  1. public boolean buildSchema(). This method guides the user through text prompts that define a database. This is done by naming the database, naming the fields in a database record, and choosing the type for each field. This information is all stored in a String Vector.
  2. void outputSchema(). This method dumps the information in the String Vector to a text file. The text file is named <dbname>.schema.

- Source 8.6 is the LightPersistence interface. The LightPersistence interface has a single function toByteArray() that converts the object to a byte array that is ready for storage in a RandomAccessFile or possibly for transmission over a network. You can think of this interface as making an object "persistent ready." Although this seems like only half the interface, it is due to the fact that the second half is best implemented as a constructor function of the object. This would be a good enhancement to the interface concept. The only other way to accomplish this would be to allow a static function in the interface, which is also currently illegal. If static methods are allowed you could have a method like this:

```
public static Object fromByteArray();
```

You could add this method as a nonstatic method but it then forces the user to declare a dummy object just to call this method. Again, the best solution is to just implement an object constructor that takes a byte array and instantiates the object from the byte array. The DbHeader class (Source 8.7) and IdxRecord class (Source 8.8) demonstrate this.

SOURCE 8.6 LightPersistence.java

```
package jwiley.chp8.database;

/** an interface to create a persistent object. */
public interface LightPersistence
{
    // a method to translate the object into the Byte array
    public byte [] toByteArray();
}
```

- Source 8.7 is the DbHeader class in the database package. Due to the length of the source this "supporting" class resides on the CD-ROM. Access the CD-ROM to view the source listing.

  —Classes.

  1. class DbHeader. A representation of a database header that stores the schema description information, a record count, and a free list (the free list is not yet implemented). This is a persistent-ready object that implements the LightPersistence interface.

  —Key methods.

  1. public DbHeader(String schemafile). This class constructor parses the schema text file and initializes the DbHeader class. It stores fldNames and fldTypes in Vectors. The fldNames data member is a Vector of Strings, while fldTypes is a Vector of Integers. You could remove fldTypes by using Run Time Type Info (RTTI) to determine the value type. This is left to you as an exercise.
  2. public DbHeader(byte bytes[]). This method is part of the implementation of LightPersistence (although not yet explicitly). This method initializes a DbHeader object from a byte array. This is used to initialize a DbHeader object from an existing database.
  3. public byte [] toByteArray(). This method must be implemented for this class to implement the LightPersistence interface. This method uses ByteArrayOutputStream and DataOutputStream to convert the DbHeader object to a byte array for persistent storage.

- Source 8.8 is the DbFiles class in the database package.

  —Classes.

  1. IdxRecord. A representation of an index record that implements the LightPersistence interface.

  —Key methods.

  1. public byte [] toByteArray(). Implements the LightPersistence interface. This method will take the index information and format it so it can be written to a file.

SOURCE 8.8 IdxRecord.java

```
// Copyright (c) 1995 by Michael C. Daconta
package jwiley.chp8.database;

import java.io.ByteArrayInputStream;
import java.io.ByteArrayOutputStream;
import java.io.DataInputStream;
import java.io.DataOutputStream;

/** index into the database. An index consists of
    the position and length of a variable-lengthed
    database record. */
public class IdxRecord implements LightPersistence
{
    /** record length. Always a fixed size. */
    public static final int REC_LENGTH = 16; // 16 bytes
    /** record position in .dat file. */
    protected long recPos;
    /** length of data record in .dat file. */
    protected long recLength;

    /** constructor. */
    public IdxRecord(long inPos, long inLength)
    {
        recPos = inPos;
        recLength = inLength;
    }

    /** accessor. */
    public long getrecPos() { return recPos; }
    /** accessor. */
    public long getrecLength() { return recLength; }

    /** construct from a byte array. */
    public IdxRecord(byte bytes[])
    {
        // translate a byte array into a header
        ByteArrayInputStream bis = new ByteArrayInputStream(bytes);
        DataInputStream dis = new DataInputStream(bis);

        try {
            recPos = dis.readLong();
            recLength = dis.readLong();
        } catch (Exception e)
          {
            System.out.println(e.getMessage());
            return;
          }
    }
```

```
    /** convert to a byte array. */
    public byte [] toByteArray()
    {
        ByteArrayOutputStream bos = new ByteArrayOutputStream();
        DataOutputStream dos = new DataOutputStream(bos);

        try {
            dos.writeLong(recPos);
            dos.writeLong(recLength);
        } catch (Exception e)
          {
            System.out.println(e.getMessage());
            return null;
          }

        return bos.toByteArray();
    }
}
```

- Source 8.9 is the DbFiles class in the database package. This source demonstrates the use of the Random Access File class and its methods; therefore, Source 8.9 is below, despite its length.

  —Classes.

  1. DbFiles. A representation of the physical file objects necessary to implement our database. This class uses RandomAccessFile for the data and index files.

  —Key methods.

  1. public boolean writeBytes(byte dataBytes[], long newDataPos, long newIdx-Pos). This function writes the bytes of the record (or persistent-ready object) to the file. It also creates and stores the persistent-ready IdxRecord.
  2. public byte [] readBytes(long newIdxPos). Given the position in the master index file, this method retrieves the persistent index record, and using that then retrieves the bytes from the data file that make up the database record.
  3. public void writeHeader(DbHeader inHeader). First makes the DbHeader class persistent-ready and then stores it in the data file. The method relocates it if it has grown too big for the "slot" it started at.

SOURCE 8.9 DbFiles.java

```
// DbFiles.java
package jwiley.chp8.database;
import java.io.File;
import java.io.RandomAccessFile;
import java.io.IOException;
import java.io.ByteArrayInputStream;
import java.io.ByteArrayOutputStream;
import java.io.DataInputStream;
import java.io.DataOutputStream;

/** class that keeps track of the actual files that make
    up the database. */
public class DbFiles
{
    /** data file. */
    protected RandomAccessFile dataFile;
    /** index file for database. */
    protected RandomAccessFile idxFile;
    /** file position in data file. */
    protected long dataPos;
    /** file position in index file. */
    protected long idxPos;

    /** accessor. */
    public long getdataPos() { return dataPos; }
    /** accessor. */
    public long getidxPos() { return idxPos; }

    /** get the length of the data file. */
    public long getdataFileLength()
    {
        long outLen = -1;
        try {
            outLen = dataFile.length();
        } catch (IOException ioe)
          {
            System.out.println("Cannot get length of data file.");
            System.exit(1);
          }
        return outLen;
    }

    /** gets the length of the index file. */
    public long getidxFileLength()
    {
        long outLen = -1;
        try {
            outLen = idxFile.length();
        } catch (IOException ioe)
```

```
        {
          System.out.println("Cannot get length of idx file.");
          System.exit(1);
        }
      return outLen;
    }

    /** constructor. */
    public DbFiles(String dbname)
    {
        try {
            // Create or Open the files
            dataFile = new RandomAccessFile(dbname + ".dat", "rw");
            idxFile = new RandomAccessFile(dbname + ".idx", "rw");

            // set initial pos at end of files
            dataPos = dataFile.length();
            idxPos = idxFile.length();

        } catch (IOException ioe)
          {
            System.out.println("Cannot create the database files.");
            System.out.println(ioe.getMessage());
            System.exit(1);
          }
    }

    /** writes a record to the database. */
    public boolean writeBytes(byte dataBytes[], long newDataPos,
                                                long newIdxPos)
    {
        try {
            // create an IdxRecord
            IdxRecord idxRec = new IdxRecord(newDataPos,
                                            dataBytes.length);

            // write IdxRecord to the idx File
            idxFile.seek(newIdxPos);

            // write the index record
            byte idxBytes[] = idxRec.toByteArray();
            idxFile.write(idxBytes,0,idxBytes.length);

            // write the data bytes to the data file
            dataFile.seek(newDataPos);
            dataFile.write(dataBytes,0,dataBytes.length);

            // store current pointers
            dataPos = dataFile.getFilePointer();
            idxPos = idxFile.getFilePointer();
        } catch (IOException e)
```

```
        {
          System.out.println("Unable to write record to DB.");
          System.out.println(e.getMessage());
          return false;
        }
      return true;
  }

  /** reads a record from the database. */
  public byte [] readBytes(long newIdxPos)
  {
      byte dataBytes[] = null;
      try {
          // read the IdxRecord
          idxFile.seek(newIdxPos);

          // read the index record from the idx file
          byte idxBytes[] = new byte[IdxRecord.REC_LENGTH];
          idxFile.read(idxBytes,0,idxBytes.length);

          // create the IdxRecord
          IdxRecord idxRec = new IdxRecord(idxBytes);

          // read the data bytes from the data file
          dataBytes = new byte[(int)idxRec.getrecLength()];
          dataFile.seek(idxRec.getrecPos());
          dataFile.read(dataBytes,0,dataBytes.length);

          // store current pointers
          dataPos = dataFile.getFilePointer();
          idxPos = idxFile.getFilePointer();
      } catch (IOException e)
        {
          System.out.println("Unable to write record to DB.");
          System.out.println(e.getMessage());
        }

      return dataBytes;
  }

  /** close a database. */
  public void close()
  {
     try {
          dataFile.close();
          idxFile.close();
     } catch (Exception e) { }
  }
```

```
    /** write the header to the database. */
    public void writeHeader(DbHeader inHeader)
    {
        byte headerBytes[] = inHeader.toByteArray();

        if (headerBytes == null)
        {
          System.out.println("Unable to write database header.");
          System.out.println("Database left in inconsistent state.");
          System.exit(1);
        }

        try {
          // read the IdxRecord
          idxFile.seek(0);

          // read the index record from the idx file
          byte idxBytes[] = new byte[IdxRecord.REC_LENGTH];
          idxFile.read(idxBytes,0,idxBytes.length);

          // create the IdxRecord
          IdxRecord idxRec = new IdxRecord(idxBytes);

          // check if need to relocate the header
          if (headerBytes.length <= idxRec.getrecLength())
          {
              this.writeBytes(headerBytes, idxRec.getrecPos(), 0);
          }
          else
          {
              // relocate the record
              long endOfData = this.getdataFileLength();
              this.writeBytes(headerBytes, endOfData, 0);
          }
        } catch (IOException ioe)
          {
           System.out.println("Unable to write database header.");
           System.out.println("Database left in inconsistent state.");
           System.exit(1);
          }
       System.out.println("Successfully wrote header to DB.");
    }
}
```

8.5 OBJECT SERIALIZATION

This category of classes allows objects to be serialized and deserialized. Serialization of an object means the object will be broken down into a byte array. The serialized form will store enough information to deserialize the object. Deserialization will reconstitute the object from its serialized form.

- **Serializable.** Used to identify a class as being serializable.
- **Externalizable.** This interface extends Serializable. This interface allows classes to provide their own implementation for serializing and deserializing.
- **ObjectInputStream.** This class extends InputStream. This class provides methods for reading an object from an input stream. This class restores objects that were written out previously using ObjectOutputStream.
- **ObjectOutputStream.** This class extends OutputStream. This class provides methods for writing an object to an output stream. Only those objects that implement the Serializable or Externalizable interfaces can be serialized using this class.
- **ObjectStreamClass.** This class contains a description of a class that can be serialized or one that is already serialized. You can think of this class as the serialized version of the class Object.
- **ObjectInput.** This interface extends DataInput. This interface is used to read objects in a machine-independent way.
- **ObjectInputValidation.** An interface that provides a callback method to allow for validation of objects within a graph.
- **ObjectOutput.** This interface extends DataOutput. This interface is used to write objects in a machine-independent way.

Source 8.10 implements a simple reminder program.

SOURCE 8.10 SimpleReminder.java

```
package jbook.chp8;

import java.io.BufferedReader;
import java.io.InputStreamReader;
import java.io.PrintWriter;
import java.io.IOException;
import java.io.FileOutputStream;
import java.io.FileInputStream;
import java.io.File;
import java.io.ObjectOutputStream;
import java.io.ObjectInputStream;

import java.util.Date;
import java.util.StringTokenizer;
import java.util.GregorianCalendar;
import java.util.Calendar;
```

```
public class SimpleReminder extends Thread
{
    BufferedReader   input;
    PrintWriter      output;
    ReminderData     reminders[];
    String           sDataFileName;

    public SimpleReminder(BufferedReader input, PrintWriter output,
                                                String sDataFileName)
    {
        this.input = input;
        this.output = output;
        this.sDataFileName = sDataFileName;

        try {
            reminders = loadReminders(sDataFileName);
        } catch (Exception e)
          {
            output.println("Error loading reminder data file." +
                           "\nError: " + e.toString());
            reminders = null;
          }
    }

    public void run()
    {
        output.println("Simple Reminder v1.0");
        output.println("Type 'help' for a list of options");

        reminders = checkReminders(reminders, output, sDataFileName);

        String sCommand = new String();

        while (true)
        {
            output.println();
            output.print("reminder>");
            output.flush();

            try {
                sCommand = input.readLine();
            } catch (IOException ioe)
              {
                output.println("Error in input data: " + ioe.toString());
                continue;
              }

            if (sCommand.equalsIgnoreCase("help"))
                printHelp(output);
```

```
        else if (sCommand.equalsIgnoreCase("add"))
            reminders = addReminder(reminders, input, output,
                                                sDataFileName);

        else if (sCommand.equalsIgnoreCase("list"))
            listReminders(reminders, output);

        else if (sCommand.equalsIgnoreCase("quit"))
            System.exit(0);

        else
            output.println("Invalid command: " + sCommand);

        reminders = checkReminders(reminders, output, sDataFileName);
    }
}

ReminderData[] checkReminders(ReminderData reminders[],
                        PrintWriter output, String sDataFileName)
{
    Date dtNow = new Date();

    if (reminders != null)
    {
        int iNumToDelete = 0;
        boolean bDeleteReminder[] = new boolean[reminders.length];

        for (int iCount = 0; iCount < reminders.length; iCount++)
        {
            if (dtNow.after(reminders[iCount].getReminderDate()))
            {
                output.println(reminders[iCount].getReminderText());
                bDeleteReminder[iCount] = true;
                iNumToDelete++;
            }
            else
                bDeleteReminder[iCount] = false;
        }

        if (iNumToDelete == 0)
            return (reminders);
        else
        {
            // collapse array
            ReminderData newReminders[] =
                    new ReminderData[reminders.length -
                                    iNumToDelete];
            int iOffset = 0;

            for (int iCount = 0; iCount < reminders.length; iCount++)
            {
```

```
                if (bDeleteReminder[iCount])
                    iOffset++;
                else
                    newReminders[iCount - iOffset] =
                                                reminders[iCount];
            }

            // write reminders to reminder file
            try {
                writeRemindersToFile(newReminders, sDataFileName);
            } catch (IOException ioe)
              {
                output.println("Error writing reminders to file." +
                               "\nError: " + ioe.toString());
                return (reminders);
              }

            return (newReminders);
        }
    }
    else
        return (reminders);
}

ReminderData[] loadReminders(String sDataFileName)
                                throws IOException, Exception
{
    File fDataFile = new File(sDataFileName);
    if (!fDataFile.exists())
        return (null);

    FileInputStream fis = new FileInputStream(sDataFileName);
    ObjectInputStream oInStream = new ObjectInputStream(fis);

    int iNumReminders = oInStream.readInt();
    if (iNumReminders > 0)
    {
        ReminderData storedReminders[] =
                                new ReminderData[iNumReminders];

        for (int iCount = 0; iCount < iNumReminders; iCount++)
        {
            storedReminders[iCount] =
                            (ReminderData) oInStream.readObject();
        }

        return (storedReminders);
    }
    else
        return (null);
}
```

```
void printHelp(PrintWriter output)
{
    output.println("Simple Reminder v1.0 Help");
    output.println("\tadd\tAdd reminder");
    output.println("\thelp\tDisplay help listing");
    output.println("\tlist\tList all reminders");
    output.println("\tquit\tQuit program");
}

ReminderData[] addReminder(ReminderData reminders[],
                           BufferedReader input,
                           PrintWriter output,
                           String sDataFileName)
{
    String sDate;
    String sTime;
    String sText;

    output.print("Date: ");
    output.flush();

    try {
        sDate = input.readLine();
    } catch (IOException ioe)
      {
        output.println("Error in input data: " + ioe.toString());
        return (reminders);
      }

    output.print("Time: ");
    output.flush();

    try {
        sTime = input.readLine();
    } catch (IOException ioe)
      {
        output.println("Error in input data: " + ioe.toString());
        return (reminders);
      }

    output.print("Text: ");
    output.flush();

    try {
        sText = input.readLine();
    } catch (IOException ioe)
      {
        output.println("Error in input data: " + ioe.toString());
        return (reminders);
      }
```

```
    Date dt = null;
    try {
        dt = parseDate(sDate, sTime);
    } catch (Exception e)
      {
        output.println(e.toString());
        return (reminders);
      }

    // add reminder to reminder array
    ReminderData newReminder = new ReminderData(dt, sText);
    int iNumReminders = 0;
    if (reminders != null)
        iNumReminders = reminders.length;

    ReminderData newReminders[] =
            new ReminderData[iNumReminders + 1];
    for (int iCount = 0; iCount < iNumReminders; iCount++)
        newReminders[iCount] = reminders[iCount];

    newReminders[newReminders.length - 1] = newReminder;

    // add reminder to reminder file
    try {
        writeRemindersToFile(newReminders, sDataFileName);
    } catch (IOException ioe)
      {
        output.println("Error writing reminder to file." +
                       "\nError: " + ioe.toString());
        return (reminders);
      }

    return (newReminders);
}

void listReminders(ReminderData reminders[], PrintWriter output)
{
    if (reminders != null)
    {
        output.println("Date\t\tTime\tText");
        output.println("—\t\t—\t—");

        GregorianCalendar calendar = new GregorianCalendar();

        for (int iCount = 0; iCount < reminders.length; iCount++)
        {
            calendar.setTime(reminders[iCount].getReminderDate());
            String sDate = (calendar.get(Calendar.MONTH) + 1) +
                          "/" + calendar.get(Calendar.DAY_OF_MONTH) +
                          "/" + calendar.get(Calendar.YEAR);
```

```
            int iMinute = calendar.get(Calendar.MINUTE);
            String sMinute = "";
            if (iMinute < 10)
                sMinute = "0" + iMinute;
            else
                sMinute = "" + iMinute;

            String sTime = calendar.get(Calendar.HOUR_OF_DAY) +
                                                    ":" + sMinute;

            String sText = reminders[iCount].getReminderText();

            output.println(sDate + "\t" +
                           sTime + "\t" +
                           sText);
        }
    }
    else
        output.println("No reminders are set");

}

void writeRemindersToFile (ReminderData reminders[],
                           String sDataFileName)
                           throws IOException
{
    FileOutputStream fos = new FileOutputStream(sDataFileName);
    ObjectOutputStream oOutStream = new ObjectOutputStream(fos);

    if (reminders != null)
    {
        oOutStream.writeInt(reminders.length);
        for (int iCount = 0; iCount < reminders.length; iCount++)
        {
            oOutStream.writeObject(reminders[iCount]);
        }
    }

    oOutStream.flush();
    fos.close();
}

Date parseDate (String sDate, String sTime) throws Exception
{
    StringTokenizer stDate = new StringTokenizer(sDate, "/");
    StringTokenizer stTime = new StringTokenizer(sTime, ":");

    int iMonth = 0;
    int iDay = 0;
    int iYear = 0;
    int iHour = 0;
```

```
        int iMinute = 0;

        try {
            iMonth = Integer.parseInt(stDate.nextToken()) - 1;
            iDay = Integer.parseInt(stDate.nextToken());
            iYear = Integer.parseInt(stDate.nextToken());
        } catch (Exception e)
          {
            throw new Exception("Invalid date format");
          }

        try {
            iHour = Integer.parseInt(stTime.nextToken());
            iMinute = Integer.parseInt(stTime.nextToken());
        } catch (Exception e)
          {
            throw new Exception("Invalid time format");
          }

        GregorianCalendar calendar = new GregorianCalendar(iYear,
                                        iMonth, iDay, iHour, iMinute);
        return (calendar.getTime());
    }

    public static void main (String args[])
    {
        BufferedReader input =
                new BufferedReader(new InputStreamReader(System.in));
        PrintWriter output = new PrintWriter(System.out, true);

        SimpleReminder simpleReminder =
                    new SimpleReminder(input, output, "reminder.dat");

        simpleReminder.start();
    }

}
```

```
package jbook.chp8;

import java.io.Serializable;
import java.util.Date;

public class ReminderData implements Serializable
{
    Date    dtReminderDate;
    String  sReminderText;

    public ReminderData (Date dtReminderDate, String sReminderText)
    {
```

```
        this.dtReminderDate = dtReminderDate;
        this.sReminderText = sReminderText;
    }

    public void setReminderDate (Date dtReminderDate)
    {
        this.dtReminderDate = dtReminderDate;
    }

    public Date getReminderDate ()
    {
        return (dtReminderDate);
    }

    public void setReminderText (String sReminderText)
    {
        this.sReminderText = sReminderText;
    }

    public String getReminderText ()
    {
        return (sReminderText);
    }
}
```

The example just shown implements a simple reminder program. You can enter a text string to be displayed at a certain time and date. If you terminate the program and start it up again later, the reminders that you entered in will still be there. This example uses object serialization to write out the ReminderData objects to a file. The key points related to object serialization are these:

- **ReminderData class.** This class implements the Serializable interface. This is all that is needed to make an object serializable.
- **loadReminders() method.** This method creates an ObjectInputStream on an existing FileInputStream. Using the readObject() method, the ReminderData objects that were stored in the file are deserialized and instantiated. Now they are ready to use in the rest of the program.
- **writeRemindersToFile() method.** This method creates an ObjectOutputStream on an existing FileOutputStream. Using the writeObject method, the ReminderData objects are serialized and written to the underlying FileOutputStream. The flush() method ensures that the ObjectOutputStream has written out all data contained in memory. The ReminderData objects are now safely stored in case the program terminates abnormally.

In this example you also see how to read and write to a file, as well as how to gather information from the console. The following points are also of interest:

- The FileInputStream and FileOutputStream classes are used to read and write data to a file.
- In the main() method a BufferedReader is constructed on top of an InputStreamReader, which in turn is constructed on the System.in variable. The System.in variable gives an InputStream to the console input. The InputStreamReader class converts the byte stream into a character stream so we can use the BufferedReader class. Using the BufferedReader.readLine() method we are able to obtain input from the console.
- In the main() method a PrintWriter is constructed on top of the System.out variable. The System.out variable gives us a PrintStream to the console output. Since the PrintStream class now supports character streams, constructing a PrintWriter is unnecessary for writing to the console. However, it is good practice to start using the new classes.

8.6 EXCEPTIONS

The io package has defined exceptions unique to I/O:

- **IOException.** This class extends Exception. A general I/O error like a disk-read or disk-write failure. For example, if a directory has the maximum number of files allowed in it (differs from OS to OS), this exception would be thrown if you attempted to create a new file in that directory.
- **InterruptedIOException.** This class extends IOException. An IO operation has been interrupted. This will be thrown if a low-priority thread is performing IO when a higher-priority thread interrupts it.
- **FileNotFoundException.** This class extends IOException. This class is thrown if you try to read a file that does not exist. You can avoid this by testing the exists() method in the File class. Source 8.10 demonstrates the use of the exists() method.
- **EOFException.** This class extends IOException. An End Of File was reached unexpectedly.
- **UTFDataFormatException.** This class extends IOException. This class is thrown if a malformed UNICODE Text Format (UTF) String has been read from a DataInputStream.
- **CharConversionException.** This class extends IOException. This is a base class for character conversion exceptions.
- **SyncFailedException.** This class extends IOException.
- **UnsupportedEncodingException.** This class extends IOException. This class is thrown if the specified encoding is not supported.

The following are exceptions specific to serialization.

- **ObjectStreamException.** This class extends IOException. This is an abstract base class for all specific object stream class exceptions.
- **InvalidClassException.** This class extends ObjectStreamException. This class is thrown when the Serialization run time detects a problem with the class.

- **InvalidObjectException.** This class extends ObjectStreamException. This is thrown by a class that is explicitly not allowing itself to be serialized.
- **NotActiveException.** This class extends ObjectStreamException. This class is thrown when serialization or deserialization is not available.
- **NotSerializableException.** This class extends ObjectStreamException. This class is thrown by the Serialization run time when a class cannot be serialized.
- **OptionalDataException.** This class extends ObjectStreamException. This class is thrown if readObject has optional data.
- **StreamCorruptedException.** This class extends ObjectStreamException. This class is thrown if the data read from the stream violates consistency checks. This could happen if the data is corrupted or has been changed by another program.
- **WriteAbortedException.** This class extends ObjectStreamException. This class is thrown during the reading of an object if one of the ObjectStreamExceptions was thrown during the writing of the object.

8.7 SUMMARY

The input/output package is a flexible, stream-based system for retrieving data from a variety of sources and outputting data to a variety of sinks. This chapter has demonstrated the power of the stream approach, a nontrivial example of RandomAccessFiles and object serialization.

CHAPTER 9

Package java.net

OBJECTIVE

This package contains classes that provide networking functionality. In this chapter you will learn how to use the socket classes to create client/server applications, and how to use URLs for accessing information via the Internet.

The java.net package provides networking classes and methods for both connecting to the Internet (internetworking) and to other computers on a local network (networking). The socket classes and methods will look very familiar to those of you who have programmed using Berkeley sockets or Winsock. The Java implementation is very easy to use because there are no complicated structures, and the exception handling allows your code to flow more smoothly because you do not have to check each statement for error codes.

9.1 INTERNETWORKING

Internetworking is the term used here for accessing the Internet. Java provides a series of classes you can use to access information on the Internet. Classes are available for URLs, handling HTTP, and handling content available on the Web. Let's look at the classes in this section.

- **InetAddress.** A class that represents an Internet address. It has methods to create and get Internet addresses. Source 9.1 demonstrates getting your host's Internet address and the address of a remote host.

SOURCE 9.1 TestInetAddress.java

```
// TestInetAddress.java
package jwiley.chp9;

import java.net.InetAddress;
import java.net.UnknownHostException;

/** Class to demonstrate the InetAddress class. */
public class TestInetAddress
{
    /** main() method to invoke from the JVM. */
    public static void main(String args[])
    {
        InetAddress myAddress=null;
        InetAddress Mystech=null;

        // get my machine's internet address
        try
        {
            myAddress = InetAddress.getLocalHost();
        } catch (UnknownHostException uhe)
          {
                System.out.println("Local host is unknown.");
                System.exit(1);
          }

        System.out.println(myAddress.toString());

        // get mystech's internet address
        try
        {
            Mystech = InetAddress.getByName("Mystech.com");
        } catch (UnknownHostException uhe)
          {
                System.out.println(uhe.toString());
                System.out.println("Mystech.com not known.");
                System.out.println("Ensure TCP/IP connection to " +
                                   "internet is up.");
                System.exit(1);
          }

        System.out.println(Mystech.toString());
    }
}
```

A run of Source 9.1 produces the following:

```
C:\jwiley\chp9>java jwiley.chp9.TestInetAddress
emobile.mystech.com/42.1.5.65
Mystech.com/42.3.0.4
```

- **URL.** This class is a representation of a Uniform Resource Locator (URL). This class allows you to create a URL by defining fields, create a URL by parsing a URL string, compare URLs, connect to a URL, getContent() of a URL object, and get a URLStreamHandler. Source 9.2 demonstrates creating and using a URL object.
- **URLEncoder.** This class is used to convert Strings into a MIME format. MIME stands for Multipurpose Internet Mail Extensions and is used to encode different file types for transmission over the Internet.
- **URLConnection.** This is an abstract class that represents an active connection to a URL. This class allows a connection to be created, to guessContentType from the file extension, to getContent() of the object, to get an InputStream from the object or an OutputStream to the object. Source 9.2 demonstrates creating an input stream to a URL, receiving the content of that URL, and writing that content to a file.

SOURCE 9.2 TestUrl.java

```
// TestUrl.java
package jwiley.chp9;

import java.net.URL;
import java.net.MalformedURLException;
import java.io.InputStream;
import java.io.FileInputStream;
import java.io.DataInputStream;
import java.io.FileOutputStream;
import java.io.IOException;

/** Class to demonstrate the use of the URL class. */
public class TestUrl
{
    /** main() method to invoke from JVM. */
    public static void main(String args[])
    {
        if (args.length < 2)
        {
            System.out.println(
                    "USAGE: java tstURL URL_string output_file_name");
            System.exit(1);
        }

        String urlString = new String(args[0]);
        String fileName = new String(args[1]);

        URL theURL = null;
        try
        {
            theURL = new URL(urlString);
        } catch (MalformedURLException mue)
```

```
        {
          System.out.println(mue.toString());
          System.exit(1);
        }

      try
      {
        byte buf[] = new byte[1000];
        InputStream input = theURL.openStream();
        FileOutputStream fout = new FileOutputStream(fileName);
        int ch;
        int count = 0;
        while (true)
        {
              int n = input.read(buf, 0, 1000);
              if (n == -1) break;
              fout.write(buf, 0, n);
              count += n;
              System.out.print(".");
              System.out.flush();
        }

        fout.close();
        input.close();
      } catch (IOException ioe)
        {
          ioe.printStackTrace();
          System.exit(1);
        }
    }
}
```

A run of this program with the command line "java jwiley.chp9.TestUrl www .mystech.com urlout1.tst" produces the file urlout1.tst with the following contents (truncated here):

```
<HTML>
<HEAD>
  <META NAME="GENERATOR" CONTENT="Adobe PageMill 2.0 Mac">
  <TITLE>Mystech Associates: Home Page</TITLE>
</HEAD>
<BODY BGCOLOR="#ffffff">

<FORM METHOD="GET" ACTION="http://altavista.digital.com/cgi-bin/query"
ENCTYPE="x-www-form-encoded">
<P><INPUT TYPE="hidden" NAME="pg" VALUE="q"><BODY><BR>
</P>
```

```
<P ALIGN=CENTER><IMG SRC="logo.gif" WIDTH="240" HEIGHT="98" ALT="Mystech
logo"
NATURALSIZEFLAG="0" ALIGN="BOTTOM"><BR>
<BR>
<STRONG>- FOR INTERNAL MYSTECH USE ONLY - </STRONG></P>

<H2>Employee News and Notes</H2>

<UL>
  <P><BR>
  <BR>

  <LI><STRONG>A New Mystech Home Page:</STRONG> Steve Bowlds has set up a
  <A HREF="http://internal-web/~www">new employee home page</A> with links
  to several Mystech projects, maps and addresses of all of our sites, and
  all of the SEI CMM briefings, documents, processes, and forms for our Level
  2 certification. The version of the home page you are now reading will
  soon be history. Please update your bookmarks. <BR>
...
```

- **HttpURLConnection.** This class extends URLConnection. This is an abstract class that provides methods and constants specific to the HTTP protocol. The HTTP protocol is one of the most popular protocols used on the Internet.
- **URLStreamHandler.** An abstract class for a URL stream handler. It should be subclassed to create stream handlers for specific protocols.
- **ContentHandler.** An abstract class to getContent() from a URL and create the object of the appropriate type.
- **ContentHandlerFactory.** An interface to create a ContentHandler for the specific MIME content type.
- **FileNameMap.** This is an interface that defines a method for mapping between a filename and a MIME type string.

9.2 NETWORKING

Sockets are very common methods of network programming. This has been implemented on Unix operating systems for many years. Socket programming should be easy to pick up if you are familiar with reading and writing to files. Once the file or socket is created, input and output streams can be created to perform input and output on either an underlying socket or an underlying file. This section describes the classes necessary for creating socket clients and servers.

- **ServerSocket.** A class that allows you to continually listen to a port and accept multiple connections from socket clients. Using threads, you could spawn off a thread for each incoming socket connection. Source 9.3 is a simple example that accepts and processes a single connection.

SOURCE 9.3 SocketWriter.java

```
// SocketWriter.java
package jwiley.chp9;

import java.net.Socket;
import java.io.OutputStream;
import java.io.InputStreamReader;
import java.io.BufferedReader;
import java.io.PrintWriter;

/** Class to demonstrate writing to a Socket. */
public class SocketWriter
{
    /** main() method to invoke from JVM. */
    public static void main(String args[])
    {
        if (args.length < 2)
        {
            System.out.println("USAGE: java socketWriter hostname port");
            System.exit(1);
        }

        String host = new String(args[0]);
        String portStr = new String(args[1]);

        try
        {
            int port = Integer.parseInt(portStr);

            // create the socket
            Socket outSock = new Socket(host,port);
            System.out.println("Socket created to " + host);

            // set up the streams
            OutputStream outStream = outSock.getOutputStream();
            PrintWriter pw = new PrintWriter(outStream, true);
            BufferedReader br = new BufferedReader(new
                                  InputStreamReader(System.in));

            // while input does not equal 'exit' output to socket
            boolean done = false;
            System.out.println("Type sentences to send. " +
                               "Type 'exit' to quit.");
            while (!done)
            {
                String line = br.readLine();
                if (!line.startsWith("exit"))
                {
                    pw.println(line);
                }
```

```
                else
                {
                    // stop reader
                    pw.println("~READER_STOP~");
                    done = true;
                }
            }

            // close the socket
            outSock.close();
        } catch (Exception e)
          {
            e.printStackTrace();
            System.exit(1);
          }
    }
}
```

A run of Source 9.3 produces:

```
c:\jwiley\chp9>java SocketReader 8001
Server Socket created to 8001
Awaiting a connection...
Connection accepted.
Java is a great technology that has been endorsed by all the major vendors.
```

- **Socket.** A class that represents a socket client. Methods in this class allow you to create a socket, get an output stream or an input stream to the socket, and close the socket. Source 9.4 demonstrates a socket client that can connect to a socket, accept input (similar to chat), and write it out to the socket. The program was run in conjunction with the socketReader used in the previous code.

SOURCE 9.4 SocketReader.java

```
// SocketReader.java
package jwiley.chp9;

import java.net.ServerSocket;
import java.net.Socket;
import java.io.InputStream;
import java.io.BufferedReader;
import java.io.InputStreamReader;

/** Class to demonstrate reading from a Socket. */
public class SocketReader
{
```

```
    /** main() method to invoke from JVM. */
    public static void main(String args[])
    {
         if (args.length < 1)
         {
            System.out.println("USAGE: java socketReader port");
            System.exit(1);
         }

         String portStr = new String(args[0]);

         try
         {
            int port = Integer.parseInt(portStr);

            // create the server socket
            ServerSocket readServer = new ServerSocket(port);
            System.out.println("Server Socket created to " + port);
            System.out.println("Awaiting a connection...");

            // wait for a connection
            Socket connection = readServer.accept();
            System.out.println("Connection accepted.");

            // set up the streams
            InputStream inStream = connection.getInputStream();
            BufferedReader br = new BufferedReader(new
                                  InputStreamReader(inStream));

            // while input does not equal 'exit' output to socket
            boolean done = false;
            while (!done)
            {
                String line = br.readLine();
                if (!line.startsWith("~READER_STOP~"))
                {
                        System.out.println(line);
                }
                else
                        done = true;
            }

            // close the server
            readServer.close();
         } catch (Exception e)
           {
            e.printStackTrace();
            System.exit(1);
           }
    }

}
```

A run of Source 9.4 produces:

```
c:\jwiley\chp9>java SocketWriter emobile 8001
Socket created to emobile
Type sentences to send. Type 'exit' to quit.
Java is a great technology that has been endorsed by all the major vendors.
exit
```

- **SocketImpl.** An abstract class that lets you define your own socket implementation for different security policies or firewalls.
- **SocketImplFactory.** An interface that creates Socket Implementations for various security policies.
- **DatagramPacket.** This class represents a datagram packet. Datagrams send information using a connectionless protocol. The datagram packet contains all the addressing information necessary to be sent to the proper host.
- **DatagramSocket.** This class is used for sending and receiving datagram packets. Note that since each datagram packet contains its own addressing information, a set of datagram packets sent from one machine to another may arrive in a different order than the order they were sent.
- **DatagramSocketImpl.** An abstract class that lets you define your own datagram implementation.
- **MulticastSocket.** This class extends DatagramSocket. This class allows the sending and receiving of IP multicast packets. This class can be used to join a multicast host on a particular port. Any packets sent would be broadcast to all other clients who have joined the host. You will also receive packets sent by other clients to the multicast host.

9.3 EXCEPTIONS

The java.net package defines exceptions unique to networking.

- **ProtocolException.** This class extends IOException. It is thrown if a socket connect gets a protocol error.
- **UnknownHostException.** This class extends IOException. The Internet address requested by a network client could not be resolved.
- **UnknownServiceException.** This class extends IOException. An unknown service exception has occurred. For example, it is thrown if a server you are connected to cannot perform the type of service that you have requested.
- **MalformedURLException.** This class extends IOException. It is thrown if a URL string could not be parsed to create a URL class.
- **SocketException.** This class extends IOException. It is thrown if an error occurs while attempting to use a socket.
- **BindException.** This class extends SocketException. This class is thrown if a ServerSocket fails to bind to the specified address or port.

- **ConnectException.** This class extends SocketException. This class is thrown if a socket fails to connect to the specified address or port.
- **NoRouteToHost.** This class extends SocketException. This class is thrown if the current network routing configuration does not provide a pathway to the specified host.

9.4 SUMMARY

The java.net chapter provides classes for both local networking (Socket, ServerSocket) and internetworking (inetAddress, URL, HttpUrlConnection). This package truly stands as one of the breakthroughs of Java. You should note that all of the examples in this chapter are extremely short. A lot of power has been packed into a small package. Combined with the io package (discussed in Chapter 8), sharing data and objects between computers is as easy as sharing data between processes on the same machine.

CHAPTER 10

The Abstract Windows Toolkit

One of the cornerstones of the Macintosh philosophy is that people should tell computers what to do and not the other way around.

—Stephen Chernicoff, *Macintosh Revealed*

OBJECTIVE

This chapter enables the reader to understand the implementation of the Abstract Window Toolkit, how to use all the major GUI elements in the AWT, and see a sophisticated GUI for a professional-style drawing program.

In 1984, the Apple Macintosh changed the face of computing by evangelizing the benefits of graphical user interfaces (GUI) to the masses. In the following years, the Massachusetts Institute of Technology created X Windows for Unix platforms and Microsoft created MS Windows for Intel-compatible PCs. The graphical user interfaces on these three platform groups have evolved and improved over the years. The Macintosh GUI has been enhanced in small and large ways, most recently by pioneering video and virtual reality on every Mac with QuickTime and QuickTime VR. The various Unix vendors have agreed upon and transitioned to a single GUI standard called the Common Desktop Environment (CDE). Microsoft has now caught up to the other two camps with its release of Windows 95. The success and market demand for graphical user interfaces are simply a validation of a common-sense principle: "A picture is worth a thousand words." There are many forms of information that can be processed faster in a graphical fashion. Second, many GUI elements can be manipulated via a mouse, which eliminates the need for advanced typing skills to use the computer. Therefore, combining the mouse with the elements of a graphical user interface brings us closer to the computer becoming an "information appliance." The introduction of sub-$500 Internet appliances that run Java applications could increase this trend as well as truly bring computing to the masses. Most homeowners do not need a $3000 Pentium to store their cooking recipes or to send e-mail to Grandma Whitaker in Florida.

The Abstract Window Toolkit (AWT) is a platform-independent interface that allows development of a GUI that runs on all major platforms. In the following sections we will describe how the AWT performs this cross-platform feat, and then demonstrate all the major AWT functionality.

10.1 UNDERSTANDING THE IMPLEMENTATION OF THE AWT

In all cross-platform products the product developer must choose between one of two strategies: a common look and feel or common functionality with a platform-unique look and feel. The first strategy of a common look and feel is much harder to implement; however, you gain the advantage of customers knowing how to work the application no matter which platform they are on. In essence, this is the strategy of the Common Desktop Environment. It is important to note, however, that CDE is possible because the various Unix flavors are all very similar and all use X Windows as the GUI backbone. Some Microsoft applications also follow this common-look-and-feel approach. The problem with the common-look-and-feel approach is that it tends to stifle new innovation on a single platform that has not yet migrated (and may never) to all supported platforms.

The AWT uses the "common functionality/specific implementation" approach. The idea is very object-oriented in that the functionality is the superclass (high-level abstraction) and each platform's specific look and feel is a subclass. This allows applications to take advantage of a platform's unique GUI and make Java applications look and feel just like other native applications. It also encourages innovation by allowing third parties to develop variations of GUI components.

The practice of modifying and replacing portions of the GUI is widespread in the Macintosh and Unix domains. For example, there are many superb alternate window managers for Unix, like the GNU window manager (GWM) and virtual window managers like FVWM. On the Macintosh, you can find virtual desktop replacements, Copland-style folders and windows, and 3D buttons. Now let's examine the specifics behind how the AWT supports this common functionality/platform-unique look and feel.

The Java AWT uses three concepts to implement common functionality/platform-unique look and feel: abstract objects, toolkits, and peers. Every GUI element supported by the AWT will have a class. Objects of that class can be instantiated. For example, a Button object can be instantiated from the Button class even though there is no physical display of a button. There is no physical display of a button because the

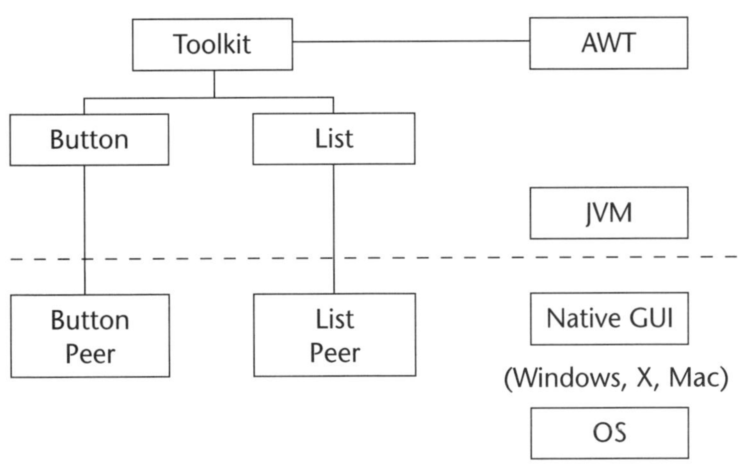

FIGURE 10.1 Java AWT and peers.

Button class in the AWT does not represent a specific look and feel. The specific look and feel would be a "Solaris button" or a "Macintosh button" or an "MS Windows button." The AWT GUI objects are platform-independent abstractions of a GUI. Just as Java byte codes are platform-independent assembly language instructions for a virtual machine, AWT objects are platform-independent GUI elements for a virtual operating system display. The toolkit is the platform-specific implementation of all the GUI elements supported by the AWT. Each toolkit implements the platform-specific GUI elements by creating a GUI "peer." Figure 10.1 shows graphically the relationship between an AWT element, a peer, and the underlying hardware. A peer is an individual platform-specific GUI element. Since every AWT GUI object is derived from the generic AWT object called a Component, every Component will have a peer. Of course, the peer implements the platform-specific behavior of the AWT component. The peer is added to the generic AWT object when the object is added to a container that has a peer.

The JDK 1.0 AWT went a long way to implementing these ideas. The JDK 1.1 and the soon to be released JDK 1.2 take the next logical step: adding new classes to make the JDK more robust. Most of the changes are targeted at software tool developers and designed to make their lives easier. Some of the enhancements include support for Cut/Paste to the clipboard, a new delegation-based event model, lightweight GUI components, popup menus, printing, and more.

Let's examine some code that demonstrates toolkits and peers.

Source 10.1 demonstrates accessing the default toolkit properties.

A run of Source 10.1 produces:

SOURCE 10.1 TestToolkit.java

```
package jwiley.chp10;

import java.awt.Toolkit;
import java.awt.Dimension;
/**
 *  TestToolkit.java
 *  A class to demonstrate the graphics toolkit.
 *  @version 1.1
 *  @author M. Daconta.
 */
class TestToolkit
{
    /** main() method to invoke from JVM. */
    public static void main(String args[])
    {
        Toolkit defTk = Toolkit.getDefaultToolkit();

        String name = System.getProperty("awt.toolkit");
        System.out.println("Toolkit name: " + name);

        Dimension screen = defTk.getScreenSize();
        System.out.println("Screen Dimension       : " +
                                    screen.toString());
        System.out.println("Screen Resolution (dpi): " +
                                    defTk.getScreenResolution());
        System.out.println("Font List.");
        String fonts[] = defTk.getFontList();
        for (int i=0; i < fonts.length; i++)
                System.out.println(i + ") " + fonts[i]);

        System.exit(0);
    }
}
```

```
C:\jdk\bin\java TestToolkit
Toolkit name: sun.awt.windows.WToolkit
Screen Dimension       : java.awt.Dimension[width=800,height=600]
Screen Resolution (dpi): 96
Font List.
0) Dialog
1) SansSerif
2) Serif
3) Monospaced
4) Helvetica
5) TimesRoman
6) Courier
7) DialogInput
8) ZapfDingbats
```

Source 10.2 demonstrates the separate creation of an AWT object from its peer. Figure 10.2 shows a button peer.

SOURCE 10.2 TestPeer.java

```
package jwiley.chp10;

import java.awt.Button;
import java.awt.peer.ComponentPeer;
import java.awt.Frame;
/**
 *  TestPeer.java
 *  A class to test the use of native peers to render the
 *  Java cross-platform GUI.
 *  @version 1.1
 *  @author M. Daconta.
 *
 * Note: getPeer() is deprecated. As of JDK version 1.1,
 * programs should not directly manipulate peers.
 */
class TestPeer
{
    /** main() method to invoke from JVM. */
    public static void main(String args[])
    {
        Button myButton = new Button("my Button");
        ComponentPeer buttonPeer = myButton.getPeer();

        if (buttonPeer == null)
        {
            System.out.println("Button peer not yet created.");
            System.out.println("Button is: " + myButton.toString());
        }
        else
        {
            System.out.println("Button Peer is Created!");
            System.out.println(buttonPeer.toString());
        }

        Frame myFrame = new Frame("my Frame");
        myFrame.add("Center", myButton);
        myFrame.pack();
        myFrame.setVisible(true);  // Here is where peer will be created.

        buttonPeer = myButton.getPeer();
        if (buttonPeer == null)
        {
            System.out.println("Button peer not yet created.");
            System.out.println("Button is: " + myButton.toString());
        }
        else
        {
            System.out.println("Button Peer is Created!");
            System.out.println(buttonPeer.toString());
        }

        ComponentPeer framePeer = myFrame.getPeer();
        System.out.println("Frame Peer is also created.");
        System.out.println(framePeer.toString());
    }
}
```

FIGURE 10.2 A button peer.

A run of Source 10.2 produces:

```
C:\jdk\bin\java TestPeer
Button peer not yet created.
Button is: java.awt.Button[button0,0,0,0x0,invalid,label=my Button]
Button Peer is Created!
sun.awt.windows.WButtonPeer[java.awt.Button[button0,4,23,104x23,label=
my Button]]
Frame Peer is also created.
sun.awt.windows.WFramePeer[java.awt.Frame[frame0,0,0,112x50,invalid,layout=ja
va.awt.BorderLayout,resizable,title=my Frame]]
```

TIP getPeer is deprecated! The JDK 1.0 contained a number of APIs that are considered "deprecated" in version 1.1. A deprecated API is one that will be either removed or superceded by another method or class. If you are compiling JDK1.0 code and you get an error stating that you should compile with the "-deprecated" switch, then you are using an older version of an API.

The getPeer method and its associated class still exist in the JDK but are deprecated. In the case of getPeer the method is no longer considered supported, and the peer class is no longer documented and its use is strongly discouraged. The preceding example only uses it for demonstration purposes.

10.2 MAJOR ELEMENTS OF THE AWT

The AWT can be divided into six major areas.

1. **Components.** The basic elements of every GUI. Components are the building blocks of GUI-based applications. GUI elements are implemented via an abstract *Component* class and its associated subclasses that implement specific GUI components. For X Windows programmers an AWT component is analogous to an X Windows widget. For Windows developers an AWT component is analogous to a CWnd object and subclasses the appropriate derived object (Cbutton, for example).

2. **Events.** A user action is translated into an Event data structure that stores the type of action and where it occurred, as well as other information. The event is then sent the JVM, via the OS. If an EventListener has been registered for this type of event then that listener is called and may perform some action.
3. **EventListeners.** Under the JDK 1.0 model events needed to be caught via an Action or EventHandler method that needed to interpret the event to determine its source and then might take action based on it. The JDK 1.1 introduces something called the Delegation Event Model (which we will see shortly). Under this new model classes register for events they would like to receive and define EventListeners which then receive these events. EventListeners and the new Delegation Event Model simplify and separate the handling of events from the GUI elements that generate them.
4. **Containers.** Components that store other components. The most common container is the window. A Panel is another very common Java AWT container that serves the purpose of grouping other components inside a window. Source 10.3 uses Panels extensively.
5. **Layout and Layout Managers.** A methodology for arranging components within a container. A layout determines where the compoment will be drawn. Layout Managers implement specific policies for laying out components. For example, the GridLayoutManager class lays out added components in a tiled grid.
6. **Painting and Updating.** Although the prefabricated AWT components are useful, you will quickly find it necessary to do custom drawing in your applications. The Java AWT provides the paint(), repaint(), and update() methods to allow you to do just that.

Let's now examine each of these elements in detail as well as develop source code that demonstrates what we have learned.

Components

GUI components are the objects that instantly come to mind when people think of what makes up a graphical user interface. Components are the buttons, menus, lists, checkboxes, and so on. A GUI could be defined simply as a collection of components arranged in a visually appealing manner.

In Java the Component class is the central element of the AWT. Figure 10.3 depicts the component hierarchy in the AWT.

Although graphical user interfaces often scare novice programmers, creating AWT components is as simple as instantiating any Java class. As in using any class in the Java standard library you simply know the constructor arguments and instantiate the object using the new operator and appropriate constructor. Source 10.3 demonstrates the instantiation and display of the majority of the AWT components.

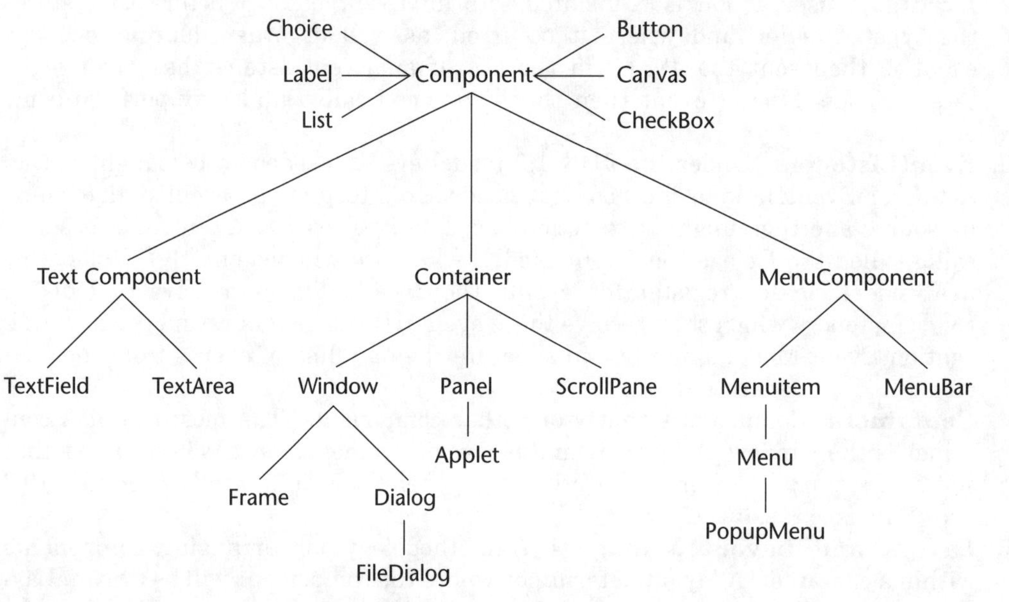

FIGURE 10.3 The Component hierarchy.

SOURCE 10.3 ComponentHolder.java

```
package jwiley.chp10;
/**
 *  ComponentHolder.java
 *  A class that demonstrates the basic AWT objects.
 *  with special support for printing
 *  @version 1.1
 *  @author M. Daconta.
 */
import java.awt.*;
import java.awt.event.*;
import java.awt.event.WindowAdapter;
import java.awt.event.WindowEvent;

/**
 * Class to demonstrate AWT components.
 */
class ComponentHolder extends Frame
implements ActionListener
{
    /** adapter class to handle window close events. */
    class ShutdownAdapter extends WindowAdapter
    {
        public void windowClosing(WindowEvent e)
        { System.exit(0); }
```

```
    }

    public void actionPerformed(ActionEvent ae)
    {
        String sCommand = ae.getActionCommand();
        if ("Exit".equals(sCommand))
        {
            dispose();
        }
          else if ("Print".equals(sCommand))
          {
              PrintJob pjob = getToolkit().getPrintJob(this,
                                          "Printing Test", null);
              // null means user canceled print job
              if (pjob != null)
              {
                  Graphics pg = pjob.getGraphics();
                  if (pg != null)
                  {
                      printAll(pg);
                      pg.dispose(); // flush page
                  }
              pjob.end();
              }
          }
    }

    /** constructor. */
    ComponentHolder()
    {
        super("AWT Basic Components");
        // Support menu for exit and print commands
        MenuBar mBar = new MenuBar();
        setMenuBar(mBar);
        Menu fileMenu = new Menu("File");
        mBar.add(fileMenu);
        MenuItem mi = new MenuItem("Print");
        mi.addActionListener(this);
        fileMenu.add(mi);
        mi = new MenuItem("Exit");
        mi.addActionListener(this);
        fileMenu.add(mi);
        /*
         *  Use a border layout for the set of panels
         */
        setLayout(new BorderLayout());
        setBackground(Color.lightGray);
        addWindowListener(new ShutdownAdapter());
            /*
             * North (or Top) panel contains
             * a button,
             * a label
             * and a checkbox.
             */
```

```
        Panel northP = new Panel();
        northP.setLayout(new FlowLayout(FlowLayout.LEFT));
        northP.add(new Button("my Button"));
        northP.add(new Label("my Label"));
        northP.add(new Checkbox("my CheckBox"));
        add("North", northP);

          /*
          *  Center panel contains
          * a list box with three items
          * a choice box with three items
          * and a white canvas
          */
        Panel centerP = new Panel();
        centerP.setLayout(new FlowLayout(FlowLayout.LEFT));
        List l = null;
        centerP.add(l = new List(5,true));
        l.addItem("listItem1");
        l.addItem("listItem2");
        l.addItem("listItem3");

        Choice c = null;
        centerP.add(c = new Choice());
        c.addItem("choiceItem1");
        c.addItem("choiceItem2");
        c.addItem("choiceItem3");
        Canvas can;
        centerP.add(can = new Canvas());
        can.setBackground(Color.white);
        can.setSize(80,80);
        add("Center", centerP);

          /*
          * The south panel contains
          * A text field
          * and a text area with scroll bars.
          */
        Panel southP = new Panel();
        southP.setLayout(new FlowLayout(FlowLayout.LEFT));
        southP.add(new TextField("my text field."));
        southP.add(new TextArea("my text Area."));
        southP.add(new Scrollbar(Scrollbar.VERTICAL));
        add("South", southP);

        pack();
        show();
    }

    /** main() method to invoke from JVM. */
    public static void main(String args[])
    {
        new ComponentHolder();
    }

}
```

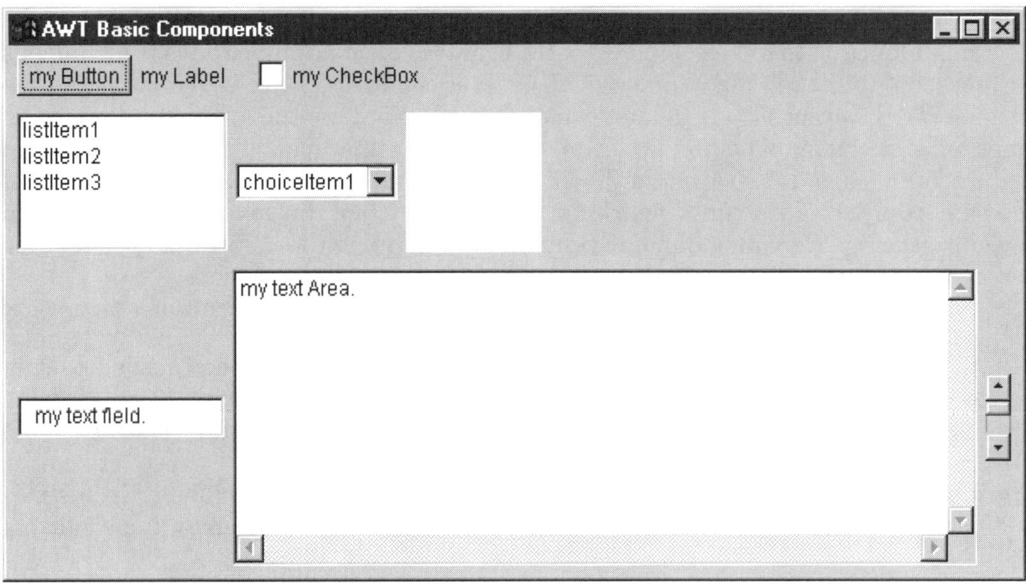

FIGURE 10.4 The AWT Components.

A run of Source 10.3 produces the output shown in Figure 10.4.

The purpose of Source 10.4 is to demonstrate the creation of various components. However, there are other constructs to display them. The creation of the components is the most trivial part of the application just shown. For example, the creation of the button is the call to

```
new Button ("my button");
```

The supporting constructs are the Frame, Panel, and FlowLayout classes. Frame and Panel are containers, while FlowLayout is a layout manager. These will be discussed in the sections to follow. For now just understand the simplicity of creating components.

AWT Events and Event Listeners

Programming graphical user interfaces introduced a new style of programming called "event-driven" programming. Although the terminology differs between X Windows, MS Windows, and the Mac OS, the methodology for event-driven programming is the same. Event-driven programming describes a new paradigm for the control flow of a program. In the event-driven paradigm your program becomes a set of event handlers that are invoked by a user-triggered event (button press, menu selection, key press, etc.). On the Macintosh and MS Windows, the application programmer actually writes the small function to retrieve and dispatch events. This main function is the infamous "event loop" (although MS Windows calls it events messages). In X Windows and the Java AWT the event loop is hidden from you. In X Windows the application programmer registers function pointers to event-handling routines (called callbacks) and then calls a function called XtAppMainLoop(). In the Java AWT events are retrieved and dispatched by the Java run time. Under the 1.0 version of the Java JDK you received events either by overriding handleEvent() or by overriding the mouseUp/down method or keyDown or one of several other methods all associated with events.

The JDK 1.0 approach had several problems. The most significant of which were:

- **Subclass a component to use its functionality.** Developers needed to subclass components to make real use of their functionality (for example, subclassing a Frame to capture events). This was a poor use of subclassing. Subclassing should be used to extend a class in some generic, meaningful way.
- **Capture events via handleEvents.** Capturing all events via handleEvents normally led to large and unwieldy switch statements, causing complex and confusing code.
- **Lack of event filtering.** Since all events filtered through a single function, application performance was degraded.

The Java JDK 1.1 introduced an entirely new event model called the Delegation Model. The purpose of the new model was twofold. First and foremost the model was designed to handle the aforementioned issues. The second purpose of the model was to simplify event processing by adhering to the following principles:

- The model should be simple and easy to use and learn.
- The separation between the GUI and the application should be clear and concise.
- The new model should be easily extendable and flexible in its use.

Several additional design goals also existed that supported runtime detection of events and backward compatibility with existing code.

The Delegation event model is based on two basic tenets: an event Source and an EventListener. Event sources are things like components, the mouse, the keyboard, and others. EventListeners are defined for each generic class of events. Events are broken into two broad classes.

- **Low-Level Events.** Low-level events are those that pertain to the keyboard, mouse, containers, or windows. Low-level events trap things like keys being pressed, mouse actions, windows being iconified or resized, and focus events.
- **Semantic Events.** Semantic events apply to higher-level ideas and are the semantics, or meaning, of an event within a given application. Events that fall into the Semantic category are Action Events, Values changing, items being selected, and so forth.

The stock Event Listener classes are all subclassed from java.util.EventListener. Semantic listener interfaces are:

- **ActionListener.** This captures events such as menu selections, button clicks, list selection changes, and so forth.
- **AdjustmentListener.** Some value was adjusted.
- **ItemListener.** Some item's state has changed.
- **TextListener.** Some text was changed.

Low-level listener interfaces are:

- **ComponentListener.** Some component has changed, (i.e., hidden, resized, moved, etc.). Normally the JDK handles these events, and these events are provided for notification only.
- **ContainerListener.** An item was added to a container. Normally the JDK handles these events, and these events are provided for notification only.
- **FocusListener.** Some component has received keyboard focus.
- **KeyListener.** Some keyboard event has occurred.
- **MouseListener.** Some component has been clicked.
- **MouseMotionListener.** The mouse has been moved or something has been dragged.
- **WindowListener.** A window has been resized, iconified, activated, deactivated, and so forth.

Source 10.4 exercises several of the event listeners provided by the new AWT Delegation model.

SOURCE 10.4 EventTester.java

```
package jwiley.chp10;

import java.awt.*;
import java.awt.event.*;
import java.util.EventObject;
import java.util.Vector;
import java.io.FileOutputStream;
import java.io.PrintWriter;
import java.io.IOException;

/**
 *  EventTester.java
 *  A class that demonstrates event firing and capturing.
 *  @version 1.1
 *  @author M. Daconta.
 */
class EventTester extends Frame implements
```

```
     ActionListener,
     FocusListener,
     KeyListener,
     MouseListener,
     MouseMotionListener,
     WindowListener,
     ItemListener
{
    /** flag to denote events should be saved. */
    private boolean capture;
    /** flag to denote events should be printed. */
    private boolean print;
    /** Vector to store events. */
    private Vector evtVector;

    /** constructor. */
    EventTester()
    {
        super("Event Tester");
        capture = print = false;
        evtVector = new Vector(100);

        MenuBar mBar = new MenuBar();
        setMenuBar(mBar);
        Menu fileMenu = new Menu("File");
        mBar.add(fileMenu);
        CheckboxMenuItem cbmi = new CheckboxMenuItem("Capture Events");
        cbmi.addItemListener(this);
        CheckboxMenuItem cbmi2 = new CheckboxMenuItem("Print Events");
        cbmi2.addItemListener(this);
        MenuItem mi = new MenuItem("Dump Events To File");
        mi.addActionListener(this);
        MenuItem mi2 = new MenuItem("Exit");
        mi2.addActionListener(this);
        fileMenu.add(cbmi);
        fileMenu.add(cbmi2);
        fileMenu.add(mi);
        fileMenu.add(mi2);
        setLocation(new Point(100,100));
        setSize(300,100);
        /*
         *  Use a border layout for a set of panels
         */
        setLayout(new BorderLayout());

            /*
             * North (or Top) panel contains
             * a button,
             * a label
             * and a checkbox.
             */
```

```
        Panel northP = new Panel();
        northP.setLayout(new FlowLayout(FlowLayout.LEFT));
        Button b = new Button("my Button");
        b.addActionListener(this);
        northP.add(b);
       Checkbox cb = new Checkbox("my CheckBox");
       cb.addItemListener(this);
        northP.add(cb);
        add("North", northP);

        // add other event listeners
        addFocusListener(this);
        addKeyListener(this);
        addMouseListener(this);
        addMouseMotionListener(this);
        addWindowListener(this);
        show();
    }

    /** utility routine. */
    public void checkCapture(EventObject eo)
    {
        if (capture)
        {
            evtVector.addElement(eo);
        }
    }

    /** ActionListener method. */
    public void actionPerformed(ActionEvent ae)
    {
        String sCommand = ae.getActionCommand();
        System.out.println("Action Performed: " + sCommand);
        if ("Exit".equals(sCommand))
        {
            dispose();
        }
        else if ("Dump Events To File".equals(sCommand))
        {
            if (evtVector.size() > 0)
            {
                try
                {
                    FileOutputStream fos =
                      new FileOutputStream("Event.txt");
                    PrintWriter pw = new PrintWriter(fos);
                    pw.println("Dumping " + evtVector.size() + " events:");
                    for (int i=0; i < evtVector.size(); i++)
                    {
                        pw.println(
                          ((EventObject)evtVector.elementAt(i)).toString());
```

```
                    }
                    fos.close();
                }
                catch (IOException ioe)
                {
                    System.out.println(ioe.toString());
                    System.out.println("Unable to dump to file.");
                }
            }
            else
            {
                System.out.println("event vector is empty.");
            }
        }
        checkCapture(ae);
    }

    /** ItemListener method. */
    public void itemStateChanged(ItemEvent ie)
    {
        String sItem = (String) ie.getItem();
        System.out.println("Item state changed: " + sItem);
        if ("Capture Events".equals(sItem) &&
             ie.getStateChange() == ie.SELECTED)
        {
            capture = !capture;
        }
        else if ("Print Events".equals(sItem) &&
                  ie.getStateChange() == ie.SELECTED)
        {
            print = !print;
        }
        checkCapture(ie);
    }

    /** FocusListener method. */
    public void focusGained(FocusEvent fe)
    {
        if (print)
            System.out.println("Gained Focus.");
        checkCapture(fe);
    }

    /** FocusListener method. */
    public void focusLost(FocusEvent fe)
    {
        if (print)
            System.out.println("Lost Focus.");
        checkCapture(fe);
    }
```

```
/** KeyListener method. */
public void keyPressed(KeyEvent ke)
{
    if (print)
        System.out.println("Key Pressed.");
    checkCapture(ke);
}

/** KeyListener method. */
public void keyReleased(KeyEvent ke)
{
    if (print)
        System.out.println("Key Released.");
    checkCapture(ke);
}

/** KeyListener method. */
public void keyTyped(KeyEvent ke)
{
    if (print)
    {
        System.out.println("Key Typed.");
        System.out.println("Key char: " + ke.getKeyChar());
    }
    checkCapture(ke);
}

/** MouseListener method. */
public void mouseClicked(MouseEvent me)
{
    if (print)
    {
        System.out.println("Mouse Clicked.");
        System.out.println("At (x,y): " + "(" +
                           me.getX() + "," + me.getY() +
                           ")");
    }
    checkCapture(me);
}

/** MouseListener method. */
public void mouseEntered(MouseEvent me)
{
    if (print)
        System.out.println("Mouse Entered.");
    checkCapture(me);
}

/** MouseListener method. */
public void mouseExited(MouseEvent me)
{
```

```
        if (print)
            System.out.println("Mouse Exited.");
        checkCapture(me);
    }

    /** MouseListener method. */
    public void mousePressed(MouseEvent me)
    {
        if (print)
            System.out.println("Mouse Pressed.");
        checkCapture(me);
    }

    /** MouseListener method. */
    public void mouseReleased(MouseEvent me)
    {
        if (print)
            System.out.println("Mouse Released.");
        checkCapture(me);
    }

    /** MouseMotionListener method. */
    public void mouseDragged(MouseEvent me)
    {
        if (print)
            System.out.println("Mouse Dragged.");
        checkCapture(me);
    }

    /** MouseMotionListener method. */
    public void mouseMoved(MouseEvent me)
    {
        if (print)
            System.out.print(".");
        checkCapture(me);
    }

    /** WindowListener method. */
    public void windowActivated(WindowEvent we)
    {
        if (print)
            System.out.println("Window Activated.");
        checkCapture(we);
    }

    /** WindowListener method. */
    public void windowClosed(WindowEvent we)
    {
        if (print)
            System.out.println("Window Closed.");
        checkCapture(we);
```

```
        System.exit(0);
    }

    /** WindowListener method. */
    public void windowClosing(WindowEvent we)
    {
        if (print)
            System.out.println("Window Closing.");
        checkCapture(we);
        dispose();
    }

    /** WindowListener method. */
    public void windowDeactivated(WindowEvent we)
    {
        if (print)
            System.out.println("Window Deactivated.");
        checkCapture(we);
    }

    /** WindowListener method. */
    public void windowDeiconified(WindowEvent we)
    {
        if (print)
            System.out.println("Window Deiconified.");
        checkCapture(we);
    }

    /** WindowListener method. */
    public void windowIconified(WindowEvent we)
    {
        if (print)
            System.out.println("Window Iconified.");
        checkCapture(we);
    }

    /** WindowListener method. */
    public void windowOpened(WindowEvent we)
    {
        if (print)
            System.out.println("Window Opened.");
        checkCapture(we);
    }

    /** main() method to invoke from the JVM. */
    public static void main(String args[])
    {
        new EventTester();
    }
}
```

A run of Source 10.4 produces three outputs: output to the screen, output to a file, and a window (see Figure 10.5). Here is the output to screen.

```
C:\java\bin\java EventTester
Item state changed: Capture Events
Action Performed: my Button
Item state changed: my CheckBox
Action Performed: my Button
Action Performed: my Button
Item state changed: my CheckBox
Item state changed: my CheckBox
Action Performed: my Button
Action Performed: my Button
Action Performed: Dump Events To File
```

Here is a small sample of the output file:

```
Dumping 21 events:
java.awt.event.ItemEvent[ITEM_STATE_CHANGED,item=Capture
Events,stateChange=SELECTED] on chkmenuitem0
java.awt.event.ActionEvent[ACTION_PERFORMED,cmd=my Button] on button0
java.awt.event.MouseEvent[MOUSE_ENTERED,(52,75),mods=0,clickCount=0] on frame0
java.awt.event.MouseEvent[MOUSE_MOVED,(52,75),mods=0,clickCount=0] on frame0
java.awt.event.MouseEvent[MOUSE_MOVED,(68,83),mods=0,clickCount=0] on frame0
java.awt.event.MouseEvent[MOUSE_MOVED,(94,91),mods=0,clickCount=0] on frame0
java.awt.event.MouseEvent[MOUSE_MOVED,(146,94),mods=0,clickCount=0] on frame0
java.awt.event.MouseEvent[MOUSE_MOVED,(160,88),mods=0,clickCount=0] on frame0
java.awt.event.MouseEvent[MOUSE_MOVED,(170,80),mods=0,clickCount=0] on frame0
java.awt.event.MouseEvent[MOUSE_EXITED,(172,72),mods=0,clickCount=0] on
frame0
java.awt.event.ItemEvent[ITEM_STATE_CHANGED,item=my
CheckBox,stateChange=SELECTED] on checkbox0
java.awt.event.ActionEvent[ACTION_PERFORMED,cmd=my Button] on button0
java.awt.event.ActionEvent[ACTION_PERFORMED,cmd=my Button] on button0
java.awt.event.ItemEvent[ITEM_STATE_CHANGED,item=my
CheckBox,stateChange=DESELECTED] on checkbox0
java.awt.event.ItemEvent[ITEM_STATE_CHANGED,item=my
```

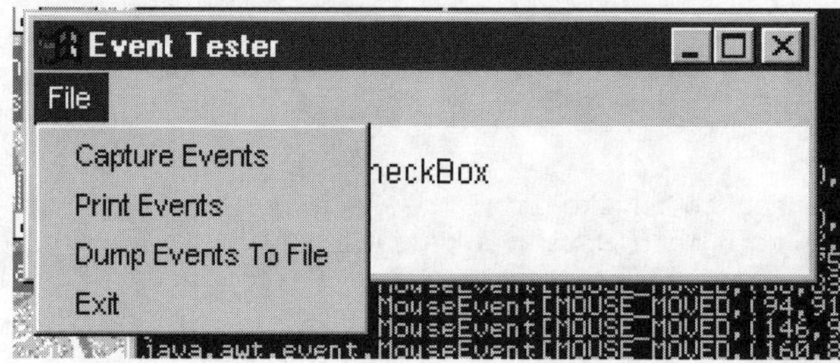

FIGURE 10.5 The Event Tester GUI.

```
CheckBox,stateChange=SELECTED] on checkbox0
java.awt.event.ActionEvent[ACTION_PERFORMED,cmd=my Button] on button0
java.awt.event.MouseEvent[MOUSE_ENTERED,(-3220,527),mods=0,clickCount=0] on
frame0
java.awt.event.MouseEvent[MOUSE_EXITED,(16,46),mods=0,clickCount=0] on frame0
java.awt.event.ActionEvent[ACTION_PERFORMED,cmd=my Button] on button0
java.awt.event.MouseEvent[MOUSE_ENTERED,(125,178),mods=0,clickCount=0] on frame0
java.awt.event.MouseEvent[MOUSE_EXITED,(124,185),mods=0,clickCount=0] on frame0
Action Performed: Exit
```

The key points to note about Source 10.4 are:

1. You will notice that several imports were required to import all the classes that make up the new event model.

```
import java.awt.*;              // For the awt as a whole
import java.awt.event.*;        // For events
import java.util.EventObject;   // for getting the string version of an event.
```

2. The example extends a frame but was used to implement the required action listeners.

```
class EventTester extends Frame implements
ActionListener,
FocusListener,
KeyListener,
MouseListener,
MouseMotionListener,
WindowListener,
ItemListener
```

3. Each action listener required a certain method be implemented, some of which is shown here.

```
/** ActionListener method. */
    public void actionPerformed(ActionEvent ae)
/** ItemListener method. */
    public void itemStateChanged(ItemEvent ie)
/** FocusListener method. */
    public void focusGained(FocusEvent fe)
/** FocusListener method. */
    public void focusLost(FocusEvent fe)
/** KeyListener method. */
    public void keyPressed(KeyEvent ke)
/** KeyListener method. */
```

Using Adapters. In addition to event listeners the AWT provides several adapters. Adapter classes are provided as a basis to extend from. That is, they implement EventListener interfaces with empty methods which the developer can override. As we have seen, many of the EventListener interfaces have many methods that need to be implemented. The java.awt.event adapter classes provide empty implementations that can be overridden to capture only the set of events required. For example, the java.awt.event.KeyAdapter class provides

```
keyPressed(KeyEvent)
keyReleased(KeyEvent)
keyTyped(KeyEvent)
```

An application that needs to capture keyboard events need only derive a subclass from the KeyAdapter class and only override those methods that were of interest.

Now that we understand components and the Delegation Event model, we can move on to those components that hold other components: Containers.

Containers

A container is a component that stores other components and arranges them inside the container according to a Layout manager. The general screen representation of a container is a rectangle; therefore, components are arranged within the container rectangle. There are two types of containers: windows and panels. A window can be thought of as a standalone container that is the primary viewport of your application. A window is a communication conduit between your application and the user. If you think of your application as a black box, then a window is the link between your application and the outside world. A panel is a section of a window. Panels allow windows to be divided into subsections that may have a different Layout manager for each subsection (Source 10.3 used panels and the next section covers panels and layouts in detail). An applet is a panel that is displayed inside the browser's window (see Chapter 12 for an explanation and demonstration of applets).

There are several types of windows and each has a different purpose. Source 10.5 demonstrates the following four window types as well as popup menus:

- **Window.** A top-level window with no borders and no menubar.
- **Frame.** A top-level window with a border that can contain a menubar. The border can have a title of the frame.
- **Dialog.** A window with a border that is normally a subwindow within an application that is used to get input from the user. There are two types of dialogs depending upon the necessity of the information required from the user or being conveyed to the user. If information from the user is absolutely necessary for the program to continue and the user cannot do anything else before providing this information, you are putting the program (and user) into a certain "mode" of operation. To do this with the AWT you specify the dialog as a "modal dialog." A modal dialog will capture all input of the application. This means that the user must respond to the

SOURCE 10.5 TestWindows.java

```
package jwiley.chp10;

import java.awt.*;
import java.awt.event.*;
/**
 *  TestWindows.java
 *  Class to demonstrate AWT windows.
 *  @version 1.1
 *  @author M. Daconta.
 */

/**
 *
 */
class TestWindows extends Frame implements ActionListener
{
    /** adapter class to catch window close event. */
    class ShutdownAdapter extends WindowAdapter
    {
        public void windowClosing(WindowEvent we)
        { System.exit(0); }
    }

    /** constructor. */
    TestWindows()
    {
        super("AWT Windows");

        MenuBar mb = new MenuBar();
        setMenuBar(mb);

        Menu fileMenu = new Menu("File");
        mb.add(fileMenu);
        MenuItem mi = new MenuItem("Frame");
        mi.addActionListener(this);
        fileMenu.add(mi);
        mi = new MenuItem("Window");
        mi.addActionListener(this);
        fileMenu.add(mi);
        mi = new MenuItem("Modeless Dialog");
        mi.addActionListener(this);
        fileMenu.add(mi);
        mi = new MenuItem("Modal Dialog");
        mi.addActionListener(this);
        fileMenu.add(mi);
        mi = new MenuItem("FileDialog");
        mi.addActionListener(this);
        fileMenu.add(mi);
```

```
        mi = new MenuItem("PopupMenu");
        mi.addActionListener(this);
        fileMenu.add(mi);

        mi = new MenuItem("Exit");
        mi.addActionListener(this);
        fileMenu.add(mi);

        // add WindowListener
        addWindowListener(new ShutdownAdapter());

        setLocation(new Point(100,100));
        setSize(200,200);
        setVisible(true);
    }

    /** ActionListener method. */
    public void actionPerformed(ActionEvent evt)
    {
        String command = evt.getActionCommand();
        if ("Exit".equals(command))
                System.exit(0);
        else if ("Frame".equals(command))
                new bareFrame();
        else if ("Window".equals(command))
                new bareWindow(this);
        else if ("Modeless Dialog".equals(command))
                new bareDialog(this,false,"Modeless Dialog");
        else if ("Modal Dialog".equals(command))
                new bareDialog(this,true,"Modal Dialog");
        else if ("FileDialog".equals(command))
                new bareFileDialog(this);
        else if ("PopupMenu".equals(command))
        {
                bareFrame bf = new bareFrame();
                barePopupMenu bp =  new barePopupMenu(bf);
                bf.add(bp);
                bp.show(bf,10,10);
        }
    }

    /** main method to invoke from JVM. */
    public static void main(String args[])
    {
        new TestWindows();
    }
}

/** adapter class for window listening. */
class DisposeAdapter extends WindowAdapter
{
    public void windowClosing(WindowEvent we)
```

```
    {
        we.getWindow().dispose();
    }
}

/** Class to demonstrate a Frame. */
class bareFrame extends Frame
{
    /** constructor. */
    bareFrame()
    {
        super("A Frame");
        setLocation(new Point(110,150));
        setSize(150,150);
        addWindowListener(new DisposeAdapter());
        setVisible(true);
    }
}


/** Class to demonstrate a Window. */
class bareWindow extends Window
{
    /** constructor. */
    bareWindow(Frame parent)
    {
        super(parent);
        setLocation(new Point(110,150));
        setSize(150,150);
        addWindowListener(new DisposeAdapter());
        setVisible(true);
    }
}

/** Class to demonstrate a dialog. */
class bareDialog extends Dialog
{
    /** constructor. */
    bareDialog(Frame parent, boolean modal, String title)
    {
        super(parent,modal);
        setTitle(title);
        setLocation(new Point(110,150));
        setSize(200,150);
        addWindowListener(new DisposeAdapter());
        setVisible(true);
    }
}

/** Class to demonstrate a FileDialog. */
class bareFileDialog extends FileDialog
{
```

```
    /** constructor. */
    bareFileDialog(Frame parent)
    {
        super(parent,"A File Dialog");
        setLocation(new Point(110,150));
        addWindowListener(new DisposeAdapter());
        setVisible(true);
    }
}

/** Class to demonstrate a PopupMenu */
class barePopupMenu extends PopupMenu
implements ActionListener
{
     barePopupMenu(Frame _parent)
     {
          super("Help");

          MenuItem item;
          item = new MenuItem("Contents");
          item.addActionListener(this);
          add(item);

          item = new MenuItem("Search for help on");
          item.addActionListener(this);
          add(item);
          addSeparator();

          item = new MenuItem("Tip O'The day");
          item.addActionListener(this);
          add(item);
          addSeparator();
          item = new MenuItem("About TestWindows.java");
          item.addActionListener(this);
          add(item);
     }

     public void actionPerformed(ActionEvent ae)
     {
          String command = ae.getActionCommand();
          if ( command.equals("Contents"))
               System.out.println("User selected contents");
          else if ( command.equals("Search for help on"))
               System.out.println("User selected search for help on");
          else if ( command.equals("Tip O'The day"))
               System.out.println("User selected Tip O'The day");
          else if ( command.equals("About TestWindows.java"))
               System.out.println("User selected About TestWindows.java");
     }
}
```

dialog. In general, you should not put the user into such modes, but let the user have as much freedom of choice as possible. An example of a modal dialog is the print dialog that most operating systems put up before allowing a print operation. The user is forced to either enter the information in the dialog or cancel the operation. The user cannot do anything else when the print dialog is present. If you want the user to enter information but also allow the user to perform other actions in the application, you create a "modeless dialog." Setting Modal to false in the AWT dialog constructor does this. An example of a "modeless dialog" would be the Find dialog, where the user enters information to search. The user is not put into a "mode" and therefore can leave the find dialog up while performing other actions in the application.

- **FileDialog.** A special-purpose dialog that is used to save a file to disk or open a file from disk. It presents the user with a listing of all the files in the current directory and allows the user to navigate up and down the directory hierarchy before deciding where to place the file (or get the file from). Once the user has chosen a directory, the dialog also allows the user to enter the filename.
- **Popup menu.** A popup menu, also sometime called a context menu, is one that is not attached to a menubar but rather "pops up" when the mouse is clicked within a window or frame or other container.

A run of Source 10.5 produces the output shown in Figure 10.6. Figure 10.6 shows an AWT popup menu. Now that we understand the different types of containers (and have seen something to contain, a popup menu) available to our programs, we can move on to how components are arranged within these containers, which brings us to the AWT Layout managers.

Layout

Layouts are especially important in AWT programming because AWT graphical user interfaces must run on a variety of platforms and operating systems. This causes problems for simple X and Y arrangement of components because components are different sizes on different operating systems. Therefore, it is best to use one of the predefined layout managers provided in the AWT. We will first discuss the relationship between Containers and Layout managers and then cover all the predefined classes that implement the LayoutManager interface.

Containers and the LayoutManager Interface. A LayoutManager is an interface that describes the methods a class must implement in order to lay out a container. By "laying out" a container, we mean a class that uses a specific methodology for arranging components within a container's rectangle (specified by its Dimension). Every container must have a LayoutManager. The default layout manager is the BorderLayout (discussed later in this section). Containers have the following methods that are specific to laying out components.

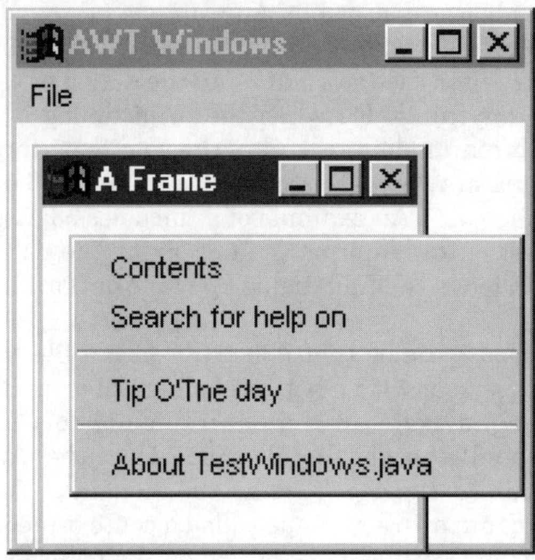

FIGURE 10.6 A popup menu.

1. **public setLayout(LayoutManager mgr).** This method sets the LayoutManager class for the container. You can set the LayoutManager to one of the predefined LayoutManagers (described later in this section) or one of your own LayoutManagers. You can also set the LayoutManager to null and lay out the components yourself by using the setBounds() method in the Component class. Setting the layout manager to null is not recommended because it makes the look of your GUI only correct for your system. Your GUI may look horrible on another operating system or hardware configuration. Source 10.6 demonstrates manually laying out components.
2. **public LayoutManager getLayout().** This method returns the current LayoutManager.
3. **protected void addImpl(Component comp, Object constraints, int index).** This method is used to add a component to the container. The constraints object is used to provide layout information for this component. If the container's LayoutManager is an instance of LayoutManager2, then the component and constraint are added to the LayoutManager in addition to the container. LayoutManager2 is an interface that provides methods for laying out components based on a constraints object. If the current layout is not an instance of LayoutManager2, the component will be added to the layout manager and the container if the constraints object is an instance of String. Otherwise, the component is added only to the container.
4. **public synchronized Component add(<variable args>).** There are five add methods with different arguments in the container. Each add method results in a call to addImpl discussed earlier.

SOURCE 10.6 tstValidate.java

```
package jwiley.chp10;

import java.awt.Frame;
import java.awt.Button;
/**
 *  tstValidate.java
 *  A example of laying out buttons manually.
 *  @version 1.1
 *  @author M. Daconta.
 *
*/

class tstValidate
{
    public static void main(String args[])
    {
        Button button1 = new Button("button One");
        Button button2 = new Button("button Two");
        Button button3 = new Button("button Three");

        Frame myFrame = new Frame("Validate tester");
        myFrame.setLayout(null);
        myFrame.add(button1); // add to container, NOT layout mgr
        myFrame.add(button2);
        myFrame.add(button3);

        // manually layout
        button1.setBounds(5,25,50,20);
        button1.validate();
        button2.setBounds(20,50,50,20);
        button2.validate();
        button3.setBounds(40,75,50,20);
        button3.validate();

        myFrame.setLocation(100,100);
        myFrame.setSize(200,200);
        myFrame.show();
    }
}
```

A run of Source 10.6 produces the window shown in Figure 10.7.

Now that you understand the relationship between layout managers and containers, let's examine the predefined layout managers in the AWT.

Predefined AWT classes that implement LayoutManager. Source 10.7 demonstrates the use of five classes that implement LayoutManager.

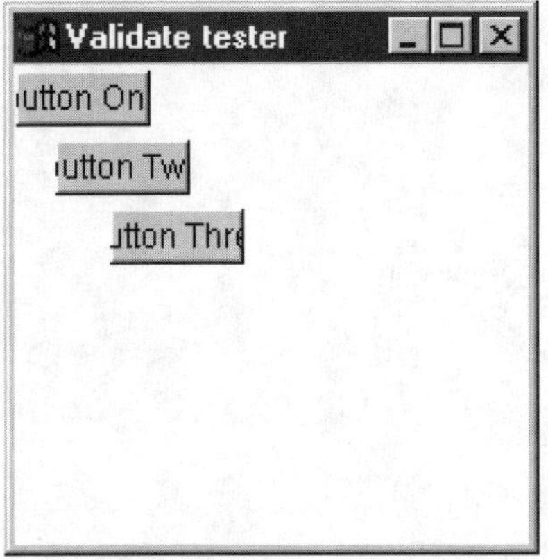

FIGURE 10.7 A manual layout.

SOURCE 10.7 LayoutWindow.java

```
package jwiley.chp10;

import java.awt.Frame;
import java.awt.Button;
import java.awt.MenuBar;
import java.awt.MenuItem;
import java.awt.Menu;
import java.awt.FlowLayout;
import java.awt.GridLayout;
import java.awt.BorderLayout;
import java.awt.GridBagLayout;
import java.awt.GridBagConstraints;
import java.awt.CardLayout;
import java.awt.Panel;

import java.awt.event.ActionListener;
import java.awt.event.ActionEvent;

class layoutWindow extends Frame implements ActionListener
{
    Button buttons[];
    CardLayout cl;

    layoutWindow()
    {
        super("Layout Tester");

        buttons = new Button[5];
        buttons[0] = new Button("One");
```

```
        buttons[1] = new Button("Two");
        buttons[2] = new Button("Three");
        buttons[3] = new Button("Four");
        buttons[4] = new Button("Five");

        // start with border Layout
        setLayout(new BorderLayout());
        add("North",buttons[0]);
        add("Center",buttons[1]);
        add("South",buttons[2]);
        add("West",buttons[3]);
        add("East",buttons[4]);

        // add the MenuBar
        MenuBar mBar = new MenuBar();
        setMenuBar(mBar);
        Menu fileMenu = new Menu("File");
        mBar.add(fileMenu);
        Menu layoutMenu = new Menu("Layouts");
        mBar.add(layoutMenu);

        MenuItem mnuExit = new MenuItem("Exit");
        mnuExit.addActionListener(this);
        fileMenu.add(mnuExit);

        MenuItem mnuItems[] = new MenuItem[5];
        mnuItems[0] = new MenuItem("BorderLayout");
        mnuItems[1] = new MenuItem("FlowLayout");
        mnuItems[2] = new MenuItem("GridLayout");
        mnuItems[3] = new MenuItem("GridBagLayout");
        mnuItems[4] = new MenuItem("CardLayout");

        for (int i=0; i < mnuItems.length; i++)
        {
            layoutMenu.add(mnuItems[i]);
            mnuItems[i].addActionListener(this);
        }

        setSize(300,300);
        setLocation(50,50);
        show();
    }

    public void actionPerformed(ActionEvent evt)
    {
        Object target = evt.getSource();
        if (target instanceof MenuItem)
        {
            String label = (String) evt.getActionCommand();
            if (label.equals("Exit"))
            {
```

```
        dispose();
        System.exit(0);
    }
    else if (label.equals("BorderLayout"))
    {
        removeAll();
        setLayout(new BorderLayout());
        add("North",buttons[0]);
        add("Center",buttons[1]);
        add("South",buttons[2]);
        add("West",buttons[3]);
        add("East",buttons[4]);
        doLayout();
        repaint();
    }
    else if (label.equals("FlowLayout"))
    {
        removeAll();
        setLayout(new FlowLayout(FlowLayout.LEFT));
        add(buttons[0]);
        add(buttons[1]);
        add(button's[2]);
        add(buttons[3]);
        add(buttons[4]);
        doLayout();
        repaint();
    }
    else if (label.equals("GridLayout"))
    {
        removeAll();
        setLayout(new GridLayout(0,2));
        add(buttons[0]);
        add(buttons[1]);
        add(buttons[2]);
        add(buttons[3]);
        add(buttons[4]);
        doLayout();
        repaint();
    }
    else if (label.equals("GridBagLayout"))
    {
        removeAll();
        GridBagLayout gbl = new GridBagLayout();
        setLayout(gbl);

        GridBagConstraints c[] = new GridBagConstraints[5];
        for (int i=0; i < 5; i++)
                c[i] = new GridBagConstraints();

        c[0].gridwidth = 1;
        c[0].gridheight = 1;
```

```
            c[0].gridx = 0;
            c[0].gridy = 0;
            add(buttons[0], c[0]);

            c[1].gridwidth = 1;
            c[1].gridheight = 1;
            c[1].gridx = 1;
            c[1].gridy = 1;
            add(buttons[1],c[1]);

            c[2].gridwidth = 1;
            c[2].gridheight = 1;
            c[2].gridx = 2;
            c[2].gridy = 2;
            add(buttons[2],c[2]);

            c[3].gridwidth = 1;
            c[3].gridheight = 1;
            c[3].gridx = 3;
            c[3].gridy = 3;
            add(buttons[3],c[3]);
            c[4].gridwidth = 1;
            c[4].gridheight = 1;
            c[4].gridx = 4;
            c[4].gridy = 4;
            add(buttons[4],c[4]);
            doLayout();
            repaint();
        }
        else if (label.equals("CardLayout"))
        {
            removeAll();
            cl = new CardLayout();
            setLayout(cl);
            Panel p[] = new Panel[5];
            Button nextButton[] = new Button[5];
            for (int i=0; i < 5; i++)
            {
                p[i] = new Panel();
                p[i].setLayout(new BorderLayout());
                nextButton[i] = new Button("Next");
                nextButton[i].addActionListener(this);
            }

            p[0].add("Center",buttons[0]);
            p[0].add("South", nextButton[0]);
            p[1].add("Center",buttons[1]);
            p[1].add("South", nextButton[1]);
            p[2].add("Center",buttons[2]);
            p[2].add("South", nextButton[2]);
            p[3].add("Center",buttons[3]);
```

```
                p[3].add("South", nextButton[3]);
                p[4].add("Center",buttons[4]);
                p[4].add("South", new Button("No More"));

                add("One",p[0]);
                add("Two",p[1]);
                add("Three",p[2]);
                add("Four",p[3]);
                add("Five",p[4]);
                cl.first(this);
                doLayout();
                repaint();
            }
        }
        else if (target instanceof Button)
        {
            String label = (String) evt.getActionCommand();
            if (label.equals("Next"))
            {
                // card Layout - next card
                cl.next(this);
            }
        }
    }

    public static void main (String args[])
    {
        new layoutWindow();
    }
}
```

- **BorderLayout.** A layout that represents a wall of components that surrounds a center component. Implemented by only having five components labeled one of "North," "South," "East," "West," and "Center." You can also specify a horizontal and vertical gap (in pixels) between components. BorderLayout is the default layout for a Frame.
- **FlowLayout.** A layout that represents components in a row. Implemented by placing components on a line from left to right. If there are too many components to fit on a single line, a new line will be created. You can also specify a horizontal and vertical gap between lines. FlowLayout is the default layout of a Panel.
- **GridLayout.** A layout that represents a simple grid with one component per cell. Implemented by specifying the number of rows and columns in your grid. All cells are equally sized. Components are placed in each cell by filling rows first.
- **GridBagLayout.** A layout that represents a very flexible grid. Implemented by a rectangular grid of cells where a component can be placed in any cell AND a com-

ponent may occupy one or more cells. This is more complicated than the other layouts but is much more powerful and flexible. We demonstrate this layout in Source 10.7 and then discuss it in detail in the GridBagLayout section.

- **CardLayout.** A layout that represents a stack of cards. Implemented by only displaying a single component at a time and allowing you to flip through components.

Source 10.7 demonstrates each of these layouts.

A run of Source 10.7 produces five different layouts as depicted in Figures 10.8 through 10.12.

From the descriptions and code just shown you should have a good idea of how to lay out components using the predefined layout managers. The GridBagLayout deserves special attention because it is both more complex and more powerful. The next section examines it in detail.

The GridBagLayout Up Close. My first experiences with the GridBagLayout class were not good ones. The little documentation available did not make sense, the GridConstraint variables did not make sense, and components would not be placed where I thought they would. I first thought that a GridBag was a grid of grids where you specified a separate grid for each component. This impression was formed because of the fact that you specified a gridheight and gridwidth for each component. This did not seem very elegant or simple to me. It seemed to violate the principle of simplicity that Java espoused.

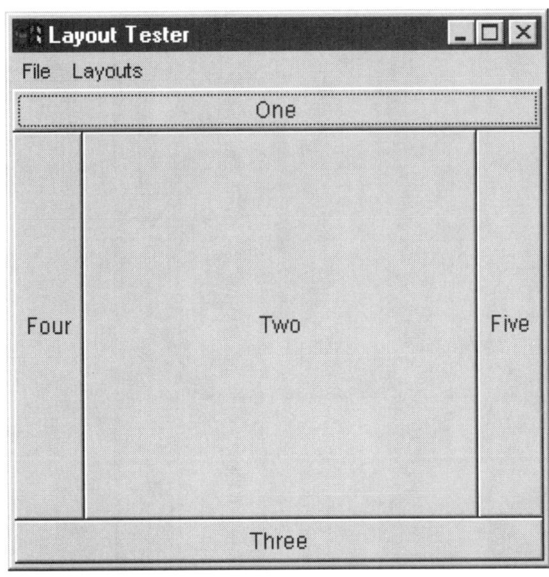

FIGURE 10.8 The BorderLayout.

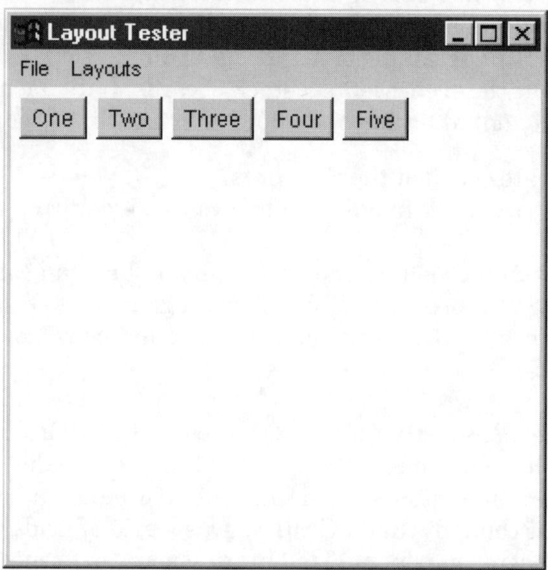

FIGURE 10.9 The FlowLayout.

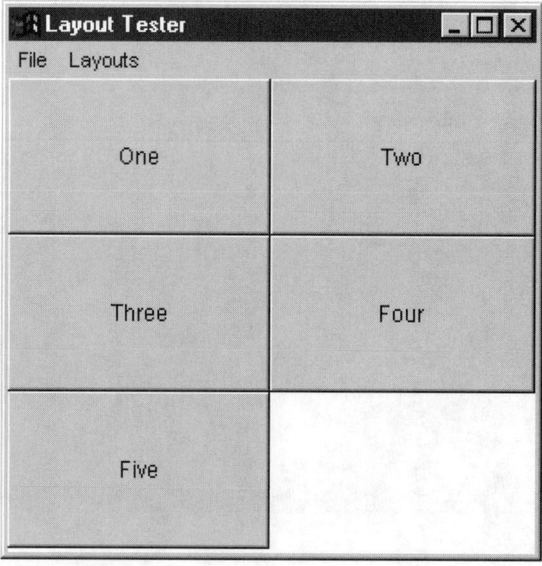

FIGURE 10.10 The GridLayout.

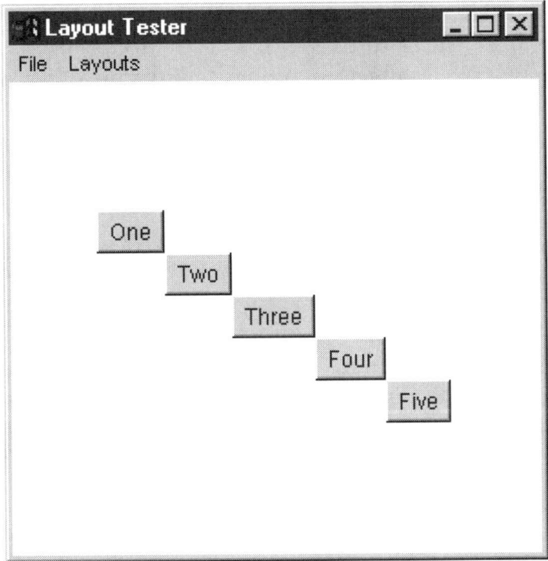

FIGURE 10.11 The GridBagLayout.

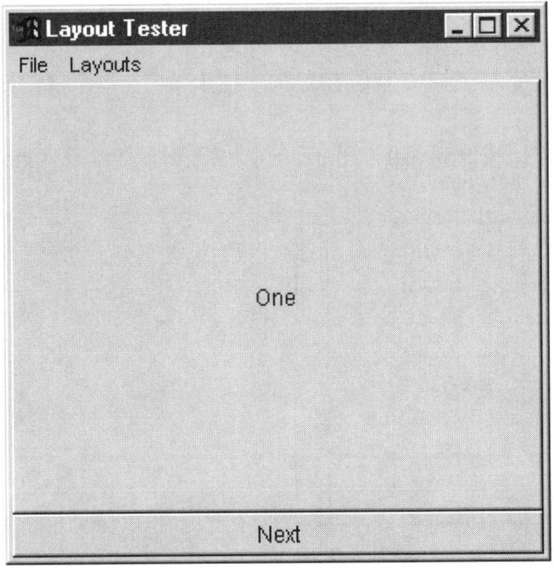

FIGURE 10.12 TheCardLayout.

Through a very fruitful e-mail exchange with Stephen Uhler of Sun Microsystems and some more experimentation, I now understand the GridBagLayout and see its power and elegance. The first thing to clear up is that a GridBag is NOT a grid of grids. It is a single grid that lets you place components anywhere in the grid. You specify where to place the component in the grid by modifying the gridx and gridy variables of the constraints for each component.

Second, a component does not have to occupy a single cell as is the case with the simple GridLayout. A component may occupy one or more cells as specified by the gridheight and gridwidth variables of the constraints for each component. The variables gridheight and gridwidth specify the width and height of a "sub-grid" within the single grid. You could also think of this as the number of cells wide and number of cells high occupied by the component. Once you have defined this display area for a component you can also specify where the component should be anchored in this display area if the display area is larger than the component (the default is CENTER). Figure 10.13 shows how I set up the GridBagLayout of Source 10.8. I wanted to use GridBagLayout in a similar fashion as a BorderLayout with the BIG exception that the GridBagLayout would not make the buttons fill the entire window. Source 10.8 demonstrates how to do this with the GridBagLayout.

A run of Source 10.8 produces Figure 10.14.

Creating Your Own LayoutManager. The layout classes provided in Java are powerful and work well for a small number of components. But what if you wanted to lay out a large number of components, such as the components for a data form? You could use the layout classes provided and break up your form into Panels. Each Panel can have its own layout, so with enough Panels you can achieve the layout you want. The GridBagLayout is flexible enough to handle complex layouts but you will find its use cumbersome. An easier way to achieve the layout you want is to create your own Lay-

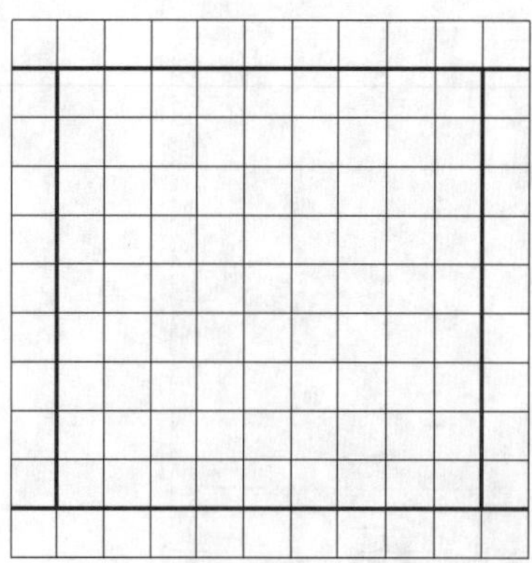

FIGURE 10.13 GridBagLayout pattern.

SOURCE 10.8 tstGridBag.java

```
import java.awt.Frame;
import java.awt.Button;
import java.awt.GridBagLayout;
import java.awt.GridBagConstraints;

class tstGridBag
{
    public static void main(String args[])
    {
        Button theButtons[] = new Button[5];
        for (int i=0; i < 5; i++)
            theButtons[i] = new Button("Button #" + (i+1));

        GridBagConstraints theConstraints[] = new GridBagConstraints[5];
        for (int i=0; i < 5; i++)
            theConstraints[i] = new GridBagConstraints();
        // create the Frame
        Frame theFrame = new Frame("Grid Bag Tester");
        theFrame.setSize(300,300);

        // set the layout of this container
        GridBagLayout gblayout = new GridBagLayout();
        theFrame.setLayout(gblayout);

        // set the constraints for each component and
        // add it to the container
        theConstraints[0].gridwidth = 11;
        theConstraints[0].gridheight = 1;
        theConstraints[0].gridx = 0;
        theConstraints[0].gridy = 0;
        theConstraints[0].weightx = 1.0;
        theConstraints[0].weighty = 1.0;
        theFrame.add(theButtons[0],theConstraints[0]);

        theConstraints[1].gridwidth = 1;
        theConstraints[1].gridheight = 9;
        theConstraints[1].gridx = 0;
        theConstraints[1].gridy = 1;
        theConstraints[1].weightx = 1.0;
        theConstraints[1].weighty = 1.0;
        theFrame.add(theButtons[1],theConstraints[1]);

        theConstraints[2].gridwidth = 9;
        theConstraints[2].gridheight = 9;
        theConstraints[2].gridx = 1;
        theConstraints[2].gridy = 1;
        theConstraints[2].weightx = 1.0;
        theConstraints[2].weighty = 1.0;
        theFrame.add(theButtons[2],theConstraints[2]);

        theConstraints[3].gridwidth = 1;
        theConstraints[3].gridheight = 9;
```

```
        theConstraints[3].gridx = 10;
        theConstraints[3].gridy = 1;
        theConstraints[3].weightx = 1.0;
        theConstraints[3].weighty = 1.0;
        theFrame.add(theButtons[3],theConstraints[3]);

        theConstraints[4].gridwidth = 11;
        theConstraints[4].gridheight = 1;
        theConstraints[4].gridx = 0;
        theConstraints[4].gridy = 10;
        theConstraints[4].weightx = 1.0;
        theConstraints[4].weighty = 1.0;
        theFrame.add(theButtons[4],theConstraints[4]);

        theFrame.setLocation(50,50);
        theFrame.show();
    }
}
```

outManager class. You can create your own layout by creating a class that implements the LayoutManager interface. Let's take a look at the methods we have to implement:

- **void addLayoutComponent(String name, Component Comp).** This method is used to add the component to the layout manager. The name variable can be used to pass in a name for the component but is commonly used to provide layout information.

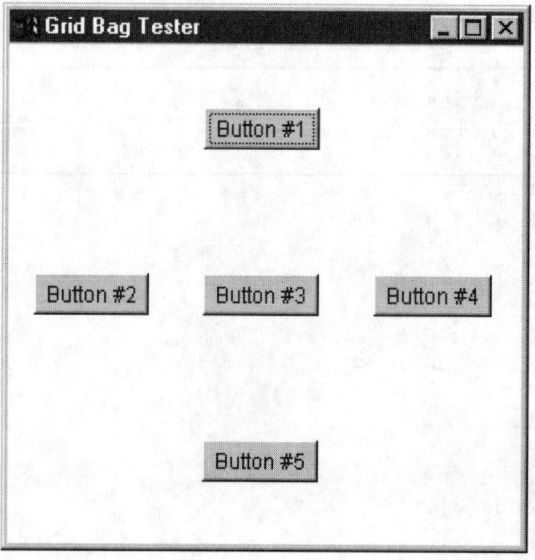

FIGURE 10.14 GridBag Tester.

- **void removeLayoutComponent(Component comp).** This method is used to remove components from the layout manager.
- **Dimension preferredLayoutSize(Container parent).** This method is used to compute the preferred size of the layout as it would be laid out in relation to the Container parent. This method is ultimately called when you use auto-size methods such as pack().
- **Dimension minimumLayoutSize(Container parent).** This method is used to compute the minimum size of the layout as it would be laid out in relation to the Container parent.
- **void layoutContainer(Container parent).** This is the most important method, this is the method that does all the work. This method should get the size of the parent and use this to compute the place of each component. You should provide a layout algorithm and call setBounds() to place each component. Depending on the algorithm you choose, you can lay out components added using the addLayoutComponent method, or you can enumerate through the components stored in the parent object.

To get a firm understanding of how to implement your own layout manager, let's look at an example. The example shown here implements a grid layout called Grid. Another grid layout you say? What about GridLayout and GridBagLayout? GridLayout and GridBagLayout are both useful, but GridLayout is too simple for most layout tasks and GridBagLayout is too complex for most tasks. The class Grid is similar to GridBagLayout but the layout information is passed in as a String, so you do not have to create and set constraint objects for every component. Source 10.9 shows the Grid class.

SOURCE 10.9

```
package jwiley.chp10;

import java.awt.*;
import java.util.Vector;
import java.util.StringTokenizer;

public class Grid implements LayoutManager
{
    Vector vCoordinates = new Vector();
    Vector vComponents = new Vector();
    int iRows;
    int iCols;
    int iXInsets;
    int iYInsets;

   public Grid(int iCols, int iRows)
   {
       This(iCols, iRows, 0, 0);
```

```
{
public Grid(int iCols, int iRows, int iXInsets, int iYInsets)
{
    if (iRows < 1)
        iRows = 1;
    else
        this.iRows = iRows;

    if (iCols < 1)
        iCols = 1;
    else
        this.iCols = iCols;

    if (iXInsets < 0)
        iXInsets = 0;
    else
        this.iXInsets = iXInsets;

    if (iYInsets < 0)
        iYInsets = 0;
    else
        this.iYInsets = iYInsets;
}

public void addLayoutComponent(String sCoordinates, Component comp)
{
    vCoordinates.addElement(sCoordinates);
    vComponents.addElement(comp);
}

public void removeLayoutComponent(Component comp)
{
    int iCount = vComponents.indexOf(comp);
    if (iCount != -1)
    {
        vCoordinates.removeElementAt(iCount);
        vComponents.removeElementAt(iCount);
    }
}

public Dimension preferredLayoutSize(Container target)
{
    int     iMaxHeight = 0;
    int     iMaxWidth = 0;

    // find out largest preferred size for width and height
    int iNumComponents = vComponents.size();
    for (int iCount = 0; iCount < iNumComponents; iCount++)
```

```
        {
            Component comp = (Component)vComponents.elementAt(iCount);
            Dimension d = comp.getPreferredSize();

            if (d.width > iMaxWidth)
                iMaxWidth = d.width;

            if (d.height > iMaxHeight)
                iMaxHeight = d.height;
        }

        // add grid getInsets
        iMaxHeight += iYInsets * 2;
        iMaxWidth += iXInsets * 2;
        // multiply by cols and rows
        iMaxHeight *= iRows;
        iMaxWidth *= iCols;

        // add target getInsets
        Insets insets = target.getInsets();

        iMaxHeight += insets.bottom + insets.top;
        iMaxWidth += insets.left + insets.right;

        return (new Dimension(iMaxWidth, iMaxHeight));
    }

    public Dimension minimumLayoutSize(Container target)
    {
        int     iMaxHeight = 0;
        int     iMaxWidth = 0;

        // find out largest preferred size for width and height
        int iNumComponents = vComponents.size();
        for (int iCount = 0; iCount < iNumComponents; iCount++)
        {
            Component comp = (Component)vComponents.elementAt(iCount);
            Dimension d = comp.getMinimumSize();

            if (d.width > iMaxWidth)
                iMaxWidth = d.width;

            if (d.height > iMaxHeight)
                iMaxHeight = d.height;
        }

        // add grid getInsets
        iMaxHeight += iYInsets * 2;
```

```
    iMaxWidth += iXInsets * 2;

    // multiply by cols and rows
    iMaxHeight *= iRows;
    iMaxWidth *= iCols;

    // add target getInsets
    Insets insets = target.getInsets();

    iMaxHeight += insets.bottom + insets.top;
    iMaxWidth += insets.left + insets.right;

    return (new Dimension(iMaxWidth, iMaxHeight));
}

public void layoutContainer(Container target)
{
    Insets insets = target.getInsets();
    int iNumComponents = vComponents.size();
    Dimension d = target.getSize();
    d.width -= insets.left + insets.right;
    d.height -= insets.top + insets.bottom;

    float fCellWidth = d.width / iCols;
    float fCellHeight = d.height / iRows;

    for (int iCount = 0; iCount < iNumComponents; iCount++)
    {
        Component comp = (Component)vComponents.elementAt(iCount);
        Dimension pf = comp.getPreferredSize(); //
        StringTokenizer st =
          new StringTokenizer((String)vCoordinates.elementAt(iCount),
                                                              ",;\t");

        int iLeft = Integer.valueOf(st.nextToken()).intValue();
        int iTop = Integer.valueOf(st.nextToken()).intValue();

        int iWidth, iHeight;
        boolean bUsePreferredSize = false;

        if (st.hasMoreElements())
        {
            String sNextElement = st.nextToken();
            if (sNextElement.equals("p"))
            {
                bUsePreferredSize = true;
                iWidth = 1;
                iHeight = 1;
```

```
                }
                else
                {
                    iWidth = Integer.valueOf(snextElement).intValue();
                    iHeight = Integer.valueOf(st.nextToken()).intValue();
                    if (st.hasMoreElements())
                    {
                        sNextElement = st.nextToken();
                        if (sNextElement.equals("p"))
                            bUsePreferredSize = true;
                    }
                }
            }
            else
            }
                iWidth = 1;
                iHeight = 1;
            }

            int x1 = 0, y1 = 0, x2 = 0, y2 = 0;

            if (bUsePreferredSize)
            {
                int iWholewidth = (int)(fCellWidth * iWidth)
                                            - (2 * iXInsets);
                int iWholeHeight = (int)(fCellHeight * iHeight)
                                            - (2 * iYInsets);
                x1 = (int)(fCellWidth * (iLeft - 1)) + insets.left
                          + iXInsets + ((iWholeWidth - pf.width) / 2);
                y1 = (int)(fCellHeight * (iTop - 1)) + insets.top
                          + iYInsets + ((iWholeHeight - pf.height) / 2);
                x2 = pf.width;
                y2 = pf.height;
            }
            else
            {
                x1 = (int)(fCellWidth * (iLeft - 1)) + insets.left
                                                  + iXInsets;
                y1 = (int)(fCellHeight * (iTop - 1)) + insets.top
                                                  + iYInsets;
                x2 = (int)(fCellWidth * iWidth) - (2 * iXInsets);
                y2 = (int)(fCellHeight * iHeight) - (2 * iYInsets);
            }

            comp.setBounds(x1, y1, x2, y2);
        }
    }
}
```

The use of the Grid class is the same as drawing blocks on a piece of graph paper. The constructors let you specify the size of your grid and optionally the spacing between each grid cell. When adding components to the grid, the component string can take a number of forms:

- **x, y** These are the x and y coordinates for the start cell of the component. By default the component's width and height are one grid cell, so using this will place the component in the specified cell.
- **x, y, p** This is the same as above, except using p will force the component to use its preferred size instead of taking up the space allocated for it.
- **x, y, width, height** x and y specify the start cell of the component and width and height specify how many cells to allocate in the horizontal and vertical directions.
- **x, y, width, height, p** This is the same as above, except using p will force the component to use its preferred size.

Figure 10.15 shows what coordinates to use to lay out the specified components. The Grid is an 8 × 8 grid.

Let me briefly go over each method and then we will use this layout to lay out the components of a frame. In addLayoutComponent I am adding the component and its layout information to their respective vectors. This layout will only lay out components that were added using the addLayoutComponent method, unlike some layouts that enumerate through components using the target variable. The removeLayout-Component simply removes the component and its associated layout information. The preferredLayoutSize and minimumLayoutSize methods will compute a Dimension

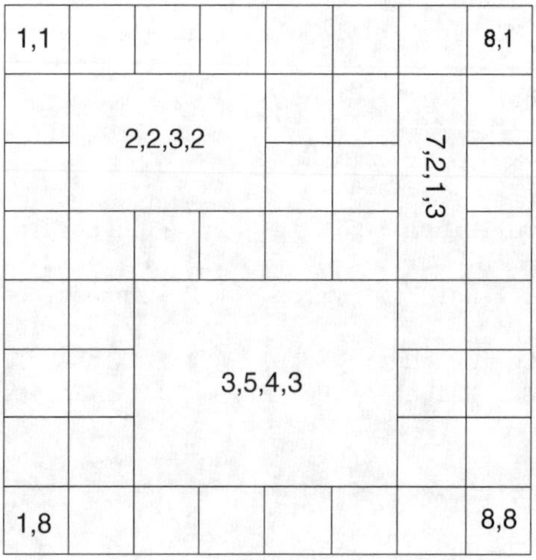

FIGURE 10.15 A custom Grid layout.

based on the component that has the largest preferredSize or minimumSize. The last method is where all the work is done. The size of each grid cell is computed and the layout information contained in the vCoordinates vector is used to lay out each component. Source 10.10 shows an example of using the Grid layout.

A run of Source 10.10 produces Figure 10.16. Try laying out the preceding form using the layout managers provided by Java. You will probably find it a very tedious process involving many panels and layouts. Using the Grid class makes laying out components easy.

SOURCE 10.10

```
package jwiley.chp10;

import java.awt.*;

public class TestGrid extends Frame
{
    TextField   txtFirstName = new TextField();
    TextField   txtMiddleName = new TextField();
    TextField   txtLastname = new TextField();
    TextField   txtAddress = new TextField();
    TextField   txtcity = new Textfield();
    TextField   txtState = new TextField();
    TextField   txtZip = new TextField();

    Button      cmdSave = new Button("Save");
    Button      cmdCancel = new Button("Cancel");

    public TestGrid (String sTitle)
    {
        super (sTitle);

        setLayout(new Grid(10,6,2,2));

        add("1,1,5,1", new Label("Personal Information"));

        add("1,2,2,1,p", new Label("Name:"));
        add("3,2,2,1", txtLastName);
        add("5,2,2,1", txtFirstName);
        add("7,2,2,1", txtMiddleName);

        add("3,3,2,1,p", new Label("Last"));
        add("5,3,2,1,p", new Label("First"));
        add("7,3,2,1,p", new Label("Middle"));

        add("1,4,2,1,p", new Label("Address:"));
        add("3,4,7,1", txtAddress);
        add("3,5,4,1", txtCity);
        add("7,5", txtState);
        add("8,5,2,1", txtZip);
```

```
        add("3,6,4,1,p", new Label("City"));
        add("7,6,p", new Label("State"));
        add("8,6,2,1,p", new Label("Zip"));

        add("10,3", cmdSave);
        add("10,4", cmdCancel);

        setSize(500,200);
        show();
    }

    public static void main (String args[])
    {
        new TextGrid("Text Grid");
    }
}
```

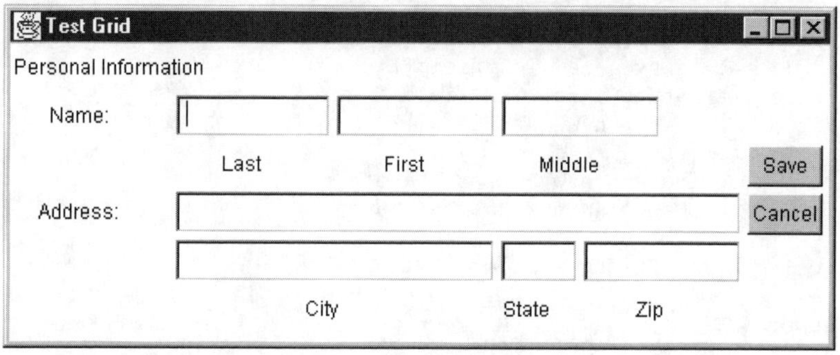

FIGURE 10.16 A test grid.

Painting and Updating

All graphical user interface systems have a concept of a graphics data structure to store context-specific information about a drawing area. This drawing area could be the whole screen, a portion of the screen (like a single component), or even a printer. The benefit of this is that it allows you to divide the physical monitor into a potentially infinite number of drawing areas (a simple example would be a graphics context per window). Each graphics context (and consequently, each drawing area) could have a different set of graphic characteristics like background color, default Font, line size, and so forth. On the Macintosh this graphics data structure is called the GrafPort (for Graphics Port). On MS Windows it is called the Device Context (DC). On X Windows, it is called GC (short for Graphics Context). Another way to think about this graphics context, devices, or ports is that they allow drawing to occur in a generic way without specifying where the drawing will occur. This makes it device-independent and allows such things as outputting to the printer by simply directing the draw routines at the printer's graphics port (or device).

In Java the Graphics context is represented by the abstract Graphics class. Just as the toolkit and peer are instantiated when the show() method is called, the Graphics context is also platform-specific and instantiated at the same time. Source 10.11 demonstrates accessing and drawing into a graphics context.

SOURCE 10.11 TestGraphics.java

```
// TestGraphics.java
package jwiley.chp10;

import java.awt.*;

/** Class to demonstrate drawing to a Graphics context. */
class myPanel extends Panel
{
    /** constructor. */
    myPanel()
    {
        setBackground(Color.white);
    }

    /** method to that draws to a graphics context. */
    void printGC()
    {
        Graphics GC = this.getGraphics();
        if (GC != null)
        {
            System.out.println("A Graphics Context exists " +
                                          "for this component.");
            System.out.println("The GC is : " + GC.toString());
            System.out.println("Would you like to draw " +
                                             "something in it?");
            System.out.println("Sure, here's a circle for you.");
            GC.setColor(Color.red);
            GC.drawOval(25,25, 50,50);
        }
        else
            System.out.println("No Graphics context for this " +
                                                 "component.");
    }
}
```

```
/** Class to demonstrate a graphics context. */
class TestGraphics
{
    /** main() method to invoke from a JVM. */
    public static void main(String args[])
    {
        Frame myFrame = new Frame("Graphics Context test");
        myFrame.setSize(125,125);
        myPanel aPanel = new myPanel();
        myFrame.add("Center",aPanel);
        myFrame.setVisible(true); // GC created
        // sleep a half sec
        try { Thread.sleep(500); } catch (Exception e) { }
        aPanel.printGC();
    }
}
```

A run of Source 10.11 produces both text output (shown here) and Figure 10.17.

```
C:\java\bin>java tstGraphics
A Graphics Context exists for this component.
The GC is : sun.awt.windows.WGraphics[0,0]
Would you like to draw something in it?
Sure, here's a circle for you.
```

One important thing to note about drawing into the graphics context like this is that if a window overlaps your window and you then click to bring your window again to the foreground, your window will not have your drawing in it. In our example, the circle would be gone and you would just see a white background. The solution to this involves a special method called the paint() method that is automatically called whenever your component is exposed (made visible).

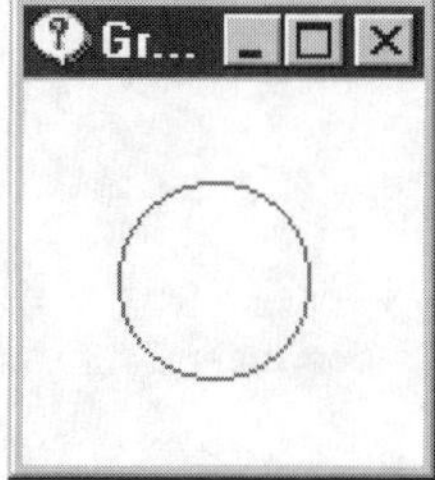

FIGURE 10.17 Drawing to a graphics context.

There are three critical "painting" methods in every component and it is very important to understand what they do and the relationship between them.

- **paint(Graphics g).** The default method in a component does nothing. You override this method to "paint" the component. This method is called when the component is first shown (with a call to show()) and then every time the window is re-exposed after having been covered by another window.
- **repaint().** With no argument, this method calls the update method of the component as soon as possible. You can also specify a number of milliseconds within which to call update().
- **update(Graphics g).** The default method repaints the background and then calls paint. The repainting of the background is what causes the infamous "animation flicker." This can be solved in two ways: dirty rectangle animation and double-buffered animation. We demonstrate dirty rectangle animation in Source 10.12. You will find dirty rectangle animation satisfactory for most of your applications unless they involve heavy animation. You perform dirty rectangle animation by using the paint() method to paint the initial background and foreground of the scene, then override update() method to paint anything that changes in the scene. This means you override update() to erase the old and paint the new. This works fine for small changes in a scene. Source 10.12 demonstrates the successful use of this technique. For heavy animation you will want to switch to double-buffered animation. This is a technique that mirrors the way animated movies work. The key is to create a full "scene" with background and foreground that is a slight change from the current background and foreground currently displayed. Then you copy this new "scene" over the old one in a single operation. This is done by overriding the update() method to call the paint() method but supplying the graphics context of an offscreen image. The paint() then does all of its painting of the current scene into the offscreen image. You then copy the offscreen image onto the current screen.

Source 10.12 demonstrates dirty rectangle animation.

SOURCE 10.12

```
// DvorakWindow.java
package jwiley.chp10;

import java.awt.*;
import java.awt.event.*;

/** Class to demonstrate dirty rectangle animation. */
class keyboardCanvas extends Canvas
{
    private Rectangle board;
    private Rectangle keys[][];
    private Rectangle spaceBar;
    private int keySize;
```

```
static String letters0[] = { "1", "2", "3", "4", "5", "6", "7", "8",
                             "9", "0", "]", "}" };
static String letters1[] = { "\", "<", ">", "P", "Y", "F", "G", "C",
                             "R", "L", "?", "+" };
static String letters2[] = { "A", "O", "E", "U", "I", "D", "H", "T",
                             "N", "S", "_" };
static String letters3[] = { ":", "Q", "J", "K", "X", "B", "M", "W",
                             "V", "Z" };

public boolean pressed[][];
public Point asciiPos[];
public boolean update;
public int updateRow, updateCol;

static String pos2String(int row, int col)
{
        String outstr=null;
        switch (row) {
                case 0:
                        outstr = letters0[col];
                        break;
                case 1:
                        outstr = letters1[col];
                        break;
                case 2:
                        outstr = letters2[col];
                        break;
                case 3:
                        outstr = letters3[col];
                        break;
        }
        return outstr;
}

public keyboardCanvas(Container parent)
{
    Dimension psize = parent.getSize();

    // initialize variables
    update = false;

    // ascii position to dvorak key
    // start at ascii 33.
    asciiPos = new Point[96];
    asciiPos[0] = new Point(0,0); asciiPos[1] = new Point(1,0);
    asciiPos[2] = new Point(0,2); asciiPos[3] = new Point(0,3);
    asciiPos[4] = new Point(0,4); asciiPos[5] = new Point(0,6);
    asciiPos[6] = new Point(1,0); asciiPos[7] = new Point(0,8);
    asciiPos[8] = new Point(0,9); asciiPos[9] = new Point(0,7);
    asciiPos[10] = new Point(1,11); asciiPos[11] = new Point (1,1);
```

```
asciiPos[12] = new Point(2,10); asciiPos[13] = new Point (1,2);
asciiPos[14] = new Point(1,10); asciiPos[15] = new Point (0,9);
asciiPos[16] = new Point(0,0); asciiPos[17] = new Point (0,1);
asciiPos[18] = new Point(0,2); asciiPos[19] = new Point (0,3);
asciiPos[20] = new Point(0,4); asciiPos[21] = new Point (0,5);
asciiPos[22] = new Point(0,6); asciiPos[23] = new Point (0,7);
asciiPos[24] = new Point(0,8); asciiPos[25] = new Point (3,0);
asciiPos[26] = new Point(3,0); asciiPos[27] = new Point (1,1);
asciiPos[28] = new Point(1,0); asciiPos[29] = new Point (1,2);
asciiPos[30] = new Point(1,10); asciiPos[31] = new Point (0,1);
asciiPos[32] = new Point(2,0); asciiPos[33] = new Point (3,5);
asciiPos[34] = new Point(1,7); asciiPos[35] = new Point (2,5);
asciiPos[36] = new Point(2,2); asciiPos[37] = new Point (1,5);
asciiPos[38] = new Point(1,6); asciiPos[39] = new Point (2,6);
asciiPos[40] = new Point(2,4); asciiPos[41] = new Point (3,2);
asciiPos[42] = new Point(3,3); asciiPos[43] = new Point (1,9);
asciiPos[44] = new Point(3,6); asciiPos[45] = new Point (2,8);
asciiPos[46] = new Point(2,1); asciiPos[47] = new Point (1,3);
asciiPos[48] = new Point(3,1); asciiPos[49] = new Point (1,8);
asciiPos[50] = new Point(2,9); asciiPos[51] = new Point (2,7);
asciiPos[52] = new Point(2,3); asciiPos[53] = new Point (3,8);
asciiPos[54] = new Point(3,7); asciiPos[55] = new Point (3,4);
asciiPos[56] = new Point(1,4); asciiPos[57] = new Point (3,9);
asciiPos[58] = new Point(0,10); asciiPos[59] = new Point (-1,-1);
asciiPos[60] = new Point(0,10); asciiPos[61] = new Point (-1,-1);
asciiPos[62] = new Point(2,10); asciiPos[63] = new Point (-1,-1);
asciiPos[64] = new Point(2,0); asciiPos[65] = new Point (3,5);
asciiPos[66] = new Point(1,7); asciiPos[67] = new Point (2,5);
asciiPos[68] = new Point(2,2); asciiPos[69] = new Point (1,5);
asciiPos[70] = new Point(1,6); asciiPos[71] = new Point (2,6);
asciiPos[72] = new Point(2,4); asciiPos[73] = new Point (3,2);
asciiPos[74] = new Point(3,3); asciiPos[75] = new Point (1,9);
asciiPos[76] = new Point(3,6); asciiPos[77] = new Point (2,8);
asciiPos[78] = new Point(2,1); asciiPos[79] = new Point (1,3);
asciiPos[80] = new Point(3,1); asciiPos[81] = new Point (1,8);
asciiPos[82] = new Point(2,9); asciiPos[83] = new Point (2,7);
asciiPos[84] = new Point(2,3); asciiPos[85] = new Point (3,8);
asciiPos[86] = new Point(3,7); asciiPos[87] = new Point (3,4);
asciiPos[88] = new Point(1,4); asciiPos[89] = new Point (3,9);
asciiPos[90] = new Point(0,11); asciiPos[91] = new Point (0,11);
asciiPos[92] = new Point(-1,-1); asciiPos[93] = new Point (-1,-1);

setBackgroud(Color.gray);
setForeground(Color.black);
int boardSize = psize.width/8 * 4;
board = new Rectangle(psize.width/8 * 2,
                      2,boardSize
                      ,80);
spaceBar = new Rectangle(psize.width/16 * 6,
                         84, psize.width/16 * 4,
                         10);
```

```
        keys = new Rectangle[4][];
        keys[0] = new Rectangle[12];
        keys[1] = new Rectangle[12];
        keys[2] = new Rectangle[11];
        keys[3] = new Rectangle[10];

        // pressed array
        pressed = new boolean[4][12];

        for (int i=0; i < 4; i++)
                for (int j=0; j < pressed[i].length; j++)
                        pressed[i][j] = false;

        keySize = boardSize/14;
        int RowStart[] = new int[4];
        RowStart[0] = psize.width/8 * 2 + keySize;
        RowStart[1] = RowStart[0] + keySize/2;
        RowStart[2] = RowStart[1] + keySize/2;
        RowStart[3] = RowStart[2] + keySize/2;

        for (int i = 0; i < 4; I++)
            for (int j=0; j < keys[i].length; j++)
                keys[i][j] = new Rectangle(RowStart[i] + (j * keySize),
                                           board.y + (20 * I),
                                           keySize, 20);

    }

    public void paint(Graphics g)
    {
        if (!update)
        {
            g.setColor(Color.black);
            g.drawRect(board.x-1,board.y-1,board.width+1,board.height+1);
            g.setColor(Color.white);
            g.fillRect(board.x,board.y,board.width, board.height);

            // space bar
            g.setColor(Color.black);
            g.drawRect(spaceBar.x-1, spaceBar.y-1, spaceBar.width+1,
                       spaceBar.height+1);
            g.setColor(Color.lightGray);
            g.fillRect(spaceBar.x, spaceBar.y, spaceBar.width,
                       spaceBar.height);
            g.setColor(Color.white);
            g.fillRoundRect(spaceBar.x+1, spaceBar.y+1,
                            spaceBar.width - 2,
                            spaceBar.height - 4, 5, 5);

            //key borders
            g.setColor(Color.black);
```

```
        g.drawLine(board.x, board.y+20, board.x + board.width,
                board.y+20);
        // shorten for Return key
        g.drawLine(board.x, board.y+40,
                board.x + (keySize * 13 + keySize/2),
                board.y+40);
        g.drawLine(board.x, board.y+60, board.x + board.width,
                board.y+60);

        // draw keys
        for (int i = 0; i < 4; i++)
            for (int j=0; j < keys[i].length; j++)
            {
                g.setColor(Color.black);
                g.drawRect(keys[i][j].x,
                        keys[i][j].y,
                        keys[i][j].width,
                        keys[i][j].height);
                g.setColor(Color.lightGray);
                g.fillRect(keys[i][j].x+1,
                        keys[i][j].y+1,
                        keys[i][j].width-1,
                        keys[i][j].height-1);

                /* *** if key pressed change
                       to yellow */
                if (!presses[i][j])
                   g.setColor(Color.white);
                else
                   g.setColor(Color.yellow);

                g.fillRoundRect(keys[i][j].x+2,
                            keys[i][j].y+2,
                            keys[i][j].width - 3,
                            keys[i][j].height - 3, 2, 2);
                // draw Letter
                g.setColor(Color.black);
                g.drawString(pos2String(i,j),
                          keys[i][j].x + keySize/4,
                          keys[i][j].y +
                            (keys[i][j].height - 4));
            }
    }
}

public void update (Graphics g)
{
    g.setColor(Color.black);
    g.drawRect(keys[updateRow][updateCol].x,
            keys[updateRow][updateCol].y,
            keys[updateRow][updateCol].width,
            keys[updateRow][updateCol].height);
```

```
        g.setColor(Color.lightGray);
        g.fillRect(keys[updateRow][updateCol].x+1,
                   keys[updateRow][updateCol].y+1,
                   keys[updateRow][updateCol].width-1,
                   keys[updateRow][updateCol].height-1);

        /* *** if key pressed change
               to yellow */
        if (!pressed[updateRow][updateCol])
           g.setColor(Color.white);
        else
           g.setColor(Color.yellow);

        g.fillRoundRect(keys[updateRow][updateCol].x+2,
                        keys[updateRow][updateCol].y+2,
                        keys[updateRow][updateCol].width - 3,
                        keys[updateRow][updateCol].height - 3, 2, 2);
        // draw Letter
        g.setColor(Color.black);
        g.drawString(pos2String(updateRow,updateCol),
                     keys[updateRow][updateCol].x + keySize/4,
                     keys[updateRow][updateCol].y +
                        (keys[updateRow][updateCol].height - 4));

    }
}

public class DvorakWindow extends Frame
{
    private int defWidth, defHeight;
    keyboardCanvas keyboard;

    class KeyCatcher extends KeyAdapter
    {
        public void keyPressed(KeyEvent ke)
        {
            int iKey = (int) ke.getKeyChar();
            if (iKey >= 33)
            {
               keyboard.update = true;
               Point keyPos = keyboard.asciiPos[iKey - 33];
               if (keyPos.x != -1)
               {
                  keyboard.updateRow = keyPos.x;
                  keyboard.updateCol = keyPos.y;
                  keyboard.pressed[keyPos.x][keyPos.y] = true;
                  keyboard.repaint();
               }
            }
        }
        public void keyReleased(KeyEvent ke)
```

```
        {
            int iKey = (int) ke.getKeyChar();
            if (iKey >= 33)
            {
               keyboard.update = true;
               Point keyPos = keyboard.asciiPos[iKey - 33];
               if (keyPos.x != -1)
               {
                  keyboard.updateRow = keyPos.x;
                  keyboard.updateCol = keyPos.y;
                  keyboard.pressed[keyPos.x][keyPos.y] = false;
                  keyboard.repaint();
               }
            }
        }
    }

    public DvorakWindow()
    {
            super("Your First Dvorak Lesson");

            setLayout(new BoarderLayout(2,2));
            setBackground(Color.lightGray);

            // get screen dimensions to size window
            Toolkit theToolkit = Toolkit.getDefaultToolkit();
            Dimension size = theToolkit.getScreenSize();
            defWidth = size.width/12 * 7;
            defHeight = size.height/12 * 3;

            MenuBar mBar = new MenuBar();
            setMenuBar(mBar);
            Menu fileMenu = new Menu("File");
            mBar.add(fileMenu);
            MenuItem exitItem = new MenuItem("Exit");
            fileMenu.add(exitItem);
            exitItem.addActionListener(
                     new ActionListener()
                     {
                          public void actionPerformed(ActionEvent ae)
                          {
                               if (ae.getActionCommand().equals("Exit"))
                               {
                                    dispose();
                                    System.exit(0);
                               }
                          }
                     } );

            setLocation(size.height/12 * 2, size.width/12 * 2);
            setSize(defWidth, defHeight);
```

```
            Label lup = new Label("The Dvorak Keyboard",Label.CENTER);
            add("North",lup);
            lup.addKeyListener(new KeyCatcher());

            // add keyboard to Panel
            keyboard = new keyboardCanvas(this);
            keyboard.setSize(defWidth,defHeight);
            //centerP.
            add("Center",keyboard);
            keyboard.addKeyListener(new KeyCatcher());

            //centerP.

            Label ldwn = new Label(
                      "Type a key to see its dvorak counterpart.",
                              Label.CENTER);
            ldwn.addKeyListener(new KeyCatcher());
            add("South",ldwn);

            addWindowListener(new WindowAdapter()
                               {
                                 public void windowClosing(WindowEvent we)
                                 {
                                      System.exit(0);
                                 }
                               });
            addKeyListener(new KeyCatcher());
            pack();
            setVisible(true);
    }

    public static void main(String args[])
    {
        new DvorakWindow();
    }
}
```

A run of Source 10.12 produces Figure 10.18.

Now that we have demonstrated dirty rectangle animation, let's discuss the premier technique for flicker-free animation: double-buffering.

Double-Buffering. Double-buffering is a drawing technique used for achieving smooth animation. The DrawRectangleFrame example from the AWT Enhancements section implements double-buffering. The concept of double-buffering is simple—never draw to the onscreen graphics object. All drawing should be done to an offscreen graphics object. After drawing to the offscreen graphics object is complete the image can be copied on to the onscreen Graphics object. Using this technique eliminates the

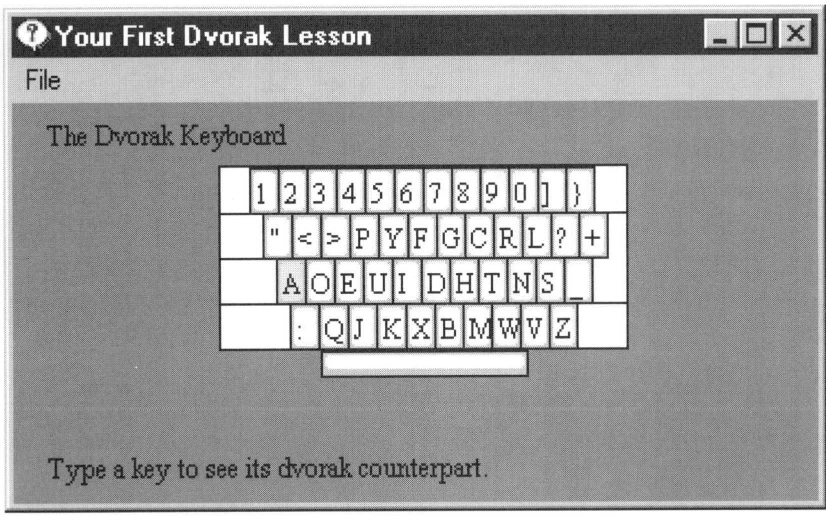

FIGURE 10.18 The Dvorak keyboard GUI.

ugly animation you see when objects are erased and then redrawn. Let's examine the steps needed to implement double buffering.

Create an offscreen graphics object. The first step to implementing double-buffering is to create an offscreen graphics object. Here is the code in the DrawCanvas class used to create an offscreen graphics object:

```
Dimension d = getSize();
offScreenImage = createImage(d.width, d.height);
offScreenGraphics = offScreenImage.getGraphics();
```

One thing that is very important is to keep the size of the two graphics objects the same. Here we create an image the same size as our canvas and then get its graphics object. If the size of our canvas changes we must create a new offscreen image the same size of the canvas and again get its graphics object. Make sure the size of the canvas is set before creating the offscreen image.

Paint to the offscreen graphics object. Now that our offscreen graphics object has been created, all drawing in our program must draw to the offscreen graphics object. Drawing to the offscreen graphics object is exactly the same as drawing to the onscreen graphics object, except the changes are not reflected on the screen. To copy the offscreen image to the screen you need to call repaint(). The repaint() method will call the update() method as soon as possible to update the screen.

Override the paint() and update() methods. The final step to implement double-buffering is to override the paint() and update() methods. Here are the paint() and update() methods from the DrawCanvas class:

```
public void paint (Graphics g)
{
    if (offScreenImage != null)
    {
        g.drawImage(offScreenImage, 0,0,this);
    }
}

public void update (Graphics g)
{
    if (rectangles != null)
    {
        for (int iCount = 0; iCount < rectangles.length; iCount++)
        {
            rectangles[iCount].draw(this, offScreenGraphics);
        }
    }
    paint(g);
}
```

The update method redraws all of the rectangles on to the offscreen graphics object. After doing this it calls the paint() method. The paint() method copies the offscreen graphics object on to the screen with a call to drawImage(). The update() method first prepares the offscreen graphics object by doing all necessary drawing. Once the offscreen graphics object is ready it is copied on the screen. This frame-by-frame copy produces smooth animation because no erasing ever takes place on screen.

10.3 AWT ENHANCEMENTS

In Java 1.1 the Abstract Window Toolkit (AWT) had some very important features added to it. These features provide access to some of the GUI components users have come to expect on their native platforms. Among these are popup menus, menu shortcut keys, context-sensitive cursors, and features everyone expects—drag and drop, cut and paste, and printing. These new features will increase the usability of Java programs and therefore allow Java to become an application programming language instead of just an applet programming language.

This section will introduce the new classes and interfaces added to the java.awt package. The drag and drop and cut and paste features are encapsulated in the java.awt.datatransfer package, and will be discussed in a later section. Let's take a look at the new classes added in Java 1.1:

- **Cursor.** This class provides access to the mouse cursor. In most GUI systems the cursor is used to provide feedback to the user. If the mouse is over a resizing handle, the cursor will change to a resize cursor. If the system is busy, the mouse will change to a wait cursor. Previously, setting the cursor was only allowed in the Frame class. Now cursor support exists for all components. To set the cursor for a component, the component's setCursor() method must be called with an instance of class Cursor. The Cursor class provides a variety of predefined cursors such as resizing cursors and wait cursors.

- **MenuShortcut.** This class is used to provide a keystroke sequence that will activate a menu item. A MenuShortcut can be associated with a MenuItem by specifying the shortcut in the MenuItem's constructor, or by calling the setShortcut() method. Providing a shortcut for a menu item lets the user activate the menu item without the mouse.
- **PopupMenu.** This class extends Menu. PopupMenu is used to display a detached menu associated with a component. Previously, all menus had to be accessed from the menubar of a Frame. Creating a popup menu is the same as creating a normal menu, the difference is how to display it. To display a popup menu it must first be added to a component using the add(PopupMenu popup) method. The add(PopupMenu popup) is a method in the Component class. To show the popup menu, use the PopupMenu show() method. This method lets you specify the origin of the popup menu. When a menu item is selected or an area outside the popup menu is clicked, the popup menu will disappear.
- **PrintJob.** An abstract class that is used to print from Java. A PrintJob object can be obtained with a call to the getPrintJob() method in the class Toolkit. The PrintJob class provides a getGraphics() method that will return a Graphics object for the printer. You can pass this in to a paint routine to draw on the printer graphics object. A call to the end() method will send the print job to the printer.
- **ScrollPane.** This class extends Container and implements Adjustable. The ScrollPane is provided for automatic scrolling of components. The ScrollPane will display scrollbars if the component contained by the scroll pane is larger than the scroll pane. Three flags are available to specify when the ScrollPane should display scrollbars. These flags are SCROLLBARS_ALWAYS, SCROLLBARS_AS_NEEDED, and SCROLLBARS_NEVER.
- **SystemColor.** This class extends Color. This class provides access to the system colors for your native environment. The SystemColor class provides variables for every aspect of a native color scheme. To access a particular color just access the variable you are interested in. Source 10.13 is an example of how to get the desktop color.

The other five classes just discussed will be demonstrated in Source 10.14. Source 10.14 implements a simple rectangle drawing program. Before we look at the code, let me briefly describe each class and what concepts to look for in each class.

- **DrawRectangleFrame.** This class provides the frame for our application. It demonstrates the use of the ScrollPane class, the MenuShortcut class, and the PrintJob class. Its main purpose is to provide a container for our DrawCanvas and to handle all of the menu events. Source 10.14 implements this object.

SOURCE 10.13 TestColor.java

```
package jwiley.chp10;

import java.awt.*;

public class TestColor
{
    public static void main (String args[])
    {
        Frame f = new Frame("Desktop Color");
        Color desktop = SystemColor.desktop;
        f.setBackground(desktop);
        f.setSize(200,200);
        f.show();
    }
}
```

- **DrawCanvas.** This class provides a drawing area for our application. It demonstrates the use of the PopupMenu class and the PrintJob class. The draw canvas also implements "double-buffering," a drawing technique used to achieve smooth animation. Double-buffering is discussed earlier in the chapter. Source 10.15 implements this object.

SOURCE 10.14 DrawRectangleFrame.java

```
// DrawRectangleFrame.java
package jwiley.chp10;

import java.awt.*;
import java.awt.event.*;

/**
 * This class is a frame that will demonstrate the following features:
 *
 * - Mouseless Operation
 * - Popup Menu
 * - Printing
 * - ScrollPane
 * - Cursor
 *
 * @author Eric Monk
 * @version 1.0
 *
 */

public class DrawRectangleFrame extends Frame
        implements ActionListener, ItemListener
{
```

```
DrawCanvas  drawCanvas = new DrawCanvas();
MenuBar     menuBar = new MenuBar();
Menu        mnuFile = new Menu("File");
Menu        mnuEdit = new Menu("Edit");
Menu        mnuColor = new Menu("Color");
Menu        mnuTool = new Menu("Tool");

MenuItem mnuPrint = new MenuItem("Print", new MenuShortcut('p'));
MenuItem mnuExit = new MenuItem("Exit");

MenuItem mnuDelete = new MenuItem("Delete", new MenuShortcut('d'));

CheckboxMenuItem mnuColorBlue = new CheckboxMenuItem("Blue");
CheckboxMenuItem mnuColorGreen = new CheckboxMenuItem("Green");
CheckboxMenuItem mnuColorRed = new CheckboxMenuItem("Red");
CheckboxMenuItem mnuColorBlack = new CheckboxMenuItem("Black");

CheckboxMenuItem mnuPointerTool = new CheckboxMenuItem("Pointer");
CheckboxMenuItem mnuRectangleTool =
       new CheckboxMenuItem("Rectangle");

public DrawRectangleFrame (String sTitle)
{
    super (sTitle);

    ScrollPane scrollPane =
        new ScrollPane(ScrollPane.SCROLLBARS_AS_NEEDED);

    Adjustable vadjust = scrollPane.getVAdjustable();
    Adjustable hadjust = scrollPane.getHAdjustable();
    hadjust.setUnitIncrement(10);
    vadjust.setUnitIncrement(10);

    drawCanvas.setSize(400,400);
    scrollPane.add(drawCanvas);

    setLayout(new BorderLayout());
    add("Center", scrollPane);

    mnuFile.add(mnuPrint);
    mnuFile.addSeparator();
    mnuFile.add(mnuExit);

    mnuPrint.addActionListener(this);
    mnuExit.addActionListener(this);

    mnuEdit.add(mnuDelete);

    mnuDelete.addActionListener(this);
```

```
        mnuColor.add(mnuColorBlue);
        mnuColor.add(mnuColorGreen);
        mnuColor.add(mnuColorRed);
        mnuColor.add(mnuColorBlack);

        mnuColorBlue.addItemListener(this);
        mnuColorGreen.addItemListener(this);
        mnuColorRed.addItemListener(this);
        mnuColorBlack.addItemListener(this);
        mnuColorBlack.setState(true);

        mnuTool.add(mnuPointerTool);
        mnuTool.add(mnuRectangleTool);

        mnuPointerTool.addItemListener(this);
        mnuRectangleTool.addItemListener(this);
        mnuPointerTool.setState(true);

        menuBar.add(mnuFile);
        menuBar.add(mnuEdit);
        menuBar.add(mnuColor);
        menuBar.add(mnuTool);

        setMenuBar(menuBar);

        setSize(300,300);
        show();
        drawCanvas.createOffScreenGraphics();
    }

    public void actionPerformed (ActionEvent evt)
    {
        Object target = evt.getSource();
        if (target == mnuExit)
        {
            dispose();
            System.exit(0);
        }

        else if (target == mnuPrint)
        {
            PrintJob printJob = getToolkit().getPrintJob(this,
                                      "Print Rectangles", null);
            drawCanvas.print(printJob);
        }

        else if (target == mnuDelete)
        {
            drawCanvas.delete();
        }
    }
```

```
public void itemStateChanged (ItemEvent evt)
{
    Object target = evt.getSource();
    if (evt.getStateChange() == ItemEvent.SELECTED)
    {
        if (target == mnuPointerTool)
        {
            mnuRectangleTool.setState(false);
            drawCanvas.setSelectToolOn();
        }
        else if (target == mnuRectangleTool)
        {
            mnuPointerTool.setState(false);
            drawCanvas.setRectangleToolOn();
        }
        else if (target == mnuColorBlue)
        {
            drawCanvas.setDrawColor(Color.blue);
            deselectColorItems(target);
        }
        else if (target == mnuColorRed)
        {
            drawCanvas.setDrawColor(Color.red);
            deselectColorItems(target);
        }
        else if (target == mnuColorGreen)
        {
            drawCanvas.setDrawColor(Color.green);
            deselectColorItems(target);
        }
        else if (target == mnuColorBlack)
        {
            drawCanvas.setDrawColor(Color.black);
            deselectColorItems(target);
        }
    }
    else
    {
        // never allow all tools to be deselected
        ((CheckboxMenuItem)target).setState(true);
    }
}

void deselectColorItems (Object oKeepSelected)
{
    if (mnuColorGreen != oKeepSelected)
        mnuColorGreen.setState(false);

    if (mnuColorBlue != oKeepSelected)
        mnuColorBlue.setState(false);
```

```
        if (mnuColorRed != oKeepSelected)
            mnuColorRed.setState(false);

        if (mnuColorBlack != oKeepSelected)
            mnuColorBlack.setState(false);
    }

    public static void main (String args[])
    {
        new DrawRectangleFrame("Draw Rectangle Program");
    }
}
```

- **DrawingObject.** This is an abstract class that represents a generic drawing object. It provides methods for drawing, resizing, and selecting the object. Source 10.16 implements this object.
- **RectangleObject.** This class extends DrawingObject and represents a rectangle. It demonstrates the use of the Cursor class. The RectangleObject implements all of the abstract methods declared in DrawingObject and therefore can be drawn, resized, or selected.

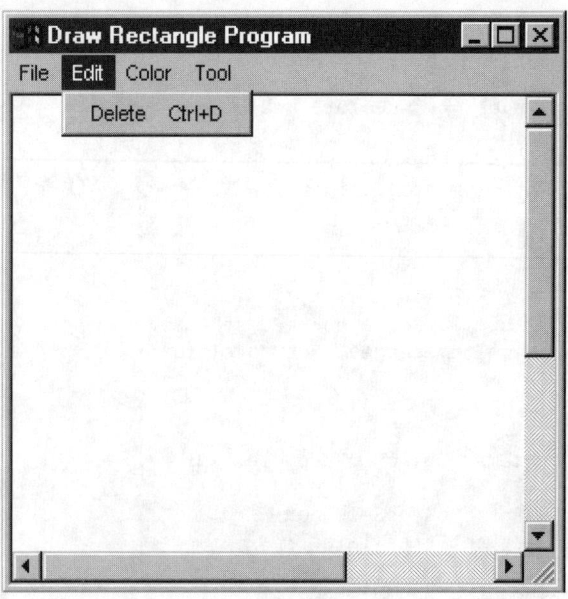

FIGURE 10.19 MenuShortcut.

SOURCE 10.15 DrawCanvas.java

```
// DrawCanvas.java
package jwiley.chp10;

import java.awt.*;
import java.awt.event.*;

public class DrawCanvas extends Canvas
    implements MouseMotionListener, MouseListener
{
    boolean             bMousePressed = false;
    DrawingObject       rectangles[];
    int                 iCurrentIndex = -1;

    boolean             bRectangleSelected = false;

    boolean             bSelectToolOn = false;
    boolean             bRectangleToolOn = false;
    public Graphics     offScreenGraphics;
    Image               offScreenImage;

    public DrawCanvas ()
    {
        addMouseListener(this);
        addMouseMotionListener(this);
        setForeground(Color.black);
    }

    public void createOffScreenGraphics()
    {
        Dimension d = getSize();
        offScreenImage = createImage(d.width, d.height);
        offScreenGraphics = offScreenImage.getGraphics();
    }
    public Graphics getOffscreenGraphics()
    {
        return offScreenGraphics;
    }

    public void setSelectToolOn ()
    {
        bSelectToolOn = true;
        bRectangleToolOn = false;
    }

    public void setRectangleToolOn ()
    {
        cleanupSelectTool();
        bSelectToolOn = false;
        bRectangleToolOn = true;
    }
```

```
public void setDrawColor (Color color)
{
    setForeground(color);
    offScreenGraphics.setColor(color);
}

public void cleanupSelectTool()
{
    if (bRectangleSelected)
        rectangles[iCurrentIndex].deselect(this);

    iCurrentIndex = -1;
    bRectangleSelected = false;
}


public void mouseDragged (MouseEvent evt)
{
    if (bMousePressed)
    {
        rectangles[iCurrentIndex].resize(this, evt.getPoint());
    }

    if (bSelectToolOn && bRectangleSelected)
    {
        if (getCursor().getType() == Cursor.DEFAULT_CURSOR)
            // move mode
            rectangles[iCurrentIndex].move(this, evt.getPoint());
        else
            // resize mode
            rectangles[iCurrentIndex].resize(this,
                                    evt.getPoint(), getCursor());
    }
}

public void mouseMoved (MouseEvent evt)
{
  if (bRectangleSelected)
  {
    // check to see if mouse is over a selection handle
    rectangles[iCurrentIndex].setHandleCursor(this, evt.getPoint());
  }
}

public void mousePressed (MouseEvent evt)
{
    if (bRectangleToolOn)
    {
        bMousePressed = true;
        iCurrentIndex = addNewRectangle(evt.getPoint());
        rectangles[iCurrentIndex].setColor(getForeground());
    }
```

```
    if (bSelectToolOn && bRectangleSelected)
    {
     rectangles[iCurrentIndex].setHandleCursor(this, evt.getPoint());
     if (getCursor().getType() == Cursor.DEFAULT_CURSOR)
        // set up for move mode
        rectangles[iCurrentIndex].setMoveAnchor(evt.getPoint());
    }
}

public void mouseReleased (MouseEvent evt)
{
    bMousePressed = false;
}

public void mouseEntered (MouseEvent evt)    {    }

public void mouseExited (MouseEvent evt)     {    }

public void mouseClicked (MouseEvent evt)
{
    if (bSelectToolOn)
    {
        if (rectangles != null)
        {
          // deselect the rectangle that is selected
          if (bRectangleSelected)
            rectangles[iCurrentIndex].deselect(this);

          iCurrentIndex = -1;
          bRectangleSelected = false;

          Point p = evt.getPoint();
          for (int iCount = 0; iCount < rectangles.length; iCount++)
          {
            if (rectangles[iCount].isBorderClicked(this, p))
            {
              rectangles[iCount].select(this);
              iCurrentIndex = iCount;
              bRectangleSelected = true;
              break;
            }
          }

          if (bRectangleSelected)
          {
            // check to see if right mouse button clicked
            if (evt.getModifiers() == InputEvent.BUTTON3_MASK)
            {
              ColorPopupMenu colorPopupMenu =
                new ColorPopupMenu(rectangles[iCurrentIndex], this,
                               rectangles[iCurrentIndex].getColor());
```

```
                add(colorPopupMenu);
                colorPopupMenu.show(this, evt.getX(), evt.getY());
            }
          }
        }
    }
}

int addNewRectangle(Point p)
{
    if (rectangles == null)
    {
        rectangles = new RectangleObject[1];
        rectangles[0] = new RectangleObject(p);
    }
    else
    {
        DrawingObject newRectangles[] =
            new DrawingObject[rectangles.length + 1];

        for (int iCount = 0; iCount < rectangles.length; iCount++)
        {
            newRectangles[iCount] = rectangles[iCount];
        }

        newRectangles[newRectangles.length - 1] =
                                new RectangleObject(p);
        rectangles = newRectangles;
    }
    return (rectangles.length - 1);
}
public void paint (Graphics g)
{
    if (offScreenImage != null)
    {
        g.drawImage(offScreenImage, 0,0,this);
    }
}

public void update (Graphics g)
{
    if (rectangles != null)
    {
        for (int iCount = 0; iCount < rectangles.length; iCount++)
        {
            rectangles[iCount].draw(this, offScreenGraphics);
        }
    }
    paint(g);
}
```

```
    public void print (PrintJob printJob)
    {
        if (printJob != null)
        {
            Graphics pg = printJob.getGraphics();
            if (pg != null)
            {
                paint(pg);
                pg.dispose();
            }
            printJob.end();
        }
    }

    public void delete ()
    {
        DrawingObject rectangleToDelete = rectangles[iCurrentIndex];

        if (bSelectToolOn && bRectangleSelected)
        {
            // remove from rectangles array
            if (rectangles.length == 1)
            {
                rectangles = null;
            }
            else
            {
              int iOffset = 0;
              DrawingObject newRectangles[] =
                  new DrawingObject[rectangles.length - 1];

              for (int iCount = 0; iCount < rectangles.length; iCount++)
              {
                  if (iCount == iCurrentIndex)
                      iOffset++;
                  else
                      newRectangles[iCount - iOffset] =
                                              rectangles[iCount];
              }
              rectangles = newRectangles;
            }

            rectangleToDelete.deselect(this);
            rectangleToDelete.erase(this);

            iCurrentIndex = -1;
            bRectangleSelected = false;
        }
    }
}
```

- **SelectionHandle.** This class contains the data needed for a selection handle. It contains a rectangle and a Cursor object. The Cursor object is used to store the resizing cursor associated with the selection handle. Source 10.17 implements this object.
- **ColorPopupMenu.** This class extends PopupMenu. It provides a list of colors that can be selected to change the color of a drawing object. Source 10.18 implements this object.

The first bolded lines show how to use MenuShortcut to provide a shortcut for the menu item. I am adding a shortcut to both the delete menu item and the print menu item. The MenuShortcut constructor actually accepts an integer keycode, but by specifying a character in single quotes Java is able to get the keycode for the character. The MenuShortcut cannot be accessed simply by pressing the character specified. Each platform has a modifier key that also needs to be pressed to invoke the shortcut. On Windows 95, the modifier is the <Ctrl> key. Figure 10.19 shows the DrawRectangleFrame with delete menu item visible. Pressing <Ctrl-d> will cause the delete code to run.

The second set of bolded lines demonstrates the use of the ScrollPane. The ScrollPane flag SCROLLBARS_AS_NEEDED is passed in to the constructor. The drawCanvas component is added to the scroll pane. Since the drawCanvas component is larger than the ScrollPane the scrollbars are displayed. If the window is resized to make the ScrollPane larger than the drawCanvas the scrollbars will disappear. The horizontal and vertical increments are set by using the Adjustable interface. Note that layout of the ScrollPane is not set. The reason for this is that the ScrollPane manages its own layout and it overrides the setLayout method so the layout cannot be set.

The last bolded line gets a PrintJob object. The getPrintJob() method is called with the current frame, a job title, and a properties object. In this case the properties object is null, but if you needed to pass information to the printer you would specify it in the properties object. The reason the getPrintJob() method needs a frame is to allow it to bring up a print dialog. The print dialog gets displayed and if the user clicks OK, a valid PrintJob object is returned. If the user cancels, null will be returned.

If you look at the first set of bolded lines you will see that drawCanvas handles the creation and display of the popup menu. First the popup menu is created and then added to drawCanvas. Adding the popup menu to drawCanvas allows the menu to be created before it is displayed. You must add a popup menu to a component before calling the show() method or an exception will be thrown. The show method is used to display the popup menu at the desired location. In the DrawCanvas class I check the mouse modifiers to determine which button was pushed. If BUTTON3 is pushed then the popup menu is displayed. The isPopupTrigger() method in the MouseEvent class should be used to check if a popup menu should be displayed. However, at the time of this writing the isPopupTrigger() method was not working properly. Figure 10.20 shows the displayed popup menu.

The second set of bolded lines demonstrates how to print in Java. A PrintJob has already been created in DrawRectangleFrame. To print all we need to do is get the printer graphics object, draw on it, and then end the print job. All of the work in printing is drawing on the printer graphics object. You can use existing paint routines to

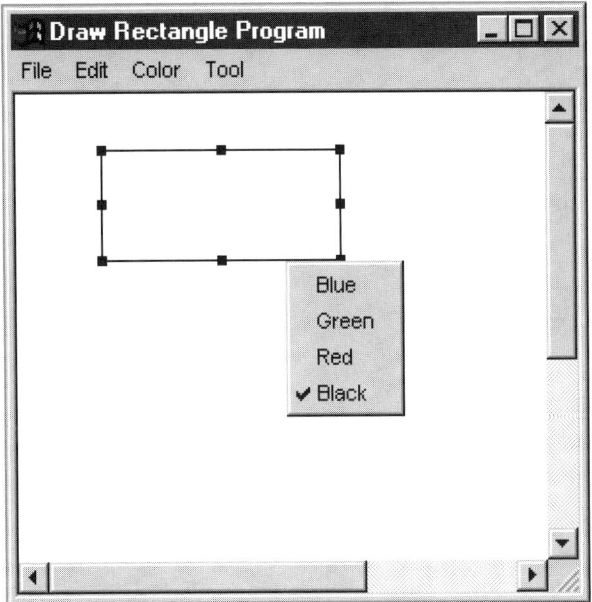

FIGURE 10.20 Popup menu.

SOURCE 10.16 DrawingObject.java

```
// DrawingObject.java
package jwiley.chp10;

import java.awt.Color;
import java.awt.Point;
import java.awt.Cursor;
import java.awt.Graphics;

public abstract class DrawingObject
{
    protected Color     color;

    public void setColor(Color color)
    {   this.color = color; }

    public Color getColor()
    {   return (color);     }

    public abstract void draw (DrawCanvas drawCanvas, Graphics g);
    public abstract void erase (DrawCanvas drawCanvas);
    public abstract void resize (DrawCanvas drawCanvas, Point p);
```

```
    public abstract void resize (DrawCanvas drawCanvas, Point p,
                                                     Cursor cursor);
    public abstract void setMoveAnchor (Point p);
    public abstract void move (DrawCanvas drawCanvas, Point p);
    public abstract boolean isBorderClicked (DrawCanvas drawCanvas,
                                                          Point p);
    public abstract void select (DrawCanvas drawCanvas);
    public abstract void deselect (DrawCanvas drawCanvas);
    public abstract void setHandleCursor (DrawCanvas drawCanvas,
                                                          Point p);
}

// RectangleObject.java
package jwiley.chp10;

import java.awt.*;

public class RectangleObject extends DrawingObject
{
    Point pAnchor;           // used for initial drawing and resizing
    Point pMoveAnchor;       // used for moving
    int x = 0;
    int y = 0;
    int width = 0;
    int height = 0;

    SelectionHandle selectionHandles[];

    public RectangleObject(Point pAnchor)
    {
        this.pAnchor = pAnchor;
        x = pAnchor.x;
        y = pAnchor.y;
        color = Color.black;
    }

    public void draw (DrawCanvas drawCanvas, Graphics g)
    {
        if (g != null)
        {
            Color colorCurrent = g.getColor();
            g.setColor(this.getColor());
            g.drawRect(x, y, width, height);
            g.setColor(colorCurrent);
        }
    }

    public void resize (DrawCanvas drawCanvas, Point p)
    {
        Graphics g = drawCanvas.getOffscreenGraphics();
        if (g != null)
        {
```

```
            g.setXORMode(Color.white);
            draw(drawCanvas, g);
            computeNewRect(p);
            g.setPaintMode();
            draw(drawCanvas, g);
        }
        drawCanvas.repaint();
    }

    public void resize (DrawCanvas drawCanvas, Point p, Cursor cursor)
    {
        Graphics g = drawCanvas.getOffscreenGraphics();
        Point pAnchor1;
        Point pAnchor2;

        if (g != null)
        {
            deselect(drawCanvas);
            g.setXORMode(Color.white);
            draw(drawCanvas, g);

            int iCursorType = cursor.getType();
            if (iCursorType == Cursor.NW_RESIZE_CURSOR)
            {
                pAnchor = new Point(x + width, y + height);
                computeNewRect(p);
            }
            else if (iCursorType == Cursor.NE_RESIZE_CURSOR)
            {
                pAnchor = new Point(x, y + height);
                computeNewRect(p);
            }
            else if (iCursorType == Cursor.SE_RESIZE_CURSOR)
            {
                pAnchor = new Point(x, y);
                computeNewRect(p);
            }
            else if (iCursorType == Cursor.SW_RESIZE_CURSOR)
            {
                pAnchor = new Point(x + width, y);
                computeNewRect(p);
            }
            else if (iCursorType == Cursor.N_RESIZE_CURSOR)
            {
                computeNewRect(new Point(x, y + height),
                               new Point(x + width, y + height), p);
            }
            else if (iCursorType == Cursor.S_RESIZE_CURSOR)
            {
                computeNewRect(new Point(x, y),
                               new Point(x + width, y), p);
            }
```

```
        else if (iCursorType == Cursor.W_RESIZE_CURSOR)
        {
            computeNewRect(new Point(x + width, y),
                           new Point(x + width, y + height), p);
        }
        else if (iCursorType == Cursor.E_RESIZE_CURSOR)
        {
            computeNewRect(new Point(x, y),
                           new Point(x, y + height), p);
        }

        g.setPaintMode();
        draw(drawCanvas, g);
        select(drawCanvas);
    }
    drawCanvas.repaint();
}

public void setMoveAnchor (Point p)
{
    this.pMoveAnchor = p;
}

public void move (DrawCanvas drawCanvas, Point p)
{
    Graphics g = drawCanvas.getOffscreenGraphics();
    if (g != null)
    {
        deselect(drawCanvas);
        g.setXORMode(Color.white);
        draw(drawCanvas, g);

        x = x + (p.x - pMoveAnchor.x);
        y = y + (p.y - pMoveAnchor.y);
        pMoveAnchor = p;

        g.setPaintMode();
        draw(drawCanvas, g);
        select(drawCanvas);
    }
    drawCanvas.repaint();
}

public void erase (DrawCanvas drawCanvas)
{
    Graphics g = drawCanvas.getOffscreenGraphics();
    if (g != null)
    {
        g.setXORMode(Color.white);
        draw(drawCanvas, g);
        g.setPaintMode();
    }
```

```
        drawCanvas.repaint();
    }

    public boolean isBorderClicked (DrawCanvas drawCanvas, Point p)
    {
        // check within a 1 pixel buffer if the border was clicked
        int iBuffer = 1;
        Rectangle r[] = new Rectangle[4];
        r[0] = new Rectangle(x - iBuffer, y - iBuffer,
                             width + iBuffer * 2,
                             iBuffer * 2 + 1);
        r[1] = new Rectangle(x + width - iBuffer, y - iBuffer,
                             iBuffer * 2 + 1,
                             height + iBuffer * 2);
        r[2] = new Rectangle(x - iBuffer, y + height - iBuffer,
                             width + iBuffer * 2,
                             iBuffer * 2 + 1);
        r[3] = new Rectangle(x - iBuffer, y - iBuffer,
                             iBuffer * 2 + 1,
                             height + iBuffer * 2);

        for (int iCount = 0; iCount < r.length; iCount++)
        {
            if (isPointInRectangle(r[iCount], p))
                return (true);
        }

        return (false);
    }

    public void select (DrawCanvas drawCanvas)
    {
        // draw selection handles
        int iNumHandles = 4;
        int iHandleSize = 5;
        int iHandleOffset = (int)((iHandleSize - 1) / 2);
        int iMiddleHandleMultiplier = 6;

        boolean bXMiddleHandles = false;
        boolean bYMiddleHandles = false;

        if (width > (iHandleSize * iMiddleHandleMultiplier))
        {
            bXMiddleHandles = true;
            iNumHandles += 2;
        }

        if (height > (iHandleSize * iMiddleHandleMultiplier))
        {
            bYMiddleHandles = true;
            iNumHandles += 2;
        }
```

```
// put handles at four corners
selectionHandles = new SelectionHandle[iNumHandles];

selectionHandles[0] =
      new SelectionHandle(x - iHandleOffset, y - iHandleOffset,
                          iHandleSize, iHandleSize,
                          new Cursor(Cursor.NW_RESIZE_CURSOR));
selectionHandles[1] =
      new SelectionHandle(x + width - iHandleOffset,
                          y - iHandleOffset,
                          iHandleSize, iHandleSize,
                          new Cursor(Cursor.NE_RESIZE_CURSOR));
selectionHandles[2] =
      new SelectionHandle(x + width - iHandleOffset,
                          y + height - iHandleOffset,
                          iHandleSize, iHandleSize,
                          new Cursor(Cursor.SE_RESIZE_CURSOR));
selectionHandles[3] =
      new SelectionHandle(x - iHandleOffset,
                          y + height - iHandleOffset,
                          iHandleSize, iHandleSize,
                          new Cursor(Cursor.SW_RESIZE_CURSOR));

if (bXMiddleHandles)
{
    int iMidPoint = x + ((int) width / 2);
    selectionHandles[4] =
        new SelectionHandle(iMidPoint - iHandleOffset,
                          y - iHandleOffset,
                          iHandleSize, iHandleSize,
                          new Cursor(Cursor.N_RESIZE_CURSOR));

    selectionHandles[5] =
        new SelectionHandle(iMidPoint - iHandleOffset,
                          y + height - iHandleOffset,
                          iHandleSize, iHandleSize,
                          new Cursor(Cursor.S_RESIZE_CURSOR));

}

if (bYMiddleHandles)
{
    int iMidPoint = y + ((int) height / 2);
    int iOffset = 3;
    if (bXMiddleHandles)
        iOffset = 5;

    selectionHandles[iOffset + 1] =
        new SelectionHandle(x - iHandleOffset,
                          iMidPoint - iHandleOffset,
                          iHandleSize, iHandleSize,
                          new Cursor(Cursor.W_RESIZE_CURSOR));
```

```
        selectionHandles[iOffset + 2] =
            new SelectionHandle(x + width - iHandleOffset,
                                iMidPoint - iHandleOffset,
                                iHandleSize, iHandleSize,
                                new Cursor(Cursor.E_RESIZE_CURSOR));

    }

    Graphics g = drawCanvas.getOffscreenGraphics();
    for (int iCount = 0; iCount < selectionHandles.length; iCount++)
    {
        g.fillRect(selectionHandles[iCount].rect.x,
                   selectionHandles[iCount].rect.y,
                   selectionHandles[iCount].rect.width,
                   selectionHandles[iCount].rect.height);
    }
    drawCanvas.repaint();
}

public void deselect (DrawCanvas drawCanvas)
{
    Graphics g = drawCanvas.getOffscreenGraphics();
    g.setXORMode(Color.white);
    for (int iCount = 0; iCount < selectionHandles.length; iCount++)
    {
        g.fillRect(selectionHandles[iCount].rect.x,
                   selectionHandles[iCount].rect.y,
                   selectionHandles[iCount].rect.width,
                   selectionHandles[iCount].rect.height);
    }

    g.setPaintMode();
    draw(drawCanvas, g);
    drawCanvas.repaint();
}

public void setHandleCursor(DrawCanvas drawCanvas, Point p)
{
  if (selectionHandles != null)
  {
    for (int iCount = 0; iCount < selectionHandles.length; iCount++)
    {
      if (isPointInRectangle(selectionHandles[iCount].rect, p))
      {
        drawCanvas.setCursor(selectionHandles[iCount].cursor);
        return;
      }
    }
  }

  drawCanvas.setCursor(new Cursor(Cursor.DEFAULT_CURSOR));
}
```

```
    boolean isPointInRectangle (Rectangle r, Point p)
    {
        if ((p.x >= r.x) &&
            (p.x <= r.x + r.width) &&
            (p.y >= r.y) &&
            (p.y <= r.y + r.height))
        {
            return (true);
        }
        else
            return (false);
    }

    void computeNewRect(Point p)
    {
        if (p.x < pAnchor.x)
        {
            x = p.x;
            width = pAnchor.x - x;
        }
        else
        {
            x = pAnchor.x;
            width = p.x - x;
        }

        if (p.y < pAnchor.y)
        {
            y = p.y;
            height = pAnchor.y - y;
        }
        else
        {
            y = pAnchor.y;
            height = p.y - y;
        }
    }

    void computeNewRect (Point pAnchor1, Point pAnchor2, Point p)
    {
        // assumption - either the x or y of the anchors is the same
        if (pAnchor1.x == pAnchor2.x)
            p.y = pAnchor1.y;
        else
            p.x = pAnchor1.x;

        this.pAnchor = pAnchor2;
        computeNewRect(p);
    }
}
```

print out components or graphics, but you will have to implement your own routines for sophisticated printing. You can also obtain the paper size and resolution using the PrintJob class.

In the RectangleObject class the Cursor class is demonstrated. Let's first take a look at the select method. The select method is responsible for creating the selection handles for the rectangle. When a selection handle is created, a cursor is associated with the handle. If you take a look at the bolded code in the select method, you will see that we are creating a new Cursor object to pass into the SelectionHandle constructor. You must pass in a predefined cursor variable when creating a cursor. In this instance we are creating a NW_RESIZE_CURSOR. In the setHandleCursor() method, all selection handles are checked to see if the mouse location is inside the selection handle. If the mouse is over a selection handle we call the setCursor() method on drawCanvas to change the cursor type. If the mouse is not over a selection handle the cursor is set to the default cursor.

In the resize() method we use the cursor one more time. By calling the getType() method on the cursor we can obtain the cursor's predefined type. By checking this type against several of the resize cursor types we can determine which direction we need to resize. If the cursor is of type NW_RESIZE_CURSOR then we want to anchor the opposite corner of the rectangle so the northwest corner can be resized.

SOURCE 10.17 SelectionHandle.java

```
// SelectionHandle.java
package jwiley.chp10;

import java.awt.Cursor;
import java.awt.Rectangle;

class SelectionHandle
{
    Rectangle rect;
    Cursor    cursor;

    SelectionHandle (Rectangle rect, Cursor cursor)
    {
        this.rect = rect;
        this.cursor = cursor;
    }

    SelectionHandle (int x, int y, int width, int height, Cursor cursor)
    {
        this.rect = new Rectangle(x, y, width, height);
        this.cursor = cursor;
    }
}
```

SOURCE 10.18 ColorPopupMenu.java

```
// ColorPopupMenu.java
package jwiley.chp10;

import java.awt.*;
import java.awt.event.*;

public class ColorPopupMenu extends PopupMenu implements ItemListener
{
    CheckboxMenuItem mnuColorBlue = new CheckboxMenuItem("Blue");
    CheckboxMenuItem mnuColorGreen = new CheckboxMenuItem("Green");
    CheckboxMenuItem mnuColorRed = new CheckboxMenuItem("Red");
    CheckboxMenuItem mnuColorBlack = new CheckboxMenuItem("Black");

    DrawingObject   drawObject;
    DrawCanvas      drawCanvas;

    public ColorPopupMenu (DrawingObject drawObject,
                           DrawCanvas drawCanvas,
                           Color colorSelected)
    {
        this.drawObject = drawObject;
        this.drawCanvas = drawCanvas;

        add(mnuColorBlue);
        add(mnuColorGreen);
        add(mnuColorRed);
        add(mnuColorBlack);

        mnuColorBlue.addItemListener(this);
        mnuColorGreen.addItemListener(this);
        mnuColorRed.addItemListener(this);
        mnuColorBlack.addItemListener(this);

        if (colorSelected == Color.blue)
            mnuColorBlue.setState(true);
        else if (colorSelected == Color.green)
            mnuColorGreen.setState(true);
        else if (colorSelected == Color.red)
            mnuColorRed.setState(true);
        else if (colorSelected == Color.black)
            mnuColorBlack.setState(true);
    }

    public void itemStateChanged (ItemEvent evt)
    {
        Object target = evt.getSource();
        if (evt.getStateChange() == ItemEvent.SELECTED)
        {
```

```
            if (target == mnuColorBlue)
                drawObject.setColor(Color.blue);
            else if (target == mnuColorGreen)
                drawObject.setColor(Color.green);
            else if (target == mnuColorRed)
                drawObject.setColor(Color.red);
            else if (target == mnuColorBlack)
                drawObject.setColor(Color.black);

            // force repaint but keep it selected
            drawObject.deselect(drawCanvas);
            drawObject.select(drawCanvas);
        }
    }
}
```

The draw rectangle program only has two tools: pointer and rectangle. If the rectangle tool is selected you can draw rectangles on the canvas by pressing the mouse button and dragging. The rectangle will be completed when the mouse button is released. You can change the current draw color by choosing a color from the Color menu.

To select a rectangle you must change to the pointer tool. If the pointer tool is active you can select a rectangle by clicking on the rectangle's border. Once the rectangle is selected you can resize it, move it, change its color, or delete it. To resize the rectangle, place the mouse over a selection handle and drag it until the desired shape is achieved. To move the rectangle drag the rectangle's border to the desired location. Clicking the right mouse button will display the popup menu for changing the rectangle's color. Finally, selecting the Delete menu item will delete the rectangle.

Loading and Drawing Images

The basics of displaying images in Java are quite simple and involve three steps:

1. Decoding a known image format (currently .gif or .jpg).
2. Loading the image into an Image object.
3. Rendering (or drawing) the image in a component.

Decoding an image means that the program understands the specifics of an image file format like the number of bits used to represent a pixel and how the pixels are stored in the file. Java currently only supports the most common image formats used on the Web, which are gif (Graphics Image Format) and jpeg (Joint Photographic Experts Group). There are many image conversion programs available to change any other format into one of these formats. The major difference between the formats is that gif images only support 256 colors while jpeg supports millions (as well as image compression). Another option is to write your own image decoder. In Java, you begin the decoding and loading process with a single method call to getImage() as shown here:

```
Toolkit tk = Toolkit.getDefaultToolkit();
Image img = tk.getImage("myImage.gif");
```

In a standalone application you use the getImage() method of the default windowing toolkit; however, the Applet class also has a getImage() method that uses the http protocol to retrieve an image. The toolkit can load the image either from the file system or using a URL. The getImage() method returns a reference to an Image, which is a subclass of Image that is a specific implementation of an image. The Image class itself is an abstract class that has a subclass for each type of image Java can decode. You should remember that since the Image class is abstract, you cannot instantiate it directly.

It is very important to understand that getImage() is an asynchronous method that returns immediately. The getImage() method starts a separate image loading thread that actually does the work. This is the best solution for images that can be retrieved from the Internet because the program should not expect to wait on what could be a slow process. The Java AWT has three interfaces that create the framework for this asynchronous image loading. The interfaces are ImageProducer, ImageConsumer, and ImageObserver. An ImageProducer object can produce a stream of pixels (data that makes up an image) to an ImageConsumer. An ImageConsumer object receives pixels from an ImageProducer. An ImageObserver receives notification of the image loading. All AWT components are image observers because the Component class implements ImageObserver and by default repaints itself each time some image data is received. You can observe this default behavior of an ImageObserver by running the Source 10.19 with the following parameters:

```
java LoadImage javabk.gif
```

This will load the image entitled javabk.gif, which must be in the same directory the LoadImage class resides. You will see a AWT frame pop up and the image get painted in sections as the pixels become available from the default ImageProducer provided with the implementation of the .gif decoder in the Java AWT. The important point to understand is that the image is being painted as soon as any pixel data is available from the image loading thread. As the program runs, you have two threads working simultaneously: the image loading thread and the screen updater thread that paints (or repaints) the component.

There are many occasions when you do not want to display an image unless it is entirely loaded. One simple example of this would be a splash screen that uses an image. You don't want the splash screen to paint piecemeal because that portrays an unfinished or clunky feel to the user; therefore, you want to make the image loading a synchronous process. In other words, you want your program to wait until the image is fully loaded before moving on. The AWT package provides an object to do just that called the MediaTracker. You can register an Image with the media tracker and then tell it to wait until the image is fully loaded. Here is a demonstration of that from Source 10.19:

```
MediaTracker theTracker = new MediaTracker(new Frame());
theTracker.addImage(theImage,0);
try
{
     theTracker.waitForAll();
} catch(Exception e)
  {
     System.out.println("Error loading image.");
     System.exit(1);
  }
```

The constructor for the MediaTracker requires a reference to an ImageObserver. Remember that all AWT components implement the ImageObserver interface. We then use two methods to add and wait for the image. The addImage() method adds the image to the image tracker (you may add many images). The waitForAll() method waits for all images added to the media tracker. There is a method to check for any errors in the image loading process called isErrorAny(); Source 10.19 also demonstrates using the media tracker when you specify the _wait flag.

TIP If your call to isErrorAny() returns true you can try and reload the image with another call to getImage(); however, you must first call the flush() method on the image. If you do not call the flush() method the loading will just fail again.

Now that we understand how to "get" an image and the nature of asynchronous image loading, we can render the image on a component. Normally, you will draw an image onto a canvas but that is not a requirement. In Source 10.19 we render the image onto a Frame. In the Graphics object there are several versions of the drawImage() method. The key parameters to the drawImage() method are the image to be drawn, the x and y coordinates in the component to begin drawing the image, and the ImageObserver to be notified if not all the data is available at this drawing. You can also specify a height and width to the image which will then cause the AWT to scale the image to the requested size. If you do not specify a height and width, the image will be drawn at its actual size. Once an image has been loaded you can get its height and width by calling getHeight() or getWidth() on the Image reference. Source 10.19 also demonstrates drawing an image. I recommend experimenting with the program by calling it with various parameters and on several different images.

SOURCE 10.19 LoadImage.java

```
/** loadImage.java */
package jwiley.chp10;

import java.awt.*;
import java.awt.event.*;
import java.io.File;

/**
 * Class that represents a window with a single image displayed in it.
 * @version 1.1
 * @author Michael C. Daconta
 */
class imageFrame extends Frame
{
    /** The image to display. */
    Image theImg;

    /** Adapter class to shutdown application when close
        box clicked on window. */
    class ShutdownAdapter extends WindowAdapter
    {
        public void windowClosing(WindowEvent we)
        { System.exit(0); }
    }

    /**
     * Constructor to create the frame.
     * @param anImg the Image to display.
     * @param sizeToImage flag to determine size of window frame. If true
     *        the frame will be sized to the image width and height.
     */
    imageFrame(Image anImg, boolean sizeToImage)
    {
        super("Image Frame");
        theImg = anImg;
        if (sizeToImage)
            setSize(anImg.getWidth(this) + 1,anImg.getHeight(this) + 1);
        else
            setSize(200,200);
        addWindowListener(new shutdownAdapter());
        show();
    }

    /** Method to paint image in window. */
    public void paint(Graphics g)
    {
        Dimension d = getSize();
        g.drawImage(theImg,0,0,d.width, d.height, this);
    }
}
```

```
/**
 * Class that wraps the main method and responds to command line args.
 */
public class LoadImage
{
    /** Main method of standalone program. */
    public static void main(String args[])
    {
        boolean fitWindowToImage=false;
        boolean waitForImageToLoad=false;

        if (args.length < 1)
        {
            System.out.println("USAGE: java loadImage " +
                               "<imageFileNmae> [-fit] [-wait]");
            System.exit(1);
        }

        // set flags if necessary
        for (int i = 0; i < args.length; I++)
        {
            if (args[i].equals("-fit"))
                fitWindowToImage = true;
            else if (args[i].equals("-wait"))
                waitForImageToLoad = true;
        }

        // check if file exists
        File imgFile = new File(args[0]);
        if (imgFile.exists())
        {
            // load the image
            Image the Image =
                (Toolkit.getDefaultToolkit()).getImage(args[0]);

            if (waitForImageToLoad || fitWindowToImage)
            {
                // create a MediaTracker
                MediaTracker theTracker = new MediaTracker(new Frame());
                theTracker.addImage(theImage,0);
                try
                {
                    theTracker.waitForAll();
                } catch(Exception e)
                  {
                    System.out.println("Error loading image.");
                    System.exit(1);
                  }

                if (theTracker.isErrorAny())
                {
                    System.out.println("Error loading image.");
                    System.exit(1);
                }
```

```
            }

            // display the image
            new imageFrame(theImage, fitWindowToImage);
        }
        else
        {
            System.out.println("Image File <" + args[0] +
                               "> does not exist.");
        }
    }
}
```

A run of Source 10.19 produces Figure 10.21.

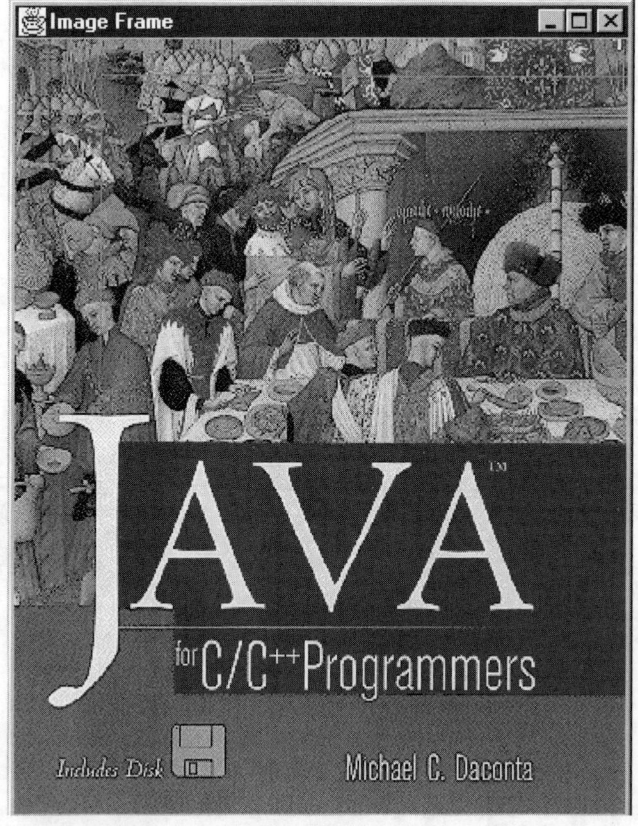

FIGURE 10.21 Image Frame.

Printing

Printing from within Java, and the AWT specifically, has been something that Java developers have been asking for, for a long time. The goal of AWT printing support is simple: provide a mechanism for printing that works within the realm of the current AWT graphics model. With the release of the JDK 1.1 came a new toolkit method, getPrintJob. getPrintJob is a class factory method for returning PrintJob object. The PrintJob object itself is an abstract object and cannot be instantiated.

The toolkit getPrintJob method is defined as shown here:

```
public abstract PrintJob getPrintJob(Frame frame,
                                     String jobtitle,
                                     Properties props)
```

and returns a Printjob that is the result of starting a print operation on the target platform.

Source 10.20 actionPerformed() shows a snippet of code from one of our previous examples (ComponentHolder.java). The snippet shows how to use the new AWT printing support.

SOURCE 10.20 actionPerformed method

```
public void actionPerformed(ActionEvent ae)
{
    String sCommand = ae.getActionCommand();
    if ("Exit".equals(sCommand))
    {
        dispose();
    }
    else if ("Print".equals(sCommand))
    {
        PrintJob pjob = getToolkit().getPrintJob(this,
                                 "Printing Test", null);

        // null means user canceled print job
        if (pjob != null)
        {
            Graphics  pg = pjob.getGraphics();
            if (pg != null)
            {
                printAll(pg);
                pg.dispose(); // flush page
            }
            pjob.end();
        }
    }
```

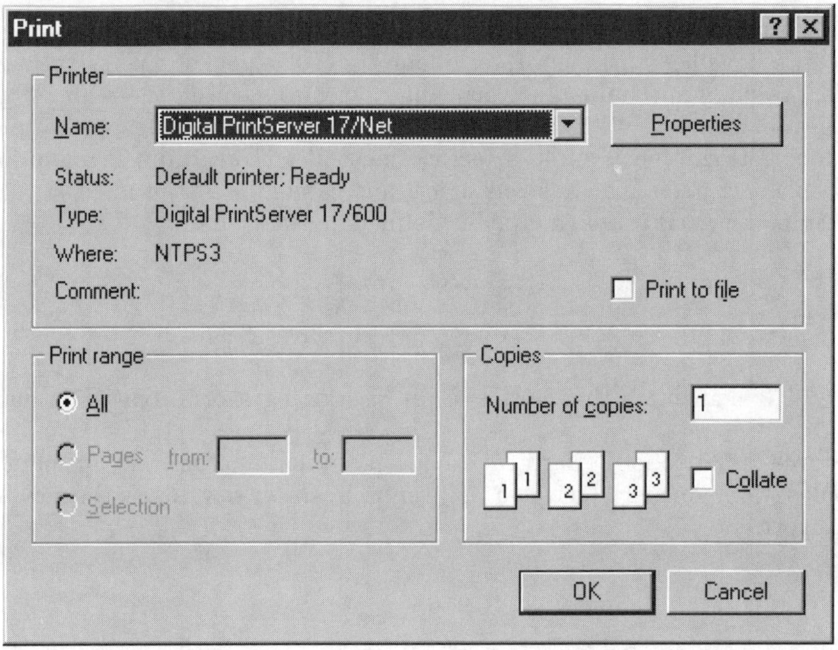

FIGURE 10.22 Printer dialog.

Figure 10.22 shows the printer dialog generated under Windows 95 when the print menu selection is chosen.

Let's examine the printing capabilities of the ComponentHolder example to better understand just how the AWT supports printing.

The actionPerformed method captured the request to print the document and we then created a print job by using the toolkit's method getPrintJob.

```
PrintJob printJob = getToolkit().getPrintJob(this,
                                    "Printing Test", null);
```

The parameters to getPrintJob are quite simple. The first is the frame associated with the print job, the second is a name for the print job, and the third is a list of print job properties. The properties argument is the least obvious of the three and allows the developer to send platform-specific information about the print job to the printer. Examples of properties might be the name of the printer, print a selection versus the entire document, the number of copies, and so on.

TIP The properties a printer supports are platform-specific. However, the getPrintJob call will fill in a properties object based on changes a user makes when the job is printed. A trick you can use to determine some of the printer properties is to print something and then change some of the printer options. The properties object should come back with property-based representations of the changes.

If the user cancels the print job then getPrintJob will return a null reference and the application can go on its way. Otherwise, the application continues by obtaining a reference to a printer graphics context.

```
Graphics pg = pjob.getGraphics();
```

The interesting thing about the getGraphics method is that it returns an everyday Graphics object and can be used anywhere a Graphics context makes sense.

TIP Printing an object versus rendering an object on the screen may be handled differently. Since the getGraphics method of the PrintJob object implements the PrintGraphics context (and is a subclass of the Graphics object), a developer can test within a paint method whether the result is going to a printer (Graphics context is instanceof PrintGraphics) and handle the process differently, perhaps printing text descriptions of objects rather than graphics when the print source is a printer.

Once we have obtained our context we need to actually cause the object to be printed. In our example we use the printAll method, which works by calling the print (or appropriate rendering methods) of each of the contained objects.

```
printAll(pg);
```

In our example the printAll method would be called for each object in the Frame's hierarchy, first calling the various panels' rendering methods and then each of the subcomponents. Finally, we flush the page to the printer with the dispose call.

```
pg.dispose(); // flush page
```

When we are finished with our print job we free its resources with the PrintJob.end method.

Page Size and Pagination. Two topics we have not given any thought to are page size and pagination. Our example was simple enough to not warrant any size or page-break manipulations. Most applications are not this simple. The PrintJob class provides two methods for getting page information.

- **int getPageResolution().** Returns the page resolution in pixels. The page resolution may or may not match the print resolution depending on how the print is set up. For example, a 600-dpi printer may be configured to print text at 300-dpi.
- **Dimension getPageDimension.** Returns the X by Y page resolution in pixels.

Note that it is the responsibility of the developer to handle pagination. Because of the simplicity of our example we didn't handle page breaks in any special way. But what we did do is gloss over something, and that is that the getGraphics method returns a context for the current page! If, for example, our application had been a word processor rather then a simple dialog we might have wished to print each page individually, in which case we would have done something like:

```
For each page in document
{
      // Get a context for THIS page.
      Graphics pg = pjob.getGraphics();
      // Render the page
      pg.dispose(); // Flush the page to the printer.
}
```

Security and Printing. As a final note about printing, printing is a potential security risk. Therefore, the getPrintJob method is controlled via the standard security principles, which means that under normal circumstances distrusted applets cannot print!

10.4 DATATRANSFER

The DataTransfer package provides a mechanism to do copy and paste operations, and drag and drop operations. Both of the aforementioned types of data transfer are standard on operating systems that employ a graphical user interface. Providing these mechanisms in Java will bring Java applications one step closer to performing like a "native" application.

Clipboard

The copy and paste operations are implemented via the Clipboard. A clipboard is an object that is used to temporarily store information. In the Java implementation, this information is encapsulated in an object. Only one object can be stored on a clipboard at any given time. The object itself can present the information it encapsulates in a variety of formats, called "data flavors" in Java. The object that encapsulates that data must implement the Transferable interface, which provides methods for examining and retrieving supported data flavors. An object implementing the Transferable interface can be placed on the clipboard with the setContents() method. The object is now available to everything that has access to that particular clipboard. Java provides a system clipboard that can be used to interface between Java applications and native applications. A Java program can get the information from the clipboard using the get-

Contents() method. The data will be returned in the requested data flavor if it is supported. Let's take a look at the classes used to implement the clipboard functionality.

- **ClipboardOwner.** An interface that provides a single method, lostOwnership(). All classes that want to set data in the clipboard must implement this interface. The lostOwnership method will be called when another ClipboardOwner is requesting access to the clipboard.
- **Transferable.** An interface that must be implemented by classes that wish to be transferred to the clipboard. The Transferable interface provides methods for examining the available data flavors supported by the object, and to request the data in the data flavor it desires. A transferable class encapsulates data to be placed on the clipboard. One of the most common things placed on clipboards is strings. The StringSelection class is provided by Java as a Transferable class that encapsulates the String data type. To make other data types available for copy and paste, you have to encapsulate the data type in a class and implement the Transferable interface.
- **Clipboard.** This class acts as a repository for a Transferable class. Only one class at a time can be placed on the clipboard. To get or set the data in the clipboard, the Clipboard class provides the getContents() and setContents() methods. To allow Java programs to interact with the native environment, a system clipboard is provided. The system clipboard can be obtained by calling the getSystemClipboard() method in the java.awt.Toolkit class.
- **DataFlavor.** This class represents a way to identify a particular data format. A particular data format is actually identified by a MIME type. The DataFlavor class itself stores the MIME type, and provides methods for comparison and manipulation of the MIME type.
- **StringSelection.** This class implements Transferable and ClipboardOwner. It is used to encapsulate a string for transferring to and from the clipboard.
- **UnsupportedFlavorException.** This exception is thrown when a particular data flavor is requested, but the Transferable object does not support it.

Source 10.21 demonstrates the use of the Clipboard. It allows for copying and pasting of strings to and from a TextArea.

SOURCE 10.21

```
// ExtendedTextArea.java
package jwiley.chp10;

import java.awt.*;
import java.awt.event.*;
import java.awt.datatransfer.*;

/**
 * This class provides Java copy and paste functionality to
 * java.awt.TextArea
```

```
 *
 * @author Eric Monk
 * @version 1.0
 */

public class ExtendedTextArea extends TextArea implements
                                  ClipboardOwner, KeyListener
{
    Clipboard   clipboard;

    public ExtendedTextArea ()
    {
        addKeyListener(this);
        clipboard = getToolkit().getSystemClipboard();
    }

    public void keyPressed (KeyEvent evt)
    {
        if (evt.isControlDown())
        {
            if (evt.getKeyCode() == KeyEvent.VK_A)  // copy command
            {
                String sCopyText = getSelectedText();
                if (sCopyText != null) {
                    StringSelection sClipboardText =
                            new StringSelection(sCopyText);
                    clipboard.setContents(sClipboardText, this);
                }
                evt.consume();
            }
            else if (evt.getKeyCode() == KeyEvent.VK_B) // paste command
            {
                Transferable clipboardData = clipboard.getContents(this);
                if (clipboardData != null)
                {
                    try
                    {
                        String sPasteText =
                                (String)clipboardData.getTransferData(
                                                DataFlavor.stringFlavor;
                        inset(sPasteText, getCaretPosition());
                    } catch (Exception e)
                      {
                        System.out.println("Error pasting data");
                      }
                }
                evt.consume();
            }
        }
    }

    public void keyReleased (KeyEvent evt)  {   }
    public void keyTyped (KeyEvent evt)     {   }
```

```
    public void lostOwnership(Clipboard clipboard, Transferable contents)
    {   }

    public static void main (String args[])
    {
        Frame f = new Frame("Test Clipboard");
        f.setLayout(new GridLayout(0,1));

        ExtendedTextArea textArea1 = new ExtendedTextArea();
        ExtendedTextArea textArea2 = new ExtendedTextArea();
        f.add(textArea1);
        f.add(textArea2);

        f.setSize(300,300);
        f.show();
    }
}
```

A run of Source 10.21 produces Figure 10.23:

```
java jwiley.chp10.ExtendedTextArea
```

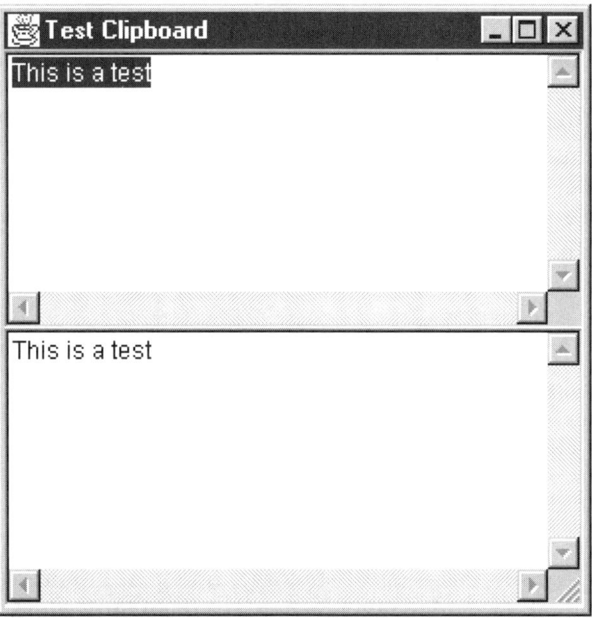

FIGURE 10.23 ExtendedTextArea clipboard example (ETA.TIF).

The ExtendedTextArea supports both copy and paste using keystrokes. To copy, select the text to be copied then press <Ctrl-A>. This will place the text on the system clipboard. To paste, position the cursor where you want the text to be pasted and press<Ctrl-B>. Any text copied from a native application can be pasted in the ExtendedTextArea, and any text copied from the ExtendedTextArea can be pasted to a native application.

The key points in Source 10.21 have been bolded. Let's take a look at each section.

- **public class ExtendedTextArea extends TextArea implements ClipboardOwner, KeyListener.** This is the declaration of the class. The important part to note here is that this class implements ClipboardOwner. Any class that wishes to set the contents of a clipboard must implement this interface.
- **public ExtendedTextArea().** This is the constructor for this class. When the constructor is executed the data member, *clipboard*, gets initialized to the system clipboard.
- **KeyEvent.VK_A.** When <Ctrl-A> gets pressed the selected text gets copied to the clipboard. Using the StringSelection convenience class we create a transferable object that encapsulates the data we want to place on the clipboard. By calling the setContents() method, we place the StringSelection object on the clipboard and assert ourselves as the owner.
- **KeyEvent.VK_B.** When <Ctrl-B> gets pressed the text on the clipboard gets pasted into the text area. First we get the Transferable object contained on the clipboard. Next we ask the object to return its data in a stringFlavor. Since the Transferable object does support the stringFlavor, the string is returned and the text can be pasted onto the text area.
- **public void lostOwnership(Clipboard clipboard, Transferable contents).** This method must be defined by classes that implement the ClipboardOwner interface. This method is called when the contents that were originally placed on the clipboard by us are about to be replaced. In this example, we do not care when we lose ownership of the data, and therefore a null definition is provided.

10.5 SUMMARY

The Abstract Window Toolkit enables Java programmers to create cross-platform graphical user interfaces. We first examined just how the Java AWT allows programmers to code to a single set of classes while supporting multiple platforms through peers. We then examined all the major features of a cross-platform GUI: components, events, containers, layouts, and painting and updating.

We went over the new event model in detail. The 1.2 event model is based on delegation. We have event sources, event listeners, and event adapters.

We examined all of the built-in layout types to include BorderLayout, FlowLayout, GridLayout, GridBagLayout, and CardLayout. We also examined how to create your own layout manager.

We then examined many significant AWT enhancements like popup menus and menu shortcuts. We looked at these in the context of a very sophisticated drawing program called DrawRectangleFrame. I encourage you to examine this code in detail and enhance it to include other drawing objects (like circles, lines, etc.).

Last, we covered printing in Java, which is also demonstrated in our DrawRectangleFrame program.

CHAPTER 11

JavaBeans

OBJECTIVE

The objective of this chapter is to introduce you to the JavaBeans architecture and classes, and then demonstrate their use through a series of examples. You will learn the difference between JavaBeans and regular Java classes with regard to class reusability. We will also demonstrate how to use the Bean Development Kit (BDK) to test your beans. Lastly, we will build and run a JavaBean that displays URLs!

Object-oriented programming languages like C++ and Java allow developers to create generic classes, which can then be reused in a variety of ways. Unfortunately, the reuse of C++ and Java classes is limited to developers; the ability to reuse classes is not easily extended to the end user of an application. In addition, most object-oriented languages do not have clear rules governing the packaging, delivery, and manipulation of reusable classes.

JavaBeans was designed to allow the creation of truly reusable software components by addressing the limitations of traditional object-oriented programming. In fact, the JavaBeans specification states: "a JavaBean is a reusable software component that can be manipulated visually in a builder tool." Any JavaBean-capable application can import, embed, and access any JavaBean, regardless of its implementation. A builder tool is an application whose purpose is to dynamically load JavaBeans and allow users to manipulate and connect JavaBeans to build an application. An example of a builder tool is the "beanbox" application provided with the Bean Developer's Kit.

The delivery of JavaBeans relies on the existing class delivery system for Java classes. JavaBeans can be located by either searching the classpath of the local machine or by requesting specific classes from a Web server. JavaBeans are packaged as a JAR file. A JAR file is a Java archive that supports zip compression. JAR files are one of the new features of Java 1.1. A JAR file contains all of the classes that implement a JavaBean, along with any other files that the JavaBean requires. The manipulation of JavaBeans is supported by two mechanisms: introspection and customization. Introspection allows a JavaBean to be examined at runtime so that its features can be presented to the end user. Features are the properties, methods, and events supported by a JavaBean. Customization allows Java beans to provide their own mechanisms to walk a bean user through various setup options and complex interactions. Customization helps an end user to manipulate a JavaBean but is not mandatory for all beans.

Consider the following example that illustrates the usefulness of JavaBeans. One programmer could develop and distribute a bean that loads and displays a URL. Once the development is complete, the programmer packages all of the relevant class files into a JAR file and distributes it.

Another programmer wishes to use this new JavaBean in an application. This programmer starts a bean builder tool (such as beanbox) and selects the JAR file containing the URL displaying bean. The toolbox of the bean builder tool will now display an icon for the URL display bean. The user selects the icon and places a URL display bean object into his or her application. A window called a property sheet displays the supported properties for the bean. By changing the values on the property sheet, the user can manipulate the behavior of the bean. For more detailed modification, a custom dialog called a customizer can be used. The full configuration of the bean can be performed without programming.

Once the bean is placed in the application and configured, the user would then continue to design the rest of his or her application, using other beans. Beans can be connected so that activating one bean can influence another. In this application, a button could refresh the URL bean's display when it is pressed.

The rest of this chapter will explain the JavaBean concepts in greater detail, and work through the example just given.

11.1 THE JAVABEANS ARCHITECTURE

The JavaBeans specification states: "a JavaBean is a reusable software component that can be manipulated visually in a builder tool." This definition of JavaBeans is intentionally very flexible. The JavaBeans designers wanted bean creation to be a simple process. Writing a bean is not much more challenging than writing a regular Java class. An important distinction between a Java class and a JavaBean is that a bean's interface is not equivalent to the interface of the class that implements it. Because of this distinction, the design of a bean must be considered from two viewpoints: that of the bean implementer and that of the bean user.

A bean is described by its *features*. A feature is a property, method, or event. Bean features are not to be confused with their Java class counterparts. Bean properties are far more complex than simple fields in a Java class, whereas methods and events are similar to their counterparts in a Java class.

There are three types of bean properties: *regular* properties, *bound* properties, and *constrained* properties. Regular properties can be read and written without restriction. Bound properties notify a series of listeners whenever they are changed. When two or more properties of different beans are bound together, the builder tool will make sure that the bound properties have the same value. Only properties with the same data type can be bound in this fashion. Defining a bound property does not actually bind it to anything, rather it declares that the property can be bound. Constrained properties also notify a series of listeners whenever they are changed, but any one of the listeners can veto the change, forcing the property to revert to its old value. Properties, including regular, bound, and constrained properties, are implemented with a pair of methods on the bean class. One method is used to read the value of the property and the other is used to write the value of the property. Bound properties throw a PropertyChangeEvent to all its PropertyChangeListeners when the value is changed. Constrained properties throw a PropertyChangeEvent to all of its VetoableChangeListeners when the value is changed. This implementation of properties is important because, unlike a Java class, a bean's properties cannot be read or written without the bean's knowledge.

JavaBean methods are very similar to Java class methods. A method is simply a function implemented by the bean. Calling a bean's method will perform some processing based on the properties of the bean.

Bean events are very similar to AWT events in Java 1.1. In fact, the AWT event system was rewritten based on the JavaBeans event system. For each event that can be fired, a class and an interface are created. The class represents the event, and any class that wishes to receive the event implements the interface. Then, two methods are implemented on the bean class. One method registers a listener for the event and the other removes a listener. When a bean needs to fire the event, it calls each listener sequentially, sending it an event object through the listener interface.

Source 11.1 is an implementation of a simple JavaBean that will display the contents of a URL. This bean has two properties: Display and URL. Display is a boolean indicating whether or not the bean should actually display the URL. GetDisplay and setDisplay provide access to the Display property. URL is a string containing the URL to display. GetURL and setURL provide access to the URL property. Reload is the only method supported by this bean. Reload retrieves the contents of the URL from a Web server. Paint is an overridden method from java.awt.Component. The paint routine allows the bean to display its contents visually. Finally, addURLLoadedListener and removeURLLoadedListener allow other beans to add or remove listeners for our bean's event, URLLoaded.

JavaBeans allows two mechanisms for associating each bean feature with the method or methods that implement it. The first mechanism is to use the JavaBeans naming and signature convention for all bean implementations. At runtime, a bean builder tool can use reflection to examine the methods of a bean, recognizing patterns

SOURCE 11.1 URLDisplay JavaBean

```
// URLDisplay.java
package jwiley.chp11;

import java.awt.*;
import java.awt.image.*;
import java.net.URL;
import java.net.MalformedURLException;
import java.util.Vector;
import java.io.BufferedInputStream;
import java.io.IOException;

/**
 * Java bean that displays URLs.  This class is very simplistic
 * it attempts to display everything as text, regardless of the
 * content.  This is a visual Bean, so it needs to extend an AWT
 * component class
 */
public class URLDisplay extends Canvas
{
    /**
     * value of the Display property
     */
    private boolean bDisplay = true;

    /**
     * value of the URL property
     */
    private String strLocation = "";

    /**
     * URL object.  This only exists if the URL property
     * is properly formatted
     */
    private URL url = null;

    /**
     * Object referred to by the URL.  This only exists if the URL
     * object exists, and it pointed to a valid location
     */
    private Object curObj = null;

    /**
     * A vector of all the listeners for our event
     */
    private Vector listeners = new Vector();

    /**
     * Read the Display property
     */
```

```
    public synchronized boolean getDisplay()
    {
        return bDisplay;
    }

    /**
     * Write the Display property
     */
    public synchronized void setDisplay(boolean bNewVal)
    {
        bDisplay = bNewVal;
    }

    /**
     * Read the URL property
     */
    public synchronized String getURL()
    {
        return strLocation;
    }

    /**
     * Write the URL property
     */
    public synchronized void setURL(String newStr)
    {
        strLocation = newStr;
        reload();
    }

    /**
     * Load (or reload) the object pointed to by the URL
     */
    public synchronized void reload()
    {
        curObj = "Loading...";

        try
        {
            url = new URL(strLocation);
            curObj = url.getContent();
            if (curObj instanceof BufferedInputStream)
            {
                boolean bStore = true;
                StringBuffer sb = new StringBuffer();
                while (((BufferedInputStream)curObj).available() > 0)
                {
                    char c = (char)((BufferedInputStream)curObj).read();
                    if (!bStore && c == '>')
                    {
                        bStore = true;
```

```
                    continue;
                }
                if (c == '<')
                {
                    bStore = false;
                    continue;
                }
                if (bStore)
                {
                    sb.append(c);
                }
            }
            curObj = sb.toString();
        }
        else if (curObj instanceof ImageProducer)
        {
            curObj =
Toolkit.getDefaultToolkit().createImage((ImageProducer)curObj);
        }
    }
    catch (java.io.IOException iox)
      {
        curObj = null;
      }

    fireEvent(curObj);
    repaint();
}

// java.awt.Component support
/**
 * Paint the object if we have it.  Paint an error
 * message otherwise.
 */
public synchronized void paint(Graphics g)
{
    if (bDisplay)
    {
        if (curObj == null)
        {
            if (url == null)
            {
                g.drawString("No URL specified", 10, 10);
            }
            else
            {
                g.drawString("There was an error loading the URL",
                             10, 10);
```

```
            }
        }
        else if (curObj instanceof String)
        {
            g.drawString((String)curObj, 10, 10);
        }
        else if (curObj instanceof Image)
        {
            g.drawImage((Image)curObj,0,0,this);
        }
        else
        {
            g.drawString("Could not display URL", 10, 10);
        }
    }
}

// event support
/**
 * Add a listener for our event
 */
public synchronized void addURLLoadedListener(URLLoadedListener l)
{
    listeners.addElement(l);
}

/**
 * Remove a listener for our event
 */
public synchronized void removeURLLoadedListener(URLLoadedListener l)
{
    listeners.removeElement(l);
}

/**
 * Fire our event to signify that we are done loading the URL
 */
public synchronized void fireEvent(Object obj)
{
    URLLoadedEvent event = new URLLoadedEvent(this, obj);
    for (int i = 0; i < listeners.size(); i++)
    {
        ((URLLoadedListener)listeners.elementAt(i)).URLLoaded(event);
    }
}
}
```

to determine the bean's features. Property implementation methods should have the following format:

```
<PropertyType> get<PropertyName>();
void set<PropertyName>(<PropertyType> newValue);
```

A similar convention is used for bean events. The methods that add and remove subscribers should have the following format:

```
void add<EventListenerName>(<EventListenerName> newListener);
void remove<EventListenerName>(<EventListenerName> existingListener);
```

Note that it doesn't matter how the event is fired. A bean's event features are determined by the events that can be registered through interfaces like these. Methods are simply implemented as usual. Anything that doesn't fit the pattern for a property or an event is considered to be a method.

In some cases, a bean developer may want to be more explicit regarding the features of a bean. Each bean can provide BeanInfo about itself. BeanInfo enumerates each bean feature and provides additional information that cannot be specified through the use of naming conventions. In particular, BeanInfo can be used to specify which properties, methods, and events are hidden, and which are intended for *expert* use only. An expert feature will not normally be visible when using a bean through an application builder such as beanbox. Bean developers need to write their own Java routines to interact with expert features. BeanInfo is very useful for specifying which methods should be exposed as part of the bean. Typically, a bean will have many methods either implemented on the bean or inherited from a superclass that should not be bean features. BeanInfo can be used to specify only the intended features.

The JavaBeans architecture allows for both visual and nonvisual beans. Visual beans should be derived from java.awt.Component or some similar class. Nonvisual beans can be derived from any class, but all beans must implement the Serializable interface. Java serialization allows JavaBeans to persist their state. Even the most complex application can be easily stored because every bean is responsible for storing itself.

TIP The BDK's test builder tool beanbox only supports visual beans. There is no currently available bean builder tool for testing nonvisual beans. Users can simulate nonvisual beans by creating beans that never paint themselves; however, all beans must currently extend an AWT class.

Icons

Beans can support four icon types: 16x16 color, 16x16 monochrome, 32x32 color, and 32x32 monochrome. Icons are used at various times by a bean builder tool to graphically represent a bean. For example, the toolbox portion of beanbox attempts to display a 16x16 color icon to the left of the bean name. If the desired icon type is not supported then the builder tool may attempt to use another type of icon. When all applicable icon types are not available, then the bean builder tool will display nothing.

TIP Icons are completely optional. The most often used icon type is 16x16 color, so if a bean only supports one icon type, it should support that one.

Customizers and Property Editors

Bean builder tools use a property sheet to allow the modification of a bean's properties. This is limiting in two ways. If a bean has a property that is an unknown or complex data type, then the property sheet will not know how to display or manipulate the value. Additionally, some properties may be dependent on one another, or should be set in a particular order.

To solve these problems, JavaBeans supports two user interface mechanisms for handling the situations. A PropertyEditor is an AWT component that can display and edit a particular data type. PropertyEditors are registered with the PropertyEditor-Manager, which associates the editor with a particular data type. The property sheet then uses that PropertyEditor for all properties of that data type.

For more complex configuration, a customizer should be used. A customizer is also an AWT component, however, it deals with one or more properties of a bean. A component can also do additional processing. For instance, a JDBC bean might have two parameters: a data source name and a table name. The table name cannot be specified until the data source is selected. A customizer might implement this by disabling the table name entry until the data source has been specified. Then, the table name could be picked from a list of the tables within that data source.

JAR Files

JAR files must be used to package and distribute JavaBeans. A JAR file can contain any number of Java classes, graphics, and any other files needed by a bean. Typically, a JAR file will contain the following: the bean's implementation class, the bean's customizer class, any property editors required by the bean, icons used by the bean, any event classes and event listener interfaces used by the bean, and any other required resources.

Refer to Chapter 1 for a detailed explanation on using the JAR utility. Here we will only explain a portion of the JAR utility's options. A simple JAR command line looks like the following:

```
jar {required flag}[optional flags] <archive name> <files ->
```

The flags that are most commonly used are "c" and "f." "c" specifies that an archive will be created and "f" specifies that the archive name will be specified.

When storing class files in a JAR file, they must be stored with their pathname intact. In other words, if a class file is in the location:

```
C:\javasrc\x\y\z.class
```

and the class is in package x.y, then the JAR utility should be executed from the c:\javasrc directory as follows:

```
cd \javasrc
jar -cf myJARfile x\y\z.class
```

or

```
jar -cf myJARfile x\y\*.class
```

A JAR file can contain any number of files, but it must contain at least one JavaBean or it will not be loaded by a bean builder tool. Each JAR file contains exactly one manifest file that contains an inventory of the class file, and other useful information. Manifest files are important because bean builder tools need to examine the manifest in order to determine which class files in the archive are JavaBeans.

Assuming that z.class is a JavaBean, the manifest for the JAR file will look like the following:

```
Name: x\y\z.class
Java-Bean: True
```

Now, if that manifest file were stored in a file named manifest.tmp, then we would use the "m" option to the JAR utility to include our manifest file in the archive:

```
jar -cfm myJARfile manifest.tmp x\y\z.class
```

For the purposes of JavaBeans, a manifest file need only specify the JavaBeans in the JAR file. No other classes need to be specified. Once the JAR file is created it can immediately be loaded into a bean builder tool such as beanbox.

Bean Builder Tools

A bean builder tool enables application developers to rapidly add beans to an application, customize each bean, then define how the beans interact with each other, all without writing any code. A builder tool usually has three areas of interest: a toolbox, a property sheet, and a design area.

The Design area is where the application is actually built. All the beans that are part of the application are visually represented in the design area (see Figure 11.1). A bean can be selected by clicking on it and, depending on restrictions imposed by a particular bean, the bean can be resized. The design area can be used to associate events of one bean with methods of another. This feature allows an application builder to define program logic without writing any code. A builder tool generates the Java code

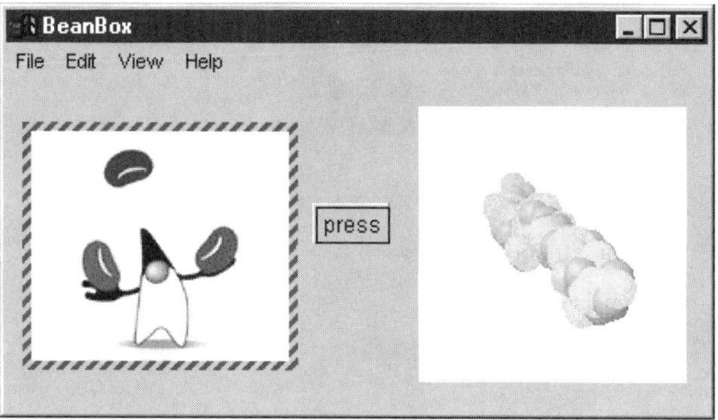

FIGURE 11.1 The BeanBox design area populated with some JavaBeans.

necessary to perform this association, then compiles it and brings it into the application dynamically. The class generated through this process is called an adapter class.

The toolbox of a builder tool lists all of the available beans (see Figure 11.2). Each bean's name, icon, or both appear somewhere on the tool. New beans can be added by

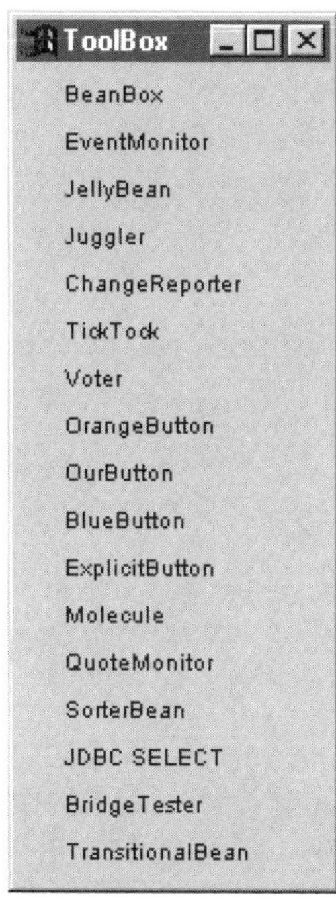

FIGURE 11.2 The beanbox default toolbox.

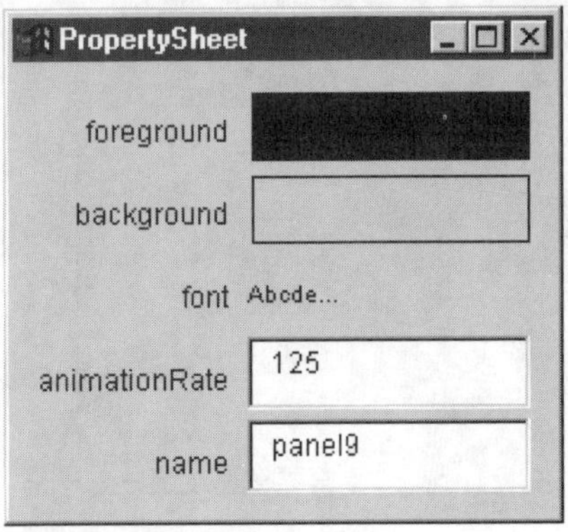

FIGURE 11.3 The beanbox property sheet for the Juggler Bean.

manually loading JAR files that contain beans. Once a JAR file is specified, any available beans specified in the manifest are automatically loaded and added to the toolbox. Users can add beans to their application by selecting the bean from the toolbox and specifying where on the design area the bean should be added.

The property sheet specifies all non-hidden, nonexpert properties for the bean currently selected in the design area. Each property is represented in a different way on the property sheet, depending on its data type (see Figure 11.3). If a data type has no PropertyEditor class defined for it, then the property is not shown. The selected bean is updated dynamically to reflect changes made on the property sheet.

11.2 THE JAVA.BEANS PACKAGE

The beans package is composed of the following interfaces, classes, and exceptions.

Interfaces

The following interfaces are used by various aspects of the JavaBeans architecture.

- **BeanInfo.** Classes that implement the BeanInfo interface provide explicit information about the structure of a JavaBean, including information about its methods, properties, and events. If the BeanInfo for a particular bean is not implemented or is incomplete, reflection will be used to obtain the required information. The SimpleBeanInfo class provides a generic BeanInfo implementation that provides no information about a bean. By overriding this class, developers can specify a part of their BeanInfo and rely on the SimpleBeanInfo implementation to implement the rest of the BeanInfo interface. This is similar to using the event adapter classes as demonstrated in Chapter 10.

- **Customizer.** A customizer is a visual object that can be used to manipulate the properties of a bean. A customizer must supply a default constructor so that it can be properly created, and it must extend java.awt.Component so that it can be displayed inside a Dialog or some other AWT container. Source 11.2 implements a customizer for the URL Display Bean we described earlier. Note how the example extends Panel and implements Customizer. This is required of all bean Customizers. Once these requirements are satisfied, the customizer can be implemented using standard AWT programming.

SOURCE 11.2 URLDisplay customizer

```
// URLDisplayCustomizer.java
package jwiley.chp11;

import java.awt.*;
import java.awt.event.ActionListener;
import java.awt.event.ActionEvent;
import java.beans.*;

/**
 * Customizer for the URLDisplay Bean.  This is a simple panel which
 * allows the user to input the URL through an alternative mechanism
 */
public class URLDisplayCustomizer extends Panel implements Customizer,
ActionListener
{
    /**
     * Instance of the URLDisplay bean being edited
     */
    URLDisplay bean;

    /**
     * Helper class for handling PropertyChangeEvents
     */
    private PropertyChangeSupport propChange = new
PropertyChangeSupport(this);

    /**
     * The TextField object on the panel.  This is used to
     * retrieve the new value of the URL property
     */
    TextField text = null;

    /**
     * Default constructor
     */
    public URLDisplayCustomizer()
    {
        setLayout(new BorderLayout());
    }
```

```
    /**
     * A Customizer method. This is called to associate a Bean instance
     * with a customizer instance
     */
    public void setObject(Object obj)
    {
     bean = (URLDisplay) obj;

     Label label = new Label("  Enter a URL:");
     add("North", label);

     text = new TextField(bean.getURL());
     add("Center", text);

     text.addActionListener(this);
    }

    /**
     * The size the customizer should be
     */
    public Dimension getPreferredSize() {
     return new Dimension(300, 50);
    }

    /**
     * AWT event handler so we know when the TextField is modified
     */
    public void actionPerformed(ActionEvent e)
    {
        bean.setURL(text.getText());
    }

    /**
     * Customizer event support
     */
    public void addPropertyChangeListener(PropertyChangeListener listener)
    {
         propChange.addPropertyChangeListener(listener);
    }

    /**
     * Customizer event support
     */
    public void removePropertyChangeListener(PropertyChangeListener listener)
    {
         propChange.removePropertyChangeListener(listener);
    }
}
```

- **PropertyChangeListener.** An interface for objects that need to "listen" for PropertyChange events fired from bound properties of JavaBeans.
- **PropertyEditor.** PropertyEditors are used by a bean builder tool to allow design-time editing of complex data types. A PropertyEditor is like a customizer, except that it acts on a single value of a particular data type rather than on an entire bean. PropertyEditors can either handle values as strings, or they can draw their own representation of the data using the printValue method. A PropertyEditor can implement its own visual tool for manipulating a property by returning a java.awt.Component from the getCustomEditor method.
- **VetoableChangeListener.** An interface for objects that need to "listen" for VetoableChange events fired from constrained properties of JavaBeans.
- **Visibility**. This interface allows beans to specify if and when they require a graphical user interface (GUI). When a GUI is not available, a bean can only be run if it specifies that it either doesn't need or doesn't want a GUI.

JavaBeans Classes

These are the main JavaBeans classes. They provide various utility functions for either bean developers or bean builder tools.

- **Beans.** A class that provides several utility methods for JavaBeans. By calling methods on the bean class, JavaBeans can manipulate the bean environment and create new beans.
- **Introspector.** A utility class that returns a BeanInfo for a particular Bean. If BeanInfo exists, it will be found and returned. Otherwise, the Introspector uses reflection to generate a BeanInfo for the Bean.
- **PropertyChangeEvent.** An EventObject that indicates a bound or constrained property is in the process of changing. In most cases, the PropertyChangeEvent object will provide access to both the old and new values.
- **PropertyChangeSupport.** A utility class that provides support for bound properties. JavaBeans can either extend this class, or contain a PropertyChangeSupport object and delegate operations to it.
- **PropertyEditorManager.** A utility class for associating PropertyEditor classes with the class they are intended to edit.
- **PropertyEditorSupport.** A utility class that provides generic support for Property editors. PropertyEditors can either extend this class, or contain a PropertyEditorSupport object and delegate operations to it. If a PropertyEditor does not rely on a default implementation for any of the PropertyEditor methods, then the use of this class is not required.
- **VetoableChangeSupport.** A utility class that provides support for constrained properties. JavaBeans can either extend this class, or contain a VetoableChangeSupport object and delegate operations to it.

BeanInfo Classes

These classes are used to implement BeanInfo.

- **BeanDescriptor.** Provides general information about a JavaBean, including the class name of the Java class that implements the bean, and a descriptive name for the bean.
- **EventSetDescriptor.** Describes all the events that a JavaBean can fire.
- **FeatureDescriptor.** A base class for method, parameter, property, and event set descriptors.
- **IndexedPropertyDescriptor.** Describes an indexed property of a JavaBean. An index property is treated like an array and can be implemented in one of two ways: the read/write functions for the property can either take an index as an argument and accept and return single objects, or they can simply accept and return arrays.
- **MethodDescriptor.** Describes a method of a JavaBean.
- **ParameterDescriptor.** Describes a parameter to a JavaBean method. ParameterDescriptors provide more information than is available through the java.lang.reflect.Method interface.
- **PropertyDescriptor.** Describes a property of a JavaBean. Bean properties are typically represented by two methods: one to set the value of the property and the other to retrieve the value of the property.
- **SimpleBeanInfo.** A default implementation for a BeanInfo. By extending this class, developers can provide as much or as little BeanInfo as desired, without having to worry about implementing all the methods of the BeanInfo interface. Source 11.3 extends SimpleBeanInfo in order to provide explicit bean info for our URL Display Bean. Note that because our bean uses the JavaBean naming conventions for all its properties, methods, and events, explicit bean info is not required. We provide it here only for completeness.

Exceptions

These are the Exception classes used exclusively by JavaBeans.

- **IntrospectionException.** This class extends Exception. It indicates that some error occurred while attempting to generate BeanInfo for a class.
- **PropertyVetoException.** This class extends Exception. It indicates that an attempt was made to set a constrained property with an invalid value.

SOURCE 11.3 URLDisplay Bean Info

```
// URLDisplayBeanInfo.java
package jwiley.chp11;

import java.beans.*;
import java.lang.reflect.Method;

/**
 * Bean info for the URLDisplay Bean
 */
public class URLDisplayBeanInfo extends SimpleBeanInfo {
    /**
     * Returns the Property list for the Bean
     */
    public PropertyDescriptor[] getPropertyDescriptors()
    {
        try
        {
            PropertyDescriptor background = new
              PropertyDescriptor("background", URLDisplay.class);
            PropertyDescriptor foreground = new
              PropertyDescriptor("foreground", URLDisplay.class);
            PropertyDescriptor font = new
              PropertyDescriptor("font", URLDisplay.class);
            PropertyDescriptor display = new
              PropertyDescriptor("display", URLDisplay.class);
            PropertyDescriptor url = new
              PropertyDescriptor("URL", URLDisplay.class);

            PropertyDescriptor ret[] =
              {background, foreground, display, font, url};
            return ret;
        }
        catch (IntrospectionException e)
          {
            throw new Error(e.toString());
          }
    }

    /**
     * Returns the index of the default property
     */
    public int getDefaultPropertyIndex()
    {
        return 4; // URL
    }

    /**
     * Returns the method list for the Bean
     */
    public MethodDescriptor[] getMethodDescriptors()
```

```
    {
        try
        {
            Method meth =
              URLDisplay.class.getMethod("reload", new Class[0]);
            MethodDescriptor reload = new MethodDescriptor(meth);
            MethodDescriptor ret[] = {reload};
            return ret;
        }
        catch (NoSuchMethodException x)
          {
            return null;
          }
    }

    /**
     * Returns the event list for the Bean
     */
    public EventSetDescriptor[] getEventSetDescriptors()
    {
        try
        {
            EventSetDescriptor loaded =
                new EventSetDescriptor(URLDisplay.class,
                                       "URLLoaded",
                                       URLLoadedListener.class,
                                       "URLLoaded");

            loaded.setDisplayName("URL Loaded");

            EventSetDescriptor ret[] = {loaded};
            return ret;
        }
        catch (IntrospectionException e)
        {
            throw new Error(e.toString());
        }
    }

    /**
     * Returns top-level information for the Bean
     */
    public BeanDescriptor getBeanDescriptor()
    {
        return new BeanDescriptor(URLDisplay.class,
URLDisplayCustomizer.class);
    }
}
```

11.3 URLDISPLAY BEAN EXAMPLE

Three of the classes (URLDisplay, URLDisplayCustomizer, and URLDisplayBeanInfo) used in our example have been defined earlier. In order to complete our example, we require two more source files that are used for the event our URL display bean fires. Source 11.4 implements the event object for our URLLoaded event. Source 11.5 contains the interface that must be implemented by all classes that wish to subscribe to our bean's event.

SOURCE 11.4 URL Loaded Event Class

```
// URLLoadedEvent.java
package jwiley.chp11;

import java.util.EventObject;

/**
 * Event class for the URLDisplay Bean.  This event indicates that
 * the Display Bean has finished loading its object.
 */
public class URLLoadedEvent extends EventObject
{
    /**
     * The object that was just loaded
     */
    private Object loadedObject;

    /**
     * Constructor, takes the Bean that fires the event and the object
     * that was loaded as arguments
     */
    public URLLoadedEvent(Object srcObj, Object urlObj)
    {
        super(srcObj);
        loadedObject = urlObj;
    }

    /**
     * Public accessor method for the loaded object value
     */
    public Object getLoadedObject()
    {
        return loadedObject;
    }
}
```

SOURCE 11.5 URL Loaded Event Listener Interface

```
// URLLoadedListener.java

package jwiley.chp11;

import java.util.EventListener;

/**
 * Interface that must be inherited by objects wishing to receive
 * URLLoadedEvents
 */
public interface URLLoadedListener extends EventListener
{
    /**
     * Method that is called when the event is fired
     */
    public void URLLoaded(URLLoadedEvent e);
}
```

Now that we have all of our source files, we should compile them with the following command:

```
cd \src\jwiley\chp16
javac *.java
```

In order to use our bean, we must first package it into a JAR file. Before we can create our JAR file, however, we must define the manifest file so that the beanbox application will know which class is the bean (shown in Source 11.6).

For convenience, the manifest file should be placed in the directory that the JAR utility will be executed from. In this case, that is the c:\src directory. The JAR utility should be executed so that the files are archived with the correct relative path.

```
cd \src
jar ñcfm URLDisplay.jar manifest.tmp jwiley\chp11\*.class
```

When the JAR utility completes, the file URLDisplay.jar should be located in the current directory.

Our bean is now ready for use in a builder tool such as beanbox. To start the beanbox, change into the beanbox directory of the Bean Developer's Kit and type:

```
run
```

SOURCE 11.6 manifest.tmp.

```
Name: jwiley/chp11/URLDisplay.class
Java-Bean: True
```

The first step in using our bean is to add it to the builder environment. This is accomplished by selecting the "loadjar..." option from the File menu. Once the URLDisplay Bean is successfully added to the toolbox, select it and click on the design area. A new URLDisplay Bean will be added to the application and its properties will be listed on the property sheet.

To use the customizer for URLDisplay, select "customize..." from the Edit menu. When you are finished, press the Done button (see Figure 11.4).

The customizer only allows us to modify the URL property of the bean. To modify the other properties, use the property sheet.

In order to illustrate the other features of our bean we will need to place additional beans in the design area. Place a Juggler bean and an ExplicitButton Bean in the design area so that they don't overlap. You do this by clicking on the bean in the toolbox, then click in the beanbox window to "drop" the bean. We are going to connect the three beans so that when the button is clicked, the URLDisplay will be reloaded. When the URLDisplay finishes updating, the Juggler will stop juggling (see Figure 11.5).

First, select the Button. Pick "events >" from the Edit menu. From the Events submenu, pick "button push", then "actionPerformed." Now the mouse will control a line that originates from the button. Move the mouse over the URLDisplay and press the button. Another menu will appear offering a choice of methods to call on the target bean. Since the URLDisplay Bean has only one method, reload, select that and press OK.

The preceding steps connect the actionPerformed button event with the reload method for our URLDisplay Bean. Whenever a user clicks the ExplicitButton Bean in our application, the URLDisplay Bean will automatically reload itself if we added additional methods to the BeanInfo for URLDisplay, and provided implementations for those methods in the class URLDisplay.

Now we'll want to do the same thing to connect the URLLoaded event of our URLDisplay Bean to the stopJuggling method of the Juggler Bean. In both cases, once the final selection is made, the beanbox writes and compiles the adapter class that handles the logic of the connection.

Finally, to see the application work, pick "Disable design mode" from the View menu and press the button. Our URLDisplay Bean only loads URLs and fires events when the

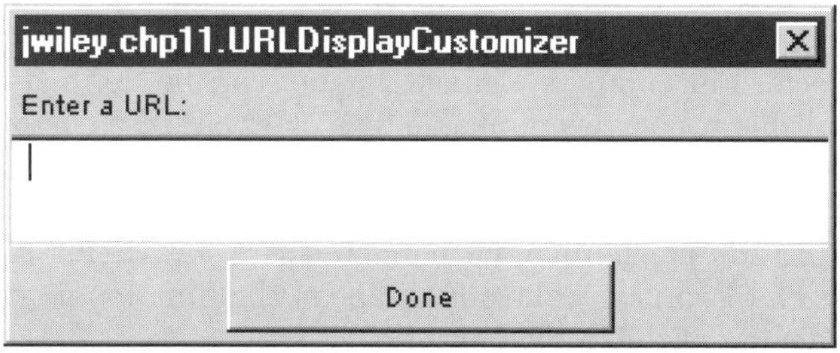

jwiley.chp11.URLDisplayCustomizer

Enter a URL:

Done

FIGURE 11.4 The URLDisplay customizer.

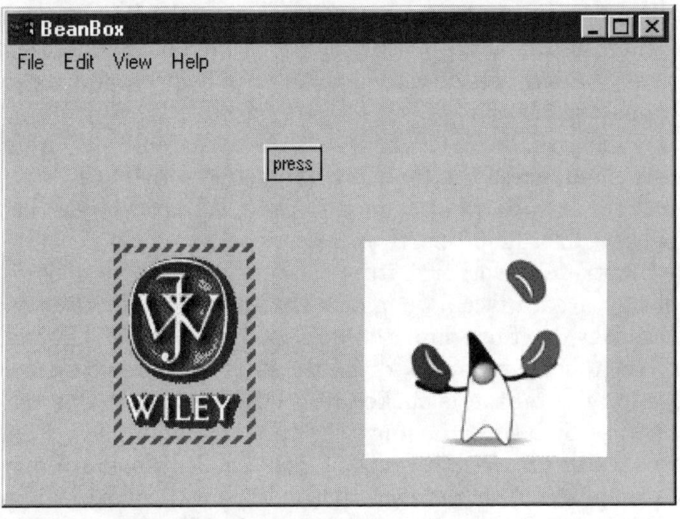

FIGURE 11.5 A sample application.

application is running. Assuming that a valid URL was entered for the URL property, a fragment of the URL should be displayed and the Juggler should stop juggling.

11.4 SUMMARY

JavaBeans is a flexible architecture for building reusable software components that can be visually manipulated in a builder tool. Beans are defined by their features including properties, methods, and events. A Bean's features can either be determined by using the reflection APIs and looking for patterns in the signature of the Bean, or by explicitly specifying the Bean's properties through the BeanInfo interface.

A Bean can be edited on a property-by-property basis using a builder tool's property sheet. Property sheet support can be added for additional data types by creating PropertyEditor objects. For complex Beans, a panel can be defined that allows the manipulation of multiple properties managed by a class called a customizer.

Beans are packaged in archives called JAR files. A manifest within the JAR file specifies which of the contents are JavaBeans and which are not. All Beans must support the Java serialization mechanism for persistence. A JavaBean is completely self-contained. The user of a Bean can take advantage of the functionality without having to worry about the details of the implementation.

CHAPTER 12

Package java.applet

OBJECTIVE

In this chapter you will learn how to create an applet and embed it in an HTML page. We will also cover the restrictions placed upon applets, the interaction between the Web browser and Java applets, and cases where applets should be used instead of Java applications.

12.1 OVERVIEW

The java.applet package consists of a single class, Applet, that is used to create Java applets. This class provides a standard interface between a graphical Java object and the browser environment in which it runs. In addition to the Applet class the applet package also contains three interfaces: AppletContext, AudioClip, and AppletStub. These interfaces are used for controlling the browser environment and handling audio clips.

What Is an Applet?

The "applet paradigm" involves two key concepts: first, an applet is a non-standalone program. In other words, an applet is NOT an application. Second, an applet is a component of the browser's GUI. That does not mean it has to be a visible component, but that is surely the most common use for applets. We will explore these two concepts in great detail. The methodology we will use to explore applets will be to transition an idea from a standalone application to an applet.

How Are Applets Used?

Applets can be classified into two main categories: applets that provide dynamic content to a Web page, and applets that act as a client to an intranet/Internet application. Let me elaborate on these two categories a bit more. Applets that provide dynamic content to a Web page consist of applets that perform simple animation, applets that play audio, and other small programs that allow for rich user interaction. Applets that act as a client to an intranet/Internet application could consist of data forms that collect information and write it to the server, or more sophisticated applications such as a spreadsheet or collaboration tool.

In the next section we will introduce the basics of programming an applet, and how it can be used to display dynamic content. After that, we will explore how to code an applet client that interacts with a server. Last, we will discuss how to use the Java Archive tool (jar) to decrease applet download time

12.2 PROGRAMMING APPLETS

Many businesses promote their goods by advertising them on an electronic scrolling message board (also known as a marquee). With the World Wide Web being pitched as an electronic marketplace a scrolling message board could come in handy for many businesses. Let's examine first how we would build a standalone application to do this, then we will transition the standalone app to an applet. The basic idea behind the application is simple: animate a single text line so that it moves across the screen. Instead of just writing an application without an awareness of how it would transition to an applet, you will see how seamlessly a well-written component fits the applet model.

Source 12.1 implements the scrolling message board. The program simply consists of the invoking of a single class. This single class will later become our applet.

SOURCE 12.1 ScrollMsg.java

```
// scrollMsg.java
package jwiley.chp12;

import java.awt.*;

public class scrollMsg extends Panel implements Runnable
{
    String theMessage;
    Font textFont;
    FontMetrics fontMetrics;
    int stepPixels;
    int oldX, oldY, newX, newY;
    int speed; // in milliseconds
```

```
public scrollMsg(String msg)
{
    setBackground(Color.lightGray);

    theMessage = msg;

    textFont = new Font("TimesRoman",Font.BOLD, 18);

    stepPixels = 6;
    speed = 15;
}

public void run()
{
        paint(this.getGraphics());
        while (true)
                repaint(speed);
}

public void paint(Graphics g)
{
    // initial background
    g.setColor(Color.black);
    g.drawRect(0,0, getSize().width,
                getSize().height);
    g.setColor(Color.white);
    g.fillRect(1,1, getSize().width - 1,
                getSize().height - 1);

    // set the font
    g.setFont(textFont);
    fontMetrics = g.getFontMetrics();

    // set initial X and Y to drawString
    oldX = newX = getSize().width -
            fontMetrics.charWidth(theMessage.charAt(0));
    oldY = newY = getSize().height/2 +
            (fontMetrics.getHeight()/2);
}

public void update(Graphics g)
{
    g.setFont(textFont);

    // Erase the old
    g.setColor(Color.white);
    g.drawString(theMessage, oldX, oldY);

    // draw the New
    g.setColor(Color.black);
    g.drawString(theMessage, newX, newY);
```

```
        // step
        oldX = newX;
        newX -= stepPixels;

        // restart?
        if (newX <= -(fontMetrics.stringWidth(theMessage)
                    - fontMetrics.charWidth(
                      theMessage.charAt(
                         theMessage.length() - 1))))
                paint(g);  // start at the beginning
    }

}

// tstMsg.java
package jwiley.chp12;

import java.awt.Frame;

public class tstMsg
{
    public static void main(String args[])
    {
        Frame myFrame = new Frame("Scrolling Message");
        scrollMsg myScroll =
            new scrollMsg("Big Sale!!! Internet terminals for $299!!!");
        myFrame.add("Center", myScroll);
        myFrame.setLocation(100,100);
        myFrame.setSize(400,100);
        myFrame.show();

        Thread animateThread = new Thread(myScroll);
        animateThread.start();
    }
}
```

A run of Source 12.1 produces Figure 12.1.

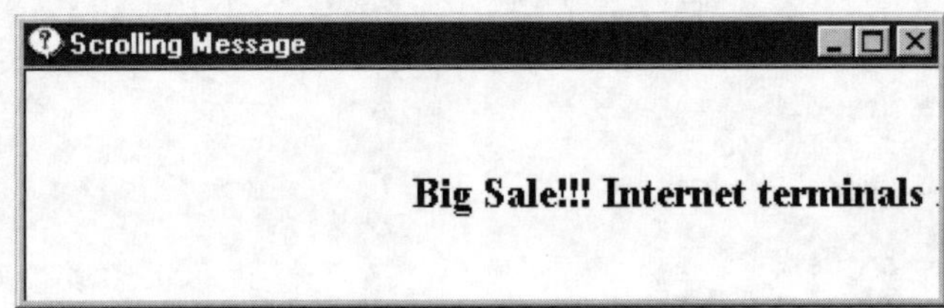

FIGURE 12.1 A scrolling message GUI.

Let's now examine Source 12.1 in detail and then discuss how we transition it into an applet. The application is composed of two classes: the scrollMsg class and the tstMsg class. The tstMsg class has the main method. Let's begin with the scrollMsg class because that is the class that will become our applet. The declaration of the class is:

```
public class scrollMsg extends Panel implements Runnable
```

The fact that this class extends Panel and implements Runnable is no accident. An applet also extends Panel. We know that a Panel is a Container that is a GUI component. So it is easy to see the correlation between an applet being a Panel in the browser and any Panel we create for a standalone application. They can almost be used interchangeably (with the exception that an applet has a few extra requirements, which we shall cover). The scrollMsg class also implements Runnable, which means that it can be the target of a Thread (run in its own execution path). This is not a requirement for an applet but it is definitely recommended programming practice for EVERY applet you create. The benefit of making your applet runnable is that your applet will run in its own execution context and not hold the browser hostage to your applet. If your applet is in its own execution context, the user is free to still choose other options on the browser; for example, jump to another Web page or quit the application.

TIP Some browsers, like Netscape, will automatically run all applets in a separate thread; however, this is not guaranteed with all browsers. It is therefore good practice to run applets in their own thread.

The implementation of scrollMsg class involves four methods. Each method is relevant to transforming the application into an applet. The four methods are:

- **public scrollMsg(String msg).** This constructor serves two purposes. The first is to initialize the object's key data members. Second, the method accepts key parameters from its caller (which is the main method of the tstMsg class). In this case, the scrollMsg class only receives one parameter, the String to scroll across our message board.
- **public void run().** This method makes the class Runnable. In our scrolling message board this method first calls paint and then enters an endless loop. Inside the endless loop it calls repaint(). All the real work is done in the paint() and update() methods.
- **public void paint(Graphics g).** This program uses the dirty rectangle animation technique to scroll the message. To do this the paint() method merely creates our initial scene. The initial scene is simply a white background.
- **public void update(Graphics g).** The animation of our scrolling text is very simple. It only requires stepping the x coordinate of where we draw the String. Update() first erases the old String, draws the new String, and then calculates the next X position.

The implementation of the tstMsg class is also relevant to the transition to an applet because the services that our tstMsg class performs in its main() method are similar to the functions that the Browser is required to perform for our applet. There are primarily three key services the tstMsg class provides for the scrollMsg class:

- **Provides a Frame.** This is the top-level window the subclass of Panel will inhabit. This is analogous to the portion of the Browser window that is provided to the applet.
- **Instantiates and initializes the scrollMsg class.** The Browser instantiates the applet without any arguments and then calls the applet's init() method. When we examine the applet source code you will see how the applet is passed information from the browser.
- **Starts the new Thread with the scrollMsg class as its target.** The Browser calls the applet's start() method to begin running the applet.

Now that we have studied our standalone application, let's see how easy it is to convert it into an applet. Before we discuss the differences, let's cover what is identical: the run(), paint(), and update() methods. Also notice how similar the class declaration is:

```
public class simpleMarquee extends Applet implements Runnable
```

As we stated previously, the Applet class extends Panel. In fact, the only difference between an Applet and a Panel is that an Applet has some additional methods that allow it to be initialized, started and stopped from another application (a Browser or the appletviewer). Those Applet methods are also the only difference between the simpleMarquee class and the scrollMsg class. Let's examine each of those methods:

- **public void init().** This method allows an applet to initialize its data members and access parameters passed to the applet from the HTML page. This method is invoked only once by the browser when the applet is loaded.
- **public void start().** This method starts the applet's execution. This method may be invoked multiple times by the browser.
- **public void stop().** This method stops the applet's execution. This method may be invoked multiple times by the browser.
- **public void destroy().** This method allows your class to perform final cleanup before the class is unloaded. An example of when to use this class would be to close file pointers or connections. It is not necessary to try to free memory since Java programs are garbage collected; therefore, most applets will not need to override this method. The applets demonstrated in this chapter do NOT override this method. This method is called only once by the browser when the applet is unloaded.

Now that we know the difference between the scrollMsg class and the simpleMarquee applet, you can examine Source 12.2 to see a working applet.

SOURCE 12.2 simpleMarquee.java

```
// simpleMarquee.java
package jwiley.chp12;

import java.applet.Applet;
import java.awt.*;

public class simpleMarquee extends Applet implements Runnable
{
    String theMessage;
    Font textFont;
    FontMetrics fontMetrics;
    int stepPixels;
    int oldX, oldY, newX, newY;
    int speed; // in milliseconds
    Thread scroller=null;

    // standard applet methods
    public void init()
    {
        theMessage = getParameter("message");
        if (theMessage == null)
                theMessage = new
                        String("A simple Marquee by Michael Daconta.");

        String speedStr = getParameter("speed");
        if (speedStr == null)
                speed = 15;
        else
                speed = Integer.parseInt(speedStr);

        textFont = new Font("TimesRoman",Font.BOLD, 18);
        stepPixels = 6;
    }

    public void start()
    {
        if (scroller == null)
        {
            scroller = new Thread(this);
            scroller.start();
        }
    }

    public void stop()
    {
        if (scroller != null)
        {
                scroller.stop();
                scroller = null;
        }
    }
```

```
    public void run()
    {
        Thread.currentThread().setPriority(Thread.NORM_PRIORITY-1);
        paint(this.getGraphics());
        while (true)
                repaint(speed);
    }

    public void paint(Graphics g)
    {
        // initial background
        g.setColor(Color.black);
        g.drawRect(0,0, getSize().width,
                    getSize().height);
        g.setColor(Color.white);
        g.fillRect(1,1, getSize().width - 1,
                    getSize().height - 1);

        // set the font
        g.setFont(textFont);
        fontMetrics = g.getFontMetrics();

        // set initial X and Y to drawString
        oldX = newX = getSize().width -
                fontMetrics.charWidth(theMessage.charAt(0));
        oldY = newY = getSize().height/2 +
                (fontMetrics.getHeight()/2);
    }

    public void update(Graphics g)
    {
        g.setFont(textFont);

        // Erase the old
        g.setColor(Color.white);
        g.drawString(theMessage, oldX, oldY);

        // draw the New
        g.setColor(Color.black);
        g.drawString(theMessage, newX, newY);

        // step
        oldX = newX;
        newX -= stepPixels;

        // restart?
        if (newX <= -(fontMetrics.stringWidth(theMessage)
                    - fontMetrics.charWidth(
                      theMessage.charAt(
                         theMessage.length() - 1))))
                paint(g);  // start at the beginning
    }

}
```

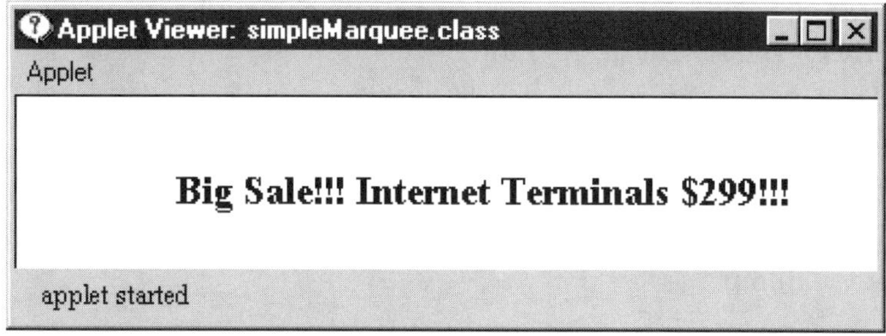

FIGURE 12.2 The simpleMarquee applet.

The HTML page for the preceding applet is:

```
<html>
<title> A simple Scrolling Marquee </title>
<hr>
<applet code="jwiley.chp12.simpleMarquee.class" width=400 height=80>
<param name=message value="Big Sale!!! Internet Terminals $299!!!">
<param name=speed value="25">
</applet>
```

When run in the applet viewer, Source 12.2 produces Figure 12.2.

Before we can feel confident about applets though, we need to briefly examine the Hyper Text Markup Language (HTML) file and the applet HTML tag, which the browser uses to load our Applet subclass.

An HTML file is a normal text file that has special tags in it that the browser treats as commands. HTML documents are divided into logical elements. Elements are marked by tags of the form

```
<TagName> ... some text  ... </TagName>
```

There are many different HTML tags and many fine books on the market on preparing HTML documents. We are only concerned with one new tag: the applet tag.

```
<applet  attributes>  </applet>  - this is the applet tag.
```

Non-Java enabled browsers will ignore this tag. HTML tags can have attributes. The applet tag has the following key attributes and may contain any number of param elements. Here are the key applet attributes:

- **codebase="path/classes".** Specify a path to search for the class. If not specified, the browser expects the class to be in the same directory the .html page was loaded from.

- **code="classname.class".** The class name. Mandatory.
- **width=#.** The width of the Panel to contain the applet. Mandatory.
- **height=#.** The height of the Panel to contain the applet. Mandatory.
- **archive="archiveList".** A listing of one or more archive files created with the jar tool.
- **alt="alternateText".** Alternate text to display if the browser understands the applet tag but does not have Java support.
- **name="appletName".** Assigns name to applet, making it possible for other applets to find it.

An applet tag can also contain a param element. A param element does not contain any text and is called an "empty element." Here is what the param element looks like:

```
<param attributes>
```

The param element can have two attributes:

- **name=parameter_name.** The name of the parameter.
- **value="value".** The value of the parameter.

That is all there is to the applet tag. The param elements are used to pass parameters into the applet. In the init() method you call the getParameter() method with the name of the parameter as the argument. The getParameter() method will return the String in the value attribute of the param element.

12.3 USING APPLETS IN CLIENT/SERVER PROGRAMS

Not only can applets be used to provide dynamic graphical content to a Web page, but as a client application delivery system. Even though an applet is only a component on a Web page, applets can run any Java code you have written with a few security-related exceptions. An applet can create new Frames and Windows so its graphical content is not limited to the space allocated on the Web page. Here is a list of limitations placed on unsigned applets:

- **Cannot access the local file system.** For security reasons an applet is not allowed to access the file system. If it could it would be able to get at valuable system files and could potentially corrupt them. This also means your applet cannot save or retrieve files on the system it is running, which limits the usefulness of applets. An applet can read files using a URL instead of a filename. In JDK 1.1, JavaSoft enabled applets to be signed, which extends their capabilities. For a discussion of signed applets see Chapter 17, "Java and Security."
- **Cannot call native methods.** A call to a native method would force a shared library to load on the local file system. Since applets cannot access the local file system, calling native methods is prohibited.

- **Can only make a socket connection to the host it was loaded from.** For security reasons an applet can only make a socket connection back to the originating host. If it was allowed to connect anywhere it wanted, it could be used to hack into other systems on the Internet and the attack would be traced back to your machine!
- **Cannot start any program on the host that is executing it.** This would require access to the file system and is therefore prevented.
- **Cannot access certain system properties.** An applet cannot access java configuration variables (java.class.path, java.home) or user variables (user.dir, user.home, user.name).
- **Windows displayed from applets contain warning text and a graphical identifier marking this window as untrusted.** In this manner, native windows can be distinguished from applet windows.

Despite these restrictions, applets are still very powerful. But in order to be powerful they must be coded with the preceding restrictions in mind. An applet is ideal for a "thin" client application. A thin client is an application that provides the user interface portion of an application, but the actual processing and work needed to be done is performed by a server application. Source 12.3 is an applet that acts as a front end for a server application.

SOURCE 12.3 SearchForm.java applet

```
// SearchForm.java
package jwiley.chp12;

import java.applet.Applet;
import java.awt.*;
import java.awt.event.*;
import jwiley.chp10.Grid;

public class SearchForm extends Applet implements ActionListener
{
    TextField   txtSearchText = new TextField();
    Checkbox    chkTitle = new Checkbox("Title");
    Checkbox    chkKeyword = new Checkbox("Keyword");
    Checkbox    chkText = new Checkbox("Text");

    Button      cmdSearch = new Button("Search");

    List        lstResults = new List();
    TextArea    txtDocumentView = new TextArea();

    Document    docs[] = null;

    public void init ()
    {
```

```
        // layout form
        setLayout(new Grid(8,8,2,2));

        add("1,1", new Label("Search:"));
        add("2,1,2,1", txtSearchText);
        add("4,1", cmdSearch);

        add("1,2", chkTitle);
        add("2,2", chkKeyword);
        add("3,2", chkText);

        add("1,4", new Label("Results:"));
        add("1,5,4,4", lstResults);

        add("6,1,2,1", new Label("Text Document:"));
        add("5,2,4,7", txtDocumentView);

        // set up event handlers
        cmdSearch.addActionListener(this);
        lstResults.addActionListener(this);
    }

    public void actionPerformed (ActionEvent evt)
    {
        SearchClient searchClient =
                new SearchClient(getCodeBase().getHost(), 8511);

        if (evt.getSource() == cmdSearch)
        {
            docs = searchClient.performSearch(txtSearchText.getText(),
                                               chkTitle.getState(),
                                               chkKeyword.getState(),
                                               chkText.getState());


            if (docs != null)
            {
                lstResults.removeAll();
                for (int iCount = 0; iCount < docs.length; iCount++)
                {
                    lstResults.addItem(docs[iCount].getTitle());
                }
            }
            else
                lstResults.removeAll();
        }
        else if (evt.getSource() == lstResults)
        {
            // find associated file name first
            if (docs != null)
            {
```

```
                String sListItem = evt.getActionCommand();
                for (int iCount = 0; iCount < docs.length; iCount++)
                {
                    if (docs[iCount].getTitle().equals(sListItem))
                    {
                        String sFileName = docs[iCount].getFileName();
                        String sDocumentText =
                            searchClient.getDocumentText(sFileName);

                        txtDocumentView.setText(sDocumentText);
                        break;
                    }
                }
            }
        }
    }
}

// SearchClient.java
package jwiley.chp12;

import java.net.Socket;
import java.io.DataInputStream;
import java.io.DataOutputStream;
import java.io.IOException;

public class SearchClient
{
    String  sHostName = "";
    int     iPort = 0;

    public SearchClient(String sHostName, int iPort)
    {
        this.sHostName = sHostName;
        this.iPort = iPort;
    }

    public Document[] performSearch (String sSearchText,
                                     boolean bTitleSearch,
                                     boolean bKeywordSearch,
                                     boolean bTextSearch)
    {
        Socket      sock = null;
        Document    docs[] = null;

        try
        {
            sock = new Socket(sHostName, iPort);

            DataInputStream disStream =
                    new DataInputStream(sock.getInputStream());
```

```
        DataOutputStream dosStream =
                new DataOutputStream(sock.getOutputStream());

        dosStream.writeUTF("<SEARCH>");
        dosStream.writeUTF(sSearchText);
        dosStream.writeBoolean(bTitleSearch);
        dosStream.writeBoolean(bKeywordSearch);
        dosStream.writeBoolean(bTextSearch);

        int iNumDocs = disStream.readInt();
        if (iNumDocs > 0)
        {
            docs = new Document[iNumDocs];
            for (int iCount = 0; iCount < iNumDocs; iCount++)
            {
                String sFileName = disStream.readUTF();
                String sTitle = disStream.readUTF();

                docs[iCount] = new Document(sFileName,
                                            sTitle);
            }
        }

        sock.close();

    } catch (IOException ioe)
      {
        System.out.println("Error in performing search." +
                           "\nError: " + ioe.toString());
      }

    return (docs);
}

public String getDocumentText (String sFileName)
{
    Socket      sock = null;
    String      sDocText = null;

    try
    {
        sock = new Socket(sHostName, iPort);

        DataInputStream disStream =
                new DataInputStream(sock.getInputStream());

        DataOutputStream dosStream =
                new DataOutputStream(sock.getOutputStream());

        dosStream.writeUTF("<GET-DOC>");
        dosStream.writeUTF(sFileName);
        sDocText = disStream.readUTF();
```

```
            sock.close();

        } catch (IOException ioe)
          {
            System.out.println("Error in getting document." +
                               "\nError: " + ioe.toString());
          }

        return (sDocText);
    }
}

// Document.java
package jwiley.chp12;

public class Document
{
    String sFileName = "";
    String sTitle = "";

    public Document (String sFileName, String sTitle)
    {
        this.sFileName = sFileName;
        this.sTitle = sTitle;
    }

    public String getFileName()
    {
        return (sFileName);
    }

    public String getTitle()
    {
        return (sTitle);
    }
}
```

The html page for the above applet is:

```
<HTML>
<BODY>
<APPLET CODE="jwiley.chp12.SearchForm"
WIDTH=600 HEIGHT=300>
</APPLET>
</BODY>
<HTML>
```

When run in the applet viewer, Source 12.3 produces Figure 12.3.

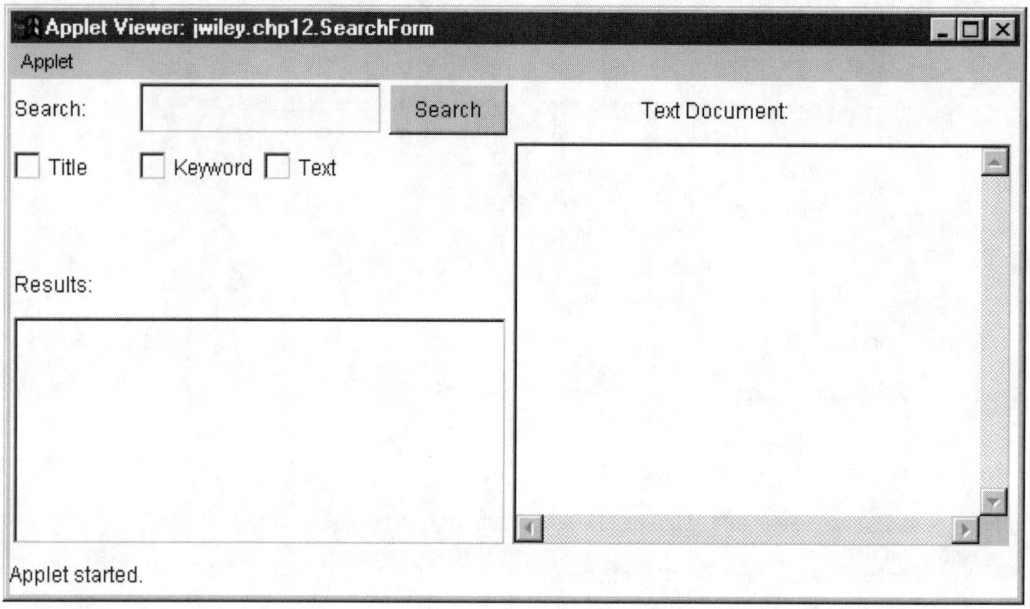

FIGURE 12.3 The SearchForm applet.

Source 12.3 consists of three classes: SearchForm, SearchClient, and Document. These three classes provide the applet client to our application. The application is a simple search engine that can be used to search documents for keywords, title text, or full body text, and return a list of hits. Double-clicking a specific document will display the document in the text window of the applet. Let's discuss the purpose of each class and the key areas within each class.

- **The SearchForm class is our applet.** In the init() method we lay out the fields used in the form and set up our event listeners. Note that this applet does not have a start(), stop(), or destroy() method. Since the applet is not doing continuous processing and no cleanup needs to be performed, the methods are not needed. Also note that this applet does not implement Runnable. Since this applet does not run in a tight loop it does not need to have its own thread.
- **The actionPerformed() method handles events generated by the Search button and the Results list.** The key point to this method is the getCodeBase().getHost() method call in the following line:

```
SearchClient searchClient =
    new SearchClient(getCodeBase().getHost(), 8511);
```

- **The getCodeBase() method returns the URL of the Web server the applet was loaded from.** Using the URL we can then get the hostname of the Web server. This is important because we need this information to create a socket connection to a program running on the server. Remember, this is a restriction of applets—you can only create socket connections back to the originating host. In this instance the getCodeBase() method will only be useful if the applet is loaded from a Web server. The rest of the actionPerformed() method is used to update the display based on results from the server.
- **The SearchClient class contains the code to create a socket back to the host and to perform a few actions.** The SearchClient has two methods: performSearch() and getDocumentText(), which pass information gathered in the applet to the server.
- **The Document class is used to identify a document.** Documents are stored in the directory the server application is running. The methods provided by the Document class allow access to the title of the document and to the filename of the document.

Source 12.4 lists the server portion of our application.

SOURCE 12.4 SearchServer.java

```
// SearchServer.java
package jwiley.chp12;

import java.net.ServerSocket;
import java.net.Socket;

import java.io.DataInputStream;
import java.io.DataOutputStream;
import java.io.IOException;
import java.io.FileInputStream;
import java.io.File;
import java.io.InputStreamReader;
import java.io.BufferedReader;

import java.util.Vector;
import java.util.StringTokenizer;

public class SearchServer extends Thread
{
    int iPort = 0;

    public SearchServer (int iPort)
    {
        this.iPort = iPort;
    }
```

```
public void run ()
{
    ServerSocket sockServer = null;

    try {
        sockServer = new ServerSocket(iPort);
    } catch (Exception e)
      {
        System.out.println("Error creating ServerSocket." +
                           "\nError: " + e.toString());
        System.exit(0);
      }


    try {
        while (true)
        {
            Socket sockConnection = sockServer.accept();
            DataInputStream disStream =
                new DataInputStream(sockConnection.getInputStream());

            DataOutputStream dosStream =
                new DataOutputStream(sockConnection.getOutputStream());

            String sCommand = disStream.readUTF();
            if (sCommand.equals("<SEARCH>"))
                handleSearch(disStream, dosStream);
            else if (sCommand.equals("<GET-DOC>"))
                handleGetDoc(disStream, dosStream);

            sockConnection.close();
        }

    } catch (IOException ioe)
      {
        System.out.println(ioe.toString());
      }

}

void handleSearch (DataInputStream disStream,
                   DataOutputStream dosStream)
{
    try {
        String sSearchText = disStream.readUTF();
        boolean bTitleSearch = disStream.readBoolean();
        boolean bKeywordSearch = disStream.readBoolean();
        boolean bTextSearch = disStream.readBoolean();

        Document docs[] = parseDocuments(sSearchText,
                                         bTitleSearch,
                                         bKeywordSearch,
                                         bTextSearch);
```

```
            if (docs != null)
            {
                dosStream.writeInt(docs.length);
                for (int iCount = 0; iCount < docs.length; iCount++)
                {
                    dosStream.writeUTF(docs[iCount].getFileName());
                    dosStream.writeUTF(docs[iCount].getTitle());
                }
            }
            else
                dosStream.writeInt(0);

        } catch (IOException ioe)
          {
            System.out.println("Error handling search." +
                               "\nError: " + ioe.toString());
          }

    }

    void handleGetDoc (DataInputStream disStream,
                       DataOutputStream dosStream)
    {
        try {
            String sFileName = disStream.readUTF();

            // get file text here
            FileInputStream fis = new FileInputStream(sFileName);
            BufferedReader input =
                new BufferedReader(new InputStreamReader(fis));

            String sDocumentText = "";
            String sLine = input.readLine();

            while (sLine != null)
            {
                if (!sDocumentText.equals(""))
                    sDocumentText = sDocumentText + "\n" + sLine;
                else
                    sDocumentText = sDocumentText + sLine;

                sLine = input.readLine();
            }

            fis.close();

            dosStream.writeUTF(sDocumentText);

        } catch (IOException ioe)
          {
            System.out.println("Error getting document." +
                               "\nError: " + ioe.toString());
          }
```

```
}

Document[] parseDocuments(String sSearchText,
                          boolean bTitleSearch,
                          boolean bKeywordSearch,
                          boolean bTextSearch)
{
    File fCurrentDir = new File(".");
    String sFiles[] = fCurrentDir.list();

    Vector vFileHits = new Vector();

    if (sFiles != null)
    {
        for (int iCount = 0; iCount < sFiles.length; iCount++)
        {
            if (sFiles[iCount].endsWith(".txt"))
            {
                String sTitle = parseDocument(sFiles[iCount],
                                              sSearchText,
                                              bTitleSearch,
                                              bKeywordSearch,
                                              bTextSearch);
                if (sTitle != null)
                {
                    Document doc = new Document(sFiles[iCount],
                                                sTitle);
                    vFileHits.addElement(doc);
                }
            }
        }
    }

    Document documentHits[] = null;

    int iNumHits = vFileHits.size();
    if (iNumHits > 0)
    {
        documentHits = new Document[iNumHits];
        for (int iCount = 0; iCount < iNumHits; iCount++)
        {
            documentHits[iCount] =
                    (Document) vFileHits.elementAt(iCount);
        }
    }

    return (documentHits);
}
```

```
String parseDocument(String sFileName,
                     String sSearchText,
                     boolean bTitleSearch,
                     boolean bKeywordSearch,
                     boolean bTextSearch)
{
    try {
        FileInputStream fis = new FileInputStream(sFileName);
        BufferedReader input =
                new BufferedReader(new InputStreamReader(fis));

        String sTitleString = input.readLine();
        if (bTitleSearch)
        {
            if (parseLine(sTitleString, sSearchText, "Title:"))
            {
                fis.close();
                return (sTitleString);
            }
        }

        String sKeywordString = input.readLine();
        if (bKeywordSearch)
        {
            if (parseLine(sKeywordString, sSearchText, "Keywords:"))
            {
                fis.close();
                return (sTitleString);
            }
        }

        if (bTextSearch)
        {
            String sTextString = input.readLine();
            while (sTextString != null)
            {
                if (parseLine(sTextString, sSearchText, null))
                {
                    fis.close();
                    return (sTitleString);
                }
                sTextString = input.readLine();
            }
        }

    } catch (IOException ioe)
      {
        System.out.println("Error parsing text file." +
                           "\nError: " + ioe.toString());
      }
```

```
            return (null);
        }

        boolean parseLine(String sLine,
                          String sSearchText,
                          String sPrefixText)
        {
            if (sPrefixText != null)
            {
                sLine = sLine.substring(sPrefixText.length());
            }

            StringTokenizer st = new StringTokenizer(sLine, " ,.:;");
            while (st.hasMoreTokens())
            {
                String sToken = st.nextToken().trim();
                if (sSearchText.equalsIgnoreCase(sToken))
                    return (true);
            }

            return (false);
        }

        public static void main (String args[])
        {
            SearchServer searchServer = new SearchServer(8511);
            searchServer.start();
        }

    }
```

The SearchServer class waits for connections and then handles the request. The SearchServer class will look for text documents located in the current directory and parse those documents according to the parameters passed in from the client. Figure 12.4 shows the SearchClient application after performing a search and retrieving the document.

Reducing Applet Download Time

When an applet is accessed on a Web page the Java interpreter running in the browser loads the class file from the Web server. Any classes your applet references are also loaded from the Web server. If your applet references many class files or uses a lot of resources, it may take the browser a significant amount of time to load all the necessary files. In addition, the browser may have to use multiple connections to load all the necessary files. To solve this problem of downloading so many files, Java has intro-

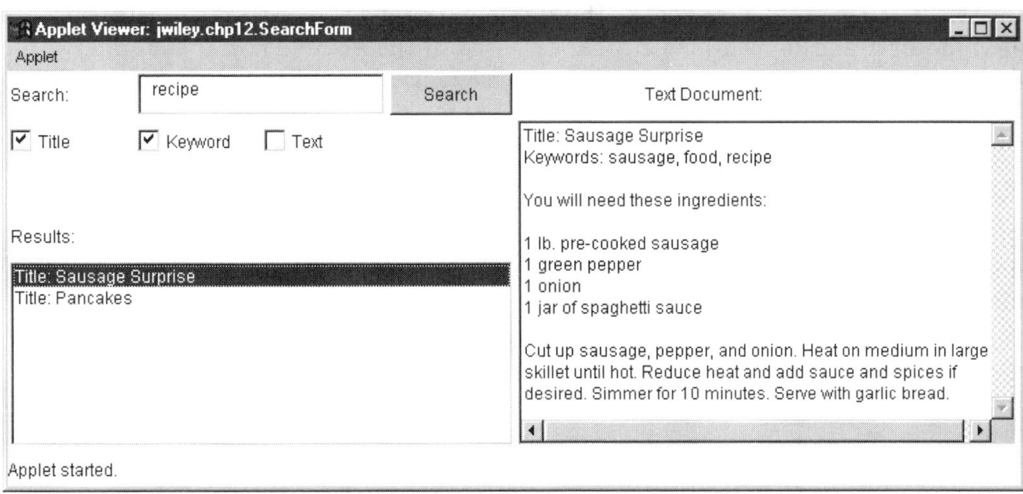

FIGURE 12.4 The SearchForm applet in action.

duced JAR files. A JAR file is an archive of Java classes and resources that is created using the jar tool. For more information on the jar tool, refer to Chapter 1.

Using an archive to store applet classes and resources significantly reduces download time for applets. Two immediate benefits are gained by using JAR files. The first is that all files needed by your applet are stored in a single archive file; therefore, only one connection needs to be opened and only one file needs to be downloaded. The second benefit is that when files are added to a JAR file they are compressed using the ZLIB compression library. This will reduce the file size and therefore speed up the download process. Let's look at an example of how to create a JAR file for an applet. The following line will create a JAR file for the SearchClient applet listed in Source 12.3.

```
jar cf search.jar jwiley\chp12\*.class jwiley\chp10\Grid.class
```

This line will create the search.jar file and add all class files from jwiley\chp12 and the Grid class in jwiley\chp10. In order to use the JAR file we must add a parameter to the applet tag in our html file. Here is the html file used to call our applet:

```
<HTML>
<BODY>
<APPLET CODE="jwiley.chp12.SearchForm" ARCHIVE="search.jar"
WIDTH=600 HEIGHT=300>
</APPLET>
</BODY>
<HTML>
```

The only difference between this file and the one used previously is the addition of the ARCHIVE parameter. Adding this parameter tells the browser to download the JAR file first and to look for necessary classes in the archive file. If the archive file does not contain all necessary classes the browser will load the class from the Web server.

12.4 SUMMARY

This chapter covered all of the concepts necessary to program applets. Applets are mini-applications that are run within a browser. Programming applets involves a new paradigm that I call “browser-driven” programming. Just as GUIs ushered in a new paradigm called “event-driven” programming, so applets now usher in browser-driven programming. Browser-driven programs just need to be designed in such a way to be controlled by the browser using several simple methods like init(), start(), stop(), and destroy().

The Applet class extends the AWT Panel class. This makes writing applets as easy as writing any awt application. We demonstrated this by transitioning an awt program to an applet (ScrollMsg.java).

We discussed how to place applets in Web pages via the applet tag. We discussed all the parameters to the applet tag in detail.

We demonstrated how to effectively use applets in client-server programming. We highlighted this with a nontrivial searchForm applet that searched a host file for text files of interest.

We then concluded the chapter with a discussion of Java archive files (JAR) and how they reduce applet download time.

CHAPTER 13

Programming with CORBA and Java

OBJECTIVE

In this chapter we will introduce the concepts of the Common Object Request Broker Architecture (CORBA), see how CORBA can be used with Java, and examine the benefits of doing so. We will also introduce the Java Interface Description Language (IDL) developers kit for CORBA and show some examples of how it can be used.

13.1 INTRODUCTION

The Web first gained real popularity with the advent of HTML. However, HTML pages provided only static data and their uses were limited. CGI and similar tools then entered the fray and provided more dynamic behavior and data, but were clumsy, slow, and forced the burden back on the server. Java has relocated the client-side processing back where it belongs, on the client. But something is still missing and that is interaction with distributed objects. Sun's JDK1.1 provides a simple RPC service, known as RMI, which goes part of the way to providing distributed objects. But as we shall see, CORBA provides a complete framework for true distributed objects for both Java objects and legacy objects.

CORBA really defines a network communications infrastructure allowing a heterogeneous distributed collection of objects to collaborate transparently. Two key components of CORBA make this possible: the interface definition language (IDL) and the Internet Inter-ORB Protocol(IIOP). Before we look at what IDL and IIOP are, let's look more closely at what CORBA is and why we might want to use it in the first place.

What Is OMG?

The Object Management Group, or OMG, is the standards body responsible for the care and feeding of the CORBA standards. The OMG is a consortium of over 500 software vendor and user organizations devoted to the open standards of distributed object technology. The OMG contains technical committees responsible for all aspects of CORBA and the Common Management Architecture, or CMA.

What Is CORBA?

CORBA is a standard architecture for describing and distributing objects around the Net. CORBA provides a way to find, access, create, and interact with objects that may be local or remote, written in Java, C, C++, or any other language appropriate for the object in question. In short, CORBA provides the structure required to take network applications to the next level and provide true distributed object-oriented programs.

Why CORBA?

We've seen a simple definition of CORBA. Why would a Java developer want to use it? Here are just a few reasons.

Provides a layer above the network, removing UPD, IP, and other transport-level concerns. The java.net package provides basic network functionality but the developer must design and implement his/her own protocols.

Designed from the bottom up for distributed object support. CORBA was designed from the beginning with distributed computing and all its features in mind.

Defines objects without regard to their implementation via IDL. CORBA's interface description language abstracts away the definition of an object from its implementation, allowing objects to be developed by separate teams using a well-defined interface. Systems that support standard object models such as Booch or OMT can easily support IDL.

Implements object in whatever language is appropriate. Separating the implementation from the interface allows for developing objects in a language appropriate for the object, supporting legacy systems in the language they were designed in. Separating the implementation from the definition also allows for multiple implementations of the same object; for example, one Database Management System (DBMS) object definition implemented on top of many DBMSs. Basically, CORBA objects can be implemented in any language and CORBA clients can be implemented in any language.

Provides location-independent access to objects. CORBA naming services allow for objects to be located where they fit best, either locally, remotely, or some combination thereof through IIOP.

Provides automatic generation of skeleton and stub code to ease development. The various development tools provided with implementations of CORBA automatically generate both the client-side stubs and the server-side skeleton classes. These classes take the drudgery out of development by providing the infrastructure for creating, destroying, and maintaining network connections.

Provides access to common CORBA services. For example:

Naming service. A service for remotely finding objects and accessing objects, alleviating the need for hardcoding addresses and URLs.
Trading Service. A service for remotely offering and finding distributed services. Services can be pooled and then queries made to find a service that fits a user's need (such as a printer or scanner).
Event notification and transaction support. Provides subscriber-based event notification and transaction-level support.
Vendor independence via CORBA2.0. CORBA2.0 specifies how objects implemented by different ORB implementations must interoperate, clearing the road for combining objects from many different vendors into a single application.

What Is IDL?

The CORBA Interface Definition Language, or IDL for short, defines the methods and attributes of an object. The key difference between CORBA IDL, RMI, and other similar tools is that IDL is a definition of an interface specification only. It presupposes no knowledge of the underlying implementation or programming language.

Strangely enough, CORBA IDL and Java bear a striking similarity, which we will examine in detail a little later. A quick comparison shows:

- Java Packages are very much like CORBA IDL modules, allowing a similar flavor for nesting namespaces.
- Java interfaces are very much like CORBA Interfaces, performing much the same function of defining an interface but not an implementation.
- Java methods are very much like CORBA operations. Both define the way a function is called, defining both its return value and its arguments.
- Java native data types are very much like CORBA native data types, but with some differences.

One of the key differences between Java and CORBA is that CORBA is language-neutral. CORBA IDL has been mapped into many languages such as C, C++, Java, and others. Idltojava, Sun's IDL compiler, maps CORBA IDL to Java interfaces. The IDL definition is quite long but we will cover the most common aspects in detail in a later section.

What Is IIOP?

With the second major release of CORBA, CORBA2.0, the OMG defined a standard that included specifications for ORB interoperability. The General inter-ORB Protocol, or GIOP, is a CORBA2.0 mandatory protocol and is required by all CORBA implementations if they wish the CORBA2.0 compliant. The Internet Inter-ORB Protocol, or IIOP, is a TCP/IP-based transport based on the GIOP protocol and is also mandatory for CORBA 2.0 compliance. Several other protocols exist, one of the key ones being DCE Common Inter-ORB Protocol, or DEC-CIOP for short. In addition to all this the CORBA2.0 also provides a specification called Interoperable Object References, or IORs, which describe how any object reference from a 2.0-compliant Object Request Broker can be used by any client of any other Object Request Broker.

What CORBA Offers to Java Developers

Before we get into how to develop applications with CORBA it's important to understand that other methods do exist to develop distributed objects, two of which are Microsoft's DCOM and Sun's RMI. Let's take a moment and examine these technologies and how they compare to CORBA.

Remote Method Invocation. RMI, or Remote Method Invocation, as we will see in Chapter 16, is a method to separate an object definition from its implementation. The idea behind RMI is to create objects whose methods can be executed on another Java VM. RMI is really just RPC for Java. In many ways, RMI is like CORBA. Both generate stub and skeleton code. Both handle the marshalling of method arguments. It's here that the similarities between CORBA and RMI end. CORBA is designed to be language-independent. RMI, on the other hand, is optimized for Java-to-Java communications. One of the main strengths of CORBA is its language independence. More often then not the purpose of an RPC call is to interact with a host of some sort of running legacy software. It's difficult at best and perhaps even impossible, even given the use of native methods, to wrap the host software in Java. Another significant advantage of CORBA is its Naming and Trading services support. CORBA is truly location-independent.

There is no question that RMI has its place. It's quick and easy and supports the development of small- to medium-size distributed applications. RMI works well in new development, where both sides can and should be written in Java. Where CORBA shines is in the building of large industrial-scale distributed objects where legacy systems are a factor and distributed naming comes into play. IDL with its ability to separate the interface from the implementation makes breaking up a project easier, and CORBA2.0 interoperability requirements make interfacing with other vendors' ORBs much simpler.

Microsoft DCOM. The Microsoft Distributed Common Object Model (DCOM) really does compare well with CORBA. As we will see in some detail in Chapter 22, COM contains its own IDL compiler. DCOM even goes one step further than CORBA in defining a binary standard for objects as well as standard interface definition. If we compare COM with CORBA, we see the following:

- DCOM has MIDL, the Microsoft Interface Definition Language, also sometimes referred to as ODL, whereas CORBA has its own Interface Description Language (IDL).

- DCOM is language-neutral just as CORBA is language-neutral.
- DCOM defines a binary standard for objects. CORBA does not. But then DCOM binaries are only standard under Windows NT and Windows 95.

However, CORBA has some features that DCOM does not. Specifically, CORBA contains a standardized API-based method of determining the location of objects. CORBA's naming and trading services provide ways for a client to determine, at run time, where an object is and a method to make queries about network services. In addition, CORBA was designed from the get-go as a distributed object management system. DCOM, on the other hand, has grown, somewhat painfully, from DDE to OLE to OLE2 and finally to DCOM and ActiveX, carrying along all its baggage and history. One of the major failings of DCOM is that it stores all remote object references in the local registry and provides no method to automate updates when object locations change. This "feature" seriously compromises the use of DCOM. DCOM does have one feature that this author would like to see become part of CORBA, interface versioning. With interface versioning two clients can access the same interface without concern for how it has evolved over time.

Installing the Sun JavaIDL Package

The early release of the JavaIDL kit for Windows 95, Windows NT, and Sun platforms did not come as part of the JDK. You will need to install the kit yourself if you wish to do actual real CORBA development. The Sun JavaIDL software package can be found at ftp://ftp.javasoft.com/pub/jdk1.1/id/. After downloading the latest JavaIDL from JavaSoft, run JavaIDL-EA-win32.EXE. Then follow these directions:

1. When prompted for the name of a folder to install, choose the directory where the JDK is installed; for example, c:\jdk1.1 under Windows 95 and Windows NT. The JavaIDL kit will install creating bin\, doc\, lib\ and examples\ directories.
2. From a DOS or Unix prompt, cd to the {JavaIDLPath}\JavaIDL\bin directory.
3. Make sure that the JDK\bin and JavaIDL\bin directories are in your path and type

```
Java installJavaIDL.class[return]
```

4. You will then be prompted. Simply follow the prompts to complete the installation.

```
Welcome to the Installation of JavaIDL for Windows NT.
Enter full path to Java interpreter executable
 (JDK 1.0.2 or higher): c:\jdk\bin\java[return]
Enter full Java classpath [f:\jdk\lib\classes.zip]:[return]
Enter JavaIdl Path [F:\jdk\JAVAIDL]: [return]
Using:
Java Interpreter: f:\jdk\bin\java
Java Classpath: f:\jdk\lib\classes.zip
JavaIDL Path: F:\jdk\JAVAIDL
Generating script...
Installation for Windows NT complete.
```

```
The script "c:\jdk\JAVAIDL\bin\nameserv.bat" can be used to start the COS
Name Server.
```

The JavaIDL kit should now be installed and ready to use.

13.2 JAVA PROGRAMMING WITH CORBA

At this point we've seen some history, covered some of the CORBA terminology, and installed the JavaIDL kit. In the following sections we will examine the CORBA architecture and how we develop CORBA clients and servers using the idltojava tool.

Those developers who have done RPC development before, or who have read Chapter 16, will see many similarities in the CORBA programming model versus other RPC models. When a client application calls a CORBA Object method, that method call is translated to its accompanying stub, which marshalls the method arguments and then passes them to the ORB core. The ORB core then transfers the data to the target machine where the implementation of the object resides and unmarshalls the arguments and calls the implementation of the method. Figure 13.1 shows this flow. Under normal circumstances a result would then be computed and returned to the caller via the ORB core.

The American Heritage Dictionary defines marshalling as "to place in methodical or proper order." In the CORBA case, placing methods arguments *in proper order* is the process of translating those arguments into a network-neutral form that can be read and processed by either end of the CORBA pipe, regardless of the underlying hardware architecture. Unmarshalling is the inverse process, that is, converting arguments back into their native architecture form. Network-neutral form is important because it allows two computers, which may have different underlying architectures, to converse without concern for little endian/big endian issues. Little endian/big endian refers to the direction bytes are layed out in a data type that consists of multiple bytes.

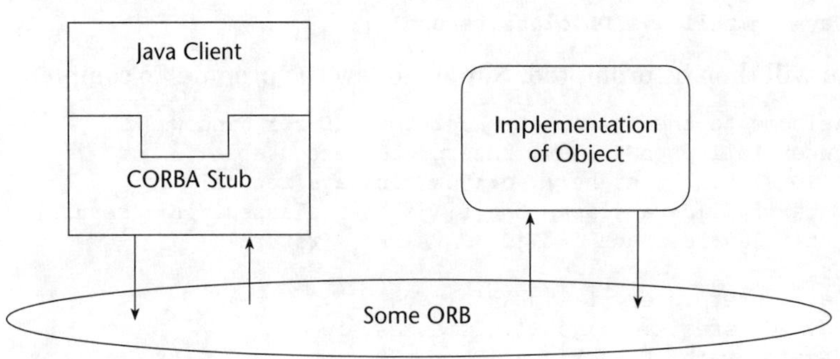

FIGURE 13.1 CORBA in action.

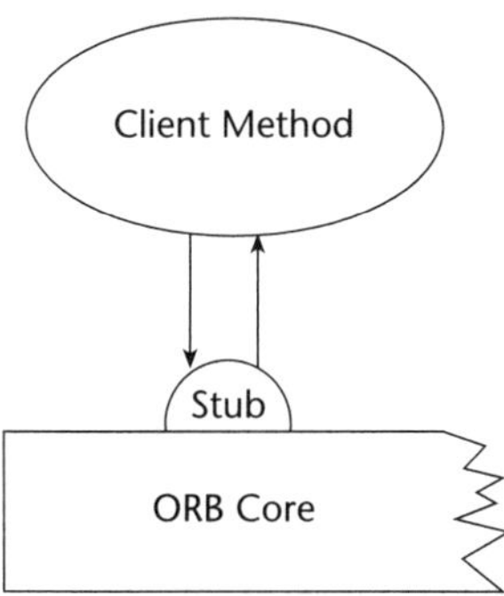

FIGURE 13.2 Calling a CORBA stub.

Figure 13.2 shows a closer view of how the client calls the IDL stub. A similar process happens on the server side, with the client stub being replaced with the server skeleton stub.

Building an Application

To build a CORBA application you need to perform the following steps:

1. Develop and compile your IDL file.
2. Develop your skeleton server functions.
3. Develop your client application.
4. Compile your application, stubs, skeleton and server functions.
5. Run a copy of the name server, server and client.

If you can remember all the way back to Chapter 1, you will recall our 99 bottles of beer example. For the next few sections we will reexamine this application in order to remote the printing of the each chorus.

IDL. The starting point of all your CORBA applications will be the Interface Description Language, or IDL. For our 99 bottles of beer example we define a simple module

SOURCE 13.1 bottles.idl

```
module Sing
{
    interface bottles
    {
        void Chorus(in string line);
    };
};
```

TABLE 13.1 idltojava Arguments

Flag	*Description*	*Default*
-flist-flags	Print the state of all –f flags	Off
-fverbose	Print details of compilation	Off
-fversion	Print idltojava tool version information	Off
-j output directory	Specifies the output directory for the generated files	Default output directory is the name of the module.
-linclude directory	Specifies include directories to be searched for other IDL files.	Default is none.
-Dsomesymbol	Define a symbol	None
-Usomesymbol	Undefine a symbol	None

called Sing. Sing contains only a single interface, aptly named bottles. And within bottles is a single operation, Chorus. The Chorus operation takes only a single parameter, the line to sing.

We compile the bottles.idl file with the following command, issued from the DOS or Unix prompt:

```
idltojava -fclient -fserver bottles.idl
```

TIP Don't forget to make sure that you have both the javaidl\bin directory and the jdk\bin directory in your command path. The idltojava tool is in the javaidl\bin directory!

The idltojava can take several arguments. We are primarily interested in the –f arguments. The remaining arguments are listed in Table 13.1. Anyone who has used a C compiler will be familiar with the idltojava arguments.

- -fclient Generate client-side stubs for IDL files supplied. The default value is off.
- -fserver Generate server-side skeleton stubs for IDL files supplied. The default value is off.

TIP You can negate or turn off any flag by prefixing it with no. For example you could turn off the c-preprocessor with the argument –fno-cpp.

Let's look one more time at our simple IDL and see the corresponding classes that were generated.

TABLE 13.2 bottles.idl Generated Code

bottles.idl	*Generated Java Classes*

<pre>module Sing
{
    interface bottles
    {
        void Chorus(in string line);
    };
};</pre>
	<pre>// bottles.java
	package Sing;
	public interface bottles
	    extends org.omg.CORBA.Object {
	    void Chorus(String line);
	}
	
	// bottlesHelper.java
	package Sing;
	public final class bottlesHelper {
	    //...
	    public static Sing.bottles
	      narrow(org.omg.CORBA.Object that)
	}
	
	// bottlesHolder.java
	package Sing;
	public final class bottlesHolder
	  implements
	   org.omg.CORBA.portable.Streamable{
	. . .
	}</pre>

The three classes provide the following methods:

- **Bottles interface.** The Bottles interface defines the methods that correspond to the operations defined in the bottles.idl file. When the client is run, the class, which implements this interface, represents the local version of the object being accessed. (See Table 13.2.)
- **Bottles helper.** The Bottles Helper class defines a set of methods necessary for CORBA to manipulate the object. The most notable method is the narrow method, which "casts" the CORBA object back to its underlying implementation. You can see from the source code that the narrow method casts the object of type org.omg.CORBA.Object to an object of type Sing.bottles.
- **Bottles holder.** The Bottles Holder class defines a set of methods that get and set the underlying arguments to the implemented Bottles class. This class also contains the methods for marshalling and unmarshalling the method arguments.

It's not necessary to understand everything about the files that the idltojava compiler produces. Except in some very rare cases, you needn't ever look at these classes. A client application can invoke a remote operation in one of two ways.

- **Static invocation.** The normal way of invoking a method, where the name, argument types, and return value of the method are known.
- **Dynamic invocation.** Dynamic invocation is much more flexible and provides a method for clients to determine what methods exist and call them. The current version of idltojava does not support dynamic invocation.

Under normal circumstances a Java application defines an instance of a variable and then uses the new operation to create an instance of that variable. Using CORBA, a client application obtains a reference to an object. These objects are normally created by another object, typically called an *object factory*. An application also needs a stub routine, which serves as the remote call proxy. Source 13.2 shows a simple example of these features.

Develop Your Client Application. The key concept behind a CORBA client is obtaining a reference to a proxy class. In Source 13.2 we see that most of the new code is concerned with obtaining this reference.

While it looks complicated at first glance the client code is really quite simple.

```
org.omg.CORBA.Object objRef =
    orb.resolve_initial_references("NameService");
NamingContext ncRef = NamingContextHelper.narrow(objRef);
```

This code obtains a reference to a "NameService" object. There could be many name services running on a given machine and the application can choose an appropriate one. In our example, we use the default name service supplied with the JavaIDL SDK, appropriately named NameService. The NamingContextHelper narrow method is the one used to narrow the generic ORB object to a reference of type NamingContext that we can use to resolve our object from a name to an actual Java object. Other ORBs would require their own helper functions to provide this service.

Once we have a reference to a naming service we can use it to obtain a reference to our object,

```
NameComponent nc = new NameComponent("bottles", "");
```

which names our component directly. This name normally matches the name of the interface defined in the original IDL file and matches the name the server binds when it starts. The second parameter is the "kind" of the object we are requesting. A server might support many different variations or flavors of the same object, all referenced via the same object but of different "kinds." Our example only has one kind so we leave this parameter blank. Again, these parameters match the ones provided by the server object.

```
bottles theChorus = bottlesHelper.narrow(ncRef.resolve(path));
```

obtains for the developer's use a reference to the proxy object. The use of resolve and narrow is much simpler than it looks. NameComponents are hierarchical objects, much like a path to a file, but a path to a file does not give us the file—only its location.

SOURCE 13.2 client.java

```
//
// Client Implementation for remote 99 Bottles of beer
//

// package jwiley.chp13;

import Sing.*;                    // Our package defining the proxy class
import org.omg.CosNaming.*;       // Support for naming service
import org.omg.CORBA.*;           // support for the CORBA objects themselves

public class client
{
    public static void main(String args[])
    {
        try
        {
            // create and initialize the ORB
            ORB orb = ORB.init(args, null);
            // get the root naming context
            org.omg.CORBA.Object objRef =
                orb.resolve_initial_references("NameService");
            NamingContext ncRef = NamingContextHelper.narrow(objRef);
            // resolve the Object Reference into our context
            NameComponent nc = new NameComponent("bottles", "");
            NameComponent path[] = {nc};
            // use the narrow method to resolve our reference
            bottles theChorus =
                bottlesHelper.narrow(ncRef.resolve(path));

            // Now use the class normally
            for (int i=99; i > 0; i--)
            {
                theChorus.Chorus(i +
                    " bottles of beer on the wall,");
                theChorus.Chorus(i + " bottles of beer.");
                theChorus.Chorus(
                    "If one of the bottles should happen to fall,");
                theChorus.Chorus(
                    i-1 + " bottles of beer on the wall.");
            }
        }
        catch (Exception e)
        {
            System.out.println("ERROR : " + e) ;
            e.printStackTrace(System.out);
        }
    }
}
```

The resolve method actually goes out to the NameServer and returns a reference to a generic object, which is then "narrowed" into a reference to a specific object type rather then a generic object. We will discuss narrowing in a later section, but for now just take for granted that it's a "cast" operation from one object type to another.

TIP Naming contexts appear complex but are in fact quite simple. Naming contexts are really a hierarchical name structure that can be used to support any of a number of naming schema (for example, x.500 or something as simple as a directory structure under Windows 95) . In our examples we use the nameserver that was provided with the JavaIDL SDK.

Server Skeleton Functions. The next step is to fill in the server functions. The server side looks quite similar to the client side and is shown in Source 13.3.

As with the client, the server is much simpler than it looks. The first section of the server is concerned with the actual implementation of the method we defined in bottles.idl.

```
class singServant extends _bottlesImplBase
```

Class singServant extends the generated Abstract class and contains the actual methods that required implementation. The new statement instantiates a new servant to handle client calls and connect it to the previously allocated ORB. Note that the allocation of the ORB object should not be confused with the Naming Service, which runs to find an object. The ORB we allocated and initialized is simply a program reference to a running Object Request Broker that the server object will connect to and announce its presence through.

```
singServant singRef = new singServant();
orb.connect(singRef);
```

The final statement of interest names our server as providing the implementation of bottles via the following statement:

```
NameComponent nc = new NameComponent("bottles", "");
```

SOURCE 13.3 server.java

```
//
// Server.java
// If successful should print 99 bottles of beer!
//
package jwiley.chp13;
import Sing.*;
```

```
import org.omg.CosNaming.*;
import org.omg.CosNaming.NamingContextPackage.*;
import org.omg.CORBA.*;

// Implement the bottles.idl methods here.
class singServant extends _bottlesImplBase
{
    public void Chorus(String line)
    {
            System.out.println(line);
    }
}

public class server
{

    public static void main(String args[])
    {
            try
            {
                    // create and initialize the ORB
                    ORB orb = ORB.init(args, null);

                    // create servant and register it with the ORB
                    singServant singRef = new singServant();
                    orb.connect(singRef);

                    // get the root naming context
                    org.omg.CORBA.Object objRef =
                    orb.resolve_initial_references("NameService");
                    NamingContext ncRef = NamingContextHelper.narrow(objRef);

                    // bind the Object Reference in Naming
                    NameComponent nc = new NameComponent("bottles", "");
                    NameComponent path[] = {nc};
                    ncRef.rebind(path, singRef);

                    // wait for invocations from clients
                    java.lang.Object sync = new java.lang.Object();
                    synchronized (sync)
                    {
                        sync.wait();
                    }

            }
            catch (Exception e)
            {
                    System.err.println("ERROR: " + e);
                    e.printStackTrace(System.out);
            }
    }
}
```

For a more in-depth discussion of the classes and methods required to use the JavaIDL ORB see the JavaIDL documentation, which is provided as a part of the JavaIDL kit.

Compile Your Classes. Once you have generated the stub and skeleton code it can be compiled with a command similar to the one here (note that the line was broken for display only).

```
f:\jdk\bin\javac -classpath
     "f:\jdk\lib\classes.zip;F:\jdk\JAVAIDL\lib\classes.zip;."
     .java generatedCodeDirectory/*.java
```

Note that in the early release of the JavaIDL, support classes were not part of the core JDK. The commands given for building the bottles example can all be found in a DOS batch procedure called build.bat in the chp13 subdirectory of the CD-ROM. Copy this directory to your hard drive and then update the build.bat file to correctly reference the location of the idltojava and javac tools. In addition, client.bat and server.bat files are provided for running the client and server. These too need to have the paths updated to match your development environment.

TIP If you are seeing compilation errors the CLASSPATH variable is most likely not set correctly to include the JavaIDL classes. Under DOS this can be done with "set CLASSPATH=<somedir>." For other operating systems see the appropriate man page on the shell in use.

Run a Copy of the Name Server, Server, and Client Functions. The final step in our example is to run the example. For this we need to open three shell or DOS windows, one each for the client, server, and naming service.

In the first window cd to the JavaIDL\bin directory and type

```
Nameserv -ORBInitialPort someportnumber.
```

where someportnumber is any TCPIP port that is available. In our examples 1000 was used but its choice was somewhat arbitrary.

In the second window cd to the chp13 directory where you build the examples and type

```
server.bat
```

This will run the server with the appropriate arguments.

In the third window cd to the chp13 directory where you build the examples and type

```
client.bat
```

This will run the client with the appropriate arguments.

If you were successful in building the application you should see output in the server window that looks something like the result shown here.

A run of Source 13.3 produces, with a run of Source 13.2:

```
99 bottles of beer on the wall,
99 bottles of beer.
If one of the bottles should happen to fall,
98 bottles of beer on the wall.
. . .
2 bottles of beer on the wall.
2 bottles of beer on the wall,
2 bottles of beer.
If one of the bottles should happen to fall,
1 bottles of beer on the wall.
1 bottles of beer on the wall,
1 bottles of beer.
If one of the bottles should happen to fall,
0 bottles of beer on the wall.
```

Object Request Brokers in Detail

Now that we've seen an example, let's look more closely at ORBS and the CORBA architecture in general. As we saw in earlier sections, object request brokers are the underlying feature of CORBA. ORBs are the mechanism by which clients can get access to CORBA services like naming and transactions. From a server's perspective, ORBS are the mechanism that services are provided to. The terms client and server are somewhat arbitrary and are often clouded. For our discussions the following terms hold:

- **Client.** A program that obtains an object reference and uses that reference as if it were a local object.
- **Object reference.** A handle to an object implemented somewhere else on the network.
- **Server.** A program that implements one or more object references.

One additional term is sometimes used, that of a *pure* client. A pure client is one that has no server-side capacities at all. In practice, pure clients are rare because most applications take on the role of both server and client. Consider for a moment a "chat" application. Clients of the chat application need to broadcast their messages (client-side functionality) and need to process messages from other clients (server-side functionality).

Stubs and Skeletons. The purpose of the CORBA stub is to adapt the client-side request into the ORB. While CORBA knows how to marshal arguments it does not know what arguments to marshal for a given method. Client-side stubs provide the argument descriptions required to complete the marshaling process. The stub makes the appropriate calls to the underlying CORBA to complete the process by passing control to a remote implementation of the method. Skeleton functions are effectively server-side stubs. The server-side ORB calls skeleton functions when a request arrives to invoke a function. Basically the ORB unmarshals the call arguments, builds an appropriate call stack, and calls the skeleton function that implements the method being invoked.

Dynamic Method Invocation. CORBA ORBs may support a second form of method invocation known as *Dynamic Invocation*. In dynamic invocation, rather than have a stub routine that defines the call signature of a method and handles marshaling of arguments, we obtain a reference to an object and then build the call stack ourselves. The current version of JavaIDL does not support dynamic invocation and so we will end our discussion of it here.

Typesafe Narrowing. Typesafe narrowing is the process whereby a CORBA object can be *narrowed* to its appropriate user-defined equivalent. Typesafe narrowing is the equivalent of Java casting for CORBA objects.

If we reexamine our client application we see that we:

1. Initialized our connection to the ORB, so we could do CORBA stuff.

   ```
   ORB orb = ORB.init(args, null);
   ```

2. Obtained a reference to the name server, so we could find our object.

   ```
   org.omg.CORBA.Object objRef =
   orb.resolve_initial_references("NameService");
   ```

We defined a name context to use to locate our object.

```
NamingContext ncRef = NamingContextHelper.narrow(objRef);
NameComponent nc = new NameComponent("bottles", "");
NameComponent path[] = {nc};
```

and then we used one of the generated helper functions to narrow the resulting object to something our class understood.

```
bottles theChorus =bottlesHelper.narrow(ncRef.resolve(path));
```

The final step in this process is typesafe narrowing and allows CORBA objects to be cast to their appropriate types.

IDL Basics

We've already seen a simple example of IDL and understand the basic principles of CORBA. To complete the picture we need a more complete understanding of IDL; specifically, we need to understand how its elements map to their Java equivalents.

Let's start by looking at the basics of IDL and then compare IDL type keywords to their Java equivalents.

Modules. IDL contains *modules* much like Java contains packages. Modules are defined as follows:

```
module moduleName { … };
```

Each module definition generates a directory under the IDL directory based on the module name. Modules may be nested to any level required, with each generating another nested subdirectory. The aforementioned example would generate a class as shown here:

```
// moduleName.java
package moduleName;
// Remainder of IDL definition.
```

Nested modules produce both nested directories and nested package descriptions. For example:

```
Module outerModule { module innerModule { …};  };
```

would produce directories

```
outerModule and outerModule\innerModule
```

and, similarly, files with packages package outerModule; and package

```
outerModule.innerModule.
```

Interfaces. Interfaces within IDL are almost identical to Java interfaces.

```
interface anInterface { … };
```

would produce

```
public interface anInterface
    extends org.omg.CORBA.Object { … };
```

in the accompanying generated Java file.

Operations. IDL defines operations within interfaces. Operations map directly to Java methods but have some additional argument qualifiers based on how the parameters are to be used. By default, operations pass their parameters by value; that is, a copy of the input parameter is passed to the underlying function. Passing by value reduces call overhead—changes to the underlying variables need not be tracked for return to the caller—but differs from the traditional Java model of call by reference. To achieve the same result as a call by reference, IDL provides three additional operation argument modifiers: in, inout, and out. In implies pass by value, and is the default and need not be specified. Out implies pass by result: changes made in the underlying method are returned to the caller. Values defined as out should NOT be used as input to the underlying implementation as there is no guarantee that the input value will be available to the implemented method. Inout most closely matches the Java model. Parameters passed as inout will contain their input value when supplied to the underlying function and return any changes made. Last, the return value of the call will be the return value of the underlying implementation.

Attributes. Attributes are like single-argument operations. They can either return or send parameters to the underlying methods. An attribute will generate both assessor and mutator methods unless marked readonly, in which case only assessor methods will be defined.

```
attribute string imReadWrite;
readonly attribute string imReadOnly;
```

Attributes can only be defined within interfaces; it makes no sense to define attributes within a module as it has no implementation. The two attributes defined previously would generate three methods: an accessor/mutator method for the read/write attribute, and an accessor only for the readonly method.

```
// Generated Java
String imReadWrite() throws org.omg.CORBA.SystemException;
void imReadWrite(String arg) throws org.omg.CORBA.SystemException;
String imReadOnly() throws org.omg.CORBA.SystemException;
```

It is important to understand that CORBA objects can be implemented in any language. Because of this there are no analogies to private and public and the other method and data access modifiers that Java programmers are so used to. This is because there is no guarantee on how these "objects" are implemented. CORBA objects could be implemented in a non-object-oriented language like C or even COBOL!

Inheritance. As we all know, inheritance is a way of extending the functionality of module without writing additional code by basically extending the definition of the parent class. Inheritance in IDL allows for one interface to extend the functionality of another and is defined as

```
Interface parent { // some methods here};
Interface child: parent { // more methods on top of the parent methods };
```

TABLE 13.3 Simple Data Types

IDL	*Java*	*Description/Differences*
Boolean	boolean	Standard meaning of boolean
Char	char	IDL char is 8 bit mapped to the 16-bit UNICODE character set
Octet	byte	Standard meaning
Short/unsigned short	short	16-bit integer
String/wstring	java.lang.string	IDL supports bounded and unbounded strings. Both mapped to Java strings.
Long/unsigned long	int	32-bit integer
Long long	Long	64-bit signed integer
Float	float	Standard IEEE float
Double	double	Standard IEEE double

IDL differs somewhat from Java in that it allows for multiple inheritance of interfaces. On the surface this appears to violate the Java principle of not allowing multiple inheritance. We must remember that IDL defines only interfaces. Likewise, Java supports multiple inheritance of interfaces. We must remember that interfaces are only signatures, and that by extending from more than one interface we are simply stating that we will implement more methods. We are NOT inheriting implementations from multiple classes. This should be obvious since there are no data members in an IDL, just accessor and mutator methods. This allows CORBA to mimic object-oriented principles even using procedural languages like C and Fortran.

IDL-to-Java Mappings. With an understanding of modules, interfaces, operations, and attributes, let's move on to the basic IDL to Java-type mappings. (Note that the mapping of Java types to IDL types has yet to be formalized. The descriptions given in this chapter match the Java IDL language mappings submitted to the OMG.)

In addition to the standard simple types, IDL also supports enum, union, and structure. Enums are handled by generating a public final class as shown here. The interval variables of the enum are mapped to the values 0,1, 2, and so forth. (While the generated code is fairly long for enums, unions, and structures, it is quite interesting to review, and so for these types we show the complete generated class.)

enum

IDL	***Java***
`enum enumExample` `{value1, value2, value3 };`	see below

IDL:

```
enum enumExample
{value1, value2, value3 };
```

Java:

```
public final class enumExample {
     public static final int _value1 = 0,
                             _value2 = 1,
                             _value3 = 2;
     public static final enumExample value1 =
           new enumExample(_value1);
     public static final enumExample value2 =
           new enumExample(_value2);
     public static final enumExample value3 =
           new enumExample(_value3);
     public int value() {
         return _value;
     }
     public static final enumExample
             from_int(int i)  throws
                org.omg.CORBA.BAD_PARAM {
           switch (i) {
             case _value1:
                 return value1;
             case _value2:
                 return value2;
             case _value3:
                 return value3;
             default:
               throw new
               org.omg.CORBA.BAD_PARAM();
           }
     }
     private enumExample(int _value){
         this._value = _value;
     }
     private int _value;
}
```

Unions. IDL supports the concept of a discriminated union as shown. The purpose of a discriminated union is to have a simple structure that may contain many different object types at run time. Compilers and calculators and similar applications might want to make use of a discriminated union. IDL unions are mapped to Java final classes. The Java class provides simple constructor and accessor methods for the discriminator and a public method for each of the values whose name is based on the original union field name.

IDL	*Java*
```union unionExample switch (short)```	

IDL

```
union unionExample switch (short)
{
      case 0: short sValue;
      case 1: long lValue;
      case 2:
      case 3:
             float fValue;
      default: boolean bBoolean;
};
```

Java

```
Public final class unionExample {
    // instance variables
    private boolean __initialized;
    private short __discriminator;
    private java.lang.Object __value;
    private short _default = 4;
    // constructor
    public unionExample() {
       __initialized = false;
       __value = null;
    }
    // discriminator accessor
    public short discriminator() throws
org.omg.CORBA.BAD_OPERATION {
       if (!__initialized) {
           throw new
org.omg.CORBA.BAD_OPERATION();
       }
       return __discriminator;
    }
    // branch constructors and get and set
accessors
    public short sValue() throws
org.omg.CORBA.BAD_OPERATION {
       if (!__initialized) {
           throw new
org.omg.CORBA.BAD_OPERATION();
       }
       switch (__discriminator) {
       case (short) (0L):
           break;
       default:
           throw new
org.omg.CORBA.BAD_OPERATION();
       }
       return ((org.omg.CORBA.ShortHolder)
__value).value;
    }
    public void sValue(short value) {
       __initialized = true;
       __discriminator = (short) (0L);
       __value = new
org.omg.CORBA.ShortHolder(value);
    }
    public int lValue() throws
org.omg.CORBA.BAD_OPERATION {
       if (!__initialized) {
           throw new
org.omg.CORBA.BAD_OPERATION();
       }
       switch (__discriminator) {
```

IDL	*Java*

```
      case (short) (1L):
         break;
      default:
         throw new
org.omg.CORBA.BAD_OPERATION();
      }
      return ((org.omg.CORBA.IntHolder)
__value).value;
   }
   public void lValue(int value) {
      __initialized = true;
      __discriminator = (short) (1L);
      __value = new
org.omg.CORBA.IntHolder(value);
   }
   public float fValue() throws
org.omg.CORBA.BAD_OPERATION {
      if (!__initialized) {
         throw new
org.omg.CORBA.BAD_OPERATION();
      }
      switch (__discriminator) {
      case (short) (2L):
      case (short) (3L):
         break;
      default:
         throw new
org.omg.CORBA.BAD_OPERATION();
      }
      return ((org.omg.CORBA.FloatHolder)
__value).value;
   }
   public void fValue(float value) {
      __initialized = true;
      __discriminator = (short) (2L);
      __value = new
org.omg.CORBA.FloatHolder(value);
   }
   public boolean bBoolean() throws
org.omg.CORBA.BAD_OPERATION {
      if (!__initialized) {
         throw new
org.omg.CORBA.BAD_OPERATION();
      }
      switch (__discriminator) {
      default:
         break;
      case (short) (0L):
      case (short) (1L):
```

IDL	*Java*
	``` case (short) (2L): case (short) (3L): throw new org.omg.CORBA.BAD_OPERATION(); } return ((org.omg.CORBA.BooleanHolder) __value).value; } public void bBoolean(boolean value) { __initialized = true; __discriminator = (short) _default; __value = new org.omg.CORBA.BooleanHolder(value); } }```

```
            case (short) (2L):
            case (short) (3L):
                throw new
org.omg.CORBA.BAD_OPERATION();
            }
            return
((org.omg.CORBA.BooleanHolder)
__value).value;
        }
        public void bBoolean(boolean value) {
            __initialized = true;
            __discriminator = (short) _default;
         __value = new
org.omg.CORBA.BooleanHolder(value);
        }
}
```

Structs. Structures are handled almost exactly like Java classes that have no methods and translate into a final class as shown. The final class generated by the IDL compiler is much simpler than a union and contains a no-arg constructor and a constructor that takes one argument for each of the structure fields.

IDL

```
struct structExample
{
      boolean aBool;
      long   aLong;
};
```

Java

```
Public final class structExample
    // instance variables
    public boolean aBool;
    public int aLong;
    // constructors
    public structExample() { }
    public structExample(boolean __aBool, int
__aLong) {
        aBool = __aBool;
        aLong = __aLong;
    }
```

Typedefs. IDL supports typedefs much like C and C++ typedefs. Typedefs based on native types such as bytes, chars, and so on, are represented in the resulting Java code in their native type. Other types are simply unwound until a native type or the underlying definition is returned. For example, the following code generates no special definitions, just additional helper functions that perform the name translations back to the original types.

IDL	*Java*

`Typedef long alongExample;`
`typedef structExample structAlias;`
	`structAliasHelper.java and`
	`alongExampleHelper.java generated but no`
	`additional type based private classes.`

Constants. Constants are handled slightly differently, based on whether they are defined inside or outside a package.

IDL	*Java*

`// Constant outside a package`
`const long aLongValue=123;`
	`Public final class aLongValue {`
	`    public static final int`
	`      value = (int)  (123L);`
	`};`

`// Constant inside a package`
`interface longInterface`
`{`
`    const long aNotherValue = 321;`
`};`
	`public interface longInterface`
	`    extends org.omg.CORBA.Object {`
	`    public static final int aNotherValue =`
	`(int)  (321L);`
	`}`

Exceptions. Exceptions are mapped in a fashion similar to structures based on the following hierarchy:

```
                    java.lang.Object
                           |
                   java.lang.Throwable
                           |
                   java.lang.Exception
                           |
                    CORBA.Exception
               /                         \
   CORBA.UserException         CORBA.SystemException
           |                              |
 Some IDL Defined Exception     pre-defined CORBA Exception
```

A user-defined exception generates a no-arg constructor and a constructor based on the exception arguments.

IDL	*Java*
`Exception aUserException { string why; };`	`public final class aUserException extends org.omg.CORBA.UserException { // instance variables public String why; // constructors public aUserException() { super(); } public aUserException(String __why) { super(); why = __why; } }`

Arrays. IDL supports arrays. Arrays are mapped directly to their underlying type. No special code is generated for arrays. If the user defined an array, he or she would then need to define the appropriate Java source. This differs from the normal generation of Java code from the IDL. Arrays can be used as type specifiers but do not generate specific initializations or other code—that is up to the Java developer. Arrays are often used in conjunction with a typedef to define a new "type" that can be used as an argument to a method.

```
typedef long longArray[10];
```

would require that the user declare an appropriate variable such as

```
Int [] longArray = new int(10);
```

Sequences. IDL supports sequences by binding them to a Java array with the same name. Bounded sequences have appropriate bounds done when the sequences are marshaled. Anywhere the sequence is used it is replaced with the generated Java type. Examples of sequences are

```
const long aBound=100;
typedef sequence <long> sequenceOfLong;
typedef sequence <long, aBound> boundSequenceOfLong;
```

13.3 NAMING SERVICE

The CORBA classes provide a set of methods that support what is known as Common Object Services or COS. COS provides methods that support directory-style naming and referencing of objects. Special objects known as *contexts* provide this service.

The JavaIDL developers kit provides a simple implementation of COS naming service. This file, run as nameserv.bat under Windows and nameserv under Solaris, provides the basic functionality defined in the COS Naming Services Specification. As we saw in our example you must start this service before any CORBA application can take advantage of the COS server. Note that the JavaIDL name service is transient; that is, any services registered with it are lost when it exits.

A detailed analysis of the COS naming service is beyond the scope of this chapter. The interested reader should refer to the Common Object Services Specification or one of the excellent references noted in the "Further Reading" section.

13.4 AVAILABLE ORBS

In addition to the JavaIDL ORB provided by Sun there exist several commercially available ORBS.

- Visibroker is a Java-based ORB available from Visigenics, Inc. Visibroker has been on the market since April 1996 and supports the full IDL language and implements all of the mandatory CORBA features. In addition, Visigenics also provides Visibroker for C++.
- OrbixWeb is a Java-based ORB available from Ionas, Inc. OrbixWeb provides a complete client-side implementation with a server-side implementation in beta and will soon be available. OrbixWeb provides a special software package for tunneling http packets called WonderWall.

In addition, the following vendors have either announced plans to ship an ORB or have one in beta.

- IBM has licensed Sun's original Joe implementation and plans to ship products based on it.
- HP has announced that it has its own ORB in alpha testing.

13.5 SUMMARY

Distributed objects are a complex concept at best. CORBA does an excellent job of breaking this idea down into manageable pieces by defining well-conceived building blocks for creating distributed objects. The JavaIDL developer's kit goes a long way to implementing this complex technology, providing the basic tools for developing a Java-based CORBA application. Readers interested in more information on CORBA, and distributed objects in general, are encouraged to seek out some of the literature in the "Further Reading" section. These excellent texts provide a much deeper look into the complexities of distributed objects.

Further Reading

Java Programming with CORBA, 1997, A. Vogel and K. Duddy, John Wiley and Sons, Inc., New York, NY.

CORBA Fundamentals and Programming, 1996, J. Siegel et al., John Wiley and Sons, Inc., New York, NY.

CHAPTER 14

Java2D

OBJECTIVE

The objective of this chapter is to introduce the Java2D package to the reader. The general capabilities of the package will be explained, and the classes and interfaces that make up the package will be examined.

14.1 INTRODUCTION

The Java2D package is part of the Java Foundation Classes, a set of classes to ease Java application development. As the name suggests, this package contains classes for generating two-dimensional graphics. Java2D provides enhanced support for images, geometric paths, fonts, colors, painting and rendering, and graphics device interrogation and support. Many of the classes in the Java2D package are intended to either supplement the related AWT classes, or to replace them entirely. As you can imagine, many of the services offered by Java2D interact with each other. For example, the color, rendering, and image services are closely related. At the time of writing, the Java2D package was not available for testing and evaluation. For this reason, there are no examples on the use of these classes. This chapter will serve as a survey of the technology. Be sure to check the Wiley Publishing Web site at www.wiley.com/compbooks/ for updated information. When the Java2D classes are available for use, examples will be posted there.

The color support in Java2D is drastically improved, and this improved support carries over into other areas. Java2D supports multiple color models, each defined by a ColorModel object. These color models in turn define a series of channels. A channel is a single value that contributes to the overall appearance of a color. For example, a typical monitor has three channels, one each for red, green, and blue. A color printer typically has three channels, one each for red, yellow, and blue. Images in Java2D are represented in terms of those channels with two separate representations. A Tile represents an image as a set of channels. A tile can be thought of as a set of layers that when placed on top of each other, become a whole image. An Image represents an image as a set of pixels, where each pixel contains its own color information.

Also new to Java2D is the concept of a geometric path. A geometric path is different than a regular image because it represents an image as a series of segments rather than a series of pixels. It is sometimes useful to consider an image as a path, especially when performing some algorithm, such as a scaling algorithm, or an algorithm that rounds the edges of a closed figure.

The font support of Java2D is likewise enhanced. Fonts no longer have a single name to identify them. The old AWT system for font naming simply used the names of the installed fonts on the host system. This resulted in platform-dependent font support. This naming scheme is still supported as the "logical font name." Two new naming schemes have been introduced, the "font face name" and the "family name." A face name refers to the actual font being used, including stylistic modifiers such as bold, underline, or strikethrough. The font's family name is the most general name of a font, and is used to identify fonts that have the same basic composition, aside from stylistic modifiers. In general, Java2D programmers should retrieve fonts using the font face name.

One final area of improvement is system interrogation and multiple device support. Java2D represents each graphics device on a system with its own GraphicsDevice object. Available configurations of each device are represented with GraphicsConfiguration objects. Each device will have one or more configuration objects. The GraphicsEnvironment object enables programmers to retrieve lists of all available devices, configurations, and fonts on a given system.

14.2 THE JAVA2D PACKAGE

Image and Image Operation Classes and Interfaces. Much of the Java2D package is focused on images and their manipulation. Images can be implemented in two ways, using either the BufferedImage class or the Tile class. A tile is comprised of a number of channels, where each channel represents the pixel color values for a particular color channel. Most Tiles have four channels, one each for red, green, blue, and the alpha value. The alpha value indicates the transparency or opaqueness of the pixel. A BufferedImage is simply a tile with an associated color model. In a BufferedImage, the number of channels in the tile must match the number of channels expected by the color model.

Images can be easily filtered to achieve various effects. This is accomplished using the BufferedImage Filter class along with an operation object. The Java2D package supplies a number of useful operations, all of which have class names ending in "Op."

AffineTransform. This class performs an affine transform, which is a linear mapping of two-dimensional coordinates. Line properties such as "straightness" and "parallelness" are preserved by this transform.

AffineTransformOp. An abstract class that applies an affine transform to an image or tile.

BilinearAffineTransformOp. This class applies an affine transformation with bilinear interpolation to an image or a tile. This transformation cannot be applied in-place, so the source and destination objects must be different. When operating on tiles, the number of channels in the source and destination tiles must be identical.

BufferedImage. This class extends java.awt.Image and represents an image with a buffer of image data.

BufferedImageOp. Any object that applies a filter to a single image, producing a single output image, implements this interface. The output image will be completely overwritten, so existing pixels in the output image do not contribute to the result. Some BufferedImageOp objects can perform the operation in-place, meaning that the input and output images can be the same object. Refer to the documentation of the specific BufferedImageOp classes for details on which can operate in-place and which cannot. BufferedImageOp classes should be used with the BufferImageFilter class in order to apply the operation to actual images.

BufferedImageFilter. This class provides Java2D programmers with a simple mechanism for applying BufferedImageOp filters to images and tiles.

ByteDiscreteChannel. A ByteDiscreteChannel represents a tile channel for one band of an image.

BytePackedChannel. A BytePackedChannel represents a tile channel for one band of an image.

Channel. Channel is an abstract class representing a tile channel. A tile channel consists of data and layout parameters that define one band of an image. Multiple channels combine to form a tile.

ChannelCombineOp. ChannelCombineOp implements an arbitrary linear combination of image components in an image, or of channels in a tile. The linear combination is specified by a matrix of floating point values. This operation can be performed in-place, so the source and destination objects can be the same.

ColorConvertOp. ColorConvertOp implements a pixel-by-pixel color conversion on the source image. This conversion can be done in-place, so the source and destination can be the same object.

ConvolveOp. This operation implements a convolution of a source image into a destination image. Each pixel in the source image is modified based on its neighboring pixels. This operation cannot perform these manipulations in-place, so the source and destination objects cannot be the same.

DiscreteChannel. A DiscreteChannel represents a tile channel for one band of an image.

IntDiscreteChannel. An IntDiscreteChannel represents a tile channel for one band of an image.

IntPackedChannel. An IntPackedChannel represents a tile channel for one band of an image.

LookupOp. LookupOp implements a filter operation based on an internal lookup table. This operation can be performed in-place, so the source and destination objects can be the same.

NearestNeighborAffineTransformOp. This class applies an affline transformation with nearest neighbor interpolation to an image or a tile. This transformation cannot be applied in-place, so the source and destination objects must be different. When operating on tiles, the number of channels in the source and destination tiles must be identical.

PackedChannel. A PackedChannel represents a tile channel for one band of an image.

RescaleOp. This class transforms an image of tile by magnifying or shrinking the object without disturbing the relative locations of the pixels and other objects within the image. This operation can be performed in-place, so the source and destination objects can be the same.

ShortDiscreteChannel. A ShortDiscreteChannel represents a tile channel for one band of an image.

ShortPackedChannel. A ShortPackedChannel represents a tile channel for one band of an image.

ThresholdOp. This class transforms an image or tile by applying a lower and upper bound to the values comprising the target object. This operation can be performed in-place, so the source and destination objects can be the same.

Tile. A tile is a collection of channels that make up an image. A tile can contain subtiles in addition to its own channel information.

TileOp. Any object that applies a filter to a single tile, producing a single output tile, implements this interface. The output tile will be completely overwritten, so existing pixels in the output tile do not contribute to the result. Some TileOp objects can perform the operation in-place, meaning that the input and output images can be the same object. Refer to the documentation of the specific TileOp classes for details on which can operate in-place and which cannot.

Geometric Path Classes and Interfaces. Java2D enables Java programmers to represent graphical objects as geometric paths. A path is a set of line segments and curves rather than a set of pixels.

Path. The Path interface provides methods to manipulate geometric path objects.

BezierPath. This class represents a path constructed only with lines and Bezier curves. All geometric paths, no matter how complex, can be reduced to a Bezier Path. If a Java2D routine cannot perform a function on a complex path, it converts it to a BezierPath in order to complete the function.

BezierPathEnumerator. This class is used to enumerate the elements of a BezierPath. The enumerator can only be traversed once.

Stroke. The Stroke interface enables a Graphics2D object to convert a stroking primitive to a path that represents the boundaries of that stroking primitive.

BasicStroke. This class represents a stroked graphics primitive. A stroke is defined by attributes that define the shape of the pen, starting and ending points for path segments, and decorations that are applied to endpoints and points where two path segments meet.

Font Classes and Interfaces. Java2D offers improved support for fonts. Classes encapsulate the various font technologies and Java2D provides support for various complex rendering issues.

Font. The Font class represents a font in the Java2D system. This class is designed to eventually replace java.awt.Font. Fonts encapsulate two concepts: characters and glyphs. A character is a symbol that represents letters or numbers in a particular writing system. A glyph is the shape that represents that letter or number.

FontDescriptor. FontDescriptor provides information about a specific font as well as capabilities to generate a list of all fonts currently available to the system.

FontDesignMetrics. This class is used to store detailed information about the glyphs used by a particular Font object. This information includes measurements of the glyphs and hints to display the glyphs.

FontFeatures. FontFeatures are special attributes of fonts and are associated with specific characters or glyphs. FontFeatures include kerning, glyph substitution, small caps, rare ligatures, and demibold.

GlyphMetrics. GlyphMetrics provide information necessary to properly place a glyph.

GlyphMetricsHV. This class extends the functionality of GlyphMetrics by providing vertical metrics as well as horizontal metrics.

GlyphSet. A GlyphSet is the lowest-level representation of a glyph used by a font.

MultipleMaster. This interface represents Type 1 Multiple Master Fonts.

OpenType. This interface represents OpenType and TrueType fonts.

StyledString. This class simplifies the process of displaying a string by coordinating font and glyph layout with the text drawing process.

TextHitInfo. This class allows a programmer to detect where within a text field or text area a user has clicked. This information allows the programmer to easily place an insertion carat or otherwise locate a specific location within the target string.

TextLayout. The TextLayout class extends StyledString and adds more layout abilities along with hit test support.

Color Classes and Interfaces. Java2D provides support for multiple color models, each representing colors using a different mechanism.

Color. This class is designed to eventually replace java.awt.Color and is based on the sRGB standard, a proposed RGB color standard. A Color is defined by four values, one each for red, green, and blue, and one for the alpha value of the color.

ColorModel. ColorModel is an abstract class containing methods for converting pixel values to Color components. This class is designed to eventually replace java.awt.ColorModel.

ColorSpace. ColorSpace is an abstract class used to identify the specific color space of a Color Object. In addition, the methods of this class can be used to convert Colors between different color spaces.

ComponentColorModel. ComponentColorModel is used to represent most color models in the Java2D system. It can handle an arbitrary ColorSpace and an array of color components associated with that ColorSpace.

DirectColorModel. This class is designed to eventually replace java.awt.DirectColorModel and is used to represent pixels that have RGB color values embedded directly in the pixel representation.

ICC_ColorSpace. This class extends the abstract class ColorSpace and implements a color space based on the ICC Profile Format Specification.

ICC_Profile. This class stores color profile data based on the ICC Profile Format Specification.

ICC_ProfileGray. This class extends ICC_Profile and represents a specific greyscale color profile.

ICC_ProfileRGB. This class extends ICC_Profile and represents a specific RGB color profile.

IndexColorModel. This color model represents the color of a pixel as an index into a table of available colors.

PackedColorModel. The PackedColorModel class implements a color model where the color information is encoded within the bits of the pixel.

Transparency. This interface defines the transparency modes for Java2D classes.

Painting and Rendering Classes and Interfaces. Java2D provides a variety of utility classes for drawing on graphical devices. These classes implement various functions for modifying the contents of graphical devices, or for generating new content.

AlphaComposite. This class combines source and destination pixels, blending color and transparency effects.

Composite. A Composite, together with potentially multiple CompositeContexts combines the colors of a drawing operation with those already existing on a Graphics2D object. Composite objects are immutable to avoid undefined behavior resulting from a composite being modified after it has been assigned to a Graphics2D object.

CompositeContext. A CompositeContext maintains state for composition operations. In a multithreaded environment, each Composite object will have multiple CompositeContexts.

GradientPaint. This class provides programmers with a mechanism to perform simple gradient fills of a shape. A gradient fill colors an object starting with an initial color at the starting point, then modifying the color linearly as the fill progresses to the endpoint of the fill with the target color.

Paint. Objects implementing the Paint interface define how color patterns are generated for the stroke and fill methods of Graphics2D objects. Paint objects are immutable to avoid undefined behavior resulting from a Paint object being modified after it has been assigned to a Graphics2D object.

PaintContext. A PaintContext maintains state for a paint operation. In a multithreaded environment, each Paint object will have multiple PaintContexts.

TexturePaint. The TexturePaint class allows a Java2D programmer to fill a shape or area with a specific image. During this operation, the image is copied, so it is advisable to use small images with this class.

Transform. The Transform interface is implemented by objects that can perform geometric transformations of 2D coordinates. All transform objects must be cloneable because Graphics2D objects clone their Transform object when they are cloned.

TransformChain. A TransformChain is an object that combines multiple transforms into a single operation. Individual transforms are added to the chain in specific positions, and the TransformChain preserves this order. Transform objects are cloned as they are added, so modifications to the original transform objects have no effect on the chain.

TransformChainEnumerator. This enumerator is used to examine the elements of a TransformChain. Each transform in a chain is represented by an element in its associated enumeration.

System Information and Other Classes. These classes allow Java2D programmers to determine what devices are available, and what the capabilities of those devices are. Other classes in this section represent primitive graphics objects, and provide utility classes for other Java2D operations.

ByteLookupTable. A lookup table object that contains byte data for multiple tile channels or image components.

Graphics2D. This is the main class for the Java two-dimensional rendering subsystem. This class extends java.awt.Graphics and provides users with four new capabilities. Using this new system, programmers can more easily define and manipulate path geometry, coordinate transformations, color management, and text layout.

GraphicsConfiguration. A GraphicsConfiguration represents the characteristics of a graphics device, such as a printer or screen. Each device can have multiple GraphicsConfiguration objects associated with it, one for each state the graphics device can be in. For example, each resolution and color combination of a video card would be represented by its own Graphics Configuration object.

GraphicsDevice. A GraphicsDevice object represents an object that is available for use in a graphics environment. Each device has one GraphicsDevice object, and each available mode of that device is represented with a separate GraphicsConfiguration object. Typically, a GraphicsDevice will be a screen or a printer.

GraphicsEnvironment. The GraphicsEnvironment object details all of the graphical resources available on a single machine. This can be either the local machine or a remote machine. Resources include graphics devices and fonts.

TileImageConsumer. An extension of ImageConsumer, this interface is implemented by objects that wish to retrieve an Image from an ImageProducer.

Kernel. A Kernel object is a matrix describing how a pixel should be modified during a filter operation. The kernel details how the current value and values of the surrounding pixels impact the result.

LookupTable. LookupTable is an abstract class that implements a lookup table object. A lookup table can contain multiple tile channels or images.

Point2D. A Point2D object represents a location in two-dimensional Cartesian coordinates (x,y) where each coordinate is specified as a floating point number.

Rectangle2D. Like java.awt.Rectangle, Rectangle2D represents a rectangle with a point and size. The significant difference between Rectangle and Rectangle2D is that Rectangle2D uses floats for the point and size values, where Rectangle uses integers.

ShortLookupTable. A lookup table object that contains short data for multiple tile channels or image components.

Exception Classes. Java2D provides for classes that represent specific exceptional conditions.

IncompatibleTransformException. This exception indicates that a transformation was attempted with invalid transform objects.

NoSuchProfileDataException. This exception indicates that an attempt to access data in an ICC_Profile object failed because that data did not exist.

NoninvertibleTransformException. A NoninvertibleTransformException indicates that a transform object was used in an operation that required the inverse of the transform object, and that object was not invertible.

TileFormatException. This exception is thrown when invalid layout information is found within a tile.

14.3 USING THE JAVA2D CLASSES

This section will examine the interaction between some of the Java2D classes. We will examine how images are created, and how filtering operations can be applied to images.

Creating an image is easily achieved by using one of the constructors for BufferedImage. We chose a constructor that allows us to specify the width and height of the image and use a predefined color model.

```
BufferedImage  image = new BufferedImage(
               60, 60, BufferedImage.TYPE_INT_ARGB_PRE);
```

Now that we have an image object, we can retrieve a Graphics2D object from it, and proceed to draw directly into that graphics object.

```
Graphics2D graphics = image.createGraphics();
```

At this point we want to create a two-dimensional closed figure and add it to our new image. We begin by constructing a BezierPath object. A Bezier path is a geometric path where each segment is either a straight line or a Bezier curve. When we create the path, we need to specify the winding rule. The winding rule is used to determine what region is inside a path and what region is outside a path. The two winding rules are even/odd and non-zero. Even/odd traverses the path, alternating marking enclosed regions as interior or exterior. The non-zero approach marks a point and then creates a ray extending from that point to infinity. Then, each intersection of the ray and the path is examined. At each point of intersection, the direction of the path is calculated (either right to left or left to right). Finally, if the number of intersections traveling in each direction is equal, then the initial point was outside the path, otherwise it was inside the path. We will be creating a simple path for which the two algorithms generate the same result.

```
BezierPath path = new BezierPath(BezierPath.EVEN_ODD);
```

Now we will construct our path. We will use the moveTo method to add our initial point to the path, then add a few line segments and a curve, before using the closePath method to close our Path. Whenever we specify coordinates, we are expected to use floating point values. This extra precision is very useful when generating paths through complex algorithms. Since we are generating our path by hand, we will use whole numbers only.

```
path.moveTo(10.0, 10.0);
path.lineTo(10.0, 50.0);
path.curveTo(23.0, 55.0, 36.0, 45.0, 50.0, 50.0);
path.lineTo(50.0, 10.0);
path.closePath();
```

In order to enhance our image, we will define a new rule for painting that uses the GradientPaint object. This will fill our path with a progression of colors, starting with blue at the left, and ending with red at the right.

```
GradientPaint paint = new GradientPaint(10.0, 10.0, Color.blue
                                        50.0, 10.0, Color.red);
```

Now that we have created all of our objects, we can add our painting rule to our image and draw our path.

```
graphics.setPaint(paint);
graphics.fillPath(path);
```

14.4 SUMMARY

In this chapter, we examined the features of the Java2D package, part of the Java Foundation Classes. Java2D extends the AWT package, adding additional support for colors, images, fonts, and painting. In addition, Java2D adds support for geometric paths and system interrogation as well as enhanced image filtering capabilities.

We examined every class and interface in the package and then worked through an example that used some of the different classes in the package.

Java2D was not publicly available at the time of writing. Be sure to check our Web site for updates and examples.

CHAPTER 15

Package java.math

OBJECTIVE

This chapter discusses the two classes contained in this package, BigInteger and BigDecimal, and how they can be used.

15.1 OVERVIEW

The java.math package consists of two classes: BigInteger and BigDecimal. These classes are capable of storing very large precision numbers. All other math functionality still exists in the java.lang.Math class. BigInteger should be used by applications that use very large integers, such as an encryption program that generates and compares keys. BigDecimal should be used to store very high precision decimal numbers, such as the amount of time that has elapsed since the universe began.

Since these classes are not Java primitives, normal arithmetic (add, subtract, multiply, divide) are done via methods in the class. The methods for arithmetic operation only accept another instance of the same class; In other words, a BigInteger can only be added to a BigInteger. This means that you cannot do arithmetic operations with a primitive type (such as an int) and a BigInteger or BigDecimal. Primitive types must be converted to a BigInteger or BigDecimal to be used in arithmetic operations with other BigIntegers or BigDecimals. An example is shown in Source 15.1.

SOURCE 15.1 MixBigIntWithPrimitive.java

```
// MixBigIntWithPrimitive.java
package jwiley.chp15;

import java.math.BigInteger;

/** class to demonstrate BigIntegers. */
public class MixBigIntWithPrimitive
{
    /** main() method to invoke from JVM. */
    public static void main (String args[])
    {
        int         iMultiplier = 2;
        BigInteger  bi = new BigInteger("123123123123123123123123");

        System.out.println(iMultiplier + " * " + bi + " = " +
            bi.multiply(new BigInteger(String.valueOf(iMultiplier))));
    }
}
```

A run of Source 15.1 will produce the following output:

```
2 * 123123123123123123123123 = 246246246246246246246246
```

In the example just given we converted iMultiplier to a BigInteger by first converting it to a String, and then using the String as an argument to the BigInteger contructor. Once iMultiplier was a BigInteger it could be used in the operation with bi. Source 15.2 shows some more examples of BigInteger and BigDecimal.

SOURCE 15.2 TestMath.java

```
// TestMath.java
package jwiley.chp15;

import java.math.BigInteger;
import java.math.BigDecimal;

/** Class to demonstrate operations on BigIntegers and
    BigDecimals. */
public class TestMath
{
    /** main() method to invoke from JVM. */
    public static void main (String args[])
    {
        BigInteger bi1 = new BigInteger("123456789123456789");
        System.out.println("BigInt1: " + bi1);
```

```
        BigInteger bi2 = new BigInteger("54235892340857328023480");
        System.out.println("BigInt2: " + bi2);

        System.out.println();
        System.out.println("BigInt1 * BigInt2 = " + bi1.multiply(bi2));
        System.out.println("BigInt2 / BigInt1 = " + bi2.divide(bi1));
        System.out.println("BigInt1 + BigInt2 = " + bi1.add(bi2));
        System.out.println("BigInt1 - BigInt2 = " + bi1.subtract(bi2));
        System.out.println();

  BigDecimal bd1 = new
BigDecimal("123456789.123456789123456789");
        System.out.println("BigDecimal1: " + bd1);

        BigDecimal bd2 = new
BigDecimal("523423425245345.0083458982792834");
        System.out.println("BigDecimal2: " + bd2);

        System.out.println("BigD1 * BigD2 = " + bd1.multiply(bd2));
        System.out.println("The result as a double: " +
   (bd1.multiply(bd2)).doubleValue());
    }
}
```

A run of Source 15.2 will yield the following results:

```
BigInt1: 123456789123456789
BigInt2: 54235892340857328023480

BigInt1 * BigInt2 = 6695789123647728341850496630618557405720
BigInt2 / BigInt1 = 439310
BigInt1 + BigInt2 = 54236015797646451480269
BigInt1 - BigInt2 = -54235768884068204566691

BigDecimal1: 123456789.123456789123456789
BigDecimal2: 523423425245345.0083458982792834
BigD1 * BigD2 = 64620175432792007360354.8101766884198111165878835537850026
The result as a double: 6.4620175432792E22
```

The preceding example gives you an idea of the capabilities of BigInteger and BigDecimal. These two classes also come with numerous methods to convert BigInteger and BigDecimal values into primitive variable types. BigInteger also provides methods for bit manipulation and bit operations. BigDecimal provides support for different rounding implementations. To summarize, these classes give you math support for numbers that cannot be stored as a double or a long.

15.2 SUMMARY

In this chapter we have demonstrated the use of two new classes, BigInteger and BigDecimal. These classes allow you to create and mathematically manipulate numbers of any precision. We also demonstrated how to convert the "Big" numbers into primitive data types.

CHAPTER 16

Remote Method Invocation (RMI)

OBJECTIVE

This chapter introduces and explains Remote Method Invocation, the Java mechanism for remote object communication. RMI is examined from the ground up, and the required tools are examined both in their function and their use. Finally, two examples show how to use RMI to build applications.

16.1 INTRODUCTION

Remote Method Invocation (RMI) is the Java 1.1 mechanism that enables objects running in different virtual machines to communicate with each other, whether or not they reside on the same machine. RMI is similar in concept to Remote Procedure Calls (RPCs). A remote procedure call is a function call that originates on one machine, is executed on another, then returns to the first.

Why Use RMI?

RMI is designed to facilitate the remote communication between two Java objects. For this reason, RMI is best used for communication between two Java applications or a Java application and a Java applet. Due to the design of RMI, such communications can be implemented with very little code. In addition, RMI takes advantage of object serialization, so Java objects can easily be passed between remote objects.

If a Java applet or application communicates with a non-Java application, then it is not advisable to use RMI. In these cases, it is wiser to implement a more general remote communication mechanism such as CORBA, or alternatively, to implement a custom communications protocol for that application. When writing a Java client to interface with an existing server, it is usually simplest to implement the server's protocol in Java.

TIP: Byte Ordering When implementing a communications protocol in Java other than RMI, you will likely have to pay attention to the byte order of the protocol. Java uses network byte order, which places the most significant bytes first. Be sure to know the byte order used by the communications protocol before starting your implementation.

Figure 16.1 illustrates a program that updates fields in a database located on the same machine. The program probably has a function or two that it can call to perform the actual update. At some point, it may be desirable to move the database to a new machine, perhaps a high-performance database server. Since a server machine can run many applications, but has only one console, it no longer makes sense for an application to run on the same machine as the database it updates. RPCs allow a programmer to replace one set of functions in a program that are performed locally with a new set of functions that have the same calling syntax, but actually perform their work on a remote machine.

In any RPC, there is a *client* and a *server*. A client is a program that issues the request for a remote procedure call. A server is a program that provides functions that implement the functionality of one or more remote procedures. The server implements one or more functions, and the client calls those functions remotely. Figure 16.2 shows our same database application divided into client and server pieces.

The implementation of an RPC typically relies on machine-generated *stubs*. A stub is a portion of code that implements the remote communications involved in a remote procedure call. There are two kinds of stubs, *client stubs* and *server stubs*. A client stub defines a function that matches the signature of the remote function. The body of a client stub sends the function name and argument list through a network protocol to the server process. When the server responds, the client stub receives a package containing a return value. The client stub unpacks the return value and returns it to the

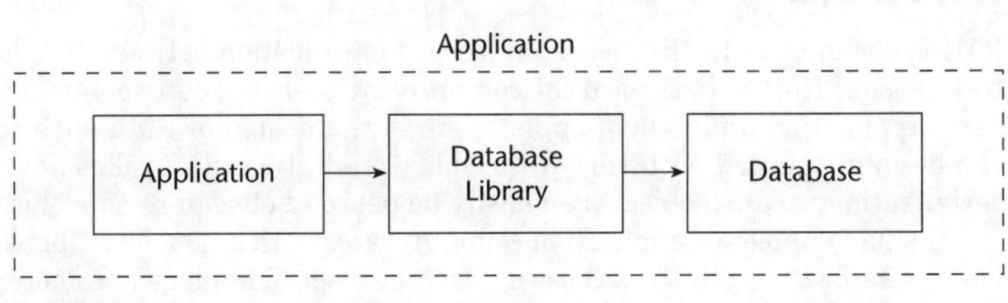

FIGURE 16.1 An application accessing a local database.

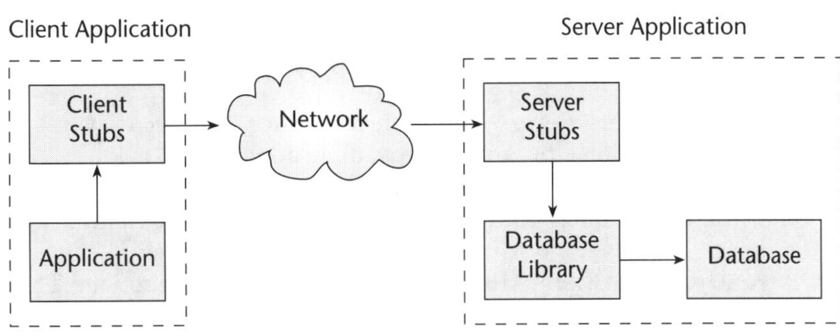

FIGURE 16.2 An application accessing a remote database using RPCs.

calling function. A developer calling the stub need not understand the complex process of sending and receiving Remote Procedure Calls; he or she can simply call the client stub routine as if it were a normal function. A server stub provides the second half of an RPC's functionality. When the server process receives a request, it sends the request package to the server stub. The server stub then unpacks the arguments and calls the function written by the developer. The server packages the return value from that function and sends it back to the client. Developers can write the functionality of a remote function as if it were any other function. The server stub handles all the complexity of receiving and responding to Remote Procedure Calls.

Like RPCs, RMI communications feature a client and a server. The server object implements a remote interface that defines the methods available for invocation. The client requests a reference to the remote interface through a naming service called the Java Remote Object Registry, and calls methods on that interface. Because client and server stubs are used, clients can call remote methods as if they were local methods. Likewise, server objects can implement remote methods as if they were normal methods. The RMI subsystem and stubs provide all the required functionality to send the invocation request to the server object, and return with the response.

16.2 THE RMI PACKAGES

There are four packages that contain the RMI classes: java.rmi, java.rmi.dgc, java.rmi.registry, and java.rmi.server. Because of the complexity and interdependence of the RMI classes, it is not possible to illustrate the use of individual classes through examples. In addition, the use of the RMI classes requires additional tools that are new additions to the JDK. After this section on the contents of the RMI packages, separate sections will discuss the tools, and work through some examples.

java.rmi. The main RMI package contains classes and interfaces that are used in all aspects of RMI.

- **Remote.** An interface used to identify RMI objects. All remote objects must implement this interface.
- **Naming.** This object is used to bind Uniform Resource Locators (URLs) to RMI server objects.
- **RMISecurityManager.** This object defines the security restrictions for Java server applications. It cannot be used for applets.
- **AccessException.** This class extends RemoteException. This exception indicates that the RMI request could not be satisfied because it violated Java access restrictions.
- **AlreadyBoundException.** This class extends Exception. This exception indicates that a request was made to bind a server object to a registry using a name that is already in use.
- **ConnectException.** This class extends RemoteException. This exception indicates that an error occurred while attempting to connect to either the RMI registry or the server object.
- **ConnectIOException.** This class extends RemoteException. This exception indicates that an error occurred while attempting to connect to either the RMI registry or the server object.
- **MarshalException.** This class extends RemoteException. This exception indicates that an unexpected condition occurred while attempting to serialize an RMI request or response.
- **NoSuchObjectException.** This class extends RemoteException. This exception indicates that the requested object could not be found.
- **NotBoundException.** This class extends Exception. This exception indicates that a server object was requested using a name that isn't bound to any server object.
- **RMISecurityException.** This class extends SecurityException. This exception indicates that the RMI security restrictions would have been violated by the request.
- **RemoteException.** This class extends Exception. This exception is a base class for most other RMI exceptions.
- **ServerError.** This class extends RemoteException. This exception indicates that the server object encountered an error.
- **ServerRuntimeException.** This class extends RemoteException. This exception indicates that the server object threw an exception that was not caught.
- **StubNotFoundException.** This class extends RemoteException. This exception indicates that a required stub or skeleton class was not found while attempting to invoke a remote method.
- **UnexpectedException.** This class extends RemoteException. This exception indicates that an unexpected condition occurred during the remote method invocation.
- **UnknownHostException.** This class extends RemoteException. This exception indicates that the host specified in an RMI request could not be found.

- **UnmarshalException.** This class extends RemoteException. This exception indicates that an unexpected condition occurred while attempting to deserialize an RMI request or response.

java.rmi.dgc. The RMI distributed garbage collection package contains classes and interfaces that are used to implement the garbage collection on remote objects.

- **DGC.** The server-side interface of the distributed garbage collection system.
- **Lease.** A lease object represents a remote object reference.
- **VMID.** A global identifier, unique across all Java Virtual Machines.

java.rmi.registry. The RMI registry package implements classes and interfaces used in the implementation of and the interaction with remote object registries.

- **Registry.** An interface that describes registry services. An object that implements the Registry interface is used to associate RMI clients with RMI server objects.
- **RegistryHandler.** An interface used by the internal representation of a Remote Object Registry.
- **LocateRegistry.** This is a utility class used for locating and interacting with one or more Remote Object Registries.

java.rmi.server. The RMI server package implements classes and interfaces that are used only in the implementation of RMI server objects. RMI server objects are those objects that receive and respond to remote requests.

- **LoaderHandler.** Objects that load remote classes implement this interface.
- **RMIFailureHandler.** Objects that implement socket failure recovery implement this interface.
- **RemoteCall.** This interface is used internally by RMI stub and skeleton classes.
- **RemoteRef.** This interface represents a remote object.
- **ServerRef.** This interface represents the server side of a remote object.
- **Skeleton.** This interface is used internally by RMI skeleton classes.
- **Unreferenced.** Remote objects that implement this interface will receive notification when there are no more remote references to it.
- **LogStream.** This object is used to implement an activity log for the RMI subsystem.
- **ObjID.** This object is used to give remote objects unique identifiers within a Java Virtual Machine. ObjIDs are assigned to remote objects when they are exported.
- **Operation.** An operation is used to represent an RMI method.
- **RMIClassLoader.** This object is used to load objects over the network.
- **RMISocketFactory.** This object creates sockets for RMI client and server operations.
- **RemoteObject.** RemoteObject implements generic object behavior for remote objects.
- **RemoteServer.** RemoteServer provides a base implementation for remote server objects.

- **RemoteStub.** RemoteStub is a base class for all client stubs.
- **UID.** An identifier that is unique for a particular host.
- **UnicastRemoteObject.** Provides a base implementation for a remote object and handles all of the initialization and communications required. Remote objects should extend this class. Remote objects that do not extend this class will need to at a minimum call the exportObject method of this class in order to properly initialize the object.
- **ExportException.** This class extends RemoteException. This exception indicates that some error occurred while attempting to export a remote object.
- **ServerCloneException.** This class extends CloneNotSupportedException. This exception indicates that a clone operation failed on the server side of an RMI call.
- **ServerNotActiveException.** This class extends Exception. It indicates that the server was not active.
- **SkeletonMismatchException.** This class extends RemoteException. This occurs when the skeleton associated with a server object doesn't match the interface of the server object. This usually happens when the class is changed without regenerating the RMI stubs.
- **SkeletonNotFoundException.** This class extends RemoteException. The skeleton class required for an RMI server object was not found. Typically, this happens when the stubs were never generated, or the stub files are in the incorrect location. Skeleton class files should occupy the same directory as the server objects they correspond to.
- **SocketSecurityException.** This class extends ExportException. A socket error occurred while attempting to export a remote object.

16.3 USING THE RMI TOOLS

JDK 1.1 (http://java.sun.com/products) provides two new tools that must be used in order to properly create and deploy an RMI application. A program named "rmiRegistry" implements the Remote Object Registry, while a program named "rmic" implements the RMI stub generator. Both tools can be found in the bin directory of the JDK 1.1 installation. This section explains how to use both tools, and works through two examples that demonstrate use of the tools and the implementation of an RMI application.

The Java Remote Object Registry (rmiregistry)

One of the more complex tasks performed in an RPC system is the location of the server by the client. Generally, an RPC server is always running. It is a client's responsibility to find and connect to the server. RMI solves this problem with an application called the Remote Object Registry. The Remote Object Registry, or RMI Registry, stores a list of server object names called a *namespace*. Each entry in the namespace is associated with a running Java object that implements some remote methods.

When the RMI Registry is started, its namespace is empty. The Registry only stores information about server objects that are part of a running Java application and therefore currently available for use. Because the list of objects managed by the registry changes dynamically, it makes little sense to store information on disk. The RMI Registry has the ability to store information about objects on any machine, so it also makes no sense for the registry to search for and locate running objects. The duty of updating the registry therefore falls on the shoulders of the server object. When a server application initializes, the first thing it should do is create and register all of its RMI server objects.

In order to provide easy access to RMI Registries, Java provides the class java.rmi.Naming. The Naming class implements some methods for interacting with an RMI Registry. In particular, the bind and rebind methods are used to bind a server object to a specific name. An RMI Registry can only associate a single-server object with a particular name. The fundamental difference between bind and rebind is that bind will throw an exception if the designated name is in use, whereas rebind will replace the object already in the registry with the new object.

TIP: Using Rebind Exclusively It is often convenient to write RMI applications that use only rebind. This usage is potentially risky, because rebind will replace existing objects regardless of the type. If a name is in use by two different server objects that both use rebind exclusively, then only one will actually bind to the name, but neither will report an error. There are two approaches to avoiding this issue: either guarantee that your server objects register themselves using unique names, or verify that the currently registered object (if any) is of the same type as the server that wishes to rebind to the name.

The Remote Object registry is started by running the application rmiregistry as follows:

```
rmiregistry [options]
```

The only currently available command line parameter accepted by rmiregistry is a port number. If no port number is specified on the command line, then the registry will use a default port. Overriding the default value complicates RMI applications.

Argument	*Description*
<port number>	The machine port number the registry should use for communications. Specifying a value on the command line overrides the default port number.

TIP: Windows 95 Users A server object can only register itself to a Remote Object Registry if it has a working Internet connection. Attempting to register server objects, even if the registry is running on the same machine, will fail during the bind or rebind operations.

The RMI Stub Generator (rmic)

As mentioned previously, machine-generated stubs are responsible for the complex network communication aspects of a Remote Method Invocation including argument *marshaling*. Marshaling is the process of packaging all information concerning a Remote Method Invocation into the RMI network format. A client stub implements the same remote interface as the server object, but instead of implementing the methods, it marshals the method requests and sends them to the server application. The server stub receives the package, demarshals it, and calls the actual method on the server object.

In order to generate stubs for the correct methods, the stub generator must know which class it is generating stubs for. The stub generator does not work on source files; it only works on class files. When you execute the stub generator you must specify the full class name, including the package specification (if any). Assuming there are no errors, the stub generator produces two class files; for a class named "myRMIClass" the stub generator will produce "myRMIClass_Stub.class" and "myRMIClass_Skel .class."

The _Stub or stub class is the client stub, and the _Skel or skeleton class is the server stub. When a server application registers an object with the RMI Registry, the skeleton class is actually registered. When a client application or applet requests a server object, an instance of the stub class is created and connected to the server application. Figure 16.3 shows the interaction between all these classes.

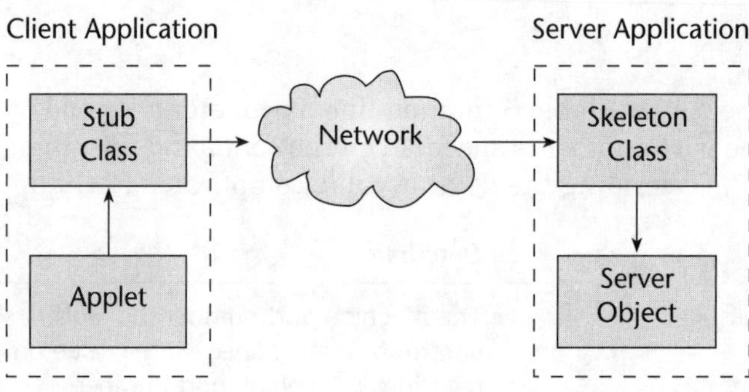

FIGURE 16.3 Client class communicating with server class through stubs.

RMI is simple to implement because most of the complexity is hidden in the stub and skeleton classes. Developers can transform a normal Java object into an RMI server object by applying a few simple modifications and generating stubs. The client invokes methods on the server object through a Java interface, so there are even fewer modifications required there.

The RMI stub generator is started by running the application rmic as follows:

```
rmic <class name> [options]
```

Rmic, the RMI stub generator, requires the name of a class for which to generate stubs. The name specified must include the package specification for the class if any exists. There are also many optional command line arguments detailed in the following table.

Argument	*Description*
<class name> (required)	A Java class to build stubs for. This class must be located somewhere in the classpath, and must implement at least one remote interface.
-classpath <path>	Overrides the environment setting of the Java classpath. <path> is a semicolon-delimited list of Java class locations.
-d <directory>	Specifies the root directory of the class hierarchy. This is the directory where the stub and skeleton class files will be created.
-depend	Forces the compiler to consider recompiling any referenced class it encounters while compiling. By default the Java compiler only considers recompiling classes referenced by source files it encounters, not those in class files it encounters.
-g	Compiles the stub and skeleton classes with debug information.
-keepgenerated	Prevents the stub generator from deleting the temporary source files it creates. By default the stub generator deletes these files after they have been compiled.
-nowarn	Prevents the compiler from displaying warning messages.
-O	Optimizes the stub and skeleton classes for speed. This may produce larger class files.
-show	Runs the GUI version of rmic.
-verbose	Causes the compiler to display additional information when compiling the stub and skeleton classes.

TIP: Not All Classes Can Be Used to Generate Stubs You can only use rmic to generate stubs for classes that implement an interface that extends java.rmi.Remote.

Calling from Client to Server

Developing a basic client-server application using RMI is actually quite simple. This section will detail the five major steps involved in creating a simple RMI application. An example is given to illustrate the steps and provide the exact syntax. The sample application implements a counter object as the server. This server object will implement one method called getCount. Calling getCount will increment the server's counter and return the new value. An applet calls getCount when it initializes, then displays the value returned from the server. This RMI application could be used on a Web page to indicate the number of visitors who have accessed the page.

- Create a Java interface defining the methods you wish to implement. This interface should extend java.rmi.Remote. Every method in the interface should be declared to throw a java.rmi.RemoteException exception. If the interface does not satisfy these two criteria, then the stub generator will produce an error and fail to produce stubs for the server object. Source 16.1 defines the interface our simple basic RMI application will use.
- Create a class that implements this new interface and is derived from java.rmi .server.UnicastRemoteObject as shown in Source 16.2. Because the constructor of UnicastRemoteObject is declared to throw a java.rmi.RemoteException, all server objects must implement a constructor that also throws a RemoteException. At some point, an instance of the server object must be created and bound to the server. In our example, we implement a main routine directly on our server object. The main routine sets the system security manager, creates an instance of our server object, and then registers itself with the registry using the Naming class. Note that the registry must be running on the same machine as the server application in order for this code to work.
- Create an applet that locates the server object, casts it to the server interface, and calls a method on that interface. Source 16.3 implements an applet that communicates with our newly created server object.
- Compile the interface, the server object, and the applet. Simply change into the directory where the source files reside and type:

  ```
  javac *.java
  ```

SOURCE 16.1 Simple Counter Server Interface

```
// File: SimpleCounterServer.java
package jwiley.chp16;

public interface SimpleCounterServer extends java.rmi.Remote
{
    public int getCount() throws java.rmi.RemoteException;
}
```

SOURCE 16.2 Simple Counter Server Implementation

```
// File: SimpleCounterServerImpl.java
package jwiley.chp16;

import java.rmi.*;
import java.rmi.server.UnicastRemoteObject;

public class SimpleCounterServerImpl
     extends UnicastRemoteObject
        implements SimpleCounterServer
{
    private int iCount;

    public SimpleCounterServerImpl() throws java.rmi.RemoteException
    {
        iCount = 0;
    }

    public int getCount() throws RemoteException
    {
        return ++iCount;
    }

    public static void main(String args[])
    {
     // Create and install the security manager
     System.setSecurityManager(new RMISecurityManager());

     try
     {
            SimpleCounterServerImpl server = new SimpleCounterServerImpl();
            System.out.println("SimpleCounterServer created.");
            Naming.rebind("SimpleCounterServer", server);
            System.out.println("SimpleCounterServer registered.");
     } catch (Exception x)
       {
         x.printStackTrace();
       }
    }
}
```

- Run rmic on the server object to generate the two stubs. The exact syntax of this step can vary depending on the classpath of the machine. Assuming that our compiled classes are accessible through the classpath, we would type:

  ```
  rmic jwiley.chp16.CounterImpl
  ```

To run the preceding example, we need to start the registry, the server application, and the client applet, in that order. In order to view the applet, we need an

SOURCE 16.3 Simple Counter Client Implementation (Applet)

```
// File: SimpleCounterApplet.java
package jwiley.chp16;

import java.awt.*;
import java.rmi.*;

public class SimpleCounterApplet extends java.applet.Applet {

    String message = "";

    public void init() {

    try {
        SimpleCounterServer server =
          (SimpleCounterServer)Naming.lookup("//" +
          getCodeBase().getHost() + "/SimpleCounterServer");
        message = String.valueOf(server.getCount());

     } catch (Exception x) {
         System.out.println("HelloApplet: an exception occurred:");
         x.printStackTrace();
     }
    }

    public void paint(Graphics g) {
     g.drawString("Number of visitors to this web page: " + message,
                  10, 10);
    }
}
```

HTML page. Source 16.4 is a simple HTML file that does little more than host our applet.

Now that we've created the four files and run the stub generator, we can test the application.

SOURCE 16.4 SimpleCounterApplet's HTML Page

```
<HTML>
<center><h1>Counter Example</h1></center>
<p>
<applet codebase=".."
        code="jwiley.chp16.SimpleCounterApplet"
        width=300 height=100> </applet>
</HTML>
```

First, start the RMI registry by typing:

```
rmiregistry
```

TIP: "Start" Command for Windows 95/NT Users To start a process in a new window under Windows 95 or NT simply prepend "start" to your normal command line. For example, to start the Remote Object Registry in a new window type:

```
start rmiregistry
```

Now start the server application by typing:

```
java jwiley.chp16.SimpleCounterServerImpl
```

Wait for the server to indicate that it has registered itself with the registry. When the server is ready to receive requests, you should see the following in the console window for the server object:

```
SimpleCounterServer created.
SimpleCounterServer registered.
```

Once these messages have appeared, start the client applet by typing:

```
Appletviewer SimpleCounter.html
```

When the applet initializes, it should display the number 1. By reloading, restarting, or cloning the applet you can witness the counter incrementing. Figure 16.4 shows what the appletviewer will look like when it has been reloaded once:

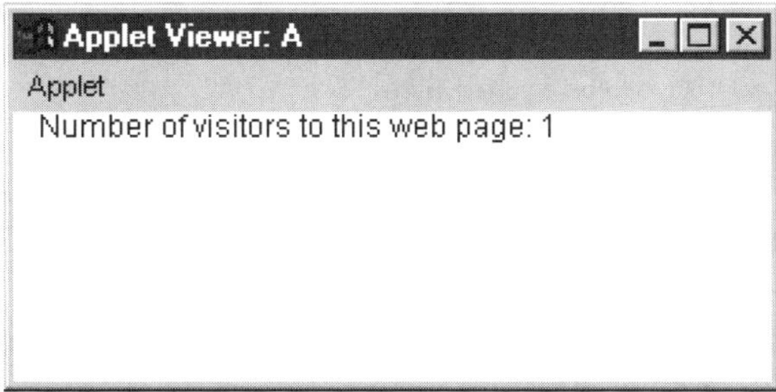

FIGURE 16.4 The SimpleCounterApplet after a successful call against SimpleCounterServerImpl.

TIP: Misplaced Stubs and Skeletons On some versions of the JDK, rmic places the stub and skeleton classes in the working directory when it should place them in the same directory where the source class is located. If this happens, simply move the files into the correct location.

Calling from Server to Client

Many times it is useful to have the client register with a server for future notification. Because RMI takes advantage of object serialization, this is easy to do and does not require the services of the Remote Object Registry. It is often useful for a client to register itself with a server application in order to receive asynchronous messages or notifications. This is accomplished by implementing a second remote interface, this time for the client application. A method is implemented on the server object that takes an argument of that interface's type. The client object calls this new method on the server object to register itself. The server method stores the interface reference for later use. The method invocation completes, but the server application retains a reference to the client. Now the server can call remote interfaces on the client application whenever it needs to.

The structure of this example is almost identical to our first RMI example. Source 16.6 is our new server object interface, Source 16.7 implements our server object, Source 16.8 implements the client applet, and Source 16.9 provides an HTML page to

SOURCE 16.5 "Callback" Counter Client Interface

```
// File: CallbackCounterClient.java
package jwiley.chp16;

public interface CallbackCounterClient extends java.rmi.Remote
{
    public void setCount(int iCount) throws java.rmi.RemoteException;
}
```

SOURCE 16.6 "Callback" Counter Server Interface

```
// File: CallbackCounterServer.java
package jwiley.chp16;

public interface CallbackCounterServer extends java.rmi.Remote
{
    public void registerForCount(CallbackCounterClient client) throws
                java.rmi.RemoteException;
}
```

SOURCE 16.7 "Callback" Counter Server Implementation

```
// File: CallbackCounterServerImpl.java
package jwiley.chp16;

import java.rmi.*;
import java.rmi.server.UnicastRemoteObject;

public class CallbackCounterServerImpl
        extends UnicastRemoteObject
        implements CallbackCounterServer
{
    private int iCount;

    public CallbackCounterServerImpl() throws java.rmi.RemoteException {
        iCount = 0;
    }

    public void registerForCount(CallbackCounterClient client)
                throws RemoteException {
        client.setCount(++iCount);
    }

    public static void main(String args[])
    {
     // Create and install the security manager
        System.setSecurityManager(new RMISecurityManager());

     try {
            CallbackCounterServerImpl server = new
              CallbackCounterServerImpl();
            System.out.println("Server object created");
            Naming.rebind("CallbackCounterServer", server);
            System.out.println("Server object registered");
     } catch (Exception x) {
            x.printStackTrace();
     }
    }
}
```

host the applet. The important addition to the example is Source 16.5, which describes the RMI interface of the client object. Because the applet is now itself an RMI object, you will need to generate stubs for it as well as for the server object.

This example performs exactly the same function as the first RMI example. When the applet initializes, it makes an RMI call to the server object to see how many times the server has been called. In this case, however, the server object does not return the number of calls, but instead calls back to the client through a second RMI call to send the call count to the client. This example then discards the remote reference, because

SOURCE 16.8 "Callback" Counter Client Implementation (Applet)

```
// File: CallbackCounterApplet.java
package jwiley.chp16;

import java.awt.*;
import java.rmi.*;
import java.rmi.server.UnicastRemoteObject;
import java.io.Serializable;

public class CallbackCounterApplet extends java.applet.Applet implements
               CallbackCounterClient, Serializable
{
    String message = "";

    public void setCount(int iCount) throws java.rmi.RemoteException
    {
        message = String.valueOf(iCount);
    }

    public void init()
    {
        try
        {
            System.out.println("Exporting object");
UnicastRemoteObject.exportObject(this);

            System.out.println("Getting server object");
            CallbackCounterServer server =
              (CallbackCounterServer)Naming.lookup("//" +
              getCodeBase().getHost() + "/CallbackCounterServer");

            System.out.println("Invoking remote method");
            server.registerForCount(this);
        }
        catch (Exception x)
        {
            x.printStackTrace();
     }
    }

    public void paint(Graphics g)
    {
        g.drawString("Number of visitors to this web page: " + message, 10,
10);
    }
}
```

SOURCE 16.9 CallbackCounterApplet's HTML Page

```
<HTML>
<center><h1>Counter Example</h1></center>
<p>
<applet codebase=".."
        code="jwiley.chp16.CallbackCounterApplet"
        width=300 height=100> </applet>
</HTML>
```

it is no longer useful. If we wanted the server object to update all clients whenever the count changed, then the server would need to maintain a list of all the client objects that have ever called it. When the count changes, the server would iterate through the list, renotifying every client with the new count value.

16.4 SUMMARY

RMI allows Java objects running on one Java Virtual Machine to interact with objects running on another. This allows programmers to develop distributed applications without going through the rigors of writing their own communication libraries. RMI is very similar to RPC technology that has been available for quite some time. RMI uses classes called stubs to perform the communications required by a Remote Method Invocation. The Java Developer's Kit provides a tool named rmic to generate these stubs.

In order to take advantage of RMI, a programmer typically writes at least two Java classes and one interface. The interface describes the methods that can be invoked remotely. One class implements the remote method as part of the server object, the other implements a client object that calls the remote method.

The Java Developer's Kit also provides an application called the Remote Object Registry, or rmiregistry. The Remote Object Registry tracks all running objects capable of satisfying RMI requests. When a client object makes an RMI request, it checks with a registry to locate an available server object.

The classes that implement Remote Method Invocation are located in four packages: java.rmi, java.rmi.server, java.rmi.registry, and java.rmi.dgc. Of all the classes in all four packages, the most often used are java.rmi.Naming, which allows client and server objects to access the registry, and java.rmi.server.UnicastRemoteObject, which is used to initialize server objects and prepare them to receive RMI requests.

We saw how RMI can be used to implement a simple Web server page counter. Two implementations were shown, illustrating the two most common uses of RMI: calling from client to server, and calling from server to client.

CHAPTER 17

Java and Security

OBJECTIVE

This chapter introduces the basic concepts of security and how they apply to Java. Specifically, this includes the Java Security Model (the Java Sandbox), Applet and application security, Digital Signatures and JAR Files, the Java Cryptography Interface, and Java Access Control Lists (ACLs).

17.1 INTRODUCTION

The Internet has radically changed the computer landscape. The days of monolithic systems that worked individually or only marginally together are gone. Over the next few years distributed computing will become the norm. In fact, it could be argued that distributed computing is already here. With the advent of the Internet comes an entirely new set of problems, both for the developer and for the provider of security. Years ago you could provide security with simple virus checking and some due diligence. As long as users were vigilant and didn't bring hordes of shareware to work each day it was possible to scan and control the introduction of viruses, Trojan Horses, and other security risks. Today's security provider needs to provide security against an active foe, a foe that is motivated by financial gains, informational gains, or just for the fun of it.

The Internet has completely changed the security landscape. Today, with the advent of e-mail, Java, ActiveX, and similar technologies, a virus could arrive without anyone's knowledge. In the past a user knew what he or she was bringing to work. We have entered a new age for security, that of the *netborne* virus. A netborne virus is much like a real airborne virus; it can and will attack your machine without any active participation on the part of the user. Simply looking at a Web page could introduce a virus into your machine.

There are several levels at which a machine may be attacked, some of which are (loosely in order of severity):

- **Annoyance.** These types of attacks include displaying obscene messages, playing annoying sounds, and the like. The cost of this type of attack is low. It normally costs little in productivity or lost monies.
- **Denial of service.** These types of attacks are motivated by a belief that "if I can't use it then neither should you." Like annoyance attacks, denial of service attacks cause little real loss. Examples of these types of attacks are applications that gobble all available CPU cycles, or generate an infinite number of windows.
- **Invasion of privacy.** These types of attacks include reading your e-mail and modifying messages. Attacks of this nature have the potential to cause real loss of money, productivity, or both.
- **Theft of data and/or services.** With the advent of electronic commerce, theft of data and services has become quite real. This type of attack normally involves stealing someone's credit card number or illegally using some sort of service, such as phone lines.
- **System modification.** This attack is potentially the worst. Attacks of this kind involve destruction of data, hidden corruption of data, or corruption of system files and settings.

Costs of Security

Security has real costs, and not just hardware and software costs, but loss of productivity and usability. It's a fine line that the security provider must walk. Security measures must be strict enough to provide real value but not so strict as to constrain use of software and hardware. Be aware, very aware, of the impact of security measures on the user. Measures that are so restrictive that the user acts to avoid them are counter-productive.

There are three principles that must be examined when attempting to implement a security policy, each of which has associated cost. The first is to maximize the difficulty of a potential attack, where the cost is that of hardware and software. The second is to minimize the impact on users, where the cost factor is productivity. And the last is to minimize the chance of a security breach, where the cost is loss of data, services, or both. All in all these three concepts must be balanced so that the security put into place has the most "bang for the buck."

TIP When thinking about security always keep *the principle of least security* in mind. The principle of least security dictates that we look for a solution that is the least restrictive. Only requiring the level of security necessary to get the job done, never more, and never less!

Concepts of Security

Security, Java security or any other, really encompasses four major areas. Java, with its sandbox, introduces a fifth concept.

- **Authentication.** Authentication is the first step in security. Each time you enter a password to join some sort of computing environment you are being authenticated. Authentication is a safeguard that ensures only trusted users have access to the system.
- **Authorization.** Authorization is the process of granting certain individuals or systems the right to access resources.
- **Confidentiality.** Confidentiality is the process of hiding from prying eyes those things that you would rather not have seen. With more and more commerce being done on the Web it's important to able to encrypt reliably sensitive information such as trades, credit card numbers and any other sensitive or proprietary data.
- **Containment.** The Java Virtual Machine Sandbox is an example of containment. Security containment is the process whereby applications are only allowed to perform certain functions. For example, Java applets are not allowed to access the file systems of the host machine. You can think of this as a built-in authorization policy. Protected Domains are a new security concept that may change this somewhat by granting classes and applets permissions based on the protected domain they reside in.
- **Auditing and non-repudiation.** Auditing is just that, producing an audit trail (log file) of the set of operations a user or application has performed. Java does not currently provide any support for auditing; however, work is under way to add auditing support.

Roles in Security

There are various roles that must be examined when thinking about security. Each takes a slightly different approach and requires different tools and techniques.

- **Clients.** Clients are what we are normally thinking of when we think security. Clients are the users and processes that load the Web pages that contain Java applets. As we shall see in the next section, the Java sandbox and its components primarily protect clients.
- **Network.** The network is the intermediary through which all network traffic flows. A smart attacker might use a network sniffer or other device to attempt to read e-mail messages or pick up passwords. Technologies like encryption and firewalls protect the network.
- **Servers.** The last piece in the network puzzle is servers. Most of the security measures we historically think about were designed to secure and protect the server. With the introduction of commerce on the Net, server security takes on a new and more critical role.

Security in the Java Environment

Up to this point we really haven't examined Java's role in security, just security in general. Java takes a multifaceted view of security. First, the Java language itself has features that influence security. By eliminating memory-related bugs, Java applications are more robust. Known problems with memory have been taken advantage of in the past by hackers by intentionally overwriting areas of memory, resulting in data being corrupted or malicious code being introduced into an otherwise "safe" application. By making the language strongly typed it becomes difficult, if not impossible, to spoof one class into another. By checking array bounds at run time, many previous methods for attaching viruses to legitimate programs have been eliminated. Other language features also contribute to the overall security in Java. The Java language is only the first step of many steps necessary in creating a secure environment. The most well known security aspect of Java is the Java Sandbox, a general environment for containing applications. The next line of defense is the Java class loader, followed by the Java bytecode verifier, and the last line of defense is the Java Security Manager. As we shall see in detail in the next few sections, Java handles each of the previously mentioned security areas. Specifically, Authentication through the Security Manager classes, Authorization through Digital signatures, Confidentiality via the Java Cryptography Extensions, and Containment via the Java Sandbox. The only area not specifically covered by a Java Security policy is Auditing and Non-repudiation, and work is being done to support this as well! Let's look at the security put in place by each of these Java environment components.

The Java Sandbox. There are two approaches to the problem of execution-time security. The first is the more traditional virus-checker-based approach where each program is scanned once for strings that represent viruses. The Java Virtual Machine takes a different approach known as *containment*. Containment is the process of running an application within a bounded environment. Within that environment only certain actions are allowed. This is the basis for the Java Sandbox. The analogy is that a sandbox is an area in the machine where your program can run (or play) safely without harming other programs or the machine.

As we are all aware, Java allows users to download and run applications. When an applet is run by the JVM it is run in what is commonly called the Java Sandbox. The minimum operations allowed by the Sandbox are for the applet run (use the CPU), get input (use the keyboard and mouse), and reply with output (use the monitor). Specifically, this means that applets are not allowed to do any of the following:

- *Read, write, delete, or get information about files.* For obvious reasons, file IO must be restricted.
- *Read any but a few selected attributes of the system.* Knowledge of certain system attributes could be taken advantage of. For example, a hacker could significantly shorten the time it takes to obtain access to a machine if he or she knew a valid username.

- *Connect to any network port on the client.* Since the applet is now executing on the inside of a firewall, connecting to any port on the client machine could be a breach of security. A malicious Java applet could, at a minimum, start sending nasty e-mail.
- *Connect to any network port except those on the machine where the applet was loaded.* Similar reasons to those of a client.
- *Load any sort of dynamic link library (DLL) or shared library.* DLLs and shared objects are not controlled by the Java Sandbox and could wreak havoc on a user's machine.
- *Start any other program or script.* The implications here are obvious.
- *Create an unlabeled popup window.* This is perhaps the least obvious of all the restrictions. But imagine an unlabeled popup requesting the user to enter a password and then transferring it back to the host. If nothing else, labeling all windows alerts the user as to where the window originated.
- *Cause the Java Virtual machine to exit with an error.* This could potentially allow the sharp hacker to exploit weaknesses in the browser.

There are other more subtle reasons for some of the Sandbox constraints but these are the most notable. The next line of defense is the Java Class Loader.

The Java Class Loader. The Java Class Loader's primary purpose is to locate and load classes as they are called for. In addition to loading classes, the class loader manages two or more *namespaces*. Namespaces allow variables, classes, packages, and the like to be separated based on where they were loaded from. Each namespace allows the class loader to enforce different security policies for the same class. The class loader performs three major functions:

- Fetch or load an applet from a remote machine.
- Manage one or more namespaces, each of which can have its own security policy.
- Invoke the class verifier on each class as it's loaded.

The Java Class Verifier. As we all know, Java code is compiled into an architecture-neutral form known as bytecode. As a final precaution, before a class is run it must pass through the Java Class Verifier. The purpose of the verifier is to examine the bytecodes for the following features

- *The compiled code is correctly formatted.* This is to protect against manual editing of class files.
- *Check for stack overflow and underflow.* Many hackers have taken advantage of array overflows. On November 2, 1988, Robert Morris Jr. developed a program called the "Internet Worm," which took advantage of memory overruns in the Unix Finger and sendmail daemons, and for a short time spread wildly over the Internet.
- *Check that no illegal data conversions occur.* Such illegal conversion might allow classes access to data it shouldn't have access to.

- *Check that all bytecodes have the correct number and type of arguments.* Missing or extra arguments could attempt to access data outside the normal method boundaries.
- *Check that all data members have appropriate privacy restrictions.* That is that private code is private, protected is protected, and so on.

The Java Security Manager. Earlier we mentioned that a Java class playing in the Sandbox has all of its calls monitored, and that certain calls may be disallowed based on where the class was loaded. The Java Security Manager handles all of this. The Security Manager's job in life is to monitor code as it's executing and apply the defined security policy to that code. For example, denying untrusted applets access to the IO subsystem, but granting trusted applets or applications the same access. Among other things, the Java Security Manager has the following responsibilities.

- Deny or grant network requests such as open a socket connection.
- Monitor accesses to system resources such as the IO subsystem.
- Manage the creation of new class loaders and namespaces.
- Manage and maintain threads.
- Control access to Java classes and packages, some of which might be able to perform sensitive system functions.

An important thing to note about the Java Security Manager is that it is the one thing that is not constant within a browser. Most implementations of the Security Manager are based on the original template code provided by Sun. As a whole, the Security Manager can be thought of in much the same way that the kernel on any given computer is thought of. When an application requests that a file be opened, the actual file open is processed by the kernel. If the user has access to the file system and directory where the file is located, then the file can be opened. If the user does not have access, then the file open request is denied. The Java Security Manager acts much the same way, granting and denying access to critical system resources based on attributes of the class in question.

TIP To this point we have spoken about Java applets and referred repeatedly to applets being loaded remotely. But applets are not the only thing that Java supports. Java supports applications as well. Local applications are granted access to the underlying file system and operating system functions based on the system privileges granted the user running the application. The Sandbox and Security Manager do not come into play at all, and the application can and often performs operations that would be denied to a remotely running applet.

We have now seen and understand some of the security threats. What can we do to protect our machines, or data, and our products and services from the malicious individuals out there? A first line of defense against unknown applications and applets is *Digital Signatures*.

17.2 DIGITAL SIGNATURES

Digital signatures are a first step in authenticating that an applet came from a trusted party. The Sandbox provides another valuable service by protecting us from applets that either inadvertently or intentionally attempt to compromise the integrity and security of our computers. But sometimes the security of the Sandbox keeps legitimate applications from doing real and useful work. Consider a word processor. I'm using one now, but how useful would it be if it could not save my work when I was done? If you could only guarantee that a Java applet came from a known and respectable source, then we might consider relaxing the security policies just a little bit and allow our applications a little more power and flexibility. Digital Signatures let you do just that.

Java Archive Files (JAR files) are archives of class files and resources that also support *Digital Signatures*. Digital Signatures perform authentication using a *Certificate*. Certificates are files, either generated locally (as we shall see in a moment), or provided to a developer via an external body, which validates that you are who you say you are. You can think of Digital Signatures and certificates like a passport for your code, a passport that can be either accepted or denied.

Java Archive Files (JAR)

Before we can begin using Digital Signatures we need something that can be signed. We could sign classes but that would require a huge overhead in both class format changes and additional API support to sign the classes. So, if not classes, what then? The answer is Java Archive files, or as they are more commonly called, JAR files.

JAR files are a platform-independent way to package class files, html files, sound files, and other applet or application components into a single package that can be downloaded as a single transfer to the client. This eliminates multiple connections back to the server for every class the applet needs to import. JAR files have the added benefit of being compressed, and thereby saving precious download time.

Before we move on there are two definitions that are important to understand.

- **Identities.** Identities are those people and companies with whom we do business every day. These are the entities that we are familiar with and would normally accept software from. For our purposes, an identity will always have a public key.
- **Signers.** Signers can do just that, sign files. Signers are special identities that have, in addition to their public key, a private key. Signers use their public and private keys in combination to apply Digital Signatures to files. Note that in this

instance public key and private key pairs are being used to sign a file, as opposed to other uses where the pair could be used to encrypt a file.

Creating a JAR file. The JDK, version 1.1 or better, contains a utility that allows users to create JAR files from one or more class files, HTML files, and the like. The syntax of JAR is reminiscent of the Unix tape archive (tar) command and is shown here:

```
jar {ctx}[vfm0M] [jar-file] [manifest-file] files ...
```

The options to JAR are (note that one of c, t, or x must be specified):

- **-c** Create a new archive.
- **-t** Display the table of contents of a JAR.
- **-x** Extract the named file or all files from the archive.
- **-v** Generate detailed (verbose) output to standard error.
- **-f** Specify a filename.
- **-m** Include manifest information from the named file.
- **-0** Do not compress. Note that if you wish to use the JAR file on the CLASSPATH it must not be compressed.
- **-M** Do not create a manifest file for the entries.

JAR examples. To create a JAR file, named myClasses.jar, which can be used on the CLASSPATH and contains all the class files in the current directory, type:

```
jar -cf0 myClasses.jar *.class
```

To create a JAR file containing all the classes in the current directory plus all the subdirectories that can be used on the CLASSPATH, enter the following:

```
jar -cf0 myClasses.jar .class somedirectory\*.class
```

To list all the files in a JAR file, enter the following:

```
jar -tf somefile.jar
```

Including the JAR on a Web Page. In order to support JAR files a minor addition needed to be made to the HTML applet tag. Source 17.1 shows an example of the additional keyword.

The primary difference from the applet tag we all know and love is the addition of the archive modifier. Following the archive modifier with the quote-delimited name of the archive specifies the name of the archive. As always, the directory name is relative to the location of the Web page. For example, if the Web page being loaded was

SOURCE 17.1 Sample APPLET Tag

```
<applet code=some.class
archive="somedirectory/somefile.jar" width=100 height=100>
<param name=param1 value="value1">
</applet>
```

www.somesite.com then the jar file above would be found in www.somesite.com/somedirectory/somefile.jar. The sharp reader will also note that even though we have specified an archive, we still need to specify the name of the starting class using the code keyword, with the one big difference being that the class is loaded from the archive.

When additional classes are required, the archive is searched first, and then a search is made of the directories relative to the CODEBASE modifier (the default behavior pre-JDK1.1).

TIP Multiple JAR files may be transferred by separating the jars in the archive statement by commas, for example:

```
<applet code=some.class
archive="archive1.jar, archive2.jar, archive3.jar " width=100
height=100>
<param name=param1 value="value1">
</applet>
```

loads archive1.jar, then archive2.jar, and so on.

Signing JAR files. Once you have created a JAR file it can be digitally signed. There are five steps to signing a JAR file. While the process of signing a JAR file may appear complex at first, keep in mind that you only need to generate your certificate once. The first three steps generate a public key/private key pair and an X.509 certificate; the last two steps use the certificate to sign a jar file. The X.509 standard published by the International Telecommunication Union (ITU) defines the format and fields required in a "certificate." Such a certificate can be used to authenticate a file, or individual, or other entity. (Users interested in the X.509 standard can find numerous references at the Swedish University Web page at http://ftp.sunet.se/pub/security/tools/crypt/pem/standards/.)

The five steps to signing a JAR file are:

1. Create an Identity with which to sign the JAR file.
2. Generate a Digital Signature Algorithm (DSA) key pair for the identity in step 1.
3. Generate an identity certificate.
4. If you haven't already, build the JAR file.
5. Calculate the Digital Signature and attach it to the JAR file.

In the chapter source directory chp17 are two DOS batch files, createkeys.bat and signfile.bat, which performs the steps shown. These batch files are provided as a simple convenience. There is no reason that the developer could not run the commands himself. Now let's discuss each of these steps in detail.

Create an identity. In order to sign a JAR file, an identity must exist for the signer in the identity database. An identity can be added as follows:

```
javakey -cs ASaganich true
```

This command creates an identity in the identity database by the name of ASaganich that can sign JAR files. The complete list of arguments to javakey is shown in Table 17.1. Specifying true for the given identity implies that we will trust all applets from this identity in the future.

The javakeys database is stored by default in a file known as identitydb.obj. For obvious reasons, this file should be placed in a secure location. The default is for the database to be stored in the JDK installation directory. You can manipulate the location and name of this file by changing an entry in the security properties file, called java.security. That file resides in the JDK security properties directory, in {jdk\installdir}\lib\security. For example, if you wanted to place the file into a location called f:\my\security\database you would add an entry that looks like identity.database=f:\\my\\security\\database\\identitydb.obj. Note the extra slashes, they are required under Windows 95 and Windows NT. Unix users should use the appropriate file-naming conventions for Unix.

Generate a DSA Key Pair. The next step in signing a JAR file is to generate a public key/private key pair for the identity specified in step 1. Again, we use javakey to generate the pair, only this time we specify the –gk arguments as follows.

```
Javakey -gk ASaganich DSA 512 ASaganich.pub ASaganich.pri
```

This command tells javakey to generate a public key and private key for the specified identity using the DSA algorithm and a key length of 512 bits. While there is no theoretical limit on key length, practical limitations, based on CPU speed and memory, dictate that key sizes be kept in the 128- to 512-bit range, with longer keys providing better security but slowing the application while shorter keys provide better performance but less security.

TIP Storing keys as files is risky business. Anyone who has your private key can spoof your identity. So, when storing key information take particular care to keep it confidential.

Generate a certificate. Once you have generated a key pair and stored them into the database you need to generate a certificate that contains all the remaining information

TABLE 17.1 javakey Arguments

Argument	*Description*	*Default*
-c identity [truelfalse]	Create a new identity in the database. True specifies that the identity is trusted	False
-cs signer [truelfalse]	Create a new signer in the database. True specifies that the signer is trusted. Signers may sign Java files. In the future we will accept as trusted all applets signed by this identity.	False
-t idOrSigner [truelfalse]	Change the trust level for the signer or identity specified.	False
-l	List all the identities and signers in the javakey database.	N/A
-ld	Same as l argument only lists detailed information	N/A
-li identity or signer	List information for a specified identity or signer.	N/A
-r identity or signer	Remove the specified identity or signer from the database.	N/A
-ik identity SomeKeySourceFile	Import the public key file SomeKeySourceFile and associate it with identity. Note that the file must be in X509 format.	N/A
-ikp signer publickeyfile privatekeyfile	Same as ik only imports a pair of files for the signer identified.	N/A
-ic IdentityOrSigners certificatefile	Import a certificate file and associate it with the signer or identity given. If the identity already exists, javakey confirms that the certificate file matches the public key already in the database; otherwise, the association between the public key and the identity is made.	N/A
-ii IdentityOrSigner	Sets information for a specified entity. Enter data as requested and finish with a line ending with two periods.	N/A
-gk signer algorithm keysize [public key file] [private key file]	Generate a key pair for the signer given using the algorithm and keysize specified. If a public key file and a private key file are given, then the public and private keys will be written to those files. Javakey currently supports DSA and RSA keys.	N/A
-g ...	Shortcut for the –gk command.	N/A
-gc certificatedirectivefile	Generate a certificate based on the input certificate file.	N/A
-dc certificatefile	Display the certificate stored in the given file.	N/A
-ec IdentityOrSigner certificatenumber certificatefile	Export the selected certificate for the specified identity or signer to the file specified. User –ld or –li to obtain the certificate numbers assigned by javakey.	N/A
-ek IdentityOrSigner publickeyfile [privatekeyfile]	Export the public key file for the specified identity or signer, and optionally the private key file.	N/A
-gs directivefile jarfile	Sign the specified JAR file using the information specified in the directive file.	N/A

required for signing a JAR file. Source 17.2 shows an example certificate with a lifetime of one year. The certificate file itself contains information that you supply about the *issuer* of the certificate. The issuer is typically the same as the signer, although other organizations are starting to provide certificates. In addition, the certificate contains information about the person or entity whose public key is being authenticated, and information about the certificate itself (e.g., its expiration date, etc.). The actual directive file is a simple ASCII document that can be edited with any text editor. The directive files given could be used as simple templates to generate your own directives.

Generate the certificate file (in our case, ASaganich.x509),

```
Javakey -gc cert_directive_Asaganich
```

which produces output

```
Generated certificate from directive file cert_directive_ASaganich.
```

In addition to the certificate directive file itself, javakey uses the private key in the database to produce the x509 certificate using the out.file directive. (For more information about the format of certificate files, see the JavaSoft Web site or the online documentation with the JDK at http://java.sun.com/products.)

SOURCE 17.2 Sample certificate directive

```
# cert_directive_ASaganich
# Sample certificate for the ASaganich identity

# the id of the signer
# the issuer and the signer do not have to match.
# for our example they do.
issuer.name=ASaganich

# the cert to use for the signing
issuer.cert=1

# the id of the subject
subject.name=ASaganich

# the components of the X500 name for the subject
subject.real.name=ASaganich
subject.org.unit=Java for C/C++ Programmers
subject.org=John Wiley and Sons, Publishing
subject.country=US

# Various parameters: start and end date for validity and expiration
# of the certificate. Serial number. File to which to output the certificate.
start.date=1 Jan 1997
end.date=31 Dec 1997
serial.number=1000
out.file=ASaganich.x509
```

Generate the JAR file. Generating the certificate is the last real step in signing a JAR file. The remaining two steps will be repeated over and over for each new JAR file that is signed by the identity we have just created. Generate the jar file as follows:

```
jar -cf signedTestJar.jar testJar.class testJar.html
```

You can now sign the jar file with the signing directive shown in Source 17.3.

Sign the JAR file. The last step is to apply the signature to the JAR file. We use the signature file shown in the prior figure to identify which identity to sign the jar with. It is possible for more than one identity to sign a JAR file, but each signature must be in a separate file.

```
javakey -gs sign_directive_ASaganich signedtest.jar
```

which produces output

```
Creating entry: META-INF\SIGAS.SF
Creating entry: META-INF\SIGAS.DSA
Adding entry: testjar.class
Adding entry: testjar.html
Signed JAR file signedTestJar.jar using directive file
sign_directive_ASaganich.
```

Finally, you can test the JAR file by using appletviewer and the testjar.html file found in the chp17 directory. Using applet viewer you can test the application by executing the html page testJar.html. Source 17.4 shows a Java applet that queries the

SOURCE 17.3 Sample signature directive.

```
# Sample signature directive
# Jar signing directive. This is the directive file used by javakey to
# sign a jar file.

# Which signer to use. This must be in the system"s database.
signer=AnIdentity

# Cert number to use for this signer. This determines which
# certificate will be included in the PKCS7 block. This is mandatory
# and is 1 based.
cert=1

# Cert chain depth of a chain of certificate to include. This is
# currently not supported.
chain=0

# The name to give to the signature file and associated signature block
signature.file=SigAS
```

SOURCE 17.4 testJar.java

```
/**
 * testJar.java
 * Under normal circumstances this applet would raise a security exception.
 *
 * @version Version 1.0
 * @author  Al Saganich
 *
 */

import java.awt.*;
import java.io.*;
import java.lang.*;
import java.applet.*;
import java.util.Enumeration;
import java.util.Properties;

public class testJar extends Applet
{
    int pos = 10;
    final int totalOpen = 10;
    final int totalProtected = 3;
    String openKeys[] = new String[totalOpen];
    String protectedKeys[] = new String[totalProtected];

    public void init()
    {
        openKeys[0] = new String("java.version");
        openKeys[1] = new String("java.vendor");
        openKeys[2] = new String("java.vendor.url");
        openKeys[3] = new String("java.class.version");
        openKeys[4] = new String("os.name");
        openKeys[5] = new String("os.arch");
        openKeys[6] = new String("os.version");
        openKeys[7] = new String("file.separator");
        openKeys[8] = new String("path.separator");
        openKeys[9] = new String("line.separator");
        protectedKeys[0] = new String("user.name");
        protectedKeys[1] = new String("user.home");
        protectedKeys[2] = new String("user.dir");

    }

public void paint(Graphics g)
{
    int y = 10;

    g.drawString("Attempting to access open system properties", 10,
                 y+=10);
    System.out.println("Attempting to access open system properties");
    for (int i = 0; i < totalOpen; i++)
    {
```

```
        try
        {
            String value = System.getProperty(openKeys[i]);
            g.drawString(openKeys[i] + ":= "" + value + """, 10, y+=10);
            System.out.println(openKeys[i] + ":= "" + value + """);
        }
        catch (SecurityException e)
        {
            g.drawString("System.getProperty(" +openKeys[i] +
                    "): caught security exception", 10, y+=10);
            System.out.println("System.getProperty(" +openKeys[i] +
                    "): caught security exception");
        }
        catch (Exception e)
        {
            g.drawString("System.getProperty(" +openKeys[i] +
                    "): caught exception" + e , 10, y+=10);
            System.out.println("System.getProperty(" +openKeys[i] +
                    "): caught exception" + e );
        }
    }
    g.drawString("Attempting to access protected system properties", 10,
            y+=10);
    System.out.println("Attempting to access protected system properties");
    for (int i = 0; i < totalProtected; i++)
    {
        try
        {
            String value = System.getProperty(protectedKeys[i]);
            g.drawString(protectedKeys[i] + ":= "" + value + '"", 10,
                    y+=10);
            System.out.println(protectedKeys[i] + ":= '" + value + "'");
        }
        catch (SecurityException e)
        {
            g.drawString("System.getProperty(" +protectedKeys[i] +
                   "): caught security exception", 10, y+=10);
            System.out.println("System.getProperty(" +protectedKeys[i] +
                   "): caught security exception");
        }
        catch (Exception e)
        {
            g.drawString("System.getProperty(" +protectedKeys[i] +
                 "): caught exception" + e , 10, y+=10);
            System.out.println("System.getProperty(" +protectedKeys[i] +
                 "): caught exception" + e );
        }
    }
  }
}
```

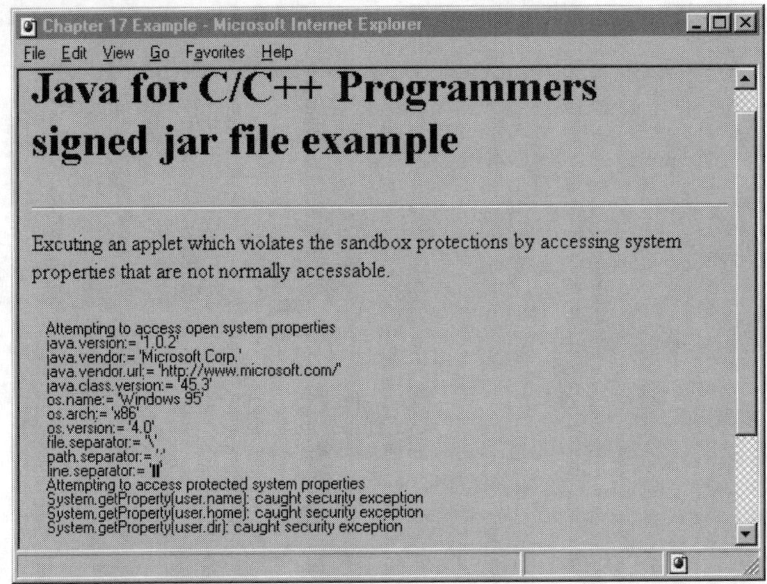

FIGURE 17.1 testJar failure.

system for a set of protected and unprotected system attributes. Without a signed JAR file the protected attributes cause a security exception. On the other hand, if the applet is run via a signed JAR file, then the protected attribute accesses are allowed.

A run of testJar.html (via Microsoft Internet Explorer v3.02, which does not support signed JAR files) produced Figure 17.1.

As the figure shows, the last three requests failed with security errors. Running the same file from within the HotJava browser, which supports signed JAR files, produces Figure 17.2.

We've seen in detail how to create an archive file. Now that we understand the process, the question becomes, when do we use an archive file, and conversely, when do we not use one? At first glance it appears to make sense to JAR everything in sight. After all, JAR files have several benefits like small size due to compression and are transferred in a single http request. For small applets using a limited number of classes this approach is in fact a valid one. But what about larger projects? What about a project with many classes, some of which are hardly ever used? Before you JAR all the files in your applet, think about which are commonly used and which are not? Does the overhead of downloading all the files at once make sense?

One of the areas that we specifically did not discuss is how keys and certificates are managed and transferred between different parties. In the financial industry, it is

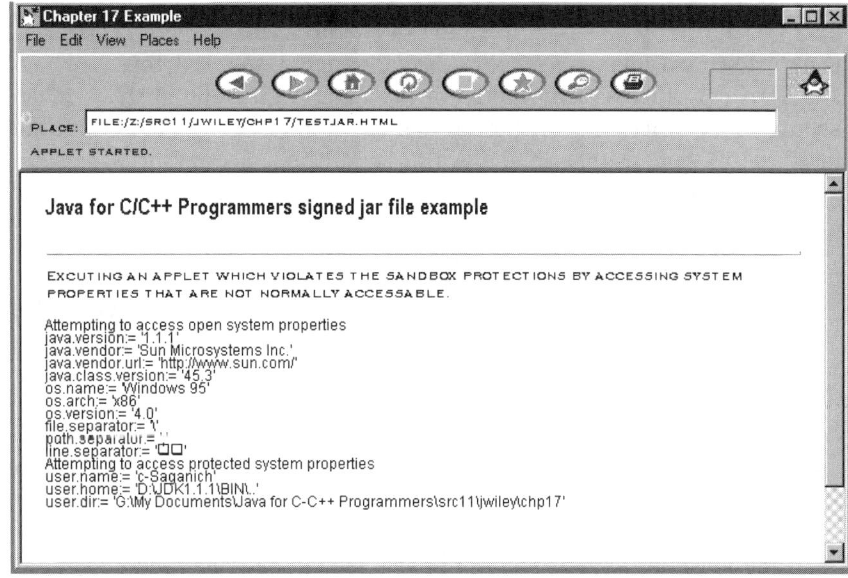

FIGURE 17.2 testJar success.

not uncommon to use secure bonded couriers to deliver sensitive documents. Registered mail and similar services could also be used. Today it is the problem of the users of security to determine how keys and certificates are transferred from one location to another. However, these certificates have generated an entirely new industry; an industry centered on the generation, management, and delivery of certificates and keys. Verisign, Inc. (http://www.verisign.com) is an example of such a company and provides certificates for use with Microsoft's Authenticode, JAR files, and other cryptography users.

Digital Signatures really boil down to the issue of trust. Who on the network do you trust? The user and developer alike need to examine closely who is trusted. Just because an application comes with a nice neat Digital Signature doesn't mean you should trust the source. We trust our coworkers and our bankers and others implicitly. But a flashy Digital Signature is not a guarantee that the applet won't do anything bad. Always be careful who you trust! A perfect example of this is the Internet Exploder ActiveX control. On June 17, 1996, Fred McLain posted an ActiveX control signed with his personal key, which was provided by Verisign.com. The control would, when loaded, shut down a Windows 95 computer that supported green or power-saving modes. More on the ActiveX Exploder can be found at http://www.halcyon.com/mclain/ActiveX/Welcome.html.

17.3 JAVA.SECURITY PACKAGE

The java.security API is a new part of the java core API. The classes and interfaces of the java.security package cover a broad range of security topics. The current release of the JDK contains API methods for creating digital signatures, message digests, and secure hash functions. In the following sections we will introduce the concepts of the java security package, and see examples of the concepts in use.

The java.security class is built around two core concepts; specifically, Providers and Engines.

- **Providers.** The core JDK includes a single Cryptography Package Provider, or CPP for short. However, the architecture is such that any number of CPPs may be used. CPPs provide or implement specific security algorithms and policies. The JDK ships with a default provider, SUN. The SUN provider contains an implementation of DSA (Digital Signature Algorithm) and implementations of Message Digest 5 and Secure Hashing Algorithms; both of which will be detailed in a later section.
- **Engines.** Cryptography engines are the implementations of the algorithms and interfaces provided by CPPs. The purpose of the engine classes is to provide a way to use the basic security classes without regard to who implemented them or how they were implemented. Applications request the specific type of algorithm they wish to use without regard to how the algorithm was implemented. With this type of architecture, the underlying algorithms may be replaced in the future with faster or more robust versions, without affecting the developer.

  Six sets of classes make up the java.security core as it ships today. They are:

- **Provider classes.** These classes implement a specific set of algorithms.
- **The Security class.** The Security class manages the provider classes.
- **Message Digest class.** This class provides implementations of the MD5 and SHA-1 algorithms. Message digests are ways to digitally stamp a message or file with a "fingerprint." Such a fingerprint can be used to tell if a message was modified or tampered with in some way.
- **Signature classes.** Signature classes provide a way to apply a Digital Signature to a file. Currently supported are the RSA and DSA algorithms. Digital Signatures are a way to sign a file using a private key so that the recipient can read a short signature and verify the authenticity and integrity of a message to be sure who sent the message and that it was not altered during transfer.
- **KeyGenerator classes.** These classes are support for the signature classes that require the use of public key/private key pairs.
- **Key Management classes.** These provide ways to manage keys associated with real identities much like we saw in the prior sections.

Provider Classes

Cryptography Package Providers (CPPs) ultimately supply all algorithms and implementations. Providers are implemented via the provider class, which implements a way by which multiple security providers may be searched for a specific implementation of an algorithm.

TIP While it is beyond the scope of this chapter to delve deeply into how providers are actually implemented and configured into the JDK, it is still important to know that many different security providers can exist and the developer/system manager can specify the search order of these providers. This provides a robust and extensible architecture that can take advantage of improvements and advancements in the security classes as they become available.

Each engine class in the java.security API provides a getInstance method that allows the developer to select an algorithm and optionally a provider. When providers are installed, they are installed in a specific *preference* order. This preference order defines how algorithms will be supplied. For example, if provider A and provider B both provide an RSA algorithm, but provider B is higher in the preference order, then provider B's algorithm will be chosen over provider A's. For example, if we wanted an implementation of an RSA algorithm and were not interested in which provider supplied it, we could obtain a copy as follows:

```
Signature rsa = Signature.getInstance("RSA","");
```

If no provider existed for the RSA algorithm a NoSuchAlgorithmException would be raised. Such a call is an example of a *factory method*. Factory methods are static class methods that return instances of objects that implement the request. (Those interested in more information on providers—for example, how to install new providers or indicate preference order—should see the JDK online documentation under the heading *Java Cryptography Architecture*.)

Information about installed providers can be obtained by using the getProviders method. Information about a specific provider can be obtained via the getName, getVersion, and getInfo methods on any instance of a provider returned by the getInstance method. Source 17.4 demonstrates this.

SOURCE 17.4 getProviders.java

```
/**
 *  A class that prints all the currently installed security providers
 *  @version 1.1
 *  @author A. Saganich
 *  @see java.security.Provider
 */
import java.security.*;  // We use the security and provider classes
```

```
class getProviders
{
     public static void main(String args[])
     {
          Provider[] providers = Security.getProviders();

          System.out.println("Getting information about " +
                              providers.length + " Provider(s)\n");

          for (int i = 0; i < providers.length; i++)
          {
               System.out.println( "Provider " + i + " name   " +
                                   providers[i].getName());
               System.out.println( "Provider " + i + " version  " +
                                   providers[i].getVersion());
               System.out.println( "Provider " + i + " info   " +
                                   providers[i].getInfo());
          }
     }
}
```

A run of Source 17.4 produces

```
C:\java\bin\java  getProviders
Getting information about 1 Provider(s)

Provider 0 name  SUN
Provider 0 version  1.0
Provider 0 info  SUN Security Provider v1.0, DSA signing and key generation,
SHA-1 and MD5 message digests.
```

Security Classes

The purpose of the security class is to manage security providers. The security class is a final class with only static methods and is never instantiated. The java.Security class is the root of all security under the JDK. Methods on the security class can only be called for an application running locally or an applet that was packaged in a JAR file and signed by an entity known to the system where the applet is being run. (See the prior sections in this chapter for more information about signing JAR files.)

Source 17.5, GetNamedProvider.java, exercises some of the methods in the security class. Note that while the methods for adding a security provider dynamically are included here, they are beyond the scope of this chapter and are only shown for completeness.

SOURCE 17.5 getNamedProvider.java

```
package jwiley.chp17;
import java.security.*;
import java.util.Enumeration;

/**
 *  getNamedProvider returns the provider information for
 *  the provider given.
 *  @version 1.1
 *  @author A. Saganich
 *  @see java.Security.
 */
class getNamedProvider
{
     public static void main(String args[])
     {

          if ( args.length < 1)
          {
               System.out.println(
                    "Usage: getNamedProvider provider1 provider2 ...\n");
               System.exit(0);
          }
          // Note that provider properties are provider specific
          // The generate security properties are listed below.
          // security.provider.1
          // system.scope
          // identity.database
          //
          System.out.println("General system security properties");
          System.out.println("Property security.provider.1 =" +
                Security.getProperty("security.provider.1"));
          System.out.println("       system.scope =" +
                Security.getProperty("system.scope"));
          System.out.println("       identity.database =" +
                Security.getProperty("identity.database"));
          System.out.println("\n");

          for (int i = 0; i < args.length; i++)
          {
               String providerName = args[i];
               System.out.println("Getting information about " +
                    providerName);

               Provider provider = Security.getProvider(providerName);
               System.out.println( "Provider name  " +
                                   provider.getName());
               System.out.println( "Provider version  " +
                                  provider.getVersion());
               System.out.println( "Provider info  " +
                                   provider.getInfo());
```

```
            System.out.println("\n");
            //
            // Print all the security properties.
            //
            System.out.println( "Provider properties");
            for (Enumeration e = provider.propertyNames();
                  e.hasMoreElements() ;)
            {
                 String propertyName = (String)e.nextElement();
                 System.out.println("\t " + propertyName);
            }
        }
    }
}
```

A run of Source 17.5 produces the following output:

```
C:\java\bin\java getNamedProvider SUN
General system security properties
Property security.provider.1 =sun.security.provider.Sun
        system.scope =sun.security.provider.IdentityDatabase
        identity.database =f:\jdk\lib\security\identitydb.obj

Getting information about SUN
Provider name  SUN
Provider version  1.0
Provider info  SUN Security Provider v1.0, DSA signing and key generation,
SHA-1 and MD5 message digests.


Provider properties
      Alg.Class.DSA
      Alg.Alias.MessageDigest.SHA
      Alg.Alias.Signature.SHA/DSA
      Alg.Alias.KeyPairGenerator.1.3.14.3.2.12
      MessageDigest.SHA-1
      Alg.Alias.Signature.SHAwithDSA
      MessageDigest.MD5
      Alg.Alias.Signature.1.3.14.3.2.13
      PublicKey.X.509.DSA
      Alg.Alias.Signature.SHA1withDSA
      Alg.Alias.Signature.SHA-1/DSA
      Signature.DSA
      KeyPairGenerator.DSA
      PrivateKey.PKCS#8.DSA
      Alg.Class.1.3.14.3.2.12
      Alg.Alias.KeyPairGenerator.OID:1.3.14.3.2.12
      Alg.Alias.Signature.OID:1.3.14.3.2.13
      Alg.Alias.Signature.DSS
```

Message Digest Class

Message Digests are really just sophisticated hash codes that can be applied to files, text, or any byte stream, and produce a "digest" that can be used to verify that the data was not changed or tampered with. Message digests are commonly used on either end of any kind of "pipe." The send side of the pipe generates the message digest using a known algorithm, and the receiving end regenerates the digest. If any data corruption occurred during transfer, then the message digests will differ.

The Message Digest class is an example of an Engine class. To use it you must first obtain an instance for a specific message digest algorithm via the getInstance function.

Message Digests have two features that make them useful,

- It is computationally intractable to find another input stream that can generate the same message digest.
- The generated digest itself should show nothing about the input it was generated from.

The Calculate Digest class shown in Source 17.6 generates a digest using the selected algorithm and an input file.

SOURCE 17.6 CalculateDigest.java

```
import java.io.*;
import java.security.*;
/**
 * This class takes an algorithm and a file name and
 * generates a message digest based on the combination.
 * For instructional purposes the use of the message digest functions
 * was broken into three parts.
 *          Creating the digest
 *          Updating the digest with the file contents
 *      and then
 *          Generating the result.
 * <pre>
 *          CalculateDigest digest = newCalculateDigest("MD5","Somefile");
 *          digest.Calculate();
 *         byte[] result = digest.Result();
 * </pre>
 *  @version 1.1
 *  @author A. Saganich
 *  @see java.Security.MessageDigest
 *
 */
class CalculateDigest
{
```

```
    String              algorithm;
    FileInputStream     file;
    MessageDigest       md;

    CalculateDigest(String inalgorithm, String infileName)
    throws FileNotFoundException
    {
        algorithm = inalgorithm;
        // May throw file not found.
        file = new FileInputStream(infileName);
    }

    public void Calculate() throws NoSuchAlgorithmException, IOException
    {
        byte data[] = new byte[512];
        int ctRead;
        md = MessageDigest.getInstance(algorithm);
        while(true)
        {
            ctRead = file.read(data);
            if ( ctRead <= 0) break;
            md.update(data);
        }
    }
    public byte[] Result()
    {
        return md.digest();
    }
}
```

The three steps to creating the digest are:

1. Obtain an instance of the message digest based on an algorithm.

```
md = MessageDigest.getInstance(algorithm);
```

2. Update the digest object with the data.

```
md.update(data);
```

3. Generate the digest.

```
return md.digest();
```

We can see message digests in action in Source 17.7.

SOURCE 17.7 generateDigest.java

```
import java.io.*;
import java.security.*;
/**
 *  generateDigest outputs a digest of the file given using
 *  the algorithm supplied.
 *  @version 1.1
 *  @author A. Saganich
 *  @see java.Security.
 */

class generateDigest
{

    public static void main(String args[])
    {
        if ( args.length < 2)
        {
            System.out.println("Usage: generateDigest AlgorithmName
                                  fileToBeDigested\n");
            System.exit(0);
        }

        System.out.println("Attempting to generate message digest");
        System.out.println("\t          using " + args[0]);
        System.out.println("\t          on file " + args[1]);

        try
        {
            CalculateDigest digest = new
                      CalculateDigest(args[0],args[1]);
            digest.Calculate();
            byte[] result = digest.Result();
            System.out.println("Resulting message digest = '" +
                          result + "'");;
        }
        catch (NoSuchAlgorithmException e)
        {
            System.out.println("Algorithm "+ args[0] + " not found!");
        }
        catch (FileNotFoundException e)
        {
            System.out.println("File "+ args[1] + " not found!");
        }
        catch (IOException e)
        {
            System.out.println("IO error on file "+ args[1]);
        }
    }
}
```

A run of Source 17.7 produces the following output:

```
java jwiley.chp17.generateDigest MD5 generateDigest.java
Attempting to generate message digest
            using MD5
            on file generateDigest.java
Resulting message digest = "[B@1ea81d"
```

The key points of CalculateDigest class are within the Calculate and Result methods.

The Calculate method takes the selected algorithm (any of the message digests from getNamedProviders can be used) and the input file and uses the MessageDigest factory object to first create a message digest object:

```
md = MessageDigest.getInstance(algorithm);
```

and then iterates over the blocks of the input file running them through the message digest update method.

```
md.update(data);
```

When the entire file has been processed, the result digest byte string can be retrieved with the digest method.

```
return md.digest();
```

The problem with message digests is that they use known algorithms that, while unique, still need to be known by both the original generator of the message and the recipient who needs the data. Signatures, on the other hand, use public key/private key pairs to sign data. If the keys are kept intact then the sender and the receiver can be sure that the message was not tampered with during transfer. In addition, since the message digest algorithms are well known, the digest lends nothing to validating who sent the data. As a result, message digests are best used when data integrity is important but content is not likely to be tampered with.

Signature Class

Signature classes solve the "known commodity" problem that exists with message digests. Since they are built on public key/private key pairs there is no "known commodity" for the hacker to use to regenerate the signature.

There are two features of signature algorithms that make them useful:

- Using the public key, the data, and the signature, the recipient can verify both the sender and the integrity of the data.
- Given the signature and the public key it is computationally intractable to generate the private key. That is to say that given the current state of technology, regarding both hardware and software, it is not possible to generate a private key

within a reasonable amount of time with the hardware available today. And that time is measured in *years* of processing time, not just days or even months.

Key Management. Before we can use the Signature class we need to understand a little more about keys and how the java.security package uses them.

As we saw when signing JAR files, the JDK supports the concept of *cryptographic keys*. Cryptographic keys are generated in pairs via the use of special algorithms. The sender of data would use a *private* key to sign a message. The recipient of the message would use the message itself, the signature, and the sender's *public* key to validate the integrity of the data as well as the recipient. It is interesting to note that this is the reverse process of encrypting files using public key encryption. While the private key is kept closely guarded, the public key is known externally and available to anyone who wishes to receive messages based on the private key.

The java.security package provides classes and methods for generating, storing, and retrieving keys.

- **KeyPairGenerator.** The KeyPairGenerator class is used to generate a key pair based on an input algorithm. The KeyPairGenerator class is an Engine class. Instances are obtained using getInstance and specifying an algorithm. Once an instance has been obtained the instance is initialized. Because all key generation algorithms are not the same, two types of initialization methods are provided. The first is for generic initialization, the second is for algorithm-specific initialization. Specific initialization comes into play where the initialization values passed to an algorithm do not conform to a common set. For example, almost all algorithms use both strength and randomness when calculating keys. In addition to these two, the DSA requires a signature format as input to its initialization.
- **KeyPair.** The KeyPair class is a simple holder class that is used to contain both a public key and a private key. KeyPair objects use two methods for obtaining the public and private keys they contain.

  —getPrivate() returns the private key stored in the KeyPair object.
  —getPublic() returns the public key.

We have already seen a utility to generate and store keys, javakey. In addition to the generation of keys, a set of classes exist that also support adding, deleting, and other manipulations on identities and their keys. These classes are:

- **Identity.** A Java class equivalent of identities as they were discussed in the signing JAR files section.
- **IdentityScope.** A subclass of the identity object that can futher refine an identity based on scope. For example, you can refine the scope of a given name from just the name, to the name within a department, to the name within a department within an organization.
- **Signers.** As we saw with JAR files, identities are further refined to indicate signers. As you remember, signers were identities that could sign "things." The Signer

class further refines the identity class to support signers in Java applications. The Signer class has methods like setKeyPair and getPrivateKey.

- **SecureRandom.** The SecureRandom class generates good-quality random numbers and will be used to seed the process of key generation.

With the concepts of keys firmly in mind let's move on to the Signature class.

Using the Signature Class. Unlike the Message Digest class the signature class is *modal*. That is, an instance of a signature class object can be in any of three states. Those states are:

- **UNINITIALIZED.** The signature object was obtained but nothing more.
- **SIGN.** The signature object has been instructed that it is going to be used to generate a signature.
- **VERIFY.** The signature object has been instructed that it is going to be used to verify a signature.

Source 17.8 shows an example of exercising the Signature class functions and the associated support classes.

SOURCE 17.8 generateSignature.java

```
import java.io.*;
import java.security.*;
/**
 * This class exercises the java.Security.Signature class and
 * its support classes
 * For instructional purposes the use of the signature functions
 * was broken into three parts.
 *          Creating the a signature key set
 *          Generate a signature
 *      Verify the signature
 * <pre>
 * CalculateSignature signatureTest = new
 *                  CalculateSignature(args[0],args[1]);
 * byte[] signature = signatureTest.Sign(args[1]);
 * boolean result = signatureTest.VerifySignature(args[1],signature);
 * </pre>
 *  @version 1.0
 *  @author A. Saganich
 *  @see java.Security.MessageDigest
 *
 */
class CalculateSignature
{
     int                     keymodulus = 1024; // Small number for speed
     String                  algorithm;
```

```
KeyPair             keys;
Signature           signature;

/**
 * Construct the object
 */
CalculateSignature(String inAlgorithm, String inFileName)
throws FileNotFoundException, NoSuchAlgorithmException
{
     algorithm = inAlgorithm;

     // May throw file not found.
     FileInputStream        file = new FileInputStream(inFileName);
     KeyPairGenerator keyGenerator =
              KeyPairGenerator.getInstance(algorithm);
     // We could provide a byte array to SecureRandom
     // but for simplicity let it seed itself.
     keyGenerator.initialize( keymodulus, new SecureRandom());

     // Now generate a pair of keys
     keys = keyGenerator.generateKeyPair();
     // and get a signature object instance
     signature = Signature.getInstance(algorithm);
}
/**
 * Verify a signature
 */
public boolean VerifySignature(String inFileName,
                               byte[] verifySignature)
throws FileNotFoundException,IOException,InvalidKeyException,
       SignatureException
{
     FileInputStream        file = new FileInputStream(inFileName);
     byte data[] = new byte[512];
     int ctRead;
      // Get the publicKey
     PublicKey publicKey = keys.getPublic();

     // Use it to initialize (move to the VERIFY state)
     signature.initVerify(publicKey);
     while(true)
     {
          ctRead = file.read(data);
          if ( ctRead <= 0) break;
          signature.update(data);
     }
     return signature.verify(verifySignature);
}

/**
 * Generate a signature
```

```
     */
    public byte[] Sign(String inFileName)
    throws FileNotFoundException,
           NoSuchAlgorithmException, IOException, InvalidKeyException,
           SignatureException
    {
        FileInputStream       file = new FileInputStream(inFileName);
        byte data[] = new byte[512];
        int ctRead;
        // Get the private key and generate a signature.
        PrivateKey privateKey = keys.getPrivate();

        // Use it to initialize (move to the SIGN state)
        signature.initSign(privateKey);
        while(true)
        {
            ctRead = file.read(data);
            if ( ctRead <= 0) break;
            signature.update(data);
        }
        return signature.sign();
    }
}
/**
 *  generateSignature outputs a signature of the file given using
 *  the algorithm supplied.
 *  @version 1.0
 *  @author A. Saganich
 *
 *  @see java.Security.KeyPairGenerator
 *  @see java.Security.KeyPair
 *  @see java.Security.SecureRandom
 */

class generateSignature
{
    public static void main(String args[])
    {
        if ( args.length < 2)
        {
            System.out.println("Usage: generateSignature
                                AlgorithmName fileToBeSigned\n");
            System.exit(0);
        }

        System.out.println("Attempting to generate and use a signature");
        System.out.println("\t          using " + args[0]);
        System.out.println("\t          on file " + args[1]);
```

```
        // Open the file first
        // It takes forever to generate a key pair and we don"t want to
        // wait and then discover that the input file is not there!
        try
        {
             System.out.println("Generating a key pair please be patient
                                 this may take a while");
             CalculateSignature signatureTest = new
                            CalculateSignature(args[0],args[1]);
             // Get the signature

             System.out.println("Generating signature from file and
                                  private key");
             byte[] signature = signatureTest.Sign(args[1]);
             System.out.println("Verifying generated signature with
                                  public key");
             boolean result =
                    signatureTest.VerifySignature(args[1],signature);
             System.out.println("Test comparison yielded "+ result +
                           "(Should be true).");
        }
        catch (FileNotFoundException e)
        {
             System.out.println("Cannot find file " + args[1]);
             System.exit(0);
        }
        catch (NoSuchAlgorithmException e)
        {
             System.out.println("Unknown algorithm " + args[0]);
             System.exit(0);
        }
        catch (InvalidKeyException e)
        {
             System.out.println("Error initializing signature object!");
             System.exit(0);
        }
        catch (SignatureException e)
        {
             System.out.println("Error processing signature object!");
             System.exit(0);
        }
        catch (IOException e)
        {
             System.out.println("Unexpected IO Exception!");
             System.exit(0);
        }
    }
}
```

A run of Source 17.8 produces the following output:

```
Attempting to generate and use a signature
            using DSA
            on file generateSignature.java
Generating a key pair please be patient this may take a while
Generating signature from file and private key
Verifying generated signature with public key
Test comparison yielded true(Should be true).
```

The generateSignature example contains three distinct parts. The first is to generate a public key/private key pair. The second is to generate a signature on a file using the private key portion of the key pair. The third is to then use that signature and the original file and the public key to verify the signature. Under normal circumstances the key pair would not be generated each time, as the example does for completeness, but rather would be generated once and the public key provided to interested parties. The message signature would then be generated and attached to a message, the message sent to an interested party, and that person would use the public key to validate the signature.

With these ideas in mind, let's examine the example.

1. The first step is to generate a public key/private key pair. The CalculateSignature object does this by using a KeyPairGenerator object.
   First create the key pair generator using a supported algorithm. Again, see getKnownProviders.java for a list of valid algorithms. Notice that both the KeyPairGenerator object and the Signature objects are factory objects and cannot be instantiated directly.

   ```
   KeyPairGenerator keyGenerator =
       KeyPairGenerator.getInstance(algorithm);
   ```

   We then initialize the algorithm using a strength (keymodulus) and a Randomness:

   ```
   keyGenerator.initialize( keymodulus, new SecureRandom());
   ```

   Next we generate the keypair using the initialized key generator.

   ```
   keys = keyGenerator.generateKeyPair();
   ```

   Our last initialization is to obtain a signature object using the given algorithm. This object will be used in a fashion similar to our message digest example, but with the addition of the private portion of the key pair to generate a signature.

   ```
   signature = Signature.getInstance(algorithm);
   ```

   Again, you would normally only generate the key pair once and then store it for later use, giving the public key to those people who would like to validate messages. Only the signature object would normally be created. It would then be fed a known private key to generate a signature or a known public key, file, and signature to validate one.

2. The next step is to generate the signature using the key pair from step 1. As you can see, the code is almost identical at this point to our message digest example.

   First, obtain the private key portion of the key from the previously generated key pair:

```
PrivateKey privateKey = keys.getPrivate();
```

   and use that key to initialize the signature object.

```
signature.initSign(privateKey);
```

   Next, use the signature object and the input file to generate a signature by passing blocks of data to the update() method and then finally returning the result via the sign() method.

```
while(true)
{
     ctRead = file.read(data);
     if ( ctRead <= 0) break;
     signature.update(data);
}
     return signature.sign();
```

   At this point the message would normally be transferred via some medium to the recipient. It's interesting to note that under normal circumstances a message digest would be used to validate that the file and its associated signature were transferred successfully!

3. The message, when received, would then be validated. The VerifySignature() method works in a similar fashion to the Sign() method. It takes a key, this time the public key, and then initializes a signature object with it. And then runs the file through the signature object, block by block, and then finally uses the attached signature to compare against the result to determine if the signature was valid.

```
Load the public key
PublicKey publicKey = keys.getPublic();
```

   Initialize the signature object with the key.

```
signature.initVerify(publicKey);
```

   Feed the file to the signature object, one block at a time.

```
while(true)
{
     ctRead = file.read(data);
     if ( ctRead <= 0) break;
     signature.update(data);
}
```

   Finally, validate the result against the original signature.

```
return signature.verify(verifySignature);
```

TIP Generating key pairs is a tremendously time-consuming process! Source 17.8 ran for almost 90 seconds on a Dual Pentium Pro running at 200Mhz consuming 100 percent of the CPU for the entire run! For this reason and no other, it makes sense to generate key pairs once and store them for future use!

17.4 JAVA CRYPTOGRAPHY ENGINE (JCE)

The Java Cryptography Engine, or JCE as it is more commonly known, is an extension of the Java Cryptography Architecture. The JCE provides support for the critical cryptography feature known as encryption. While digital signatures authenticate (or validate) the source of code or data, the JCE will provide the architecture to effectively protect content (the code or data) from unauthorized viewing or use. The basic concepts of encryption can be understood in the context of several definitions.

- **Encrypt** or **Encryption.** Encryption is the process of taking input data (normally referred to as cleartext or just clear) and a key and, with the assistance of a *cipher*, translating, or encrypting, the data into a meaningless stream of data known as ciphertext.
- **Decrypt** or **Decryption.** Decryption is the inverse of Encryption, which is taking ciphertext in combination with a key and recreating the original unencrypted text.
- **Cipher.** A cipher is an object, method, or algorithm capable of encryption or decryption.

Using the JCE is very similar to signing/verifying using signatures. First a key Pair is generated or loaded and then a cipher is selected. The cipher object is then initialized to either encrypt or decrypt and used to process text. The steps in using the cipher are as follows

1. Generate or load a key pair (the steps for generating a key pair are shown).

```
KeyPairGenerator keyGenerator =
KeyPairGenerator.getInstance(algorithm);
keyGenerator.initialize( keymodulus, new SecureRandom());
KeyPair keys = keyGenerator.generateKeyPair();
```

2. Using the getInstance method of the Cipher class, obtain a cipher.

```
Cipher cipher = Cipher.getInstance("DES") or
Cipher cipher = Cipher.getInstance("DES", "CBC","PKCS#5")
```

3. Initialize the cipher for encryption or decryption.

```
cipher.initEncrypt(keys)
```

or

```
cipher.initDecrypt(keys)
```

4. Encrypt or decrypt the data.

```
byte[] cipherText = cipher.crypt(some clear text);
```

or

```
byte[] clearText = cipher.crypt(some cipher text);
```

As you can see, the process is simple and straightforward with a few gotcha's. First, the getInstance() method of the Cipher class can take two arguments that we haven't seen before. To understand these arguments it's important to understand a few more terms; specifically, the modes that the Cipher class works in.

In addition to cipher algorithms, ciphers work in one of several *modes*. Each cipher mode determines how the cipher algorithm will operate. The actual workings of these algorithms is beyond the scope of this chapter, but simple descriptions of the algorithms are given. Two modes are supported by the JCE today:

- **CBC or Cipher Block Chaining.** Cipher Block Chaining is the process of encrypting a block by feeding back into the algorithm the previously encrypted/decrypted block. That is, outputting the current block and using it as input to the next operation ECB or Electronic Cookbook Mode. Electronic cookbook mode simply feeds blocks of data one at a time to the algorithm and outputs encrypted or decrypted blocks.
- **CFB or Cipher Feedback Mode.** CFB is the most complex of the three algorithms and combines Cipher Block chaining with a sophisticated feedback mechanism using some number of the most significant bits of the prior block and a bit vector and feeds the original text, the previously encrypted (or decrypted) block, and the bit vector into the algorithm for the next block.

The specifics of each of these modes is described in the National Institute of Standards and Technology (NIST) Federal Information Processing Standard (FIPS) 81. This specification is available directly from the National Institute of Standards for a nominal fee. Developers interested in more information about this standard should check out the NIST Web page at www.nist.gov/welcome.html.

In addition to modes, ciphers also support different methods of block padding. Padding is simply the process of extending a block of text to a given length. It's rare that the length of the data is divisible by the key size used to encode it. As such, the last block will need to be padded. Two padding modes are supported by the JCE today. They are:

- PKCS#5—Public Key Cryptography Standard #5
- PEM—Privacy Enhanced Mail

TIP The Java Cryptography extensions are considered to be munitions and are covered by export restrictions. For this reason the JCE is provided separately from the normal Java Security classes. Before you write classes that use the JCE you should think about whether those applications will be exportable outside the United States.

Before we move on to ACLs, let's finish out the section with a simple example that encrypts and decrypts a file.

SOURCE 17.9 tstCipher.java

```
import java.io.*;
import java.security.*;
/**
 * This class exercises the java.Security.Cipher class and
.* its support classes.
 * For instructional purposes the use of the Cipher functions
 * was broken into three parts.
 *     Creating the  key set
 *     Encrypt using the key
 *     Decrypt using the key and the Cipher text.
 *     Validate that the two files match
 *
 * <pre>
 *              CipherText cipherTest = new CipherText(Some
 *                                    algorithm,inputfilename);
 *              String encryptedName = cipherTest.Encrypt(inputfilename);
 *              String decryptedName = cipherTest.Decrypt(encryptedName);
 *              boolean result =
 *                   signatureTest.Validate(inputfilename,decryptedName);
 * </pre>
 *  @version 1.0
 *  @author A. Saganich
 *  @see java.Security.MessageDigest
 *
 */
class CipherText
{

    String     algorithm;
    Key        key;
    Cipher     cipher;

    /**
     * Construct the object
     */
    CipherText(String inAlgorithm, String inFileName)
    throws FileNotFoundException, NoSuchAlgorithmException
    {
        algorithm = inAlgorithm;

        // May throw file not found.
        FileInputStream        file = new FileInputStream(inFileName);
        KeyGenerator keyGen = KeyGenerator.getInstance(inAlgorithm);
        // We could provide a byte array to SecureRandom
        // but for simplicity let it seed itself.
```

```
        // Now generate a pair of keys
        keyGen.initialize(new SecureRandom());
        key  = keyGen.generateKey();
        cipher = Cipher.getInstance(inAlgorithm);
    }
    /**
     * Encrypt a file
     */
    public String Encrypt(String inFileName)
    throws
        FileNotFoundException,IOException,InvalidKeyException,
        SignatureException,
        KeyException
    {
        FileInputStream         inFile = new FileInputStream(inFileName);
        FileOutputStream        outFile = new
FileOutputStream(inFileName+".ciphertext");
        byte cleartext[] = new byte[512];
        int ctRead;

        // Use it to initialize (move to the VERIFY state)
        System.out.println("Initialising cipher");
        cipher.initEncrypt(key);
        while(true)
        {
            ctRead = inFile.read(cleartext);
            if ( ctRead <= 0) break;
            byte[] ciphertext = cipher.crypt(cleartext);
            outFile.write(ciphertext);
        }
        outFile.close();
        inFile.close();
        return inFileName+".ciphertext";
    }

    /**
     * Decrypt a file
     */
    public String Decrypt(String inFileName)
    throws FileNotFoundException,
           NoSuchAlgorithmException, IOException, InvalidKeyException,
           SignatureException,
           KeyException
    {
        FileInputStream         inFile = new
              FileInputStream(inFileName+".ciphertext");
        FileOutputStream        outFile = new
              FileOutputStream(inFileName+".cleartext");

        System.out.println("Input is from " +inFileName+".ciphertext");
        System.out.println("Output is to " +inFileName+".ciphertext");
        byte ciphertext[] = new byte[512];
        int ctRead;
```

```
        cipher.initDecrypt(key);
        while(true)
        {
            ctRead = inFile.read(ciphertext);
            if ( ctRead <= 0) break;
            byte[] cleartext = cipher.crypt(ciphertext);
            outFile.write(cleartext,0,cleartext.length);
        }
        outFile.close();
        inFile.close();

        return inFileName+".cleartext";
    }

    public boolean CompareFiles(String fileA, String fileB)
    throws FileNotFoundException,IOException
    {
        FileInputStream        inFileA = new FileInputStream(fileA);
        FileInputStream        inFileB = new FileInputStream(fileB);
        byte dataA[] = new byte[512];
        byte dataB[] = new byte[512];
        int ctReadA;
        int ctReadB;
        while(true)
        {
            ctReadA = inFileA.read(dataA);
            ctReadB = inFileB.read(dataB);
            if ( ctReadA != ctReadB)
                return false;
            else if (ctReadA <= 0)
                break;
            for ( int i = 0; i < ctReadA; i++)
            {
                if (dataA[i] != dataB[i])
                    return false;
            }
        }
        inFileA.close();
        inFileB.close();

        return true;
    }
}
/**
 *  generateSignature outputs a signature of the file given using
 *  the algorithm supplied.
 *  @version 1.0
 *  @author A. Saganich
 *
 *  @see java.Security.KeyPairGenerator
 *  @see java.Security.KeyPair
```

```
 *  @see java.Security.SecureRandom
 */

class tstCipher
{
    public static void main(String args[])
    {
        if ( args.length < 2)
        {
            System.out.println(
                "Usage: tstCipher AlgorithmName fileToBeCiphered\n");
            System.exit(0);
        }

        System.out.println(
                "Attempting to generate a key and cipher text");
        System.out.println("\t          using " + args[0]);
        System.out.println("\t          on file " + args[1]);

        // Open the file first
        // It takes forever to generate a key pair and we don't want to
        // wait and then discover that the input file is not there!
        try
        {
            System.out.println(
                "Generating a key pair please be patient this may
                 take a while");
            CipherText cipherTest = new CipherText(args[0],args[1]);
            // Get the signature

            System.out.println("Generating cipher from file and key");
            String encryptedName = cipherTest.Encrypt(args[1]);
            System.out.println("Decrypting " + encryptedName );
            String decryptedName = cipherTest.Decrypt(args[1]);
            System.out.println(
                "Validating decrypted result vs original");
            boolean result =
                 cipherTest.CompareFiles(args[1],decryptedName);
            System.out.println("Test comparison yielded "+ result +
                            "(Should be true).");
        }

        catch (KeyException e)
        {
            System.out.println("Unexpected KeyException " + e);
            System.exit(0);
        }
        catch (FileNotFoundException e)
        {
            System.out.println("Cannot find file " + args[1]);
            System.exit(0);
```

```
        }
        catch (NoSuchAlgorithmException e)
        {
             System.out.println("Unknown algorithm " + args[0]);
             System.exit(0);
        }
        catch (SignatureException e)
        {
             System.out.println("Error processing signature object!");
             System.exit(0);
        }
        catch (IOException e)
        {
             System.out.println("Unexpected IO Exception!");
             System.exit(0);
        }

    }
}
```

A quick review of tstCipher.java shows a large number of similarities between our message digest and signature examples. Some differences do exist, however, and we will point them out as we examine the code in detail.

As with the signature example we need to start with a key to base our cipher on. A key is generated as follows:

1. Use the KeyGenerator factory object to generate a KeyGenerator object based on the algorithm selected. This differs from our signature example in that we do not generate a public key/private key pair but rather a single key that is used for both encryption and decryption.

   ```
   KeyGenerator keyGen = KeyGenerator.getInstance(inAlgorithm);
   ```

2. We then initialize the generator based on a random number sequence.

   ```
   keyGen.initialize(new SecureRandom());
   ```

3. And then finally generate the key.

   ```
   key  = keyGen.generateKey();
   ```

Before we can encrypt or decrypt an object we need a cipher. The cipher, in combination with the key, is all the preparation required to begin the encrypt/decrypt process.

```
cipher = Cipher.getInstance(inAlgorithm);
```

Cipher objects can be used in one of two ways, either to encrypt data or to decrypt it. Once we have obtained a cipher and have a key we can continue the encrypt/decrypt process. Remember that cipher objects are symmetric. That is, a cipher may be used to encrypt or decrypt data depending on how it is initialized. The initDecrypt method and initEncrypt methods initialize the cipher for one action or the other.

```
cipher.initDecrypt(key);
cipher.initEncrypt(key);
```

We can then encrypt or decrypt blocks of data by using the crypt method.

```
byte[] cleartext or ciphertext = cipher.crypt(
                                 ciphertext or cleartext);
```

Two additional classes exist that we have not yet discussed but bear noting. The Cipher class is normally used to encrypt/decrypt blocks of memory data. The java.security.CipherInputStream can be used to input filter to read an encrypted file and takes as input a file stream and a cipher. Data is either encrypted or decrypted based on the way the cipher was initialized. Data can be read one byte at a time or a block at a time. In addition, the java.security.CipherOutputStream performs the same function for output. Like the CipherInputStream class, the CipherOutputStream class takes a cipher and an output stream and, again, either encrypts or decrypts the data that passes through it. Updating the tstCipher.java example to use CipherOutputStream and CipherInputStream is left as an exercise for the reader.

17.5 JAVA AND ACLS

With the release of the JDK 1.1 came a new concept within the java.security package, that of an Access Control List (or ACL for short). Acls, pronounced Ack-els, can be used to selectively grant and deny access to objects, resources, and files via Permissions. In general, the concept of an ACL is simple. An ACL contains one or more ACL Entries that grant or deny principles or entities access to resources. Principles may be gathered together within Groups and access to a resource granted or denied to that group.

The central interfaces responsible for managing ACLs are:

- **java.security.acl.Acl.** An Access Control List is a structure that contains one or more access AclEntrys.
- **java.security.acl.AclEntry.** Either grant or deny access to a resource based on the principle and whether the AclEntry is positive or negative. Positive AclEntrys grant access, negative AclEntrys deny access.
- **java.security.acl.Owner.** The Owner interface allows managing the entries within an Acl. Only the owner of an Acl may change its contents. An Acl may have more than one owner.

- **java.security.acl.Permission.** A permission is used to define the ways a resource may be accessed. Examples of permissions are read, write, create, delete, etc.

The rules for managing ACLs are straightforward.

- If there is no ACLEntry for a given principle then that principle is said to have an empty permission set.
- There can be at most one positive and one negative ACLEntry for each principle.
- Entries may cancel each other out. For example, if a principle has both a negative and a positive ACL for a resource, then the two permissions cancel each other out and the end result is the empty permission set.
- Individual-level permissions take precedence over group-level permissions. For example, if an individual has access to a resource, but the group that individual belongs to does not have access, then the individual may access the resource. Likewise, if the group was granted access but the individual was denied access, then that individual would not be given access to the resource.

The java.security package defines the various Acl interfaces but does not provide any implementation. The sun.security.acl package provides a default implementation of the Acl, AclEntry, Owner, Permission, and Group classes via the AclImpl, AclEntryImpl, OwnerImpl, PermissionImpl, and GroupImpl classes.

The testAcl example, shown in Source 17.10, exercises the various Acl classes by creating a fictitious corporation that contains two groups, finance and research. The Company BitsRus contains a number of resources, some of which can be accessed by everyone, some of which can be accessed only by finance, and some by only research. Our corporation contains the following resources.

- **Printers.** Printer can be accessed by everyone.
- **FinancialRecords.** FinancialRecords can only be accessed by members of the financial group with the exception of SneakyEmployee who, while a member of the financial group, appears to be a spy for a rival organization (BytesRus) and cannot access financial records.
- **Research.** Members of the research group can create, read, write, and update research. Members of the financial group may read research but nothing more. Again, Sneaky is also denied access to Research.

BitsRus is staffed by a number of researchers and financial personnel, as well as the CEO and CFO who can access anything.

SOURCE 17.10 tstAcl.java

```
import java.security.*;
import java.security.acl.*;      // The Acl and AclEntry interfaces
import sun.security.acl.*;       // The sun implementation.
import java.util.Enumeration;

/**
 * public class testAcl
 * @author A. Saganich
 * @version 1.0
 *
 * the testAcl class exercises the Principal, permission, group,
 * Acl and AclEntry classes.
 *
 *  @see java.security.acl.Acl
 *  @see java.security.acl.AclEntry
 *  @see java.security.acl.Principal
 *  @see java.security.acl.Group
 *  @see java.security.acl.Permission
 */
public class TestAcl
{

     // the employees
     Principal ceo                = null;
     Principal cfo                = null;

     Principal researcher1 = null;
     Principal researcher2 = null;

     Principal accountant1 = null;
     Principal accountant2 = null;
     Principal sneakyEmployee= null;

     Principal employees[]   = new Principal[7];

     Permission read       = new PermissionImpl("Read");
     Permission write      = new PermissionImpl("Write");
     Permission create     = new PermissionImpl("Create");
     Permission delete     = new PermissionImpl("Delete");

     // The groups they belong to.
     Group      financialGroup  = null;
     Group      researchGroup   = null;

     // The resources the users may access
     Acl            printers          = null;
     Acl            financialRcrds    = null;
     Acl            researchInfo      = null;
     TestAcl()
     {

          ceo = new PrincipalImpl("CEO"); employees[0] = ceo;
          cfo = new PrincipalImpl("CFO"); employees[1] = cfo;
```

```
researchGroup  = new GroupImpl("Pure R&D");
researcher1     = new PrincipalImpl("Software Developer");
employees[2] = researcher1;
researcher2     = new PrincipalImpl("Software Manager");
employees[3] = researcher2;
researchGroup.addMember(researcher1);
researchGroup.addMember(researcher2);
researchGroup.addMember(ceo);
researchGroup.addMember(cfo);

accountant1     = new PrincipalImpl("Accounting");
employees[4] = accountant1;
accountant2     = new PrincipalImpl("Bookkeeping");
employees[5] = accountant2;
sneakyEmployee= new PrincipalImpl("Mr Spy");
employees[6] = sneakyEmployee;
financialGroup = new GroupImpl("Finance");
financialGroup.addMember(accountant1);
financialGroup.addMember(accountant2);
financialGroup.addMember(sneakyEmployee);
financialGroup.addMember(ceo);
financialGroup.addMember(cfo);

// Now create the acls which match resources.
printers        = new AclImpl(ceo,"Printers");
financialRcrds  = new AclImpl(cfo,"Financial Records");
researchInfo    = new AclImpl(ceo,"Research Information");

// And add entries for each

try
{
     AclEntry entry = new AclEntryImpl(researchGroup);
     entry.addPermission(read);
     entry.addPermission(write);
     entry.addPermission(create);
     entry.addPermission(delete);
     Printers.addEntry(ceo,entry);
     researchInfo.addEntry(ceo,entry);
     entry = new AclEntryImpl(financialGroup);
     entry.addPermission(read);
     researchInfo.addEntry(ceo,entry);

}
catch (NotOwnerException e)
{
     System.out.println(
     "Unexpected error adding research permissions" + e);
}
try
{
```

```
        AclEntry entry = new AclEntryImpl(financialGroup);
        entry.addPermission(read);
        entry.addPermission(write);
        entry.addPermission(create);
        entry.addPermission(delete);

        printers.addEntry(ceo,entry);
        financialRcrds.addEntry(cfo,entry);

        // Except sneaky he's denied!
        entry = new AclEntryImpl(sneakyEmployee);
        entry.addPermission(read);
        entry.addPermission(write);
        entry.addPermission(create);
        entry.addPermission(delete);
        entry.setNegativePermissions();
        financialRcrds.addEntry(cfo,entry);

        // Grant read access to the research group.
        entry = new AclEntryImpl(financialGroup);
        entry.addPermission(read);
        financialRcrds.addEntry(cfo,entry);

        // Except sneaky!
        entry = new AclEntryImpl(sneakyEmployee);
        entry.addPermission(read);
        entry.setNegativePermissions();
        researchInfo.addEntry(ceo,entry);


    }
    catch (NotOwnerException e)
    {
        System.out.println(
        "Unexpected error adding financial permissions" + e);
    }
}

// list the permissions in the acl"s
public void listPermissions()
{
    if ( printers != null )
    {
         for (int i = 0; i < 7; i++)
         {
             System.out.println("Printer permissions for " +
              employees[i]);
             Enumeration e = printers.getPermissions(employees[i]);
             while (e.hasMoreElements())
             {
                 System.out.println("'" + e.nextElement() + "'");
```

```
                    }
                }
            }
            if ( financialRcrds != null )
            {
                for (int i = 0; i < 7; i++)
                {
                    System.out.println("financialRcrds permissions for "
                     + employees[i]);
                    Enumeration e =
                          financialRcrds.getPermissions(employees[i]);
                    while (e.hasMoreElements())
                    {
                        System.out.println("'" + e.nextElement() + "'");
                    }
                }
            }
            if ( researchInfo != null )
            {
                for (int i = 0; i < 7; i++)
                {
                    System.out.println("researchInfo permissions for " +
                     employees[i]);
                    Enumeration e =
                          researchInfo.getPermissions(employees[i]);
                    while (e.hasMoreElements())
                    {
                        System.out.println("'" + e.nextElement() + "'");
                    }
                }
            }
        }

        // List the members of the two groups.
        public void listGroups()
        {
            if ( financialGroup != null)
            {
                System.out.println("Members of the financial group");
                Enumeration e =financialGroup.members();
                while (e.hasMoreElements())
                {
                    System.out.println(e.nextElement());
                }
            }
            if ( researchGroup != null)
            {
                System.out.println("Members of the research group");
                Enumeration e =researchGroup.members();
                while (e.hasMoreElements())
                {
                    System.out.println(e.nextElement());
                }
            }
```

```
    }
    static public void main(String args[])
    {
        TestAcl testAcl = new TestAcl();
        //testAcl.listGroups();
        testAcl.listPermissions();
    }
} // end class testAcl
```

A run of Source 17.10 produces the following output.

```
Printer permissions  for CEO
"Read"
"Write"
"Create"
"Delete"
Printer permissions  for CFO
"Read"
"Write"
"Create"
"Delete"
Printer permissions  for Software Developer
"Read"
"Write"
"Create"
"Delete"
Printer permissions  for Software Manager
"Read"
"Write"
"Create"
"Delete"
Printer permissions  for Accounting
"Read"
"Write"
"Create"
"Delete"
Printer permissions  for Bookkeeping
"Read"
"Write"
"Create"
"Delete"
Printer permissions  for Mr Spy
"Read"
"Write"
"Create"
"Delete"
financialRcrds permissions  for CEO
"Read"
"Write"
"Create"
```

```
"Delete"
financialRcrds permissions  for CFO
"Read"
"Write"
"Create"
"Delete"
financialRcrds permissions  for Software Developer
financialRcrds permissions  for Software Manager
financialRcrds permissions  for Accounting
"Read"
"Write"
"Create"
"Delete"
financialRcrds permissions  for Bookkeeping
"Read"
"Write"
"Create"
"Delete"
financialRcrds permissions  for Mr Spy
researchInfo permissions  for CEO
"Read"
"Write"
"Create"
"Delete"
researchInfo permissions  for CFO
"Read"
"Write"
"Create"
"Delete"
researchInfo permissions  for Software Developer
"Read"
"Write"
"Create"
"Delete"
researchInfo permissions  for Software Manager
"Read"
"Write"
"Create"
"Delete"
researchInfo permissions  for Accounting
"Read"
researchInfo permissions  for Bookkeeping
"Read"
researchInfo permissions  for Mr Spy
```

One of the important things to note about Source 17.10 is that while our spy is granted access to financial records, as a part of the financial group, he is denied that same access on an individual basis.

The key points of Source 17.10 are:

Defining the principles who will own and have access to our resources.

```
Principle ceo = null;
ceo = new PrincipleImpl("CEO");
```

Creating a group for a set of principles.

```
researchGroup  = new GroupImpl("Pure R&D");
```

And adding principle to that group.

```
researchGroup.addMember(ceo);
```

Next we need to define the resources the principles should have access to. Each is identified by an individual Acl. Note that we choose an owner for the Acl. Only owners may change permissions associated with an Acl.

```
printers  = new AclImpl(ceo,"Printers");
```

In addition we defined a set of permissions that could be applied to resources.

```
Permission read = new PermissionImpl("Read");
```

And we assigned permissions to principles (or groups) via AclEntries.

```
AclEntry entry = new AclEntryImpl(researchGroup);
entry.addPermission(read);
```

In addition, we can deny access to a resource by negating a permission as we did with Sneaky.

```
entry = new AclEntryImpl(sneakyEmployee);
entry.setNegativePermissions();
financialRcrds.addEntry(cfo,entry);
```

And we proved out that our Acls did in fact act the way we expected by printing their contents using enumerations.

```
Enumeration e =financialGroup.members();
Enumeration e = printers.getPermissions(employees[i]);
```

17.6 THE FUTURE OF JAVA SECURITY

One of the future directions for Java Security is the *Java Protected Domain*. The concept of a Java Protected Domain is simple. A domain defines the protections/restrictions associated with a class or application. Each application/class executes in only one domain. Each application has two attributes associated with it that define how it will execute within a domain, a signer (which may be null if the application was not signed), and a location (defined by the URL the application was loaded from). On the platform where the application runs a set of permissions are defined for all known domains, with a "default" permission set for the unknown domains.

The Java Protected Domain concept is unique in that it allows the Java Sandbox concept to be extended and systematically relaxed in a controlled fashion. Under the Protected Domain concept, at least one domain always exists, that of the *System Domain*. The system domain is in control of system resources and is in place today in the form of the Java Sandbox. A system manager could develop additional domains and grant selective access to those system resources, or other resources, via the new domain. Basically, Protected Domains resolve some of the issues within the Java Sandbox by treating applets and applications uniformly, and allowing multiple protection levels based on origin and developer of application. Basically, the Java Protected Domain architecture extends the Java Sandbox by:

- Allowing system managers finer grain control based on permissions.
- Allowing system managers to selectively grant and deny access to system resources.
- Allowing system managers to selectively grant and deny access to network resources.
- Providing a new security definition called the "Extended Java Sandbox," which allows signed but otherwise unknown applications to read and write to a file area known as the "sandbox." Note that applications cannot be run from this area and no other permissions are granted.

The Java Protected Domain architecture is simply and robustly solving some of the existing problems with security, the most common being the "keys to the castle" problem. Both Java with signed JAR files and ActiveX with signed Cabinet files have a "keys to the castle" problem. Under both of these systems, applications are either restricted to the Java Sandbox or have the "keys to the castle." That is to say a signed and accepted application can access any and all resources available on a system. The Java Protected Domain architecture resolves this issue by selectively granting access to both resources and objects. Domains can be defined so that specific groups can access specific resources. For example, one might define an R&D domain that has access to R&D resources but is denied access to sensitive financial data. The financial data would only be available to members of the financial domain. And even within a domain, based on the signer, applications might have more or less permission to access objects; for example, allowing all access for the company president but only selected access for the secretary of the finance department.

17.7 SUMMARY

We have seen the threat, and examined the tools at our disposal to combat that threat. Let's reiterate the key items to keep in mind when planning for security and developing applications that take advantage of it.

- *Always, always, always keep the cost of the implementation in mind.* Not just the actual monetary costs for hardware and software, but the related costs as well—especially those costs associated with lost productivity.
- *Apply the Principle of least security.* Don't sign applets that don't use critical resources.
- *Always use the latest versions of Browsers, class libraries, and other such products.* These products are constantly being updated to take advantage of the latest security methods and to plug security-related holes.
- *Never underestimate your opponent.* Most often the best you can hope for is to make it cost- or time-ineffective to the attacker. The only system that is truly secure is the one that's locked in a vault. But remember, that same machine is of dubious worth.

FURTHER READING

www.cert.org—CERT.

http://java.sun.com/sfaq—The Sun security frequently access questions list.

www.nist.gov/welcome.html—The NIST Home page.

CHAPTER 18

Package java.sql

OBJECTIVE

This chapter will give an overview of Java Database Connectivity (JDBC), which is implemented in the java.sql package. JDBC is the mechanism Java applications and applets use to perform database access.

18.1 OVERVIEW

The java.sql package contains all the classes that make up Java Database Connectivity (JDBC). JDBC allows the java developer to access relational databases directly from Java code, a much needed feature for business application development. Prior to JDBC, the only way to access a database from a Java program was to do the database access in C, and use native methods to interface the C code with Java. JDBC is intended to be a low-level API that is powerful enough to exploit most features available on commercial relational databases, but is simple enough to be used by all levels of programmers. Before we get started looking at some examples, let's briefly review the concept of tables, relational databases, and Structured Query Language (SQL).

Tables

A table consists of two parts—its schema and the data it contains. The schema of a table describes the name and type of data fields it can store. Table 18.1 shows the schema for a table named Books. Looking at the schema, we see that this table has

TABLE 18.1 Schema for Table Books

Field Name	*Data Type*
BookId	Integer
Title	Character (20)
Author	Character (30)
NumPages	Integer

four data fields. Each field has an associated data type that determines the type of data the field can contain. The schema of a table also contains information on indexes. Indexes can be used to link tables together, enforce constraints on a data field or set of fields (e.g., keep them unique), and to speed up data access.

Data contained by a table is stored in units called records. Each record contains data for each field defined in the table's schema. Table 18.2 shows the data stored in the Books table. The table contains four records, and each record stores data as defined by the table's schema. Please note that data fields are often referred to as columns and records are often referred to as rows.

Relational Databases

A relational database can contain many tables. Relational databases let you specify relationships (either implicit or explicit) between one or more tables in the database. Using an SQL statement, you can recall data fields from more than one table using a relationship between the tables. Imagine that we have a table called libraries that stores the library name, a book Id, and the number of copies for a particular book. The book Id in this table can relate to the Books table defined earlier. In order to find the names and number of copies for each library book we have to link the tables together. Since the book Id field is the same in each table it will be used as our linking criteria.

TABLE 18.2 Books Table

BookId	*Title*	*Author*	*NumPages*
1	AirFrame	Michael Crichton	347
2	Green Eggs and Ham	Dr. Seuss	62
3	The Vampire Lestat	Anne Rice	550
4	Chaos: Making a New Science	James Gleick	317

Here is an SQL statement that will recall data from both the Libraries table and the Books table:

```
SELECT Libraries.LibraryName, Books.Title, Libraries.NumBooks FROM
Libraries, Books WHERE Libraries.BookId = Books.BookId
```

Structured Query Language

Structured Query Language, or SQL, is a standard syntax for accessing and updating relational databases. SQL is important in JDBC programming because you must use SQL statements in your method calls. SQL statements are normally used to recall and update data in a database, but they can also be used to create and delete tables, create and delete indexes, and perform other system database functions. Here are some examples of SQL statements:

```
SELECT BookId, Title FROM Books

DELETE FROM Books WHERE BookId = 1
```

The first statement is a select statement and is used to get data from the database. The SQL keywords are in capital letters. This particular query will select the fields BookId and Title for all rows. The second statement will delete the records in the Books table where BookId equals one.

JDBC-ODBC Bridge

The examples in this chapter make use of the JDBC-ODBC bridge. The JDBC-ODBC bridge translates JDBC calls into ODBC calls, therefore allowing access to any database that has an ODBC driver. Of course, using the bridge will limit you to a Microsoft Windows platform for application development. There are already many JDBC drivers available that do direct database access, and all major database vendors have committed to producing JDBC drivers that will do direct access. Some JDBC drivers will allow applets to do direct database access. This can be accomplished because the JDBC driver information is accessed in the form of a URL. The JDBC driver will handle the transmission of the data over the network, so no native libraries will be loaded.

ODBC stands for Open Database Connectivity and is used on Microsoft Windows platforms for database access. Currently, almost every database vendor has an ODBC driver for their database, so using the JDBC-ODBC bridge will give you access to almost every type of database.

18.2 JDBC BASICS

Here is a simple example of accessing a database using JDBC. It includes all the necessary steps for opening a connection to the database and retrieving data.

SOURCE 18.1 SimpleQuery.java

```
package jwiley.chp18;

import java.sql.DriverManager;
import java.sql.Connection;
import java.sql.Statement;
import java.sql.ResultSet;
import java.sql.SQLException;

/**
 * Class to demonstrate the use of basic jdbc functionality
 *
 * @author  Eric Monk
 */

public class SimpleQuery
{
    public static void main (String args[])
    {
        try
        {
            // Load database driver
            Class.forName ("sun.jdbc.odbc.JdbcOdbcDriver");
        } catch (ClassNotFoundException cnfe)
          {
            System.out.println(cnfe.toString());
            System.exit(0);
          }

        try
        {
            // Establish connection
            String sUrl = "jdbc:odbc:ExampleDb";
            Connection con = DriverManager.getConnection(sUrl);

            // Create and send statement
            String sQuery = "SELECT Author, Title, NumPages " +
                            "FROM BOOKS";
            Statement stmt = con.createStatement();
            ResultSet rslt = stmt.executeQuery(sQuery);

            // Process data
            while (rslt.next())
            {
                String sAuthor = rslt.getString("Author");
                String sTitle = rslt.getString("Title");
                int    iNumPages = rslt.getInt("NumPages");

                System.out.println(sTitle + " by " + sAuthor +
                                " has " + iNumPages + " pages.");
```

```
            }

            // Cleanup
            rslt.close();
            stmt.close();

        } catch (SQLException sqle)
          {
            while (sqle != null)
            {
                System.out.println ("SQLState: " +
                                    sqle.getSQLState ());
                System.out.println ("Message:  " +
                                    sqle.getMessage ());
                System.out.println ("ErrorCode:   " +
                                    sqle.getErrorCode ());
                sqle = sqle.getNextException ();
                System.out.println ("");
            }
          }
    }
}
```

A run of Source 18.1 using the data in Table 18.2 will yield the following results:

```
AirFrame by Michael Crichton has 347 pages.
Green Eggs and Ham by Dr. Seuss has 62 pages.
The Vampire Lestat by Anne Rice has 550 pages.
Chaos: Making a New Science by James Gleick has 317 pages.
```

Let's examine each JDBC statement in detail. The following statement loads the JDBC Driver class and registers it with the DriverManager. The class sun.jdbc.odbc .JdbcOdbcDriver implements the Driver interface, and is the class that will handle the JDBC to ODBC translation.

```
Class.forName ("sun.jdbc.odbc.JdbcOdbcDriver");
```

The following two statements identify the database and establish the connection to the database.

```
String sUrl = "jdbc:odbc:ExampleDb";
Connection con = DriverManager.getConnection(sUrl);
```

The first statement is a JDBC URL. A JDBC URL consists of three parts:

```
jdbc:<subprotocol>:<subname>
```

The jdbc portion of the URL is the protocol, just as http would be the protocol for accessing an HTML document. Subprotocol is used to further identify how to talk to the database. In our example odbc is the subprotocol, but the subprotocol could be a network naming service or a proprietary protocol. The subname provides information to identify the database. The ODBC driver name in our example is ExampleDb.

The second statement establishes the connection with the database. The DriverManager class will query registered drivers to see which drivers can handle the protocol indicated in subprotocol. In our example, the Driver class JdbcOdbcDriver knows how to handle the odbc subprotocol, so that is the class used to establish the connection to the database.

The following statements execute a query against the database and return the results of that query.

```
String sQuery = "SELECT Author, Title, NumPages " +
                "FROM BOOKS";
Statement stmt = con.createStatement();
ResultSet rslt = stmt.executeQuery(sQuery);
```

First, we allocate a Statement object. The statement object allows us to send SQL directly against the database. Second, we use the Statement executeQuery method to return data in a ResultSet object. The ResultSet object contains methods to fetch the individual data elements returned from the database.

Next we process the ResultSet to obtain the data. The ResultSet object acts as a cursor, meaning only one row of data is available at a time. Calling the next() method for the first time will position the cursor at the first row of data. Each subsequent call to next() will move to the next row of data. When there are no more rows next() will return false.

```
while (rslt.next())
{
    String sAuthor = rslt.getString("Author");
    String sTitle = rslt.getString("Title");
    int    iNumPages = rslt.getInt("NumPages");

    System.out.println(sTitle + " by " + sAuthor +
                      " has " + iNumPages + " pages.");
}
```

The ResultSet interface provides multiple getXXX methods for accessing data, where XXX stands for the variable type. We are using the getString and getInt methods in this example, which will return a String and int, respectively. There are also two implementations of each getXXX method, one that accepts a String (column name) and another that accepts an int (column index). Here we are accessing the data using the column names since they were explicitly declared in the Select statement. If you do not explicitly declare the column names in your Select statement it is recommended to use column indexes to access individual columns. The reason for this is because there is no guarantee what the column names will be, especially in a query that may return the same field name from different tables. When accessing data using column indexes the first column has an index of 1, the second an index of 2, and so on.

Now that we are done processing the results it is time to clean up. We first close the result set and then close the statement. This will free up resources allocated by the database driver.

```
rslt.close();
stmt.close();
```

Lastly, we must provide some exception handling for our program. Almost all of the methods defined in java.sql throw SQLException. The information stored in the exception is useful for debugging and includes driver-specific error codes.

```
        } catch (SQLException sqle)
          {
            while (sqle != null)
            {
                System.out.println ("SQLState: " +
                                    sqle.getSQLState ());
                System.out.println ("Message:  " +
                                    sqle.getMessage ());
                System.out.println ("ErrorCode:   " +
                                    sqle.getErrorCode ());
                sqle = sqle.getNextException ();
                System.out.println ("");
            }
          }
```

Providing an exception handler allows us to clean up, or to handle transactions gracefully. SQLExceptions can be chained together to provide multiple errors back to the user. The getNextException() method is used to get the next exception in the chain. The getSQLState(), getMessage(), and getErrorCode() methods all provide more detailed information about the error.

Now that we have seen an example, let's examine the classes and interfaces in the java.sql package. One thing to keep in mind is that all of the major functionality in JDBC is provided by interfaces. Objects that implement these interfaces are returned by the JDBC driver for use in your program.

- **DriverManager.** This class is used for managing JDBC drivers. JDBC drivers should register themselves automatically when they are loaded. The getConnection() method will look for an appropriate driver using the information provided and return a Connection object.
- **Driver.** This is an interface that represents a JDBC driver.
- **DriverPropertyInfo.** This class should only be used by advanced programmers. This class is used to examine and supply properties for opening a connection.

- **Connection.** This is an interface used to represent a connection to a database. A connection can be obtained with a call to the getConnection() method in the DriverManager class. Once a connection is opened, SQL statements can be executed.
- **Statement.** This is an interface used to execute SQL statements against the database. The statement will allocate enough space to handle results from the database. SQL statements sent via the executeQuery() method will return a ResultSet object.
- **PreparedStatement.** This class extends Statement. PreparedStatement is used to store precompiled SQL statements. Precompiled SQL is used for more efficiency when executing the same call more than one time. A PreparedStatement object can be created with a call to prepareStatement() in the Connection interface.
- **CallableStatement.** This class extends PreparedStatement. This class is used to execute stored procedures. A CallableStatement object can be created with a call to prepareCall() in the Connection interface.
- **ResultSet.** This class provides access to the data returned from an SQL query. Methods exist to get data in a variety of data types, and to enumerate through all returned rows.
- **Date.** This class extends java.util.Date. This class allows JDBC to identify this as a SQL DATE value.
- **Time.** This class extends java.util.Date. This class allows JDBC to identify this as a SQL TIME value.
- **Timestamp.** This class extends java.util.Date. This class allows JDBC to identify this as a SQL TIMESTAMP value.
- **Types.** This class defines constants used to identify SQL types.
- **SQLException.** This class extends Exception. SQLException provides information on database errors. SQLExceptions can be chained together to return multiple errors. The getNextException() method is used to return the next exception in the chain.
- **SQLWarning.** This class extends SQLException. SQLWarning provides information on database warnings. SQLWarnings can be chained together to return multiple warnings. The getNextWarning() method is used to return the next warning in the chain.
- **DataTruncation.** This class extends SQLWarning. DataTruncation is used to report warnings occuring because data was truncated during a read or write. The original size and the actual size of the data can be obtained by using the getDataSize() and getTransfersize() methods.

18.3 DATABASE UPDATE AND TRANSACTIONS

Our next example will show you how to use transactions in JDBC. Transactions allow multiple SQL statements to be grouped together in a manner such that if all the statements complete successfully, any changes made to the database will be made permanent. If any of the statements in the transaction fail, any changes made to the database during the current transaction will be undone. The act of "undoing" parts of a transaction is called "rollback."

In the example contained in Source 18.2, we try to add information to two different tables, but we want them to act as a single transaction. If one of the insert statements contained invalid data, the statement would fail and therefore trigger a rollback on the database.

SOURCE 18.2

```
package jwiley.chp18;

import java.sql.DriverManager;
import java.sql.Connection;
import java.sql.Statement;
import java.sql.ResultSet;
import java.sql.SQLException;
import java.sql.DatabaseMetaData;

/**
 * Class to demonstrate jdbc transactions
 *
 * @author  Eric Monk
 */

public class AddBook
{
    public static void main (String args[])
    {
        if (args.length != 3)
        {
            System.out.println("Usage: java AddBook <author> " +
                               "<title> <num pages>");
            System.exit(0);
        }

        try
        {
            // Load database driver
            Class.forName ("sun.jdbc.odbc.JdbcOdbcDriver");
        } catch (ClassNotFoundException cnfe)
          {
            System.out.println(cnfe.toString());
            System.exit(0);
          }

        try
        {
```

```
// Establish connection
String sUrl = "jdbc:odbc:ExampleDb";
Connection con = DriverManager.getConnection(sUrl);

DatabaseMetaData dbmd = con.getMetaData();
boolean bSupportsTransactions =
        dbmd.supportsTransactions();

if (bSupportsTransactions)
{
     int iTransactionIsolationLevel =
             con.getTransactionIsolation();
     if (iTransactionIsolationLevel ==
             Connection.TRANSACTION_NONE)
     {
         // try to set a higher TRANSACTION LEVEL
         boolean bSupportsTransLevel =
             dbmd.supportsTransactionIsolationLevel(
             Connection.TRANSACTION_READ_COMMITTED);
         if (bSupportsTransLevel)
             con.setTransactionIsolation(
             Connection.TRANSACTION_READ_COMMITTED);
     }
}

Statement stmt = con.createStatement();

try {
    if (bSupportsTransactions)
    {
        // begin transaction
        con.setAutoCommit(false);
    }

    // Get new AuthorId
    String sQuery = "SELECT MAX(AuthorId) AS Max_AuthorId " +
                    "FROM AUTHORS";
    ResultSet rslt = stmt.executeQuery(sQuery);

    int iNewAuthorId = 0;
    while (rslt.next())
    {
        iNewAuthorId = rslt.getInt("Max_AuthorId") + 1;
    }

    // Add to Authors
    String sInsertStmt = "INSERT INTO AUTHORS " +
                         "(AuthorId, Author) VALUES (" +
                         iNewAuthorId + ", "" + args[0] + "")";
    int iStatus = stmt.executeUpdate(sInsertStmt);
```

```
            // Get new BookId
            sQuery = "SELECT MAX(BookId) AS Max_BookId FROM Books_II";
            rslt = stmt.executeQuery(sQuery);

            int iNewBookId = 0;
            while (rslt.next())
            {
                iNewBookId = rslt.getInt("Max_BookId") + 1;
            }

            // Add to Books_II
            sInsertStmt = "INSERT INTO BOOKS_II (BookId, AuthorId, " +
                          "Title, NumPages) " +
                          "VALUES (" + iNewBookId +
                          ", " + iNewAuthorId +
                          ", "" + args[1] + "", " + args[2] + ")";
            iStatus = stmt.executeUpdate(sInsertStmt);

             if (bSupportsTransactions)
             {
                 // commit transaction
                con.commit();
            }

            rslt.close();

        } catch (SQLException sqle1)
          {
            if (bSupportsTransactions)
            {
                // rollback transaction
                con.rollback();
            }
            throw new SQLException(sqle1.getMessage());
          }

        // Cleanup
        stmt.close();

    } catch (SQLException sqle2)
      {
        System.out.println(sqle2.toString());
      }

  }
}
```

In this example, the program takes data entered on the command line and tries to insert it into the database. Since no validation is done on the data, an improper value can cause one of the insert statements to fail.

The first thing to note is a reference to a new interface: DatabaseMetaData. DatabaseMetaData provides information about the database itself, such as support for transactions, information on catalogs, primary keys, and so forth. Here we use DatabaseMetaData to see if the database we are connected to supports transactions.

```
DatabaseMetaData dbmd = con.getMetaData();
boolean bSupportsTransactions = dbmd.supportsTransactions();
```

If the database does support transactions we want to make sure it has an appropriate Transaction Isolation Level. For our example, anything other than TRANSACTION_NONE will enable transactions for our database connection. First we ask the database whether it will support a particular isolation level, then set it to that level if it does support it.

```
if (bSupportsTransactions)
{
    int iTransactionIsolationLevel =
           con.getTransactionIsolation();
    if (iTransactionIsolationLevel ==
           Connection.TRANSACTION_NONE)
    {
        // try to set a higher TRANSACTION LEVEL
        boolean bSupportsTransLevel =
                  dbmd.supportsTransactionIsolationLevel(
                  Connection.TRANSACTION_READ_COMMITTED);
        if (bSupportsTransLevel)
            con.setTransactionIsolation(
                  Connection.TRANSACTION_READ_COMMITTED);
     }
}
```

The following statement will enable us to start performing transactions. We have to turn the auto commit feature off or else every statement will be committed to the database immediately after it executes. With the auto commit feature off, any statements executed will act as a transaction until either commit() or rollback() is called. Once one of these methods has been called, a new transaction will begin for subsequent database updates.

```
con.setAutoCommit(false);
```

The next statement demonstrates a database update. Instead of using the executeQuery() method we use the executeUpdate() method. The executeUpdate() method will return the number of rows affected by the statement.

```
String sInsertStmt ="INSERT INTO AUTHORS " +
                     "(AuthorId, Author) VALUES (" +
                    iNewAuthorId + ", "" + args[0] + "")";
int iStatus = stmt.executeUpdate(sInsertStmt);
```

Next, the commit statement will end the transaction and make changes to the database permanent.

```
con.commit();
```

If an error occurs, an exception is thrown so the rollback method can be called to restore the database to its original state.

```
con.rollback();
```

18.4 META DATA

In addition to letting you access and update data in the database, JDBC also provides a way to analyze the schema of a table and the schema of a database. Two interfaces are provided to give you access to the schemas: ResultSetMetaData and DatabaseMetaData. Here is a brief description of the two classes:

- **ResultSetMetaData.** This class lets you examine the properties and columns for a ResultSet. A ResultSetMetaData object can be returned with a call to getMetaData() in the ResultSet interface. Methods are available for determining the properties of the result set as well as examining the columns in the result set. Source 18.3 demonstrates the use of this class.
- **DatabaseMetaData.** This class lets you examine the properties and tables of the database. A DatabaseMetaData object can be returned with a call to getMetaData() in the Connection interface. The getTables() method will return a ResultSet with a description of all the tables in the database. There are many other methods available to access specific database properties.

Source 18.3 demonstrates the use of the ResultSetMetaData interface. The SimpleMetaData class contains the same source code as Source 18.1 except for the bolded areas.

SOURCE 18.3

```
package jwiley.chp18;

import java.sql.DriverManager;
import java.sql.Connection;
import java.sql.Statement;
import java.sql.ResultSet;
import java.sql.ResultSetMetaData;
import java.sql.Types;
import java.sql.SQLException;

/**
 * Class to demonstrate the use of basic jdbc functionality
 *
 * @author  Eric Monk
 */

public class SimpleMetaData
{
    public static void main (String args[])
    {
        try
        {
            // Load database driver
            Class.forName ("sun.jdbc.odbc.JdbcOdbcDriver");
        } catch (ClassNotFoundException cnfe)
          {
            System.out.println(cnfe.toString());
            System.exit(0);
          }

        try
        {
            // Establish connection
            String sUrl = "jdbc:odbc:ExampleDb";
            Connection con = DriverManager.getConnection(sUrl);

            // Create and send statement
            String sQuery = "SELECT * FROM BOOKS";

            Statement stmt = con.createStatement();
            ResultSet rslt = stmt.executeQuery(sQuery);

            ResultSetMetaData rsmd = rslt.getMetaData();
            int iColumnCount = rsmd.getColumnCount();

            System.out.println("Field\tType");
            System.out.println("——-\t—");
            for (int iCount = 1; iCount <= iColumnCount; iCount++)
            {
```

```
                int iWidth = rsmd.getColumnDisplaySize(iCount);
                String sName = rsmd.getColumnName(iCount);
                int iType = rsmd.getColumnType(iCount);

                String sType = null;
                switch (iType)
                {
                    case Types.TINYINT:
                    case Types.SMALLINT:
                    case Types.INTEGER:
                    case Types.BIGINT:
                        sType = "Integer";
                        break;

                    case Types.CHAR:
                    case Types.VARCHAR:
                        sType = "Char";
                        break;
                }

                String sDescription = sType;
                if (sType.equals("Char"))
                    sDescription = sDescription + "(" + iWidth + ")";

                System.out.println(sName + "\t" + sDescription);
            }

            // Cleanup
            rslt.close();
            stmt.close();

        } catch (SQLException sqle)
          {
            while (sqle != null)
            {
                System.out.println ("SQLState: " +
                                    sqle.getSQLState ());
                System.out.println ("Message:  " +
                                    sqle.getMessage ());
                System.out.println ("ErrorCode:   " +
                                    sqle.getErrorCode ());
                sqle = sqle.getNextException ();
                System.out.println ("");
            }
          }

    }
}
```

A run of Source 18.3 will produce Table 18.1.

Notice that our SQL statement has changed from specifying individual data fields to using an asterisk. An asterisk will cause the database to return all the rows in the table. After we execute our query we get the meta data with this statement:

```
ResultSetMetaData rsmd = rslt.getMetaData();
```

Now that we have an instance of ResultSetMetaData we can examine the data fields of the table. First we get the number of columns in the result set by calling the getColumnCount() method. Now we can loop through all the data fields and get their type. Using the getColumnDisplaySize(), getColumnName(), and the getColumnType() methods we find out information about each data field. To translate the column type field into a string we compare it to the predefined types in the Types class. The Types class contains variables for all the different numbers getColumnType() could return. The switch statement in Source 18.3 contains only a portion of the predefined types.

18.5 SUMMARY

This chapter describes the basics of relational database technology as well as a detailed demonstration of all the major concepts of the Java Database Connectivity API that is contained in the SQL package. We covered basic concepts like tables, schema, and the Structured Query Language (SQL). We also walked through examples of accessing and updating a book database.

CHAPTER 19

Internationalization and Resources

OBJECTIVE

Today computers exist in every country in the world. With each country come one or more languages and dialects. Through the use of locales and Java resource bundles developers can internationalize their application and tailor it to the country and language where it is being displayed. This chapter details the process of writing international applications and the support provided by the JDK 1.2 for doing so.

As the Internet grows it reaches further and further. Countries that were unreachable or difficult to reach can now be reached in the blink of an eye (or the blink of a 28.8 modem!). Never before has such a large amount of information been available to so many people in so many diverse countries and speaking so many different languages.

With the advent of the JDK 1.2 Java developers can now write applications that not only perform a specific function but can determine the native language of the computer they are being run on and tailor the application to that language. The JDK 1.2 provides support for Locales and Resource Bundles and by combining the two, developers can write an application whose display is tailored not only to the type of application but also takes advantage of the knowledge of geo-political boundaries.

Before we begin writing international applications it's important to understand a little better about what an application really is. Typically, an application is made up of four parts.

- **GUI.** The portion of the application that the user sees. Most of our internationalization effort will be in the GUI aspects of a program. From our perspective, the GUI of an application contains its buttons and menus and the like.

- **Data.** Most object-oriented texts will tell you that the data defines the application. In fact, the data defines the underlying objects and data structures. However, the behind-the-scenes data is rarely seen by the user and requires little, if any, internationalization.
- **Application logic.** The logic of the application defines how the data is manipulated. The logic should never be internationalized. That is the way the application works and it should never be changed based on how the GUI of the application is presented.
- **Errors, messages, and text.** The final area of application are its messages, errors, and general displays of information. The display of these items is the second area where we need to consider internationalization.

Most applications are developed with little regard to the four parts just described. Application logic is strewn about within the applications. Strings, errors, and messages of all kinds are peppered throughout the application. There is little, if any, separation between the GUI and the underlying logic it represents. Such an application is difficult, if not impossible, to internationalize without significant effort. However, if we consider internationalization from the start it's straightforward to write international applications.

- *Separate the GUI from the applications logic.* By separating the GUI from the application logic the business rules of the application and the presentation of those rules are disentangled. This allows the GUI to be internationalized without changes to the underlying fundamental aspects of the application. The JDK 1.1 event model makes this possible and even easy.
- *Separate the strings, messages, and text of the application into a resource bundle.* By using resource bundles as containers for strings, etc., all the non-GUI aspects of an application that might need internationalization are contained in a single easy to manage and update location.
- *Format the dates, numbers, and messages of an application using the format classes and methods.* Dates, numbers, and messages are often formatted differently based on local custom. Dates may be formatted mm/dd/yyyy in the United States but other countries format dates differently. The correct use of some of the new JDK formatting methods isolates formatting issues and allows the JDK to handle them for you!

With these ideas in mind, let's examine how we might handle writing a simple international application. Source 19.1 shows a very simple applet that displays several settings; specifically, current and current time as well as several text strings that should also be internationalized.

SOURCE 19.1 English.java

```
package jwiley.chp19;
import java.applet.Applet;
import java.awt.Graphics;
import java.awt.*;
import java.awt.event.*;

/**
 * public class English
 * @author A. Saganich
 * @version 1.1
 *
 *  Sample applet which we will develop into an international application
 *
 */

public class English extends Applet
{

    class ButtonHandler implements ActionListener
    {
        public ButtonHandler()
        {
        }

        public void actionPerformed(ActionEvent ae)
        {
            String sCommand = ae.getActionCommand();
            if ("Yes".equals(sCommand))
            {
                System.out.println("User hit 'Yes' button");
            }
            else if ("No".equals(sCommand))
            {
                System.out.println("User hit 'No' button");
            }
            else if ( "Maybe".equals (sCommand))
            {
                System.out.println("User hit 'Maybe' button");
            }
        } // end ActionPerformed
    } // end NumberHandler implements ActionListener

    public void init()
    {
```

```
        Panel topPanel = new Panel();
        topPanel.setLayout(new GridLayout(1,2));
        Label label = new Label("Currency is:",Label.LEFT);
        topPanel.add(label);
        Label currency = new Label("Dollars",Label.RIGHT);
        topPanel.add(currency);
        add("North",topPanel);

        Panel middlePanel = new Panel();
        middlePanel.setLayout(new GridLayout(1,2));
        label = new Label("Today is:",Label.LEFT);
        middlePanel.add(label);
        Label date = new Label("30-July-1997",Label.RIGHT);
        middlePanel.add(date);
        add("Center",middlePanel);

        ButtonHandler bh = new ButtonHandler();
        Button b;
        Panel buttonPanel = new Panel();
        buttonPanel.setLayout(new GridLayout(1,3));
        buttonPanel.add(b = new Button("Yes"));
        b.addActionListener(bh);
        buttonPanel.add(b = new Button("No"));
        b.addActionListener(bh);
        buttonPanel.add(b = new Button("Maybe"));
        b.addActionListener(bh);
        add("South",buttonPanel);
    }

    /**
     * Simple main method to test the applet.
     */
    static public void main(String args[])
    {
        class ShutdownAdapter extends WindowAdapter
        {
            public void windowClosing(WindowEvent e)
            { System.exit(0); }
        }
         FramemyFrame    = new Frame("English");
         myFrame.addWindowListener(new ShutdownAdapter());
         English English = new English();
         myFrame.setSize(300,150);
         myFrame.add("Center",English);
         English.init();
         English.start();
         myFrame.show();
    }
}
```

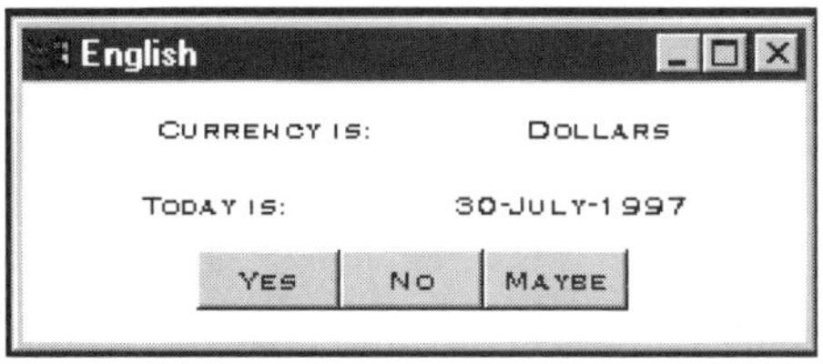

FIGURE 19.1 English version.

Figure 19.1 shows the result of running Source 19.1.

While straightforward and to the point, this application contains a number of problems that would need to be resolved. Each of these is discussed here.

Each of the buttons is labeled explicitly with English.

```
buttonPanel.add(b = new Button("Yes"));
```

Each button is then tested against its English name.

```
String sCommand = ae.getActionCommand();
if ("Yes".equals(sCommand))
```

In addition to the buttons each of the labels was hard coded with English, for example.

```
Label label = new Label("Currency is:",Label.LEFT);
```

One of the less obvious problems is that the source has strings peppered throughout. In the following sections we will examine each of these problems and present a solution with a completely internationalized application as the result.

19.1 LOCALES

The first step in writing an international application is to support *locales*. A locale is simply a political or geographic region that shares a language and a set of common customs. Java supports a number of locales, which can be found on many Web sites including http://www.ics.uci.edu/pub/ietf/http/related/iso639.txt and http://www.chemie.fu-berlin.de/diverse/doc/ISO_3166.html. We can query for the current locale with the getLocale() method from the applet class. Source 19.2 shows the beginnings of an internationalized applet that supports French, German, the United States, and the United Kingdom.

SOURCE 19.2 testLocale.java

```
package jwiley.chp19;
import java.applet.Applet;
import java.awt.Graphics;
import java.awt.Frame;
import java.util.Locale;
import java.awt.event.WindowEvent;
import java.awt.event.WindowAdapter;

/**
 * public class TestLocale
 * @author A. Saganich
 * @version 1.1
 *
 * Sample applet to exercise the use of Locales.
 *
 * @see java.util.Locale;
 */

public class TestLocale extends Applet
{

     Locale current;
     private Locale supported[] =
     {
          Locale.US,
          Locale.UK,
          Locale.FRENCH,
          Locale.GERMAN
     };

     /** Determine what the current locale is */
     public void init()
     {
          current = getLocale();
     }

     /**
     * Display the currently supported locales
     * And test if the current locale is supported.
     */
     public void paint(Graphics g)
     {
          int y = 10;
          int which = -1;
          g.drawString("Current locale is " + current.getDisplayName() ,
                    10, y+=10);

          g.drawString("Supported locales are: ", 10, y+=10);
          for ( int i = 0; i < supported.length; i++)
          {
```

```
                g.drawString(supported[i].getDisplayName(), 20, y+=10);
                if (current.equals(supported[i]) )
                    which = i;
            }

            if (which != -1)
                g.drawString("Current locale is supported as " +
                                which, 10, y+=10);
            else
                g.drawString("Locale " + current.getDisplayLanguage() +
                                " is unsupported", 10, y+=10);

        }
        /**
        * Simple main method to test the applet.
        */
        static public void main(String args[])
        {
            class ShutdownAdapter extends WindowAdapter
            {
                public void windowClosing(WindowEvent e)
                { System.exit(0); }
            }

              FramemyFrame    = new Frame("TestLocale");
              myFrame.addWindowListener(new ShutdownAdapter());
              TestLocale TestLocale = new TestLocale();
              myFrame.setSize(300,150);
              myFrame.add("Center",TestLocale);
              TestLocale.init();
              TestLocale.start();
              myFrame.show();
         }
    }
```

Figure 19.2 shows the result of running Source 19.2.

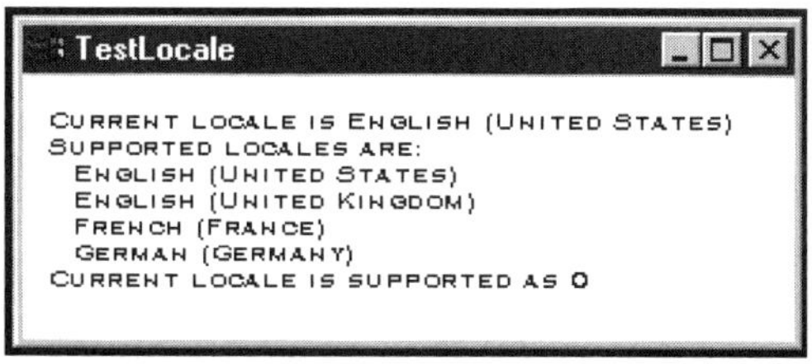

FIGURE 19.2 TestLocale.

The TestLocale application begins our trip down the internationalization road by choosing a set of supported locales. Our application chose to support English, French, and German (mostly because the author knows speakers of those languages) and defined a set of supported locales.

These locales were stored in a simple array. See the JDK documentation for a complete list of locale constants.

```
private Locale supported[] =
{
     Locale.US,
     Locale.UK,
     Locale.FRENCH,
     Locale.GERMAN
};
```

Once we have defined our supported locales we can determine the current locale with the getLocale method. getLocale can be found in a number of JDK classes including Applet and Component. We then compare the current locale against the supported set with the following code.

```
if (current.equals(supported[i]) )
```

If for some reason the current locale is not supported, we might default to English as the standard.

The locale class contains a number of methods for determining supported language, reporting ISO country codes, getting the country name, as well as many others.

Now that we know what locale we need to use how can we make use of this information to internationalize our applet? Enter resources and resource bundles.

19.2 RESOURCES

We've seen locales and now know how to determine what should be internationalized, but how do we store and manage these resources? The text, buttons, errors, and messages that make up the user interface of an application are its "resources." Resources typically include:

- GUI element labels
- Date and time display formats
- Currency and number formatting
- Error messages and messages in general
- Sounds and other images

The Java JDK1.1 provides a new base class used for handling resources known as a ResourceBundle. ResourceBundle is an abstract base class that has two subclasses derived from it, ListResourceBundle and PropertyResourceBundle.

- **ListResourceBundle.** An abstract base class that is normally subclassed further to contain key-value pairs for resources.
- **PropertyResourceBundle.** Contains `property` class based objects and is NOT an abstract class.

Typically, a developer subclasses ListResourceBundle to supply resources or loads properties, via a property file, into a PropertyResourceBundle. With the general concepts of resources firmly in mind, let's look at how to use a resource bundle.

Using Resource Bundles

To use resource bundles you must first define one or more classes that contain the resources you wish to internationalize. You then use the ResourceBundle base class as a class factory to return the resources applicable to a given language. Sources 19.3 and 19.4 show the English and German versions of the resource bundles necessary for internationalizing English.java.

SOURCE 19.3 MyResources.java

```
package jwiley.chp19;
import java.util.ListResourceBundle;

/**
 * public class MyResources
 * @author A. Saganich
 * @version 1.1
 *
 * Sample class to exercise the use of ListResourceBundles.
 *
 * @see java.util.Locale;
 * @see java.util.ListResourceBundle;
 */

public class MyResources extends ListResourceBundle
{
     public Object[][] getContents()
     {
          return contents;
     }
     static final Object[][] contents =
     {
          { "yes",        "Yes"} ,
          { "no",         "No"},
          { "maybe",      "Maybe"},
          { "today",      "Today is:"},
          { "language",   "Language"}
     };
}
```

SOURCE 19.4 MyResources_de.java

```
package jwiley.chp19;
import java.util.ListResourceBundle;

/**
 * public class MyResources_de
 * @author A. Saganich
 * @version 1.1
 *
 * Sample applet to exercise the use of ListResourceBundles.
 *
 * @see java.util.Locale;
 * @see java.util.ListResourceBundle;
 */

public class MyResources_de extends ListResourceBundle
{
     public Object[][] getContents()
     {
          return contents;
     }
     static final Object[][] contents =
     {
          { "yes",        "Ja"} ,
          { "no",         "Nein"},
          { "maybe",      "Vielleicht"},
          { "today",      "Heute ist"},
          { "language",  "Sprache"}
     };
}
```

Source 19.5 makes use of these resource bundles, and the French version as well, by displaying all the translated information from each bundle.

SOURCE 19.5 TestResources.java

```
package jwiley.chp19;
import java.applet.Applet;
import java.awt.Graphics;
import java.awt.Frame;
import java.awt.event.WindowEvent;
import java.awt.event.WindowAdapter;
import java.util.Locale;
import java.util.ResourceBundle;
import java.util.Enumeration;

/**
 * public class TestResources
 * @author A. Saganich
 * @version 1.1
```

```
 *
 * Sample applet to exercise the use of Locales and ResourceBundles.
 *
 * @see java.util.Locale;
 */

public class TestResources extends Applet
{

    Locale current;
    private Locale supported[] =
    {
        Locale.US,
        Locale.UK,
        Locale.FRENCH,
        Locale.GERMAN
    };

    /** Determine what the current locale is */
    public void init()
    {
        current = getLocale();
    }

    /**
    * Display the currently supported locales and the associated resources
    * And test if the current locale is supported.
    */
    public void paint(Graphics g)
    {
        int y = 10;
        for ( int i = 0; i < supported.length; i++)
        {
            y = dump(supported[i],y,g);
        }

    }
    int dump(Locale locale, int y,Graphics g)
    {
        g.drawString("Locale:" + locale.getDisplayName() , 10, y+=10);
        g.drawString("Known resources are ", 10, y+=10);
        ResourceBundle myResources =
            ResourceBundle.getBundle("MyResources",locale);
        for (Enumeration e = myResources.getKeys();e.hasMoreElements() ;)
        {
            String key = (String)e.nextElement();
            String value = (String)myResources.getObject(key);
            g.drawString("Key:"+key+"="+value, 20, y+=10);
        }
        return y;
    }
```

```
    /**
     * Simple main method to test the applet.
     */
    static public void main(String args[])
    {
         class ShutdownAdapter extends WindowAdapter
         {
              public void windowClosing(WindowEvent e)
              { System.exit(0); }
         }

           FramemyFrame     = new Frame("TestResources");
           myFrame.addWindowListener(new ShutdownAdapter());
           TestResources TestResources = new TestResources();
           myFrame.setSize(250,350);
           myFrame.add("Center",TestResources);
           TestResources.init();
           TestResources.start();
           myFrame.show();
    }
}
```

Figure 19.3 shows the result of running Source 19.5.

```
TestResources

Locale:English (United States)
Known resources are
  Key:maybe=Maybe
  Key:language=Language
  Key:today=Today is:
  Key:yes=Yes
  Key:no=No
Locale:English (United Kingdom)
Known resources are
  Key:maybe=Maybe
  Key:language=Language
  Key:today=Today is:
  Key:yes=Yes
  Key:no=No
Locale:French (France)
Known resources are
  Key:no=Non
  Key:maybe=Petêtre
  Key:yes=Oui
  Key:language=Langue
  Key:today=Aujourd'hui c'est
Locale:German (Germany)
Known resources are
  Key:no=Nein
  Key:maybe=Vielleicht
  Key:yes=Ja
  Key:language=Sprache
  Key:today=Heute ist
```

FIGURE 19.3 TestResources.

There are many key points to understand about resource bundles. Let's start with the resource bundles themselves.

Loading Resource Bundles Before we look at the internals of a resource bundle you need to understand the way resource bundles are loaded. A resource bundle is typically a family of resources, each one representing a given type of resource and an appropriate locale. In our example, we supported three languages: English (UK and US), German, and French. The names of the associated resource bundles were MyResources.java(English), MyResources_fr.java(French) and MyResources_de.java(German). The choice of these names was far from arbitrary. Basically a resource bundle family is named as follows:

1. family name + "_" + localeLanguage +"_"+ localeCountry + "_" + localeVariation
   or
2. family name + "_" + localeLanguage
   or
3. family name + "_" + defaultLanguage +"_"+ defaultCountry + "_" + defaultVariation
   or
4. family name + "_" + defaultLanguage

The getBundle method of the ResourceBundle class then attempts to load classes based on the conventions just given and in the order specified, stopping when a class is found and loaded using the given locale. If no resource bundle can be found a MissingResourceException is thrown. In our example we load and display all the resources for each of the supported languages using the following code:

```
ResourceBundle myResources =
     ResourceBundle.getBundle("MyResources",locale);
for (Enumeration e = myResources.getKeys();e.hasMoreElements() ;)
{
     String key = (String)e.nextElement();
     String value = (String)myResources.getObject(key);
     g.drawString("Key:"+key+"="+value, 20, y+=10);
}
```

While we will not detail an example, PropertyResourceBundles are loaded in exactly the same fashion as ListResourceBundles, with the exception that instead of searching for a class, the getBundle method searched for a file ending in .properties.

Creating Resource Bundles We've seen an example of how to use a resource bundle after it's been developed, but how do we create resource bundles in the first place?

Let's examine Source 19.3 more closely. First, each user-defined resource bundle must be subclassed from ListResourceBundle and requires that the abstract method getContents be implemented. The simplest way to implement a ListResourceBundle is to embed an array of objects as was done in Sources 19.3 and 19.4. Other methods are certainly possible, your mileage may vary.

Our example only placed strings into our resource bundles. However, there is no reason that you could not place other objects into your bundles. For example, if two languages differed on the definition of PI you might insert a double entry like { "PI", new Double(3.14)}. In fact, since both the key and the value are Java objects, they can contain anything object.

Source 19.6 shows how our original application changes when we use resource bundles.

SOURCE 19.6 International.java

```
package jwiley.chp19;
import java.applet.Applet;
import java.awt.*;
import java.awt.event.*;
import java.util.Locale;
import java.util.ResourceBundle;
import java.util.Enumeration;

/**
 * public class International
 * @author A. Saganich
 * @version 1.1
 *
 * Sample applet using Locales and Resource bundles for internationalization.
 *
 */
public class International extends Applet
{
     Locale current;
     ResourceBundle myResources;
     private Locale supported[] =
     {
          Locale.US,
          Locale.UK,
          Locale.FRENCH,
          Locale.GERMAN
     };
      class ButtonHandler implements ActionListener
     {
          public ButtonHandler()
          {
          }
          public void actionPerformed(ActionEvent ae)
          {
               Button pushed = (Button)ae.getSource();
               String sCommand = ae.getActionCommand();
```

```
            if ("Yes".equals(sCommand))
            {
                System.out.println("User hit 'Yes' button");
            }
            else if ("No".equals(sCommand))
            {
                System.out.println("User hit 'No' button");
            }
            else if ( "Maybe".equals (sCommand))
            {
                System.out.println("User hit 'Maybe' button");
            }
        } // end ActionPerforned
    } // end NumberHandler implements ActionListener

    public void init()
    {
        current = getLocale();
        int which = -1;
        for (int i = 0; i < supported.length;i++)
        {
            if ( current.equals(supported[i]))
            {
                which = i;
                break;
            }
        }
        // Default to english if not found.
        if ( which == -1)
            current = supported[0];
            myResources = ResourceBundle.getBundle("MyResources",current);

        Panel topPanel = new Panel();
        topPanel.setLayout(new GridLayout(2,2));
        Label label =
            new Label(myResources.getString("language"),Label.LEFT);
        topPanel.add(label);

        label = new Label(current.getDisplayLanguage(),Label.RIGHT);
        topPanel.add(label);
        label = new Label(myResources.getString("curr"),Label.LEFT);
        topPanel.add(label);
        Label currency =
            new Label(myResources.getString("currValue"),Label.RIGHT);
        topPanel.add(currency);
        add("North",topPanel);
        Panel middlePanel = new Panel();
        middlePanel.setLayout(new GridLayout(1,2));
```

```
        label = new Label(myResources.getString("today"),Label.LEFT);
        middlePanel.add(label);
        Label date = new Label("31-July-1997",Label.RIGHT);
        middlePanel.add(date);
        add("Center",middlePanel);
        ButtonHandler bh = new ButtonHandler();
        Button b;
        Panel buttonPanel = new Panel();
        buttonPanel.setLayout(new GridLayout(1,3));
        buttonPanel.add(b = new Button(myResources.getString("yes")));
        b.addActionListener(bh);
        buttonPanel.add(b = new Button(myResources.getString("no")));
        b.addActionListener(bh);
        buttonPanel.add(b = new Button(myResources.getString("maybe")));
        b.addActionListener(bh);
        add("South",buttonPanel);
    }

    /**
     * Simple main method to test the applet.
     */
    static public void main(String args[])
    {
        class ShutdownAdapter extends WindowAdapter
        {
            public void windowClosing(WindowEvent e)
            { System.exit(0); }
        }
          FramemyFrame    = new Frame("International");
          myFrame.addWindowListener(new ShutdownAdapter());
          International international = new International();
          myFrame.setSize(300,150);
          myFrame.add("Center",international);
          international.init();
          international.start();
          myFrame.show();
    }
}
```

Adding resource support to our application was a simple process. First we imported the required packages for locale and resource bundle support.

```
import java.util.Locale;
import java.util.ResourceBundle;
```

Next we defined a resource bundle variable.

```
ResourceBundle myResources;
```

In the applet's init method we determined the current locale and loaded the corresponding resource, defaulting to English if the locale was unknown.

```
current = getLocale();
int which = -1;
for (int i = 0; i < supported.length;i++)
{
     if ( current.equals(supported[i]))
     {
          which = i;
          break;
     }
}
// Default to english if not found.
if ( which == -1)
     current = supported[0];
myResources = ResourceBundle.getBundle("MyResources",current);
```

And finally, each of the buttons, labels, and other GUI elements that should be locale-specific were loaded from the resource bundle.

```
label = new Label(myResources.getString("curr"),Label.LEFT);
. . .
Label currency =
          new Label(myResources.getString("currValue"),Label.RIGHT);
```

Figure 19.4 shows the result of running our newly internationalized application on a computer running the German version of Windows 95.

While everything looks correct there is still a problem with this application. When Java applications were developed in English it was common to use an class implemented from ActionListener to capture events. The ActionListener class, in our case a class known as ButtonHandler, was developed that took the input event and

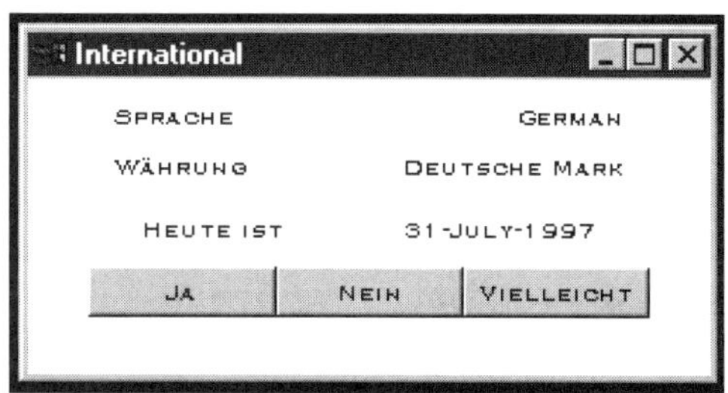

FIGURE 19.4 German.

used it as the source for determining what function to perform. This was done as shown here.

```
class ButtonHandler implements ActionListener
{
    public ButtonHandler()
    {
    }
    public void actionPerformed(ActionEvent ae)
    {
        Button pushed = (Button)ae.getSource();
        String sCommand = ae.getActionCommand();
        if ("Yes".equals(sCommand))
        {
        System.out.println("User hit 'Yes' button");
        }
    . . .
}
```

The problem with this code is that it depends on the label associated with the button. If the button label changes, as it did when the German version of the resource bundle was used, the test failed when the Ja (yes) button was pressed. We can solve this problem simply by using the setActionCommand method of the Button class to assign a meaningful name to the button, separate from its label. The following snippet of code shows this technique.

```
button b = new Button(myResources.getString("yes")
b.setActionCommand("YesButton");
b.addActionListener(buttonHandler);
```

TIP Both buttons and menu items support the setActionCommand method. Other GUI elements support other similar constructs. Check the JDK documentation for the GUI element you are using to determine if it will be affected by internationalization and if so, take appropriate steps to circumvent such errors!

19.3 DATA FORMATTING

The final area that needs consideration when developing international applications is data formatting. Many forms of data are displayed differently from locale to locale. Dates are the most commonly affected data element, but numbers (often in the form of currency) also change. In addition, sentence structure and word order often differ between languages, making it troublesome to construct messages by simply concatenating strings. The JDK provides several class factory style objects, each geared to handling a specific type of formatting.

Date Formatting

The JDK provides a class, DateFormat, which can be used to format dates in a locale-specific manner. The following snippet of code shows an example of how one might format date/times by locale.

```
DateFormat df = DateFormat.getDateTimeInstance(DateFormat.LONG,
                                         DateFormat.LONG,currentLocale);
Date date = new Date();
TimeZone tz = TimeZone.getTimeZone("EST");
df.setTimeZone(tz);
String sDate = df.format(date);
```

Number Formatting

Number formatting is similar to date formatting but simpler. The JDK provides the NumberFormat class to handle the process of formatting numbers and currencies. The following snippet of code shows how one might format numbers and currencies.

```
double aDouble = 12345678.0129;
NumberFormat currFormatter =
NumberFormat.getCurrencyInstance(currentLocale);
NumberFormat nf = NumberFormat.getInstance(currentLocale);
String sCurrency = currFormatter.format(aDouble);
String sDouble = nf.format(aDouble);
```

Message Formatting

Many messages are simple text that can be stored in a resource bundle and then retrieved and displayed at run time. However, other messages might be longer and require modification before display. Consider a disk-space monitoring application. While it might be possible to store in a resource bundle all the possible disk device names and then grab the correct one, it would be much simpler to store a single message with a "hole" that can be filled in at run time with the correct disk instance name. Messages are both the simplest and most complex formatting task developers need to work with. This is because there are not "common" types of messages that can be coded ahead of time and then used at run time.

Messages are formatted by taking an array of objects and a formatting string and then replacing the "holes" in the format string with the contents of the replacement objects. In its simplest form, MessageFormat can be used as follows:

```
Object[] arguments =
{
     new Integer(7),
     new Double(5),
     "Some Text"
};
String sFormatted = MessageFormat.format(
     "An integer {0}, followed by a double{1}, followed by a string{2}.",
```

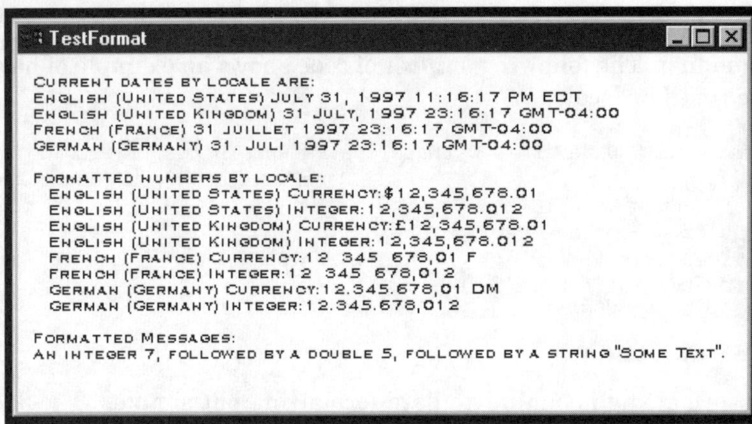

FIGURE 19.5 TestFormat output.

The format method of the MessageFormat class takes two arguments, the format string and the array of arguments. Under normal circumstances the format string would come from a resource bundle and the array arguments populated at run time with appropriate values.

The MessageFormat class is a very powerful class that can format strings, numbers, dates, and currencies in a variety of ways. See the JDK documentation for more information about the MessageFormat class and formatting complex expressions.

Figure 19.5 shows the result of applying these formatting classes and methods to some simple data.

19.4 SUMMARY

The Internet is large and grows larger every day. No longer can developers assume that English only is enough. In this chapter, we have seen how to specify locales and support resource bundles, allowing for robust internationalized applications that can adapt to the location that they are run from. Such an application is made even more robust through appropriate use of Date, Time, Number, and Message formatting.

We have only begun to scratch the surface of Java development. As the Internet grows and matures, international applications will become more and more important. This chapter has hopefully given you some insights into the internationalization process and some leads as to what classes and methods are available to build the next generation of internationalized Java applications.

CHAPTER 20

Package javax.servlet

OBJECTIVE

This chapter will provide an overview of The Java Servlet Development Kit (JSDK). We will examine the purpose of the JSDK, the contents of the JSDK package, and show you how to write your own servlets.

Almost every Java developer has written a Java applet to provide dynamic content to a Web page. But how do you provide dynamic content from your Web server? Until now, there were only two ways: CGI and proprietary APIs provided by your Web server. Now there is a third way: The Java Servlet Development Kit (JSDK). The JSDK lets you extend a Java-enabled Web server with servlets. Servlets are server-side components written in Java. Since servlets are written in Java they are platform independent, but they are also designed to be protocol independent. Even though servlets are protocol independent, the HTTP protocol is implemented within the JSDK due to its popularity. You can use servlets anywhere you used CGI before or anywhere you need dynamic content. Servlets can be used to process forms, interact with a database, or even act as a middle tier in a three-tier architecture.

There are several reasons to switch to servlets for server-side processing instead of using CGI. Here are the major reasons:

- **Performance.** There are two areas where servlets have a performance advantage. First, since servlets run under a JVM they have built-in support for threads. Since creating a thread is less expensive than creating a new process, creating a new servlet is less expensive then executing a CGI program. Second, once a servlet is loaded it remains in memory waiting for a new request. CGI programs have to load every time a request is made.

- **Server-side includes.** The SERVLET tag can be embedded in an HTML file, triggering a servlet to be run. The output of the servlet will be placed in the HTML file where the SERVLET tag was. Therefore, server-side includes provide a mechanism for dynamic HTML.
- **Cross-platform.** Since servlets are written in Java, all servlets will be cross-platform.
- **Java.** This is the best reason. You get to program in Java instead of C or some scripting language.

The JSDK can be downloaded from Javasoft at http://jserv.javasoft.com/products/java-server/sdk/. The JSDK comes with everything you need to start developing servlets. It includes API documentation, source code for the javax.* and sun.* packages, sample servlets, and a testing utility. It also comes with information on how to run servlets with several popular Web servers, such as Netscape Fasttrack, Microsoft IIS, and Apache.

The rest of this chapter will focus on the content of the JSDK and instruction on how to write your own servlets. First we will look at the development/testing environment and run some sample servlets. Next we will go over the javax.servlet and javax.servlet.http packages. Finally, we will see a servlet that presents a mini Web site, one that provides database interaction and forms processing.

Note: The Java Servlet API is a *Standard Java Extension API*. Since it is an extension to Java it is not included with standard Java libraries. It is included in this book to demonstrate that Java can and should be used for server-side processing.

20.1 SERVLET ENVIRONMENT

You should already have downloaded and installed the Java Servlet Development Kit. The README file included with the kit gives platform-specific instructions on setting up the environment to run servlets. The two main things you need to do are to modify your path and classpath variables:

- **ClassPath.** To compile servlets, the <jsdk-home>\lib\classes.zip path has to be added to your classpath variable, where <jsdk-home> is the root of the JSDK installation.
- **Path.** To test your servlets, the <jsdk-home>\bin path has to be added to your path variable, where <jsdk-home> is the root of the JSDK installation.

A standalone server called the ServletRunner is included in the JSDK to test servlets. The ServletRunner will be invoked by executing the file srun. Srun lets you set several options, including the port to listen on, the servlet directory, and others. Servlets can be accessed from your browser by specifying the servlet directory and the servlet's class name. To see if your environment is set up to run servlets, start the ServletRunner, open your browser, and go to the following URL: http://<hostname>:8080/servlet/HelloWorldServlet, where <hostname> is the hostname of your Web server. You should see something similar to Figure 20.1.

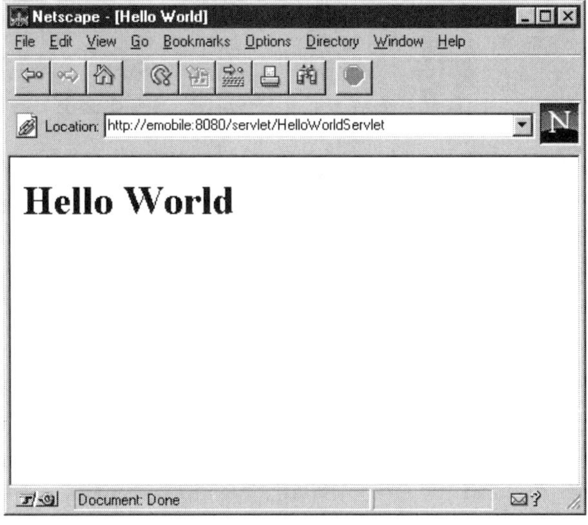

FIGURE 20.1 HelloWorldServlet.

Besides using the ServletRunner, you can also test your servlets using your own Java-enabled Web server. Consult the JSDK documentation to find out how to run servlets with your Web server. If you successfully ran the HelloWorldServlet then you are ready to start developing your own servlets. The next section will describe the classes necessary to create a servlet, and also provides a few example servlets.

20.2 SERVLET PACKAGES

This section describes the classes in the javax.servlet package and the javax.servlet.http package. The sun.* packages are not discussed here, but complete documentation is included with the JSDK.

package javax.servlet

- **Servlet.** This is an interface that all servlets must implement. This interface provides methods for initializing and destroying the servlet, responding to requests, and getting configuration and servlet information. Most servlets will not implement this interface directly, they will subclass GenericServlet or HttpServlet instead. If the servlet cannot extend one of these two classes, this interface will have to be implemented directly.
- **ServletConfig.** This is an interface that is used to pass information to a servlet when it is initialized. The init() method in the Servlet interface accepts a Servlet-

Config object as an argument. Methods are provided to retrieve the ServletContext and any initialization parameters.

- **ServletContext.** This interface should be implemented by Web Servers that can run servlets. The methods provided in this interface provide information about the environment of the servlet. A log method is also provided to write messages to the servlet log file.
- **ServletRequest.** This interface provides methods for getting data from a client request. Methods are provided for obtaining an input stream, for getting content information, getting the protocol, getting parameters, and others. A servlet developer should not have to implement this interface, but should know how to use the methods to obtain information.
- **ServletResponse.** This interface provides methods for sending data in response to a client request. Methods are provided for obtaining an output stream, and for setting the content type and length. Servlet developers do not have to implement this interface, but should know how to use the methods to send data back to the client.
- **GenericServlet.** This class implements both the Servlet and ServletConfig interfaces. This class is provided to make writing servlets easier, you just have to subclass GenericServlet and override the service method to write your own servlet. The GenericServlet provides a default implementation for init() and destroy(). These methods can be overridden to perform more specific initialization or cleanup.
- **ServletInputStream.** This is an abstract class that extends java.io.InputStream. It only provides one method, readLine(), used for getting information from the client.
- **ServletOutputStream.** This is an abstract class that extends java.io.OutputStream. Several print() and println() methods are provided to make sure Java data types are properly converted for the specific protocol being used. Using these methods lets you send information back to the client.
- **ServletException.** This class extends java.lang.Exception and is thrown to indicate a servlet problem.
- **UnavailableException.** This class extends ServletException and is thrown to indicate that a servlet is temporarily unavailable. You can specify whether the servlet is temporarily unavailable or permanently unavailable. If the servlet is temporarily unavailable, you can set the number of seconds the servlet expects to be temporarily unavailable.

package javax.servlet.http

- **HttpServletRequest.** This in an interface that represents an HTTP request. The methods provided by this interface allow you to get HTTP-specific header information. Many of the methods provided by HttpServletRequest directly correspond with CGI variables. The getQueryString() method returns the same text available in the CGI variable QUERY_STRING. Six other methods also correspond to CGI variables.

- **HttpServletResponse.** This is an interface that represents an HTTP response. Methods are available for sending statuses and errors. The common HTTP status and error codes are defined as public variables for your convenience.

HttpServlet. This is an abstract class that extends GenericServlet. You should subclass HttpServlet to easily implement your own servlets. The doGet() method is provided to respond to an HTTP GET request, and the doPost() method is provided to respond to an HTTP POST request. You should override these methods to perform your own processing for GET and POST requests. To handle other requests you will need to override the service() method.

HttpUtils. This class is a collection of HTTP utilities. The parsePostData() method is used to parse FORM data passed in from an HTTP POST request. The parseQueryString() method will parse parameters in the query string and return a Hashtable of key/value pairs. One other method, getRequestURL(), is provided to obtain the URL used by the client for the current request.

HttpServlet Example

The following is an example of writing your own servlet. As you can see, it is very easy to receive requests and respond to them using the HttpServlet class. The real work in writing servlets is implementing the processing to be done by the service() method, or possibly the doGet() and doPost() methods.

SOURCE 20.1 MyFirstServlet.java

```
// MyFirstServlet.java
import java.io.IOException;

import javax.servlet.*;
import javax.servlet.http.*;

/**
 * This class demonstrates a simple servlet
 *
 * @author Eric Monk
 * @version 1.0
 */
public class MyFirstServlet extends HttpServlet
{
    public void service(HttpServletRequest req, HttpServletResponse res)
                            throws ServletException, IOException
    {
        res.setContentType("text/html");

        ServletOutputStream out = res.getOutputStream();
```

```
        out.println("<HTML>");

        // head
        out.println("<HEAD>");
        out.println("<TITLE>My First Servlet</TITLE>");
        out.println("</HEAD>");

        // body
        out.println("<BODY>");
        out.println("<H2>My First Servlet</H2>");
        out.println("<P>This is my first servlet.</P>");
        out.println("<P>Request URI: " + req.getRequestURI() + "</P>");
        out.println("<P>Servlet Path: " + req.getServletPath() + "</P>");
        out.println("</BODY>");
        out.println("</HTML>");
    }
    public String getServletInfo() {
        return "My first servlet";
    }
}
```

As seen in Source 20.1 there are five basic points to writing a servlet:

- **subclass HttpServlet.** Extending HttpServlet means you only have to implement one method, service(), to create your servlet. Servlet initialization and destruction are handled automatically.
- **override the service() method.** This method will be called to handle any request sent to your servlet. This method should read the client request and send back a response.
- **read the client request.** The client request will be available as an HttpServletRequest object. You can get specific information about the request by executing methods in the HttpServletRequest object. In Source 20.1 we examine some information in the request by calling the getRequestURI() and getServletPath() methods.
- **send the response.** Based on the client request, you should construct the necessary response. You can send the response back by using methods in the HttpServletResponse object. The setContentType() method should be called to set the appropriate MIME type for the response, and accessing the ServletOutputStream in the HttpServletResponse object will allow data to be sent back to the client. In Source 20.1 we get the ServletOutputStream from the response object, and print HTML back to the client.
- **override the getServletInfo() method.** This method is used to obtain information about the servlet. This method does not have to be overridden, but it is good practice so servlet administrative tools can get information about the servlet.

FIGURE 20.2 MyFirstServlet.

Accessing the servlet from a browser is displayed in Figure 20.2.

20.3 SERVLET TAG

The SERVLET tag lets you include servlets in an HTML file. When the servlet tag is encountered the specified servlet will be invoked and the output will be placed where the servlet tag was. The servlet tag is only processed if the HTML file has an extension of .shtml. The syntax of the SERVLET tag is:

```
<servlet name=ServletName code=ServletCode.class codebase=ServletCodeBase
initParam1=initArg1 initParam2=initArg2 ...>
<param name=param1 value=val1>
<param name=param2 value=val2>
.
.
.
</servlet>
```

If your server does not support servlets, the servlet tag will be ignored. Let's take a look at an example.

SOURCE 20.2 CountServlet.java

```
// CountServlet.java
import java.io.IOException;

import javax.servlet.*;
import javax.servlet.http.*;

/**
 * This class demonstrates server-side includes, i.e. the SERVLET tag
 *
 * @author Eric Monk
 * @version 1.0
 */
public class CountServlet extends HttpServlet
{
     public void service(HttpServletRequest req, HttpServletResponse res)
                             throws ServletException, IOException
     {
          res.setContentType("text/html");

          ServletOutputStream out = res.getOutputStream();

          String sStartNum = req.getParameter("start");
          String sEndNum = req.getParameter("end");

          try
          {
               int iStartNum = Integer.parseInt(sStartNum);
               int iEndNum = Integer.parseInt(sEndNum);

               for (int iCount = iStartNum; iCount <= iEndNum; iCount++)
               {
                    out.println("<P>" + iCount + "</P>");
               }
          } catch (NumberFormatException nfe)
            {
               out.println("Error: " + nfe.toString());
            }
     }

     public String getServletInfo() {
          return "Count servlet";
     }
}
```

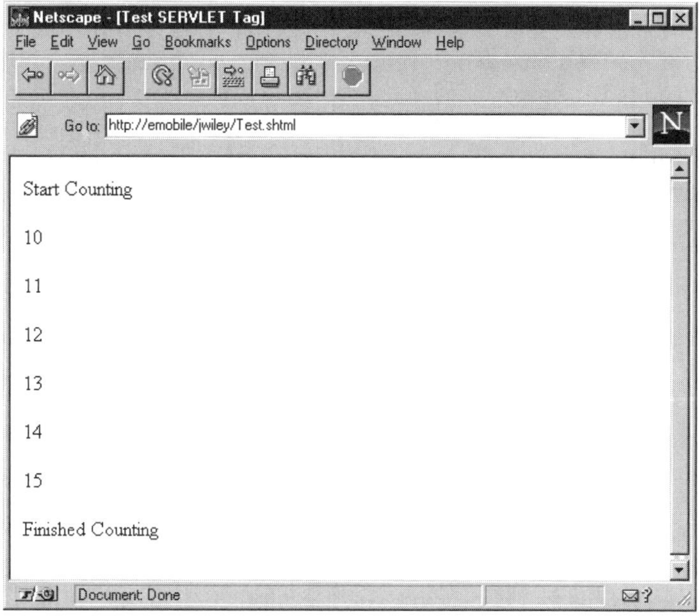

FIGURE 20.3 Example of SERVLET tag.

The HTML listed here will produce Figure 20.3. This example cannot be tested with the ServletRunner that comes with the JSDK, because the ServletRunner will not handle files. To test this example you must use a Java-enabled Web server.

```
<HTML>
<HEAD>
<TITLE>Test SERVLET Tag</TITLE>
</HEAD>
<BODY>
<P>Start Counting</P>
<SERVLET CODE=CountServlet.class>
<PARAM NAME=start VALUE=10>
<PARAM NAME=stop VALUE=15>
</SERVLET>
<P>Finished Counting</P>
</BODY>
</HTML>
```

Server-side includes using the SERVLET tag can be useful for simple dynamic content. But much more power can be achieved by calling the servlet directly from the browser. The next section presents a mini Web site that is handled by one servlet.

20.4 SERVLET WEB SITE EXAMPLE

The example discussed in this section is a servlet that handles all requests and responses for a mini Web site. The premise for this example is an online book service, which allows you to list books, search for books, or add a new book. This example makes extensive use of JDBC, and uses the Books Table defined in Chapter 18. In addition, the example demonstrates how to process an HTML form, how to generate dynamic HTML, and even contains a small amount of JavaScript. Let us begin by describing the classes that compose the servlet and a brief description of the jwiley.chp20.html package.

The following classes compose the servlet that handles our mini Web site.

- **DatabaseServlet.** This class extends HttpServlet and is the main class in our servlet. It is responsible for establishing and closing the connection to the database, and it also handles HTTP GET and HTTP POST requests.
- **BooksExampleHomePage.** This class is an HTML page and represents the main page for our web site. From here you can search, add a book, or list all books.
- **BooksSearchForm.** This class is an HTML form used to pass search information back to DatabaseServlet.
- **SearchResultsPage.** This class is an HTML page that displays books meeting the criteria of a search. By clicking on a book title, you can view the detailed information for the book.
- **BooksDetailPage.** This class is an HTML page that displays the detailed information for a book. From here you can save or delete the book's information.
- **MessagePage.** This class is an HTML page that displays an error or status message.
- **BookRecord.** This class encapsulates the data for a single book record.

In addition to the classes just described, the jwiley.chp20.html package contains many classes for creating HTML pages and components. These classes will not be discussed in detail here but are available on the enclosed CD. This package was created to encapsulate common HTML tags or components as Java objects. This facilitates the creation of dynamic HTML and code reuse.

Servlets should be designed to run in a mutlithreaded environment; this means you need to synchronize methods or statements that might cause a potential resource conflict. In this example, great liberty was taken by synchronizing both the doGet() and doPost() methods. To gain the advantage of multithreading, more specific synchronization should be done.

To access the Books Online homepage (the DatabaseServlet), go to the following URL in your browser: http://<hostname>:8080/servlet/DatabaseServlet. Your browser should look like Figure 20.4.

You can play around with the Web pages, but notice that every link calls DatabaseServlet either without parameters or with a query string attached. DatabaseServlet handles all interaction for the Web site. Let's look at the code for each class and highlight the key points in each class.

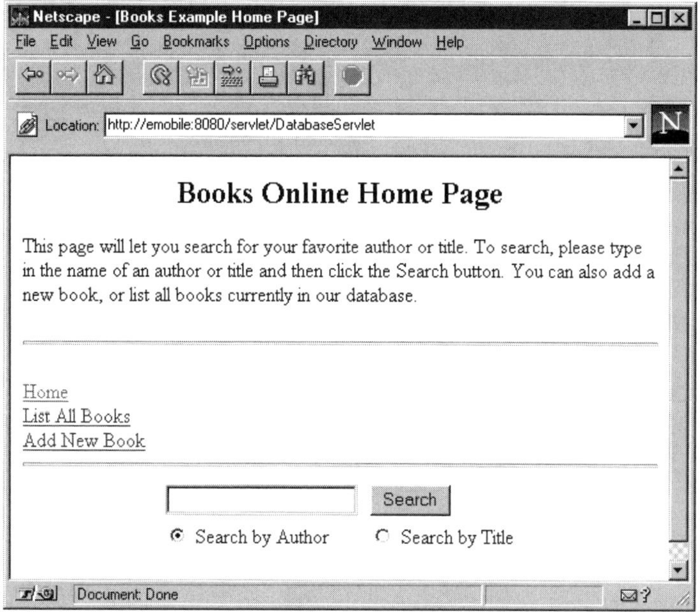

FIGURE 20.4 Books Online home page.

SOURCE 20.3 DatabaseServlet.java.

```
// DatabaseServlet.java
import java.io.IOException;
import java.util.Enumeration;
import java.util.Vector;
import java.sql.*;

import javax.servlet.*;
import javax.servlet.http.*;

import jwiley.chp20.*;
import jwiley.chp20.html.HtmlPage;

/**
 * This servlet demonstrates some of the power that can be
 * achieved using servlets. This servlet interacts with the
 * database, handles HTML form processing, and constructs
 * dynamic HTML.
 *
 * @author Eric Monk
 * @version 1.0
 */
```

```
public class DatabaseServlet extends HttpServlet
{
    private Connection con;
    private Statement stmt;

    public void init (ServletConfig config) throws ServletException
    {
        super.init(config);

        try
        {
            // Load database driver
            Class.forName ("sun.jdbc.odbc.JdbcOdbcDriver");
        } catch (ClassNotFoundException cnfe)
          {
            String sErrorMsg = "Error loading database drivers. " +
                               "Error: " + cnfe.toString();
            log(sErrorMsg);
            throw new UnavailableException(this, sErrorMsg);
          }

        try
        {
            // Establish connection
            String sUrl = "jdbc:odbc:ExampleDb";
            con = DriverManager.getConnection(sUrl);
            stmt = con.createStatement();
        } catch (SQLException sqle)
          {
            String sErrorMsg = "Could not establish database connection.";
            log(sErrorMsg);
            logSQLException(sqle);
            throw new UnavailableException(this, sErrorMsg);
          }
    }

    public void destroy ()
    {
        try
        {
            // Close database connection
            stmt.close();
            con.close();
        } catch (SQLException sqle)
          {
            log("Could not close database connection.");
            logSQLException(sqle);
          }
        super.destroy();
    }
```

```
    private void logSQLException (SQLException sqle)
    {
        while (sqle != null)
        {
            log("SQLState: " + sqle.getSQLState ());
            log("Message: " + sqle.getMessage ());
            log("ErrorCode: " + sqle.getErrorCode ());
            sqle = sqle.getNextException ();
        }
    }
synchronized protected void doGet(HttpServletRequest req,
                                  HttpServletResponse res)
                                  throws ServletException, IOException
{
    res.setContentType("text/html");

    String sServletAddress = req.getServletPath();
    ServletOutputStream out = res.getOutputStream();

    // parse query string
    String sQueryString = req.getQueryString();
    if (sQueryString == null)
    {
        BooksExampleHomePage homePage =
                new BooksExampleHomePage(sServletAddress);
        out.print(homePage.getHtml());
    }
    else
    {
        // look for command parameter
        String sCommand =
            req.getParameter(BooksExampleHomePage.COMMAND_CONST);
        if (sCommand == null)
        {
            BooksExampleHomePage homePage =
                new BooksExampleHomePage(sServletAddress);
            out.print(homePage.getHtml());
        }
        else
        {
            // handle command parameter
            if (sCommand.equals(BooksExampleHomePage.LIST_ALL_COMMAND))
            {
                String sql = "SELECT * FROM Books";
                HtmlPage resultsPage =
                       handleSearch(sql, sServletAddress);
                out.print(resultsPage.getHtml());
            }
            else if (sCommand.equals(
                       BooksExampleHomePage.SEARCH_COMMAND))
            {
```

```
                String sSearchParam = req.getParameter("searchParams");
                String sSearchText = req.getParameter("SearchText");

                String sWhereClause = null;
                if (sSearchParam.equals("author"))
                {
                    sWhereClause = " WHERE (Author";
                }
                else if (sSearchParam.equals("title"))
                {
                    sWhereClause = " WHERE (Title";
                    }
                    sWhereClause = sWhereClause + " Like '%" +
                                            sSearchText + "%')";

                    String sql = "SELECT * FROM Books" + sWhereClause;

                    HtmlPage resultsPage =
                          handleSearch(sql, sServletAddress);
                    out.print(resultsPage.getHtml());
                }
                else if
(sCommand.equals(BooksExampleHomePage.GET_COMMAND))
                {
                    String sBookId = req.getParameter("bookid");
                    String sql = "SELECT * FROM Books WHERE BookId = "
                                                          + sBookId;
                    try
                    {
                        ResultSet rslt = stmt.executeQuery(sql);

                        // Process data
                        if (rslt.next())
                        {
                            BookRecord record = new BookRecord();
                            record.setBookId(rslt.getInt("BookId"));
                            record.setTitle(rslt.getString("Title"));
                            record.setAuthor(rslt.getString("Author"));
                            record.setNumPages(rslt.getInt("NumPages"));

                            BooksDetailPage detailPage =
                              new BooksDetailPage(sServletAddress,
                                   record);
                            out.print(detailPage.getHtml());
                        }
                        else
                        {
                            String sMessage =
                                "Could not find specified record.";
```

```
                        MessagePage message =
                            new MessagePage(sServletAddress,
                                         "Error", sMessage);
                        out.print(message.getHtml());
                    }
                    rslt.close();

                } catch (SQLException sqle)
                  {
                    String sMessage = "A database error has
                        occurred.";
                    MessagePage message =
                        new MessagePage(sServletAddress, "Error",
                                    sMessage + "<BR>Error: " +
                                    sqle.toString());
                    out.print(message.getHtml());
                    logSQLException(sqle);
                  }
            }
            else if (sCommand.equals(BooksExampleHomePage.NEW_COMMAND))
            {
            // get form in new mode
            BooksDetailPage newBook =
                    new BooksDetailPage(sServletAddress, null);
            out.print(newBook.getHtml());
        }
    }
  }
}

synchronized protected void doPost(HttpServletRequest req,
                              HttpServletResponse res)
                              throws ServletException, IOException
{
    res.setContentType("text/html");

    String sServletAddress = req.getServletPath();
    ServletOutputStream out = res.getOutputStream();

    // look for command parameter
    String sCommand =
        req.getParameter(BooksExampleHomePage.COMMAND_CONST);
    if (sCommand == null)
    {
        BooksExampleHomePage homePage =
                new BooksExampleHomePage(sServletAddress);
        out.print(homePage.getHtml());
    }
    else
    {
```

```
        // handle command parameter
        if (sCommand.equals(BooksExampleHomePage.SAVE_COMMAND))
        {
             String sBookId = req.getParameter("bookid");
             String sTitle = req.getParameter("title");
             String sAuthor = req.getParameter("author");
             String sNumPages = req.getParameter("numpages");

             if (sTitle.equals("") || sAuthor.equals("") ||
                                      sNumPages.equals(""))
             {
                  String sMessage = "The following fields are required:"
                                          + " Title, Author, NumPages";
                  MessagePage message =
                    new MessagePage(sServletAddress, "Error", sMessage);
                  out.print(message.getHtml());
                  return;
             }

             try
             {
                  int iNumPages = Integer.parseInt(sNumPages);
             } catch (NumberFormatException nfe)
               {
                  String sMessage = "Num Pages must be an integer. " +
                                  "Click back to correct the error.";
                  MessagePage message =
                    new MessagePage(sServletAddress, "Error", sMessage);
                  out.print(message.getHtml());
                  return;
               }
             String sql = null;
             sBookId = sBookId.trim();

             if (sBookId.equals("0") || sBookId.equals(""))
             {
                  String sQuery = "SELECT MAX(BookId) AS " +
                                  "Max_BookId FROM Books";
                  String sNewBookId = "1";
                  try
                  {
                       ResultSet rslt = stmt.executeQuery(sQuery);
                       if (rslt.next())
                        sNewBookId = "" + (rslt.getInt("Max_BookId") + 1);
                  } catch (SQLException sqle)
                    {
                       String sMessage = "A database error has occurred."
                                          + " Could not get new BookId";
                       MessagePage message =
                            new MessagePage(sServletAddress, "Error",
                                            sMessage + "<BR>Error: " +
```

```
                                          sqle.toString());
                    out.print(message.getHtml());
                    logSQLException(sqle);
                }

                // new record
                sql = "INSERT INTO Books VALUES (" +
                                             sNewBookId + ", '" +
                                             sTitle + "', '" +
                                             sAuthor + "', " +
                                             sNumPages + ")";
            }
            else
            {
                // existing record
                sql = "UPDATE Books SET Title='" + sTitle + "', " +
                    "Author='" + sAuthor + "', NumPages=" + sNumPages +
                    " WHERE BookId=" + sBookId;
            }

            try
            {
                int iStatus = stmt.executeUpdate(sql);
                MessagePage message =
                    new MessagePage(sServletAddress, "Success",
                                 "Successfully saved the title.");
                out.print(message.getHtml());
            } catch (SQLException sqle)
              {
                String sMessage = "A database error has occurred.";
                MessagePage message =
                    new MessagePage(sServletAddress, "Error",
                                    sMessage + "<BR>Error: " +
                                    sqle.toString());
                out.print(message.getHtml());
                logSQLException(sqle);
            }
        }
        else if (sCommand.equals(BooksExampleHomePage.DELETE_COMMAND))
        {
            String sBookId = req.getParameter("bookid");
            String sql = "DELETE FROM Books WHERE bookid=" + sBookId;

            try
            {
                int iStatus = stmt.executeUpdate(sql);
                MessagePage message =
                    new MessagePage(sServletAddress, "Success",
                                 "Successfully deleted the title.");
                out.print(message.getHtml());
            } catch (SQLException sqle)
```

```
                {
                    String sMessage = "A database error has occurred.";
                    MessagePage message =
                        new MessagePage(sServletAddress, "Error",
                                        sMessage + "<BR>Error: " +
                                        sqle.toString());
                    out.print(message.getHtml());
                    logSQLException(sqle);
                }
            }
        }
    }

    private HtmlPage handleSearch(String sql, String sServletAddress)
    {
        try
        {
            ResultSet rslt = stmt.executeQuery(sql);
            Vector vRecords = new Vector();

            // Process data
            while (rslt.next())
            {
                BookRecord record = new BookRecord();
                record.setBookId(rslt.getInt("BookId"));
                record.setTitle(rslt.getString("Title"));
                record.setAuthor(rslt.getString("Author"));
                record.setNumPages(rslt.getInt("NumPages"));

                vRecords.addElement(record);
            }

            BookRecord records[] = null;
            if (vRecords.size() > 0)
            {
                records = new BookRecord[vRecords.size()];
                for (int iCount = 0; iCount < records.length; iCount++)
                    records[iCount] =
                            (BookRecord)vRecords.elementAt(iCount);
            }

            SearchResultsPage resultsPage =
                    new SearchResultsPage(sServletAddress,
                                          records,
                                          "all titles");
                rslt.close();
                return(resultsPage);

        } catch (SQLException sqle)
          {
            String sMessage = "A database error has occurred.";
```

```
            MessagePage message =
                new MessagePage(sServletAddress, "Error",
                                sMessage + "<BR>Error: " +
                                sqle.toString());
            logSQLException(sqle);
            return (message);
        }
    }

    public String getServletInfo() {
        return "Database servlet";
        }

    }
```

The DatabaseServlet class extends HttpServlet in order to handle HTTP requests. This class overrides the init(), destroy(), doGet(), and doPost() methods. Each method performs some critical processing required by the servlet.

- **init.** This method opens the database connection. If getting the database connection fails an UnavailableException is thrown to indicate the servlet will be unavailable. The init() method of the superclass is also called to perform any default initialization required by the servlet. Using the log() method, the servlet can log any errors or message to the log file specified in the servlet.properties file.
- **destroy.** This method closes the database connection. If an error occurs it is logged in the servlet log file. The destroy() method of the superclass is also called to perform any default cleanup.
- **doGet.** This method handles an HTTP GET request. The getParameter() method is called to determine the value of the Command variable. Based on this value, the appropriate Web page is generated and returned to the client. All Web pages in this example implement the HtmlComponent interface, which consists of a single method, getHtml(). The getHtml() method returns a String containing the HTML for that component.
- **doPost.** This method handles an HTTP POST request. The getParameter() method is called to determine the value of the Command variable. Based on this value the appropriate action is performed. This method is called to process an HTML form. The names and values of the fields on the HTML form can be accessed with the getParameter() or getParameters() methods. After getting the value of the form fields the appropriate database action can be taken, such as a save or delete.

Source 20.4 lists the rest of the source files used in the example. Most of the source files build a Web page by creating HTML components. All links created point back to the DatabaseServlet, but contain specific parameter information depending on the action to be performed. The BooksExampleHomePage, SearchResultsPage, and BooksDetailPage all include something noteworthy.

- The BooksExampleHomePage and the SearchResultsPage both use the BooksSearchForm as a component on their Web page. Since the BooksSearchForm is a Java class, it can be used on any number of pages simply by creating a new instance and adding it to the page.
- The BooksDetailPage contains two interesting points. The first is that it is an HTML form that specifies the HTTP "POST" method as the requesting method. This means when the form is submitted it will be handled by the doPost() method in DatabaseServlet instead of the doGet() method. The second point is that it uses JavaScript to perform the actual submit for the form. When the Save or Delete button is pushed, the JavaScript function doSubmit is called with the appropriate action. The specified action gets stored in the hidden form variable Command, and then the form is submitted for processing. Figure 20.5 shows the BooksDetailPage in action.

TIP Due to the length of the source listing, the following supporting classes reside on the CD-ROM: Search Results Page, Books Detail Page, and Message Page. See the CD-ROM to view these source listings.

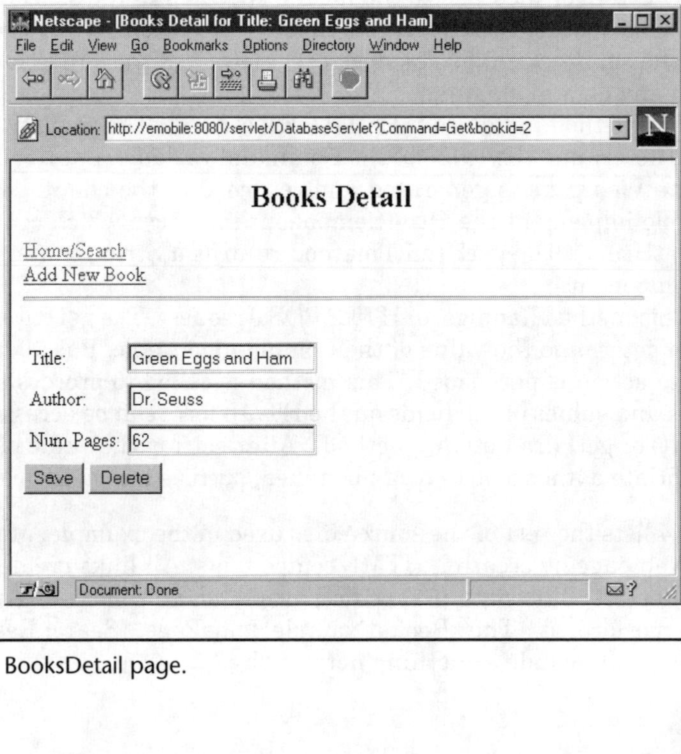

Netscape - [Books Detail for Title: Green Eggs and Ham]

File Edit View Go Bookmarks Options Directory Window Help

Location: http://emobile:8080/servlet/DatabaseServlet?Command=Get&bookid=2

Books Detail

Home/Search
Add New Book

Title: Green Eggs and Ham
Author: Dr. Seuss
Num Pages: 62
Save Delete

Document: Done

FIGURE 20.5 BooksDetail page.

SOURCE 20.4 BookExampleHomePage.java

```
// BooksExampleHomePage.java
package jwiley.chp20;

import jwiley.chp20.html.*;

/**
 * This class represents the home page for the
 * Books Online example
 *
 * @author Eric Monk
 * @version 1.0
 */
public class BooksExampleHomePage extends HtmlPage
{
     public static String COMMAND_CONST = "Command";

     public static String NEW_COMMAND = "New";
     public static String SAVE_COMMAND = "Save";
     public static String DELETE_COMMAND = "Delete";
     public static String GET_COMMAND = "Get";
     public static String SEARCH_COMMAND = "Search";
     public static String LIST_ALL_COMMAND = "ListAll";

     String sServletAddress;

     public BooksExampleHomePage (String sServletAddress)
     {
          super();
          this.sServletAddress = sServletAddress;

          HtmlHead head = new HtmlHead("Books Example Home Page");

          // Body
          HtmlBody body = new HtmlBody();
          HtmlText title = new HtmlText("Books Online Home Page", "H2");
          title.addFormatTag("CENTER");
          body.addComponent(title);

          String sOverview =
               "This page will let you search for your favorite " +
               "author or title. To search, please type in the name " +
               "of an author or title and then click the Search button. " +
               "You can also add a new book, or list all books currently " +
               " in our database.";
          HtmlText overview = new HtmlText(sOverview, "P");
          body.addComponent(overview);
          body.addHtml("<HR SIZE=2>");

          BooksSearchForm searchForm = new BooksSearchForm(sServletAddress);
          body.addComponent(searchForm);
```

```
        setHead(head);
        setBody(body);
    }
}

// BooksSearchForm.java
package jwiley.chp20;

import jwiley.chp20.html.*;

/**
 * This class represents an HTML form for searching
 * available books
 *
 * @author Eric Monk
 * @version 1.0
  */
public class BooksSearchForm extends HtmlForm
{
    public BooksSearchForm (String sServletAddress)
    {
        super("BooksSearchForm", sServletAddress, "GET");

        // create anchors/links
        HtmlAnchor aHome = new HtmlAnchor("",
                           new HtmlText("Home"),
                           sServletAddress);

        String sListAllBooksLink = sServletAddress + "?" +
                                BooksExampleHomePage.COMMAND_CONST + "=" +
                                BooksExampleHomePage.LIST_ALL_COMMAND;
        HtmlAnchor aListAllBooks = new HtmlAnchor("",
                                  new HtmlText("List All Books"),
                                  sListAllBooksLink);

        String sNewBookLink = sServletAddress + "?" +
                             BooksExampleHomePage.COMMAND_CONST + "=" +
                             BooksExampleHomePage.NEW_COMMAND;
        HtmlAnchor aNewBook = new HtmlAnchor("",
                             new HtmlText("Add New Book"),
                             sNewBookLink);

        // add anchors to form
        addComponent(aHome);
        addHtml("<BR>");
        addComponent(aListAllBooks);
        addHtml("<BR>");
        addComponent(aNewBook);

        // create table
        HtmlTable table = new HtmlTable();
        HtmlTableRow rows[] = new HtmlTableRow[2];
```

```
        HtmlTableCell cells[][] = new HtmlTableCell[2][2];

        rows[0] = new HtmlTableRow();
        rows[1] = new HtmlTableRow();

        HtmlTextInput searchText = new HtmlTextInput("SearchText", "");
        HtmlSubmitButton submit =
                    new HtmlSubmitButton("SearchButton", "Search");

        HtmlRadioButton searchAuthors =
                   new HtmlRadioButton("searchParams",
                                       "author",
                                       "Search by Author",
                                       true);
        HtmlRadioButton searchTitle =
                   new HtmlRadioButton("searchParams",
                                       "title",
                                       "Search by Title",
                                       false);

        HtmlHiddenInput command =
                   new HtmlHiddenInput(BooksExampleHomePage.COMMAND_CONST,
              BooksExampleHomePage.SEARCH_COMMAND);

        cells[0][0] = new HtmlTableCell(searchText);
        cells[0][1] = new HtmlTableCell(submit);
        cells[1][0] = new HtmlTableCell(searchAuthors);
        cells[1][1] = new HtmlTableCell(searchTitle);

        rows[0].addCell(cells[0][0]);
        rows[0].addCell(cells[0][1]);
        rows[1].addCell(cells[1][0]);
        rows[1].addCell(cells[1][1]);

        table.addRow(rows[0]);
        table.addRow(rows[1]);

        // add table to form
        addHtml("<HR SIZE=2>");
        addHtml("<CENTER>");
        addComponent(table);
        addHtml("</CENTER>");
        addComponent(command);
    }
}

// BookRecord.java
package jwiley.chp20;

/**
 * This class encapsulates the data for a book record
 *
```

```
 * @author Eric Monk
 * @version 1.0
 */
public class BookRecord
{
     int iBookId = 0;
     String sTitle = "";
     String sAuthor = "";
     int iNumPages = 0;

     public BookRecord () { }

     public BookRecord (int iBookId, String sTitle,
                         String sAuthor, int iNumPages)
     {
          this.iBookId = iBookId;
          this.sTitle = sTitle;
          this.sAuthor = sAuthor;
          this.iNumPages = iNumPages;
     }

     public int getBookId ()       {   return (iBookId);    }
     public String getTitle ()     {   return (sTitle);     }
     public String getAuthor ()    {   return (sAuthor);    }
     public int getNumPages ()     {   return (iNumPages);  }

     public void setBookId (int iBookId)
     { this.iBookId = iBookId; }

     public void setTitle (String sTitle)
     { this.sTitle = sTitle; }

     public void setAuthor (String sAuthor)
     { this.sAuthor = sAuthor; }

     public void setNumPages (int iNumPages)
     { this.iNumPages = iNumPages; }
}
```

20.5 SUMMARY

In this chapter we learned that servlets can be used to implement server-side processing. Servlets can be created with the The Java Servlet Development Kit, which is an extension to Java. We examined the classes needed to implement a servlet, and created some sample servlets. We also examined server-side includes by looking at the SERVLET tag. Creating a servlet is relatively straightforward, but to make a useful servlet requires a lot of forethought and good Java programming.

CHAPTER 21

The Java Media Framework

OBJECTIVE

This chapter details the Java Media Framework, which specifies an event-driven architecture for the development of applications that support both video and audio. These applications include playback,video capture, and videoconferencing. We introduce the basic concepts of the Java Media Framework and how they relate to developing multimedia applications.

21.1 INTRODUCTION

The Java Media Framework unleashes the power of both audio and video. With the new framework Java developers are no longer limited to simple AU (AUdio file) and GIF (Graphics Interchange Format) files, but can now take advantage of QuickTime, AVI (Audio Video Interleave), and MPEG (Motion Picture Experts Group) 1 and 2, and MIDI (Musical Instrument Digital Interface) file formats. The Java Media Framework provides full-featured support for manipulating audiovisual files. Support is provided for starting, stopping, synchronizing, and similar actions on "media" files. The current release of the Framework does not include support for Videoconferencing and Capture but is designed to support these features in a future release. The main feature and classes of the Java Media Framework are:

- **Media Display.** The local or remote playback of "multimedia data" includes sound and video from AU, MIDI, GIF, AVI, and MPEG formats, in both streaming and nonstreaming formats.
- **Media Capture.** Supports all of the Media Display capabilities as well as support for media capture through local devices such as digital cameras and microphones.

Version 1.0 of the Java Media Framework does not support Media Capture but has been designed to support it in a future release.

- **Media Conferencing.** Includes the two features just described plus support for telephony-based applications to allow for the realtime capture, transfer, and display of video and audio data. Version 1.0 of the Java Media Framework does not support Media Conferencing.

In addition to the basic functionality as described earlier, the Java Media Framework can be used in three ways. The first, as a *client* application or applet, allows the developer to display/play audiovisual files and control playback. This chapter will concentrate on the use of the Java Media Framework for developing client applications and applets. The second and third, enhancement and design, allow for enhancing existing players to add additional functionality and designing new players. For more information on designing players from scratch or enhancing existing players, see the online documentation from http://Java.sun.com/packages or www.intel.com.

Streaming Playback

Java media players can present two forms of data, typically called push and pull.

- **Pull data.** With pull data, all packets making up the media file are guaranteed to have been received prior to playing. Pull data is what we have always considered "normal" media. Download the data and then display it; that is, the clip cannot be played until it has been completely received.
- **Push data.** With push data, a player may begin playing a media clip before it has been completely downloaded. However, unlike pull data based applications, push data applications must be concerned with additional error conditions such as holes in the data, underflow, network errors, and so forth. Push data also limits the control that the user has over the display. Push data does not allow resetting the clip to the beginning, fast forwarding, and so forth, and applies better to broadcast and Video on Demand (VoD) style applications.

Elements of the Java Media Framework

The Java Media Framework is based on the following elements, which will we examine in detail in the following sections.

- **Manager Class.** A class factory style object that can be called to create "players" for different media files via the createPlayer() method and a valid URL to a media file. The Manager class allows additional players to be added "behind the scenes" with no changes to existing code, much like the security and cryptography classes of Chapter 17. The Manager class is a final class and cannot be instantiated.
- **Player class.** An object created by the Manager.createPlayer() method that can be used to stop, start, and manipulate a media file.

- **ControllerListener Interface.** An interface that defines the methods required for a Java Media Application to capture "media-specific" events.
- **ControllerUpdate method.** A method defined in the ControllerListenerInterface that is called each time a media event occurs. This method allows an application to control the way a player acts.
- **Controller Listener Events.** The events that define the state changes within a player.
- **Visual and Control Components of a player.** A media player has a set of components that represent and control the clip being displayed.

21.2 A TRIVIAL PLAYER

Source 21.1 shows a very simple class that we will dissect in order to understand the basics of how the Java Media Framework can be used to construct applications.

SOURCE 21.1 Trivial Player.java

```
import java.applet.*;       // For applet
import java.awt.*;          // for layout etc
import java.net.*;          // for URL
import java.io.IOException; // for IO Exceptions
import java.media.*;        // for the Java media class
import chp3.Warning;        // for our Warning/error message class

/**
 *  TrivialPlayer.java
 *  A class that creates a trivial media player
     which plays a clip in an infinite loop
 *  @version 1.0
 *  @author A.J. Saganich Jr.
 */
public class TrivialPlayer
     extends Applet
     implements ControllerListener
     //  requires controllerUpdate(ControllerEvent event) be implemented
{
     Player         aPlayer   = null;
     Component      vc        = null;
     boolean    fRunning  = false;         // Not initially running

     /**
      * Read the name of the media file and then begin processing
      */
     public void init()
     {
          String inputFile = null;
          URL inputURL     = null;
          Warning msg      = null; // Create one if we need it.
```

```
        // Use a border based layout
        setLayout(new BorderLayout());

        /**
         * the inputFile parameter contains the name
         * of the media file to play.
         */
        inputFile = getParameter("inputFile");
        if ( null == inputFile)
        {
             System.out.println("Invalid media file parameter");
             msg = new Warning("inputFile",
                         "Must set value of inputFile in web page!");
             return;
        }

        System.out.println("Running on file: "+ inputFile);
        try
        {
             // Create an url from the file name and the url to the
             // document containing this applet.
             inputURL = new URL(getDocumentBase(), inputFile);
             // Create a player that corresponds to the input type.
             aPlayer = Manager.createPlayer(inputURL);
             // If the player was created then we want
             // to listen to its events.
             if(aPlayer != null)
             {
                  aPlayer.addControllerListener(this);
             }
             else
             {
                  System.out.println("Could not create aPlayer for " +
                                      inputURL);
                  msg = new Warning("createPlayer",
                        "Could not create aPlayer on given input!");
             }
        }
        catch (MalformedURLException e)
        {
             System.out.println("Invalid media file URL!");
             msg = new Warning("MalformedURLException",
                  "Could not create aPlayer on given input!");
        }
        catch(IOException e)
        {
             System.out.println("IO exception creating aPlayer for" +
                             inputURL);
             msg = new Warning("IOException",
                         "Could not create aPlayer on given input!");
        }
    }
```

```
/**
 * Start method
 * Note that this method attempts to start the prefetch of the
 * clip but does not start the player playing.  When the prefetch
 * completes the a event will be generated and the controllerUpdate
 * method called which will start the clip playing.
 */
public void start()
{
     if (aPlayer != null)
          aPlayer.prefetch();
}

/**
 * Stop method
 * stop the player playing, if allocated, and release its resources.
 */
public void stop()
{
     if (aPlayer != null)
     {
          fRunning = false;
          aPlayer.stop();
          aPlayer.deallocate();
     }
}

/**
 * controllerUpdate method
 * required by the ControllerLister interface
 * called whenever a media event occurs
 */
public synchronized void controllerUpdate(ControllerEvent event)
{
     System.out.println("ControllerUpdate entered!");
     System.out.println("\twith event " + event.toString());
     // When the aPlayer is Realized, get the visual component
     // and add it to the Applet
     if (event instanceof RealizeCompleteEvent)
     {
          if ((vc = aPlayer.getVisualComponent()) != null)
               add("Center", vc);

          // force the applet to draw the component
          validate();
     }
     else if (event instanceof PrefetchCompleteEvent)
     {
          aPlayer.start();
          fRunning = true;
     }
```

```
        else if (event instanceof EndOfMediaEvent)
        {
            aPlayer.setMediaTime(0);
            if ( true == fRunning)
                aPlayer.start();
        }
        else
        {
            // Some other event occured
        }
    } // End method controllerUpdate
} // End class TrivialPlayer
```

A run of Source 21.1 produces the following output:

```
C:\jwiley.chp21\Appletviewer Trivial.htm
Running on file: Sample.avi
ControllerUpdate entered with event java.media.TransitionEvent@1ce0ad
ControllerUpdate entered with event java.media.TransitionEvent@1ce118
ControllerUpdate entered with event
. . .
java.media.StopByRequestEvent@1ce37e
ControllerUpdate entered with event java.media.TransitionEvent@1ce399
ControllerUpdate entered with event java.media.DeallocateEvent@1ce3ca
```

A visual output of Source 21.1 looks something like Figure 21.1.

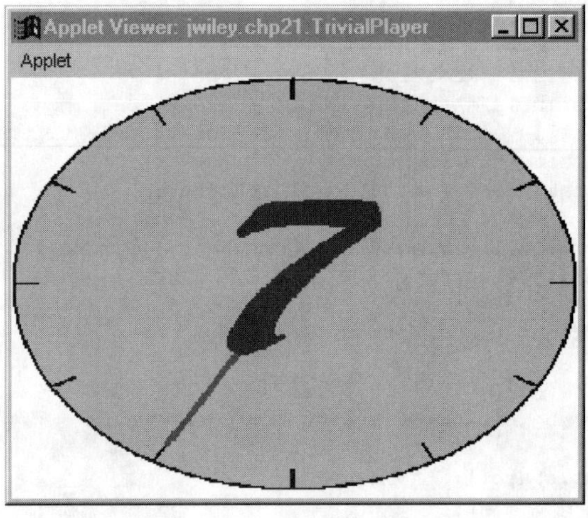

FIGURE 21.1 TrivialPlayer.

While this example is named TrivialPlayer.java it is hardly trivial! In fact, it implements all the requirements of a Java Media Framework Application! Let's look at the code closely so that we can understand what exactly was involved in creating this application.

The first thing of importance is to import the media classes themselves.

```
import java.media.*;
```

Our applet implements the ControllerListener interface. This interface defines the controllerUpdate() method that allows the applet to catch Java Media Framework player events.

```
public class TrivialPlayer … implements ControllerListener
```

The application then defines a player. The Player class and the controllerUpdate() method are used in concert to control the visual and auditory functions of the video or sound clip.

```
Player aPlayer = null;
```

Using the class factory method createPlayer() on the java.media.Manager object we can create a player for the given audio or video clip.

```
aPlayer = Manager.createPlayer(inputURL);
```

If the player was sucessfully created, then we add a listener for its events. This listener will allow us to capture events associated with player state changes, such as reaching the end of a clip, or that the player has been realized (more on that in a moment).

```
aPlayer.addControllerListener(this);
```

The start and stop methods are the logical places to start and stop the clip running, and if we were performing a simple animation based on a set of loaded GIF or JPG files this would in fact be the case. But with an Audio/Video file, which needs to be physically downloaded before it can be run, one additional step takes place called *Prefetch*. Prefetch is the process of getting the clip from the host. On slow links this may take a while, and we will see in a later section how to track it for the user. While the player takes care of the process we still cannot start the clip playing until it's completely downloaded. So our start method doesn't start the clip playing but rather starts the clip "prefetching," and then we wait for the prefetch to complete.

```
aPlayer.prefetch();
```

Because we might play the clip over and over we don't just stop the clip in the stop method, we also deallocate any resources it might have used as well. So our stop method looks like:

```
aPlayer.stop();
aPlayer.deallocate();
```

If we were simply stopping or pausing playback we would skip the call to deallocate().

The remainder of our example centers around the controllerUpdate method, shown in Source 21.2.

The controller update() method catches all the events that occur relative to the player. Because of the simple nature of the example, we need only trap the three events described here:

- **RealizeCompleteEvent.** An important part of the process of displaying a clip (either visually or audibly) is that the player has been *realized*. A player has been realized when all its components are ready for use. In the context of our example, the only thing we need to do is get the visual component of the player and then add

SOURCE 21.2 The controllerUpdate Method

```
public synchronized void controllerUpdate(ControllerEvent event)
{
     System.out.println("ControllerUpdate entered!");
     System.out.println("\twith event " + event.toString());
     // When the aPlayer is Realized, get the visual component
     // and add it to the Applet
     if (event instanceof RealizeCompleteEvent)
     {
          vc = aPlayer.getVisualComponent();
          if (vc != null)
               add("Center", vc);
          // force the applet to draw the component
          validate();
     }
     else if (event instanceof PrefetchCompleteEvent)
     {
          aPlayer.start();
          fRunning = true;
     }
     else if (event instanceof EndOfMediaEvent)
     {
          aPlayer.setMediaTime(0);
          if ( true == fRunning)
               aPlayer.start();
     }
     else
     {
          // Some other event occured
     }
} // End method controllerUpdate
```

it to our applet. Realization is one of several player "states" we will discuss in the next section.

```
aPlayer.getVisualComponent();

add("Center", vc);
```

- **PrefetchCompleteEvent.** As previously noted, a media clip needs to be prefetched before it can be seen or heard. The PrefetchCompleteEvent signals that the clip is now available and is started running with

```
APlayer.start();
```

- **EndOfMediaEvent.** This event signals that we have reached the end of playback of our clip. For the purposes of the example, we simply start the clip over by resetting the player time back to 0 and then calling start again.

```
aPlayer.setMediaTime(0);

aPlayer.start();
```

setMediaTime simply resets the current time of the clip back to its starting point. As you can see from the run of TrivialPlayer, many other events occurred, many of which we will examine as this chapter progresses.

Certain file formats can be played as they are being downloaded. These formats are called "streamable." Streamable files can be played as soon as a certain amount of the file has been downloaded. Streamable files play like any other clip except that they may generate an additional event, underflow. Underflow is just the opposite of overflow. An underflow event occurs when playback reaches the end of a downloaded section, but not the end of the media clip. Overflow occurs when frames arrive faster than they can be displayed. We will see how to handle streamable files and underflow a little later in this chapter. As it stands today, the Media Player framework can handle display of up to 30 frames/second, making overflow not a problem.

States of a Player

A Java media application typically goes through six states, five of those occur before the clip actually begins playing. These states are:

- **Unrealized.** An unrealized player is much like an uninitialized variable. It exists but is not ready for use. The unrealized state is the state a player is in after it has been created, with a call to createPlayer(), but before any other action has taken place.
- **Realizing.** A player is realizing when it is determining what resources are required and gathering those resources. Additional resources may be acquired

during the prefetching state if an *exclusive use* resource is required. An exclusive use resource is one that cannot be shared.

- **Realized.** A realized player has gathered all its resources, with the exception of exclusive use resources, has available all the controls required for playback control, and is ready to fetch the clip for playback.
- **Prefetching.** A player that is prefetching gathers any exclusive use resources it may require. It then prepares its clip or media for presentation and does anything else that is required prior to presenting the clip.
- **Prefetch complete.** Once all preparation tasks have been completed, a player is said to be in the prefetch complete state.
- **Started.** A player that is started is normally playing its associated clip. A player might not be started if its start time was manipulated prior to playback.

As a player moves from state to state it posts transition events to the control listener object associated with it. As we saw in Source 21.1, the control listener method can capture and act on these events.

Not all player methods are available for use in all states. Most of the valid states for a method are intuitive based on the method name. If for some reason a player method is executed when the player is in an invalid state, then either a NotRealizedError or a NotPrefetchedError may be thrown. See the *Java Media Players Guide* for a complete list of all the player methods and the states they apply to.

Visual Components

Source 21.1 shows a simple player without any controls; however, the Java Media Framework provides a default set of controls for both Audio and Video events. In our prior example, when we caught the RealizeCompleteEvent event, the application added the visual component of the clip to the applets frame. By default the framework provides a "VCR/Tape player" style of control interface, which you can of course override. Source 21.3 shows a more complete example of the controllerUpdate method that handles adding the visual controls associated with a media player. As we can see, very little needed to be changed to support some standard controls. We simply added a Component variable, so we could access the look and feel of the control if we so desired, and then in the RealizeCompleteEvent we used the getControlPanelControl() method to return the controls. Figure 21.2 shows the default visual controls.

Up to this point we have concentrated on applications that are visual in nature, displaying a VCR-like interface for controlling the application. There is one additional control type, geared directly at audio controls, called a GainControl. Gain controls control the audio "gain" of an application and can be obtained by using the getGainControl() method on a player. If a gain control doesn't exist, the method will return null; otherwise, it will return the instance of the control. Figure 21.3 shows an example of a gain control. The current release of the Java Media Framework did not support MIDI files. See the latest release of the Framework from www.intel.com for more information on Gain controls and supported visual and sound formats.

SOURCE 21.3 The controllerUpdate Method with Controls

```
// Player2.java
...
    Component  controls  = null;
...
    public synchronized void controllerUpdate(ControllerEvent event)
    {
        System.out.println("ControllerUpdate entered!");
        System.out.println("\twith event " + event.toString());
        // When the aPlayer is Realized, get the visual component
        // and add it to the Applet
        if (event instanceof RealizeCompleteEvent)
        {
            vc = aPlayer.getVisualComponent();
            if (vc != null)
                add("Center", vc);

            controls = aPlayer.getControlPanelComponent();
            if ( controls != null)
            {
                controls.setBackground(Color.lightGray);
                add("South", controls);
            }

            // force the applet to draw the image and the controls
            validate();
        }
        else if (event instanceof PrefetchCompleteEvent)
        {
            aPlayer.start();
            fRunning = true;
        }
        else if (event instanceof EndOfMediaEvent)
        {
            aPlayer.setMediaTime(0);
            if ( true == fRunning)
                aPlayer.start();
        }
        else
        {
            // Some other event occured
        }
    } // End method controllerUpdate
```

FIGURE 21.2 Default visual controls.

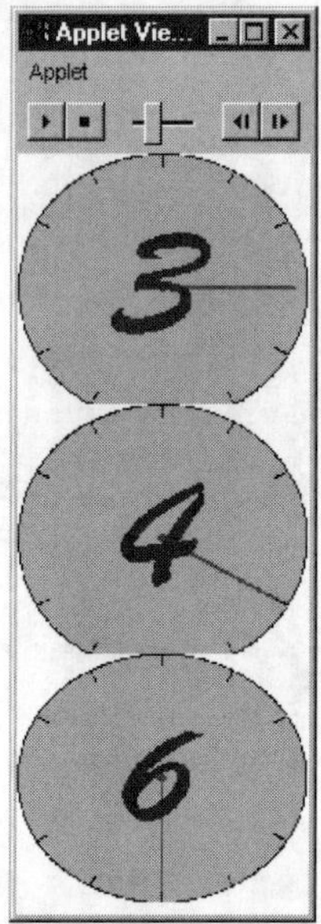

FIGURE 21.3 Default gain control.

CachingControl

There is one additional control that we have not yet addressed called the CachingControl. Since it may take a while for a clip to download from the remote host, we would like to display some sort of visual indicator of the download progress. The CachingControl is a built-in control that has its own event, the CachingControlEvent, which can be used to monitor the progress of a clip download. We can make use of the caching control as follows:

Add a new variable to the application that will be used to represent the progress of the download.

```
Component     progressIndicator = null;
```

Then, in the controllerUpdate() method, catch the CachingControlEvent and handle it as follows:

```
CachingControlEvent  cce  = (CachingControlEvent) event;
CachingControl       cc   = cce.getCachingControl();
long             elapsed  = cce.getContectProgress();
long             total = cce.getContentLength();
// If it doesn't exist add it.
if (progressIndicator == null )
```

```
{
     progressIndicator = cce.getProgressBarComponent();
     if (progressIndicator != null)
     {
          add("South", progressIndicator);
          validate();
     }
}

// Destroy it when the clip is downloaded
if (progressIndicator && elapsed == total)
{
     remove (progressIndicator);
     progressIndicator =null;
     validate();
}
```

The code itself is really simple and almost self-explanatory. We simply capture the CachingControllerEvent event and then add the progress indicator if it is not present. When the download completes, we simply delete the progress indicator.

21.3 TIMEBASES AND PLAYER TIME

One of the more important aspects of media players is that of a *Timebase*. For all practical purposes, a timebase is a clock. The Java Media documentation states that "*A **TimeBase** is a constantly ticking, monotonically increasing, source of time.*" A timeBase and clock differ in that a clock can be set, reset, and changed, but a timebase can never change nor be stopped.

You can obtain the system master timeBase via a call to the java.media.Manager object method getSystemTimeBase(). This timebase is often based on the system clock. Players have a variety of methods that are concerned with time in one way or another.

- getTimeBase() and setTimeBase() either return the current timebase or define a new timebase.
- setStartLatency() returns the worst case latency of a player. The latency of a player is the amount of time it will take for the first frame of a clip to be displayed after the start method has been called.
- setMediaTime() and setRate() set the start time and the rate, or speed, of a media clip.
- getDuration() returns the length of a media clip in nanoseconds.
- setStopTime() sets the end time of a clip.

Source 21.4 makes use of several of these methods as well as demonstrates how to capture and process the events of multiple players with a single controllerUpdate method. This source demonstrates the issues involved in controlling multiple players without using some of the built-in methods that make such control easier. At this point, we avoid those methods to better demonstrate the concepts.

SOURCE 21.4 Player3.java

```
package jwiley.chp21;

import java.applet.*;       // For applet
import java.awt.*;          // for layout etc
import java.net.*;          // for URL
import java.io.IOException; // for IO Exceptions
import java.media.*;        // for the Java media class

/**
 *  Player3.java
 *  A class that creates a set of media player each playing in a infinite
 *  loop.  Sort of like row, row, row your boat only each runs at a
 *  different speed with the first running at normal or 1/1 time.
 *  The second running at 1/2 time etc.  A start time could have been
 * set with setMediaTime instead to make all the players play in sync
 * but starting at different intervals.
 *
 *  @version 1.0
 *  @author A.J. Saganich Jr.
 */
public class Player3
     extends Applet
     implements ControllerListener
     //  requires controllerUpdate(ControllerEvent event) be implemented
{
     private static final
     int         ctPlayers   = 3;
     Player      players[]   = null;
     Panel       playerPanel = null;
     Component   vc          = null;
     Component   controls    = null;

     /**
      * Read the name of the media file and then begin processing
      */
     public void init()
     {
          String inputFile = null;
          URL inputURL     = null;

          /**
           * the inputFile parameter contains the name
           * of the media file to play.
           */
          inputFile = getParameter("inputFile");
          if ( null == inputFile)
          {
               System.out.println("Invalid media file parameter");
               return;
          }
```

```
        System.out.println("Running on file: "+ inputFile);
        // Create an url from the file name and the url to the
        // document containing this applet.
        try
        {
             inputURL = new URL(getDocumentBase(), inputFile);
        }
        catch (MalformedURLException e)
        {
             System.out.println("Invalid media file URL!");
        }

        // Create the players
        try
        {
             players = new Player[ctPlayers];
             // Create a player that corresponds to the input type.
             for (int i = 0; i < ctPlayers; i++)
             {
                  players[i] = Manager.createPlayer(inputURL);
                  if(players[i] != null)
                  {
                       // All the controllers use the same controlUpdate
                       players[i].addControllerListener(this);
                  }
                  else
                  {
                       System.out.println(
                            "Could not create player for " + inputURL);
                  }
             }

             // build a panel for the clips
             playerPanel = new Panel();
             playerPanel.setLayout(new GridLayout(ctPlayers,1));
             // n x 1 grid( a stack)


             // Use a border based layout for the whole thing
             setLayout(new BorderLayout());
             add ("Center",playerPanel);



        }
        catch(IOException e)
        {
             System.out.println("IO exception creating aPlayer for" +
                                 inputURL);
        }
   }
```

```
/**
 * Start method
 * Note that this method attempts to start the prefetch of the
 * clip but does not start the player playing.  When the prefetch
 * completes the a event will be generated and the controllerUpdate
 * method called which will start the clip playing.
 */
public void start()
{
     for ( int i = 0; i < ctPlayers; i++)
     {
          if ( players[i] != null)
                players[i].prefetch();
     }
}

/**
 * Stop method
 * stop the player playing, if allocated, and release its resources.
 */
public void stop()
{
     fRunning = false;
     for ( int i = 0; i < ctPlayers; i++)
     {
          if (players[i] != null)
          {
               players[i].stop();
               players[i].deallocate();
          }
     }
}

/**
 * controllerUpdate method
 * required by the ControllerLister interface
 * called whenever a media event occurs
 */
public synchronized void controllerUpdate(ControllerEvent event)
{
     // Determine which player caused the event
     Player which = (Player)event.getSource();
     int iWhich;
     for (iWhich = 0; iWhich < ctPlayers; iWhich++)
          if ( which == players[iWhich]) break;

     System.out.println("ControllerUpdate with event " +
                           event.toString() + " for " + iWhich);

     // When the aPlayer is Realized, get the visual component
     // and add it to the Applets panel
     if (event instanceof RealizeCompleteEvent)
     {
```

```
            // force the applet to draw the image and the controls
            playerPanel.add(which.getVisualComponent());
            // first player goes normal speed (1/1)
            // second goes half speed (1/2)
            // third goes 1/3 speed etc
            which.setRate((float)(1.0/(iWhich+1.0)));
            if ( iWhich == 0)
            {
                // The first is the master and all its controls are
                // in terms of it.
                controls = players[0].getControlPanelComponent();
                if ( controls != null)
                {
                    controls.setBackground(Color.lightGray);
                    add("North", controls);
                }
            }

            validate();
        }
        else if (event instanceof PrefetchCompleteEvent)
        {
            //
            //Are they all complete?
            //
            int i;
            for ( i = 0 ; i < ctPlayers; i++)
            {
                if (players[i].getState() != Player.Prefetched )
                    break;
            }
            //
            // then start them
            //
            if ( i == ctPlayers)
            {
                for ( i = 0 ; i < ctPlayers; i++)
                {
                    players[i].start();
                }
            }
        }
        else if (event instanceof EndOfMediaEvent)
        {
            which.setMediaTime(0);  // Go back to the beginning
            which.start();
        }
        else if ( event instanceof StartEvent)
        {
            if ( which == players[0])
            {
```

```
                // Note that we skip the first its already started.
                for ( int i = 0+1 ; i < ctPlayers; i++)
                {
                    players[i].start();
                }
            }
        }
        else if ( event instanceof StopByRequestEvent)
        {
            // Note that we skip the first, don't want to get into an
            //  infinite loop of generating and catching start events!
            if ( which == players[0])
            {
                for ( int i = 0+1 ; i < ctPlayers; i++)
                {
                    players[i].stop();
                }
            }
        }
        else
        {
            // Some other event occured
            // Adding fast forward and rewind events is left as an
            // exercise to the reader.

        }
    } // End method controllerUpdate
} // End class Player3
```

The most interesting points of this example are shown here.

For each player added we use the same controllerUpdate() method.

```
players[i].addControllerListener(this);
```

In controllerUpdate() we extract from the event the player that generated the error with getSource.

```
Player which = (Player)event.getSource();
```

We can then act on individual player events without needing more then a single controllerUpdate() method. Another approach would have been to derive a class that contains a player and catches its own controllerUpdate events within the derived class.

A player's rate can only be set after it has been prefetched, so we set the rate of each player in the RealizeCompleteEvent code as follows:

```
which.setRate((float)(1.0/(iWhich+1.0)));
```

In the same event we also display the controls for the first player, which will be used as the master controller for all other players. This is done normally by simply getting the default control panel and adding it to the frame.

```
controls = players[0].getControlPanelComponent();
. . .
    controls.setBackground(Color.lightGray);
    add("North", controls);
```

Since our example calls for starting each player at the same time, we wait for all prefetches to complete by checking the current state of each player.

```
if (players[i].getState() != Player.Prefetched )
```

Source 21.4 also handles two new events, the StopByRequestEvent event and the StartEvent, which map to the VCR controls Stop (or pause) and Start (after a pause). The StopByRequest event cascades the stop to all the slaved players. Likewise, the StartEvent is cascaded to all the slaved players. The Rewind and Fastforward events are left as exercises for the reader.

Media Synchronization

An additional use of a player's timebase is synchronization. Two players can be synchronized together by setting the second player's timebase to that of the first. For example:

```
PlayerSlave.setTimeBase(PlayerMaster.getTimeBase());
```

In Source 21.4, the tracking and managing of the states of each player made the application complex; however, there is a simpler method to accomplish the same thing that depends on the addController() and removeController() methods in the player class. Before we rewrite Player3.java to use these two methods, we need to understand the relationship between a Controller and a Player. As we saw before, a clock defines basic timing and synchronization methods. A Controller extends the Clock class to support handling resources and adds the necessary methods for events. Players build on Controllers to add support for basic GUI controls for playback. As a result, each Player has a default controller associated with it.

As we saw earlier, each player has an associated timebase. When a player is running, the internal media is mapped to its timebase. For one or more players to be synchronized, an application needs to map the players to the same timebase. The addController() and removeController() methods allow multiple players to be mapped and controlled by a single controller using that controller's timebase.

One of the basic concepts of a media player is that of *Media Time*. A player's media time represents the point in the player's clip that the media is presenting. A media time, unlike a TimeBase, can be manipulated; that is, stopped, started, reset, and so on.

Source 21.5 shows how you might use one player to control others.

SOURCE 21.5 Player4.java

```
package jwiley.chp21;

import java.applet.*;        // For applet
import java.awt.*;           // for layout etc
import java.net.*;           // for URL
import java.io.IOException; // for IO Exceptions
import java.media.*;         // for the Java media class

/**
 *  Player4.java
 *  This example demonstrates the use of a single player to control other
players.
 *
 *  @version 1.0
 *  @author A.J. Saganich Jr.
 */
public class Player4
     extends Applet
     implements ControllerListener
{
     private static final
     int        ctPlayers   = 3;
     Player     players[]   = null;
     Panel      playerPanel = null;
     Component  vc          = null;
     Component  controls    = null;
     boolean    fRunning    = false;        // Not initially running

     /**
      * Read the name of the media file and then begin processing
      */
     public void init()
     {
          String inputFile = null;
          URL inputURL     = null;

          /**
           * the inputFile parameter contains the name
           * of the media file to play.
           */
          inputFile = getParameter("inputFile");
          if ( null == inputFile)
          {
               System.out.println("Invalid media file parameter");
               return;
          }

          System.out.println("Running on file: "+ inputFile);
          // Create an url from the file name and the url to the
          // document containing this applet.
```

```
try
{
     inputURL = new URL(getDocumentBase(), inputFile);
}
catch (MalformedURLException e)
{
     System.out.println("Invalid media file URL!");
}

// Create the players
try
{
     players = new Player[ctPlayers];
     // Create a player that corresponds to the input type.
     for (int i = 0; i < ctPlayers; i++)
     {
          players[i] = Manager.createPlayer(inputURL);
          if ( players[i] == null )
          {
               System.out.println("Could not create player for "
                + inputURL);
          }
     }
     // We only need capture events on the master.
     if(players[0] != null)
     {
          players[0].addControllerListener(this);
     }

     // Realize all the players
     int i;
     for (i = 0;  i < ctPlayers; i++)
     {
          players[i].realize();
     }

     // Wait for them all to realize
     while (true)
     {
          for (i = 0;  i < ctPlayers; i++)
          {
               if (players[i].getState() != Player.Realized)
                    break;
          }
          if ( i == ctPlayers ) break;
     }

     // build a panel for the clips
     playerPanel = new Panel();
     playerPanel.setLayout(new GridLayout(ctPlayers,1));
```

```
            // Use a border based layout for the whole thing
            setLayout(new BorderLayout());
            add ("Center",playerPanel);
            // Add them to the panel and make player[0]
            // control all others
            for (i = 0;  i < ctPlayers; i++)
            {
                 playerPanel.add(players[i].getVisualComponent());
                 if (i != 0)
                      players[0].addController(players[i]);
            }
       }
       // Using the addController method may throw an
       //  IncompatibleTimeBaseException exception
       catch( IncompatibleTimeBaseException e )
       {
            System.out.println("Unexpected TimeBase exception " + e);
       }
       catch(IOException e)
       {
            System.out.println("IO exception creating aPlayer for" +
                               inputURL);
       }
  }

  /**
   * Start method
   * Note that this method attempts to start the prefetch of the
   * clip but does not start the player playing.  When the prefetch
   * completes the a event will be generated and the controllerUpdate
   * method called which will start the clip playing.
   */
  public void start()
  {
       players[0].prefetch();
  }

  /**
   * Stop method
   * stop the player playing, if allocated, and release its resources.
   */
  public void stop()
  {
       players[0].stop();
       players[0].deallocate();
  }

  /**
   * controllerUpdate method
   * required by the ControllerLister interface
   * called whenever a media event occurs
   */
  public synchronized void controllerUpdate(ControllerEvent event)
  {
```

```
        System.out.println("ControllerUpdate with event " +
                                    event.toString());

        // When the aPlayer is Realized, get the visual component
        // and add it to the Applet
        if (event instanceof RealizeCompleteEvent)
        {
            // force the applet to draw the image and the controls
            controls = players[0].getControlPanelComponent();
            if ( controls != null)
            {
                controls.setBackground(Color.lightGray);
                add("North", controls);
            }
            validate();
        }
        else if (event instanceof PrefetchCompleteEvent)
        {
            players[0].start();
        }
        else if (event instanceof EndOfMediaEvent)
        {
            players[0].setMediaTime(0);
            players[0].start();
        }
        else
        {
            // Some other event occured

        }
    } // End method controllerUpdate
} // End class Player4
```

Most of the differences between Player3.java and Player4.java are in the init method. A player must be realized before it can pass control to another player. So the loop shown here simply waits for each player to realize.

```
while (true)
{
    for (i = 0;  i < ctPlayers; i++)
    {
        if (players[i].getState() != Player.Realized)
            break;
    }
    if ( i == ctPlayers ) break;
}
```

Once the players have been realized we set the controller for the second and subsequent players with the add controller method.

```
players[0].addController(players[i]);
```

The remainder of the application is much like our first example. Only now, when the application is stopped or started, all players stop or start. Player4.java is simple, straightforward, and much less complicated than our prior application.

21.4 SUMMARY

The Java Media Framework is a robust framework that provides Java support for a much broader range of audio and video file formats. While we detailed examples of client-side usage of the JMF, there also exist APIs for extending the default players and adding new players. The interested user should read the documentation found at http://java.sun.com/products/Java-media. and the Intel site at www.intel.com/ial/jmedia. Both contain a wealth of information about not only the Java Media Framework but other works in progress.

CHAPTER 22

Java, ActiveX, and COM

OBJECTIVE

In this chapter we will learn about the Component Object Model and ActiveX, see how Java applications can make use of COM, and how Java applications can be exposed as COM objects.

22.1 INTRODUCTION

Before we begin our examination of Java, ActiveX, and COM, it's important to understand one thing. ActiveX and COM are Microsoft technologies and require the use, for the most part, of Microsoft products and tools. While ActiveX is being ported and made available on many platforms, it is still primarily Windows only. (For the remainder of this chapter we assume that the reader is somewhat familiar with Microsoft Visual J++ 1.1 or better and has access to a computer running the Visual J++ development environment.)

COM and ActiveX are large topics on which many books have been written. The purpose of this chapter is not to make anyone an ActiveX expert but rather to introduce the basic elements of the Component Object model, and then transition those to ActiveX, and finally show how an ActiveX control can be used in Java. And, conversely, how a Java applet can act as an ActiveX control.

ActiveX extends Java in many different ways. ActiveX allows a software engineer to take advantage of the many existing COM objects. Objects, which, if you use any Windows products at all, you have probably been using for a long time. Using ActiveX and Java you can place directly into your Java applet that spreadsheet control you have been so happily using for ages. Or use Visual Basic as the scripting language to control how your Java applet works. Or, conversely, you can make your Java application appear as an ActiveX control and use it within Visual Basic, Borland C++, Delphi, or other ActiveX-enabled tools. Among other things, ActiveX allows you, the developer, to develop in the language you are most comfortable with and still integrate that development effort into your Java applet!

The Component Object Model

The Component Object Model is a vast topic, but the underlying theme throughout is the *Windows Object*. A Windows Object is different from a C++ object in subtle and not so subtle ways. For example, a Windows Object will never grant you access to its data accidentally. *That is, a Windows Object can expose its data through "properties" but never accidentally, only by design.* While Windows objects can and often are implemented in C++ it is by no means a requirement. Each and every Windows Object has an *interface* and its associated code and data. Beneath it all, an *interface* is just a way for two objects to communicate.

ActiveX interfaces and Java interfaces are not the same things. ActiveX and COM objects in general, are referenced through one or more *interfaces*. These are not the same interfaces the Java developers are familiar with. As you will remember, Java interfaces contain no code and describe how an object implements a definition. On the other hand, ActiveX interfaces contain both the definition of the interface and the actual code and data that implement it.

But what exactly is COM anyway? Well, COM is really the underlying protocol that connects two processes. Once connected, COM drops out of the picture. Distributed COM, or DCOM as it's more commonly known, is simple COM extended to the Net. But how does this work? Each and every COM object supports a simple interface called Iunknown (and usually at least one additional interface). When an application wishes to use a COM object, the application queries the IUnknown interface to determine if an interface exists that both sides can agree on. Each of these interfaces, typically, supports a given way that object may be used. Interfaces, and pointers to interfaces, are normally just pointers to arrays of functions that make up how an object acts. Under COM an object's data is NEVER visible and can only be manipulated via its provided interface functions. In many ways, COM objects are used much like Java objects. An instance of an object is created. That object is queried to determine what interfaces it supports, and an appropriate interface is selected. At this point your application, or ActiveX control for that matter, can use the COM object for whatever it was intended for.

Why Use COM?

We've seen the COM Model, but why use COM in the first place? Here are just a few of the reasons.

- **Cross Platform.** COM is either available or soon to be available on the Macintosh, SUN hardware, and various mainframes.
- **Clients only use interfaces, implementations may differ.** Because of the way COM objects are developed the internals of the object are always hidden. They can only be accessed via their methods.
- **Independent component versioning.** COM Objects are versioned so that one object may have several versions of the same interface, yet still work with older code.
- **Language and compiler independent.** COM Objects can be developed in whatever language the developer chooses, whether it's Visual Basic, Visual C++, C, Delphi, or another. COM defines a binary interoperability standard rather than a language-based standard.
- **Location independent.** COM objects are location independent and may be distributed across many machines via DCOM.
- **Because it's easy!** COM Objects work seamlessly within Visual J++ because COM classes look to Visual J++ as if they were Java classes.

ActiveX

Just what is ActiveX? Many people are under the impression that ActiveX is just another name for Object Linking and Embedding (OLE). While this is true in a way, ActiveX and OLE are both based on the COM specification, in the stricter sense they are very different. Active X began life as OLE Automation. OLE Automation allowed one program to be "automated" by another. ActiveX then grew to become a set of technologies targeted at distributed computing via the Internet. ActiveX and OLE now serve two very different functions. ActiveX, on the one hand, is a very much slimmed down OLE that has been optimized for speed, size, and automation. ActiveX really provides the functionality of OLE automation controls but makes them lightweight and efficient and easier to download by requiring less supporting code. OLE, on the other hand, is optimized for integration with applications and general usability, requiring much more support in the way of software on the target computer but allowing for greater diversity. In fact, ActiveX is really a set of technologies.

ActiveX Elements. There are five major areas where ActiveX plays a role. They are:

- **Controls.** ActiveX controls are just like other controls except that they are typically much more interactive.
- **Documents.** ActiveX documents are the feature most people are familiar with. ActiveX documents allow the Web site developer to embed Microsoft Word, Excel, or other OLE-aware documents into a Web page.
- **Scripting.** ActiveX scripting is that feature of ActiveX that allows either a Java applet or an ActiveX control to be controlled by an outside source. Visual J++ is the first, and currently only, development environment that allows two Java applica-

tions to be scripted together. This is provided through the Java Virtual Machine in the Microsoft Internet Explorer 3.0.

- **Automation.** ActiveX automation is one of the two areas where we will look more closely. Automation allows your Java application to control the way an ActiveX control functions, as we will see in the USECOM example.
- **Server Framework.** The ActiveX server framework is a new technology that allows Web servers to add specific functionality (such as Security, etc.) via ActiveX.

For the remainder of this chapter we will look at how an ActiveX control or component can be used from Java and touch briefly on how a Java applet can be used as an ActiveX control.

ActiveX and Other Platforms. One of the concerns of programmers everywhere is portability. Java was built from the ground up to be portable. One of the first thoughts that came to my mind when I first encountered ActiveX was "it's proprietary." When OLE was first announced it was clearly Microsoft-only, as was OLE2. When ActiveX was announced the feeling was the same, just another Microsoft extension that was proprietary. However, on October 1, 1996, the Cambridge, Massachusetts-based Open Group took control of the ActiveX technologies from a willing Microsoft. This effectively placed ActiveX into the open.

The Open Group, together with Microsoft, then released the list of ActiveX core technologies that are expected to be the framework of the ActiveX of tomorrow. These technologies are:

- **Component Object Model (COM)** and **DCOM.** The underlying distributed object model for ActiveX.
- **Microsoft Remote Procedure Call (MS-RPC).** A compatible implementation of DCE/RPC. Provides scalability, marshaling, and privacy support.
- **NTLM Standard Security Provider Interface (SSPI).** Allows secure invocation of components.
- **Structured Storage.** Rich, transaction-based, hierarchical file format. Enables applications to share files across applications and platforms.
- **Registry.** Provides a database of COM components and their configuration information.
- **Monikers.** Provides for persistent, intelligent names.
- **Automation.** Allows objects to expose functionality to high-level programming languages and scripting environments.

Several companies have committed to bringing these technologies, or at least a subset, to other platforms. Metrowerks (a provider of Macintosh development tools) and Macromedia have both stated their intent to bring ActiveX to the Mac. Other companies, such as Bristol Technologies and Mainsoft, have expressed an interest in bringing ActiveX to Unix.

22.2 USING ACTIVEX OBJECTS IN JAVA

Now that we have a better understanding of ActiveX and COM in general, let's look at an example of how to use an ActiveX control from within a Java application. As was previously mentioned, from Java's point of view ActiveX controls are just Java objects and can be created and manipulated exactly like any other Java object. Visual J++ provides a very simple example of using ActiveX with its JavaCallingCom project, and it will be our starting point in using ActiveX from Java (see Source 22.1).

TIP The JavaCallingCom sample comes complete on the Visual J++ CD-ROM. To work with the project you will need to copy it to your hard drive. Using Find/File from the Windows 95 or Window NT4.0 start menu, search for JavaCallingCom on the Visual J++1.1 CD-ROM. When found, copy the directory to your hard drive. Once you have copied the project open the .dsw file and choose Rebuild All from the Visual J++ Build menu. This will create a runnable version of the project.

SOURCE 22.1 usecom.java

```
//**********************************************************************
// usecom.java:     Applet
//**********************************************************************
import java.applet.*;
import java.awt.*;
import usecomframe;

// import the classes from the type library
import comserver.*;

// Helper class for holding a bunch of values
class BeepValue
{
     String name;
     int value;
}

//==========================================================================
// Main Class for applet usecom
//==========================================================================

public class usecom extends Applet
implements ActionListener, ItemListener
{
```

```
// the interface to the COM object
ICOMBeeper m_beeper;

// user interface components
List m_list;
Label m_label;
Button m_button;

// a list of names and values
static final int countNames = 6;
BeepValue m_nameList[];

. . .

public void init()
{
    resize(240, 200);

    // Create the components for the user interface
    setLayout(null);
    m_label = new Label();
    m_list = new List();
    m_list.addItemListener(this);
    m_button = new Button();
    m_button.addActionListener(this);
    add(m_label);
    add(m_list);
    add(m_button);

    // Place the components in the applet
    m_list.reshape(50, 50, 120, 80);
    m_label.reshape(50, 130, 100, 15);
    m_button.reshape(60, 160, 100, 30);

    // Create the COM object
    m_beeper = new CCOMBeeper();

    // Create the list of names and values
    m_nameList = new BeepValue[countNames];
    for(int i = 0; i < countNames; i++)
        m_nameList[i] = new BeepValue();

    // Fill the list of names and values using the COM object
    // Set the current sound using the constants from
    // the type library
    m_beeper.putSound(BeeperConstants.Default);
    // ICOMBeeper.getSoundName returns a string for
    // the current sound
```

```
        m_nameList[0].name = m_beeper.getSoundName();
        // Get the associated number back as well
        m_nameList[0].value = m_beeper.getSound();

        // Repeat for the rest of the constants
        m_beeper.putSound(BeeperConstants.Asterisk);
        m_nameList[1].name = m_beeper.getSoundName();
        m_nameList[1].value = m_beeper.getSound();
    . . .
        // Use the list of names to populate the list
        for(int i = 0; i < countNames; i ++)
            m_list.addItem(m_nameList[i].name);
        // Adjust the user interface for the components
        m_label.setAlignment(Label.CENTER);
        m_button.setLabel("Play the Sound");

        // Set the current sound to the first value
        setBeeperSound(0);
        m_list.select(0);
    }

    . . .
    public void actionPerformed(ActionEvent ae)
    {
        // Play the selected sound
        m_beeper.Play();
    }
    public void itemStateChanged(ItemEvent ie)
    {
        // Update the selection
        List l = (List)m_list;
        setBeeperSound(l.getSelectedIndex());
    }

    // Helper function to update based on the list selection
    void setBeeperSound(int index)
    {
        // get the value from the list of names and values
        int i = m_nameList[index].value;
        // echo the value in the label component
        m_label.setText("Sound number: " + i);
        // set the current sound
        m_beeper.putSound(i);
    }
}
```

The Usecom example uses the new JDK1.1 event model. This was achieved by downloading and installing the beta version of the new JVM and associated SDK from the Microsoft Visual J++ Web page (at www.microsoft.com/visualj/) on top of Visual J++ 1.1.

Examining Usecom.java

As you can see from Source 22.1, calling the beeper object from Java is a very straightforward process. The code looks identical to that of a "regular" Java application. Let's look at each of the lines so that we understand what is actually going on. Figure 22.1 shows a run of the usecom example.

First we have the import statement **import comserver.*;** This looks just like your normal import, and in fact it is. Under normal circumstances the import statement causes the compiler to look for a .JAVA or a .CLASS file. Visual J++ does exactly that. In addition, if it does not find one it begins searching for an ActiveX control (such as OCXs, ActiveX-aware DLL's, etc.) and runs The Java Type Library Wizard internally to produce a .CLASS file. Seamlessly integrating ActiveX into your application, or JavaTLB, reads an ActiveX-aware DLL, OCX, TLB, EXE, or similar 'thing' and creates an import .CLASS file, which Visual J++ can handle. This seamlessly integrates ActiveX and Java. We will look at JavaTLB briefly in a later section.

The import comserver class, shown in Source 22.2, defines three objects: the comserver/ICOMBeeper class, the comserver/CCOMBeeper class, and a support class with some integer values. The actual beeper object is defined with the statement

```
ICOMBeeper m_beeper;
```

which defines an interface to an m_beeper object. It is important to remember that COM objects are referenced via these interfaces, but created with the actual object! We then allocate an object with the statement

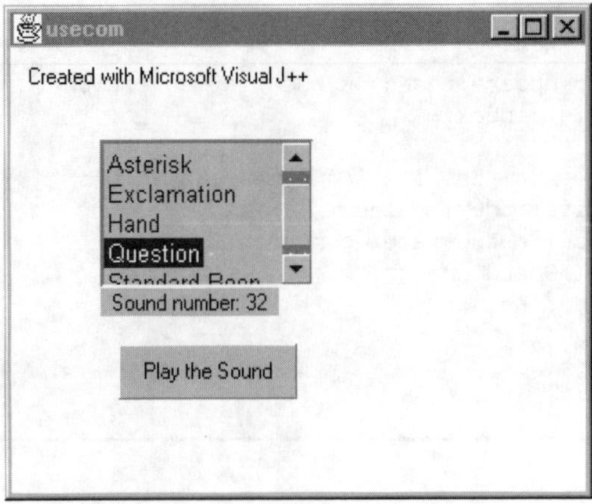

FIGURE 22.1 Usecom window.

```
m_beeper = new CCOMBeeper();
```

Again, note that we defined m_beeper to be of type ICOMBeeper, but then created a CCOMBeeper class object. As we can see from Source 22.2 the comserver class has an object and at least one interface. It may have many interfaces, in which case we would have chosen the one that suited our needs.

When Java Type Library Wizard is run on a DLL, OCX, or similar objects, either specifically or automatically by Visual J++, it creates a summary.txt file under %winsysdir%\Java\TrustLib\{objectname}. This file describes all the interfaces and properties of the COM class that can be used from a Java Application.

The remainder of the code for working with the beeper class is in the handleEvent method. The usecom application beeps whenever the Play The Sound button is pressed. Users may select a different sound to play by choosing another sound from the dropdown list of sounds supported.

Pressing the button causes the method play to be run.

```
m_beeper.Play();
```

Making a new selection ultimately results in a call to

```
m_beeper.putSound(i);
```

The comserver COMBeeper class also contains two methods for querying for the name and number of supported sounds. These are used to create the dropdown list of values.

SOURCE 22.2 Summary.txt file for Comserver.dll

```
public interface comserver/ICOMBeeper extends com.ms.com.IUnknown
{
    public abstract java.lang.String getSoundName();
    public abstract void Play();
    public abstract void putSound(int);
    public abstract int getSound();
}
public class comserver/CCOMBeeper extends java.lang.Object
{
}
public interface comserver/BeeperConstants extends com.ms.com.IUnknown
{
    public static final int Default;
    public static final int Asterisk;
    public static final int Exclamation;
    public static final int Hand;
    public static final int Question;
    public static final int StandardBeep;
}
```

TIP When you run the Java Type Library Wizard you will always be presented with a text file, shown in the output window, which describes the interface(s) of the ActiveX control you are working on. Always look at this file to determine which object is the "real" object and which are just the interfaces to that object. In most cases, the actual object will be shown as having superclass java.lang.Object and the interface's superclass com.ms.com.IUnknown, making it fairly easy to determine what to create versus how to use an object.

Handling COM Exceptions

ActiveX objects, and COM components in general, can cause exceptions just like any other object. An earlier predecessor to comserver, javabeep.dll, would beep five times, and on the sixth time raise an exception. This object would throw a com.ms.com .ComException after its fifth beep. This problem could easily be solved by simply catching the exception as shown in the following code, deleting the old and "used up" object, and allocating a new "fresh" one.

```
try
{
     m_Beeper.Beep();
}
catch(com.ms.com.ComException e)
{
     // Release the Beeper object by setting m_Beeper=null
     m_Beeper=null;
     // Create a new Beeper object
     m_Beeper = (IBeeper) new Beeper();
     m_Beeper.Beep();
}
```

ComExceptions are used to wrap the HRESULT normally returned by a COM or ActiveX object. ComExceptions are derived from RunTimeExceptions, so it is the responsibility of the developer to catch and deal with COM errors. Since ComExceptions extends RunTimeExceptions you may use all the normal exception methods to determine what happened. (See Section 3.4 for a detailed explanation of exception handling in Java.)

Visual J++ Tools

Visual J++ is really a group of tools for Java Application development. In the prior sections we discussed how Java interfaces with COM objects, but gave little time to the tools involved. Without going into too much detail about Visual J++ itself, we do need a brief introduction to some of the tools.

RegSvr32. RegSvr32 is a simple tool for registering COM classes or, as they are more often referred to as, *components*. First off, why register COM components in the first place? Each and every "remote object" technology needs to announce to the world that it has a service to provide. As we saw in Chapter 13, CORBA uses Object Request Brokers (ORBs), such that a CORBA server registers with an ORB to announce the availability of a service. Java RMI, as we saw in Chapter 16, uses the Remote Object Registry Server, rmiregistry. The Windows registry provides this service for COM components and holds information about the configuration of a machine and the COM objects it knows about. In order for a COM component to be known and usable by Windows, certain information must be known and available, such as its location, what interfaces it supports, how it is created, and so on. Most software registers its own components when it is installed. For those that do not, RegSvr32.exe can perform that service.

RegSvr32 is a tool for registering Server DLLs. Comserver.dll, from our prior example, is a server DLL. Since it was not "installed" by any software we need to register it by hand.

Under Windows 95 you would find the RegSvr32 application in the Windows\system directory. Under Windows NT it can normally be found int %winsysdir%\system32. To run RegSvr32 to register a dll from a dos prompt, type the following:

```
%winsysdir%\system{32 for NT}\regsvr32 file name.
```

in our case,

```
C:\winnt\system32\regsvr32 comserver.dll
```

after which your class would be registered with the system and almost ready for use. All we need to do is run the Java Type Library Wizard to create the import class for our Java application.

Java Type Library Wizard. Once you have registered a class with the system, Visual J++ can make use of it. After you have registered your class you make it available to Java via the Java Type Library Wizard. Java Type Library Wizard is the tool that actually creates the Import class for your Java applet as well as a text file that shows the file interface. Figure 22.2 shows the Java Type Library Wizard.

When run, the Java Type Library Wizard outputs two lines in the Java Type Library Tab of the Visual J++ output window. The first is the name of the generated Import class, in our case, comserver.*. The second is the name of the summary text file that contains the interface and class definitions for the class in question.

The result of running Java Type Library Wizard on comserver.dll after registering it with RegSvr32 looks like this:

```
import comserver.*;
C:\WINNT\java\trustlib\comserver\summary.txt(1): Class summary information
created
Tool returned code: 0
```

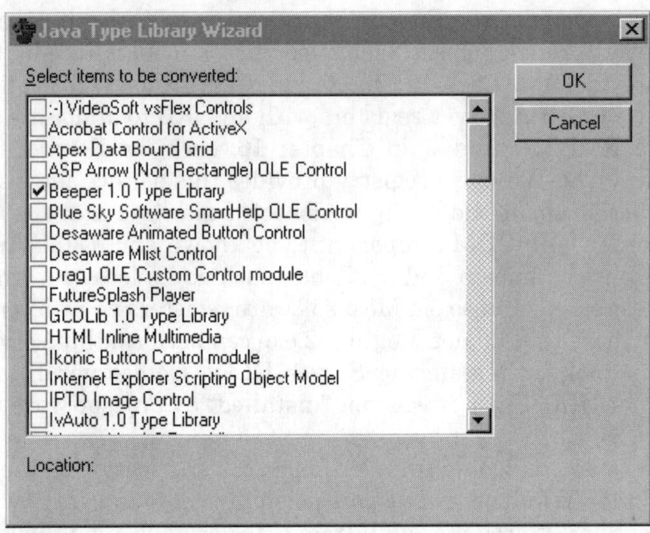

FIGURE 22.2 Java Type Library Wizard.

that just because you can see a control within Java Type Library Wizard doesn't automatically mean you can use it. Many controls were created before the existence of Java and either do not provide the necessary interfaces or use data types foreign to Java. These classes will produce warnings when the Java Type Library Wizard is run against them and may or may not produce a usable class. So, let the buyer beware! Look carefully at what Java Type Library Wizard generates.

OLE/COM Object Viewer. There is one other tool that the Visual J++ developer will find helpful, the OLE/COM Object viewer. This tool allows the developer to look into a COM object and see what interfaces it supports, as well as what methods and enums these interfaces work on. Figure 22.3 shows the result of running the OLE/COM Object viewer on comserver.dll and selecting the BeeperConstants enum.

Once you have started the OLE/COM Object viewer, you can view the interfaces associated with a server DLL directly by clicking on the icon directly. When prompted, enter the fully qualified path to the comserver.dll file. If you are successful, you will be presented with a dialog similar to Figure 22.3.

Mapping COM Types to Java Types

The classes and methods exposed by the ActiveX and COM objects are listed clearly in the summary text created when Java Type Library Wizard is run on a given class. However, it's often helpful to understand the conversion between COM types and their

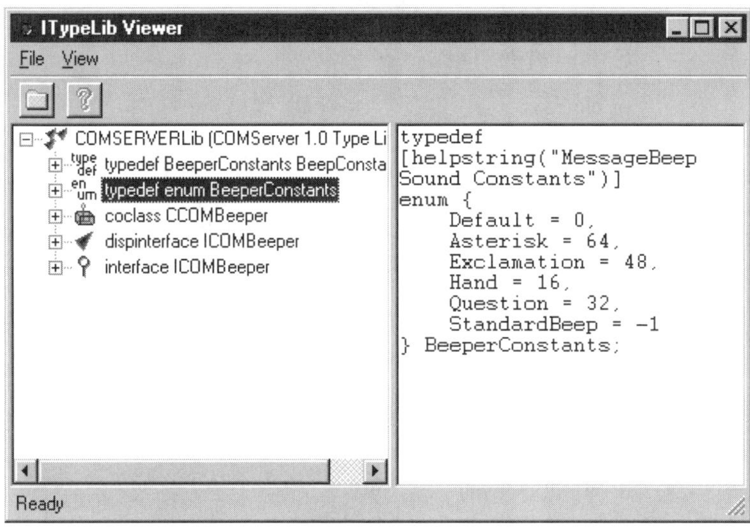

FIGURE 22.3 OLE/COM Object viewer.

associated native Java types. And, as COM has a class concept, it's important to understand how COM classes and associated concepts map to their Java counterparts.

Mapping COM Classes to Java Equivalents. The object description language of the COM. model supports five class or library-specific constructs. The following library elements and the associated constructs are described in Table 22.1. (It should be noted that this section is meant more as a guide than a definition. When developing Java applications that use COM objects, it's always important to look at the summary.txt file generated by the Java Type Library Wizard to see exactly what was generated. Not all constructs supported by COM are supported by Java.)

The Object Definition Language can be compiled by the Microsoft Interface Definition Language compiler or the MkTypLib utility. (For more information on either of these tools or a complete description of the Object Definition Language (ODL) syntax and language, refer to the *Microsoft Interface Definition Language (MIDL) Programmer's Guide and Reference*. Available through the WIN32 SDK, or see the Visual J++ online book *Java and COM*.)

Mapping COM Data Types to Java Equivalents. As with COM Libraries and classes, most COM data types have Java equivalents. Table 22.2 lists the Java equivalents for COM data types.

Any ODL type not listed is currently unsupported in Java and will generate an error when the class using the type is run through the Java Type Library Wizard.

TABLE 22.1 COM to Java Class Mappings

COM	*Java Equivalent*	*Description*
Coclass	public class	A "normal" everyday class.
Interface	public interface	The methods that can be applied to a given class. Normally, the keyword interface is applied to a set of functions that can act on a given object. Note that generated methods do not include those inherited from the IUnknown or Idispatch. You can access these methods by strategic casts of your class object.
Dispinterface	public interface	A special kind of COM interface known as a Dispatch interface. Dispatch interfaces are used to get and set properties of an object. Normally, these properties can also be accessed via the Idispatch::Invoke method of the object.
typedef (struct, enum, or union only)	public final class	Normal typedef. Works almost identically to a C or C++ typedef.
Module	public final class containing static final members	A specific class construct under COM that defines a final class with externally visible member variables. Modules typically describe a set of function calls, which are normally packaged together in a DLL rather than a class.

Note that you can still use the class, just not any methods that do not have a Java equivalent for the various parameters.

Often COM classes will take arguments of type *variant*. The variant class is really a wrapper around a variant structure which allows a single object to contain values of many types. For all practical purposes you can think of the variant class as a large union which can store most, if not all, the Java data types. Variants are primarily used to pass variables to interfaces that are derived from IUnknown where the exact data type of the parameters is either unknown at compile time or may change. (For more information on the Variant class, see the Class variant section in the Visual J++ online manual package com.ms.com.)

Java Applications Exposed via COM

One of the benefits of COM within Visual J++ is that applications and applets can expose public methods so they can be called from other programming languages or from within JavaScript. This opens the entire world of Java to Visual Basic, Visual C++, and other COM-enabled applications. In the next few sections we will explore how to create a COM callable class from a Java applet.

TABLE 22.2 COM-to-Java Type Mappings

ODL/COM Type	*Java Type*
Boolean	Boolean
char	Char
double	Double
int	Int
int64	Long
float	Float
long	Int
short	Short
unsigned char	Byte
BSTR	class java.lang.String
CURRENCY/CY	long (divide by 10,000 to get the original value as a fixed-point number)
DATE	double
SCODE/HRESULT	int, See the section titled *Handling COM Exceptions*
VARIANT	class com.ms.com.Variant More on variants in a moment.
IUnknown *	interface com.ms.com.Iunknown
IDispatch *	class java.lang.Object
SAFEARRAY(*typename*)	class **com.ms.com.SafeArray**
typename *	single-element array of *typename*
void	void

Running the Java ActiveX Wizard. You expose your Java class to the COM world by first creating the class and then running The Java ActiveX Wizard. Selecting ActiveX Wizard for Java from the Tools menu of Visual J++ runs the Java ActiveX Wizard. You will be presented with a screen that looks similar to Figure 22.4.

Step 1: **Generate the IDL.** The first step in running the ActiveX Wizard for Java is to enter the name of a valid Java class. Enter the name of a Java class or use the Browse button to select an appropriate .CLASS file. Note that by default the Wizard will fill in the name of the current class you are working on. In addition to giving the name of the file to convert you can also supply an existing IDL, or Interface Description Language, file. There are many good reasons for specifying an existing IDL file. For example, you've already run the ActiveX Wizard and want to reuse the existing IDL file. Or perhaps you've edited the IDL to remove methods you do not want to expose. In either case, either select an existing IDL file or allow Visual J++ to create one for you and press the next button.

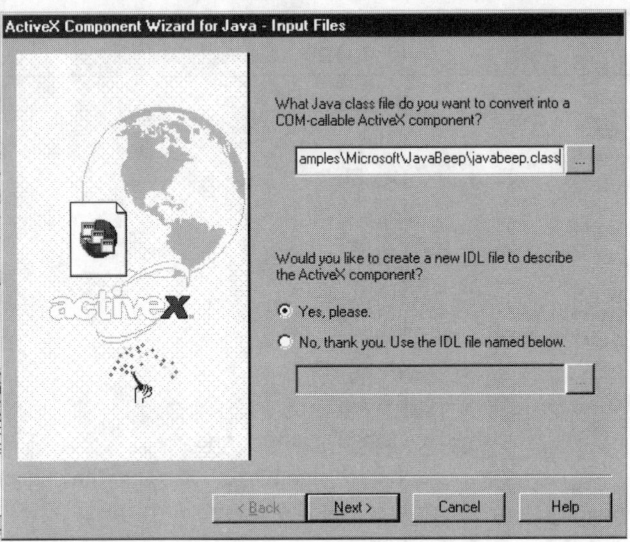

FIGURE 22.4 Step 1: define the IDL.

TIP There are a few things you should know about the ActiveX Wizard for Java. First, the wizard assumes that the input .java class has the same name as the .CLASS file you are converting. In addition, the wizard does not expose any methods of the class your class extends. If you wish to expose these methods you need to write your own wrappers and expose them as methods of the class being converted. And lastly, if the Wizard does not understand a construct in your class it may not convert it. A full definition of the IDL is available under books online, supplied with Visual J++.

Step 2: **Assign a CLSID.** The second step in converting your Java class to a COM class is assigning a class ID, or as they are typically written, CLSIDs. Class IDs are the mechanism by which COM users identify your class. In fact, if you have run the Wizard before, Visual J++ may prompt you with the existing ID even though you requested a new one. The second action step 2 can perform is to register your class. Once you have generated an ID and assigned it to your class you need to make it known to the system. We saw a flavor of this with RegSvr32 and now perform a similar action by selecting "yes, please" register my class now. The Wizard will then gen-

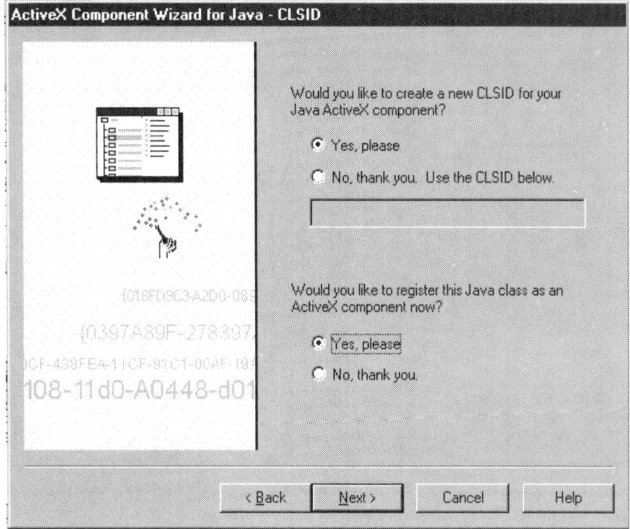

FIGURE 22.5 Step 2: Specify a CLSID.

erate a file that can be input to regedit and used to register your class. If you choose "no, thank you," then you will register the class yourself later.

TIP A special note to users of Visual Basic: If you plan on calling your Java object from Visual Basic then you may want to generate a new class ID every time. The ActiveX wizard does not absolutely guarantee binary compatibility from run to run. If you update your class often, either test it from Java and then finally generate the COM callable version, or generate a new class ID each time.

Step 3: **Generate the final type library.** The final step in converting our class is to generate a type library from the IDL of step 1. The type library defines the interfaces, methods, enums, and so forth, that are available for the caller's use. Figure 22.6 shows this step.

The first selection allows you to select either dispinterfaces or dual interfaces. A dispinterface is the simplest way to connect to a COM object and the only way supported by Visual Basic and the current version of the Microsoft Java VM. A dual interface contains both an IDispatch interface and a virtual function table. Choose the default and then select the Next button.

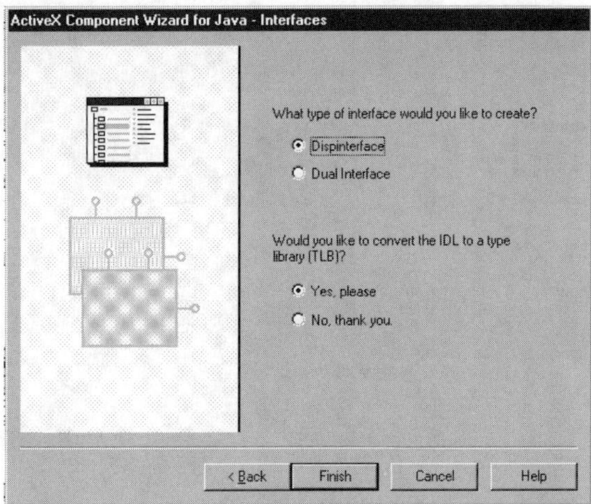

FIGURE 22.6 Step 3: Generate the type library.

TIP We've seen how to generate a type library, but how do we know when to NOT generate a type library? The only good reason not to create a type library is if you wish to change the IDL associated with a class to remove a method. In this case, select "no, thank you" and then, after modifying the IDL, rerun the Wizard.

Step 4: **Modify your Java class to contain the CLSID.** There is one additional step required before you can use your Java class, and that is the addition of the CLSID to the original Java source. Figure 22.7 shows the class ID you need to add to your Java class. This step is the final glue that links your Java class to its COM type library and registration information.

Final Review. We've seen the steps and discussed each, but for the sake of completeness let's review each one:

1. Create the Java class, potentially exposing by hand superclass methods we wish to expose.
2. Run the ActiveX Wizard for Java.
   a. Generating or specifying an IDL file.
   b. Generating or specifying a CLSID and additionally registering the class.
   c. Generating the type library and producing the updates to the original Java class.
3. Add the generated class ID as shown here:

```
// From within your Java class
private static final String = CLSID("12345678-1234-123456780000");
```

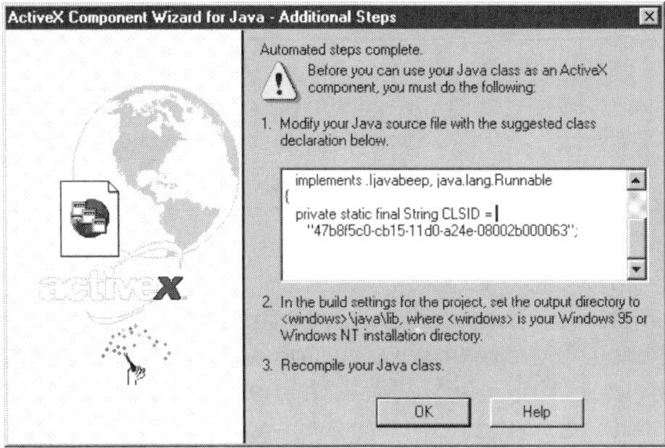

ActiveX Component Wizard for Java - Additional Steps
Automated steps complete.
Before you can use your Java class as an ActiveX component, you must do the following:
1. Modify your Java source file with the suggested class declaration below.
implements .Ijavabeep, java.lang.Runnable
{
private static final String CLSID =
"47b8f5c0-cb15-11d0-a24e-08002b000063";
2. In the build settings for the project, set the output directory to <windows>\java\lib, where <windows> is your Windows 95 or Windows NT installation directory.
3. Recompile your Java class.
OK
Help
activeX

FIGURE 22.7 Updating your source with a CLSID.

4. Set the output directory of your build to be %winsysdir%\java\lib or copy your class there.
5. Rebuild your Java class.

That's it! Your Java class can now be embedded in an HTML page using the <OBJECT> tag or can be called for any COM-aware development environment!

TIP According to the April 1997 Microsoft Developers Network, CD CLSID, or as they are sometimes called, GUID, are globally unique IDs. These IDs are generated using any of several methods, for example, guidgen.exe or the ActiveX class wizard, and are guaranteed to be unique. According to the documentation "GUIDGen.exe never produces the same number twice, no matter how many times it is run or on how many different machines it is run on." The exact algorithm is not published, perhaps by design, but appears to use the CPU ID as part of the 128-bit identifier.

22.3 SUMMARY

As we have seen, ActiveX programming lends itself nicely to both being called from Java and making Java COM callable. Because of the nature of how COM classes are implemented they very naturally complement Java. The Microsoft Visual J++ development environment is an excellent tool for the first-time Java developer. It demonstrates how easy it really is to call ActiveX controls, examine their interfaces, and handle their exceptions. All from within native Java code!

SOURCE 22.3 An HTML tag to check the version of Internet Explorer supported on a target machine.

```
<OBJECT
CLASSID="clsid:08B0E5C0-4FCB-11CF-AAA5-00401C608500"
CODEBASE="http://www.microsoft.com/java/IE30Java.cab#Version=1,0,0,1">
</OBJECT>
```

One final note: you should always make sure that any pages that are available to the outside world and use COM can only be run on a page that supports COM integration. You can do this by inserting the HTML tag shown as Source 22.3 into your page.

The purpose of this tag is to check the version of Microsoft Internet Explorer or that the current browser supports ActiveX and COM. Under Internet Explorer if the version is not current, an attempt is made to download the current version from http://www.microsoft.com.

Further Reading

Many fine books are available from John Wiley and Sons on the topic of making your Web pages *active*; two of which are *The ActiveX Sourcebook* by Coombs, Coombs, and Brewer, or *ActiveX Web Programming* by Adam Blum. Both are excellent sources of material on integrating ActiveX into your Web pages. For more information on Visual J++ itself see *The Microsoft Visual J++ 1.1 Sourcebook* by Jay Cross and Al Saganich. The Visual J++ Sourcebook is a great resource for developing Java applications using the Microsoft Visual J++ toolset.

CHAPTER 23

The Java Foundation Classes

OBJECTIVE

This chapter explains and demonstrates the Java Foundation Classes (JFC), a high-level set of sophisticated graphical user interface components layered on top of the AWT. We begin with the purpose of the JFC, examine how it is implemented, and then work through several example programs that highlight some of the major components.

The Java Foundation Classes are a set of prebuilt classes that provide Java applications and applets with the building blocks for a sophisticated graphical user interface (GUI). The JFC is intended to level the playing field so that any Java program has a look and feel (L&F) that is as good as, or better than, any currently available graphical user interface on a specific platform. The overriding theme of the JFC is that a programmer will not be forced to sacrifice a first-class GUI to get the benefits of cross-platform execution. Examples of sophisticated components provided by the JFC are trees, image buttons, borders, tabs, tables, progress bars, scroll panes, and much more! Figure 23.1 is a screen shot of the program called the "SwingSet" that demonstrates all of the JFC components (the JavaSoft project name for the Foundation Classes was "swing").

23.1 A NEW APPROACH TO CROSS-PLATFORM GUIS

The Abstract Window Toolkit used a peer paradigm to implement a cross-platform user interface. The use of an operating-system-specific or "native" peer for each AWT component created a "native" look and feel for Java applications; however, this also restricted the available AWT components to a set of native peers that existed on all

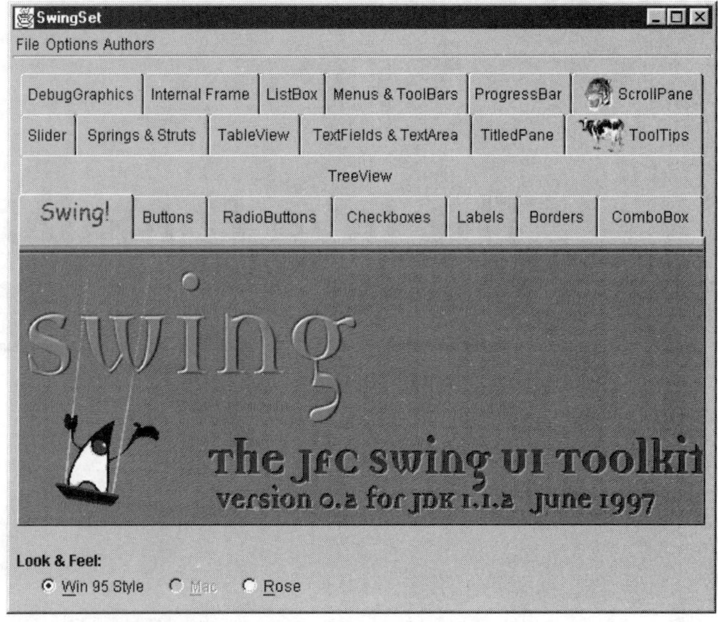

FIGURE 23.1 The SwingSet.

supported platforms. This forced the AWT into a least-common-denominator look and feel. Many companies began to patch this least-common-denominator weakness by creating custom components by extending the Canvas component. JavaSoft set out to fix the inherent weakness of the "native"-look-and-feel approach while at the same time ensuring robust cross-platform applications.

JavaSoft polled customers for what types of graphical user interfaces they wanted on their applications. The respondents fell into one of three categories: some who wanted a native look and feel for each platform the application ran on, many who wanted a common look and feel across platforms, and some large companies that wanted a "corporate" look and feel customized for their company. In response to this, JavaSoft designed a paradigm that could support all three customer bases.

To support a "common look and feel," JavaSoft improved upon the building of custom components by allowing the creation of AWT components without any native peer counterpart. These are called "lightweight" components because they are pure Java and have no operating-system-specific resources to restrict them (or weigh them down). Therefore, the existing peer interface is considered to use "heavyweight" components. We will demonstrate building a lightweight component in Java and highlight the benefits of doing so.

A user-specific (corporate or individual) look and feel can be accomplished by allowing the entire user interface to be designated at run time or switched "on the fly". JavaSoft calls this a "pluggable look and feel." To accomplish this JavaSoft implemented all of the new JFC components using the Model View Controller paradigm, which separates the nonvisual functionality of the component (model) from the control (user input) and view (look and feel) of the component. All JFC components follow this MVC paradigm and combine it with UI interfaces, dynamic object loading and dynamic resource loading to allow the look and feel of a component to be loaded or switched at run time. JavaSoft groups and encapsulates this sophisticated behavior into a UIManager class and UIFactory classes (one Factory per specific look and feel). Of course, there is a default UIFactory so that you do not have to worry about pluggable look and feel unless you want to. We will examine a demonstration of switching the look and feel of an application at run time.

23.2 LIGHTWEIGHT COMPONENTS

The foundation that all the Java Foundation Classes are built upon is the support of lightweight components in the AWT. Simply stated, this means that to create a new GUI component you can now subclass Component or Container directly instead of subclassing Canvas or Panel as was previously done. Prior to JDK 1.1 the only way to create a new custom component was to subclass Canvas or Panel, which created a corresponding native window as its peer. This one-to-one correspondence between a new component and a native window consumes operating system resources (as well as virtual machine resources), is not consistent across operating systems, and the native windows are opaque. An opaque native window means that you cannot create a transparent component (like a nonrectangular component) unless the background matches the opaque window color.

In Source 23.1, CapacityMeter.java, I demonstrate the creation of a lightweight component by subclassing Component. The custom component is a small circular progress meter where a pie wedge grows as the "capacity" increases. A full circle is 100 percent capacity.

SOURCE 23.1 CapacityMeter.java

```
// capacityMeter.java
package jwiley.chp23;

import java.awt.*;
import java.awt.event.*;
import java.io.File;

/**
 * A LightWeight, custom component.
 * This CapacityMeter is a variation of a progress meter
 * (also known as a guage).  Since it is circular it is
 * more compact than a typical progress meter.
 */
public class CapacityMeter extends Component
{
```

```
/** Current setting of meter current/max = percentage filled. */
private double current;
/** Maximum value of meter setting. */
private double maximum;
/** Color of Wedge that indicates percentage complete. */
private Color wedgeColor;
/** Color of pie face. */
private Color pieColor;
/** Color of top shaded edge. */
private Color pieLightEdge;
/** Color of Bottom shaded edge. */
private Color pieDarkEdge;
/** Debug flag. */
private boolean debug=false;
/** Dimensions of control. */
private Dimension cmDim;

/** mutator method .*/
public void setDebug(boolean flag) { debug = flag; }

/** mutator method.  Also causes an update of the pie face.
    This control uses Dirty rectangle animation. */
public void setCurrent(double curCapacity)
{

    current = curCapacity;
    update(this.getGraphics());
}

/** Constructor. */
public CapacityMeter(double fullCapacity)
{
    this(fullCapacity, Color.gray, Color.gray.brighter(),
                       Color.gray.darker(),
                       Color.red, new Dimension(110,110));
}

/** Constructor that allows different colors and a custom size. */
public CapacityMeter(double fullCapacity, Color pieFace,
                     Color pieTop, Color pieBottom, Color wedgeFace,
                     Dimension theDim)
{
    if (debug)
        System.out.println("Invoked CapacityMeter(int fullCapacity)");
    setBackground(Color.lightGray);
    maximum = fullCapacity;
    pieColor = pieFace;
    pieLightEdge = pieTop;
    pieDarkEdge = pieBottom;
    wedgeColor = wedgeFace;
    cmDim = theDim;
}
```

```
/** Preferred size to tell the layout manager. */
public Dimension getPreferredSize()
{
    if (debug)
        System.out.println("Invoked preferredSize()");

    return cmDim;
}

/** minimum size for this control. */
public Dimension getMinimumSize()
{
    if (debug)
        System.out.println("Invoked minimumSize()");

    return cmDim;
}

/** How to paint the component. In our control,
    this paints the background. To avoid flicker the
    "foreground" is painted in the update() method.
    Another way to do this is to use double-buffered
    animation - see the section on Double-buffering. */
public void paint(Graphics g)
{
    if (debug)
        System.out.println("Invoked paint(Graphics g)");
    Rectangle r = getBounds();
    if (debug)
        System.out.println("getBounds(): " + r);

    int innerX=5, innerY=5;
    int outerX=2, outerY=2;
    int innerSubtract=9, outerSubtract=4;

    // outer will be two 180 degree wedges
    g.setColor(pieLightEdge);
    g.fillArc(outerX, outerY, r.width - outerSubtract,
              r.height - outerSubtract,
                   226, -182);
    g.setColor(pieDarkEdge);
    g.fillArc(outerX, outerY, r.width - outerSubtract,
              r.height - outerSubtract,
               225, 180);


    // inner
    g.setColor(pieColor);
    g.fillOval(innerX, innerY, r.width - innerSubtract,
               r.height - innerSubtract);
```

```
        update(g);
    }

    /** How to update only a portion of the component. */
    public void update(Graphics g)
    {
        // dirty rectangle animation
        Rectangle r = getBounds();
        int innerX=5, innerY=5;
        int outerX=2, outerY=2;
        int innerSubtract=9, outerSubtract=4;
        if (current > 0)
        {
            // calculate percentage
            double perc = (current/maximum) * 100;

            // calculate degrees
            int degrees = (int) ((360 * perc)/(double)100);

            // wedge
            g.setColor(wedgeColor);
            g.fillArc(innerX, innerY, r.width - innerSubtract,
                     r.height - innerSubtract,
                      270, -degrees);

        }
    }

    /** This method overrides the default implementation (in Component)
        and will force the size and shape of the component to
        stay circular,
        be centered in the component area (which will be affected by
        resizing the window), and always stay the size set at construction.
        You may want to comment out this method and see what happens. */
    public synchronized void setBounds(int x, int y, int w, int h)
    {
        int centerX=0, centerY=0;
        if (w > cmDim.width)
            centerX = x + ((w - cmDim.width)/2);
        else
            centerX = x;
        if (h > cmDim.height)
            centerY = y + ((h - cmDim.height)/2);
        else
            centerY = y;
        super.setBounds(centerX,centerY,cmDim.width,cmDim.height);
        if (debug)
            System.out.println("Invoked setBounds(" + x + "," + y + ","
                                                  + w + "," + h + ")");
    }
```

```
    /** Main method to invoke from JVM for unit testing. */
    public static void main(String args[])
    {
        if (args.length < 1)
        {
            System.out.println("USAGE: java CapacityMeter bkgrndFile");
            System.exit(1);
        }

        BackgroundFrame tstFrame = new BackgroundFrame(args[0]);

        try { Thread.sleep(2000); } catch (Exception e) { }

        CapacityMeter cm = null;

        while ((cm = tstFrame.getCapacityMeter()) == null)
            try { Thread.sleep(2000); } catch (Exception e) { }

        for (int i=0; i < 100; i++)
        {
            cm.setCurrent(i);
            try { Thread.sleep(500); } catch (Exception e) { }
        }
    } // end of main()
} // end of class CapacityMeter

/** Frame class used in testing.  Primary purpose of the class is
    to override frame so we could draw an image in the background
    to show the transparency of lightweight components.  Of course,
    for a circular component this is essential! */
class BackgroundFrame extends Frame
{
    /** Image to draw in the background. */
    Image img;
    /** Capacity meter in this frame. */
    CapacityMeter cm;

    /** Simple adapter to shutdown the application when the
        window close box is clicked. */
    public class ShutdownAdapter extends WindowAdapter
    {
        public void windowClosing(WindowEvent we)
        {
            System.exit(0);
        }
    }

    /** accessor for capacity meter. */
    public CapacityMeter getCapacityMeter() { return cm; }

    /** Constructor. */
    public BackgroundFrame(String sBackgroundFileName)
```

```
    {
        super("Capacity Meter Test");
        // add a capacity Meter
        cm = new CapacityMeter(100);
        cm.setDebug(false);
        add("Center", cm);

        File f = new File(sBackgroundFileName);
        if (f.exists())
        {
            img =
(Toolkit.getDefaultToolkit()).getImage(sBackgroundFileName);
            MediaTracker mt = new MediaTracker(this);
            mt.addImage(img,0);
            try
            {
                mt.waitForAll();
            } catch (Exception e)
              { /* do nothing - img will be null */ }
            if (mt.isErrorAny())
            {
                System.out.println("Error loading image.");
                img = null;
            }
        }
        else
            System.out.println(sBackgroundFileName + " does not exist.");

        setSize(300,300);
        setLocation(50,50);
        addWindowListener(new ShutdownAdapter());
        show();

        try { Thread.sleep(500); } catch (Exception e) { }
    }

    /** paint method. *NOTE*: the call to super.paint(g) is necessary
        to paint lightweight components in this container. */
    public void paint(Graphics g)
    {
        Dimension d = getSize();
        if (img != null)
            g.drawImage(img, 0, 0, d.width, d.height, this);
        super.paint(g);
    }

    /** avoid flicker. */
    public void update(Graphics g)
    {
        paint(g);
    }
}
```

To run Source 23.1, we type:

```
java jwiley.chp23.CapacityMeter mandrill.jpg
```

This command produces Figure 23.2.

There are several key points to note about Source 23.1 that also apply to creating Lightweight components in general:

- As stated before, you subclass either Component or Container.
- You must implement a paint() method for your component. You explicitly "paint" using drawing primitives for the look and feel of your component.
- You override getPreferredSize() and getMinimumSize() to instruct the LayoutManager how much space your component requires.
- One very crucial difference between heavyweight and lightweight components is how your paint() method gets called. For lightweight components, the container manages the painting of the components and will call the paint method of any lightweight components it contains. Therefore, if you override the paint() method of the container as the BackgroundFrame class does, you must include a call to super.paint() in order to have your lightweight components painted.
- Notice that BackgroundFrame will draw an Image as our background. Since lightweight components can have transparent areas (anything outside of our explicit commands in paint()), our circular component is indeed circular. If we had subclassed Canvas, you would have seen a white rectangle bounding our capacity meter. The bounding box of the component is still rectangular but since the component's edges are transparent we do not see the bounding box. Demonstrating the ability for transparent parts of a component was the purpose of the BackgroundFrame.

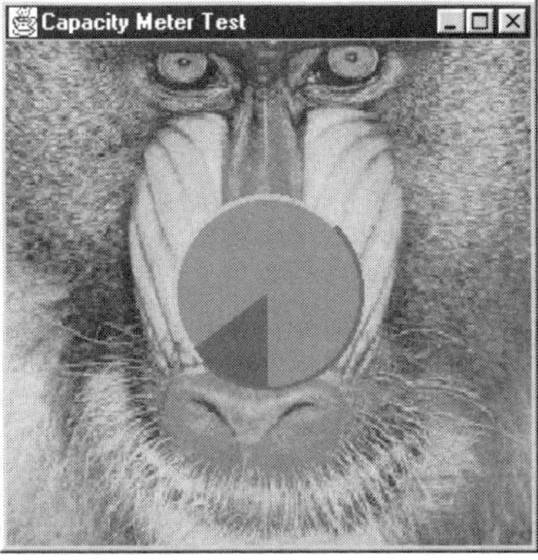

FIGURE 23.2 A circular capacity meter.

Since lightweight components are 100-percent pure Java, they are rendered exactly the same on all supported platforms. This provides a "common look and feel" across platforms and allows developers to guarantee a consistent interface across platforms for their Java applications or applets. Now let's examine the architectural foundation of a "pluggable" look and feel.

23.3 USER INTERFACE FACTORY

An object factory is a common technique (called a design pattern) used to isolate a generic capability from implementation-specific details. Good examples of object factories are the Socket class and the JDBC Connection class. Although the Socket class hides this fact, the idea behind an object factory is that instead of instantiating a class directly, you use an object factory to generate a specific implementation of an object that has generic capabilities (defined via an interface or abstract class). In other words, you are interested in the generic capabilities and want those capabilities tailored or targeted at a specific implementation at run time. For example, you receive a Connection object by a call to DriverManager.getConnection(String url, String user, String password). This gives the programmer a standard frontend interface while the actually implementation can be "plugged in" and generated dynamically at run time via the object factory. The Java Foundation Classes make use of this same pattern for generating a specific "pluggable" look and feel at run time. Let's examine the UIFactory in detail and then see a demonstration of it in action.

Before you can understand the UIFactory class you first need to understand the architecture of a JFC component. A JFC component is:

- Lightweight (as just described).
- Uses the Model View Controller design pattern. More specifically, every JFC Component is divided into a class that contains a model and an interface that defines the View/Controller requirements for this type of visual component. You create the model when you instantiate a JFC Component. For example, to create a JFC button you type: JButton button = newJButton("Hello World");
- Every JComponent subclass has a corresponding component interface; for example, JButton has a UI interface called ButtonUI.
- Each UIFactory class will have a UI class that implements the component's user interface in a specific way. For example, the Windows 95 factory is called the BasicFactory and it has a button implementation called BasicButtonUI.

Now that you understand the relationship between a UI Factory and a JFC Component let's examine some of the characteristics of a subclass of UIFactory. You will have a UIFactory for every specific look and feel that your java applications can switch between. Of course, you can lock your users into a specific look and feel if you want to. Each UIFactory implementation provides the following capabilities:

- Creates an instantiation of a UI object when requested by a JFC Component. For example, the BasicFactory will instantiate a UI object of type BasicButtonUI when requested by the instantiation of a JButton. We will see this demonstrated in Source 23.2.

- Returns factory-wide property definitions. Done by each UIFactory having a corresponding properties file.
- Returns images, fonts, and other resources.
- Installs new UI objects in a Container if the default Factory changes. We will see a demonstration of this in Source 23.2.

Since you can have multiple UI Factories, these are managed by a UIManager class. The UIManager class manages the list of installed UIFactory classes.

Now we are ready to examine a simple example that creates some JFC Components and switches their look and feel on the fly from a Windows 95 look and feel to a "Rose" look and feel. Source 23.2, SimplePanel.java, demonstrates this.

SOURCE 23.2 SimplePanel.java

```
/** SimplePanel.java */
package jwiley.chp23;

import java.awt.*;
import java.awt.event.*;
import com.sun.java.swing.*;

/**
 * An application that displays a JButton and two JRadioButtons.
 * The JRadioButtons determine the look and feel used by the application.
 */
public class SimplePanel extends JPanel {
    static JFrame frame;
    static String basic = new String("Win95");
    static String rose = new String("Rose");

    /** Constructor. */
    public SimplePanel()
      {
          super(true);

         // start out with Win95 UIFactory
        try
        {
            UIManager.setUIFactory("com.sun.java.swing.basic.BasicFactory",
                                   (Container)frame);
        } catch (ClassNotFoundException cnf)
          {
            System.err.println("Could not load Win95 factory.");
          }

        setLayout(new BorderLayout());
         setBackground(Color.lightGray);
```

```
// Create a button.
JButton button = new JButton("Hello, world");
button.setKeyAccelerator('h');

// Create the glyphs for radio buttons
ImageGlyph radio = new ImageGlyph("jwiley\\chp23\\offbut.jpg");
ImageGlyph radioSelected = new
          ImageGlyph("jwiley\\chp23\\onbut.jpg");

// Create some radio buttons with image glyphs
JRadioButton testButton = new JRadioButton("Radio1");
testButton.setSelected(true);
JRadioButton test2Button = new JRadioButton("Radio2");
ButtonGroup testGroup = new ButtonGroup();
testGroup.add(testButton);
testGroup.add(test2Button);

JRadioButton basicButton = new JRadioButton(basic, radio);
basicButton.setKeyAccelerator('b');
basicButton.setActionCommand(basic);
basicButton.setSelected(true);
basicButton.setSelectedGlyph(radioSelected);

JRadioButton roseButton = new JRadioButton(rose, radio);
roseButton.setKeyAccelerator('r');
roseButton.setActionCommand(rose);
roseButton.setSelectedGlyph(radioSelected);

// Group the radio buttons.
ButtonGroup group = new ButtonGroup();
group.add(basicButton);
group.add(roseButton);

// Register a listener for the radio buttons.
RadioListener myListener = new RadioListener();
roseButton.addActionListener(myListener);
basicButton.addActionListener(myListener);

JPanel centerP = new JPanel();
centerP.setLayout(new FlowLayout(FlowLayout.LEFT,5,5));
JPanel southP = new JPanel();

centerP.add(button);
centerP.add(testButton);
centerP.add(test2Button);

// controls
southP.add(basicButton);
southP.add(roseButton);
```

```
        // add Panels
        add("Center", centerP);
        add("South", southP);
    }


    /** An ActionListener that listens to the radio buttons. */
    class RadioListener implements ActionListener
    {
         public void actionPerformed(ActionEvent e)
         {
              String factoryName = null;

              if (e.getActionCommand() == rose)
                   factoryName = "com.sun.java.swing.rose.RoseFactory";
              else
                   factoryName = "com.sun.java.swing.basic.BasicFactory";

            try
            {
               UIManager.setUIFactory(factoryName, (Container)frame);
                    frame.pack();
            } catch (ClassNotFoundException cnf)
              {
                   System.err.println("Could not load factory: "
                                                          + factoryName);
              }
         }
    }

    /** main() method to invoke from JVM. */
    public static void main(String args[])
    {
         WindowListener l = new WindowAdapter()
         {
             public void windowClosing(WindowEvent e)
             {System.exit(0);}
         };

         frame = new JFrame("Simple Example");
         frame.setLayout(new BorderLayout(5,5));
         frame.addWindowListener(l);
         frame.add("Center", new SimplePanel());
         frame.pack();
         frame.setLocation(50,50);
         frame.setVisible(true);
    }
}
```

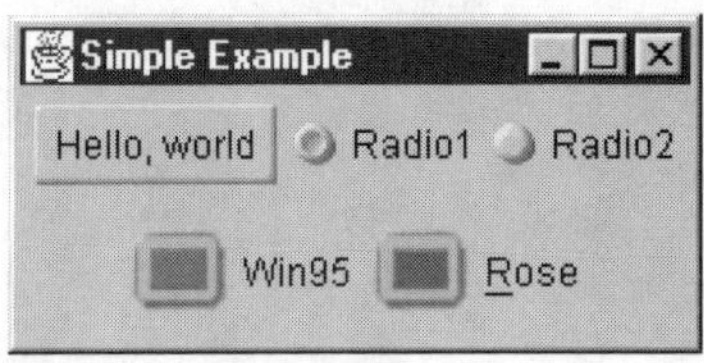

FIGURE 23.3 A panel with a pluggable interface.

A run of Source 23.2 produces Figure 23.3.

Source 23.2 should give you a good appreciation for how simple using JFC Components is as well as the simplicity of switching from one UIFactory to another. Using JFC Components is nearly identical to using heavyweight AWT Components. You just instantiate the components, set some "options" on the component by calling class methods, and then add the component to a parent container. There are a few other important points to note about Source 23.2:

- The program sets the initial UIFactory with a call to UIManager.setUIFactory (String, Container). This is also how the program will switch to another UIFactory in response to choosing one of the two radio buttons. One radio button is labeled Windows 95 and the other is Rose.
- Creating JFC Components is identical to creating an AWT Component and as simple as instantiating an object. In this simple program all we create is one button, two radio buttons (these components are just in the application to see how their appearance changes when we switch UIFactories), and two radio buttons that use Image Glyphs (we will discuss glyphs next). These image radio buttons are the buttons that we attach an event listener to in order to switch the UIFactory.
- We create two Image Glyphs by using the ImageGlyph constructor with the full path of an image. An ImageGlyph is a class optimized to load and "reload" small pictures on graphical components. All glyphs are cached so they are only loaded once. Glyphs also load synchronously (not worth the overhead of asynchronous loading) and are serializable.

Now you should feel comfortable with how the JFC has achieved both a common look and feel (using lightweight components) and a pluggable look and feel using UIFactories. Now let's examine the list of JFC components available to spruce up our applications. After that we will jump in to a few specific examples.

23.4 JFC COMPONENTS

The Java Foundation Classes are composed of a large set of classes and interfaces at your disposal. We will discuss all of the major graphical components available at the time of this writing. You can expect the graphical components to grow and you can view an updated list on our Web site. For a graphical demonstration of all of these components, see the swingset application and other demos on the CD-ROM. Here are the current key components:

JBorder, JBezelBorder, JEmptyBorder, JTitledBorder. These components provide visible borders around other components.

JButton. A lightweight, pluggable version of the familiar AWT Button. Note that all JFC Components are subclasses of JComponent. JButton allows many more variations of a button like an image button and variable placement of text. You will find that all the JFC Components, even one similar to ones in the AWT, are generally much more flexible and better looking. The model for this component is the ButtonModel. This is shared by JButton, JCheckbox, and JRadioButton.

JCanvas. A lightweight, pluggable version of the familiar AWT Canvas.

JCheckbox, JCheckboxMenuItem. A lightweight, pluggable version of Checkbox and Checkbox Menu Item.

JChoice. A lightweight, pluggable version of a choice drop-down menu (also called a combo box). In the JFC, JChoice is provided for compatibility with the existing AWT and is a subclass of JComboBox.

JComboBox. A custom combo box (allows glyphs), an editable combo box, and classic combo box. The model for this component is the ComboBoxDataModel.

JComponent. All JFC Component's subclass JComponent that extends java.awt .Container.

JFrame. A lightweight, pluggable version of the AWT Frame.

JInternalFrame. A "sub-frame". This allows frames within frames. This enables Java applications to create the familiar Windows Multiple Document Interface (MDI) type application.

JLabel. A lightweight, pluggable version of the AWT label. As other JFC Components, this is much more flexible, allowing various placement of the text and even images. JLabel has no model.

JLayeredPane. A component that is similar to a container but maintains layers like overlays.

JList, JListBox. A lightweight, pluggable version of the AWT List. JList has two models: ListDataModel and ListSelectionModel. JListBox is designed to make it very easy to view the common collection types (like arrays, vectors, and hashtables).

JMenu, JMenuBar, JMenuItem. Lightweight pluggable version of menu and menu items. The JFC Menu Items allow images on a menu and menu item.

JPanel. A lightweight, pluggable version of the AWT panel.

JPopupMenu. A menu that can "popup" anywhere on the screen. The best example is the right click contextual popup menu in Windows, which was also recently added to MacOS 8 via a ctrl-click.

JProgressBar. A new component to present a graphical view of some action's completion progress. This uses the same model as JSlider and JScrollBar, the BoundedRangeModel.

JScrollBar, JScrollPane, JViewPort. JScrollBar is a lightweight, pluggable version of the AWT scrollbar. JScrollBar is intended to be a replacement for the AWT scrollbars. The model for this component is the BoundedRangeModel. JViewPort displays a view that is potentially larger than the viewport. The JScrollPane combines JScrollBars with a JViewPort and maps them accordingly.

JSeparator. A lightweight, pluggable menu separator.

JSlider. A control that allows the user to select a value from a bounded range via dragging a selector knob. Similar to how a scrollbar operates. The model for this component is the same model as the ScrollBar, the BoundedRangeModel.

JTabbedPane. A tabbed pane displays a set of labels that resemble file folders and lets the user store any component under that tab. When the user selects that tab the component opens or comes to the front. The model for this component is the SingleSelectionModel.

JTable. This component resides in its own package called Table as it has numerous support classes and interfaces. A table is a graphical element to display relational data in a two-dimensional format (rows and columns). This is perfect for display of a database table, as you will see in Source 23.4.

JTextComponent, JTextArea, JTextField. These components reside in their own package called Text as they have numerous support classes and interfaces. The JTextComponent goes far beyond the TextComponent in the AWT by providing the building blocks for a fully internationalized text editor. It does this with the help of several other classes like a Document interface, DocumentListener, DocumentEvent, and various view classes and interfaces. There are two good examples of this that come with the JDK; an example of a Java-based notepad (similar to Microsoft's notepad.exe), and a Java-based StylePad that demonstrates stylized texts (Rich Text Format) and images in a document.

JTimer. A simple timer that delivers an actionPerformed() method at a set interval. You create the timer, add an ActionListener, and a delay between calls. This could be used for an animation class to display the next frame or any other time-based operations.

JTitledPane. A container that has an optional title and border around its contents. This class does not have a separate model.

JToolTip, JToolTipManager. Allows a tip to pop up when the mouse "hovers" for a predetermined time over a component. JComponent and all subclasses (by default) support creating these tips. The JToolTipManager controls the behavior of how all tool tips get displayed for the system.

JTree. This class displays hierarchical data in an outline format. The most common Tree is the tree used in Windows Explorer to navigate Microsoft Windows' file systems. JTree supports a more generic model that includes that type of view. The support classes are the TreeModel, the ListSelectionModel, and the TreeNode class. The TreeNode class is a simple data structure for storing hierarchical data. A JTree component will provide a default view for a TreeNode structure. This is demonstrated in Source 23.3. We will discuss the JFC Trees in more detail in the next section.

Other features of the JFC:

Collection classes. These are nongraphical classes that store sets or "collections" of data. New collection classes augment the collection classes that already exist like arrays, Vectors, and HashTable. There will be classes that provide better search time like a balanced binary tree class called a TreeTable. There will also be a generic linked list class and interfaces to iterate through and compare nodes in any collection. The collection classes provide some of the same functionality as the C++ Standard Template Library.

Custom Cursors. Custom cursors will be provided by adding a method (and OS-specific implementation) to the Toolkit class. The method will be: Cursor create-CustomCursor(Image cursor, Point hotSpot, String name).

Drag and Drop. This is a complex set of classes and OS-specific code to allow a graphical element to be dragged (the DragSource class) over one or more potential targets called Drop targets. Once the element is dropped, either a copy or move will occur, or a negotiated data transfer will occur based on what the source can deliver and what the target can accept.

Event Queues. The JFC provides an enhanced and open EventQueue above the limited event queue mechanism in the AWT. The new Event Queue API allows you to filter events, get events, post events, and have multiple components listening to the event loop by registering with it.

Keyboard Navigation. All JFC graphical components support the keyboard UI for mouseless operation. JFC has a keyboard action registry where each component can register a set of keys and associated actions.

Repaint Batching. This is a much more sophisticated way of determining the absolute minimum amount of components/subsections of components that need repainting. The technique uses a DirtyRegionManager interface to keep track of "dirty" (areas in need of a repaint) regions. There is one DirtyRegionManager interface per component because each component is unique in how and how much of itself needs to be repainted. JComponent has convenience methods to make this simple.

Undo/Redo. JFC provides a straightforward mechanism to enable all components with the ability to undo/redo an event. There are various interfaces and classes to support these operations.

Now that we have completed an overview of the complete scope of the Java Foundation Classes, we are ready to see some more specific and nontrivial examples. The next section provides a program that uses the JTree component.

23.5 A JTREE EXAMPLE

A tree provides an outline view of hierarchical data. Our example demonstrates how easy it is to quickly build a graphical view of any hierarchical data by turning a hierarchical text file into a graphical tree display.

Source 23.3 TocTreePanel, uses a JTree to create a graphical table of contents.

SOURCE 23.3 TocTreePanel.java

```
/** TocTreePanel.java */
package jwiley.chp23;

import com.sun.java.swing.*;
import com.sun.java.swing.tree.*;
import com.sun.java.swing.event.*;

import java.awt.*;
import java.awt.event.*;
import java.io.*;

import java.util.Vector;

/**
 * Class that generates a Tree from a hierarchically formatted text
 * file.
 * @author Michael C. Daconta
 */
public class TocTreePanel extends JPanel implements TreeSelectionListener
{
    /** Debug variable. */
    public static boolean debug;

    /** Tree to generate. */
    DefaultMutableTreeNode dynamicTree;

    /** Graphical Tree Outline. */
    JTree jt;

    /** List Selection Model. */
    TreeSelectionModel tsm;

    /** Tree Model. */
    TreeModel jtm;

    /** Accessor. */
    public DefaultMutableTreeNode getDynamicTree() { return dynamicTree; }

    /** utility method to determine what level this node is at by
        counting white space characters.  The simplest way to format
        the text file is to use one tab per level. */
    private int countWhiteSpace(String sBuf)
```

```
    {
        for (int i=0; i < sBuf.length(); i++)
            if (sBuf.charAt(i) != '\t' &&
                sBuf.charAt(i) != ' ')
                return i;
        return -1; // error
    }

    /** Utility inner class to store both the position and a
        reference to the DefaultMutableTreeNode at that position. */
    class LevelNode
    {
        /** position of node. */
        public int iPosition;
        /** Tree node at that position. */
        public DefaultMutableTreeNode node;

        /** constructor. */
        LevelNode(int iPos, DefaultMutableTreeNode t)
        { iPosition = iPos; node = t; }
    }

    /** Utility method to find the parent of the current node.
        The algorithm is to start with the end of the Vector and
        find out where this node "fits".  A fit is when this
        nodes position is greater than the previous one. */
    private DefaultMutableTreeNode findParent(Vector levels, int nodePos)
    {
        int iLast = levels.size();
        // start from the bottom
        for (int i = (iLast - 1); i >= 0; i–)
        {
            LevelNode ln = (LevelNode) levels.elementAt(i);
            if (nodePos > ln.iPosition)
                return ln.node;
        }
        return null; // error
    }

    /** Utility method to parse a "Toc" file.  File where each new
        level is indicated by indenting that word.  One word per line. */
    private DefaultMutableTreeNode parseTableOfContents(FileInputStream fis)
throws IOException
    {
        DefaultMutableTreeNode outNode = null;
        int iCurLevel = 0;
        Vector vLevels = new Vector();
        BufferedReader br = new BufferedReader(
                            new InputStreamReader(fis));
        String sLine = null;
        while ( (sLine = br.readLine()) != null)
```

```
        {
            if (debug) System.out.println("Line: " + sLine);

            // get position of token
            int pos = countWhiteSpace(sLine);
            DefaultMutableTreeNode aNode = new
DefaultMutableTreeNode(sLine.trim());
            vLevels.addElement(new LevelNode(pos, aNode));

            if (outNode == null)
            {
                outNode = aNode;
            }
            else
            {
                // find who to add this node to
                DefaultMutableTreeNode parent = findParent(vLevels, pos);
                if (parent != null)
                {
                    parent.add(aNode);
                }
            }
        }

        return outNode;
    }

    /** Constructor. */
    public TocTreePanel(String sTocFile) throws IOException
    {
        setLayout(new BorderLayout());

        // check if file exists
        File f = new File(sTocFile);
        if (f.exists())
        {
            FileInputStream fis = new FileInputStream(sTocFile);
            dynamicTree = parseTableOfContents(fis);
            fis.close();
        }
        else
            throw new IOException(sTocFile + " does not exist.");

        if (dynamicTree != null)
        {
            // create a JTree
            jt = new JTree(dynamicTree);
```

```
            // get the Tree Model
            jtm = jt.getModel();

            // listen to the selections
            tsm = jt.getSelectionModel();
            tsm.setSelectionMode(TreeSelectionModel.SINGLE_TREE_SELECTION);
            tsm.addTreeSelectionListener(this);

            // create a scrollPane
             JScrollPane scrollpane = new JScrollPane();
             scrollpane.getViewport().add(jt);

             add("Center", scrollpane);
        }
        else
            throw new IOException(sTocFile + " is empty.");
    }

    public void valueChanged(TreeSelectionEvent tse)
    {
        // get the path selected
        TreePath tp = tse.getPath();
        // get the leaf node of the path
        Object o = tp.getLastPathComponent();
        // for now, just print out the leaf node (a String)
        System.out.println(o);
    }

    /** Main method for unit testing. */
    public static void main(String args[])
    {
        if (args.length < 1)
        {
            System.out.println("USAGE: java TocTreePanel tocFile");
            System.exit(1);
        }

        TocTreePanel.debug = true;

        try
        {
            TocTreePanel tp = new TocTreePanel(args[0]);
        } catch (IOException ioe)
          {
            ioe.printStackTrace();
          }
        System.exit(0);
    }
}
```

TocTreePanel is a scrollable panel that contains a JTree. The panel will add scrollbars if the tree expands larger than the panel size. There are several key points to note in Source 23.3.

- The majority of the program is concerned with creating the TreeNode data structure. The parseTableOfContents() method will parse a hierarchically formatted text file (one line per node, indent to denote a child) and create a TreeNode structure. A TreeNode structure is very simple. It starts with a root node and enables you to add children recursively (i.e., children can optionally have children of their own). TreeNode also has methods to enumerate the contents in either breadth-first or depth-first order (these are very common tree traversal orders). A TreeNode can have any user object attached. What will get rendered is the user object's toString() representation (this is the default UI rendering, which can be customized). In the preceding code, dynamicTree is the reference to the root node of the TreeNode tree.
- A JTree is the JFC Component that combines the data model with the pluggable UI to create our interactive graphical tree control. JTree hides many implementation details from the user by providing a constructor that accepts a TreeNode structure. This TreeNode constructor also uses the TreeNode structure to create a default data model. JTree also has a constructor that accepts an object that implements the TreeDataModel interface.
- The key to understanding the JTree object, and all the JFC Components, is understanding that they implement the model view controller paradigm (MVC) and how they implement it. In the JFC implementation the View and Controller are integrated together. The data model is separate. The JTree has a data model called the TreeDataModel. As we discussed earlier, the JTree constructor will create a JTreeDataModel given a TreeNode structure. We can retrieve the model created via a call to getModel(). We retrieve the model because we will query it later on when handling a selection from the user. The JTree also has a ListSelectionModel (a default is also created in the JTree constructor), which can control the model. The ListSelectionModel is the same one used for a ListBox. It returns an index range selected from a list of values with stable indexes. So, the key to understanding JTree is to understand that it is a class that integrates several cooperating classes split among models, controls, and views. Do not try and understand it as a single, simple entity. You need to learn the roles each "partner" class plays in relation to displaying and controlling some data model.
- We make the class implement the ListSelectionListener interface and register it with the ListSelectionModel. The ListSelectionInterface has a single method called valueChanged(). In our example, we determine if a node was selected (instead of just tree expansion), and then print out the String value of the node.

Source 23.4, TocFrame.java, is simply a standalone frame to host our TocTreePanel.

SOURCE 23.4 TocFrame.java

```
/** TocFrame.java */
package jwiley.chp23;

import com.sun.java.swing.*;
import com.sun.java.swing.tree.*;

import java.awt.*;
import java.awt.event.*;
import java.io.IOException;

/**
 * Simple Frame to demonstrate a dynamic use for a
 * JTree.
 * @author Michael C. daconta
 * @see TocTreePanel
 */
public class TocFrame extends Frame
{
    /** Simple adapter class to shutdown the application
        when the close button is pushed. */
    class ShutdownAdapter extends WindowAdapter
    {
        public void windowClosing(WindowEvent we)
        { System.exit(0); }
    }

    /** Constructor.
     * @param sTocFile Name of ".toc" file.
     */
    public TocFrame(String sTocFile)
    {
        super(sTocFile);
        TocTreePanel tp = null;
        try
        {
            tp = new TocTreePanel(sTocFile);
            add("Center", tp);
        } catch(IOException ioe)
          { }

        addWindowListener(new ShutdownAdapter());

        setSize(200,200);
        setLocation(50,50);
        setVisible(true);
    }
```

```
    /** Main() method to invoke from the JVM. */
    public static void main(String args[])
    {
        if (args.length < 1)
        {
            System.out.println("USAGE: java TocFrame tocFile");
            System.exit(1);
        }

        new TocFrame(args[0]);
    }
}
```

To run Source 23.4 we type:

```
java  TocFrame book.toc
```

which produces Figure 23.4.

Now let's examine another nontrivial JFC Component: the JTable Component.

23.6 A JTABLE EXAMPLE

One of the most logical uses for a JTable is to display a relational database table. We will demonstrate this exact use in this section. The JTable supports resizable and reorderable columns. The design of the JTable is identical to the design of the JTree in that it has a data model and a selection model. In fact, the selection model is identical to the JTree's selection model. JTable has one extra model, a ColumnDataModel (for example, to describe the width a column should be displayed). Also similar to the JTree is that the JTable almost always resides inside a JScrollPane. To accommodate

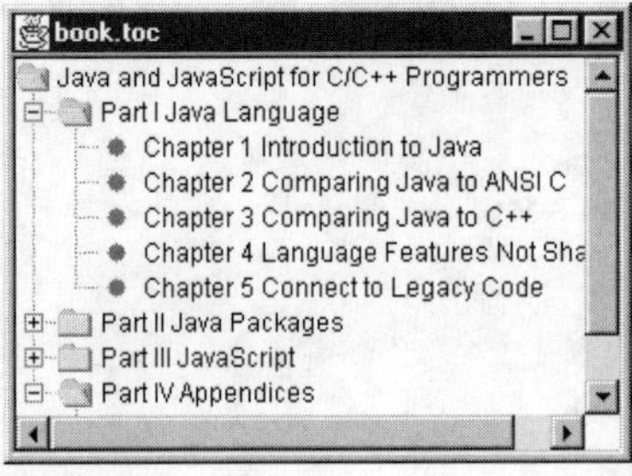

FIGURE 23.4 Graphical table of contents for this book.

this, there is a separate object for the column headings called JTableHeader, whereas the data is viewed via the JTable object.

Sources 23.5 and 23.6 represent an example to graphically display any database table in a Frame. You will see that the majority of code and key to understanding how to use the JTable is in Source 23.5, DatabaseTableDataModel.java. Setting up the data model correctly is the key to using this component correctly.

SOURCE 23.5 DatabaseTableDataModel.java

```
/** DatabaseTableDataModel.java */
package jwiley.chp23;

import java.sql.*;
import java.util.Vector;
import com.sun.java.swing.*;
import com.sun.java.swing.table.*;

/**
 * DataModel for the JTable component.
 * @author Eric Monk
 * @author Mike Daconta
 */
public class DatabaseTableModel extends DefaultTableModel
{
    /** column headings. */
    private String[]    sColumnHeadings;

    /** Constructor to build data for JTable by querying any jdbc
      *  table.
      * @param sDatabaseURL - url connection to database in jdbc format.
      * @param sTable - table name to query.
      */
    public DatabaseTableModel (String sDatabaseURL, String sTable) throws
Exception
    {
        try
        {
            // Load database driver
            Class.forName ("sun.jdbc.odbc.JdbcOdbcDriver");
        } catch (ClassNotFoundException cnfe)
          {
            throw new Exception("Error initializing database driver. " +
                                "Error: " + cnfe.toString());
          }

        // getMetaData - column headings
        // get all data from table
```

```
try
{
    // Establish connection
    Connection con = DriverManager.getConnection(sDatabaseURL);

    // Create and send statement
    String sQuery = "SELECT * FROM " + sTable;

    Statement stmt = con.createStatement();
    ResultSet rslt = stmt.executeQuery(sQuery);
    ResultSetMetaData rsmd = rslt.getMetaData();

    int iNumColumns = rsmd.getColumnCount();
    sColumnHeadings = new String[iNumColumns];

    for (int iCount = 0; iCount < sColumnHeadings.length; iCount++)
        sColumnHeadings[iCount] = rsmd.getColumnName(iCount + 1);

    setColumnIdentifiers(sColumnHeadings);

    // Process data
    while (rslt.next())
    {
        String sDataForRow[] = new String[sColumnHeadings.length];

        for (int iCount = 0; iCount < sColumnHeadings.length; iCount++)
        {
            sDataForRow[iCount] = rslt.getString(iCount + 1);
        }

        addRow(sDataForRow);
    }

    // Cleanup
    rslt.close();
    stmt.close();
    con.close();

} catch (SQLException sqle)
  {
    while (sqle != null)
    {
        System.out.println ("SQLState: " +
                            sqle.getSQLState ());
        System.out.println ("Message:  " +
                            sqle.getMessage ());
        System.out.println ("ErrorCode:   " +
                            sqle.getErrorCode ());
        sqle = sqle.getNextException ();
```

```
        }
        throw new Exception ("Database error has occurred. " +
                             "Error: " + sqle.toString());

      }
   }

   /** accessor to get the column headings. */
   public String[] getColumnHeadings()
   {
      return (sColumnHeadings);
   }

}
```

In order to understand the DatabaseTableModel you must examine the TableDataModel interface because its main purpose is to map a JDBC table to that interface. The TableDataModel interface has two methods:

```
public int getRowCount();
public Object getValueAt(Object columnIdentifier, int rowIndex);
```

The getRowCount() method is used to determine how many rows the JTable should display. If this method returns zero, there is no data to display. Therefore, you must insure that you return the correct row count. You could go through the trouble of creating the data in your data model but your JTable would still display nothing if the getRowCount() method returns a zero.

The getValueAt() method is called by the JTable to retrieve the value at a specified column and row. By default, it displays the toString() representation of the object; however, you can customize this with a specific renderer. For example, to display a boolean value as a checkbox you set the renderer like this:

```
newColumn.setCellRenderer(new JValueRenderer(new JCheckbox()));
```

Knowing that it is these two methods that define our table data, all we need to do is create two data structures that satisfy those criteria. For the preceding two methods the data to support it is an integer to store the number of rows and a two-dimensional array of data objects as the cells of the JTable. It is important to understand that it does not have to be a two-dimensional array. Your only requirement is to be able to return the data provided a column and row index. Since it is your data model, you can store the data in any format you deem appropriate. That could be a single linked list of elements if that is most appropriate for your data collection. One example of when you would want to do this is to implement a sparse matrix where it is too wasteful to declare a two-dimensional array. It is easy to understand that this is exactly what a spreadsheet of 1000 × 1000 cells does. We create the data for the data model in the constructor.

The DatabaseTableDataModel constructor queries a JDBC table. It retrieves the metadata on the table to create the column headings for the JTable. It then retrieves all of the rows from the JDBC table and stores them in a vector. When retrieving the rows it counts the number of rows and updates the iNumRows variable, which is returned in the call to getRowCount(). It then stores each row as an array of strings into the data model. The getValueAt() method simply returns the string value at that row and column in the two-dimensional array. That is all there is to creating the data model for our table.

Source 23.6, TestTableFrame.java, demonstrates creating the JTable, placing it in a ScrollPane, and adding it and the TableHeader into the Frame.

A run of Source 23.6 produces Figure 23.5.

There are four key items to note about Source 23.6:

- We first create the data model. Our data model can be any class that implements the TableDataModel interface. The TableDataModel interface is used for two-dimensional immutable data. For a data model that allows editing you create a class that implements the EditableTableDataModel interface.
- We then create the JTable like this:

```
JTable table = new JTable(dataModel);
```

- We then create a JTableColumn object for each column. This is a separate class so we can set the width, set the resizability (whether to allow it or not), and optionally change the renderer (a JContainer that implements the CellRendered interface). A good enhancement to this program would be to get the column widths from the JDBC result metadata and set column widths according to that information. This is left for the reader as an exercise.
- The last thing to do is to create a JScrollPane, JViewport, set the viewport to the JTable, and then add the scroll pane and column header to the frame. The JViewport holds a view (any component) that may optionally be larger than the viewport. It is this JViewport that supports the scrolling via a setViewPosition() method; of course, this is “manual” scrolling. To make the scrolling operation simple, the JScrollPane class is a composite class that consists of a main viewport, row and column heading viewports, horizontal and vertical scrollbars, and components for the deadspace between scrollbars.

This concludes our demonstration of the JTable Component. This is a very powerful component that is simple to integrate into your applets and applications.

Source 23.6 TestTableFrame.java

```
/** TestTableFrame.java */
package jwiley.chp23;

import com.sun.java.swing.*;
import com.sun.java.swing.table.*;

import java.awt.*;
import java.awt.event.*;

/**
 * Frame to test the JTable component.
 * @author Eric Monk
 */
public class TestTableFrame extends JFrame
{
    /** constructor. */
    public TestTableFrame (String sTitle)
    {
        super(sTitle);

        // create data model
        DatabaseTableModel dataModel = null;

        try {
            dataModel =
                  new DatabaseTableModel("jdbc:odbc:ExampleDB",
                                                        "Books");
        } catch (Exception e)
          {
            System.out.println("Cannot get data model. Error: "
                                                     + e.toString());
            System.exit(0);
          }

        // create column model
        DefaultTableColumnModel dtcm = new DefaultTableColumnModel();

        // create columns
        String[] sColumnHeadings = ((DatabaseTableModel)
dataModel).getColumnHeadings();

        for (int iCount = 0; iCount < sColumnHeadings.length; iCount++)
        {
            TableColumn column = new TableColumn(sColumnHeadings[iCount]);
             column.setWidth(100);
            dtcm.addColumn(column);
        }
```

```
     // create table
        JTable table = new JTable(dataModel, dtcm);

        // Put the table and header into a scrollPane
        JScrollPane scrollpane = JTable.createScrollPaneForTable(table);
        getContentPane().add("Center", scrollpane);

        addWindowListener(new WindowAdapter()
                          {
                            public void windowClosing(WindowEvent we)
                            { System.exit(0); }
                          });
        setSize(500, 300);
        show();
    }

    /** main method to invoke from the JVM. */
    public static void main (String args[])
    {
        new TestTableFrame("Test Table Frame");
    }
}
```

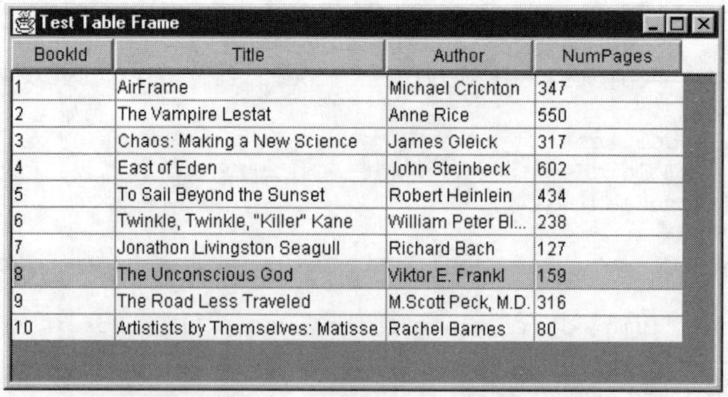

Test Table Frame

BookId	Title	Author	NumPages
1	AirFrame	Michael Crichton	347
2	The Vampire Lestat	Anne Rice	550
3	Chaos: Making a New Science	James Gleick	317
4	East of Eden	John Steinbeck	602
5	To Sail Beyond the Sunset	Robert Heinlein	434
6	Twinkle, Twinkle, "Killer" Kane	William Peter Bl...	238
7	Jonathon Livingston Seagull	Richard Bach	127
8	The Unconscious God	Viktor E. Frankl	159
9	The Road Less Traveled	M.Scott Peck, M.D.	316
10	Artistists by Themselves: Matisse	Rachel Barnes	80

FIGURE 23.5 A JTable view of a book database.

23.7 SUMMARY

In this chapter we explained and demonstrated all of the major concepts of the Java Foundation Classes. Using this knowledge, you are equipped to provide a professional-looking graphical user interface on all of your applets and applications. Specifically, we have covered:

- How the JFCs support a native look and feel, common look and feel, and pluggable look and feel.
- How to implement the common look and feel via lightweight components. We also implemented a capacity meter as a lightweight component.
- How to implement a pluggable look and feel by understanding and using the User Interface Factory. We examined an example that used the UIFactory.
- A list of all of the JFC Components and what they provide for your user interface.
- An in-depth example of a JTree.
- An in-depth example of a JTable.

You are now ready to create exciting JFC applications!

CHAPTER 24

Comparing JavaScript to Java

"I won't go so far as to call it a network operating system, but it's beginning to look like one."

Jim Clark, Chairman, Netscape Communications Corp.

OBJECTIVE

This chapter explains the difference between a scripting language and a programming language. We will show you the key elements of JavaScript and how it compares to Java. Lastly, we will examine useful examples of JavaScript scripts.

24.1 INTRODUCTION

JavaScript is not Java. It is important not to confuse the two. JavaScript is a scripting language and Java is a programming language. Both are interpreted languages; however, Java is also a compiled language. In general, a scripting language controls high-level operating system functionality (of which running programs is just one aspect) and a programming language creates programs. JavaScript is currently focused on Web scripting and not Operating System (OS) scripting; however, Sun and Netscape have indicated that it could evolve toward a cross-platform OS scripting language.

Every major operating system (Unix, MVS, VMS, Mac OS, and DOS) has one or more scripting languages to assist in the automation of common operating system tasks. Scripting languages have evolved over the years. They started as simply a packaging of OS commands in a file with a few control flow constructs added to allow repetition (loops) and decision points (if statement). DOS batch files are the most common and simplest form of this type of scripting. In fact, the name "batch file" stands for a "batch" of commands to be executed sequentially. Over the years, scripting languages have evolved in two directions: first in expanding the capabilities of the scripting language, and second, in the number of "system objects" that the language can access and manipulate. The best examples of powerful scripting languages are on the Unix operating system. Languages like tcl and Perl have such extensive capabilities that they rival programming languages in everything except speed of execution. The Mac OS has meshed the scripting language concept with the event-driven programming paradigm by including OS events (called Apple Events) in the application event queue. This allows "scriptable applications" that allows scripting to be extended to an application's internal functions. This also allows Macintosh applications to be active participants in the scripting process by sending AppleEvents to communicate with or control other applications. Now that we have a general idea of the purpose of a scripting language, let's examine the major characteristics of the JavaScript scripting language.

JavaScript is the first major Internet scripting language. It is important to understand that the Internet and World Wide Web are its initial and primary focus. There are currently five major characteristics of JavaScript:

- *A script can be as simple as a sequence of commands.* You do not have to use functions or methods. This goes back to scripting as a "batch" of commands. Of course, for longer scripts you should use functions and methods. Currently in JavaScript, methods are just functions that are assigned to a property in an Object.
- *There is no static typing of variables.* A variable can hold primitive types, string, arrays, objects, and even functions.
- *Only a small subset of Java keywords are supported.* The subset mostly consists of the flow control keywords; however, all the Java keywords are reserved for future use.
- *The JavaScript predefined objects are currently all browser type objects (document, forms, form elements, frames, window, etc.).* This contrasts to OS scripting languages that deal with files, directories, pipes, and so forth. The JavaScript predefined objects will grow to accommodate these; however, only after the security issues have been solved.

You leverage existing knowledge of Java since JavaScript is based on Java.

- *JavaScript will evolve towards Java.* You will notice that all of the Java keywords are reserved for future use. Of course, understand that even as JavaScript moves closer to Java, there is still the fundamental difference between a scripting language and a programming language. The two will never meld into one and that's a good thing. As an example, one of the future changes for JavaScript is adding UNICODE support.

As the Internet becomes the focal point of all today's applications, the browser will become the central component of the client's software. Therefore, more and more operating system functions will be performed by the browser. This will make JavaScript evolve more towards a cross-platform OS scripting language.

Now that we understand the fundamental difference between Java and JavaScript and the major characteristics of JavaScript, we are ready to study the details. This chapter refers to JavaScript 1.1, which is implemented by Netscape Navigator 3.x and Microsoft Internet Explorer 3.x.

You will see a fair amount of HTML in this next chapter. Unfortunately, I would be severely straying from the focus of this book if I detoured myself into HTML. Luckily, HTML is fairly easy. Source 24.1 is a skeleton HTML file that every one of the following examples began with. The LANGUAGE parameter of the script tag indicates what language is used for the page's script. "JavaScript" refers to JavaScript 1.0, and is supported by Netscape Navigator 2.0 and higher. In general, you can specify a specific version by appending the version number to the language parameter. To indicate JavaScript 1.1, set the LANGUAGE parameter to be "JavaScript1.1." Also, by structuring HTML comment tags as shown in Source 24.1, you can prevent non-JavaScript browsers from attempting to interpret the scripts.

TIP The LANGUAGE parameter is used by the browser to determine if it can interpret the script or not. It is still the responsibility of the script writer to ensure that the script adheres to the JavaScript specification for that version.

The SCRIPT tag supports one additional parameter not used in these examples, the SRC tag. The SRC tag allows the page author to specify a separate file that contains the JavaScript code for a page. This option is very useful when multiple pages share the same code. JavaScript source files should have the .js file extension, and the Web server must be configured to serve those files with the "application/x-javascript" mime type.

SOURCE 24.1 skeleton.html

```
<HTML>
<TITLE>  </TITLE>
<BODY>
<SCRIPT LANGUAGE="JavaScript">
<!- hide from old browsers

<!- done hiding ->
</SCRIPT>

</BODY>
</HTML>
```

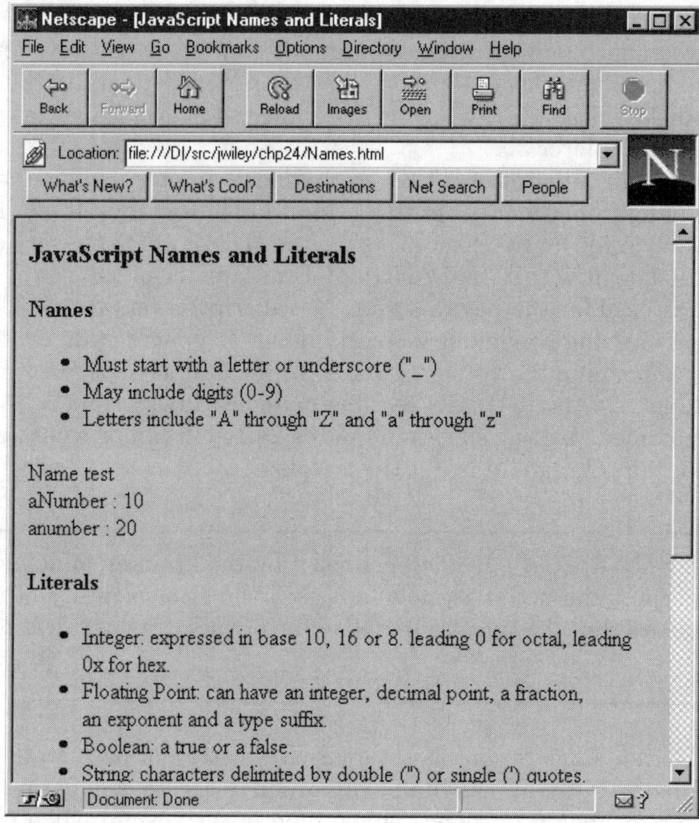

FIGURE 24.1 JavaScript names and literals.

24.2 JAVASCRIPT NAMES AND LITERALS

JavaScript variable names and literals are very similar to Java's. Their main differences concern the representation of data. For instance, Java strings are UNICODE and JavaScript strings are not. In addition, Java features several numeric data types of varying precision. JavaScript has only two: whole numbers and real numbers. Figure 24.1 provides the details on JavaScript names and literals.

For the rest of this chapter, I will be using the screen shots of the Web pages for a dual purpose. They will both present the key information for the chapter as well as simultaneously demonstrate those key points with code. The screen shots will be followed by the source code. Source 24.2 both generates the Web pages as well as tests their concepts. After presenting the source, I will highlight any points that are not intuitive or need to be stressed.

SOURCE 24.2

```
<HTML>
<TITLE> JavaScript Names and Literals </TITLE>
<BODY>
<H3> JavaScript Names and Literals </H3>

<H4> Names </H4>
<UL>
<LI> Must start with a letter or underscore ("_") </LI>
<LI> May include digits (0-9) </LI>
<LI> Letters include "A" through "Z" and "a" through "z" </LI>
</UL>

<SCRIPT LANGUAGE="JavaScript">
<!- hide from old browsers
document.writeln("Name test <BR>");
var a_persons_name = "mike";
var _int32 = 65545;
var aNumber = 10;
var anumber = 20;
document.writeln("aNumber : " + aNumber + "<BR>");
document.writeln("anumber : " + anumber + "<BR>");

var this_is_a_very_long_javaScript_name_that_is_very_very_descriptive = true;
<!- done hiding ->
</SCRIPT>

<H4> Literals </H4>
<UL>
<LI> Integer: expressed in base 10, 16 or 8.  leading 0 for octal, leading 0x
for hex. </LI>
<LI> Floating Point: can have an integer, decimal point, a fraction, <BR>
     an exponent and a type suffix. </LI>
<LI> Boolean: a true or a false. </LI>
<LI> String: characters delimited by double (") or single (') quotes.  <BR>
     Can also use \n,\t,\r,\a,\f,\b.</LI>
</UL>

<SCRIPT LANGUAGE="JavaScript">
<!- hide from old browsers
document.writeln("Literal Test <BR>");
var anInt = 252;
var PI = 3.14159;
var bigFloat = 3.2e10;
var done=false;
var name="Michael Daconta";
var lines="Mary had a little lamb \nwhose fleece was white as snow";
document.writeln("anInt : " + anInt + "<BR>");
document.writeln("PI : " + PI + "<BR>");
document.writeln("bigFloat: " + bigFloat + "<BR>");
```

```
document.writeln("done: " + done + "<BR>");
document.writeln("name: " + name + "<BR>");
document.writeln("<PRE>lines: " + lines + "</PRE><BR>");
<!— done hiding —>
</SCRIPT>

</BODY>
</HTML>
```

Source 24.2 is very intuitive. The only item to point out is the similarity to Java in allowing variable names of unlimited length. I encourage all programmers to make good use of that feature. It is always important to remember that the maintenance phase of an application's life cycle is by far the longest phase.

24.3 JAVASCRIPT KEYWORDS AND OPERATORS

JavaScript currently only uses 11 of the 50 Java keywords. This is mostly due to JavaScript not performing any static typing of variables (eliminates all the types, and type modifiers). JavaScript's object model is also much simpler and there currently is no support for exceptions or inheritance. It is doubtful that JavaScript will ever be object-oriented the way Java is. There is just no need for it in a scripting language. More important are the five new keywords that JavaScript has added. These are:

- **var.** Declares a variable. You can also optionally assign the variable a value.
- **function.** Declares a JavaScript function. You can declare parameters to the function. All function arguments are passed by value. You can return a value from a function using the return keyword.
- **in.** Used within a for loop to allow you to iterate through the properties of an object. Here is an example that would print the properties of the car object:

```
for (i in car)
     document.writeln("car[" + i + "] = " + car[i] + " ");
```

- **with.** Similar to the with keyword in Ada, this keyword establishes an object as the default object for the ensuing block of code. For example:

```
with car {
     // car is the default object for these statements
}
```

- **typeof.** Similar to the instanceof keyword in Java. Used to determine the type of an object at run time. For example:

```
typeof <target>
```

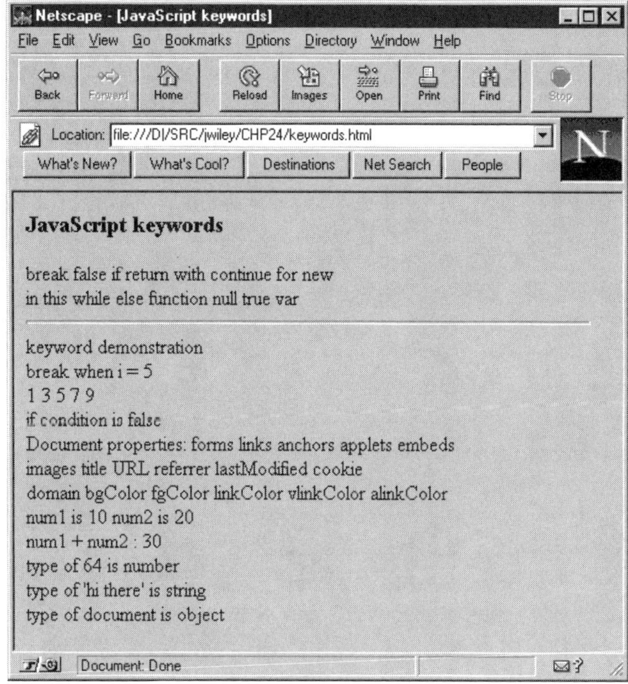

FIGURE 24.2 JavaScript keywords and operators.

Figure 24.2 lists all the current JavaScript keywords and demonstrates their functionality.

Source 24.3 generates the Web page in Figure 24.2 as well as demonstrates all of the JavaScript keywords.

SOURCE 24.3

```
<HTML>
<HEAD>
<TITLE> JavaScript keywords </TITLE>
</HEAD>

<BODY>
<H3> JavaScript keywords </H3>

break   false   if      return   with       continue   for    new<BR>
in      this    while   else     function   null       true   var<BR>
```

```
<HR>
<SCRIPT LANGUAGE="JavaScript">
<!— hide from non-netscape
document.writeln("keyword demonstration <BR>");
// break and while
var i = 10;
while (i-- > 0)
     if (i == 5)
          break;
document.writeln("break when i = " + i + "<BR>");

// continue and for
for (var j=0; j < 10; j++)
{
     if ((j % 2) == 0)
          continue;
     else
          document.write(" " + j + " ");
}
document.writeln("<BR>");

// else and false
if (false)
     document.writeln("if condition is true <BR>");
else
     document.writeln("if condition is false <BR>");

// function, in, null and var
function writeProps()
{
     var count=0;
     document.write("Document properties: ");
     if (document != null)
          for (props in document)
          {
               count++;
               if (count % 6 == 0)
                    document.writeln("<BR>");
               document.write(" " + props + " ");
          }
     document.writeln("<BR>");
}

writeProps();

// return, this, true and with
function add(num1, num2, print)
{
     var result = 0;
     with (document) {
          if (print == true)
```

```
            writeln("num1 is " + num1 +
                    " num2 is " + num2 + "<BR>");
        result = num1 + num2;
    }
    return result;
}

tot = add(10,20, true);
document.writeln("num1 + num2 : " + tot + "<BR>");

// typeof
document.writeln("type of 64 is " + typeof 64 + "<BR>");
document.writeln("type of 'hi there' is " + typeof 'hi there' + "<BR>");
document.writeln("type of document is " + typeof document + "<BR>");
<!- done hiding ->
</SCRIPT>
</BODY>
</HTML>
```

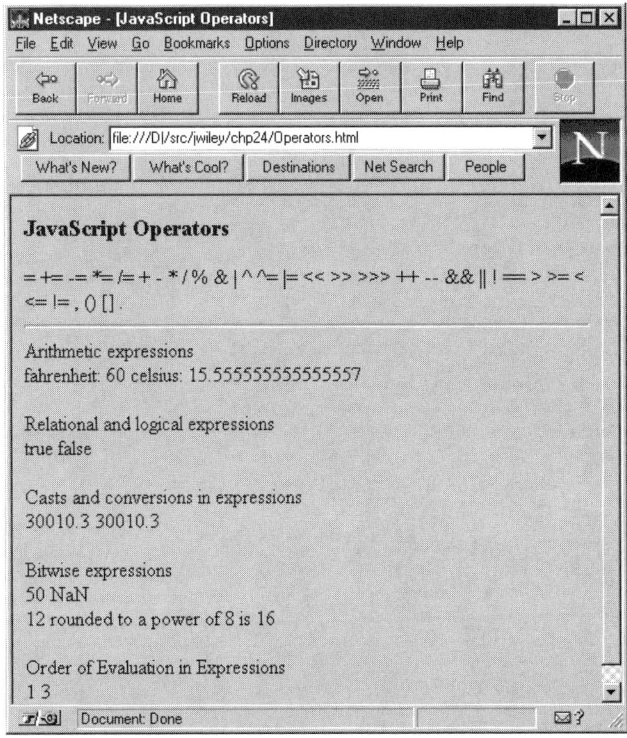

FIGURE 24.3 JavaScript operators.

There are two points of interest in Source 24.3:

- **function writeProps().** Iterates through all the properties of the JavaScript document object. The document object is covered in detail in the section on JavaScript Predefined Objects.
- **function add().** Uses document as its default object (via the with keyword). The function writeln() is a method of document. This allows us to just use writeln() instead of document.writeln().

JavaScript supports all of the Java operators. Figure 24.3 shows the Java operators and the results of examples using the operators are shown in Source 24.4.

Source 24.4 should be familiar because it is similar to the Java program we wrote to test Java expressions (see Source 2.6).

SOURCE 24.4

```
<HTML>
<HEAD>
<TITLE> JavaScript Operators </TITLE>
</HEAD>

<BODY>
<H3> JavaScript Operators </H3>

=  +=  -=  *=  /=  +  -  *  /  %  &  |  ^  ^=
|=  <<  >>  >>>  ++  –  &&  ||  !  ==  >  >=
<  <=  !=  ,  ()  []  .

<HR>
<SCRIPT LANGUAGE="JavaScript">
<!– hide for non-netscape
document.writeln("Arithmetic expressions <BR>");

var fahr=60.0, celsius=0;
celsius = (5.0/9.0) * (fahr-32.0);
document.writeln("fahrenheit: " + fahr + " celsius: " +
                  celsius + "<BR>");
document.writeln("<BR>");
document.writeln("Relational and logical expressions <BR>");
document.writeln(fahr > 20.0);
document.writeln(((fahr < 20.0) && (true)));
document.writeln("<BR>");

document.writeln("<BR>");
document.writeln("Casts and conversions in expressions<BR>");
var age=10;
var gpa = 0.0;
gpa = age;
var salary=30000.3;
age = gpa + salary;
```

```
document.writeln(gpa + salary);
document.writeln(age);
document.writeln("<BR> <BR>");

document.writeln("Bitwise expressions<BR>");
document.writeln(100 >> 1);  // division by 2
document.writeln(age << 1);  // multiplication by 2
document.writeln("<BR>");
var memoryBlock = (12 + 7) & ~7;
document.writeln("12 rounded to a multiple of 8 is " +
                    memoryBlock + "<BR>");
document.writeln("<BR>");

document.writeln("Order of Evaluation in Expressions<BR>");
var a = 5 & 1 + 2;
document.writeln(a);
a = (5 & 1) + 2;
document.writeln(a);
document.writeln("<BR>");
<!— done hiding ->
</SCRIPT>
</BODY>
</HTML>
```

It is comforting to know that JavaScript implements all the powerful operators so well known from C, C++, and now Java. Also, like Java, JavaScript overloads the + operator for string concatenation.

24.4 STRINGS, OBJECTS, AND ARRAYS

Figure 24.4 lists the key properties and methods of the JavaScript String object and then demonstrates Objects and Arrays. The string object is very intuitive but objects and arrays will need further explanation.

Source 24.5 generates the Web page shown in Figure 24.4 and demonstrates its key concepts. Pay careful attention to the code that demonstrates objects and arrays.

Let me explain the JavaScript objects and arrays in more detail. A JavaScript object is a dynamic associative array of property names and values. Lisp programmers will note the similarity of a JavaScript object to a Lisp symbol (we see another similarity with the JavaScript eval function discussed in section 24.4). The object is dynamic in that you do not have to specify the number of properties it has at creation. You create an object with the new keyword and a constructor function. The properties of an object are defined in its constructor function as in the Coordinate() function used in Source 24.5. In addition, properties can be dynamically added, either to a single object or to all objects of a specific type. Adding a property, either in a constructor or in other parts of a script, is as simple as assigning a value. If you assign a value to a property

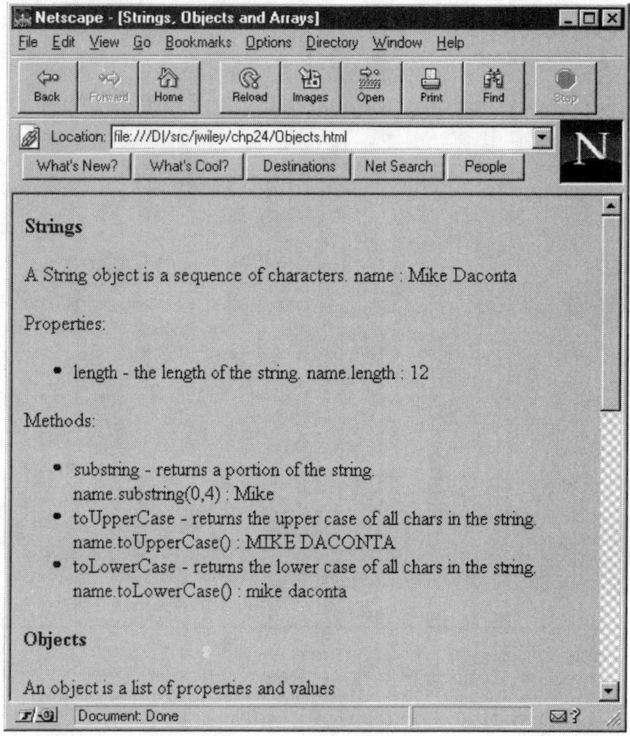

FIGURE 24.4 Strings, objects, and arrays.

that does not exist, then the property is automatically created and added to that object. Once the object has been created, we can add properties dynamically by specifying the property and assigning it a value. This is done using the dot operator like this:

```
coord.name = "First Point ;
```

In order to add a property to all objects of a type, you must specify the Object name, then property "prototype" as follows:

```
Coordinate.prototype.type = "cartesian"
```

This adds the property "type" to all coordinate objects and initializes its value to the string "cartesian."

This created both a property name "name" and a value "First Point" attached to our object. It is important to note that a property could itself be another object. A property

SOURCE 24.5

```
<HTML>
<TITLE> Strings, Objects and Arrays </TITLE>
<BODY>

<SCRIPT LANGUAGE="JavaScript">
<!— hide from old browsers
document.writeln("<H4> Strings </H4>");
var name = "Mike Daconta";
document.writeln("A String object is a sequence of characters.");
document.writeln("name : " + name + "<BR> <BR>");
document.writeln("Properties: ");
document.writeln("<UL>");
document.writeln("<LI> length - the length of the string.");
document.writeln("name.length : " + name.length + "</LI>");
document.writeln("</UL>");
document.writeln("Methods: ");
document.writeln("<UL>");
document.writeln("<LI> substring - returns a portion of the string.<BR>");
document.writeln("name.substring(0,4) : " + name.substring(0,4) + "</LI>");
document.writeln("<LI> toUpperCase - returns the upper case of all chars in
the string.<BR>");
document.writeln("name.toUpperCase() : " + name.toUpperCase() + "</LI>");
document.writeln("<LI> toLowerCase - returns the lower case of all chars in
the string.<BR>");
document.writeln("name.toLowerCase() : " + name.toLowerCase() + "</LI>");
document.writeln("</UL>");

document.writeln("<H4> Objects </H4>");
document.writeln("An object is a list of properties and values <BR>");

function Coordinate(x, y)
{
    this.x = x;
    this.y = y;
}

function addCoord(x2, y2)
{
    this.x += x2;
    this.y += y2;
}

function writeCoord()
{
    document.writeln(" x : " + this.x);
    document.writeln(" y : " + this.y + "<BR>");
}
```

```
var coord = new Coordinate(10,20);
coord.addCoord = addCoord;
coord.writeCoord = writeCoord;

document.writeln("A coordinate Object: <BR>");
coord.writeCoord();
document.writeln("A call to coord.addCoord(10,10) <BR>");
coord.addCoord(10,10);
coord.writeCoord();
// Add a property to all Coordinate objects
Coordinate.prototype.type = "cartesian"
// Add a property to a single Coordinate object
coord.name = "First Point"

document.writeln("<H1> Arrays </H1>");
document.writeln("A 2 dimensional array<BR>");
var intArray = new Array(4);
for (i=0;  i < intArray.length; i++)
     intArray[i] = new Array((i * 4),(i * 4) + 1,(i * 4) + 2, (i * 4) + 3);

for (i = 0; i < intArray.length; i++)
    for (j = 0; j < intArray[i].length; j++)
        document.writeln("intArray[" + i + "][" + j + "] is " +
intArray[i][j] + "<BR>");

document.writeln("<BR>Reverse Sorted array of strings<BR>");

var stringArray = new Array("Java", "For", "C/C++", "Programmers")
stringArray.sort();
stringArray.reverse();
document.writeln(stringArray.join());

<!— done hiding —>
</SCRIPT>
</BODY>
</HTML>
```

can also be a function. In fact, this is the way that object methods are "created." You assign the JavaScript function to one of the object's properties. The benefit this gives you is that this keyword points to the current object, which you can use inside the function to make it behave like an object method. If you iterate through the properties of your object (using the for ... in expression) you will notice that the function property holds the actual text of the function. The last point to understand about objects is that you can optionally iterate through the properties using the index number of the property.

However, you need to be careful when you do this in conjunction with assigning a new value to the property so that you don't accidentally assign an incorrect value to a property (like assigning a number to your method property).

Contrary to C++ and C, but similar to Java, JavaScript implements arrays as a special type of object. As we have shown previously, the properties of a JavaScript object can be treated as an array. Although any object can be used as an array in this fashion, the JavaScript array object adds some additional functionality, and makes the meaning of your code more explicit. Using nested arrays, you can create multidimension arrays, and JavaScript supplies some utility methods that make array manipulations much simpler. For instance, you can sort or reverse an array in JavaScript using a single method call (as demonstrated in Source 24.5). An array can be initialized with either an initial size, or with a list of initial values.

24.5 JAVASCRIPT PREDEFINED OBJECTS

JavaScript has predefined browser objects. Figure 24.5 depicts the current Object hierarchy supported by JavaScript. These predefined JavaScript objects have properties and methods the JavaScript programmer can access and call to add client-side functionality to Web pages. The navigator, window, location, history, and document objects always exist. The other objects (such as forms, text fields, anchors, etc.) only exist if they exist in the HTML document being displayed.

All of the predefined objects just discussed should be familiar to html authors as well as being self-explanatory. It is not the focus of this book to demonstrate the use of every JavaScript object. We are examining the language in comparison to Java programming and its importance in complementing Java programming. As such, we will demonstrate two of the objects that always exist: the document and window class. Many of the other objects are demonstrated in the Form Validation example in Section 24.6. Now let's examine the Window object.

The JavaScript window object refers to the browser window that displays the html document. Figure 24.6 explains all the properties and methods of the window object. It also demonstrates all of the window methods by attaching JavaScript functions to the button click event of the button object.

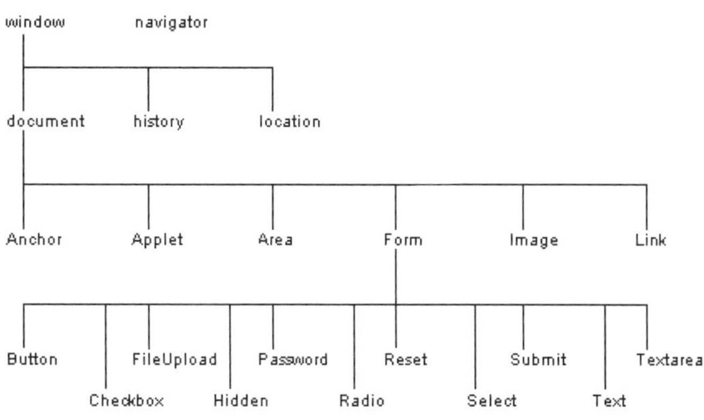

FIGURE 24.5 Object hierarchy.

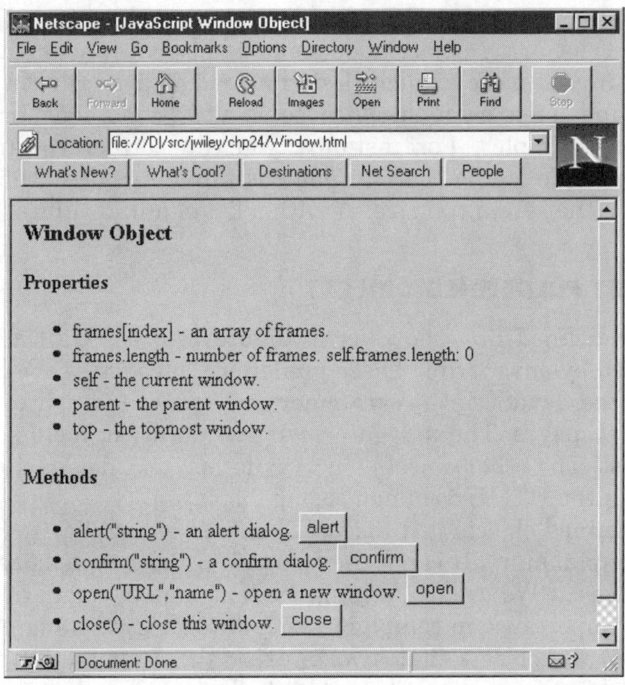

FIGURE 24.6 JavaScript window object.

Figure 24.7 depicts the window that appears when the user clicks the Alert button shown in Figure 24.6.

Source 24.6 generates Figure 24.6. The code is very straightforward and merely calls the window object methods.

One thing that is important to notice about Source 24.6 is the fact that the calls to the window methods do not need to be preceded by an object. Since these objects create new windows, they are actually more like independent functions than methods. Now let's examine the document object.

FIGURE 24.7 JavaScript alert.

SOURCE 24.6

```
<HTML>
<HEAD>
<TITLE>
JavaScript Window Object
</TITLE>
</HEAD>

<BODY>
<H3> Window Object </H3>
<H4>   Properties </H4>
<UL>
<LI>      frames[index] - an array of frames. </LI>
<LI>      frames.length - number of frames.
<SCRIPT LANGUAGE="JavaScript">
<!— hide for non-netscape
          document.write("self.frames.length: " +
                         self.frames.length);
<!— done hiding —>
</SCRIPT> </LI>
<LI> self - the current window. </LI>
<LI>      parent - the parent window. </LI>
<LI>      top - the topmost window. </LI>
</UL>

<H4>   Methods </H4>
<SCRIPT LANGUAGE="JavaScript">
<!— hide for non-netscape
function showAlert()
{ alert("This is an alert"); }

function showConfirm()
{ confirm("This is a confirm"); }

function doOpen()
{
     open(document.location.toString(),
          "Another window");
}
<!— done hiding —>
</SCRIPT>
<FORM>
<UL>
<LI>      alert("string") - an alert dialog.
<INPUT TYPE="button" VALUE="alert"
     onClick=showAlert()> </LI>
<LI>      confirm("string") - a confirm dialog.
<INPUT TYPE="button" VALUE="confirm"
     onClick=showConfirm()> </LI>
<LI>      open("URL","name") - open a new window.
```

```
<INPUT TYPE="button" VALUE="open"
         onClick=doOpen()> </LI>
<LI>      close() - close this window.
<INPUT TYPE="button" VALUE="close"
     onClick=close()> </LI>
</UL>
</FORM>
</BODY>

</HTML>
```

The document object represents the current html document being displayed. Figure 24.8 and Figure 24.9 list the document properties and object as well as display information about the current document loaded.

Sources 24.7 and Source 24.8 generate the Web pages shown in Figures 24.8 and 24.9. One of the very interesting things about the document object is the ability to

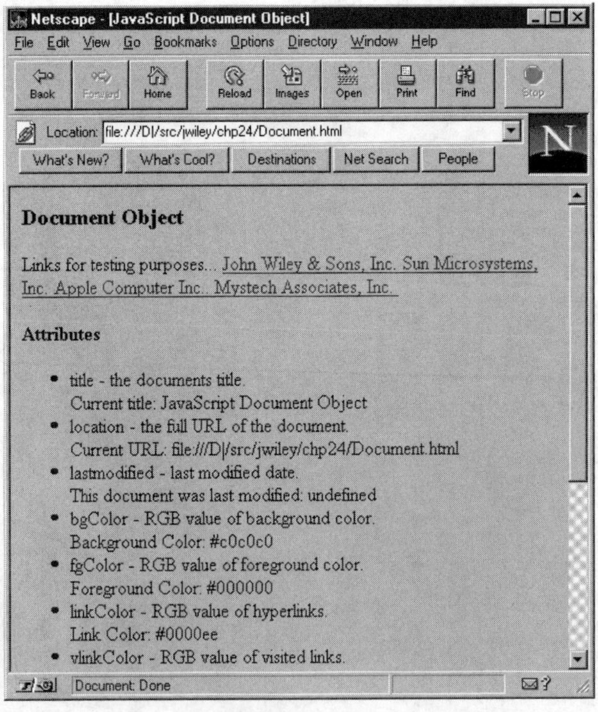

FIGURE 24.8 JavaScript document object.

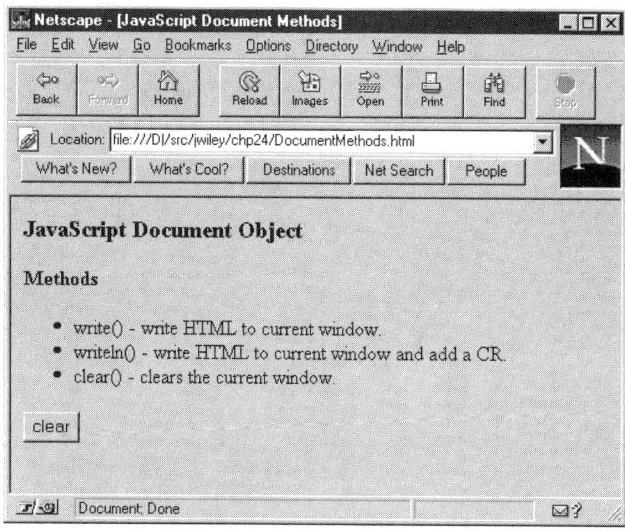

FIGURE 24.9 JavaScript document methods.

SOURCE 24.7

```
<HTML>
<TITLE> JavaScript Document Object </TITLE>
<BODY>
<SCRIPT LANGUAGE="JavaScript">
<!- hide from old browsers

<!- done hiding ->
</SCRIPT>

<H3> Document Object </H3>

Links for testing purposes...
<A HREF="http://www.wiley.com"> John Wiley & Sons, Inc. </A>
<A HREF="http://www.sun.com"> Sun Microsystems, Inc. </A>
<A HREF="http://www.apple.com"> Apple Computer Inc.. </A>
<A HREF="http://www.mystech.com"> Mystech Associates, Inc. </A> <BR>

<SCRIPT LANGUAGE="JavaScript">
<!- Hide from old browsers
document.writeln("<H4> Attributes </H4>");
document.writeln("<UL>");
document.writeln("<LI>   title - the documents title.<BR>");
document.writeln("         Current title: " + document.title + "</LI>");
```

```
document.writeln("<LI>   location - the full URL of the document.<BR>");
document.writeln("        Current URL: " + document.location + "</LI>");
document.writeln("<LI>   lastmodified - last modified date.<BR>");
document.writeln("        This document was last modified: " +
document.lastmodified + "</LI>");
document.writeln("<LI>    bgColor - RGB value of background color.<BR>");
document.writeln("         Background Color: " + document.bgColor +
"</LI>");
document.writeln("<LI>    fgColor - RGB value of foreground color. <BR>");
document.writeln("         Foreground Color: " + document.fgColor +
"</LI>");
document.writeln("<LI>    linkColor - RGB value of hyperlinks. <BR>");
document.writeln("         Link Color: " + document.linkColor + "</LI>");
document.writeln("<LI>    vlinkColor - RGB value of visited links. <BR>");
document.writeln("         Visited Link Color : " + document.vlinkColor +
"</LI>");
document.writeln("<LI>    alinkColor - RGB value of activated links.<BR>");
document.writeln("         Activated Link Color : " + document.alinkColor +
"<LI>");
document.writeln("<LI>    forms[index] - Array of form objects in source
order.<BR>");
document.writeln("         # of Forms : " + document.forms.length +
"</LI>");
document.writeln("<LI>    links[index] - Array of link objects. <BR>");
document.writeln("         # of links : " + document.links.length +
"</LI>");
document.writeln("<LI>    anchors[index] - Array of anchor objects.<BR>");
document.writeln("         # of anchors : " + document.anchors.length +
"</LI>");

document.writeln("</UL>");
<!— done hiding —>
</SCRIPT>
<A HREF="DocumentMethods.html"> Document Object Methods </A>
</BODY>
</HTML>
```

write HTML right into the current document. This has been demonstrated in every source code listing in this chapter. This "on-the-fly HTML" has many potential uses and is a very powerful capability of JavaScript. The primary method for doing this is the document.writeln() and document.write() methods. Source 24.7 and Source 24.8 demonstrate these methods.

Source 24.8 was necessary simply to present the information in a separate window as shown in Figure 24.9.

As we have demonstrated, the JavaScript predefined objects give you the ability to access information about the browser window, the current document being displayed, and the HTML elements in that window. As the language evolves, the number of pre-

SOURCE 24.8

```
<HTML>
<TITLE> JavaScript Document Methods </TITLE>
<BODY>

<H3> JavaScript Document Object </H3>

<SCRIPT LANGUAGE="JavaScript">
<!— hide from old browsers
document.writeln("<H4> Methods </H4>");
document.writeln("<UL>");
document.writeln("<LI>   write() - write HTML to current window. </LI>");
document.writeln("<LI>   writeln() - write HTML to current window and add a
CR. </LI>");
document.writeln("<LI>   clear() - clears the current window.</LI>");
document.writeln("</UL>");
<!— done hiding ->
</SCRIPT>
<FORM>
<INPUT TYPE="button" VALUE="clear" onClick=document.clear()>
</FORM>
</BODY>
</HTML>
```

defined objects will grow and so will the power and utility of the JavaScript language. The next section will discuss other features of JavaScript language like scripting events, cookies, and the use of the built-in eval function.

24.6 SPECIAL OBJECT METHODS

There are two methods that exist on every object and have special meaning: toString and assign. ToString is called when JavaScript needs to convert an object to a string, and assign is called on an object immediately before an attempt is made to overwrite it.

A toString method takes no arguments and returns a string. The properties and methods of the associated object can be accessed through this keyword. Typically, objects cannot convert themselves to strings. Results of converting objects to strings will vary depending on the version of JavaScript implemented by the browser. Source 24.9 shows the difference between an object with a toString method and without. Here, we again work with our coordinate object from Source 24.5.

An assign method takes a single argument that is the result of the right side of the assignment operation and returns no value. The default version of the assign operator allows the target object to be completely replaced. Once an assign method is supplied, assignment operations will be used to modify the left side of the assignment operation instead of replacing it. Individual fields of an object can be modified as usual, but the object itself cannot be replaced or discarded.

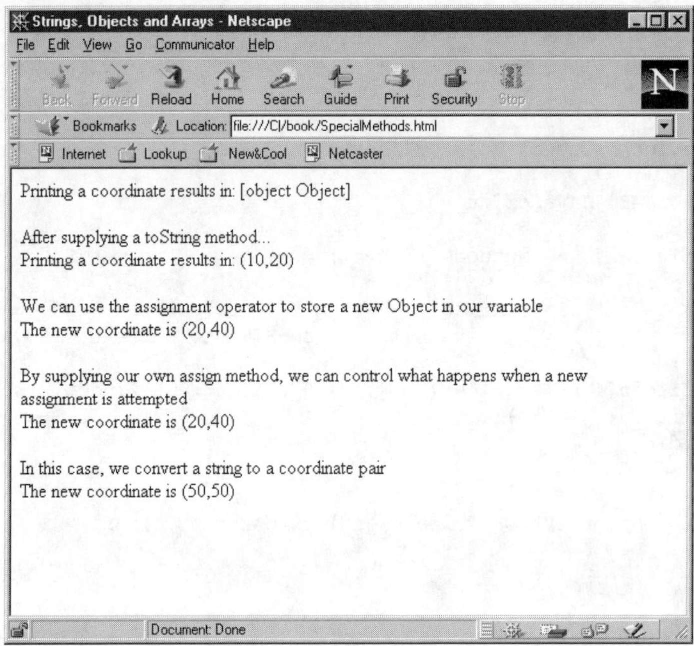

FIGURE 24.10 Special JavaScript methods.

Assign can be overridden to accomplish a variety of tasks. Firstly, as in Source 24.9 it can be used to prevent an object from being overridden entirely. By implementing an assign routine that does nothing, one can discard all assignment attempts. Additionally, to detect unintentional assignments, one can create a JavaScript alert box to indicate when an assignment attempt occurs. Finally, assign can be overridden to allow objects of one type to be assigned to objects of another. For instance, as shown at the very end of Source 24.9, assign can be used to allow strings to be assigned to coordinate objects. Source 24.9 produces Figure 24.10.

SOURCE 24.9

```
<HTML>
<TITLE> Strings, Objects and Arrays </TITLE>
<BODY>

<SCRIPT LANGUAGE="JavaScript">

<!— hide from old browsers
```

```
function Coordinate(x, y)
{
     this.x = x;
     this.y = y;
     this.addCoord = addCoord;
     this.writeCoord = writeCoord;
}

function addCoord(x2, y2)
{
     this.x += x2;
     this.y += y2;
}

function writeCoord()
{
     document.writeln(" x : " + this.x);
     document.writeln(" y : " + this.y + "<BR>");
}

var coord = new Coordinate(10,20);

document.writeln("Printing a coordinate results in: " + coord + "<BR>");

function coordString()
{
     return "(" + this.x + "," + this.y + ")";
}

Coordinate.prototype.toString = coordString;
document.writeln("<BR>After supplying a toString method...<BR>");
document.writeln("Printing a coordinate results in: " + coord + "<BR>");

function coordAssign(obj) {}

document.writeln("<BR>We can use the assignment operator to store a new
Object in our variable<BR>");
coord = new Coordinate(20, 40);
document.writeln("The new coordinate is " + coord + "<BR>");

coord.assign = coordAssign;

document.writeln("<BR>By supplying our own assign method, we can control
what happens when a new assignment is attempted<BR>");
document.writeln("In this case, we ignore all assignments, and our original
Object remains stored in our variable<BR>");
coord = new Coordinate(40, 80);
document.writeln("The new coordinate is " + coord + "<BR>");

function newAssign(obj)
{
```

```
        this.x = parseInt(obj);
        this.y = parseInt(obj);
}

coord.assign = newAssign;
document.writeln("<BR>In this case, we convert a string to a coordinate
pair<BR>");
coord = "50";
document.writeln("The new coordinate is " + coord + "<BR>");

<!— done hiding —>
</SCRIPT>
</BODY>
</HTML>
```

24.7 OTHER JAVASCRIPT FEATURES

To round out our presentation of JavaScript, there are additional features that are key to the interactivity of the language. These are events, the eval function, cookies, and data tainting.

JavaScript Events

We have seen examples of JavaScript events in the previous sources. For example, in Source 24.8 you see the line: <INPUT TYPE="button" VALUE="clear" onClick=document.clear()>. There are two points to understanding the code: First, onClick is a method of the button object that is run when the button receives a mouse click in the browser. The events the browser will pass on are predefined for different html elements. Here is a list of the JavaScript event handler methods:

- **onAbort (images).** Method run when the user aborts the loading of an image by clicking on a hyperlink or pressing the Stop button.
- **onFocus (windows, frames, form elements).** Method run when the target element receives the input focus. Similar to the Java AWT gotFocus event.
- **onBlur (windows, frames, form elements).** Method run when the target loses the input focus. Similar to the Java AWT lostFocus event.
- **onSelect (text fields).** Method run when text in a field is selected.
- **onChange (lists, text fields).** Method run when the text field's value is changed or the selection in a listbox changes.
- **onSubmit.** Method to run when the form is submitted.
- **onClick (buttons, hyperlinks).** Method run when a button or link is clicked.
- **onError (documents, images).** Method run when a document or image fails to load.
- **onLoad (documents).** Method run when the navigator finishes loading the document.

- **onMouseOut (imagemaps, links).** Method run when the user moves the mouse pointer away from an image map or link.
- **onMouseOver (hyperlinks).** Method run when a user moves the mouse pointer over a hyperlink
- **onReset (forms).** Method run when the user hits the reset button on a form.
- **OnSubmit (forms).** Method run when the user presses the Submit button on a form.
- **OnUnload (documents).** Method run when the user leaves a page.

Now that we know the predefined event methods, we understand that the code:

```
<INPUT TYPE="button" VALUE="clear" onClick=document.clear()>
```

is assigning the document.clear() function to the onClick method of the button in our form. It is important to note that you can assign any valid JavaScript commands to the onClick method as long as you enclose them within quotes (i.e., a string of commands). You will understand this better after we discuss the eval function.

The eval Function

This function gives the JavaScript programmer access to the JavaScript interpreter. The eval function will evaluate any valid JavaScript expression, to include JavaScript functions. This is a powerful tool that is well-known to Lisp programmers. One of the cool things this lets you do is generate code on-the-fly (i.e., in response to form input or selections by the user) and executed on-the-fly. Of course, since you are generating that code on-the-fly it is infinitely flexible. Source 24.10 demonstrates a simple use of the eval function and generates the Web page shown in Figure 24.11.

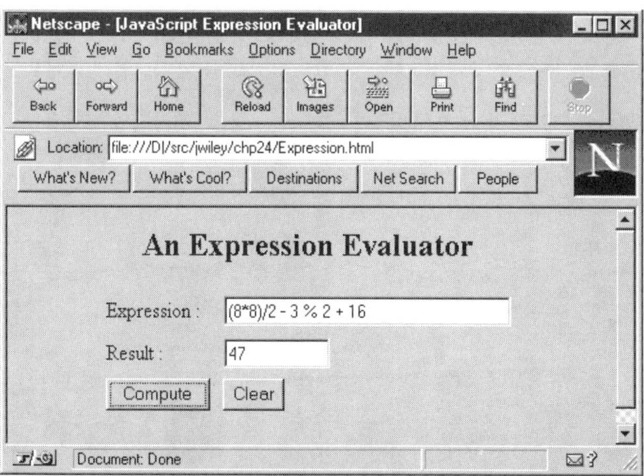

FIGURE 24.11 JavaScript expression evaluator.

SOURCE 24.10

```
<HTML>
<HEAD>
<TITLE> JavaScript Expression Evaluator </TITLE>

<SCRIPT LANGUAGE="JavaScript">

<!— hide the script tag's contents from old browsers

function computeForm(form)
{
     // if expression field empty - error
     if ( (form.expression.value == null ||
         form.expression.value.length == 0) )
     {
          alert("Expression field empty.");
          return;
     }

  // else evaluate and put result in result
  var theresult = eval(form.expression.value);
  form.result.value = theresult;
}

function clearForm(form)
{
     form.expression.value="";
     form.result.value="";
}

<!— done hiding —>
</SCRIPT>

</HEAD>

<BODY>
<CENTER>
<H2> An Expression Evaluator </H2>

<FORM method=post>
<TABLE>
<TR>
<TD> Expression : </TD>
<TD> <INPUT TYPE="text" NAME=expression SIZE=30> </TD>
</TR>
<TR>
<TD> Result : </TD>
<TD> <INPUT TYPE="text" NAME=result SIZE=10> </TD>
</TR>

<TR>
<TD> <INPUT TYPE="button" VALUE="Compute" onClick=computeForm(this.form)>
</TD>
```

```
<TD> <INPUT TYPE="button" VALUE="Clear" onClick=clearForm(this.form)> </TD>
</TR>
</TABLE>
</FORM>
</CENTER>
</BODY>
</HTML>
```

TIP The event model in JavaScript 1.2 is substantially different from the event model in JavaScript 1.1 and JavaScript 1.0.

Using JavaScript as a URL

For simple JavaScript commands, you can specify a URL that executes a JavaScript fragment. These URLs take the form:

```
javascript:<script>
```

For example, suppose you wanted to reimplement a Reload button as a link on a page. The following HTML fragment will perform the task.

```
<A HREF="javascript:history.go(0)">Reload</A>
```

Alternatively, you could place a "back" link on a page with the following:

```
<A HREF="javascript:history.go(-1)"Back</A>
```

Cookies

In a traditional Web application, all information comes from the Web server in the form of HTML pages. A Web server has no knowledge of what client is requesting a particular page, and cannot determine if that client has requested a page in the past. Because of these limitations, HTTP (the communications protocol used by the World Wide Web) is called a "stateless" protocol. JavaScript allows developers to add state information to their Web application through the use of cookies. Using JavaScript and cookies, an HTML page can store information about a user, then retrieve that information the next time the user returns to that page.

A cookie is a piece of information that is stored on the client machine as part of an HTML application. Using cookies, a JavaScript application can maintain state within a single browser session or optionally between multiple sessions by setting an optional expiration date. A cookie has the following form:

```
<name>=<value>; expires=<date>
```

The expiration field of a cookie is optional. If an expiration date is required, the date should be specified in Greenwich Mean Time (GMT) format. The JavaScript Date object features a method toGMTString, which will translate a date into the correct format.

The value of a cookie can be any string as long as the length of the entire cookie is less than 4K. If a value contains special characters such as semicolons, spaces, or commas, then the JavaScript function encode() should be used to translate the string into a storable format. In these cases, unencode() will translate the string back into its original form.

The document.cookie property is used to save and retrieve cookies. The following JavaScript function will save a cookie with the specified name, value, and expiration date:

```
Function SaveCookie(name, value, expiration)
{
     document.cookie = name + "=" + encode(value) + "; expiration=" +
expiration.toGMTString;
}
The cookie can be retrieved as follows:
Function GetCookie(name)
{
     start = document.cookie.indexof(name + "=");
     if (start != -1)
          end = document.cookie.indexof(";", start);
          if (end == -1)
               end = document.cookie.length;
          return unencode(document.cookie.substring(start, end);
}
```

Data Tainting

Probably the most complex JavaScript concept is data tainting. Data tainting is used to prevent one JavaScript page from sending information from another page back to the server. Because a single browser session can consist of several windows with multiple frames on each window, it is possible for a rogue script to examine features of other pages. An HTML form cannot send information from another page that is tainted back to the server. A form can send information on its own page back to the server regardless of taint. When data tainting is disabled in the browser, two pages cannot examine each other using JavaScript at all.

In order to prevent abuse, there are many complex rules regarding the transfer of "taint" from one object to another. For instance, copying a tainted value to a new variable taints the new value. Using a tainted variable as an input argument to a function taints the entire script that function is defined in. In general, there is nothing a script can do with a tainted value from another script unless the user intervenes somehow. When an attempt to send tainted data is made, the user is notified and prompted to proceed or cancel the current operation.

In general, taint settings cannot be modified, and most properties are tainted by default. However, using the JavaScript functions taint and untaint, programmers can copy tainted or untainted data with the desired taint setting on the newly created object. For almost all applications, the default taint settings should not be overridden.

Now that we have covered all the major elements of JavaScript, we are ready to see a demonstration of how we would use this language to enhance our World Wide Web sites.

A Form Validation Script

Currently, JavaScript will have an immediate effect in three areas of Web authoring: performing mathematical calculations on Web pages, writing HTML on the fly, and validating fields and forms before sending data to the Web server. In the examples already shown, we have examined performing mathematical calculations and on-the-fly HTML. Now we complete this chapter with a simple example of field and form validation.

Source 24.11 demonstrates field and form validation using JavaScript. The idea is simple—we have a JavaScript function tied to every form element we want validated and a JavaScript function invoked before the data is submitted. Since the majority of input that needs to be validated is text input, the functions consist mostly of traversing and validating characters in the string. As the JavaScript string methods grow in number, this process will get easier. Source 24.11 generates the Web page shown in Figure 24.12.

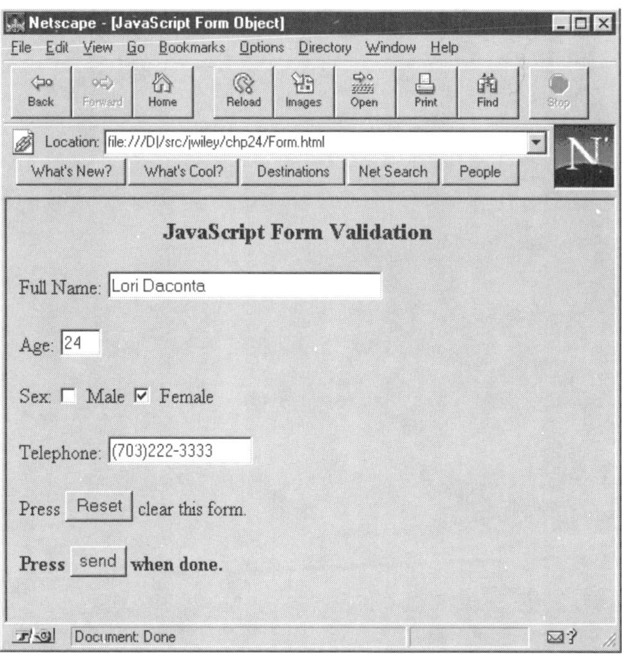

FIGURE 24.12 JavaScript form object.

SOURCE 24.11

```
<HTML>
<TITLE> JavaScript Form Object </TITLE>
<BODY>
<SCRIPT LANGUAGE="JavaScript">
<!— hide from old browsers

function checkName(form)
{
     if (form.fullname.value.length == 0)
          return;

    // check for all alpha
     for (var i=0; i < form.fullname.value.length; i++)
     {
          var ch = form.fullname.value.substring(i, i+1);
          if ((ch >= "A" && ch <= "Z") ||
               (ch >= "a" && ch <= "z") ||
               (ch == " ") )
          {
               continue;
          }
          else
          {
               alert("Invalid name.  Please re-enter");
               form.fullname.value="";
               return;
          }
     }
}

function checkAge(form)
{
     if (form.age.value.length == 0)
          return;

    // check for all numbers
     for (var i=0; i < form.age.value.length; i++)
     {
          var ch = form.age.value.substring(i, i+1);
          if (ch < "0" || ch > "9")
          {
               alert("Invalid age.  Please re-enter");
               form.age.value="";
               return;
          }
     }

     var num = 0 + form.age.value;
     if (num < 0 || num > 120)
     {
```

```
            alert("Invalid age.  Please re-enter");
            form.age.value="";
            return;
        }
}

function checkPhone(form)
{
        if (form.phone.value.length == 0)
            return;

        if (form.phone.value.length > 13)
        {
            alert("Invalid phone num. Please re-enter in this format: (###)###-
####");
            form.phone.value="";
            return;
        }

      // check for all numbers
        for (var i=0; i < form.phone.value.length; i++)
        {
            var ch = form.phone.value.substring(i, i+1);
            if ( (ch < "0" || ch > "9") && ( ch != "(" && ch != ")" && ch != "-
"))
            {
                alert("Invalid phone number.  Please re-enter");
                form.phone.value="";
                return;
            }
        }
}

function checkSex(form)
{
        // insure both are not checked
        if (form.msex.status == true &&
            form.fsex.status == true)
        {
            alert("Cannot be both sexes.");
            return false;
        }
        return true;
}

function checkForm(form)
{
        if (!checkSex(form))
        {
            alert("Cannot be both sexes. Form NOT submitted.");
            return;
        }
```

```
     if ( (form.fullname.value.length == 0) &&
           (form.age.value.length == 0) &&
           (form.phone.value.length == 0) &&
           (form.msex.status == false &&
            form.fsex.status == false)  )
     {
          alert("All fields must be filled in. Form NOT submitted.");
          return;
     }

     // if we got here - submit it!

}

function clearForm(form)
{
     form.fullname.value="";
     form.age.value="";
     form.phone.value="";
}

<!— done hiding —>
</SCRIPT>

<CENTER>
<H3> JavaScript Form Validation </H3>
</CENTER>

<FORM>
<p> Full Name: <INPUT TYPE="text" NAME=fullname SIZE=30
onChange=checkName(this.form)> <BR>

<p> Age: <INPUT TYPE="text" NAME=age SIZE=3 onChange=checkAge(this.form)>
</BR>

<p> Sex: <INPUT TYPE="checkbox" NAME=msex VALUE="Male"
onClick=checkSex(this.form)> Male
              <INPUT TYPE="checkbox" NAME=fsex VALUE="Female"
onClick=checkSex(this.form)> Female

<p> Telephone: <INPUT TYPE="text" NAME=phone SIZE=15
onChange=checkPhone(this.form)> <BR>

<p> Press <INPUT TYPE="button" VALUE="Reset" onClick=clearForm(this.form)>
clear this form.
<p> <STRONG> Press <INPUT TYPE="button" VALUE="send"
onClick=checkForm(this.form)> when done. </STRONG>

</FORM>
</BODY>
</HTML>
```

24.8 JAVASCRIPT 1.2

JavaScript 1.2 offers significant enhancements over JavaScript 1.1, although it may be some time before JavaScript 1.2 is widely used. Currently the only browser that supports JavaScript 1.2 is Netscape Communicator 4.0. JavaScript 1.2 adds many additional object methods and utility functions, but the most significant changes involve the event model. This section will explain these changes, and illustrate the new concepts with examples

The New Event Model

All event handlers now have access to an event object. The event object represents the event itself, and allows JavaScript to provide more detailed information about the event itself. The properties of the event object are:

- **Type.** This property is a string that represents the type of event being fired. This property is available for all events.
- **Target.** This property is an object and is the object for which the event was fired. This property is available for all events.
- **LayerX.** This property is a number and has different meanings depending on what event was fired. For resize events, this value is the new width of the object being resized. For all other events, this value is the horizontal position of the cursor relative to the target object when the event was fired. The value of LayerX is always identical to the value of X.
- **LayerY.** This property is a number and has different meanings depending on what event was fired. For resize events, this value is the new height of the object being resized. For all other events, this value is the vertical position of the cursor relative to the target object when the event was fired. The value of LayerY is always identical to the value of Y.
- **PageX.** This property is a number that represents the horizontal position of the cursor relative to the entire page. This property is available for all events.
- **PageY.** This property is a number that represents the vertical position of the cursor relative to the entire page. This property is available for all events.
- **ScreenX.** This property is a number that represents the horizontal position of the cursor relative to the screen. This property is available for all events.
- **ScreenY.** This property is a number that represents the vertical position of the cursor relative to the screen. This property is available for all events.
- **Which.** This property is a number and has different meanings depending on which event was fired. For mouse events involving the mouse button such as click, mousedown, or mouseup, this value indicates which mouse button was pressed. For events involving keyboard usage, this number identifies the key involved in the event.
- **Modifiers.** This property is a string and specifies which modifier keys are being held down when a mouse click or keyboard event occurs. For other events this property has no meaning. Possible values are ALT_MASK, CONTROL_MASK, SHIFT_MASK, and META_MASK.

- **Data.** This property is an array of strings and is only available for the dragdrop event. Each element in the array contains the URL of a dropped object in the dragdrop event.

The event object is not the only change to the event subsystem in JavaScript 1.2. Additional events have been added, and the mechanism for registering event handlers has changed. Finally, there are new processes that event handlers can implement so that more complex event routing can be implemented.

In JavaScript 1.2, in addition to the existing event registration process, you can register an event handler that will receive the event before the target object does. The window, document, and layer objects can all intercept events through the new registration process. A layer is a new dynamic HTML feature in Navigator 4.0 that allows you to group objects on an HTML page into a single unit, and perform action on that entire unit in a single step. In these scenarios, the higher-level object will receive all the events for every object it contains. Registering an event handler in this fashion is a two-step process. First, you must notify an object that you wish to handle its events, then you must register a function to perform the event handling. In order to notify the system that you wish to handle events, call the captureEvents method on an object. This routine takes one argument that specifies which events you wish to capture. The input arguments for this method are defined as constants on the Event object. The bitwise OR operator can be used to combine multiple event capture statements into one as follows:

```
window.captureEvents(Event.CLICK | Event.MOUSEDOWN);
```

Now, the actual event handler function needs to be registered with that same object as follows:

```
window.onClick = clickHandlerFunction;
window.onMouseDown = mouseDownHandlerFunction;
```

An event handler should be declared to take a single argument. At run time, the JavaScript interpreter will pass in an event object through this argument. An event handler routine can respond to the event in four ways. A return value of true indicates that the system can continue processing the event in its normal fashion. A return value of false indicates that the system should attempt to abort whatever process fired this event. For example, if the event is a click event associated with a link, the link will not be loaded in the browser. Calling routeEvent will let the system attempt to find another event handler to handle this event. When calling routeEvent, be sure to pass in the event object as a argument. RouteEvent takes no other arguments. Finally, an event handler can explicitly call handleEvent on some other object. This can be used to pass the event along to the target object or to pass the event to a different object entirely.

Events can be unregistered by calling the releaseEvent method on the original object.

Figure 24.13 shows a JavaScript page that utilizes the 1.2 event system. Source 24.12 is a source code listing for that page.

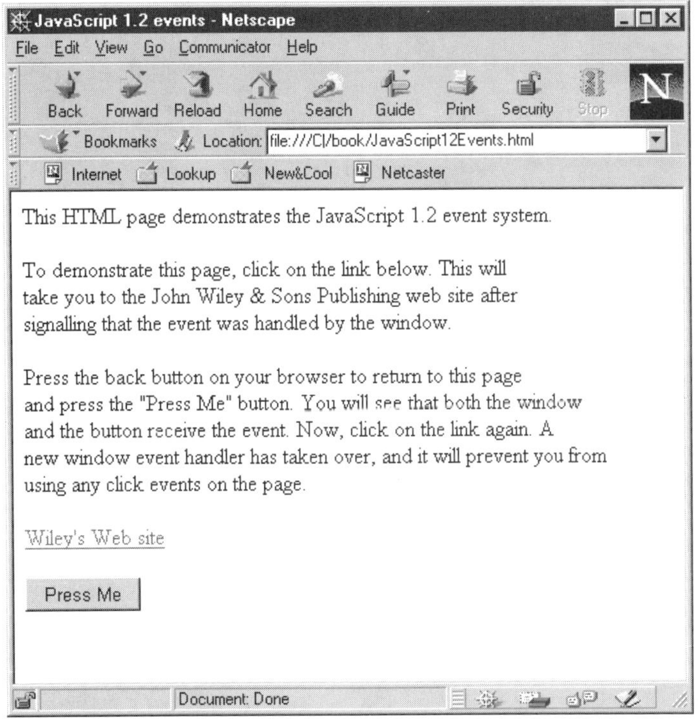

FIGURE 24.13 JavaScript 1.2 event system.

SOURCE 24.12

```
<HTML>
<TITLE> JavaScript 1.2 events <./TITLE>
<BODY>

This HTML page demonstrates the JavaScript 1.2 event system.<BR>
<BR>
To demonstrate this page, click on the link below.  This will<BR>
take you to the John Wiley & Sons Publishing web site after<BR>
signalling that the event was handled by the window.<BR>
<BR>
Press the back button on your browser to return to this page<BR>
and press the "Press Me" button.  You will see that both the window<BR>
and the button receive the event.  Now, click on the link again.  A<BR>
new window event handler has taken over, and it will prevent you from<BR>
using any click events on the page.<BR><BR>
```

```
<SCRIPT LANGUAGE="JavaScript1.2">
<!— hide from old browsers

function clickHandler(e)
{
    alert("A " + e.type + " was fired and passed on to the target!");
    e.target.handleEvent(e);
}

function clickHandler2(e)
{
    alert("A " + e.type + " was fired and rejected!");
    return false;
}

function buttonHandler(e)
{
    alert ("Switching event handlers...");
     window.onClick = clickHandler2;
    return true;
}

window.captureEvents(Event.CLICK);
window.onClick = clickHandler;

<!— done hiding —>

</SCRIPT>

<A HREF="http://www.wiley.com'>Wiley's Web site</A>

<FORM>
<INPUT TYPE=BUTTON VALUE="Press Me" onClick=buttonHandler (event)><BR>
</FORM>

</BODY>
</HTML>
```

New Methods

A series of new methods have been added to JavaScript 1.2 to simplify the development process and provide more internal services. Programming is made simpler because more functionality is provided for the developer.

- *Array objects have two new methods, slice and concat.* Concat is used to combine two arrays. Slice performs the opposite function, breaking a single array into two pieces.
- *The document method now features a getSelection method.* This method can be called to determine what text has been selected by the user.

- *The Navigator object now supports the preference method.* The preference method can be used to get and set user preferences for the browser.
- *String objects support a great deal of additional methods.* CharCodeAt returns the ISO-Latin-1 numeric value of the character at the specified location. FromCharCode constructs a string from a list of numbers that correspond to ISO-Latin-1 numeric values. Concat and slice perform the same functions they perform for arrays. Concat joins two strings to form a single string while slice breaks a single string into two pieces. Match, replace, and search all take regular expressions as input and modify the string object being invoked. Match tests to see if the string satisfies the regular expression. Search tests to see if the string or any substring satisfies the regular expression. Replace replaces any substrings that satisfy the regular expression. Finally, substr returns a substring of a specified number of characters starting at the designated starting point.
- *The window object has been greatly expanded as well.* Back, forward, home, and stop methods have been added to provide easy access to the navigation menu items of the same names. MoveBy and moveTo both move the window. MoveBy moves the window the amount specified, starting at the current position, moveTo moves the window to an absolute position. ResizeBy and ResizeTo and ScrollBy and ScrollTo allow JavaScript to resize or scroll a window in a similar manner. A find method has been added to search the current page for a specific string.
- *Three additional methods have been added to frame and window objects.* SetInterval allows JavaScript to register a function that executes at a regular interval, specified in milliseconds. ClearInterval disables a function registered through SetInterval. Finally, print activates the browser's print features for the object it is called on.

Figure 24.14 shows a JavaScript page that utilizes some of the new 1.2 methods. Source 24.13 is a source code listing for that page.

New Properties

JavaScript 1.2 has added some new properties, primarily on the window object.

- *The Function object now supports an arity property that indicates the number or arguments expected by the function.*
- *The Navigator object supports two additional properties, both intended to make handling JAR files easier.* The language property indicates which localized version of Netscape Navigator is currently in use. The platform property indicates what platform Navigator is currently running on.
- *The Window object supports many additional properties.* InnerHeight and innerWidth specify the size of the window's content area. OuterHeight and outerWidth specify the size of the window's outer boundary. PageXOffset and page YOffset specify the x and y position of the window's viewed page. All of the other properties are objects that allow JavaScript programmers to have greater control of the

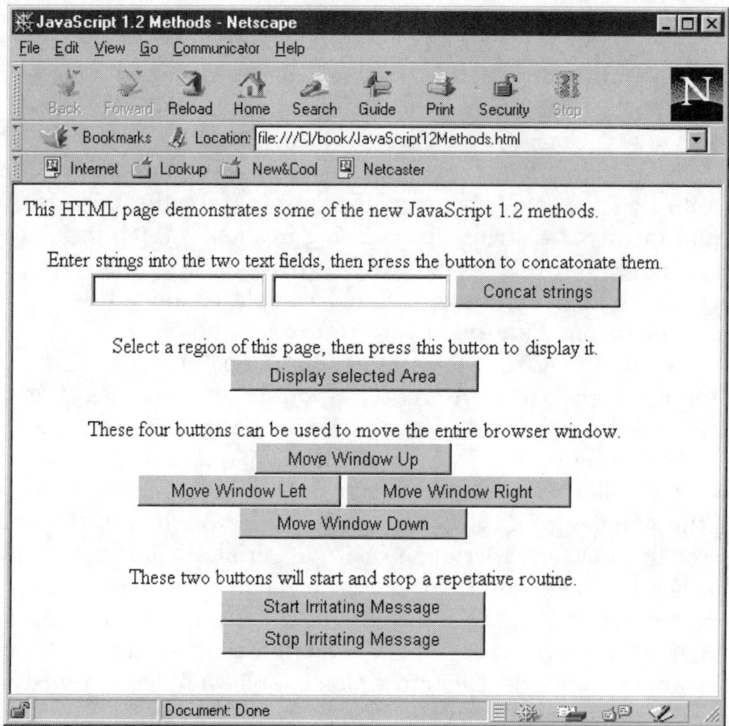

FIGURE 24.14 JavaScript 1.2 methods.

SOURCE 24.13

```
<HTML>
<TITLE> JavaScript 1.2 Methods </TITLE>
<BODY>

This HTML page demonstrates some of the new JavaScript 1.2 methods.<BR>
<BR>

<SCRIPT LANGUAGE="JavaScript1.2">
<!- hide from old browsers

nID = 0;
function startReps()
{
    alert("hi")
     nID = window.setInterval('alert("Please press the other
button!")',1500);
}
```

```
function stopReps()
{
    window.clearInterval(nID);
}

<!— done hiding —>
</SCRIPT>

<FORM>
<CENTER>
Enter strings into the two text fields, then press the button to
concatanate them.<BR>
<INPUT TYPE=TEXT SIZE=15 NAME=text1>
<INPUT TYPE=TEXT SIZE=15 NAME=text2>
<INPUT TYPE=BUTTON VALUE="Concat strings"
onClick=alert(text1.value.concat(text2.value))><BR>
<BR>Select a region of this page, then press this button to display it.<BR>
<INPUT TYPE=BUTTON VALUE="Display selected Area"
onClick-alert(document.getSelection())><BR>
<BR>These four buttons can be used to move the entire browser window.<BR>
<INPUT TYPE=BUTTON Value="Move Window Up" onClick=window.moveBy(0,-10)><BR>
<INPUT TYPE=BUTTON Value="Move Window Left" onClick=window.moveBy(-10,0)>
<INPUT TYPE=BUTTON Value="Move Window Right"
onClick=Window.moveBy(10,0)><BR>
<INPUT TYPE=BUTTON Value="Move Window Down"
onClick=window.moveBy(0,10)><BR>
<BR>These two buttons will start and stop a repetitive routine.<BR>
<INPUT TYPE=BUTTON Value="Start Irritating Message"
onClick=startReps()><BR>
<INPUT TYPE=BUTTON Value="Stop Irritating Message" onClick=stopReps()><Br>
</CENTER>
</FORM>

</BODY>
</HTML>
```

visual appearance of the browser being used to view their documents. The locationbar, menubar, personalbar, scrollbar, statusbar, and toolbar objects all allow JavaScript to show or hide the user interface elements of the same names.

24.9 SUMMARY

We have discussed all of the major elements of JavaScript 1.1 and 1.2. We covered the syntax of JavaScript, including expressions, operators, and built-in functions. We also covered the object model used by JavaScript, and learned of all the objects that already exist in the JavaScript environment. We then moved on to create our own objects to extend JavaScript's capabilities.

Both the JavaScript 1.1 and 1.2 event models were introduced. We saw how in JavaScript 1.1 programmers must individually set event handlers for each object, but in 1.2 we can assign single event handlers for entire pages.

That concludes our discussion of JavaScript. As the language evolves, I will post regular updates to my Web pages. Now you should feel confident in understanding the fundamental difference between JavaScript and Java, as well as how they will complement each other.

CHAPTER 25

Interfacing Java and JavaScript

OBJECTIVE

The reader will learn how to create and invoke Java objects from a JavaScript script. Important details and restrictions will be discussed, and an example will illustrate the concept. Then we will examine the other direction, accessing JavaScript functions from Java.

25.1 CALLING JAVA FROM JAVASCRIPT

JavaScript is not just a simple scripting language based on Java. JavaScript can actually be used to interact with Java objects. Much in the same way that Java can access native routines through the JNI interface to solve more complex problems, JavaScript can access Java through the Netscape technology called LiveConnect.

Calling from JavaScript to Java presents several problems. How can a script locate an existing Java object? How can a script create new objects? What should a script do when a Java exception is thrown? And finally, how can an untyped JavaScript variable be converted into a strongly typed Java variable? As we will soon see, the JavaScript developer is mostly shielded from these complex issues; however, understanding these issues is helpful because it can lead to a better script design and faster debugging.

25.2 ACCESSING JAVA OBJECTS FROM JAVASCRIPT

Conceptually, applets are the simplest Java objects for JavaScript to communicate with. When a script is executing, the applet is already loaded and running. In addition, applets are placed in an HTML page using the applet tag, and we've already seen that any tag can be accessed through JavaScript using the document object. Using the NAME parameter with an applet makes it easier to retrieve the applet, especially when there are multiple applets on a page. Once we store the applet object in a JavaScript variable, we can access all methods and properties on the applet object as if it were a generic JavaScript object. Even protected and private methods and properties can be accessed.

```
<APPLET CODE=someApplet NAME=myApplet WIDTH=100 HEIGHT=100> </APPLET>
<SCRIPT>
var theApplet = document.applets["myApplet"];
</SCRIPT>
```

If the applet is the first (or only) applet on the page, then it can also be accessed using:

```
var theApplet = document.applets[0];
```

Before we continue, it is important to note the second way to access Java objects. JavaScript can create Java objects in the same way it creates its own objects using the new keyword. Simply substitute Java syntax for the JavaScript constructor method as follows:

```
var javaString = new java.lang.String();
```

If the Java object being created supports multiple constructors, then they can be accessed by supplying valid arguments. The following creates a Java string using the constructor that takes an initial string:

```
var javaInitializedString = new java.lang.String("Initial Value");
```

Once a Java object reference has been acquired, calling its methods from JavaScript is as easy as calling its methods in Java. However, since JavaScript does not support exceptions, methods that are called in this fashion should not throw any exceptions. If an exception is thrown, then JavaScript will report the error and halt the script. A better approach (when interacting with JavaScript) is for Java methods to signal error conditions through the return value.

Data Translation

The translation of variables between JavaScript and Java is an important topic. Whenever a Java method or constructor is called from JavaScript, all arguments are copied from their JavaScript representation to a corresponding Java representation. When the method completes execution, its return value is copied from its Java representation to a corresponding JavaScript representation. Because all arguments and return values are copied, no arguments can be passed by reference.

JavaScript supports four main data types: strings, numbers, booleans, and objects. Java, on the other hand, supports many data types including: boolean, byte, short, int, long, float, double, strings, and objects. In both cases, strings are really objects but are handled specially by the language; hence the separation. Strings and booleans are fairly intuitive, since they have corresponding data types in the two languages. Numbers and objects are a little more complex.

JavaScript numbers can be converted to any of the Java numeric types (byte, short, int, long, float, or double). Because data is converted only in the context of a function call, the signature of the method can be examined in order to determine the correct type. When a JavaScript number is used as an argument to a Java method, the JavaScript number will always be converted to the correct type, which can result in truncation. In addition, for overloaded Java methods, JavaScript will call the first method for which the conversion is successful. In cases where multiple methods could be applied (for instance, one takes a short argument, the other takes a long argument), the first method encountered will be used. Translating numbers from Java to JavaScript is much simpler. All Java numeric types are converted to the generic JavaScript number.

Object conversion is similarly complex because of the number of possible circumstances. When translating a JavaScript object to a Java object, the object will usually be translated to a netscape.javascript.JSObject unless the object is a wrapper for a Java object. JSObject is a Java class provided by Netscape that can represent any JavaScript object. JavaScript objects that wrap Java objects are converted to their native Java type. Consider the following code fragment:

```
var jsImage = document.images[0];
var jURL = new Java.net.URL();
var anApplet = document.applets[0];
anApplet.someMethod(jsImage, jURL);
```

In the call to someMethod, the variable jsImage will be converted to a netscape.javascript.JSObject because it is a JavaScript object. The variable jURL will be converted to a java.net.URL object because it is really just a JavaScript wrapper for a Java object.

Translating a Java object to a JavaScript object is very similar. Most objects are simply given a JavaScript wrapper and undergo no special conversion. Java JSObjects are converted to their native JavaScript object type.

Because both languages represent arrays as special types of objects, JavaScript arrays are represented as JSObjects in Java, and Java arrays are given a JavaScript wrapper in JavaScript.

25.3 JAVASCRIPT TO JAVA EXAMPLE

Source 24.10 showed how JavaScript is used to validate the input of an HTML form. In this example, we want to transfer the validation rules from JavaScript to Java. Our reasoning for this is fairly straightforward: Java supports some additional methods for working with strings that are not available in JavaScript. In particular, we want to take advantage of methods such as Character.isDigit() and Integer.parseInt().

Examining Source 25.1 shows some important changes we have made to our HTML document. An APPLET tag has been added. This applet implements our validation rules. In the script section of the page, three validation rules (checkName, checkAge, and checkPhone) have been modified to call their Java counterparts. In order to keep our JavaScript-to-Java interaction simple, the Java validation rules accept strings as arguments and return booleans indicating whether or not the input was accepted. Our Java logic doesn't need to be JavaScript aware, and doesn't need to take any JavaScript-specific actions in validating the data.

Source 25.2 is the Java applet that implements the validation rules. The Java routines use the exact same algorithm used by the JavaScript routines from Source 24.10; the routines have only been modified to use Java syntax and take advantage of some useful Java APIs.

Source 25.2 generates the Web page shown in Figure 25.1.

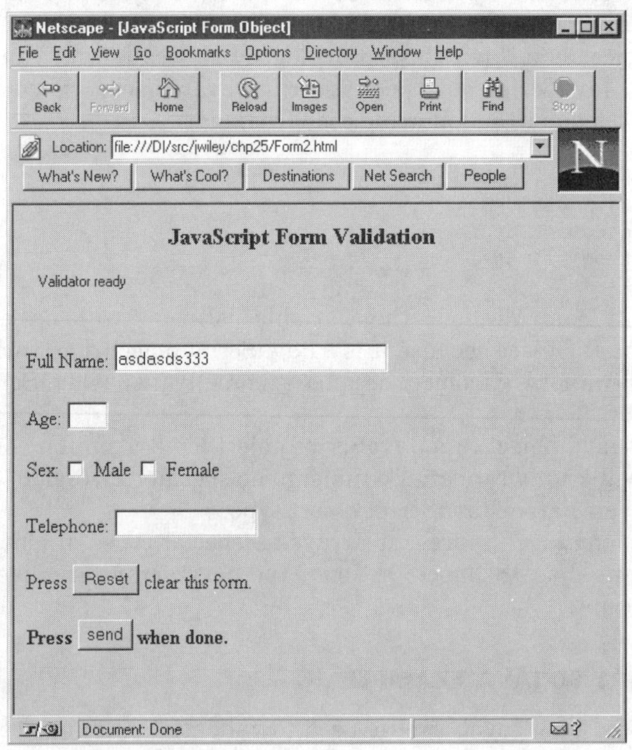

FIGURE 25.1 Our new HTML form.

SOURCE 25.1

```
<HTML>
<TITLE> JavaScript Form Object </TITLE>
<BODY>
<SCRIPT LANGUAGE="JavaScript">
<!— hide from old browsers

function checkName(form)
{
     var Validate = document.applets["Validator"];
     if (!Validate.validateName(form.fullname.value))
     {
          alert("Invalid name.  Please re-enter");
          form.fullname.value="";
          return;
     }
}

function checkAge(form)
{
     var Validate = document.applets["Validator"];
     if (!Validate.validateAge(form.age.value))
     {
         alert("Invalid age.  Please re-enter");
         form.age.value="";
         return;
     }
}

function checkPhone(form)
{
     var Validate = document.applets["Validator"];
     if (!Validate.validatePhoneNumber(form.phone.value))
     {
          alert("Invalid phone num. Please re-enter in this format: (###)###-
####");
          form.phone.value="";
          return;
     }
}

function checkSex(form)
{
     // insure both are not checked
     if (form.msex.status == true &&
          form.fsex.status == true)
     {
          alert("Cannot be both sexes.");
          return false;
     }
     return true;
}
```

```
function checkForm(form)
{
     if (!checkSex(form))
     {
          alert("Cannot be both sexes. Form NOT submitted.");
          return;
     }

     if ( (form.fullname.value.length == 0) &&
           (form.age.value.length == 0) &&
           (form.phone.value.length == 0) &&
           (form.msex.status == false &&
            form.fsex.status == false)  )
     {
          alert("All fields must be filled in. Form NOT submitted.");
          return;
     }

     // if we got here - submit it!

}

function clearForm(form)
{
     form.fullname.value="";
     form.age.value="";
     form.phone.value="";
}

<!— done hiding —>
</SCRIPT>

<APPLET CODEBASE="../.."
        CODE=jwiley.chp25.ValidationApplet
        NAME="Validator"
        WIDTH=100
        HEIGHT=100> </APPLET>

<CENTER>
<H3> JavaScript Form Validation </H3>
</CENTER>

<FORM>
<p> Full Name: <INPUT TYPE="text" NAME=fullname SIZE=30
onChange=checkName(this.form)> <BR>

<p> Age: <INPUT TYPE="text" NAME=age SIZE=3 onChange=checkAge(this.form)>
</BR>

<p> Sex: <INPUT TYPE="checkbox" NAME=msex VALUE="Male"
onClick=checkSex(this.form)> Male
```

```
            <INPUT TYPE="checkbox" NAME=fsex VALUE="Female"
onClick=checkSex(this.form)> Female

<p> Telephone: <INPUT TYPE="text" NAME=phone SIZE=15
onChange=checkPhone(this.form)> <BR>

<p> Press <INPUT TYPE="button" VALUE="Reset" onClick=clearForm(this.form)>
clear this form.
<p> <STRONG> Press <INPUT TYPE="button" VALUE="send"
onClick=checkForm(this.form)> when done. </STRONG>


</FORM>
</BODY>
</HTML>
```

SOURCE 25.2

```
// ValidationApplet.java
package jwiley.chp25;

import java.applet.Applet;
import java.awt.Graphics;

/**
 * Applet that implements logic to validate form input
 * A JavaScript page can use these routines instead
 * of implementing the logic itself
 */
public class ValidationApplet extends Applet
{
    /**
     * Checks the format of a string that is a person's name
     */
    public boolean validateName(String strName)
    {
        int len = strName.length();

        if (len  == 0)
            return true;

        for (int i = 0; i < len; i++)
        {
            char c = strName.charAt(i);

            if (!Character.isSpace(c) && !Character.isDigit(c))
                return false;
        }
```

```
        return true;
    }

    /**
     * Checks the format of a string that represents a phone number
     */
    public boolean validatePhoneNumber(String strPhoneNum)
    {
        int len = strPhoneNum.length();

        if (len  == 0)
            return true;

        if (len  > 13)
            return false;

        for (int i = 0; i < len; i++)
        {
            char c = strPhoneNum.charAt(i);

            if (!Character.isDigit(c) && (c != '(' && c != ')' && c!= '-'))
                return false;
        }

        return true;
    }

    /**
     * Checks the format of a string that represents a person's age
     */
    public boolean validateAge(String strAge)
    {
        int len = strAge.length();
        int realAge;

        if (len  == 0)
            return true;

        try
        {
            realAge = Integer.parseInt(strAge);
        }
        catch (NumberFormatException x)
          {
            return false;
          }
```

```
        if (realAge < 0 || realAge > 120)
            return false;

        return true;
    }

    /**
     * Overridden from java.awt.Component.  We want to display
     * some text here so that users know when the applet has
     * loaded.
     */
    public void paint(Graphics g)
    {
        g.drawString("Validator ready", 10, 10);
    }
}
```

25.4 JAVA-TO-JAVASCRIPT EXAMPLE

In our second example, we take the conversion of our JavaScript form validator one step further. Before, we used JavaScript helper functions to pass the strings into the Java applet and present errors to the user. In our second example, we put all of the form validation logic in the Java applet. Again, the exact same form validation is taking place, however, now Java code is examining the JavaScript objects, presenting error messages, and clearing the values of invalid fields.

The structure of Sources 25.3 and 25.4 in the example is the same as in Source 25.1 and 25.2. The only important difference is the addition of the MAYSCRIPT parameter to the applet tag in our HTML page. Unless you specify the MAYSCRIPT parameter for an applet, it will not be allowed to use JavaScript and any attempts to do so will result in a JSException being thrown. Running Source 25.3 generates the Web page shown in Figure 25.2.

In order to compile this example, you must have the Netscape package in your classpath. This package can be found in the archive in the directory java\classes of your Netscape installation. The netscape.javascript package contains two classes, JSObject and JSException. JSObject represents a JavaScript object in Java while JSException is used to indicate a JavaScript error in Java. The filename has the form java_<ver> where <ver> is the version number. For Netscape Navigator 3.01, the file is named java_301.

SOURCE 25.3

```
<HTML>
<TITLE> JavaScript Form Object </TITLE>
<BODY>
<CENTER>
<H3> JavaScript Form Validation </H3>
</CENTER>

<FORM NAME=jsForm>
<p> Full Name: <INPUT TYPE="text" NAME=fullname SIZE=30> <BR>

<p> Age: <INPUT TYPE="text" NAME=age SIZE=3> </BR>

<p> Sex: <INPUT TYPE="checkbox" NAME=msex VALUE="Male"> Male
         <INPUT TYPE="checkbox" NAME=fsex VALUE="Female"> Female

<p> Telephone: <INPUT TYPE="text" NAME=phone SIZE=15> <BR>
</FORM>

<APPLET CODEBASE="../.."
        CODE=jwiley.chp25.ValidationApplet2
        NAME="Validator"
        WIDTH=100
        HEIGHT=60
        MAYSCRIPT> </APPLET>
</BODY>
</HTML>
```

SOURCE 25.4

```
// ValidationApplet.java
package jwiley.chp25;

import java.applet.Applet;
import java.awt.Graphics;
import netscape.javascript.*;
import java.awt.*;
/**
 * Applet that implements logic to validate form input
 * A JavaScript page can use these routines instead
 * of implementing the logic itself
 */
public class ValidationApplet2 extends Applet
{
    Button bSubmit;
    Button bReset;
```

```
    public void init()
    {
        setLayout(new BorderLayout());
        bSubmit = new Button("Submit");
        add("South", bSubmit);
        bReset = new Button("Reset");
        add("North", bReset);

    };

    public boolean action(Event evt, Object what)
    {
        if (evt.target == bSubmit)
        {
            JSObject window = JSObject.getWindow(this);
            JSObject doc = (JSObject)window.getMember("document");
            JSObject form = (JSObject)doc.getMember("jsForm");
            validateForm(form);
        }

        if (evt.target == bReset)
        {
            clearForm();
            return true;
        }

        return false;
    }

    /**
     * Checks the format of a string that is a person's name
     */
    public boolean validateName(JSObject form)
    {
        JSObject jsName = (JSObject)form.getMember("fullname");
        String strName = (String)jsName.getMember("value");
        int len = strName.length();

        if (len  == 0)
            return true;

        for (int i = 0; i < len; i++)
        {
            char c = strName.charAt(i);

            if (!Character.isSpace(c) && !Character.isDigit(c))
            {
                JSObject.getWindow(this).eval("alert('Invalid name.  Please
re-enter');");
                jsName.setMember("value", "");
```

```
                return false;
            }
        }

        return true;
    }

    /**
     * Checks the format of a string that represents a phone number
     */
    public boolean validatePhoneNumber(JSObject form)
    {
        JSObject jsPhone = (JSObject)form.getMember("phone");
        String strPhoneNum = (String)jsPhone.getMember("value");
        int len = strPhoneNum.length();

        if (len  == 0)
            return true;

        if (len  > 13)
        {
            JSObject.getWindow(this).eval("alert('Phone numbers must be of
the form (###)###-####');");
            jsPhone.setMember("value", "");
            return false;
        }

        for (int i = 0; i < len; i++)
        {
            char c = strPhoneNum.charAt(i);

            if (!Character.isDigit(c) && (c != '(' && c != ')' && c!= '-'))
            {
                JSObject.getWindow(this).eval("alert('Phone numbers must be
of the form (###)###-####');");
                jsPhone.setMember("value", "");
                return false;
            }
        }

        return true;
    }

    /**
     * Checks the format of a string that represents a person's age
     */
    public boolean validateAge(JSObject form)
    {
        JSObject jsAge = (JSObject)form.getMember("age");
        String strAge = (String)jsAge.getMember("value");
        int len = strAge.length();
```

```
        int realAge;
        if (len  == 0)
            return true;

        try
        {
            realAge = Integer.parseInt(strAge);
        }
        catch (NumberFormatException x)
          {
            JSObject.getWindow(this).eval("alert('Invalid age.  Please re-
enter.');");
            jsAge.setMember("value", "");
            return false;
          }

        if (realAge < 0 || realAge > 120)
        {
            JSObject.getWindow(this).eval("alert('Invalid age.  Please re-
enter.');");
            jsAge.setMember("value", "");
            return false;
        }

        return true;
    }

    public boolean validateSex(JSObject form)
    {
        Boolean bMale =
(Boolean)((JSObject)form.getMember("msex")).getMember("status");
        Boolean bFemale =
(Boolean)((JSObject)form.getMember("fsex")).getMember("status");

        if (bMale.booleanValue() && bFemale.booleanValue())
        {
            JSObject.getWindow(this).eval("alert('Cannot be both sexes.');");
            return false;
        }

        return true;
    }

    public boolean validateForm(JSObject form)
    {
        if (!validateName(form) ||
            !validatePhoneNumber(form) ||
            !validateAge(form) ||
            !validateSex(form))
        {
            return false;
```

```
        }
        // make sure we've filled it all in
        String strName =
(String)((JSObject)form.getMember("fullname")).getMember("value");
        String strPhone =
(String)((JSObject)form.getMember("phone")).getMember("value");
        String strAge =
(String)((JSObject)form.getMember("age")).getMember("value");
        Boolean bMale =
(Boolean)((JSObject)form.getMember("msex")).getMember("status");
        Boolean bFemale =
(Boolean)((JSObject)form.getMember("fsex")).getMember("status");

          if (strName.length() == 0 ||
            strPhone.length() == 0 ||
            strAge.length() == 0 ||
            (!bMale.booleanValue() && !bFemale.booleanValue()))
        {
            JSObject.getWindow(this).eval("alert('All fields must be filled
in.  Form NOT submitted');");
            return false;
        }

        Object[] args = new Object[0];
        form.call("submit", args);

        return true;
    }

    public void clearForm()
    {
        JSObject window = JSObject.getWindow(this);
        JSObject doc = (JSObject)window.getMember("document");
        JSObject form = (JSObject)doc.getMember("jsForm");

        ((JSObject)form.getMember("fullname")).setMember("value", "");
        ((JSObject)form.getMember("phone")).setMember("value", "");
        ((JSObject)form.getMember("age")).setMember("value", "");
    }
}
```

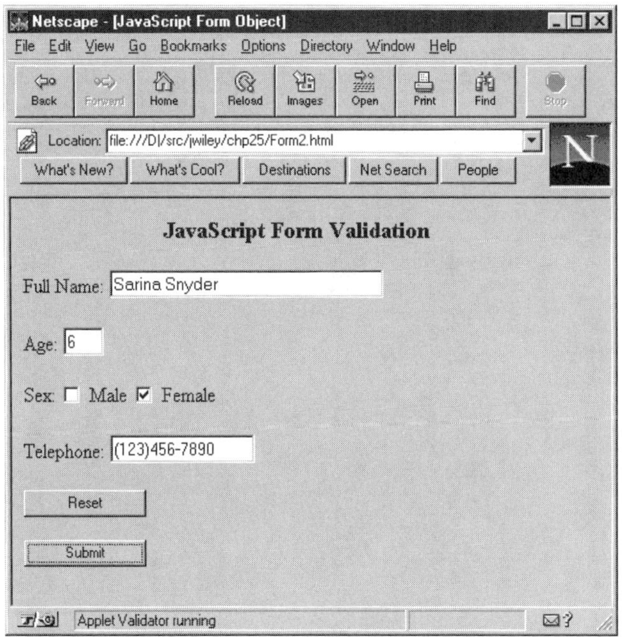

FIGURE 25.2 Our final HTML form.

25.5 SUMMARY

Java and JavaScript can easily communicate with each other using the LiveConnect interface. Primitives in one language are converted to primitives in the other, whereas objects in one language are copied and placed in an object wrapper. Java classes and objects can be accessed natively in JavaScript merely by specifying their names. To access JavaScript objects from Java, however, you must use the netscape.javascript class JSObject, which allows generic access to JavaScript objects.

What's on the CD-ROM?

This document is a supplement to the Autoplay extender application that should run when you insert the *Java 1.2 and JavaScript for C/C++ Programmers* companion CD-ROM. It contains information about the directory structure and content of the CD-ROM. If for some reason the autoplay program does not start simply click on the My Computer icon within My Computer and then double click the program autorun.exe.

The CD-ROM contains the following directories and components.

All book source code can be found in
{cdrom}:\Exploded Source
Windows 95/NT Source code install.
{cdrom}:\Examples\setup.exe

Adobe Acrobat pdf files containing.
{cdom}:\Supplements\

appendix.pdf	Appendix of Java and JavaScript reserved words as well as useful URLs.
coding.pdf	A bonus chapter on coding conventions and standards. Contains an additional sample.

Shareware/Freeware tools:
{cdrom}:\Tools

jdk111.exe	Bill Bercik of Dippybird's Windows JDK Help file.
jgl3_0_0.exe	Objectspaces JGL 3.0 container classes for Windows.
jgl3_0_0_tar.gz	Objectspaces JGL 3.0 container classes for Unix.
voyager1_0_1.exe	Objectspaces CORBA Orb for Windows.

voyager1_0_1_tar.gz	Objectspaces CORBA Orb for Unix.
sc_12.exe	Supercede Try-and-Buy demo version 1.2.
wingdis_demo.zip	Wing Softwares Java decompiler demo in zip format.
wingdis_demo_tar.Z	Wing Softwares Java decompiler demo in tar.Z format.
wingeditor.zip	Wing Softwares Wingeditor in zip format.
wingeditor_tar.Z	Wing Softwares Wingeditor in tar.Z format.
js10Win32.exe	Java Studio V1.0 for Windows.
JS1_0_intel-S2.tar.Z	Java Studio V1.0 for x86 Unix.
JS1_0_sparc-S2.tar.Z	Java Studio V1.0 for Sparc 2.
jws20Win32.exe	Java WorkShop V2.0 for Windows.
jws2_0_intel-S2.tar.Z	Java WorkShop V2.0 for x86 Unix.
jws2_0_sparc-S2.tar.Z	Java WorkShop V2.0 for x86 Sparc 2.

{cdrom}:\Tools\Adobe\ar32e30.exe
Adobe Acrobat Reader for Win32 v2.0

{cdrom):\Tools\TextPad\SETUP.EXE

Keith Mcdonalds TextPad editor version 3.1
Also included are the internation and Win16 versions of TextPad.

HARDWARE REQUIREMENTS

Windows 95, Windows NT 4.0, Solaris for Sparc2 or X86.
486, Pentium, Sparc2 or better which supports Javasoft JDK 1.1.4 or better.
16 MB RAM memory.
10 MB disk space for examples.
Additional software tools may require disk space as well.

USER ASSISTANCE AND INFORMATION

The software accompanying this book is being provided as is without warranty or support of any kind. Should you require basic installation assistance, or if your media is defective, please call our product support number at (212) 850-6194 weekdays between 9 A.M. and 4 P.M. Eastern Standard Time. Or, we can be reached via e-mail at: wprtusw@wiley.com. Al Saganich can be reached via e-mail at: ASaganich@Aol.com. Michael C. Daconta can be reached via e-mail at MikeDacon@Aol.com.

To place additional orders or to request information about other Wiley products, please call (800) 879-4539.

Index

What is JAVA-SIG?

Java-SIG (special interest group) is an international association of people who work with Java. Java-SIG serves as a conduit of information between Java developers and programmers across the world.

Come visit us in early 1998 at:

http://www.java-sig.com

CUSTOMER NOTE: IF THIS BOOK IS ACCOMPANIED BY SOFTWARE, PLEASE READ THE FOLLOWING BEFORE OPENING THE PACKAGE.

This software contains files to help you utilize the models described in the accompanying book. By opening the package, you are agreeing to be bound by the following agreement:

WILEY